ALICE
MUNRO

Writing Her Lives

ALICE MUNRO

Writing Her Lives

A BIOGRAPHY

ROBERT THACKER

EMBLEM
McClelland & Stewart

Cloth edition published 2005
Emblem edition with new chapter published 2011

Emblem is an imprint of McClelland & Stewart Ltd.
Emblem and colophon are registered trademarks of McClelland & Stewart Ltd.

Library and Archives Canada Cataloguing in Publication

Thacker, Robert
Alice Munro : writing her lives : a biography / Robert Thacker.

Includes bibliographical references and index.
ISBN 978-0-7710-8510-9

1. Munro, Alice, 1931-. 2. Munro, Alice, 1931 – Criticism and interpretation. 3. Authors, Canadian (English) – 20th century – Biography. I. Title.

PS8576.U57Z885 2011   C813'.54   C2010-907896-9

We acknowledge the financial support of the Government of Canada through the Book Publishing Industry Development Program and that of the Government of Ontario through the Ontario Media Development Corporation's Ontario Book Initiative. We further acknowledge the support of the Canada Council for the Arts and the Ontario Arts Council for our publishing program.

Typeset in Garamond
Printed and bound in the United States of America

McClelland & Stewart Ltd.
75 Sherbourne Street
Toronto, Ontario
M5A 2P9
www.mcclelland.com

1 2 3 4 5   15 14 13 12 11

For Debbie, Mike, and Sue:

Friends of a Lifetime

The walnuts drop, the muskrats swim in the creek.
— "A Real Life" (1992) *Open Secrets*

Some of these stories are closer to my own life than others are, but not one of them is as close as people seem to think.
— "Introduction" to *The Moons of Jupiter* (1986)

The story must be imagined so deeply and devoutly that everything in it seems to bloom of its own accord and to be connected, then, to our own lives which suddenly, as we read, take on a hard beauty, a familiar strangeness, the importance of a dream that can't be disputed or explained. Everything is telling you: Stop. Hold on. Here it is. Here too. Remember.
— "Golden Apples" (1999) *The Georgia Review*

Contents

ALICE
MUNRO

Writing Her Lives

PROLOGUE
Alice Munro, August 1974

This ordinary place is sufficient, everything here is
touchable and mysterious.
– "Everything Here Is Touchable and Mysterious" (1974)

On August 18, 1974, CBC Radio aired a long interview with Alice Munro conducted by Harry J. Boyle on its *Sunday Supplement* program. Munro's third book – *Something I've Been Meaning to Tell You: Thirteen Stories* – had been published by McGraw-Hill Ryerson the previous spring, and she was just about to take up a year's position as writer-in-residence at the University of Western Ontario. The year before, Munro had returned to Ontario from British Columbia after making for herself what she later described for one of her characters as "a long necessary voyage from the house of marriage," leaving James Munro, her husband of twenty-two years, in the Victoria house where he still lives.[1] Their daughters, Sheila, twenty, Jenny, seventeen, and Andrea, seven, were at varying stages of independence and dependence. Munro was worried about how the breakup would affect them, especially Andrea, but was pressing ahead. Her new life involved no real plan beyond leaving British Columbia for Ontario. Alice Munro had decided to come home.

"Home," despite more than twenty years on the west coast, was still Ontario. Specifically, it was Wingham, Huron County, Ontario – the place Alice Ann Laidlaw had left for marriage to James Armstrong Munro and a shared life in Vancouver at the very end of 1951. She was then twenty years old and had completed two years on scholarships at the University of Western Ontario; he was twenty-two, had a general arts B.A. from Western and a job at Eaton's department store in Vancouver. Within two years of the marriage, Sheila was born, followed within another two by Catherine, who died the day of her birth; Jenny was born in 1957 and, after a longer interval, Andrea followed in 1966.

Throughout her domestic life as a young wife and mother, Alice Munro wrote. Before she was married, Munro had published stories in Western's undergraduate literary magazine, *Folio*, and she had made contact with Robert Weaver, an arts producer at the CBC, who bought and broadcast Munro's "The Strangers" in October 1951. This was the first of a succession of stories broadcast there, and throughout the 1950s these were complemented by magazine publication in *Mayfair*, the *Canadian Forum*, *Queen's Quarterly*, *Chatelaine*, and the *Tamarack Review*. The 1960s saw more commercial and little magazine

publication, with the *Montrealer* emerging then as Munro's most frequent venue, and the possibility of a book gradually became real. *Dance
of the Happy Shades* was published by Ryerson Press in 1968, winning
Munro's first Governor General's Award and, three years later, in 1971,
Lives of Girls and Women appeared from McGraw-Hill Ryerson.

To this point Munro's writing was solitary, personal, private,
something she did not talk about nor, really, much share with Jim
Munro, although throughout their years together he remained supportive of her writing. When stories were finished, they went out to be
considered for broadcast or publication. They often came back.
Throughout most of Munro's time living in British Columbia, as she
later wrote, Robert Weaver was "almost the only person I knew who
had anything to do with the world of writing." This changed as time
passed and Munro's stories continued to appear, but for a long time
Weaver – who besides his work at the CBC also held the leading editorial post at the *Tamarack Review* – was, she wrote, "one of the two – or
possibly three – people who took my writing seriously." Yet a writer was
what she really was, engaged always in a "wooing of distant parts of"
herself, as one of her narrators characterizes the process. That was her
"real work." Yet to the world, she was a housewife and a mother. After
Jim quit his job at Eaton's and the family moved to Victoria to open
Munro's Books in 1963, Alice was known there as the wife of the man
who ran the bookstore. Only gradually did the people she knew there
learn that Munro wrote – for a long time very few people in Victoria
were aware that she had published anything.[2]

But all this changed in the early 1970s when Munro began her
"long voyage from the house of marriage" and headed east to Ontario
to stay, going home to the place she started out from. To make it easier
on the children, Munro's leave-taking from Victoria was prolonged. It
involved departures and returns – for a time she lived elsewhere in
Victoria, going home to prepare meals and be with her daughters. She
spent much of the summer of 1972 in Toronto with Andrea, and in
1973, she and her daughters were in Nelson, in the British Columbia
interior, while Munro taught a summer-school course in creative
writing at Notre Dame University. That fall she was living in London

with Jenny, commuting once a week into Toronto to teach at York University. She was also preparing *Something I've Been Meaning to Tell You* for the press.

Something would prove to be Munro's last book with McGraw-Hill Ryerson. She had remained with Ryerson with some misgivings after a large U.S. firm, McGraw-Hill, bought it in 1970; this decision to stay was made largely out of loyalty to Audrey Coffin, her Ryerson editor who had moved to McGraw-Hill Ryerson. Unlike its predecessor, *Lives of Girls and Women*, *Something* offers no pretense of a single point of view – it is an eclectic collection of stories, including "The Found Boat," which dates from Munro's 1950s attempts to write a conventional novel, along with some of the most singular, striking stories she has ever written, such as "Material" and "The Ottawa Valley." The former offers a caustic critique of a writer's pretensions while at the same time celebrating that person's genuine gift ("an act of magic . . . an act, you might say, of a special, unsparing, unsentimental love. A fine and lucky benevolence").3

"The Ottawa Valley," the last story written for *Something*, is the second of a succession of Munro stories confronting the looming fact of her mother, Anne Clarke Chamney Laidlaw, who died in early 1959 after an almost twenty-year struggle with Parkinson's disease. That affliction had asserted its symptoms by the summer of 1943 ("'Is your arm going to stop shaking?'") when Laidlaw took her two daughters, Alice and Sheila, to visit her relatives near Carleton Place in the Ottawa Valley. As in the story, it was here that Alice, then eleven or twelve, suffered the humiliation of a broken elastic in her underwear just before church at St. John's Anglican, Innisville. Also as in the story, Mrs. Laidlaw sacrificed her own safety pin, to her daughter's humiliation, so her own slip showed. Munro focuses on this episode, and as the story ends she steps back to assert that "the problem, the only problem is my mother. And she is the one of course that I am trying to get; it is to reach her that this whole journey has been undertaken."4

During 1973 Munro also worked on "Home," most often seen as a story but much more a memoir – significantly, its initial title was "Notes for a Work." Like "The Ottawa Valley," it also deals with

Munro's family and shows her willing to step outside her narrative guise to comment directly on the realities and truths she had rediscovered and was trying to convey. "Home" was finished in 1973 and published in an anthology of new Canadian stories in 1974 but was excluded from *Something*. In it, Munro deals directly with her father, Robert Eric Laidlaw, and his declining health but she also describes her own feelings on her return home to Wingham – where her father still lived with his second wife, Mary Etta Charters Laidlaw, in the same house where Alice had grown up. Munro comments defensively on the life she was then living in London, "a life of a typewriter and three rooms and odd adventures," a life "incomprehensible" to her stepsister, who lives nearby on a farm. On the way to the Wingham hospital, to which Robert Laidlaw has to drive himself since Alice does not drive, she writes that "we follow slowly that old usual route. Victoria Street. Minnie Street. John Street. Catherine Street. The town, unlike the house, stays very much the same, nobody is renovating or changing it. Nevertheless it has faded, for me. I have written about it and used it up. The same banks and barber shops and town hall tower, but all their secret, plentiful messages drained away."[5]

"I have written about it and used it up," . . . "their secret, plentiful messages drained away." Munro decided to leave "Home" out of her third book largely because of her sensitivity over its depiction of her stepmother and father, each still living. But another reason was her own dissatisfaction, she has remarked since, with her intrusions as author into what might be seen as the story's fictional surfaces. The correct phrase is "might be seen" here because this is a central issue in the art of Alice Munro: her stories mostly begin in "real life," as she said in her interview with Harry Boyle and has freely admitted throughout: "There is always a starting point in reality." In "Material," for instance, Munro wrote, "When I was pregnant with Clea we lived in a house on Argyle Street." When Alice Munro was pregnant with Sheila, she and Jim lived in a house on Argyle Street in Vancouver; a more recent story, "Cortes Island," has the young narrator, a new bride, living on Arbutus Street, where they lived before that.[6] As Munro also told Boyle, the episode in "The Ottawa Valley" with the safety pin did happen. The details offered in "Home," from the people and circumstances depicted, to the route taken to the Wingham hospital – the streets named would be either taken or passed when driving from the Laidlaw farm to the Wingham hospital – are factually exact. So too are the circumstances of that story's narrator: she feels sensitive over the life she was then leading in London – one her stepsister must see as "incomprehensible" with "no work: nothing she could even call work, no animals to look after or vegetables to harrow and dig."

More crucially, there is the fact of Wingham itself. The town is the place that Munro, writing in October 1973 about a visit made earlier that month (though during the previous summer she also had visited Wingham regularly), asserts that she "has written about . . . and used . . . up," the "secret, plentiful messages" Wingham's outward signs had held for her had now "drained away." In one sense this was true: the Wingham of mind and memory, the place recalled from the west coast since 1952, separated by time and distance, in Munro's previous work – in stories like "Walker Brothers Cowboy" or "Images" or "Boys and Girls" from *Dance of the Happy Shades*, in the whole of *Lives of Girls and Women*, and even in some of the stories in *Something*, like "Winter Wind" – that remembered Wingham may well have been "used up." Yet in "Home," back there in Wingham in October 1973, Munro was looking at the place anew, so it was not at all used up, only different.

In "Home" the narrator explains her previous relation to Wingham, and to her remembered home there: "Now that I am living a hundred miles away I come home every two months or so. Before that, for a long time, throughout my marriage, I lived thousands of miles away and would go without seeing this house for years at a time. I thought of it then as a place I might never see again. I was greatly moved by the memory of it. I would walk through its rooms in my mind." Looking at it now, her mother long dead, "reminders of my mother in this house are not easy to find. Though she dominated it for so long, filled it with astonishing, embarrassing hopes, and her dark and helpless, justified complaint."[7]

The presence of "Home" in Munro's work is crucial as this book begins: it confirms its author's imaginative grappling with her "home place." That phrase is Wright Morris's; he used it as the title for a book Munro very much admires. Returning to Ontario, she found her home place lying before her in 1972–73 as a mature woman in her early forties, having left it a very young woman of twenty. Munro returned home as an author of some accomplishment and renown (especially since *Lives of Girls and Women* was just then showing every sign of marked success), having left it as a gifted student writer. Most of all, "Home" shows Alice Munro wondering over, and trying to find new ways into, her home place as material: though worried that she may have "used up" Wingham, that all the town's "secret, plentiful messages" had been "drained away" by her long-distance rememberings, she rediscovered anew her home place, a place where "everything was touchable and mysterious."

☙

This was the Alice Munro who walked into the studio for her interview with Harry Boyle for *Sunday Supplement* to discuss *Something I've Been Meaning to Tell You*. It is more casual conversation than interview, really. And at over forty minutes in length, Boyle had time to meander. A journalist, broadcaster, columnist, and novelist, Harry Boyle was a wholly appropriate choice for the assignment the CBC gave him – or, more accurately, that he assigned to himself – that day. Like Munro, he was a native of Huron County from St. Augustine, in West Wawanash Township – and like her also he attended high school in Wingham. As he noted at the outset, he saw the young Alice Munro in Wingham during the 1940s where he was working at his first job in radio at CKNX, the local station. Along with other Wingham children, Munro performed recitations and scripted pieces on the radio, so she certainly knew Boyle, whether he specifically knew her then or not.

While Boyle is at pains to focus on several of the stories in *Something* – the title story, "Material," "The Spanish Lady," and "The Ottawa Valley" come in for the most discussion – the interview speaks eloquently to the culture of the people among whom Boyle and Munro grew up, and still owe allegiance to, more than anything else. Boyle compliments Munro for her ability to retain, and "celebrate," "the essential mystery of individuals." Talking about the culture of Huron's Scots and Irish people, farmers and others who worked on the land, they agree that small towns in Huron "make a drama out of life. You're a character in the whole drama." To this, Munro remarks that "even the town loonie" has his role to play. More tellingly, she recalls that people were encouraged "not to aim too high": " 'Who do you think you are?' they used to ask," she says. And while they do not quite exactly agree, both feel that there are elements of the macabre, what Munro calls "a Canadian Gothic," in the life of rural southwestern Ontario. People were always being maimed in horrible accidents, living with untreated disease, singling themselves out by some excessive behaviour. Borne of "dispossessed peoples" fleeing eviction or poverty or famine or religious persecution in Europe during the nineteenth century, the people who live in Huron County evince both "enormous energy" and, Boyle and Munro agree, considerable sexual repression. They are the people Munro knows, they have provided her characters she has created, characters whose culture is rooted, and defined by, Huron County – this place where everything is both "touchable and mysterious."

Among the listeners to Boyle's interview that August day in 1974 were three people who were to have a huge impact on Munro's life and career. One had already figured in Alice Munro's career; another was about to do so in the years just to come; and a third brought about Munro's move back to Huron County to live – a move she has said she had "never anticipated," and one that proved "a big shock to the system." The first, Audrey Coffin, Munro's editor at Ryerson and then McGraw-Hill Ryerson, heard the interview and later wrote that she "heard that Boyle interview on CBC – it was much better than I'd thought – really satisfying." The second, Douglas M. Gibson, editorial director of the trade division at Macmillan of Canada, later wrote to Munro, "Last week I had the eerily pleasant experience of having my reading of *Something I've Been Meaning to Tell You* interrupted by your radio conversation about the book with Harry Boyle." Gibson then mentions that, as "Harry's editor for the past three books," he has discussed many of the same topics with Boyle himself, and in his letter compliments the interview and *Something*. Finally getting to the real reason for his letter, Gibson also writes, "I'd very much like to meet you, if that could be arranged." He says that he's available in Toronto, but in any case "I'm sure that I could be easily persuaded to visit London."[8]

The third, and most important, person to hear Munro's conversation with Boyle that August day was Gerald Fremlin, a physical geographer and the editor of *The National Atlas of Canada*. After a career in the civil service in Ottawa, Fremlin had retired to his native Clinton, Ontario, to look after his elderly mother. Years before, when he was a student at Western, he had been among the contributors whose writing had been published along with Alice Laidlaw's in *Folio*. Fremlin was also someone Alice had her eye on before she connected with Jim Munro – she tried to submit her first story for *Folio* directly to Fremlin, whom she thought was an editor, in the hope of attracting his attention. That did not happen, but Fremlin was mightily impressed by Munro's writing when it appeared in *Folio* and the next summer sent her a fan letter praising her work. By then Jim Munro was very much in evidence and everyone at Western knew it. Several years older and a veteran, Fremlin graduated and went to work. But for the fan letter, the two lost touch. Yet listening to Munro's conversation with Boyle in August 1974 as he drove between Ottawa and Clinton, he could not miss Munro saying at one point, "Even since I've come back the past year to live here."

Picking up on this comment, Fremlin contacted Munro, and their connection was re-established. Given the elderly Mrs. Fremlin's situation, the only way the two could have had a relationship was for Alice to go to Clinton, just thirty-five kilometres southwest of Wingham – back to Huron County, back to the people she grew up among and had long written about from British Columbia, back to the place where her father still lived in Wingham.

Returning home to Ontario in 1973, really returning home to Huron County in 1975, Alice Munro was about to effect a transformation in her writing – one brought on, most certainly, by that homecoming. That transformation, in turn, brought about a coequal change in her writing career: just over a year after the Boyle interview, Munro was writing to Gibson from Clinton, Ontario – he had been persuaded to come to London for their meeting and she was working on a Macmillan book project he was editing. Munro worked with Gibson and Macmillan throughout 1975 on the projected book and, though it was never published, that connection brought her next book, *Who Do You Think You Are?* in 1978 to Macmillan, with Gibson as her editor. He remains her editor in Canada, since Munro followed him in 1986 to McClelland & Stewart to inaugurate Douglas Gibson Books with her sixth collection, *The Progress of Love.*

Though she did not hear the Boyle interview that August day in 1974, Virginia Barber, a New York literary agent seeking new clients in Canada, was by late 1975 planning to approach Alice Munro in the hope of becoming her agent. Munro hired her in 1976.[9] In one of her first acts in that capacity, Barber was able to get Charles McGrath, a young man who had become a fiction editor at the *New Yorker* in January of 1976, to have a look at some of the stories Munro had written since her return home. McGrath and his colleagues in the *New Yorker* fiction department were immediately enraptured: they quickly bought "Royal Beatings" and "The Beggar Maid," publishing each during 1977. By year's end, Munro had a right-of-first-refusal contract with the *New Yorker* for 1978, a contract she has renewed each year since. There have been almost fifty Munro stories in the *New Yorker* since those first two. Given such interest, by the end of 1978 Munro also had a book contract in New York from Alfred A. Knopf, the revered publisher of fine literary work.

∂

When Alice Munro walked into a CBC studio in 1974 to talk to Harry Boyle, she was already, in Mordecai Richler's sardonic phrase, "World Famous in Canada." Her long apprenticeship as a writer concluded – her first book awarded a Governor General's prize, her second becoming a 1970s feminist *cri de coeur* – her return home to Ontario begun, though not fully accomplished, Munro had reached a critical moment as a person, as a family member, and as a writer. Having left her life in British Columbia, having returned to an Ontario recognizably the same, though much changed during her absence, Alice Munro was forty-three years old and, really, on her own for the first time. What she had been before in each guise would change, yet what she would yet become was not clear. As a result of the Boyle interview broadcast, Munro made contacts that transformed her life and her career. Moving back to Huron County to join Gerald Fremlin, Alice Munro found her material – the people, land-scape, culture, and history of her home place – the same, yet, given age, perspective, experience, and understanding, very different. And connect-ing with Douglas Gibson and Virginia Barber – each of whom saw the real potential of her fiction – Munro found a way to reach a larger audi-ence. She was still what she had always been as a writer: driven, intuitive, always uncertain about her writing, continually trying to improve it, to make it perfect. That is how she wrote. But walking into that CBC studio to talk to Huron County-born and -raised Harry Boyle in August 1974, Alice Munro took a critical step toward becoming the writer she became over the next thirty years. Writing "Home," moving back to the mysteri-ous, touchable place she had left behind in 1951, the place that she had recalled, imagined, and detailed in the intervening years from British Columbia, now confronting it anew with its surfaces and depths still there, resonant, Alice Munro had come home.

PART ONE

Everything Here Is Touchable

I

Ancestors, Parents, Home

It's the fact you cherish.
– "What Do You Want to Know For?" (1994)

Ancestors: "A Better Place Than Home"

The part of Ontario Alice Munro returned to in 1973 was one that her own ancestors had pioneered. Each side of her family – one Scots Presbyterian, the Laidlaws, the other Irish Anglican, the Chamneys – arrived in Upper Canada at the beginning of the great emigration from Britain that followed the end of the Napoleonic wars. As Munro herself has detailed in a 1997 essay entitled "Changing Places," her first ancestor, James Laidlaw (1763–1829), left Scotland for Canada in June 1818 with two of his sons, Walter and Andrew, his daughter, a grandson, and a pregnant daughter-in law, Agnes, who gave birth to a daughter not long after their ship had left Leith. The Laidlaws landed at Quebec in August and travelled upriver to York, now Toronto. Munro writes, "This family had lived in the Scottish Borders and particularly the Ettrick Valley – called in the old days the Ettrick Forest – for centuries."[1] The family remained in York for a time before taking up land grants in Halton County, about thirty miles to the west of York, in Esquesing Township near Georgetown.

Among the Laidlaw relatives left behind in Scotland was a cousin, James Hogg (1770–1835), the poet, whose mother, Margaret Laidlaw, was well known for having passed the oral traditions of the Scottish Borders on to Walter Scott. Seeing a letter from James Laidlaw written to his eldest son, Robert, from York, Hogg had it published in the March 1820 number of *Blackwood's Magazine*, along with one of his own. Hogg describes James Laidlaw as "a highly respected shepherd of this country, and as successful as most men in the same degree of life; but for a number of years bygone he talked and read about America till he grew perfectly unhappy; and, at last, when approaching his sixtieth year, actually set off to seek a temperary home and grave in the new world; but some of his sons had formed attachments at home, and refused to accompany him." Laidlaw's letter, dated York, September 9, 1819, was intended in part to entice these remaining sons, Robert and William, to North America. The father details the differences he has found between Upper Canada and Scotland, much to Canada's credit, writing of a "Mr. Macgill" who is "a very ricth man, and has befriended me more than all the farmers in Esther Ettrick or yearrow [w]ould have Dun."[2] In "Changing Places," Munro draws on her great-great-great-grandfather's letter – as published, and on Hogg's too – and on other unpublished letters in her possession from some of these relatives that have been passed down to her by her paternal grandmother, Sarah Jane "Sadie" Code Laidlaw.

In her essay Munro details the circumstances of one of the lingering Laidlaw sons, William, his wife, Mary, and their family. They did eventually emigrate to North America, but not until 1836, when they left the Scottish Highlands of Invernesshire and travelled by way of New York to Will County, Illinois. That is, William came after everyone in the family who had gone to Upper Canada years before had given up expecting him, and after his father, James, was dead. William and Mary had four sons, the youngest of whom was a newborn when the family emigrated. Thomas Laidlaw (1836–1915) proved to be Alice Munro's great-grandfather and her first direct ancestor to settle in Huron County. As Munro details in "Changing Places," the family was not long in Illinois because William, who had found work on "a canal being built" linking "Lake Michigan with the Illinois River," died of cholera on January 5, 1839. "He was forty years old. On the same day, no doubt in the same sod house, his daughter Jane was born." Mary Laidlaw appealed for help to her relatives in Upper Canada and, the next spring, she and her children were brought there by one of her husband's brothers. So they find themselves "bound to the family after all," and destined "not to become Yankees as their father must have wished."[3]

♫

Munro's essay "Changing Places" is important as an example of the parallel tracks of Alice Munro's life, Alice Munro's texts. Probably no more than most professional writers of fiction, yet nonetheless very precisely and so verifiably, Alice Munro has drawn on the factual details of her life – where she has been, whom she has known, her roots, what has happened, how things have turned out – in the fiction she has published. As she told Harry Boyle in 1974 and has freely admitted throughout her career, "There is always a starting point in reality." For Munro, those starting points are first noticed, then probed, and then sharply detailed as she intuitively articulates them. As "Changing Places," a historical essay that offers no hint of fiction, makes clear, Alice Munro is always able, often stunningly so, to take a web of human connections and, by the way her story is told, by finding *her* way into *her* material, to discover and articulate its mysteries. Concluding her text, Munro stands back and looks at what she has done with her own sense of awe at the way things are, and with her own understanding of them. This process is described well at the end of "Powers," in *Runaway*, when Nancy wishes "not so much to live in the past as to open it up and get one good look at it." Munro's method is one of taking some image or idea that interests her, asking, "How can you get your finger on it, feel that life beating?", because she wants to know "What does this mean, what can be discovered about it, what is the rest of the story?"4 So taking up "Changing Places" at the beginning of a biography of a writer of fiction who, throughout her career, has always placed herself on that very-dotted line between "fact" and "fiction" requires some initial explanation.

In 1982 Munro asked through the title of an essay, "What Is Real?" The same question might be asked of a 2002 *New Yorker* piece she published in one of its fiction issues called "Lying Under the Apple Tree." It was identified there as a memoir, but in its first paragraph there is a disclaimer (one that, though written in Munro's voice, was added by her editor at the magazine) that says "(To disguise some people and events, I have allowed myself a certain amount of invention with names and details)."5 Such distinctions indicate this writer's methods and direction because, though here writing about something that really happened, Munro imagined "names and details." They are, in other words, fiction. By tracing in the pages that follow the facts of Alice Munro's cultural inheritance and life, and by recognizing the symbiotic relationship between those facts and the texts that Munro has produced, this book looks both forward and backward, and both outside of the texts as well as inside them. When Alice Munro wrote "Changing Places," she probed the historical facts of her father's family through what was public (the Hogg-Laidlaw exchange in *Blackwood's*), through what was private (the letters she received from her grandmother), and through what she was able to deduce and shape herself (the text she produced).

In another instance, "Working for a Living," Munro published a memoir about her parents that had its beginnings as a fictional story about a protagonist very like herself, a person who left university without completing her degree. That story was finished and submitted to the *New Yorker*, where it was declined. Upon revision, it became a memoir, and was again declined by the magazine in that form. The first submission was rejected because the editors did not think it worked as a story; they passed on the memoir because the *New Yorker* had already run too many like it.[6] It was, however, published as the first piece in the inaugural issue of *Grand Street* in 1981. By reversing Munro's usual method – fiction becoming memoir rather than facts becoming fiction – "Working for a Living" shows how close the two modes in Alice Munro's writing really are – the cherished fact is never far distant. In "Changing Places," Munro takes the history of her Laidlaw ancestors as her subject. That essay, like "Working for a Living," is the exception that proves the rule.

What this close relationship suggests is that when the lives of Munro's maternal ancestors are recounted – the Chamneys, the Codes, the Stanleys – their factual stories cannot be told without reference to what Munro does with them in fictions like "The Ottawa Valley," "Chaddeleys and Flemings: 1. Connection," and "The Progress of Love." Alice Munro's own "progress" has been one of using the factual details of her own life – at each stage of being: child, adolescent, young adult, mother and wife, single person, remarried, older person – as the litmus paper of her characters' beings. She imagines their connections and wonderings, she articulates their feelings, she creates the very sense of being that all humans feel moving from birth to death. It is indeed the fact that Alice Munro cherishes, as well as the fiction. Following Munro's own pattern, this biography traces her life and career going from the fact to the fiction and back again. Autobiography is imbedded in Alice Munro's work, autobiography always resonant with fictional imaginings ("grafted on from some other reality"), and she can be seen as always "writing her lives," the lives she has both lived and imagined.7

⋙

Munro's first maternal ancestors to leave County Wicklow, Ireland for Upper Canada – John Chamney, a distant uncle of hers, and George Code (1796–1890), her dual great-great-grandfather – arrived immediately after James Laidlaw and his family, about 1820. Just how these people travelled to Canada is not as well documented as the Laidlaws' emigration, but there are possible clues in the historical detail. That same year a George Codd was listed among the Lanark Society settlers travelling aboard the *Brock*, one of the ships furnished by the British government to carry some 1,200 emigrants from Scotland via Quebec to Upper Canada. Underwritten by the Crown, these emigration movements were a response to the depression in Britain that followed the Napoleonic Wars; in North America, they were a means of settling Upper Canada with loyal citizens after the War of 1812 with the Americans. The Lanark Society focused on settling the area around the town of Perth, north of the Rideau River in what became Lanark County, Ontario.8 An area north of Perth is still called the Scotch Line and, although Munro's ancestors from Lanark were predominantly Irish, they farmed in an area known as Scotch Corners. It is loosely defined by portions of three Lanark townships – Beckwith, Drummond, and Ramsay – abutting and partially encircled by Mississippi Lake, a broad section of the Mississippi River that flows north into the Ottawa. The name Codd – one of the variant spellings, along with Coad, or Code – was common in the Scotch Corners area. The George Codd among the Lanark Society settlers may or may not have been Munro's great-great-grandfather, but there is no doubt about his early arrival in Upper Canada.

About 1820 John Chamney, following a daughter and son-in-law out from Ireland, took up land on the Twelfth Concession road of Lanark Township just north of what became Scotch Corners. Chamney – or "Chaddeley," as Munro renders the name in her dual ancestral story, "Chaddeleys and Flemings" – derives from Cholmondeley and dates back to thirteenth-century Britain. There, and throughout references to Munro's own immediate ancestors, the name is frequently rendered Chambly, as it is in her grandparents' published wedding announcement and in her mother's birth announcement. Like many of the Irish who came to Upper Canada, the Chamneys were Protestants and farmers.[9]

George Code, Munro's dual great-great-grandfather, was born in County Wicklow, Ireland, and, after emigrating, he farmed initially in Ramsay Township before moving south into Scotch Corners. In October 1826 he married Jane Morris in Perth and they went on to raise a family of twelve children, among them Ann Code (1828–1911), their second, and Thomas Code (1844–1927), their tenth. Ann Code was one of Munro's maternal great-grandmothers, Thomas one of her paternal great-grandfathers. Born in Scotch Corners, Thomas Code as a young man went off to Huron County to farm with his oldest brother, Joseph, who ultimately settled in Wingham. Thomas returned to Scotch Corners to marry and farmed there for a time but in 1885 took his family of four daughters – among them his eldest, Sarah Jane "Sadie" Code, Munro's paternal grandmother – back to Huron to settle on a farm near Blyth in Morris Township. His sister Ann had married Edward Chamney in 1847 and, after a time in Renfrew County at a place called the Scotch Bush, they farmed on the Second Concession of Ramsay just north of Scotch Corners, raising a family of four children – three sons and a daughter. George Chamney (1853–1934), the second son, was Munro's maternal grandfather.

Edward Chamney died in April 1869 and in August of 1870 his widow Ann bought the first lot on the Tenth Concession in Beckwith Township, the farm just across the road from the site of the Scotch Corners school, which was constructed there in 1871. During 1871 a national census was taken, showing the Chamneys – the forty-year-old widow Ann and her four children, Edward (21), George (17), John (15), and Rebecca (12) – on that farm. The eldest son, Edward, did not marry until his late thirties, in 1888, and his brother George followed the same pattern, marrying Bertha Ann Stanley on New Year's Day, 1891, when he was thirty-seven. Once married, both sons brought their wives to live on the farm at Scotch Corners; Edward and family eventually moved to the next farm, leaving Ann Code Chamney (who lived on as a widow, a "relic," as she's called in one of her obituaries in 1911) and George and his family on the farm on the Tenth Concession. This farm is where Annie Clarke Chamney, Munro's mother, was born in 1898, and where she grew up.

Her mother, Bertha Ann Stanley, was born in 1867 and was the eldest daughter of John McLenaghan Stanley (1841–91) and Catherine Clarke (1838–83). Of English extraction, the Stanley family was well known in the Perth area – there is a prominent landform there still referred to Stanley's Hill. Matthew Stanley (1845–1922), John's cousin and probably his business associate for a time, ran a carriage and wagon business in Perth, establishing his business in 1866 and running it for over thirty years. Although family lore credits John Stanley, Matthew constructed a special wagon to transport "The Mammoth Cheese" that eastern Ontario cheese makers sent for display to the 1893 Chicago World's Columbian Exposition. (Through the Stanleys, too, Munro is related to George F.G. Stanley, who was a noted historian of western Canada and former Lieutenant-Governor of New Brunswick.)

Some of the circumstances of John and Catherine Stanley's marriage, and of Munro's grandmother Bertha Stanley's religiosity, are the basis of "The Progress of Love" – a story in which a wife threatens to hang herself in response to her husband's wanton behaviour. Certainly some detail regarding them, and Catherine's circumstances in particular, is apt. Catherine Clarke was the daughter of James Clarke and Ann Dougherty, who moved to Wisconsin when she was a teenager, leaving her to live with her maternal grandparents, Thomas and Mary Dougherty. Her father and a brother, Thomas, subsequently drowned in Lake Michigan while fishing.

Munro has often said that a basic cultural norm in her childhood was the enmity between Protestant and Catholic inherited from Ireland – the Orange and the Green. The Orange Lodge was a presence and she refers to "King Billy's parade" in her fiction. An illustration of this legacy in her own family is found when Catherine's grandfather, Thomas Dougherty, executed a will in 1853. He left Catherine a cow. But Dougherty also left his property to his daughter Ellen "provided she shall not at any time intermarry with any person who shall be a member or adherant or any way of or to the Roman Catholic church or persuasion."[10]

Alice Munro has been wearing Catherine Clarke's wedding ring, one that her mother inherited, since she was fifteen; she also has a sampler her great-grandmother made on her wall at home in Clinton and, in her travels, has located Clarke's grave in the Anglican cemetery in Pembroke. John and Catherine married in Lanark village in 1866; Bertha Ann was born the next year and, the year after that, a second daughter, Blanche, arrived. About 1870, Stanley and his family moved to Pembroke; the 1871 census has them living in East Pembroke village.[11] While it is not clear just what Stanley initially did there, in early 1875 the local paper announces a "New carriage shop in Pembroke, Next Door to Mill's Axe Shop." The first ad is signed "M. Stanly & Co.," so it is a reasonable surmise that Matthew Stanley, who had been in this business in Perth for almost a decade, was expanding with his cousin John involved, and throughout the summer of 1875 and into the fall the *Pembroke Observer and Upper Canada Advertiser* carries an ad reading "Stanley & Co's Carriage Factory is Again in Full Blast." Weekly from the tenth to the thirty-first of December 1875, there is an ad for "J.M. Stanley & Co Carriage Manufacturers" announcing that the company has moved "to one of the largest Factories in Central Canada," where "they are now in a position to turn out work second to none in Canada, and at rates cheaper than heretofore." In her own researches, Munro has read these ads (or others like them) and commented that the copy-writing showed imagination and creativity, "a lively sort of ad written with style."[12] John M. Stanley, who had apparently taken over the company from his cousin, most certainly had these qualities; Munro thinks he passed them on to his granddaughter, Annie Clarke Chamney, her mother.

But he had other qualities, too. Just as Munro characterizes the grandfather in "The Progress of Love," John Stanley drank and was a womanizer. Within the Chamney family, Catherine was reputed to have died of a broken heart. In any case, Catherine Clarke died in Pembroke on October 12, 1883 – on her forty-fifth birthday.[13] Her daughters – Bertha, sixteen, and Blanche, fourteen – each went to live with a married aunt, each one a sister to John Stanley. Bertha went to her aunt Nancy, who was married to John Code; Blanche to her aunt Mary, who was married to George Legerwood. For his part, John Stanley left the area and remarried; he subsequently fathered two sons, the first born less than two years after Catherine Clarke's death, by his second wife, Catherine Kennedy. By July 1888 he was apparently on his own in Seattle. In a letter dated July of that year Stanley tells his sister things are not going well for him, and in response to Blanche's query that he might visit them, Stanley writes that "it is impossible under existing circumstances, there is not the least probability of my returning [or] of my ever going back." He says that his life out west "is a little rough and at many times very lonely." By May of 1891 Stanley writes to his brother-in-law, George Legerwood, of his "sickness. I did not get better [and] have been under the doctors care for very near five months – scarcely able to walk out. I am not able to attend any business." Though the doctors say he will get better, it will take a long time. He does add that he "is so used to trouble for the last Eight years, that I do not mind it so much after all." Even so, Stanley ends, "It would have been better for me if I had died when my wife died. I have had nothing but trouble from that day to this – now I do not expect anything else but trouble – circumstances often force trouble – and they have been heaped on me." Despite his hope for a recovery, none came. John Stanley died on July 2, 1891, in Providence Hospital, Seattle, and, in August, his daughter Blanche received a letter from a Seattle lawyer charged with administering his estate. At the time of his death, Stanley had a chest of tools, some clothing, a watch, and eight dollars. Additionally, he was part owner of some real estate in Jefferson County, Washington, where he had a homestead claim on which the improvements needed for clear title had not been made, and there may have been land in Oregon too.[14]

This information, based on documents previously unknown to Munro, offers specifics on her great-grandfather's history and circumstance that, had she known it, may have caused her to change the character based on him in "The Progress of Love." There, his wife dies and he remarries, goes to the States – and eventually to Seattle – but takes the younger daughter, Beryl, with him. He prospers well enough to leave each of his daughters three thousand dollars when he dies. And that money, and what it implies, is at the heart of the story, since the narrator's mother so hated her father that upon receiving the money from her inheritance in cash she burned it in the stove. In everything but this central detail "The Progress of Love," then, is derived directly from the materials of Munro's Chamney family lore and history. Fame, its narrator, is an imagined character (Munro had a great-aunt named Euphemia, this character's given name). She is a person more like Munro herself than her mother, who was in fact daughter to Bertha Ann Stanley, the person who trained as a teacher, taught, married a farmer, and was religious. Since her father, John M. Stanley, died near destitute, she had no inherited money to burn, but Bertha must have had feelings toward her father similar to those Munro creates in "The Progress of Love."

On the first day of 1891, Bertha Ann Stanley married George Chamney, a young man described in the wedding announcement as "a rising young farmer," at her uncle John Code's home in Ramsay, where she had lived after her mother's death in 1883. After completing high school, Bertha had trained as a teacher at the Renfrew model school and then, also according to the announcement, "achieved a wide and permanent reputation as a teacher in various parts of Lanark and Renfrew Counties." During 1890 Bertha taught at Davis Mills in Alice Township near Pembroke and, the year prior, had taught at the Scotch Corners school on the Ninth Concession – the school across the road from the Chamney farm. There, according to Munro, she met George Chamney. On the day of her marriage, Bertha reinscribed a scrapbook that had belonged to her mother – it read "Mrs. John M. Stanley, Pembroke, Ont 1878." Beneath her mother's inscription is written, "Mrs. George Chamney, Scotch Corners Ont Jan 1st 1891." This book is filled with clippings from newspapers and other publications of a religious nature and other clippings giving instructions on how to be a better wife and mother. Beyond the shared inscriptions it cannot be said which woman accounted for the contents, but there is no doubt as to the continuity between them. Bertha's religiosity was not extreme; "she was a woman," Munro described her, "who had kind of taken hold of religion, of an Anglican religion, but very devout. Not fundamentalist, I think more devout in an Anglican way."[15]

Bertha and George Chamney raised a family of four children on their farm in Scotch Corners, Beckwith Township, three sons – Edward (1892–1951), John (1894–1972), and Joseph (1900–70) – and a daughter, Annie Clarke (1898–1959), Munro's mother. On the edge of the Canadian Shield, the farms of Lanark were marginal operations – an Ontario agricultural assessment in 1881 reported that those in Beckwith Township "had heavy clay, sand, and gravel with some flat, rocky soil." Describing the Chamneys' situation, Munro commented that they lived on this "hardscrabble land for a long time, but they had not much to show for it. And that was fine, they respected themselves." Though Bertha trained and went out and "achieved a wide and permanent reputation as a teacher," she did not encourage her daughter on the same path. Her religiosity was in part about submission to her husband and, in turn, their daughter, Annie, was expected to submit in the same fashion as a point of pride: she was the only daughter of the family, and the only daughter lives at home until she is married. "My daughter does not have to go out and earn her living" was what was thought and sometimes said; but what this really meant, Munro has observed, is that "my daughter has to slave at unpaid labor at home."[16]

This was the situation Annie Clarke Chamney confronted as she grew up in Scotch Corners, but she had other ideas of her own. She trained as a teacher at the Ottawa Normal School on money borrowed from one of her cousins, Myrtle Chamney, also a teacher. Then she taught in Lanark before moving to Alberta to teach for several years. Returning to Ontario for two more years of teaching in Bathurst, near her home, Annie Chamney married a cousin from Morris Township, Huron County, and had children of her own. Once she had done all this, Anne Clarke Chamney Laidlaw brought her own daughters home during the war to "The Ottawa Valley." There, in the story of that title, Anne's eldest daughter, Alice Ann, remembers that visit and recreates her first recollection of the symptoms of the Parkinson's disease that would eventually imprison her mother. More than that, Munro recreates the cultural contexts of the Ottawa Valley, her mother's people, the Chamneys and the Codes: "Now I look at what I have done and it is like a series of snapshots, like the brownish snapshots with fancy borders that my parents' old camera used to take. In these snapshots [her mother's cousin, her brother, and his wife], even her children, come out clear enough. (All these people dead now except the children who have turned into decent friendly wage earners, not a criminal or as far as I know even a neurotic among them.) The problem, the only problem, is my mother."[17]

This was the last story Munro wrote, late in 1973, that was included in *Something I've Been Meaning to Tell You*. Another late story there is "Winter Wind," and she had also written "Home" in October 1973 but decided not to include it in the book. In direct and vivid ways, these three stories reveal Alice Munro rediscovering – as a mature woman and writer – the cultural legacies left her by her family in her home place. Munro's mother's presence is only the most pressing and urgent one – more distant ancestors, like the cousins in "The Ottawa Valley" or her aunt and grandmother in "Winter Wind," reveal Munro's awareness of the web of human interconnection defined by her home place. She began exploring that web in a new way in her stories when she returned and confronted them, still there, in Ontario.

ॐ

When William Laidlaw's sons – living among Andrew and Walter Laidlaw's families in Halton County – reached their young manhood years during the late 1840s, it was clear that there was no land for them there. To farm, they would need to go to a part of the province that was still opening up, where land to homestead was still available. Since the late 1820s, the Canada Company had been developing the Huron Tract – the lands stretching west from Guelph to Lake Huron at Goderich. During the 1830s, the Huron Road had been cut and made reasonably passable, although by the end of that decade most settlement in the tract was at the western end, in and around Goderich. During the 1840s settlement continued to grow. Land was available – usually in lots of fifty or one hundred acres – for a small down payment and ten years to pay the balance. In November 1851, John and Thomas Laidlaw – William and Mary's sons, twenty-one and fifteen years old respectively – and their cousin Robert B. Laidlaw, Andrew and Agnes' youngest son, who was twenty-three, set off to the Huron Tract.

Recalling this in 1907, Robert B. Laidlaw wrote that the threesome "got a box of bed-clothes and a few cooking utensils into a wagon and started from the County of Halton to try our fortunes in the wilds of Morris Township." They got as far as Stratford and thought to take the stage to Clinton (where young Thomas Laidlaw's great-granddaughter Alice Munro now lives, more than 150 years later) but "the stage had quit running, until the road froze up," so the three young men "got our axes on our shoulders and walked to Morris." They found a place to board near their land on the Ninth and Tenth Concessions and the three set about building a "shanty" on John's property. In February, Andrew brought Mary Laidlaw, John and Thomas's mother, and their sister Jane, thirteen, to live. That summer Robert went back to Halton, returning in the fall to work on his own place. James Laidlaw, William and Mary's oldest son, also came to Morris in fall 1852. During the spring of 1853, James, John, and Robert were building a shanty for a neighbour, "and as we were falling a tree, one of its branches was broken in the falling, and thrown backwards," hitting "James on the head, and killing him instantly. We had to carry his body a mile and a quarter to the nearest house," Robert B. Laidlaw continues, "and I had to convey the sad news to his wife, mother, brother and sister. It was the saddest errand of my life. I had to get help to carry the body home, as there was only a footpath through the bush, and the snow was very deep and soft. This was on April 5, 1853." A common sort of accident during the frontier period, and frequent enough in the logging business even today, James Laidlaw's death became the basis of Munro's "A Wilderness Station," itself the basis of the feature film *Edge of Madness*.[18]

As these recollections indicate, Munro is descended from some of the first pioneers of Morris Township. Thomas Laidlaw, who came to Morris as a fifteen-year-old, and initially did most of the cooking for the threesome because he was the best of them at such things, took up a hundred acres of land on the Ninth Concession just to the northeast of the village of Blyth. His land was next to his brother Robert's, adjacent to their brother John's and not too far from their cousin Robert B. Laidlaw's, the farthest east on the Ninth Concession.[19] In 1863, at the age of twenty-six, Thomas Laidlaw married Margaret Armour and they raised a family of five children. Their first, William Cole Laidlaw (1864–1938), was Munro's paternal grandfather; he was followed by four sisters.

In the two-part "Chaddeleys and Flemings," Munro takes up family material from each side of her family – in "Connection," three of the narrator's mother's cousins visit one summer; in "The Stone in the Field," the narrator wonders over the lives of her six shy and reclusive spinster aunts, who still live together on the family farm. The visiting cousins are based partially on cousins of Anne Clarke Chamney Laidlaw, some of whom were also teachers; the spinster Fleming sisters on the farm replicate William Cole Laidlaw's four sisters, two of whom married and one of whom died in infancy. Underneath "The Stone in the Field" of that story's title lies the body of a hermit, a Mr. Black, "a one-legged fellow that built a shack down in a corner of the field across the road [from the family farm], and he died there." The lot across the road from Thomas Laidlaw's farm was owned by a William Black.

In "The Stone in the Field," Munro offers the following account, in the voice of the narrator's father, of their family's emigration to Canada:

> But it's a wonder how those people had the courage once, to get them over here. They left everything. Turned their backs on everything they knew and came out here. Bad enough to face the North Atlantic, then this country that was all wilderness. The work they did, the things they went through. When your great-grandfather came to the Huron Tract he had his brother with him, and his wife and her mother, and his two little kids. Straightaway his brother was killed by a falling tree. Then the second summer his wife and her mother and the two little boys got the cholera, and the grandmother and both the children

died. So he and his wife were left alone, and they went on clear-
ing their farm and started up another family. I think the courage
got burnt out of them. Their religion did them in, and their
upbringing. How they had to toe the line. Also their pride.
Pride was what they had when they had no more gumption.

While Munro changes the actual relations and some of the chronology
here, the details are accurate – brother killed by falling tree, both children dying of illness, the parents starting over. That is what Thomas's
brother, Robert Laidlaw, and his wife, Euphemia, had to do when their
children died in the summer of 1868, as Munro details in "Changing
Places."[20] Thomas's brother Robert was always referred to as "Little
Rob" to differentiate him from their larger cousin, Robert B. And
Euphemia, Little Rob's wife, had a name that might be shortened to
"Fame" – the name of the narrator in "The Progress of Love."

  Munro's fictions will be taken up in the pages to come as she had
occasion to publish them, yet the presence of her ancestors in the writing
that has made her reputation needs to be both acknowledged and
specified. What Munro offers by her namings – by using the facts of
her families' histories to pose the human mysteries she probes in her
fiction – is persistent tribute to what her ancestors were, what they
believed, what they did. For Munro, the facts of her families' interconnected lives pose fundamental mysteries that she needed to confront,
and then probe. In her hands – as in "Changing Places," "The Stone in
the Field," or more recently, "Working for a Living" – those facts glisten,
glow, and become articulate. In a more detailed and articulate way, they
are equivalent to this passage from an obituary of her great-grandfather
Thomas Laidlaw, published when he died in September 1915:

> The late Mr. Laidlaw was born in Scotland in the year 1836
> and came with his parents in the same year to America where
> they settled in the state of Illinois. His father died three years
> later and the widow and children moved to Halton County, Ont.
> In the year 1851 he with his mother and elder brothers (all

deceased) came to Morris and settled on lots 7 and 8, Concession 9. They were the seventh family to settle in the township. Here he endured all the privations and trials of the early settler, but through energy and with that indomitable spirit that ensures success, managed to hew out a home for himself on lot north half 8 Concession 9 where he lived until 15 years ago when he retired and has lived since in Blyth. In religion the late Mr. Laidlaw was a staunch Presbyterian and in politics Liberal.[21]

After both children of Robert and Euphemia Laidlaw died during the summer of 1868, they began their family again: they had a son, James, born in 1869, who grew up and eventually became engaged to Sadie Code, Thomas and Ann Code's eldest daughter. That family moved to Morris Township in 1885, buying the farm next to Thomas Laidlaw's on the Ninth Concession. They came, according to Munro, because Thomas Code "was a notable alcoholic," and he "needed to get away from his cronies" in Scotch Corners. "He'd taken the pledge; it did seem to work except once in a while as an old man he'd get hold of a bottle. . . . The Codes," she continued, "were Irish Protestants, Anglicans from a different, livelier tradition" than the Laidlaws. Sadie Code, the oldest of the four daughters who were reputed to be the best-looking women in Morris Township, once had a horse named after her – because she was such a high-stepper at a dance. James and Sadie never married – they had what Munro called a "disastrous engagement"; she remembers James as "a fantastically handsome old man." James and Sadie "had been in love and engaged and they had a fight and very shortly after that" Sadie married William Cole Laidlaw (1864–1938), Munro's grandfather, in January 1901. In November of that year their only child, Robert Eric "Bob" Laidlaw (1901–76), was born. Munro surmises that her grandparents "probably had nothing to do with one another after that. There was a great tension in that family."[22]

Writing about her grandmother in "Working for a Living," Munro describes the Anglicanism in which Sadie Code was raised, and continues: "Her father had been a drinker, a storyteller, a convivial Irishman. When she married she wrapped herself up in her husband's

Presbyterianism, getting fiercer in it than most; she took on the propriety competition like the housework competition, with her whole heart. But not for love; not for love. For pride's sake she did it, so that nobody could say that she regretted anything, or wanted what she couldn't have." Comparing these people, Munro turns to William Cole Laidlaw and continues: "As for the father he passed no opinions, did not say whether he approved or disapproved [of what his son Robert Eric Laidlaw decided to do with his life]. He lived a life of discipline, silence, privacy." Compared to others in the Laidlaw family, his own ancestors and cousins, William "diverged a little, learned to play the violin, married the tall, temperamental Irish girl with eyes of two colors. That done, he reverted; for the rest of his life he was diligent, orderly, silent. They prospered."

More than any other relative from outside her immediate family, Sadie Code was a presence in Alice Ann Laidlaw's childhood. When she was young, when her grandparents had retired from the farm and were living on Drummond Street in Blyth, Munro would visit them, sometimes for extended periods owing to illnesses or other circumstances at home. After her grandfather died in 1938, these visitings back and forth continued regularly; they were even sometimes noted in the weekly Wingham *Advance-Times*. After her sister Maud Code Porterfield's husband, Alex, died in 1944 – when Alice was twelve – Sadie and her sister moved into a house on Leopold Street in Wingham where they lived until Sadie died in 1966, when she was almost ninety, and Maud went into the Huron View nursing home. She died there in 1976 when she was in her late nineties, after Munro had come back to Huron and had been one of her regular visitors.

These two women appear as the keepers of family secrets in "The Peace of Utrecht," Munro's first painfully autobiographical story, one she did not even want to write. There, one of the women tells the narrator that before her death her mother escaped from the hospital into the January snow ("The flight that concerns everybody"). In "Winter Wind," these women loom large to the teenaged narrator, reminding her of ancestral inheritances and connection, drawing her back from the future she imagines away from them, reminding her that "the haunts we have contracted for are not gone without," as Munro writes in "Utrecht."[23]

Anne Clarke Chamney, Robert Eric Laidlaw: "Working for a Living"

"Working for a Living," Munro's 1981 memoir, began as a short story but became a memoir. It is a touchstone text in her biography. To write about Alice Ann Laidlaw's parents, Anne Chamney and Robert Laidlaw, before they became her parents (and William George Laidlaw's and Sheila Jane Laidlaw's, too) seems to demand Munro's own words as beginning:

> When I think of my parents in the time before they became my parents, after they had made their decision but before their marriage had made it (in those days) irrevocable, they seem not only touching and helpless, marvelously deceived, but more attractive than at any later time, as if nothing was nipped or thwarted then, and life still bloomed with possibilities, as if they enjoyed all sorts of power until they bent themselves to each other.

The mystery Munro seeks to understand is brought to a particular moment: when Annie Clarke Chamney visited her cousins the Laidlaws, cousins because of the Code connection in Morris Township, her grandmother sister to Mrs. Sadie Laidlaw's father, Thomas Code, who lived on the next farm. There she met Sadie and William's son Bob, and also saw the foxes he had begun to raise for their pelts. Munro continues:

> A young woman came to visit them, a cousin on the Irish side, from Eastern Ontario. She was a school-teacher, lively, importunate, good-looking, and a couple of years older than he. She was interested in the foxes and not, as his mother thought, pretending to be interested in order to entice him. (Between his mother and the visitor there was an almost instant antipathy, though they were cousins.) The visitor came from a much

poorer home, a poorer farm, than this. She had become a school-teacher by her own desperate efforts, and the only reason she had stopped there was that school-teaching was the best thing for women that she had run across so far. She was a popular hard-working teacher, but some gifts she knew she had were not being used. These gifts had something to do with taking chances, making money. They were as out-of-place in my father's house as they had been in her own though they were the very gifts (less often mentioned than the hard work, the perseverance) that had built the country. She looked at the foxes and did not see their connection with the wilderness; she saw a new industry, the possibility of riches. She had a little money saved, to help buy a place where all this could get started. She became my mother.[24]

Annie Clarke Chamney – she became "Anne" in 1927 when she married and moved to Wingham – had been born on September 12, 1898, on George and Bertha Chamney's farm in Scotch Corners. She was the third child of four, the only daughter. She first went to school across the road from her home, in the same one-room school where her mother had taught and then, on her own initiative, she completed high school in Carleton Place. In 1916, through what Munro calls "her own desperate efforts," she borrowed the necessary money from a cousin and entered the Ottawa Normal School to train as a teacher. Even though her mother, Bertha Stanley, had also been a teacher, Annie's parents were not willing to support these studies, preferring that she remain at home rather than work away from the farm. Such attitudes were, Munro says, a combination of pride, Bertha's religiosity, and her grandmother's deference to her husband. Annie, however, had cousins who trained as teachers – Anna Myrtle, Sarah Margaret, and Rebecca Pearl, three of her uncle Edward and aunt Mary James Chamney's five daughters. Myrtle was six years older than Annie; Sarah "Sadie," four; and Pearl just a month younger. Myrtle lent Annie the money so that she and Pearl could attend the Ottawa Normal School together. They began their studies in the fall of 1916.

Established in 1875, the Ottawa Normal School had just celebrated its fortieth anniversary, and in the fall of 1916, in the middle of World War I, it enrolled 239 students, its largest class. Like most students, Annie and Pearl Chamney studied toward their provisional certification, a year-long course that ran from mid-August to late December and from early January to late June. On graduation, they were allowed to teach for four years before returning to obtain permanent certification. The Chamneys typified their times, since during the next decade almost half of the normal-school students in Ontario were "farmers' daughters, products of country elementary and high schools. No fees were charged, and the $250 to $300 expense for room and board was within reach of most farm families with ambitions for their daughters."[25] Most female students did not return for their permanent certificate, though, since they married before that had to be done. Women predominated in the teaching ranks and held special sway in rural schools; in 1918–19 – the first year Annie Chamney taught full-time – of 111 teachers in the Carleton West-Lanark East district, only three were men who, given the war, were in short supply. Just one person, a woman, had a permanent teaching certificate, which required at least two years spent teaching and another year at normal school. The year-long provisional course required coursework on the science and history of education, and school management and organization, while students took classes in literature, grammar, composition, arithmetic, science, geography, and history. They also had instruction in reading, spelling, art, singing, hygiene, "physical culture," "nature study," agriculture, "manual training," "household science," and "manners." Students were also evaluated on their practice teaching.

Annie Clark Chamney – so her name reads on her records – was a solid student at normal school. History was her best subject, but her performance was sound throughout. In January 1917, her regular evaluations ended when she fell seriously ill and had to be hospitalized, so she was forced to break off her year in order to recuperate. Once she had recovered, Chamney obtained a teaching position at the Goulburn school number eight in Ashton, Ontario, in Beckwith Township during fall 1917 at a salary of $480 a year. According to Munro, the students here "were all religious fundamentalists and quite mad at her because she wouldn't get saved." After the new year, she returned to normal school where she completed her course and was granted an Interim Second Class certificate "valid for two years." The next year, 1918–19, Annie Chamney taught at the Beckwith school number four and lived at Prospect; her salary was $600.[26]

From 1919 to 1921, Chamney taught at school number twelve on the Twelfth Concession of Lanark Township, referred to locally as James school. During that time she became engaged to Edward James but they later broke up. In the fall of 1921, she moved to Alberta to teach and was succeeded at the James school by her cousin Sadie. That fall she taught in Woodham, Alberta, and the next year in nearby Killam. There is no record of where Chamney was during 1923–24 but the next year, 1924–25, she appears to have split the year between Park Grove and Glenora, Alberta, the first a small community east of Edmonton, the second closer to the city. Of these Alberta schools, only Killam maintained a presence in the family's history since Munro wrote a cousin that Annie "taught at Killam and one other place (rode a horse to school in one of these places, got engaged and disengaged in another)." Munro also thinks that Killam may have been the only place her mother taught in a school with more than one room – the Killam school was made of stone, with four classrooms. When Munro saw her mother's picture in a local history, she recognized the last name of one of the other teachers, knowing her to be one of her mother's friends – "they called each other by their last names, a kind of independent nickname sort of thing."[27]

Annie Clarke Chamney came back east to Lanark County in the fall of 1925 to teach at Bathurst school number nine on the Sixth Concession of that township at a salary of $1,000. She boarded with a relative, William Stanley, and his family. One of Annie's students, W. Clyde Bell, as a ten- and eleven-year-old had her as his teacher during the next two years, and remembers her as "a good teacher and a pleasant person." Additionally, she had a sense of humour. Bell recalls her telling them stories from her time in Alberta and he also remembers that she had William Stanley drive her to see a picture of the men who had made the mammoth cheese that eastern Ontario cheese makers sent to the Chicago World's Fair in 1893.[28]

At some point during her time at the Bathurst school, Annie Clarke Chamney made the trip with her father to Huron County to visit her Code relatives and, near Blyth, met Robert Eric "Bob" Laidlaw. She saw the fox farm he was starting at his parents' place and, more than its very real possibilities, she saw in Bob Laidlaw the possibility of a life different from that of a farmer's wife – the life she had been born into and hoped to avoid. In Alberta Chamney had been engaged but had broken it off, and when she taught at the James school she was also engaged and also broke that engagement. Wondering over these facts, Munro thinks her mother was "unwilling perhaps to commit herself to a life she'd known women to have," the life her own mother had had as a farmer's wife. She did not commit herself until she met Bob Laidlaw.[29]

♔

Bob Laidlaw was the only child of Sadie Code and William Cole Laidlaw, born on November 2, 1901, on the farm on the Ninth Concession near Blyth that Thomas Laidlaw had cleared during the 1850s. He was born eleven months to the day after his parents' marriage and more than three years after his future wife, Annie Clarke Chamney, was born. In "Working for a Living" Munro treats each of her parents as individuals, but she has more to say there about her father. A visit to him while he was working at the Wingham foundry is key to the fictional version. She begins with an observation about the "notable" cultural "difference between people who lived on farms and people who lived in country towns and villages," so that "farmers maintained a certain proud and wary reserve that might be seen as diffidence." She makes clear that Bob Laidlaw, as a person rather than her father, best exemplifies just what she is writing about. When he was a child, Bob Laidlaw attended the country school just down the road from his family's farm and, Munro writes, when "he had gone as far as he could go" there "he wrote a set of exams called collectively, the Entrance. He was only twelve years old. The Entrance meant, literally, the Entrance to High School, and it also meant the Entrance to the world, if professions such as medicine or law or engineering, which country boys passed into at that time more easily than later. . . . He passed the Entrance and went to the Continuation School in Blyth. Continuation Schools were small high schools, without the final fifth Form, now Grade Thirteen; you would have to go to a larger town for that."

In an earlier typescript, Munro includes details later left out of the published memoir, writing that when her father attended the Continuation school, "He always walked into Blyth, to school, with two boys who were his close friends. One was from the Eighth, or Protestant, line of Morris Township; he went on to become a bank clerk and bank manager. The other was from the Seventh, or Catholic, Line; he became a priest. They both found school more difficult than he did but they stuck with it. On Saturdays, before the other two became too preoccupied with school-work, they would all spend whatever time they had left over from chores, in the bush, along Blyth Creek."[30]

As this passage implies, Laidlaw did not keep at his education beyond the Blyth Continuation school: "He did what many boys wanted to do. He began to spend more and more days in the bush." Munro's accounting for this focuses on her father's misunderstanding of a poem he learned at the Blyth school; he heard the teacher say, "Liza Graymen Ollie Minus" instead of "Lives of Great Men all remind us," a misunderstood phrase he years later repeated to his children as a joke. Munro sees this as characteristic, because her father "had been willing to give the people of the school, and in the little town, the right to have strange language, or logic; he did not ask that they made sense on his terms. He had a streak of pride posing as humility, making him scared and touchy, ready to bow out, never ask questions. . . . He made a mystery there, a hostile structure of rules and secrets, far beyond anything that really existed. He felt a danger too, of competition, of ridicule. The family wisdom came to him then. Stay out of it." Munro's memoir is itself an exercise in biography, a tribute to her parents likely occasioned by Bob Laidlaw's death in 1976 (it was written sometime during 1979 or early 1980). It traces the trajectory of his life through its various phases, beginning with his parents and ending with his time working in the Wingham foundry. An unpublished fragment, intended as an introduction, takes Laidlaw to the end of his life, when he became a writer. Throughout, Munro describes what she here calls "the family wisdom," Laidlaw's tendency to "stay out of it." Thus she writes, speaking initially of the time the young Bob Laidlaw spent along Blyth Creek:

> My father being a Huron County farm boy with the extra, Fenimore-Cooper perception, a cultivated hunger, did not turn aside from these boyish interests at the age of eighteen, nineteen, twenty. Instead of giving up the bush he took to it more steadily and seriously. He began to be talked about more as a trapper than as a young farmer, and as an odd and lonely character, though not somebody that anyone feared or disliked. He was edging away from the life of a farmer, just as he had edged away earlier from the idea of getting an education and becoming a professional man. He was edging towards a life he probably could not clearly visualize, since he would know what he didn't want so much better than what he wanted. The life in the bush, on the edge of the farms, away from the towns; how could it be managed? Even here, some men managed it.[31]

As Laidlaw was pursuing his trapline and earning money from it, Munro notes that he "never went after girls; he grew less and less sociable." This, she says, would have pleased his mother who, though disappointed that her only child had not pursued a professional career, would have thought that "at least he was not just turning into a farmer, a copy of his father." In the manuscript version of her memoir, Munro offers another omitted passage that details her father's work and his transformation:

> Muskrats he trapped in the spring, because their fur stays prime until about the end of April. All the others were at their best from the end of October on into winter. He went out on snowshoes. The white weasel didn't attain its purity until around the

tenth of December, and was going off by the end of January. He built up deadfalls, with a figure 4 trigger, set so the boards or branches fell on the muskrat or mink; he nailed weasel traps to trees. He nailed boards together to make a square box-trap working on the same principle as a deadfall (less conspicuous to other trappers). The steel traps for muskrats were staked so the animal would drown, often at the end of a sloping cedar rail. Patience and foresight and guile were necessary. For the vegetarians he set out tasty bites of apple and parsnip; for the meat-eaters, such as mink, there was delectable fish-bait mixed by himself and ripened in a jar in the ground. A similar meat-mix for foxes was buried in June or July and dug up in the fall; they sought it out not to eat but to roll upon, reveling in that pungency of decay.

Foxes interested him more and more, though they were not so easy to get. He followed them away from the creek into the bush and out into the little rough sandy hills that are sometimes to be found at the edge of the bush, between bush and pasture, useless bits of land which grew nothing but pine trees and juniper bushes. Foxes love the sandy hills at night. He learned to boil his traps in water and soft maple bark, to kill the smell of metal, to set them out in the open with a sifting of sand over them. How do you kill a trapped fox that you don't want to shoot, because of the wound to the pelt and the blood-smell left around the trap? You stun it with the blow of a long, strong, stick, then put your foot on its heart.[32]

About 1925, such experience and his growing interest in foxes led Laidlaw to begin fur farming. During this time he met a cousin, Annie Chamney, visiting with her father from eastern Ontario. Thinking about her parents' first meeting and courtship, Munro has said that when they met, her father "would have been very idealistic about women. . . . He was an only child, he had been very shy. People liked him a lot, but he still had led a very kind of solitary life. I think Mother would have seen him as someone with whom she could have had a different life than she could have had" with the two men she had been engaged to. "And she was probably right." Munro thinks her mother "saw in him a much more interesting man, because he was, and a kinder man. He was very – he was soft-hearted in some ways."

When Annie Chamney met Bob Laidlaw, their eldest daughter asserts, she really was interested in the foxes and not just Bob, despite what Mrs. Laidlaw thought. An omitted passage in the manuscript version of "Working for a Living" has Chamney thinking, "The other trapping should be forgotten, the foxes were the thing to concentrate on." During her years of teaching, Chamney had saved "a little money . . . to help buy a place where this new enterprise could get started." The two courted and became engaged; after Chamney completed her second year teaching at the Bathurst school, they were married on July 28, 1927, at St. John's Anglican church, Innisville – the Chamneys' family church in Scotch Corners. Before that, their daughter recalls, Anne made Bob promise that he would never take a drink and, as long as Anne lived, he never did.[33]

The wedding announcement, probably written by Annie Chamney, offers considerable detail. Beginning "A very pretty wedding was solemnized," it notes that "the bride entered the church, which was prettily decorated for the occasion with white hydrangeas, leaning on the arm on her father, while [the accompanist] played and the choir sang sweetly, 'The Voice That Breath'd O'er Eden.' She was charmingly gowned in white georgette painted in pastel shades over a slip of white satin with trimming of English lace with shoes and stockings to match. Her veil of white was arranged becomingly with a wreath of orange blossoms and she carried a shower bouquet of Ophelia roses, lily-of-the-valley, and maiden-hair fern, and wore the gift of the groom, a handsome green gold watch." After the wedding dinner, which was served by "four of the bride's girl friends, . . . Mr. and Mrs. Laidlaw left for a short trip by motor, amidst showers of confetti." On this honeymoon they camped at Christie Lake, southwest of Perth, and returned to a "farewell party where about eighty guests enjoyed a most delightful evening in music and dancing. The bride was the recipient of many handsome gifts which testified to the high popularity of the bride among her many friends. . . . Mr. and Mrs. Laidlaw left on Monday by

motor for their home at Wingham, Ontario where the groom is a prosperous fox rancher and fruit farmer."34

The home the new Mr. and Mrs. Laidlaw motored toward was
one, Munro wrote in "Working for a Living," that

> had an unusual location. To the east was the town, the church
> towers and the Town Hall visible when the leaves were off the
> trees, and on the mile or so between us and the main street
> there was a gradual thickening of houses, a turning of dirt paths
> into sidewalks, an appearance of street lights that got closer
> together, so that we could say that we were at the town's fur-
> thest edge, though half a mile beyond its municipal boundaries.
> But to the west there was only one farm-house to be seen, and
> that one far away, at the top of a hill almost at the mid-point
> of the western horizon. . . .
>
> The rest of the view was a wide field and river-flats sloping
> down to the great hidden curve of the river, a pattern of over-
> lapping bare and wooded hills beyond. It was very seldom that
> you got a stretch of country as empty as this, in our thickly pop-
> ulated county.

In June 1927, the Laidlaws had bought the farm for $2,300, including
a mortgage of $1,000; it was a property of just under five acres with a
barn and a brick house built on higher ground above the surrounding
flood-prone area known as Lower Town. Munro imagined her parents
as they were about to set out on their marriage, "when they came and
picked out the place where they would live for the rest of their lives, on
the banks of the Maitland River just west of Wingham, still in Huron
County but in Turnberry Township, they were driving in a car that ran
well, on a bright spring day with the roads dry, and they themselves
were kind and handsome and healthy and trusting their luck."35

Describing her parents, Munro adopts a rueful tone that reveals
her deeply felt and long-examined understanding of her parents' lives
and struggles, both as a couple and as individuals, in the years that followed their marriage and move to Wingham. In 1982 Munro wrote to

the *Globe and Mail* correcting a characterization of her father put forward in a profile of her they had just published, asserting that "my father worked so hard, through some very hard times, and he had some quite unpredictable bad luck. At the end of his life, he became a writer. He was a brave, uncomplaining, tremendously hard-working man." In similar fashion, Munro tempers her discussion of Anne Chamney Laidlaw's sales triumph at the Pine Tree Hotel in Muskoka in "Working for a Living" with a chilling sentence, one omitted from the published version: "She did not know what treachery was already underway in her own body."[36] Her mother began showing symptoms of Parkinson's disease not too long after this triumph.

Settling into their new home along the Maitland River just west of town in August 1927, Mr. and Mrs. Robert Laidlaw certainly did not know what awaited them there – no more than anyone does. Yet looking back from her vantage of fifty years, their eldest daughter, Alice Ann, continued to do what had become her hallmark – she "lifted [them] out of life and held [them] in light, suspended in that marvelous clear jelly" she has spent her "life learning how to make." It was "an act of magic, there is no getting around it; it is an act, you might say, of a special, unsparing, unsentimental love. A fine and lucky benevolence."[37] These words are especially apt, especially poignant, as they apply to Munro's parents.

Lower Town, Wingham: "Home"

Wingham is located just over twenty kilometres northeast of Blyth, where Bob Laidlaw grew up and his parents still lived. The town developed at the point of confluence of the Middle branch of the Maitland River, which flows from the south, and the North branch, which flows from the northeast. Joined at Wingham, the river continues south and west to Lake Huron. Called the Meneseteung by the Natives, the river was renamed for an early governor general, Sir Peregrine Maitland, as the Huron Tract was opened. One of two major watersheds in Huron County, the Maitland reaches Lake Huron at Goderich, adjacent to its harbour. At Wingham it encircles the town on three sides so that, as Munro describes Jubilee in "The Peace of Utrecht," the town's buildings, and especially its distinctive town hall, can be seen from a considerable distance as Wingham is approached from the south, the river flats opening the view. Lower Wingham – located in a flood plain across the river to the west and south of the town, in Turnberry Township and not a part of the town – was settled first, in 1858. Other settlers followed over the next several years, both in Lower Wingham and on the higher ground to the east, which became Wingham proper.

Initially, Lower Wingham prospered. According to one local history, by 1879 it had "the flour mill, carding factory, a saw mill, three general stores, two hotels and one school." But in the early 1870s Wingham was chosen as the junction of the Toronto, Grey, and Bruce railway with the London, Huron, and Bruce railway; this caused rapid development there, to the detriment of Lower Wingham. When Wingham was incorporated as a village in 1874, its population stood at seven hundred, and three years later it had almost tripled to two thousand. It was incorporated as a town in 1879. Initially a service and transportation centre for surrounding farms, Wingham developed several industries over its history; the Western Foundry company, where Robert Laidlaw worked after the late 1940s, was founded in 1902 to manufacture stoves; the company offered a wide array of Huron stoves, sold through the Timothy Eaton Company catalogue and other outlets, which by 1914 included some fifteen models of ranges, stoves, and furnaces. Today, the company operates as Wescast Industries. In addition, there was Gurney's glove factory, a furniture manufacturer – making hardwood chairs – called Brown's factory when Munro was growing up, and a door manufacturer called Lloyd's. CKNX radio was granted a commercial licence in 1935, "making Wingham the only town of its size in Canada at that time to have a commercial broadcasting station."[38]

While Munro has maintained for some time that her various fictional towns – Jubilee, Dalgleish, Hanratty, Logan, Carstairs, Walley – are not models of Wingham, there is no doubt that Wingham's geography, economic bases, demographics, and cultural ethos have been shaping presences in her fictional imaginings. As the Wingham

Advance-Times advertised, its Lyceum Theatre was offering weekly features when the Laidlaws arrived in August 1927. Hanna's Ladies Shop later asserted, in an ad keyed to Easter, that "Only Quality Coats Retain Their Appearance" since "Quality, like character, is pretty hard to see at first glance." A few weeks before, the King Department Store asked, "Have you planned your Spring wardrobe?" and went on to note that "there's nothing like spring to make a success of your appearance." Originally a men's clothing store, King's had become a department store by the time the Laidlaws moved to Wingham; one of its competitors then was the Walker Store, an Ontario company with several stores across the province.[39] Munro would refer to it in "Walker Brothers Cowboy," and stores similar to Wingham's occur frequently in her other stories.

Wingham evolved into a centre that in many ways encapsulates Huron County; most people were descendants of emigrants from the British Isles and, in religion, Protestants of many sects considerably outnumbered Roman Catholics. The Baptists and Methodists built churches within a few years of the arrival of the first settlers, and other Protestant groups followed suit before the Catholics built a church and installed a priest. Given this, it is not surprising that the first fraternal lodge in Wingham – with an 1856 charter that predates the town itself – was the Orange Lodge, an openly anti-Catholic organization. There is little doubt that Wingham was a place where religion was taken seriously. Not too many years ago its Baptist church identified itself on its sign out front as a "Bible Believing, Soul Saving" church. For most of its history, Wingham was dry, and it was populated mostly by people for whom virtue came from hard work, who often felt guilt, who were quick to remember a slight but would seldom recall a compliment. Such was the world Alice Munro came to know.

Lower Town (always pronounced, Munro says, "Loretown"), was another place altogether, separate as it was from Wingham proper. Although there had once been real commerce in Lower Town, by the Laidlaws' time there was only a grocery store there. On the west bank of the Maitland, in the flats area just by the confluence, Lower Town was populated by a disparate population. Munro has characterized the area there as a "kind of little ghetto where all the bootleggers and prostitutes and hangers-on lived. Those were the people I knew. It was a community of outcasts. I had that feeling about myself." This characterization of Lower Town, when quoted in a newspaper article, brought Munro considerable criticism around Wingham in 1981, yet there is no doubt that her memories, and her characterizations, are accurate. Most of the houses in Lower Town – and especially those closer to the river – were rented (owned largely by better-off people who lived in Wingham). Every year the Maitland flooded, and stories in the Wingham *Advance-Times* dealt with these annual floods in a resigned way: "The flats, of course, were completely inundated. . . . In Lower Town the agricultural grounds were completely covered, the water being about three feet deep around the building nearest the river."[40] Farther west from the area most often affected by this flooding and living in a house set on relatively higher ground, the Laidlaws were only mildly inconvenienced by these floods, since they were cut off from their most direct route to Wingham. But there can be little doubt that those who lived in Lower Town nearer the confluence, those the Laidlaws had to pass on their way to town, were just the sort of people Munro said they were, since people of greater means would not have chosen to live there.

When she spoke to Harry Boyle in 1974, Munro commented on what she called "a Canadian Gothic" aspect to life of rural southwestern Ontario throughout her own time there and still present in 1974. If one examines the *Advance-Times* literally at random during the years Munro lived in the family home, stories confirming the sorts of occurrences she has used in her stories are frequent. Some examples: "Howick Baby Scalded to Death. . . . The 18-months-old baby pulled a pail of boiling water off the table, the water spilling over his entire body, scalding him badly" (March 23, 1939). Or "Hand Nearly Severed. . . . His hand came into contact with the saw, which bit into his wrist, slicing three-quarters of the way through and severing bones, tendons and nerves" (March 23, 1939). Or "Recluse Dies" and "Lamb Born With 7 Legs and 2 Tails"; these are offered above and below "Will Be Presented to the Queen" (April 27, 1939). "George Magee Found Dead in His Barn" (December 21, 1939). And, finally, on the same page that announces the Wingham school promotions, including Alice Laidlaw's promotion to Grade 8, there is "Six-Year-Old Child Was Badly Burned" (July 1, 1943).

Such facts confirm the world the Laidlaws were moving into when they set up housekeeping along the Maitland River west of Wingham in 1927. It is the place Munro has most remembered from her years living there, from 1931 to 1949. This stretch along the Maitland by the Laidlaws' farm is a real place certainly, but more significantly it is the place that has fed Alice Munro's imagination since she began writing there during her teenage years, and she has drawn on it ever since – an "ordinary place," her own site for her imaginings, it "is sufficient, everything here touchable and mysterious." This place – Munro's own "home place" – is multifaceted, made up of a specific physical and cultural geography, the surrounding society populated by the people Munro knew, or knew of, and infused with the culture she herself came to own, embody, and understand. And the acculturation Munro experienced was one in which her ancestors – Irish Anglicans and Scots Presbyterians alike – maintained a presence through their particular histories. Her writing derives almost wholly from that "little stretch" along the Meneseteung / Maitland River, from the surrounding Lower Town, from Wingham and Huron County more generally.

"A place that ever was lived in is like a fire that never goes out," wrote Eudora Welty, one of Munro's avowed influences. Munro's home place is just such a place – one still populated by the felt presences of people named Chamney, Code, Laidlaw, and Stanley, as well as others. The place Munro has lived in for most of her life – Huron County – is emphatically "like a fire that never goes out." It is the place Alice Munro cherishes, the one from which she has fashioned her fictions, one that still burns.[41]

2

"Particularly Clear and Important to Me"
Lower Town and Wingham, 1931–1949

There are few pleasures in writing to equal that of creating your town. . . . Solitary and meshed, these lives are, buried and celebrated.
– "An Open Letter from Alice Munro" (1974)

n 1974, Alice Munro wrote "An Open Letter" for the inaugural issue of *Jubilee*, a short-lived publication from Gorrie, Ontario, a village east of Wingham. Named after Munro's own fictional town, and carrying on its cover an image of Wingham's leading civic structures – its post office and town hall – *Jubilee* was a celebration of Munro's work and the small-town ethos. She initially began using Jubilee as a town name during the 1950s and some references were included in her first book, *Dance of the Happy Shades*, but the town of that name was used most extensively as Del Jordan's home place in *Lives of Girls and Women*. When in December 1970 Munro sent the manuscript of that book to her Ryerson Press editor, Audrey Coffin, the title she gave it was *Real Life*. In her open letter, she writes: "When I was quite young I got a feeling about Wingham – the town, of course, from which Jubilee has come – which is only possible for a child and an outsider. I was an outsider; I came into town every day to go to school, but I didn't belong there. So everything seemed a bit foreign, and particularly clear and important to me. Some houses were mean and threatening, some splendid, showing many urban refinements of life. Certain store-fronts, corners, even sections of sidewalk, took on a powerful, not easily defined, significance. It is not too much to say that every block in that town has some sort of emotional atmosphere for me, and from the pressure of this atmosphere came at last the fictional place: Jubilee."

Of Munro's various unused titles, *Real Life* is her most evocative. These two words conclude the "Baptizing" section of *Lives*, where Del achieves her most powerful epiphany – her rejection of Garnet French's attempt to dominate her – encapsulating that new understanding within herself. But more broadly, *Real Life* defines the essential feeling that Munro creates within and through her fiction: that what a reader reads here is not fiction, that this is real life – these events really happened. Or, at the very least, Munro makes her reader *feel* as if they did. Alluding in her open letter to other mythic towns found in fiction – among them Sherwood Anderson's Winesburg, Ohio, Eudora Welty's Morgana, Mississippi, and Margaret Laurence's Manawaka, Manitoba – Munro asserts just what she is about in her creation of Jubilee: "There are few pleasures in writing to equal that of creating your town, exploring the pattern of it, feeling all those lives, and streets, and hidden rooms and histories, coming to light, seeing all the ceremonies and attitudes and memories in your power. Solitary and meshed, these lives are, buried and celebrated."[1]

Real Life and Munro's creation of her own town; her remembered feelings as a child in Wingham, feelings of mystery and feelings of threat; her sense of herself as an outsider, a person from Lower Town – each of these characterizations suggests the complexity of her relation with Wingham, and the inextricable connection between her own life and her fiction. From memories of being in Lower Wingham, growing up there amid its curious circumstances, smells, sights, and people, Munro fashioned fictions derived from that "real life." Alice Munro's relationship with Lower Wingham and with Wingham, set within the cultural contexts of Huron County, has been deep and continuing throughout her career.

Childhood, Lower Town School, and Family Connections

That relationship began on July 10, 1931. The next Thursday, the Wingham *Advance-Times* announced the birth: "Laidlaw – In Wingham General Hospital on Friday, July 10th, to Mr. and Mrs. R.E. Laidlaw, a daughter – Alice Ann." She was named after her mother's dearest friend, Alice Mary Thompson, from the Ottawa Valley. In the fall, the Laidlaws had their daughter christened at the United Church in Wingham. As Catherine Sheldrick Ross, Munro's first biographer, has observed, she initially "lived the life of a sheltered, cherished only child." Munro's brother, William George, was born a few months before her fifth birthday, on March 13, 1936, and their sister, Sheila Jane, arrived the year after that, on April 1. Munro recalls wondering if news of her sister's birth was her father's April Fool's joke – it seemed to her that her brother had only just turned up.[2]

Munro's first memories derive from this time as the only child, for she remembers a trip she made with her mother to Scotch Corners sometime in 1934, when she was about three. This was one of two trips the two made there when Munro was very young. When she was about a year old, George Chamney had visited the Laidlaws in Wingham, without his wife, probably because he was ill – it was the last time he saw his daughter. He died in March 1934. By then Bertha Stanley Chamney had for some time been suffering from cancer; she was gone in less than a year after her husband's death. Visiting Scotch Corners in 1934, Munro had shared a bed with her grandmother there; more precisely, she recalls being with and watching her uncle Joe Chamney feed pigs: "I remember standing – I was too small to look over the wall of the pig-pen, but I had climbed up on the boards, and I was peering over, watching my uncle feed the pigs."3

And in "Home" Munro uses another memory from about this time, one occurring in the barn in Lower Wingham, a memory that she fictionalizes as "*the setting of the first scene I can establish as a true memory in my life. There is a flight of wooden steps going up to the loft. . . .*" This passage is in italics as Munro's authorial comment on what she had written in the story proper. She continues:

> *In the scene I remember I am sitting on one of the bottom steps watching my father milk the black and white cow. That is how I can always date the scene. The black and white cow died of pneumonia in the bad winter, which was nineteen thirty-five; such an expensive loss is not hard to remember. And since in my memory I am wearing warm clothes, something like a woolen coat and leggings, and there is a lantern hanging on a nail beside the stall, it is probably the fall, late fall or early winter of that year.*
>
> *The lantern hangs on the nail. The black and white cow seems remarkably large and shiny, at least in comparison with the red cow, a very muddy red cow, her survivor, in the next stall. My father sits on a three-legged milking stool, in the cow's shadow. I can get the rhythm of the milk going into the pail, but not quite the sound: something hard and light, like hailstones. Outside the small area of the stable lit by a lantern are the shaggy walls of stored hay, cobwebs, brutal tools hanging out of reach. Outside that, the dark of these country nights which I am always now surprised to rediscover, and*

the cold which even then must have been building into the cold of
that extraordinary winter, which killed all the chestnut trees, and
*many orchards.*4

In "Home," which among other things is another meditation on
her father, Munro unites herself with him in a single image she imaginatively calls "*the setting of the first scene I can establish as a true memory*
in my life." Thus, she suggests the way her parents – father and mother
each – moved through her memory and, eventually, through her fiction.
With occasional exceptions such as "Boys and Girls" and "Walker
Brothers Cowboy," Munro has largely left her siblings out of her fictionalized memories, yet Anne and Bob Laidlaw, and the family life they
made in Wingham after their marriage in 1927, became presences to
whom Munro returned again and again.

In "Walker Brothers Cowboy," one of the three stories Munro
wrote over the winter of 1967–1968 in response to her Ryerson editor's
request for three more stories to round out *Dance of the Happy Shades*,
she offers parents probably based to some considerable degree on the
differing personalities of Bob and Anne Laidlaw. Although Ben Jordan's
circumstances in the story are largely invented, there is no doubt that
his casual demeanour with his children owes a great deal to Bob
Laidlaw. More pointedly, Munro creates in the mother a character who
closely resembles Anne Laidlaw.

Once they had settled into their new home in Lower Town, with
the fur farm established there and growing, Anne Laidlaw set about
achieving the middle-class life to which she aspired. Having been born
in self-respecting rural poverty in Scotch Corners, having through her
own "desperate efforts" moved away and become a teacher, both in
Lanark County and in Alberta, Anne Laidlaw naturally aspired toward
Wingham and away from Lower Town. Thus Munro characterizes the
narrator's mother in "Walker Brothers Cowboy" in terms that owe
much to her own experience as her mother's child: "She walks serenely
like a lady shopping, like a *lady* shopping, past the housewives in loose
beltless dresses torn under the arms. With me her creation, wretched
curls and flaunting hair bow, scrubbed knees and white socks – all I do

not want to be." Recalling her years as the only child, Munro has said she was "the object of my mother's care in a role" that her brother and sister were not. "And her care was in shaping a person. Not the person that I wanted to be. I think that was always the conflict between us. . . . She wanted me to be smart, but a good person and the kind of person who was both socially and intellectually successful and was nice."[5]

Heading from their house to Wingham, or even to the grocery in Lower Wingham, the two would have had a walk of about a kilometre, past most of Lower Town's houses, which were more numerous closer to the river and the bridge to town. The grocery, then called the Lower Town Store, was located by the river and near the Turnberry agricultural grounds. "Uptown" Wingham – the area along Josephine Street where most of its stores were – was about twice as far from the Laidlaws'. Once Munro started school, this was the same route she walked to school and back, first to the Lower Town School by the store and the river and then, after two years there, across the bridge to Wingham to first its public and then its high school.

The Laidlaws' house was built in the 1870s when Lower Wingham and Wingham were still competing as local centres. It is made of brick and is still occupied now, over 130 years later. When the Laidlaws lived there it had two bedrooms upstairs, the stairs running up between the walls from a landing two steps up from the dining room; the dining room was on the house's north side, the living room on the south, to the right as you approached the front door. Behind the living and dining rooms was the kitchen. There was no indoor plumbing until the mid-1940s, when a bathroom was added upstairs.

The farm itself was something of an island, set off by itself between the end of the Lower Town road and the river. The road was north of the house; to the east was a large open field; to the south was the river, a river flat, and a high bank above; to the west, the direction in which the house faces, was "such a wonderful view of the landscape." Munro has said, "You saw the hills. Some were treed, some were bare, and you couldn't see another building except Roly Grain's farmhouse," off in the distance. To the south of the house was a barn, "toward the river, but the way the river is there's a river flat – this was because there was a spillway and then there's the bank of the river, which is quite pronounced." Between the barn and river, the fox pens were built on the ridge running parallel to the river, behind them a sharp drop of about thirty metres down to the river flat, and "all that land down there was pasture for whatever horses we were keeping and the cow." The fox pens were quite extensive, housing upwards of two hundred animals at various times, a world to itself with its own sounds and smells.[6] The closest neighbours were the Cruikshanks, who lived across the Lower Town road, now called Turnberry Street.

Once Anne and Bob Laidlaw took possession in 1927, they set about making it their own, working toward the prosperity asserted in their wedding announcement. Bob built the fox pens. He planted walnut trees between the house and the barn ("the walnuts drop, the muskrats swim in the creek"), and pine trees to the west as a windbreak – "Dad planted it and it's in the old pictures when they were just new and I'm a baby, so I think they were planted the same year I was born." They cultivated a vegetable garden between the house and the road and, in the field to the east, they grew hay: "We had to have hay for the animals." Inside, Bob Laidlaw built the fireplace in the living room and, for her part, Anne painted the floors and, Munro has said, even painted the linoleum to look like a rug, which they could not afford.[7] Remembering this house, or one very much like it, in "Home," Munro writes:

> Now that I am living a hundred miles away I come home every two months or so. Before that, for a long time, throughout my marriage, I lived thousands of miles away and would go without seeing this house for years at a time. I thought of it as a place I might never see again. I was greatly moved by the memory of it. I would walk through its rooms in my mind. All the rooms are small, and as usual in farmhouses, they are not designed to take advantage of the out-of-doors, but if possible to ignore it. People who worked in the fields all day may have sensibly decided that at other times they did not want to look at them.

> In my mind, then I could see the kitchen ceiling made of narrow, smoke-stained, tongue-and-groove boards, and the frame of one of the kitchen windows gnawed by a dog that had been shut in all night, before my time. The wallpaper in the front rooms was palely splotched by a leaky chimney. The floors were of wide boards which my mother painted green or brown or yellow every spring; the middle was a square of linoleum, tacks and a tin strip holding it down.

Summing up, Munro calls it "a poor man's house, always, with the stairs going up between the walls" – that is, built in the simplest way. "A house where people have lived close to the bone for a hundred years."[8]

Along with her first memories, Munro made one of her earliest friends when she was three: Mary Ross, who was just about the same age. Her father, Dr. George Ross, was one of Wingham's three dentists. She lived in town and the two mothers got Alice and Mary together to play, both at Mary's house and at Alice's. Ross remembers going to the Laidlaws' home and finding it a delight – with the land, the fox pens, and the river, there were lots of attractions to explore. For her part, Alice Ann, a name Ross still uses, delighted in the sidewalks in the town since she could ride a tricycle on them, something she could not do at home. Even when she was very young, Ross recalls, Munro could recite from memory successive verses of the traditional folk song "Barbara Allen," and she sees this as evidence of Anne Laidlaw's frequent reading to her daughter. Because Munro began her schooling at the Lower Town school, the two were not in classes together until Grade 4, after each had skipped a grade; once Munro had moved to the Wingham school, though, they went all through school together and when they were in high school, they were the top two students. In 1948, Alice and Mary shared a scholarship for middle-school French. Throughout their years together, Mary Ross was the only other Wingham student to do as well as Munro, and sometimes scored slightly better. Remembering their early connection and Alice's move from the Lower Town school to the Wingham school, Ross has said that "Mrs. Laidlaw wanted the best education possible for her children," and so "decided to send them uptown where she felt, rightly or wrongly, there were more opportunities."9

For the first two years of school, 1937 to 1939, Munro attended the Lower Town school – she completed Grades 1 and 3 there, skipping Grade 2 – "I still have trouble with subtraction," she says today. Originally the first Baptist church dating from the 1860s, the Lower Town school was, in youthful microcosm, a reflection of Lower Wingham itself. About fifty children were pupils there. The geography of West Hanratty in *Who Do You Think You Are?* – the school "which was not very far" from Flo's store – reflects that of Lower Wingham and, as Munro has frequently said, the details of the school in "Privilege" in that book come from her time at the Lower Town school: "The school . . . is the school I went to. It's the most autobiographical thing in the book. One of the more autobiographical things I have written. But that's exactly how it was."

Munro has also said that in Lower Town "there was always a great sense of adventure, mainly because there were so many fights. Life was fairly dangerous." She was herself subject to the violence, once being beaten by other kids who whacked her with shingles. And at the school, as in the area more generally, Munro writes, "religion . . . came out mostly in fights. People were Catholics or fundamentalist Protestants, honor-bound to molest each other. Many of the Protestants had been – or their families had been – Anglicans, Presbyterians. But they had got too poor to show up at these churches, so had veered off to the Salvation Army, the Pentecostals. Others had been total heathens until they were saved. Some were heathens yet, but Protestant in fights."10

As an adult Munro may speak of such happenings as "adventure," and as an artist can recall them so as to create particular effects – that last sentence is a good example of her humour, which bubbles under so much of her writing. Yet there is no question but that Munro's two years at the Lower Town school were extremely difficult for a shy, sensitive child who had been sheltered at home and who had had her parents to herself until the year before she started school. Munro has called her time at the Lower Town school "a tumultuous two years," saying further that she cannot "remember a single class or book from those years." Both socially and scholastically ambitious for her daughter, Anne Laidlaw saw to it that beginning with the fall of 1939, when Alice would be in Grade 4, she would attend school in Wingham. Munro recalls herself at school – both at Lower Town and in Wingham – as "just kind of a weird kid . . . being so nervous and so frightened, having no self-confidence." At the same time, she remembers herself as having "a lot of lofty superiority." Such feelings no doubt came from Munro's vivid imagination and, once she had begun writing in her early adolescence, from her construction of imaginary worlds, but they also connected to her sense of separateness, a sense that was amplified by the move to the Wingham school. Not living in Wingham, walking just under three kilometres each way back and forth from home, Munro had ample reason to feel herself an outsider and to define herself as one. And by the time she entered high school in 1944, her mother's Parkinson's disease (though the family did not then know what her illness was) had begun to assert its symptoms. Needed to look after things at home, Munro often stayed home from school, though her performance did not slip. "I was happier at home because I could think my thoughts," she recalled.[11]

The onset of Anne Chamney Laidlaw's disease about 1943 was the harbinger of changes within the Laidlaw family. Notably, they suffered a significant decline in their economic circumstances brought on by the drop in fur prices during the last years of the war. And given the presence of a mother in the throes of illness in Munro's writing, it is important to see Mrs. Laidlaw both before and after the disease gripped her. After the Laidlaws came to Lower Wingham, they settled in and the family grew – Alice was born in 1931, there was a miscarriage when she was about two, the other children came in 1936 and 1937. During this time, Anne Chamney Laidlaw was very much the same person who had striven to achieve an occupation for herself. While Munro describes her father as a "*wonderful* fitter-inner" who had "almost a different vocabulary for outside and inside the house," her mother asserted her difference from her Lower Town neighbours and didn't care about the consequences: "She deliberately used her correct school-teacher grammar, which set her speech apart from the rural accents of Huron county. She joined the

Book-of-the-Month Club, and acquired a set of good dishes and some pieces of antique furniture." When Anne became ill, Munro later wrote in a fragment, "this trouble was so rare as to seem my mother's own special property. There was a feeling in our family, which we never put into words, that she had somehow chosen her own affliction, that she had done this on purpose. My grandmother, talking about my mother once in some other connection, said, 'She never minded being the center of the stage.' My grandmother said this in a dry and delicate voice, which pretended to be amused, but which I recognized as damning; nothing could be worse, in the opinion of my father's family, who were full of pride and a great fear of being laughed at, or singled out in any way."[12]

"'She never minded being the center of the stage.'" Much of the evidence of Anne Chamney Laidlaw's forthrightness comes out in her eldest daughter's writing and commentary, but there are other indications as well. Anne's description of her wedding, already seen, corroborates the assessment putatively offered by her mother-in-law (who had, Munro asserts, an "almost instant antipathy" toward her cousin); another piece of writing – probably by Anne Chamney Laidlaw – was her own mother's obituary ("The late Mrs. Chamney was well known for her charitable works and was dearly beloved by old and young in every walk of life"). During the summer of 1941 she went to the Pine Tree Hotel in Muskoka to sell their best furs directly to American tourists; also during that period, ads for the Laidlaw Fur Farm, almost certainly written by her, appeared in the Wingham *Advance-Times*: "We had made specially for us beautiful silver fox muffs each with fully equipped purse inclosed. For the very special gift we think these have no rivals. Laidlaw Fur Farm" (December 12, 1940). During the war, the Laidlaws donated a fur raffled off for the benefit of the Red Cross: "The Laidlaw Fur Farm is again presenting a gift of fur to the Wingham Branch of the Red Cross. This year, it is a scarf of two Canadian mink skins, and is on exhibition in King Bros. Window" (April 1, 1943). As the war ended, "The Laidlaw Fur Farm has generously donated a scholarship," a twenty-five-dollar cash prize awarded "To Pupil With Highest Entrance Standing At Wingham Entrance Centre" (May 31, 1945). All this was Anne Chamney Laidlaw's doing.[13]

Mrs. Laidlaw also participated in the Wingham Women's Institute, a group that had intellectual and educational interests. In April 1939, she presided over the elections of new officers and was herself selected as the convenor of the standing committee on Agriculture and Canadian Industries. At that same meeting, someone read a paper titled "Our Women in Parliament," someone tap danced and another person sang, and there was another presentation on the history of the Women's Institute. Munro has said that her mother "loved the work with the Institute. The only things that were really open to women were church societies, which my grandmother belonged to, the Women's Missionary Society, and the Women's Institute, which embraced all religions and was 'For God and Country' but not too much God. And Mother loved it. She did papers, she prepared papers on . . . industries and they'd be on history or anything she could do – she just loved a job like that. And they were always admired. . . . She was good at public speaking; she enjoyed it." At the same time, Mrs. Laidlaw's involvement in the institute was something her mother-in-law disapproved of – the institute, Sadie Code Laidlaw thought, "had a lot of kind of show-offy women in it. . . . They were sort of getting out and talking about things that were maybe none of their business." Her grandmother, Munro says, was a "lively but conventional woman; she didn't approve of any attempt to show off or distinguish oneself, and that's what the Institute was because they weren't raising money for a mission." By contrast, her daughter-in-law was a quite unconventional woman.[14]

Both Mary Ross and Audrey Boe, who was Munro's high school English teacher in Grades 10 and 11, recall Mrs. Laidlaw as a person who would stop people on the street when she had a question or had something on her mind. Most often, Boe said, she had some concern connected with Alice or she would call to see how Alice was doing in school. If Alice was with her mother, Boe recalls, she would stand slightly back from the conversation. Mrs. Laidlaw was given to calling Stanley Hall, the high school principal, regularly to the same purpose. An example of Anne Laidlaw's forthrightness occurred when Munro was seven years old, in her second year at the Lower Town school. A large group of Wingham schoolchildren took the train to Stratford on

June 6 to see the King and Queen pass through during their 1939 Royal Visit. The trouble was, students had to be eight in order to go, and Munro's birthday was not until the next month. Recalling this, Munro said, "I was a big, big fan of the little princesses and the King and Queen, and already knew some of the history. And I made such a fuss at home that my mother did go to bat for me and persuaded the teacher to take me along. And then I heard the teacher talking to another teacher when we were down there – saying, 'I got this one wished on me.'" Although Munro did get to go (and Gerry Fremlin, then in high school, was there too), the children did not actually see the royal couple – their train sped through the Stratford station and the King and Queen were not in evidence. "That was the first major disappointment in my life," Munro said. During the winter of 1940–41, when Alice was nine, her mother rented a house in town and lived there with her children – the arrangement in *Lives of Girls and Women* – in order to give them "a town experience." Munro still remembers that winter fondly.

In a draft of "Changes and Ceremonies" in *Lives*, Munro offered this characterization that was most certainly based on her mother:

> My mother thinks you can solve anything by writing a letter to the principal. Or going to see him. She dresses up in a big hat and walks through the school hall talking in a voice that is not so much loud as it is carrying, a ringing voice. She used to be a teacher herself. Margaret Thomas said to me, "Who does your mother think she is, a Duchess? The duchess of Jubilee." Once she called to me on the schoolground, "Come along, don't delay," and afterwards kids would imitate the way she said it, Come-along-Del-don't delay, like someone who really enjoys the sound of her own voice. All she needed to say was, "Del" if she wanted me to come.[15]

Disappointments notwithstanding, and even though she felt herself an outsider in Wingham as she attended school there, Munro's childhood was one that most would call conventional. As well as attending school, Munro participated in local activities. On the local radio station, CKNX, for example, there was a Saturday morning show for children, and Munro, along with all the other Wingham children, was on it. They sang songs, people played the piano, others tap danced – on the radio. Munro did recitations, "mostly comic poems from the *Saturday Evening Post*, from their humour page." The children were paid with vouchers, worth five cents, and Munro still remembers buying an ice cream cone with one. This "was a big deal, you didn't have ice cream cones that often." On the way home, she dropped the ice cream on the railway tracks and still remembers her anguish; "you almost will it back into the cone. You just don't think this can have happened." Munro was on the children's show several times and, when she was a bit older, appeared on *Sunday School of the Air*, a scripted program conducted by the United Church minister, Mr. Beecroft. The children would ask questions, Mr. Beecroft would explain, and the children would respond, Munro says, with lines like "That was smart of Jesus!"[16]

Such activities were usual, especially before Anne Laidlaw became ill when Munro was twelve or thirteen. Speaking again of her grandmother, Munro has said that "she didn't approve of Mother going out of the house when we were little children," but "Mother always had a maid. We had maids until I was eight or nine – we didn't have indoor plumbing but we had girls, some of them from Lower Town. . . . Had Mother been doing it all herself with no one to look after us, she would have been penned in all the time, and she had decided not to be that." As this suggests, the Laidlaws were relatively better off in the 1930s – "We were selling furs." This continued into the war.

The Laidlaws owned a car, though it was often in questionable repair. Munro now sees this as indicative of her parents' ambitions, since most people in similar economic circumstances in those days did without. In their car the Laidlaws would make an annual trip to the beach on Lake Huron at Goderich. Munro wrote a short essay for a 1983 Ontario bicentennial volume called "Going to the Lake" in which her characteristic geographical detail is readily evident; reading its first paragraphs, one can trace the route on a map of Huron County:

We start out once a summer, on a Sunday morning, probably in July, on Highway 86, which we leave at Lucknow, or Whitechurch, or even at Zetland. We zigzag south-west, to Goderich, over the back roads, "keeping our car out of the traffic." The jolting it gets on these roads is apparently less damaging to its constitution than the reckless, competitive company of its own kind.

St. Augustine. Dungannon. A village called Nile on the map but always referred to as "the Nile." Places later easily accessible, which seem buried then, in the deep country of hills not cut up for gravel, swamps not drained, narrow dirt roads and one-lane iron bridges. Trees arch across the road and sometimes scrape the car.

The day is always hot, hot enough to make the backs of your legs slick with sweat, to make you long for a drink from a farmhouse pump. There will be dust on the roadside leaves and on the tough plantains that still grow in some places between the wheel-tracks, and a jellifying heat shimmer over the fields that makes the air look as if you could scoop it up with a spoon. Then the look of the sky, to the west, seems to change, to contain a promise of the Lake. Can we really see a difference? Do we imagine it? The subject will come up for discussion – unless my mother feels too sick, or my father too worried, or we in the back seat have been put under a disheartening rule of silence, due to a fight. Even then, we cry out, when we top a certain hill, from which you can see – at last, expectedly, and yet amazingly – the Lake. No piddling pond in the rocks and pines but a grand freshwater sea, with a foreign country invisible on the other side. There all the time – unchanging. Bountiful Lake Huron that spreads a blessing on the day. Behind the farms and fences and swamp and bush and roads and highways and brick towns.

This essay continues to detail the scene at the Goderich beach, describing the remembered scene there before returning to herself and a conclusion: "I skid past" the people on the beach, "eager to separate, get as lost as I can, plunge alone in the crowded trough of risky pleasures."[17]

Like this essay, which also exists in other versions in Munro's papers at the University of Calgary, unpublished fragments reveal that she made repeated use of childhood memories, memories born of her family's doings. One begins "I spent most of the summer of 1939 with my grandparents, in Devlin, Ontario, I slept in the bedroom over the kitchen. My window faced east, and the sun woke me early in the morning, shining past the modest steeple of the Catholic church." The east-facing bedroom window of William and Sadie Laidlaw's house on Drummond Street in Blyth, not surprisingly, looks toward the Catholic church two lots away. "My grandfather was dying then, and I suppose everybody knew that, but the process was gradual and not marked by any crisis that I could see." Like the description of the family's trip to the beach, this fragment is based on Munro's childhood, for she did spend time at her grandparents' house in Blyth – they had moved there after they had sold the farm – and she was there during the summer of William Laidlaw's final illness, although that was 1938, not 1939.

About that time too – owing to her sister Sheila's illness when she was about two – Munro stayed with her aunt Maud and uncle Alex Porterfield in Marnoch, southwest of Wingham and just east of Belgrave. Having no children of their own, the Porterfields welcomed Alice just as, when Bob Laidlaw was young, they had welcomed him. This helped Anne and Bob Laidlaw and also gave young Alice a break from the Lower Town school – there were only ten children at the local school. "They had never seen anybody like me before," Munro has said. "I would organize concerts and . . . went wild with power. . . . I had wonderful fun." Munro's uncle Alex Porterfield was the clerk of East Wawanosh Township, having taken over the job from his father on his death in 1907; father and son eventually served for seventy-three consecutive years. Alex Porterfield served also as the prototype for Uncle Craig in *Lives of Girls and Women*; when he died in 1944, his funeral was the first time she had seen a dead person whom she knew. During another extended visit to Marnoch, probably in 1941, Munro remembers sitting on the Porterfields' porch "with some kind of a bull horn and yelling at cars, 'Buy Victory Bonds,' because he was the Victory

Bond salesman for the township. Of course, I'd only get about one car an hour and it would be the neighbours laughing at me." This was before she had decided to take up writing – her first ambition at the age of eight was to be a movie star.[18]

As Munro remembered her childhood visits to her grandparents' place in Blyth and to the Porterfields', she commented that her father as a boy used to stay with Maud and Alex and wrote about his experiences there along the Maitland River at Marnoch. Robert Laidlaw's memoir, "The Boyhood Summer of 1912," was published in 1974 and was one of several such pieces that appeared in a supplement to the Blyth newspaper, the *Citizen*, before he wrote his novel, *The McGregors*. Likewise, the *Advance-Times* notes visits made back and forth between Blyth and Wingham by the Laidlaw family. Sadie Code Laidlaw made a number of such visits after her husband died in 1938 and before she moved to Wingham in 1944.

Taken together, the specific details of Munro's childhood reveal connections that sustained her as both an individual and a member of a family and a community. "Connection," Munro would come to write in the first part of "Chaddeleys and Flemings," "That was what it was all about. The cousins were a show in themselves, but they also provided a connection. A connection with the real, and prodigal, and dangerous, world."[19] So it was for Alice Laidlaw herself, growing up in Lower Town, yet connected to a web of relations, immersed in the culture and being of her home place – a wide-ranging community spreading beyond Wingham.

"Writing as a Way of Surviving as Herself": The Beginnings of a Writer in Wingham

In November 1939, when Munro was eight and had just begun Grade 4 in Wingham, Lucy Maud Montgomery paid a visit and spoke at St. Andrew's Presbyterian church there. According to the *Advance-Times*, Montgomery attracted a large audience to an evening program in which she both talked about her literary career and recited "one of her beautiful poems."[20] By the time of Montgomery's visit, Munro had read *Anne of Green Gables* while, for her part, her mother had read all of Montgomery's books. Munro was unaware of this visit until she was told about it quite recently, but hearing of it she spoke of her interest in Montgomery, saying, "I think she was boxed in by the very same things that a generation later could have boxed me in – being nice and being genteel." Munro continued, "But she had a great eye, and I think *Emily of New Moon* is one of the best books in Canada. I just loved that book." She recalls that she first read the book when she was nine or ten years old and was "pleased and troubled" by it. In her afterword to the New Canadian Library edition, Munro offers a statement about writing as a way of life, one that also gains power by applying so utterly to her own circumstances:

> But what's central to the story, and may be harder to write about than sex or the confused feelings in families, is the development of a child – and a girl child at that – into a writer. Emily says, near the end of the book, that she has to write, she would write no matter what, and we have been shown not only how she learned to write, but how she discovered writing as a way of surviving as herself in the world. . . . We're there as Emily gets on with this business, as she pounces on words in uncertainty and delight, takes charge and works them over and fits them dazzlingly in place, only to be bewildered and ashamed, in half a year's time, when she reads over her splendid creation. . . .
>
> What mattered to me finally in this book, what was to matter to me in books from then on, was knowing more about life than I'd been told, and more than I can ever tell.[21]

Munro's move from the Lower Town school to the Wingham school at the beginning of Grade 4 doubled her distance from home – she now had a walk of just under three kilometres, travelling through Lower Town, across the Lower Town bridge into Wingham, and through the town to the school at the corner of East John and Frances streets across Josephine Street, Wingham's main street. "I was eight, it was quite a walk, but I liked it," she recalled. At the time, too, Munro saw herself as "different, and different in what I considered a favourable way." She had seen herself in this way before she began school, and this sense of difference developed with the change in schools.

Munro was not initially successful in the Wingham school. She was a year younger than her classmates and clumsy with her hands. "It was terribly difficult for me to learn to write with a straight pen, which we had to do then. Dip it in the ink. I would get about half a word done and it would end in a blot." While she loved some of what they were learning then, Munro did not learn the material in the prescribed way – writing it down in notes. "I kept a notoriously untidy desk, with balls of paper crumpled up and shoved into it. The notes were all written on the board, and I couldn't finish, and then when three boards were finished he would go back – this was the Grade 5 teacher – and rub off the first board and begin writing more. I wouldn't have finished it yet, and so I would just give up, putting the paper in my desk." One of her teachers called her "Uncle Wiggly" because her handwriting wiggled so. Remembering this period, Munro says she was "always in trouble, always in trouble." When she was in Grade 5, Munro got a terrible report card that she hid and considered signing herself – "Mother had to go for a conference at the school and she was upset because she wanted me to do well and she thought it was pure wilfulness that I wasn't doing well." This trouble continued as Munro took home economics and had to learn to crochet – she was not adept at either. But Grade 7 was a bit better and, in Grade 8, when Munro was twelve, she "suddenly shone, because we had a man who didn't care if you were untidy, and who recognized if you liked the stuff he was teaching," a consideration "which had never come into it before." Munro realized that her interest in her studies would be "the way in which I could actually shine."[22] So it proved to be.

Her walks to and from school were not the only walks she took. The road leading north from her family's farm – then without a name but now called West Street – was where, she says, "I always went on my walks. I loved this road." That road led up past the Cruikshanks' abandoned first house, vacant for years, a place Munro liked to visit with her girlfriends. When she was in Grade 7, "I found a book of Tennyson's poems there. One of the Cruikshanks had been a high school English teacher and there was a book." Having found it, Munro took it home. "That was so marvellous. They were all those long poems by Tennyson, like 'Enoch Arden' and 'The Princess' and *Idylls of the King*, and 'In Memoriam A. H. H.' You know how the rhythm of Tennyson goes, it was so enrapturing when you're beginning to read poetry. Oh God, I just went crazy about it. It was a true treasure. I still know lines from those poems." About the same time that Munro discovered Tennyson, she also became aware of her potential as a student. She maintains, though, that her subsequent excellence in school was not a matter of being gifted: "I absorbed history naturally because I loved it and, in English, I soared beyond all possible requirements. But at everything else, I had to work at it – I wasn't a natural."[23]

The summer before she moved to the Wingham school, while she was still seven years old, Munro read Dickens's *A Child's History of England*. It was, she asserted in a 1962 essay, "the first book I ever read. . . . When I say that this was the first book I ever read, I don't mean to give the impression that I was dipping into English history at four and a half, or anything like that. I mean it was the first real book, and also the first book I ever *read*, in the sense that I had a private vision of what I was reading about – unexpected, incommunicable, painfully exciting." She had had whooping cough and so could not pursue her usual activities: "So I swung in my swing until I got dizzy and then for no reason in particular I took the *Child's History* out of the bookcase in the front room, and sat down on the floor and started to read." Most of her essay, "Remember Roger Mortimer," traces and comments on Dickens's handling of the kings and queens of England, the intrigue surrounding them, and her understanding of just what the author was doing; but it is especially significant in the way it offers an extended image of an Ontario child, reading, within her family:

Not until I was grown up did I discover that it came there because it had been my father's, and that it had been the first book *he* had ever read, too. I was ignorant of this because nobody asked me what I was reading, and I never told anybody; reading in our family was a private activity and there was nothing particularly commendable about it. It was a pesky sort of infirmity, like hay fever, to which we might be expected to succumb; anyone who managed to stay clear of it would have been the one to be congratulated. But once the addiction was established, nobody thought of interfering with it. A couple of years later, when I had turned into the sort of child who reads walking upstairs and props a book in front of her when she does the dishes, my mother pointed me out to some visiting aunts with a fatalistic gesture – "Another Emma McClure!" Emma McClure was a relative of ours who lived somewhere deep in the country, where she had been reading day and night for thirty-five years, with no time to get married, learn the names of her nephews and nieces, or comb her hair when she came in to town. They all looked at me pessimistically, but nobody took my book away.

Munro's reading of Dickens's book, placed within what she later calls "the isolation of my home" is revelatory: it defines her own sensibility as a reader, makes another story connection with her father, and defines the family's tentative, even sceptical, view of its idiosyncratic pleasures.[24] More particularly, "Remember Roger Mortimer" shows the intellectual direction she would herself take toward history, toward imagined stories, and above all toward "a private vision" of what she "was reading about – unexpected, incommunicable, painfully exciting."

The year Munro was in Grade 7, 1942–43, eleven years old and the year she found Tennyson, was critical for her in several ways. Following this discovery, she began writing poetry and, as a parallel activity, "was always making up stories in her mind." A memory of this story-making passion is found in "Boys and Girls," where the narrator enjoys telling stories to herself after her brother Laird falls asleep in their shared upstairs bedroom:

> Now for the time that remained for me, the most perfectly private and perhaps the best time of the whole day, I arranged myself tightly under the covers and went on with one of the stories I was telling myself from night to night. These stories were about myself, when I had grown a little older; they took place in a world that was recognizably mine, yet one that presented opportunities for courage, boldness and self-sacrifice, as mine never did. I rescued people from a bombed building (it discouraged me that the real war had gone on so far away from Jubilee). I shot two rabid wolves who were menacing the schoolyard (the teachers cowered terrified at my back). I rode a fine horse spiritedly down the main street of Jubilee, acknowledging the townspeople's gratitude for some yet-to-be-worked-out piece of heroism (nobody ever rode a horse there, except King Billy in the Orangeman's Day parade).[25]

In an interview with Thomas Tausky, a University of Western Ontario professor, Munro confirmed that this passage was based on a memory, and that when she was creating such stories they were "half and half," partly imitative of things she had read and partly imaginative. These activities gradually evolved, she remembers, into a *Wuthering Heights* imitation, a piece of writing she worked on throughout high school and was continually imagining, working out its details. Looking back, she told Tausky that "in the early stuff it would be the excitement of a plot, but with the *Wuthering Heights* imitation it was the soul of the fiction I was trying to capture on my own. . . . There was some apprehension there of what fiction is. The excitement – I think Jack Hodgins said, 'I wanted to be part of the excitement.'"

Such feelings were derived from, and confirmed by, Munro's reading of *Emily of New Moon*. But more than any single, though crucial, book Munro's development came from the ongoing acts of being read to as a preliterate child and then reading for herself. Although the Laidlaws' middle-class prosperity may have been somewhat fragile, there is no question but that Munro grew up in a literate home. A childhood friend recalls attending birthday parties for Alice at the Laidlaws' at which Mrs. Laidlaw read to all the children. Former high school teacher Audrey Boe remembers Mrs. Laidlaw's deep interest in education – always wanting to know and learn more. And she recalls Bob Laidlaw as a reader, saying that she thought he "probably read every book in the library." Given this, and not surprisingly, when Munro came to write an introduction for her *Selected Stories* in 1997, she invoked and analyzed an image seen from the window of the Wingham Public Library when she was about fifteen. Writing of this scene – a man with his horses in swirling snow "carelessly revealed" – Munro describes its effect as giving her "something like a blow to the chest." Once its moment had passed, "it was more a torment than a comfort to think about" this scene, "because I couldn't get hold of it at all." By then, Munro was seeing that scene through the eyes of a developing writer – since early adolescence she knew that was what she wanted to do.

A draft of "The Albanian Virgin" offers a narrator like Munro who lives outside the town of Logan, a town that like Wingham has its library in the town hall and also a major hotel named the Brunswick. Its narrator for a long time forgoes taking books home from the library since she had been told by another child that, living outside of town as she does, getting a library card would be too complex a process. Instead, she goes to the library and reads there, mesmerized: "The books themselves, the smell of the paper and the feel of the cover with these smooth indented pictures and letters, these objects, as well as the stories contained in them, seemed to me magical. They were magical. I didn't even want to take them home." Though the librarian encourages her to get a card, the narrator refuses. "This situation lasted 'til high school, when I got so greedy for the books that I had to swallow my pride."[26]

Thus for the young Alice Munro reading and writing involved "greed," "torment," "magic," "excitement," "a blow to the chest," and above all, "the soul of the fiction." Although she dates the writing of her first real story to the Easter holidays, when she was fifteen during an enforced holiday from school caused by an operation to remove her appendix, Munro's development as a writer began much earlier.[27] It began when she was read to by her mother (and committed stanzas of "Barbara Allen" to memory), when she discovered Dickens and read Montgomery's books (and doubtless others), when she saw her parents read, when she made up stories in imitation of Zane Grey, Hans Christian Anderson, Emily Brontë, and others, and when she discovered that collection of Tennyson's poems in the Cruikshanks' house and so wrote her own poems in imitation of them. On those long walks to and from school, she was both making up stories and, as she said, "thinking my thoughts," tracing her route from Lower Town to Wingham and back again, literally and imaginatively infusing that place with what was known and imagined, or yet to be imagined, yet to be articulated: a torment, a call, a sense of direction – everything there "touchable and mysterious." Imagining lives and stories for this, her own known population.

ॐ

If Munro's year in Grade 7, 1942–43, anticipated the academic success she would later achieve, it also happened within a context of great changes in the circumstances of the Laidlaw family. The fur business had remained a tenuous undertaking; the war had adversely affected the market and there was evidence that styles were changing. During the war, such decorative frills as furs seemed unimportant; money went into other things. Bob Laidlaw had been thinking of getting out of furs altogether. At one point, early in the war, he had thought of pelting his stock and going into the army as a tradesman. As Munro details in "Working for a Living," Anne Laidlaw suggested instead that she should go to the Pine Tree Hotel in Muskoka during the summer of 1941 and sell their best furs directly to American tourists. She did so with some real success that year, but after that summer – once the Americans were in the war themselves – such tourists stopped coming.

In June 1943 an issue of the *Advance-Times* ran a story headlined "Cows Electrocuted Entering Barn." It begins: "The fact that they were wearing rubber boots probably saved Robert Laidlaw and Lloyd Cook of town from receiving a severe shock or worse."[28] In order to feed his foxes and minks, Bob Laidlaw salvaged dead animals from local farms or took old unneeded animals and kept them until they were butchered for feed (two such horses figure in "Boys and Girls"). An electrical short in a barn had killed a cow; Laidlaw and Cook, arriving to salvage the carcass, nearly met the same fate. Had that occurred, the effect on the Laidlaw family would have been catastrophic. That same summer, just as Munro's academic circumstances were improving, Anne Chamney Laidlaw took her daughters east to Scotch Corners for a visit with her relatives there. Bill, who was seven, stayed home with his father.

The Laidlaw women stayed about six weeks in the Ottawa Valley: "It was a big family visit," Munro remembers. "We visited everybody, cousins at Carleton Place. Mother thought I should see the Parliament buildings and the Chateau Laurier, so I was taken to Ottawa one day and I got sick." Munro is not sure whether this was the result of excitement or food, but she remembers spending "the whole day in the Chateau Laurier ladies' room being sick." This visit is the basis of "The Ottawa Valley," the final story in, and also the last one she wrote for, *Something I've Been Meaning to Tell You.* It draws precisely from the details of that visit. Much of what is there, Munro has said, is autobiographical – the elastic on her underpants did break and she did insist on taking a safety pin from her mother, whose slip showed as a consequence. However, its central scene, when the narrator confronts her mother about the symptoms of her illness, is imagined. Alice Munro did not do that. Nevertheless, she does offer precise detail of Anne Chamney Laidlaw's symptoms as she remembered them. At the time, "just her left forearm trembled. The hand trembled more than the arm. The thumb knocked ceaselessly against the palm. She could, however, hide it in her fingers, and she could hold the arm by stiffening it against her body." When asked "So, are you not going to get sick at all?" the mother does not answer:

"Is your arm going to stop shaking?" I pursued recklessly, stubbornly. I demanded of her now, that she turn and promise me what I needed. But she did not do it. For the first time she held out altogether against me. She went on as if she had not heard, her familiar bulk ahead of me turning strange, indifferent. She withdrew, she darkened in front of me, though all she did in fact was keep on walking along the path that she and Aunt Dodie had made when they were girls running back and forth to see each other; it was still there.[29]

Another feature of "The Ottawa Valley" is Munro's quotation from the definition of Parkinson's disease in a commonly found medical encyclopedia – she cites her source. When Anne Laidlaw started showing symptoms of "Parkinson's disease or shaking palsy," as it is described by Fishbein, the family did not know what it was; in fact, it took about three years from the onset of symptoms to get a clear diagnosis. Even then there was nothing to be done – it was incurable. This fact exacerbated an already difficult situation: at the time, the family's economic circumstances were already faltering, and they would continue to deteriorate during Munro's high school years. Bob Laidlaw's near accident in June 1943 also reveals the family's vulnerability – as Munro said to Catherine Ross when first told about the incident, one she had never known of, her father "may not have wanted us to know. If he had died, we would have been destitute." More pointedly, the onset of Anne's Parkinson's disease came just as Munro had reached puberty and was realizing her vocation as a writer. Recalling those times, Munro commented that "the lack of money and Mother's illness coming at the same time was pretty bad. But in adolescence I was very self-protected, I was ambitious and a lot of the time I was quite happy. But I ignored this. I knew it, but I didn't want to be tainted by tragedy. I didn't want to live in a tragedy."[30]

Munro describes her high school years, 1944 to 1949: "We were just very, very poor as far as cash flow went. But we had some nice furniture and we had a lot of books and we had magazines Dad brought home from the foundry. So it was always a culturally rich life." By this time they had an indoor toilet and running water too. The Laidlaws ate from their garden and they had milk; they kept a cow that Munro milked from the time she was twelve – to get out of the house – until it wandered off and drowned in the river when she was fifteen. Munro continues,

> We had eggs. But we'd heat the house with sawdust, which was the cheapest fuel you could buy. A horrible smell, but it was cheaper than wood, so we did that. I never had a boughten dress, or clothes. But then a lot of kids I went to high school with didn't have either. Many of us were in the same boat except for that thin upper crust of people, whose fathers were doctors and dentists and merchants, and they were in a different class altogether. So that was a terrible sort of time in our family, though I didn't take it too seriously at the time. Because the business failed, Dad had to go to work at the foundry job, which they had never anticipated.

Although she felt separate from the family circumstances, Munro could also see their downward direction and recognized her position as the oldest daughter.

Thinking her thoughts, imagining her stories, self-protected, walking back and forth from school, beginning her writing, Munro says she "took over the housework and I was very proud of keeping the house clean, keeping our standard of living from sinking, when Mother couldn't do it. I ironed all the clothes, I ironed everybody's pajamas . . . it amazes me now that I was so . . . but it was part of keeping our respectability – of living up to a middle-class level, that was important to me."[31] As this comment suggests, Anne Laidlaw's ambitions were not lost on her eldest daughter, who acted on them during her high school years.

After the death of her great-uncle Alex Porterfield in January 1944, her great-aunt Maud and her grandmother Sadie Laidlaw bought a house on Leopold Street in Wingham and moved there to be close to, and to help, the Laidlaw family. The two sisters became a regular part of Munro's high school years and, as she remembered them later in her writing, became figures in "The Peace of Utrecht" and "Winter Wind." The latter story offers, Munro says, her most precise characterization of the two women living in Wingham during her high school years.

"Red Dress – 1946": High School

The April 6, 1944, issue of the Wingham *Advance-Times* carried a headline reading "Capacity Crowd at School Concert," "Three Act Operetta Well Presented" over a story that describes the two performances of the annual town hall concert given by the pupils of the Wingham Public School: "A capacity house enjoyed the entertainment which seems to be better each year." The school "presented 'The Operetta,' 'The Magic Piper' . . . based on the old familiar story of 'The Pied Piper of Hamelin', where the piper comes to the rescue of the citizens of Hamelin, who are plagued with rats and with his 'Magic Pipe' takes the rats to the river where they are all drowned." The story continues and, in the way of small towns and local papers, details the production and names all the performers. Toward the end of the story, just after the listing of the clown rat and his accompanying rats are the "Town's Folk Dancers," two of whom are Mary Ross and Alice Laidlaw, then in Grade 8. When Munro came to detail this experience herself in *Lives of Girls and Women* – there the operetta is *The Pied Piper* and Del Jordan, though initially passed over, is eventually cast as a peasant dancer – she writes that "the operetta was the only thing at school, now. Just as during the war you could not imagine what people thought about, worried about, what the news was about, before the war, so now it was impossible to remember what school had been like before the excitement, the disruption and tension, of the operetta."[32]

Between 1944 and 1949, the *Advance-Times* includes regular mentions of Alice Munro's public life as a high school student in Wingham. A few months after the account of the operetta, her name is listed among those students from Wingham who had passed the high school Entrance; though students from other towns are listed there as having

passed the test with honours, no student from Wingham is so designated. In March of 1945, when Munro was in Grade 9, she is listed as
having participated in the high school's "Easter Literary." *O Canada!*
was sung, two students sang a duet entitled "Marching to the Rhythm
of the Boogie Woogie Beat," and "Alice Laidlaw then gave a reading of
'Civilization Smashes Up' by the American humorist, Ellis Parker
Butler." There were other performances, Mary Ross was a member of
the cast in a "French playlet entitled 'Pour Acheter un Chapeau,'" there
were "critics remarks" given by one of the teachers, and the "meeting
closed with the singing of *God Save the King*."[33] Remembering this,
Munro said that she "once gave a reading and nearly died of fear, my
heart was just really pounding. I was sick with nerves, and I was like
that all through my adolescence." Her reactions were such that this was
her last appearance in a literary event. Nor was she elected a society
officer. Part of this was her shyness, though her long walk home and
her responsibilities there made after-school obligations difficult for her.

Instead, Alice Laidlaw is listed in the paper as among the highest-
scoring students in the Wingham High School. Reflecting the work
ethic Munro has written about and spoken of as characteristic of the
Scots-Irish of Huron County, and an accepted journalistic practice at
the time, each student's final test grades were printed each term in the
Advance-Times. At the end of Grade 9, for instance, Munro was promoted to Grade 10 with the second-highest score, 80.7 per cent, with
Mary Ross at 84.4 per cent. They were the only students to score above
80 (June 28, 1945). The next year, they were listed along with another
student obtaining "Class I (75% and over)" ranking as they were
promoted to Grade 11 (June 27, 1946). Munro slipped slightly as the
students were promoted to Grade 12 – Ross scored over 75 per cent on
all of her subjects, Donna Henry, another good friend, was just behind
with first-class marks save a second-class in English, while Alice Laidlaw
had all firsts but for a third-class mark in algebra (June 26, 1947).
Munro regained her second-place standing as the students were passed
to Grade 13, although mathematics remained her bane – she obtained
a third-class mark in geometry along with firsts in everything else. Ross,
for her part, continued to earn all firsts (June 23, 1948).

In "Red Dress – 1946" – the year in the title biographically precise to the year Munro was in Grade 11, since its dance is on a Christmas theme – Munro draws on her high school experiences to recreate what certainly look like her own feelings of being "sick with nerves." In a long paragraph in which the narrator explains why she hates each subject she is taking, hating them because of her feelings of inadequacy or ineptitude, Munro offers characteristically funny and appalling description. The narrator hates English, for example,

> because the boys played bingo in the back of the room while the teacher, a stout, gentle girl, slightly cross-eyed, read Wordsworth at the front. She threatened them, she begged them, her face red and her voice as unreliable as mine. They offered burlesqued apologies and when she started to read again they took up rapt postures, made swooning faces, crossed their eyes, flung their hands over their hearts. Sometimes she would burst into tears, there was no help for it, she had to run out into the hall. The boys then made loud mooing noises; our hungry laughter – oh, mine too – pursued her. There was a carnival atmosphere of brutality in the room at such times, scaring weak and suspect people like me.
>
> But what was really going on in the school was not Business Practice and Science and English, there was something else that gave life its urgency and brightness. That old building, with its rock-walled clammy basements and black cloakroom and pictures of dead royalties and lost explorers, was full of the tension and excitement of sexual competition, and in this, in spite of daydreams of vast successes, I had premonitions of total defeat. Something had to happen, to keep me from that dance.

"Red Dress – 1946" begins "My mother was making me a dress." While its prime focus is on the dynamic of the dance and how the narrator navigates it, the story also treats the narrator's mother's expectations for her daughter. The mother, who is "not really a good sewer," "liked to make things. That is different." Unlike the narrator's aunt and grandmother, who were proficient in "the fine points of tailoring," the narrator's mother "started off with an inspiration, a brave and dazzling idea; from that moment on, her pleasure ran downhill." Munro then details a succession of outfits the mother had made for her daughter, variously garish, that the narrator had worn when she "was unaware of the world's opinion." One teacher – who probably chaperoned the dance on which this story is based, since she taught dancing in her physical education classes – remembers Munro in a red velvet dress very like the one described in the story. When the dance is over and the narrator has succeeded in it – even being walked home the considerable distance out from the town by a boy who bestowed a kiss "with the air of one who knew his job when he saw it" – she looks in the kitchen window of the house and sees her mother "sitting with her feet on the open oven door, drinking tea out of a cup without a saucer. She was just sitting and waiting for me to come home and tell her everything that had happened." When the narrator saw her mother there, she remembers, "with her sleepy but doggedly expectant face, I understood what a mysterious and oppressive obligation I had, to be happy, and how I had almost failed it, and would be likely to fail it, every time, and she would not know."[34] So the story ends.

"Red Dress – 1946" was first published in 1965 in the *Montrealer*, so it was written after Anne Chamney Laidlaw's death in February 1959. Mrs. Laidlaw's illness is not present in "Red Dress – 1946," yet her dressmaking abilities – such as they were, in contrast with those of Aunt Maud, who was a professional seamstress before she married, and Sadie Laidlaw – and some of her personal history are evident. Her expectations for her daughter's social success, and the daughter's "oppressive obligation" to be happy, are the quite usual ones, irrespective of traceable biographical facts. "Red Dress – 1946," really, is a mother-daughter story untouched by the effects of disease; Munro imagined her mother, as well she might wish to, without it.

Anne Chamney Laidlaw's illness and her gradual decline coloured all of her daughter's high school years. Learning of Mrs. Laidlaw's condition, the people of Wingham generally rallied with awareness and sympathy, although it was soon recognized that there was not a great deal anyone could do. A major effect of the Parkinsonism was that Anne Laidlaw gradually lost her ability to speak clearly, although her mind was fine. The doctors were not able to give her anything to help control the tremors. As the condition advanced, when Mrs. Laidlaw called people on the telephone, she had difficulty making herself understood. Still, she continued to go out; sometimes she would spend a night or two with Donna Henry's mother in town both for the company and to give Bob Laidlaw a break. To those who knew the Laidlaws, it was evident that being isolated in Lower Town away from Wingham proper was very difficult for her as an interested, active, gregarious woman. That had always been the case, but once she became sick her need for social contact became more pronounced.

For Munro, the overall social situation of her high school years seems to be accurately presented in "Red Dress – 1946." The high school in Wingham was farther east, and up a hill, from the public school – so Munro's already long walk to and from home was slightly extended. In another draft of "Changes and Ceremonies" from *Lives of Girls and Women*, this one called "I Am the Daughter of a River God," Munro details the route as she walked from Wingham to Lower Town:

> Lonnie and I walked home together, always the same way, down the hill from the High School, along two blocks of the main street, and out Victoria Street past the glove factory, the junkyard, some deteriorating houses, in one of which bad women had lived, when we were young and the war was on, but we never saw them, only the dark-green blinds and geraniums growing in their windows. We crossed the narrow silver bridge, hung like a cage over the Wawanash river. Here was the end of town, no more street-lights, and the sidewalk turned into a plain dirt path. There was a grocery-store, Agnew's, covered with haphazard signs and insubstantial looking as a cardboard box stood on end, then the Flats Road running past the old fair-grounds and the widely separated houses, small, commonplace, covered with sheets of painted tin or, since the wartime prosperity, with imitation brick, with their yards, henhouses, apple trees, small

barns and broken-down trucks. Every house we called by name, Miller's, Beggs', Castle's, and so on, and each had a look of the people who lived in them, Miller's having the tightly shut-up, evil look of a bootlegger's, and Boyd's, where two children died in accidents, one falling into the wash-water and one shot by Denny Boyd practicing with a hunting rifle, had a look of falling-apart hopelessness and carelessness turning hopelessly into disaster.

Munro's geography here traces her exact route, one she walked twice each school day for ten years, but for the one winter spent in town. She did so observing and understanding the people and conditions she saw along the way, she recognized the social differences between Wingham and Lower Town. Given such a route, and given Munro's sharp familiarity with the people she saw along the way, she came to know and understand both parts of her town. In 1994, when Peter Gzowski asked her how she could create the interior of a bootlegger's place so realistically in "Spaceships Have Landed," she replied that she had been in one before she was eighteen. She might also have said that she had been walking by one twice a day since she was eight.

During the winter Munro would sometimes be caught in town by bad weather – Wingham, close to Lake Huron, is prone to massive lake-effect snows – and would have to stay overnight there at her grandmother and aunt's house on Leopold Street or with the Beecrofts, the United Church minister and his wife. She once wrote that "the storms that come on this country are momentous productions, they bury the roads and fences, and curl drifts up to the porch eaves, and whip the bare trees around and howl across the open fields; they will rattle and blind you." During the spring, too, there would be floods, so Munro would sometimes be cut off by water, or unable to get into town because of the high water surrounding the Laidlaws' place. (The 1947 and 1948 floods when Munro was in Grades 11 and 12 remain legendary – publications that chronicle the town's history are filled with pictures of "The Flood." Munro has recalled those years: "I remember seeing people out in their boats to feed their chickens that were roosting on top of the hen house.

It was quite dramatic.") When the way home was clear, Munro always had work to do to maintain the household – when she was in high school her brother and sister were still young, so basic housework was her responsibility. Mary Ross has observed that she and their friends were aware that Alice Ann had to do things at home that they did not but that Alice Ann never talked about it, either out of embarrassment or a certain secretiveness owing to Mrs. Laidlaw's situation.

Given this, Munro did not much participate in the dances held at the high school and, on special occasions, at the Wingham Armory, where the high school held its gym classes. The circumstances detailed in "Red Dress – 1946" – everyone getting dressed up, girls going to the dance with other girls, boys with boys, the pairing up – were just as the dances were conducted then. Mary Ross remembers regularly encouraging Alice Ann to plan to stay at her house in town, to go together to the dance, but says that Munro did so only a few times.

Generally, social life among the students did not involve much dating. Munro was included in a mixed social group at the high school – though because of distance and responsibilities at home she was on its fringes – that regularly did things together: movies, skating parties, and the like. In any case, Munro was not involved in any dating during these years. When she published *Dance of the Happy Shades* her father commented to one of Munro's high school teachers that he had not been aware that she had even had a boyfriend. The story that led to his observation may well have been "Red Dress – 1946," although "An Ounce of Cure" would also qualify. Munro did have a boyfriend the summer she was sixteen, in 1947, but that was in the Ottawa Valley; she won a prize at school that gave her some money and she used it to visit her relatives in Scotch Corners. There she connected with and spent time with the hired man (really a boy a few years older) from the farm across the road from the Chamneys.

During the summer of 1948, the year Munro turned seventeen, she worked away from home as a maid for a well-to-do family that had a home in Forest Hill, in Toronto, and a cottage on an island in Georgian Bay, near Pointe au Baril. This experience occasioned her first visit to downtown Toronto, on a day off from the family's home, and inspired two stories: "Sunday Afternoon," which first appeared in the *Canadian Forum* in 1957 and subsequently in *Dance of the Happy Shades*; and "Hired Girl," which was in the *New Yorker* in 1994 and has not been reprinted.

The latter story offers the circumstances of Munro's employment, pretty much as it occurred; her employer, Mrs. Montjoy, "had picked me up at the station in Pointe au Baril and brought me to the island. I had got the job through the woman in the Pointe au Baril store, an old friend of my mother's – they had taught school together. Mrs. Montjoy had asked this woman if she knew of a country girl who would take a summer job, and the woman thought I would be about the right age, and trained to do housework." The real-life woman who had made the connection did run a store in Pointe au Baril, and she had taught at the Lower Town school; she had relatives in Wingham. In "Sunday Afternoon," Munro creates the circumstances of the home in Forest Hill. ("There was a guy who made a pass at me in the kitchen," she recalled, and also said, "It was time I found out" about such things.) In that story a cousin "took hold of" Alva, the maid, "lightly, and spent some time kissing her mouth." This leaves Alva, as the story ends, with "a tender spot, a new and still mysterious humiliation."

But in "Hired Girl," Munro quite precisely recreates her circumstances and a narrator who seems a close self-portrait. When the hired girl, Elsa, arrives on the island, named Nausicaä, Mrs. Montroy tells her that the name is from Shakespeare; knowing better, the narrator almost corrects her, but does not. She realizes her position. And at one point she comments, in a passage that certainly reflects Munro's circumstances at home in Wingham at the time,

> The work that I had to do here was nothing new for me. Like most country girls of my age, I could bake and iron, and clean an oven. This was the reason, in fact, that Mrs. Montjoy had sought out a country girl. In some ways the work was not as hard as it was at home. Nobody tracked barnyard mud into the kitchen, and there were no heavy men's clothes to wrestle through the wringer and hang on the line.

After she's worked there the summer, having learned much about her employers' lives, little of it edifying, she asks Mrs. Montjoy about the circumstances of her daughter's death, details she already well knows, just to hear the mother's account and see her manner. Even so, "I thought myself blameless, beyond judgment, in my dealings with Mrs. Montjoy. Because I was young and poor and knew about Nausicaä. I didn't have the grace or fortitude to be a servant." This story ends with Munro's recreation of herself then, in 1948, and with an affirmation of Munro's passion for reading, for words: "Reading this, I felt as if I had been rescued from my life. Words could become a burning-glass for me in those days, and no shame of my nature or condition could hold out among the flares of pleasure." Here Munro is remembering herself as she was during the summer of 1948, driven to read and to write, knowing just what she wanted to do.

During these years Munro was a presence in the young lives of the Cruikshank girls, Julie and Jane, who lived across the road and for whom she babysat with some regularity. Like the Laidlaws, the Cruikshanks also lived far out on the Lower Town Road, did not really fit in to Lower Town and so were not seen as part of that place. Julie, who would have been three or four during Munro's last years of high school, remembers Alice as "a totally exotic creature" who delighted them by telling them an ongoing serial story when she came to look after them. "I would wait with huge anticipation until my parents went out again," she recalls. Munro would ask Julie, the older of the two sisters, where she had left off before "and then she'd pick up and carry on again . . . this was a kind of never-ending story," which delighted the girls. The stories themselves, she recalls, were geared to the mind of a four-year-old, for they had princesses in them and sometimes they acted them out. (Such stories bore some resemblance, certainly, to the *Wuthering Heights*-like novel Munro was working on then.) Cruikshank, who went on to become a cultural anthropologist and a university professor, credits Munro's stories with inspiring her own academic interest in narrative.[35]

ᔓᓭ

Such considerations notwithstanding, Munro's "real life" – the phrase she used in *Lives of Girls and Women* and, altered slightly, again in "Miles City, Montana" as "real work" – was in her imagination as she developed as a writer. In "Miles City," the narrator speaks of her "real work" as "a sort of wooing of distant parts of myself" and that, most clearly, was what Alice Laidlaw was doing as she walked to and from school, as she walked north from her home past the Cruikshanks' toward their abandoned house, as she "thought her thoughts." She was always reading and making up stories, partly imagined and partly as imitation of something she had read, the *Wuthering Heights* novel real and compelling, her own version written and imagined during those years. At that time too Munro was writing poetry and even submitted poems to *Chatelaine*, the Canadian women's magazine, during 1945– 46 – mercifully, she says now, none were ever published; "they all came back," Munro has said, "and a good thing too. They were pretty bad."

The effects of this were evident to all who knew her. As Munro has said, by the time she was fourteen she was "totally serious" about her writing. The year before, she had Audrey Boe for Grade 10 English, and she had her again in Grade 11. Boe, who was from Toronto and a graduate of the University of Toronto, had come to Wingham to teach in the fall of 1943; she subsequently married a man who worked in the foundry office, stopped teaching, and raised a family in Wingham. Over the years she kept track of Munro's career and describes herself as her "first fan." Boe gave writing assignments in her classes and, once they were handed in, she would read the best ones to the class. Munro's were always read and they were always singular. Even though she wrote about "the normal things of everyday," Mary Ross remembers, they were quite different from, and far more accomplished than, what other students wrote. They were of a different level altogether, making a commonplace subject interesting. As Munro herself said, as a student of English she "soared beyond all possible requirements." The other students saw this quality in her; indeed, when Mary Ross came to write her "Prophet's Address" detailing future expectations for her classmates, she envisioned Alice Laidlaw as a successful writer: "Her greatest short, short novel which had swept her to fame in '53 was 'Parkwater's Passionate

Pair'" and she now ensures the success of a magazine called "Candid Confessions." (Her name on its cover was spelled "Alys," Munro's preferred spelling then.) For their part, many of Wingham's adults also saw Alice's potential. Ross describes her father as being particularly sympathetic to Alice since he recognized what a struggle these years had been for her – her family's economic circumstances, the distance from town, Mrs. Laidlaw's illness, and Munro's additional household responsibilities. The Beecrofts, Ross remembers, were of the same mind.[36]

Audrey Boe recalls approaching Munro when she was alone in her Grade 11 classroom and telling her she must find a way to go to university. Others had done the same thing, so by the time she had reached her final high school years Munro knew about scholarships and was aiming at them. At the time, only a very small percentage of graduating students (and few girls) went to university, but Munro's academic achievements clearly marked her, despite her family's economic circumstances, as one for whom university was quite possible. There was no question of the family's financial support – Bob Laidlaw was unable to provide any and, although Aunt Maud and Sadie Laidlaw might have helped, it was understood that they would eventually help Alice's brother Bill as "the academic star of the family." They did understand Alice's going, though, and did not disapprove. They did worry that Alice, who had never had a boyfriend, so far as they knew, would never marry. The general view expressed then was that a young girl would be on her own (or on her way to getting married) once she was eighteen.

So Munro decided on a plan – the same plan pursued by Del Jordan in *Lives of Girls and Women* – for obtaining scholarships that would take her to university. She hoped she would get into the University of Western Ontario, in London. "These were competitive scholarships, so you had to get the best in a certain category." Midway through Grade 12, Munro began studying German; it was not offered at her school but the French teacher – Miss MacGregor – agreed to stay after school to tutor her. "I had started it because I could look ahead – I knew what the categories for scholarships were," and "if I didn't take three languages other than English, I would have to take a math and I knew I couldn't get scholarship marks on that. My math teacher agreed."

Thus as she completed Grade 13, Munro wrote the provincial exams in eleven subjects – composition and literature papers in English, French, German, and Latin plus Botany, History, and Zoology. She obtained first-class marks in all these papers save German authors and German composition, in which she obtained seconds. "I really wasn't up on it enough to get a first," Munro recalls, but writing the German exams saved her from mathematics. Along with ten other students who had "obtained standing in eight or more subjects," Munro earned "the Honor Graduation Diploma"; as the highest-scoring student, she was named valedictorian of her class.37

Even so, after she took these tests Munro was worried about the outcome. For purposes of scholarships at the University of Western Ontario, a student had to specify the papers she wished to be judged on. Munro had indicated English, French, Latin, and History. She knew she had missed a question on the French literature paper, and she felt certain that this lapse would keep her from obtaining the needed scholarship. She was so concerned, in fact, that she "started reading the *Globe and Mail* for ads for teachers. . . . At the time, teachers were scarce enough that the little far-off country schools and even schools [in Huron County] would accept a Grade 13 graduate without any training to be a teacher at all. They specified Catholic or Protestant, and that was that. Being a Protestant with Grade 13, I got a school in Oxdrift, Ontario" – in the northwest part of the province near Dryden, a very long way away. She was to be paid $1,100, much of it held back until the year was completed. "I had the contract on the dining room table ready to sign when I heard from Western that I had the scholarship."

The *Advance-Times* detailed the awards Munro received, as well as her exam results, and it did so with some evident civic pride:

> Congratulations to Miss Alice Laidlaw, who has been awarded a University of Western Ontario Scholarship for the highest standing in six Grade XIII papers including English, History, French and one other paper. This scholarship has a value of $50 cash with tuition of $125 a year for two years or

a total value of $300. She also qualified for the school scholar-
ship of tuition up to $125 a year for two years ($250 value) for
obtaining an average of 75% on eight Grade XIII papers. Alice
ranked first in English of all students applying for the University
of Western Ontario. She has been awarded a Dominion-
Provincial Bursary with a value of $400 per year. In eleven
papers of Grade XIII Alice obtained nine firsts and two seconds.
We wish her every success in the course in Journalism at the
University of Western Ontario.

Accepting all this – and while they amounted to an impressive net
amount, these awards ensured only two years' study for a hardscrabble
scholarship student – Alice Ann Laidlaw went off to university in
London. In December, during the first Christmas holiday, she and her
classmates who had also gone off – Mary Ross, for instance, was attending the University of Toronto – returned home for their high school commencement. As valedictorian, Alice Laidlaw gave another speech, this
one a fit conclusion to her academic successes in Wingham, though
beyond its delivery the *Advance-Times* reports nothing of what she said.
Munro recalls that she wore a dark blue taffeta dress that she had bought
by selling her blood, and that she said "the usual things," though she also
said that "high school wasn't the greatest time in your life." She was not
nervous since she had been to university in London – she was already out
of Wingham, and its standards didn't matter so much any more. The
commencement was a two-evening affair in the town hall; in addition to
the handing out of diplomas and the acknowledgement of scholarships
and awards, it included a student production of *Pride and Prejudice*, the
play Munro later used in "An Ounce of Cure." Listing Alice Laidlaw's
scholarships takes up most of the scholarship report in the paper, and she
is followed by the person who won the Laidlaw Fur Farm Scholarship for
the highest score on the Entrance examination.[38]

Years later when Munro had returned home to Huron County to
live, she drew on memories of returning to Wingham from university
in London in the draft fictional version of "Working for Living." In this

case, Jubilee had become Dalgleish, and Munro's protagonist Janet thinks of the town she has just returned to – "where she was known" – as it contrasts with the university city and the life of a college student she has just left:

> The waste, the frivolity, the shamefulness of that life seemed clear to her, particularly as she looked out at the ploughed fields, the golden stubble, the red and yellow woods, the dipping and sunny and nostalgic landscape that had replaced the city street. She was going to be a writer, very soon.
>
> In order not to lose more of this feeling, she did not go into her house but set her books and suitcase and coat inside the porch door. The kitchen beyond was dark, the lights had not been turned on anywhere, which meant that her mother was probably asleep. Her mother slept odd hours, and was often most wakeful in the middle of the night[.] Her sickness had removed her from the ordinary course of life.

"She was going to be a writer, very soon." Alice Ann Laidlaw had set off to London to begin university in the usual way, even though, she knew then, her real intention was to be a writer like her character. Janet comes home from university knowing that her real focus is on the place she came from, the place that she would write about to become the writer she sought to be. Just as Alice Munro was to do.

After she describes in "An Open Letter" the feeling she had for Wingham when she was a child, Munro finds an illustration, a correlative, for that feeling in another piece of art, writing,

> There is a painting by Edward Hopper that says much better what I am trying to say here. A barber-shop, not yet open; the clock says seven and it must be seven in the morning, yes, a cool light, fresh morning light of a hot summer day. Beside the barber-shop a summer-heavy darkness of trees. The plain white slight shabby barber-shop, so commonplace and familiar; yet

everything about it, in the mild light, is full of a distant, murmuring, almost tender foreboding, full of mystery like the looming trees.

So in the fall of 1949 Alice Laidlaw left Lower Town, left Wingham, left the only home place she had known, for London and the University of Western Ontario. Apart from visits over the years, she has never come back to stay, though she has lived nearby since 1975. Alice Munro was nevertheless destined ever and always to return in her imagination to Wingham, to her home place, a place "full of mystery like the looming trees."[39] She has probed its mysteries, perpetually recreating her town and its people – "Solitary and meshed, these lives are buried and celebrated" – in the stories she has written and continues to produce.

PART TWO

Becoming Alice Munro

3

"My Name Now Is Alice Munro, and I Am Living in Vancouver"

Friendship, Loveship, Courtship, Marriage, Family, 1949–1960

Helen had won a scholarship and gone off to university, and at the end of two years, to her own bewilderment, she was married, and going to live in Vancouver.

– "Places at Home" ("The Peace of Utrecht")

Although the notice of Munro's scholarships in the *Advance-Times* makes her situation sound quite positive, and these awards certainly allowed her to move away from Wingham, her university scholarship support was in fact barely enough for subsistence. Once she got to London, Munro worked at two library jobs and, for extra money, sold her blood for fifteen dollars a pint. During these two years, getting enough to eat was a problem – one classmate said she thought Alice subsisted on "apples and iron pills" and her father wondered how she managed to live. But apart from what her scholarships allowed day to day, they confined Munro more significantly by their extent: they covered only those two years of a four-year program. So when she quit university and married James Munro in 1951 after completing just two years, as she told Thomas Tausky, "it wasn't that I opted out of university. It was that I had a two-year scholarship and couldn't go on. There was no money."

But in another way, Munro *had* opted out of university. By the time she left Western to marry, Munro had moved beyond the gratification brought by academic success. While she was at Western, her writing "was getting so much in the way" of her academic work, she recalls, "that's all I wanted." During her two years at university, Munro spent about half her time writing and the rest looking after her classes, working at both the public and the university libraries and, in a way she had not done before, having a social life. She also made two contacts – with James Munro and, much more distantly, with Gerald Fremlin – that would prove to shape the trajectory of her life. The April 1950 issue of *Folio*, Western's undergraduate literary magazine, included Munro's first published story, "The Dimensions of a Shadow." It was followed there by Fremlin's story, "An Ear to a Knot Hole." A senior, Fremlin had contributed poems, both comic and serious, to every issue of *Folio* but one since spring 1947, and the issue in which his story followed Munro's also featured two of his poems. Given this presence in *Folio*, Alice Laidlaw thought during her first year to bring her initial submission to the magazine to Fremlin directly. She hoped, as she has said, that he would immediately fall for her. He did not. Instead, he sent her down the hall to the actual editor, who eventually accepted her story for publication.

The contributor's note in that issue of *Folio* refers to Munro as an "eighteen-year-old freshette, whose story in this issue is her first published material. Graduate of Wingham High School. Overly modest about her talents, but hopes to write the Great Canadian Novel some day." As with Mary Ross's "Prophet's Address" in Wingham, this note confirms Munro's very clear, and very serious, commitment to her writing. Even during Munro's first year at Western, people who knew the magazine were talking about Alice Laidlaw as *Folio*'s "find." Such was her evident potential.[1]

Folio published two more stories by Alice Laidlaw during her time at university, but by the spring of 1951 she was in correspondence with Robert Weaver at the CBC about her submissions to a radio program called *Canadian Short Stories*. In May he wrote to her requesting revisions to a story called "The Strangers" and, once she had made them, he bought the story for fifty dollars. Initially slated for broadcast on June 1, the story was preempted by the release that day of the Massey Commission report on National Development in the Arts, Letters and Sciences – an ironic coincidence given Munro's subsequent reputation. "The Strangers" was ultimately broadcast on October 5 during the first broadcast of the fall schedule. Weaver, who championed Canadian writing and Canadian writers through the CBC from the late 1940s on, and through the *Tamarack Review* from the 1950s through the 1980s, was to be among *the* critical people in Alice Munro's career, the one person she knew from the larger world of writing who helped to sustain her through her first two decades of serious writing. During the 1950s, Munro submitted fourteen stories to Weaver, some accepted and broadcast, others rejected. Throughout, he encouraged, helped, supported, and made suggestions. With Weaver's encouragement, Munro started sending her stories to magazines. The first story she sold for publication appeared in the Canadian magazine *Mayfair* in November 1953; it was followed during the decade by contributions to the *Canadian Forum*, *Queen's Quarterly*, *Chatelaine* (which had rejected

Munro's submitted poems during her teenage years) and, in its second issue, the *Tamarack Review*.

During the spring of 1952 when Weaver was about to broadcast the second story he had bought from Laidlaw – "The Liberation" – he received a letter from the author. Then living at 1316 Arbutus Street, Vancouver, she writes, "I don't like to bother you about this, but I wonder if it would be too much trouble to give my new name and address when the author's name is mentioned. I have been married since the story's acceptance; my name now is Alice Munro, and I am living in Vancouver." When the story was broadcast on June 13, however, Munro was still identified as "Alice Laidlaw" "of London Ontario."[2] She was, of course and a bit perversely, both persons – for, though she had left Wingham and London and Ontario and would only visit there during the next twenty years, she was still and would continue to be "from" Ontario. In ways she most probably did not intend when she wrote to Robert Weaver in May of 1952, her name really *was* "Alice Munro" – she was living in Vancouver, imagining Ontario.

"The Twin Choices of My Life": University of Western Ontario, 1949–1951

Founded in 1878, the University of Western Ontario served in 1949 as the regional university in southwestern Ontario just as, in the east, Queen's University fulfilled a similar role for that part of the province. The University of Toronto, by contrast, liked to cast itself as the provincial institution and also, in many ways, the national university. When Munro arrived in London in the fall of 1949, Western enrolled over four thousand students in all of its programs and associated colleges; about half that number would have been undergraduates in the university itself. At the time, Western was reaching the end of a post-war influx of veterans that had taxed its capacities; during 1946–47, for example, veterans made up just under half of Western's students. Throughout the late 1940s these men "dominated the student unions and newspapers" –

Gerald Fremlin, who was approached by Munro, was a veteran of the Royal Canadian Air Force and the war and sent her to another RCAF veteran, John Cairns. Such older and more experienced students "brought a degree of seriousness and maturity that served as a counterweight to the more jejune aspects of student culture." At the same time, there was what intellectual historian A.B. McKillop calls a resurgence of "the cult of domesticity" after the war – he cites advertisements in *Maclean's* magazine as an indication, since those "aimed at the woman as homemaker rose from about forty percent in 1939 to over seventy percent in 1950." Although the war years had seen a surge in women's attendance at Canadian universities, that increase was reversed with the war's end – women made up considerably less than a third of students in arts and sciences at Canadian universities at the beginning of the 1950s.[3]

Recalling her university years, Munro says that she loved her time there, "being in that atmosphere, having all those books, not having to do any housework. Those are the only two years of my life without housework." Not that she has greatly minded such work, either before university or after, but those two years at Western stand singular in her memory: "to have that concentration of your life, that something else was the thing you got up in the morning to do, and it was all reading and writing, studying." Munro enrolled initially in the journalism program as something of a cover, so that she would not have to say that she wrote fiction – though, given the contributor note in the April 1950 *Folio* that has her major as Honours English "with an emphasis on creative writing," it was not much of a cover. The journalism program required English, and that first year Munro also took English history (which she says she already knew backwards), economics, French conversation, and psychology. Those enrolled in programs like journalism – that is, with some sort of applied focus – were put in the same sections of these courses and were seated alphabetically. Thus Alice Laidlaw met Diane Lane – a first-year pre-business student from Amherstburg – who became a friend and roommate.

Both students had come from small towns, neither had much money (though Laidlaw was the more strapped), and each, initially, roomed with someone she knew from home. During that first year, each found that she was not enjoying the association with her original roommate. So the two took to spending time together at the public library, where Munro had a part-time job two or three afternoons a week sorting and reshelving books (as she also did at the Lawson library on campus on Saturday afternoons). Eventually, Munro moved into the same rooming house as Lane – the upstairs of a house belonging to Mr. and Mrs. Charlie Buck at 1081 Richmond Street – where she lived through her second year. Mr. Buck's brother Tim was the leader of the Communist Party of Canada and had been in jail. The Bucks "rented the entire upstairs of their house, and it was a place where vaguely intellectual non-sorority-type girls lived." Munro recalls that "we were all fairly poor, and we all cooked these messes we made on hotplates." Socially, at the time, she remembers, "Western was fraternity, sorority. Not too serious." That second year was "interesting, but fun, because I was then with people at University who were more or less like me." Munro captures some of this in an unpublished draft story called "The Art of Fiction," which draws on her time at Western. The narrator writes, "During my university years I lived in a house which was not really very big and which sheltered seven other girls, a landlady who wove her own skirts and belonged to a Bell Ringers Society, and a periodically confined lovesick Siamese cat."4

During their first year, both young women took the same English 20 – a survey of British literature – class from Robert Lawrence and, through him, they came to the attention of the English department. Just as in high school, Munro made her mark by what she wrote: as a student she did not have much to say in class, but Lawrence read "The Dimensions of a Shadow," a story she wrote that became her first publication. The English department was seeking students for its honours program, and both Laidlaw and Lane were successfully recruited. Munro recalls that some time during that first year she was approached by Professor Murdo MacKinnon about switching to English. By that time, she remembers, she had "run afoul of economics" so she asked him if she would have to take more economics. No, he replied, she would need only to pick up the Latin she had missed that first year. So she shifted to English for her second year. That year she took aesthetics from Carl Klinck, eighteenth-century British literature from Brandon Conron, a course in drama from Eric Atkinson ("the best course I took"), French poetry, Greek literature and translation, and another course in English history "from a dreadful man" who "read from notes." Although Munro says she spent about half of her time at Western writing, she did very well in her courses – apart from economics. At the end of her second year, she won a prize for the highest marks in English.[5]

During her first year at Western, Alice Laidlaw was sitting across from another student in the Lawson library. He was eating some candy, a piece of which he accidentally dropped on the floor. This young man had had his eye on Laidlaw and, looking at the candy on the floor as he was wondering what to do, he heard her say, "I'll eat it." Thus Alice Ann Laidlaw met James Armstrong Munro. Jim Munro was from Oakville, the eldest son of Arthur Melville Munro, a senior accountant at the Timothy Eaton company in Toronto, and his wife, Margaret Armstrong Munro. Just under two years older than Alice, Jim was in his second year studying Honours History when he met her. Growing up in Oakville and through high school, he was interested in the arts; he listened to opera and classical music, took art classes, and acted in plays. Jim had seen Alice around the university and had noticed her, but did not know anything about her; he did not know that she was a writer until, when he asked around about her, he was told that Alice Laidlaw "was *Folio*'s new find." Recalling himself then, Jim Munro says he was "full of poetry and romantic notions" – he remembers then being under the influence of a book, *The Broad Highway* by Jeffrey Farnol, about a young man who falls for a high-spirited girl. He mirrored the story when he met Alice Laidlaw – "I really fell hard for her."[6]

Describing Alice Laidlaw when she was a student at Western, Doug Spettigue, a classmate, recalls that "she was shy and small and had a very white face, freckle-sprinkled, and chestnut hair. . . . You thought you could stare right through those quiet eyes and the girl would disappear. But she didn't. There was an unexpected strength there, and even then a confidence that some of the rest of us, noisier, may have envied." For his part, Jim Munro is remembered from that time as also being shy, a bit awkward, and handsome. He had a great friend, Donald

Dean, who wore a tam and played the bagpipes. He was more of a "true eccentric" than Jim Munro was, and the two were often together. Jim Munro was one of the theatre crowd among the students, a group Spettigue, another member, describes with verve: "We would have scorned to work at our courses but we worked passionately for the Players' Guild and the Hesperian Club and for *Folio*. . . . We acted and directed and even wrote plays, we built and tore apart sets endlessly both in the old Guild Room and the Grand Theatre. We lived for the successive issues of *Folio*, to admire ourselves and envy our friends in print."

After their meeting in the library in Alice's first year, she and Jim began seeing each other. They became a couple that year and were engaged at Christmas 1950. At Western they participated in the activities of the arts crowd; their eldest daughter, Sheila, writes that her mother wrote an adaptation of Ibsen's *Peer Gynt* "for a production put on by the Players' Guild" and she and Jim once "attended a literary evening hosted by a young professor," Jim Jackson, who "read one of her stories, 'The Man Who Goes Home,' about a man who takes the train home to the town he is from." He does this repeatedly and, each time, he refuses to venture into the town once he reaches the station: he has a cup of coffee and takes the next train back to the city. He knows that the Maitland he might find will not be the Maitland he remembers.

Among the members of the audience that literary evening was Gerry Fremlin, who by then had graduated and was working in London; he was there with his girlfriend. After Munro's story was read, "he raised his hand and asked her why she hadn't called the town Wingham." Sheila Munro also writes that her mother "thought of Gerry as something of a Byronic figure on campus, dark and lean." Another classmate recalls Fremlin at Western as "a raging, unconventional guy . . . the village atheist of the Arts Faculty." Fremlin's atheism was outspoken in classes (he remembers as much); the same classmate recalls him publicly taking on the well-known theologian Reinhold Niebuhr when he spoke at Western, although Fremlin does not recall doing so. Like Alice, Fremlin had begun in the journalism program but he later switched to English and philosophy. After working for a time in Toronto and London, he did graduate work at Western, receiving an M.A. in geomorphology. In 1955 he joined the geography branch of the Department of Energy, Mines, and Resources in Ottawa as a geographer, becoming its chief in 1971. After serving as editor of *The National Atlas of Canada* (1974), Fremlin left the civil service and returned home to Clinton, Ontario. During this time he never married.7

This brief encounter at the literary evening is notable, given Munro and Fremlin's later relationship, but the question he addressed to her that evening about "The Man Who Goes Home" is one that has been asked repeatedly during Munro's career about the settings of her stories. However, a letter he wrote to her the following summer suggests something of the growing appreciation of her writing around Western. It "was all about my writing," she recalls, "a really, really appreciating, insightful letter . . . one of the best I ever got." Fremlin saw Munro as a real writer, complimenting her work, comparing her to Chekhov – "but since I was seeing Jim already, it didn't say anything about coming to Muskoka to see me."

The predominant feature of Munro's writing while she was at Western is seen in the three stories she published in *Folio*. The first of these was "The Dimensions of a Shadow." Owning a typewriter, Diane Lane volunteered to type it for her and, once it had been successfully submitted to John Cairns, his reaction caused a small scene. According to Sheila Munro, Fremlin remembers Cairns "running down the hall after reading the story, waving it in his hand and shouting 'You've got to read this. You've got to read this.'" The story concerns Miss Abelhart, a small-town teacher who, pathetically, is revealed to have an infatuation with one of her male students; she was, Munro writes, "not ugly or absurd, in herself, only a little dried and hollowed, with straw hair tightly and tastelessly curled, and skin somewhat roughened, as if she had been for a long time facing a harsh wind. There was no blood in her cheeks, and something like dust lay over her face. People who looked at her knew she was old, and had been old always. She was thirty-three." Miss Abelhart is distracted and disaffected as the story begins, so she avoids her usual temperance meeting at the church, walking off into the town by herself, thinking of the boy in her Latin class – "In four days the school would be closed, and he would be gone." She walks toward the school and meets the boy; they talk and he admits that he reciprocates her feelings for him. At one point she asks him, "Did you ever think that once in her life, a woman has the right to have someone look at her and not see anything about her, just her, herself? Every woman has a right, no matter how old or ugly she is." The point of view shifts as the conversation concludes and it is revealed that Miss Abelhart is really alone, talking to a hallucination – Munro leaves her "alone in bottomless silence."

This revelation is effected by three high school girls who walk by Miss Abelhart and overhear her speaking aloud to the boy she imagines before her, whom the reader at the time thinks is real – "The three girls whom she had seen earlier in the evening walked past them. They were giggling together and glancing furtively from the corners of their eyes. The boy did not even look at them." Later, realizing that Miss Abelhart is talking to an imaginary person, one of them exclaims, "Jesus Christ! That's it! She thought there was somebody right there beside her!"

After she had learned that the story was accepted, Munro remembers that her father was "almost as excited as I was." But then the story came out and had "swear words" – "Jesus Christ!" – in it. This was "very hurtful" to her mother, grandmother, and aunt, Munro recalls, and it offended Jim's mother too, for he had shown his mother the story. Bob Laidlaw, for his part, understood why she had used the expression, but did not think it was a good idea. He would subsequently refer to it as "that expression which you used." Thus Munro began offending certain Huron County proprieties with her very first published story.[8]

As the summary of "The Dimensions of a Shadow" suggests, Munro's techniques are more than a bit forced. The same might be said of her third *Folio* story, "The Widower," which was subsequently seen and rejected by Weaver at the CBC. It concerns a man who, after his wife dies, discovers that he is not very bereft after all. Between these two, Munro published "Story for Sunday" in the December 1950 *Folio*. Unlike the others, it offers a young girl's point of view, one closer to Munro's own. Evelyn is a fifteen-year-old who "had never walked home from a dance with a boy," but the week before, after Sunday school, the superintendent had taken her in his arms and kissed her. This man, named Mr. Willens, works "in the office, down at the factory." His touch has transformed Evelyn. She returns to Sunday school the next week, and as she enters the church "her whole body came alive in a new way and tingled with faint excitement." Positioning herself to reenact their kiss of the previous week, Evelyn is stymied – she finds Willens's attentions are now focused on another, Myrtle Fotheringay, the church pianist. So what Willens had done the previous week, she sees, "was all quite meaningless." Rebuffed, Evelyn turns "to the face of the immaculate Christ . . .", and the story ends with this evasive ellipsis.9

Of the three stories Munro published as an undergraduate in *Folio*, "Story for Sunday" is the strongest in that it derives from her own point of view and range of experience; by contrast, the other two stories are wooden, more conventional and forced despite their strength in physical description. The ending of "Story for Sunday" is forced – the shift from adolescent rapture to religious fervour neat but unlikely – but there is a genuine quality to Evelyn's feelings that is lacking in the other two narratives.

Perhaps the most interesting thing about "Story for Sunday," especially at this juncture in Munro's career, is that when she came to write one of her most ambitious stories of the 1990s, "The Love of a Good Woman," she decided to name the roué character "Mr. Willens." As that story begins, Munro writes that "for the last couple of decades, there has been a museum in Walley, dedicated to preserving photos and butter churns and horse harnesses and an old dentist's chair and a cumbersome apple peeler and such curiosities as the pretty little porcelain-and-glass insulators that were used on telegraph poles. . . . Also there is a red box, which has the letters D.M. WILLENS, OPTOMETRIST printed on it, and a note beside it, saying, 'This box of optometrist's instruments though not very old has considerable local significance, since it belonged to Mr. D.M. Willens, who drowned in the Peregrine River, 1951. It escaped the catastrophe and was found, presumably by the anonymous donor, who dispatched it to be a feature of our collection.'"

Like the first Mr. Willens, this one also preys on vulnerable females for physical gratification, but unlike that one, the second Mr.

Willens is also derived from another, intermediary figure in Munro's work. During the mid-1970s she was working on a text for a book of photographs, mostly vignettes of a paragraph to two pages in length; one of these is called "Hearse" and begins, "The most successful seducer of women that there ever was in that country was Del Fairbridge's uncle, the older undertaker brother, retired." Since the book was never completed and published, Munro used much of it in *Who Do You Think You Are?* There this fellow is transformed slightly and turns up in "Wild Swans," another story of a young woman vulnerable to an older man's advances: the "little man" who comes into Flo's store "had been an undertaker, but he was retired now. The hearse was retired too. His sons had taken over the undertaking and bought a new one. He drove the old hearse all over the country, looking for women." He had been heard, "singing, to himself or somebody out of sight in the back. *Her brow is like the snowdrift / Her throat is like the swan.*"[10] His reappearance as Willens, an optometrist who makes house calls on women home alone in "The Love of a Good Woman," is made the more interesting by his date of death – murdered in the midst of adultery when caught by the woman's husband "in the spring of 1951." That is, at about the same time as the first Mr. Willens was created. It is almost as if Munro returned to Willens to give him what he deserved – and coincidental dates continue in the story: Mrs. Quinn, his putative partner in adultery, dies of a kidney problem on Alice Munro's twentieth birthday, July 10, 1951.

During the summer of 1950 Munro had a job as a waitress at the Milford Manor hotel on Lake Muskoka in the tourist region of Ontario that bears that lake's name. In a draft unpublished story titled "Is She as Kind as She Is Fair?", probably written some time later in the 1950s, Munro attempts to make fiction of this experience. It shows her developing a narrative posture toward her personal material – what might be called a wry, distant wonder at the mysteries of being – that later became characteristic. That posture is wholly absent from the *Folio* stories – they all too clearly strive to create particular effects – but it emerged as Munro wrote and published during the 1950s and into the 1960s. One draft of "Is She as Kind as She Is Fair?" begins

Between my first and second years at college I worked as a waitress in a summer hotel in Muskoka. It was called the Old Pine
Tree, and it was a chalet-type firetrap three storeys high, painted
dark green and hung with balconies and baskets of petunias. It
was not what people call "the better sort of place", although I
don't suppose it was among the worst; you got your orange juice,
which was canned, in a plain saucer without any cracked ice
around it, and you got to share the beach, the tennis court and
the dance-hall with the hired help. We got a lot of moderate-
income honeymooners, often a depressing sight as they munched
their way resolutely through breakfast, their eyes lifting occasionally, not to meet, but to blink at the prospect of another
staring day, in the anxious country between courtship and
domesticity. We got office-girls too, and girls who worked in
stores, arriving in pairs to spend their holidays, and entering the
dining-room, the first night, in full makeup, earrings, and
flowered sheer; not again.

The story focuses on the waitresses, their difficult relations with the
cooks, with a person named Bill, "the mental defective," and generally
deals with the romances and other human relations going on around
the hotel during the summer. At one point two of the waitresses are
locked out of their room because their roommate, Dodie, is "doing it"
with one of the other workers, Joey. Munro works through one girl's
hesitancy over phrasing – she tries out "having intercourse," to which
her roommate replies, "Screwing?" Evie, the hesitant girl, wonders:

That was what Evie was thinking of. Her wish to see somebody
doing it had always run parallel to her wish to see somebody dead – that is, she had wished and not wished at the same
time, with alternating violent curiosity and superstitious fear.
Though given a chance to battle it out, curiosity would almost
certainly have won. And now without anybody seeing or preparing her she had seen it. She was glad she had come to the door
first, and not Mareta, for if Mareta had pushed her back and

told her what was happening she could not have said let me look, I want to see too.

She thought of Joey's small body with the t-shirt pulled up and the pants around his ankles, his flat white buttocks and narrow back, he was like a child held between Dodie's thick freckled legs. She couldn't remember Dodie's face, or the back of Joey's head, nothing but the amazing bodies, locked and jerking. The impression remained that Joey was an instrument, Dodie had stuck him in there, she hung on to him and made him do it but she was really doing it to herself. Who would have guessed the fragility, the defencelessness of Joey in such a situation, or the strength of Dodie?

By way of an answer to this question, Munro later writes, "This was a nymphomaniac, Evie thought. Such a phenomenon deserved her closest attention, but did not readily reward it."[11]

The wondering, the seeing, the questioning, the realization. These qualities are evident in these passages, which focus on occurrences that are utterly commonplace – yet seen and written of by Munro, such commonplaces are transformed into occasions for mystery, for understanding. They find their point of departure in her experience ("There is always a starting point in reality," she told Boyle in 1974), and Dodie is based on a person Munro knew that summer, but it is how she transforms such remembered people that is her hallmark.

In this story Munro has the waitresses reading romance stories as they sun themselves in the afternoons by the lake; some of them began with their next year's university texts but those were soon put aside. The summer she was in Muskoka Munro tried her hand at writing such commercial stories.[12] She found she did not believe in them enough – their hope, what they offered those who bought and read them. She was already too cynical to write them with success, with the necessary conviction. That balance, between belief and hope and romance on the one hand, and what is real on the other, is evident in "Is She as Kind as She Is Fair?", especially when she meditates on the relation between Dodie and Joey – her insight, even early on, is as caustic as it is humane.

And as she describes the honeymooning couples "in the anxious country between courtship and domesticity" in her draft story, Munro offers a knowing perspective on their circumstances. Well she should, since by the time she wrote "Is She as Kind as She Is Fair?" Munro was herself married. Speaking to Thomas Tausky in 1984, she explained that once she had earned her scholarships to Western she "had to come to university" since, at home, there was no money even "to come to London to look for a job." And once her two years at university had passed, there "was no money then to do anything but get married. . . . I could either stay in Wingham or get married." Even if she went home to Wingham, her most likely prospect was to marry a farmer there. There was also her mother's situation. And by the time she was in university, Munro also knew that she was an artist, so her dilemma was compounded. Talking to Tausky about her early attraction to *Wuthering Heights* and the story she wrote in high school in imitation of Brontë, and connecting it with what she later did in creating Del Jordan's circumstances in *Lives of Girls and Women*, Munro saw then "that these were the twin choices of my life . . . marriage and mother-hood or the black life of the artist." Although the first choice was to predominate during the 1950s, Alice Munro ultimately chose both.

Once they met toward the end of Alice's first year, she and Jim Munro began their own version of what she would later characterize as "friendship, courtship, loveship, marriage." Jim Munro had enrolled in a training program of the Royal Canadian Navy for university students and spent the summer Alice was in Muskoka in British Columbia. This led to his resolve to move there after he finished university. And once he fell hard for Alice Laidlaw, Jim also decided to switch from history to the general arts program at Western – it would allow him to take courses in English and other subjects and, more significantly, he would be able to graduate a year earlier than he had previously planned, in 1951. Jim could then find a job so he and Alice could marry.

When they got engaged at Christmas 1950, Jim went to Wingham and asked Robert Laidlaw for Alice's hand in marriage – Mrs. Laidlaw's suggestion, Jim recalls. When their final year at Western was over, Alice went home to Wingham and then took off for a time with Diane Lane working at a job intended to make them lots of money. Arranged by a neighbour in St. Thomas, Ontario – Lane's father, an Anglican minister, had moved to a new church there – the two young women were hired to remove the suckers that fed on the tobacco plants in the neighbouring fields. They were singularly unsuccessful at that work, which was difficult, dirty, and tedious, and they abandoned it after a time. Jim, who had graduated with a general arts degree in English and History, did another period of Navy training and, once he got out, began working in Vancouver for the Timothy Eaton department store – the same Canada-wide company his father worked for in Toronto.

In December Jim Munro came back east to marry Alice Laidlaw. The wedding was "a quiet ceremony at the home of the bride's parents," according to the *Advance-Times*, held on December 29, 1951, and conducted by Dr. W.A. Beecroft, the United Church minister. The announcement continues:

> Given in marriage by her father, the bride wore an afternoon dress of wine velvet, with matching accessories and corsage of Lester Hibbard roses. She was attended by her sister, Miss Sheila Laidlaw, wearing a dress of sapphire blue velvet similar in style to the bride's dress, with matching accessories and corsage of Pink Delight roses. Mr. Donald Dean of Tillsonburg was best man and Miss Diane Lane of St. Thomas played the wedding music.
>
> After the ceremony, a wedding dinner was served to the bridal party and the immediate families in the Brunswick Hotel. Following the dinner the bride and groom left for Toronto to travel by train to Vancouver. Mr. and Mrs. Munro will live in Vancouver.

Diane Lane, who came up to Wingham before the wedding to help Alice with its preparations, recalls the ceremony as "about as modest a wedding as you could have." Along with the Laidlaws, Lane, and Dean, only Mr. and Mrs. Munro attended. Lane played Handel's *Largo* – a piece Alice requested as one of Jim's favourites – and Bill Laidlaw, who was then fifteen, arranged for tin cans trailing from the wedding

couple's car as they drove away, something Jim did not much appreciate. Alice and Jim were very happy, she recalls, and Jim in particular
was most evidently "deeply infatuated."13

Yet given the disparity of social backgrounds involved in the union
and especially given Anne Chamney Laidlaw's condition, all was not
entirely well. Mrs. Laidlaw was at the time "so noticeably ill" – as Lane
remembers her – and her speech was so badly affected that only family
members could consistently understand her. Looking at a wedding
photograph including her mother, Munro told Catherine Ross that
"she looked quite nice in the picture. She had a fixed look, which is a
characteristic of Parkinsonians, very masklike." Munro looked at her
wedding photographs at other times and tried to use them in what
appears a draft version of "Chaddeleys and Flemings: 2. The Stone in
the Field" in one of her longhand notebooks; it is entitled "Old Mr.
Black" and it begins:

> People don't spend much time looking at wedding pictures, par-
> ticularly when the marriage itself no longer exists. I have a
> picture of myself and my first husband that deserves some atten-
> tion. I am twenty, my husband is twenty-two. I am wearing a
> home-made velvet dress and hat. My husband is wearing a new
> suit, too large even when you take into account the baggy styles
> of the early fifties. Our attitudes to the undertaking are reflected
> in our faces – his stricken but shining with conviction, mine
> pale, resolute, sullen. Our parents on either side look un-
> comfortable. My wedding had come at a time when our family
> had had a patch of ill-luck so shocking that it makes other people
> turn away in embarrassment, my mother sick with an incurable
> disease (there she is with her slightly crazy eyes and her stiff pose
> and her beautiful Irish skull), my father with his business in
> ruins trying to support us by working as a night-watchman
> in the local foundry, our skid into poverty coinciding naturally
> with a skid from the middle class through the bottom of the
> middle class into the working class. And it was not as if there

hadn't been hopes and possibilities. My father owned a set of golf clubs. A few years before my mother had furnished the living-room where this picture was taken with an idea of creating a Victorian parlour, with uncomfortable needle-pointed chairs and settee, a painted hanging-lamp and fine gilt-framed mirror (our sheets and towels were worn almost to pieces, we had no refrigerator, fly-stickers hung over our kitchen table; that is the picture)[.]

What Munro has written here — as only she can — is a precise description of the moment captured in this photograph. Likely written during the late 1970s (the adjacent material is connected to *Who Do You Think You Are?*), perhaps just after her father's death and perhaps as "Working for a Living" was coming to the fore in her imagination, what Munro writes here is a precise, unadorned reminiscence. She continues, shifting to Jim's parents:

Into such squalor and elegance & illness & ill-luck & pretension come my husband's parents, perfectly normal well-behaved people of the upper middle class to whom exaggerations of all kinds were distressing. Plenty here for them to behave well about. They had never reason to think their son would marry anyone but the daughter of a family like themselves, or if he did take up with a girl from a little backwoods town, her father would at least be the leading citizen of the town, a judge or a doctor or at worst a merchant. How had this happened, they must have asked themselves a dozen times that day, how did their son even come to meet the daughter of a night-watchman who lived in a house with no garbage pickup and flies blackening the back door. At the University, that was how, where the new Provincial Govt's munificences opens the Gothic doors a crack, lets in a dribble of the children of the poor who are brash & brainy & scornful & lucky too sometimes under their meekness in ways their betters can't suspect.

No doubt owing to her own perspective on this scene – written, as she says, when the marriage it commemorates was over, her mother and likely her father dead – Munro starkly analyzes the commemorated moment's meaning, the differences between the two principals and their two families, not really known then, but intimately familiar by the time Munro writes. She focuses on an item in the photo, an antique gun that does appear by the Laidlaws' mantel in Wingham in the actual wedding photo, and continues:

> Well, in a corner of the picture, propped up in the old-fashioned parlour, there is a gun, an elegant old muzzle-loader with a bayonet on the end. That's part of my mother's decorating and in itself has some complicated meaning, guns were no longer a natural article in parlours, of course; the gun was displayed for its antique elegance, and its history. When asked, we said it had been used in the War of 1812. My future mother-in-law and her friends would never have had a gun in their living-rooms (their living-rooms were all very much alike – comfortable, creamy, chintzy, pleasant) – and neither would any of the members of our family, who tended toward ferny curtains & plastic-covers on brocade-like furniture. I did not know anyone else who would have a gun in the living-room and for once I was not in opposition to my mother. I liked the gun there and valued its history (though I had got it all wrong, one of the things I'm coming to).
>
> So there is a gun included in my wedding-pictures. If I had been marrying a boy of my own background there could have been jokes about this but in the circumstances nobody mentioned it. I don't mean that there was a specifically awkward circumstance, such as pregnancy; just that everything was awkward, and sad, and ill-omened. It was not a wedding any sort of jokes could be made about. It was a wedding nobody wanted except the bride & groom, and they clung to it in spite of drastic misgivings. I clung to it too; make no mistake, if anybody had advised me not to go through with it I would have eloped, to show them.

Munro's commentary on her wedding photograph breaks off here, for she shifts her focus, saying, "When I was about ten or eleven years old I went with my father when he had to fix the fences on the fifty acres we owned."[14] The draft then breaks off altogether. Yet what remains of "Old Mr. Black" is as direct and clear-sighted an articulation of the social and personal contexts animating the Laidlaw-Munro wedding as might be imagined – Munro's description recreates the day she literally became Alice Munro starkly, abjectly, precisely. She had made her choice: her name became Alice Munro, and she and her new husband went off to start their new life together in Vancouver.

"I Certainly Hope That You Will Continue Writing"

Sometime in 1951, while she was still at Western and engaged to Jim Munro, Alice Laidlaw wrote to Robert Weaver in the Talks and Public Affairs section of the Canadian Broadcasting Corporation in Toronto. A native of Niagara Falls, a war veteran, and a graduate of the University of Toronto, Weaver had joined the CBC in late 1948 to organize and produce its literary programs. He replaced James Scott, who returned to his native Seaforth (fairly close to Wingham) primarily to write but also to teach creative writing at Western. Among the programs Weaver inherited was one called *Canadian Short Stories*, a weekly fifteen-minute program of readings of original stories. When he arrived it had been on the air since 1946 and was undistinguished, so Weaver set about soliciting stories from across the country. He also drew on his own contacts at the University of Toronto (Henry Kreisel and James Reaney were classmates, so their work came in) and elsewhere. Having produced *Canadian Short Stories* himself, James Scott was a source, too, since he was involved with young writers at Western – he put Doug Spettigue in touch with Weaver and may well have done the same with Munro. She recalls hearing that a classmate, Bill Davidson, had sent a story to Weaver. Doug Spettigue did so as well, since one of his was broadcast in July 1951. By May of that year Alice had begun a correspondence with Weaver over her own submissions.

Connecting with Robert Weaver was a key moment for Alice Munro, even a very lucky one. Luck and timing did have roles to play in her career's unfolding, and hearing about *Canadian Short Stories* was one such moment. Weaver's "main concern" was "to promote literature through the medium of radio" and, as he wrote in the June 1949 CBC program guide, "one of the chief aims" of *Canadian Short Stories* was to "discover and develop new talent." At the same time, Weaver was acting on his own initiative: his was a classic case of a person defining and extending his own position. He went well beyond what was expected of him by his superiors and so made a contribution to Canadian letters that extended the scope of what the corporation did in fostering Canadian writing. After almost a decade of this, he extended his radio work with his editorial direction of the *Tamarack Review*. Setting about all this in 1948, Bob Weaver – as everyone still calls him – became what Robert Fulford has called "a one-man national literary network." Somehow, Fulford has said, Weaver "caught on at the CBC and stayed there for the rest of his career"; he "seized upon this position at the CBC to become the friend, advocate, the explorer, the discoverer of Canadian writers." Weaver made a point of travelling across the country, making regular trips to the west coast and to Montreal and points east. When he stopped, he would have parties in his hotel rooms, inviting all the local writers and others with literary connections. Through such gatherings, writers, editors, and critics met and came to know one another so Weaver was able to function as "a one-man national literary network" indeed.

In the conclusion to his 1984 thesis on Weaver's contributions to Canadian literature, Mark Everard anticipates this book by writing that the "biographer of Alice Munro . . . would be both ungracious and historically inaccurate if he did not examine in some detail the editorial relationship that was largely responsible for keeping Munro interested in writing" in the years before her first book, *Dance of the Happy Shades,* was published.[15] That relationship began apparently when the Canadian Writers' Service – an agency run by Cybil Hutchinson, who had been an editor at McClelland & Stewart – submitted "The Man Who Goes Home" to Weaver early in 1951. That was the same Munro story Jim

Jackson had read at the literary evening in London, and Weaver rejected it, but on May 18 he wrote to her at 1081 Richmond Street about two other stories, "The Widower" and "The Strangers." He rejected "The Widower" but, contingent on Munro's willingness to shorten "The Strangers" – *Canadian Short Stories* required pieces not longer than 2,100 words – offered to buy it. He hoped to broadcast it on June 1, so the cuts had to be done quickly. Weaver suggests how to do this, but his most indicative comments are his criticisms of "The Widower": "Here you have failed to rise above somewhat common-place and tedious material." The three stories he has seen suggest to him that Munro tends to understate her material. "This is something which a great many of our writers could learn to their benefit, but when this method is followed in a story like 'The Widower,' which is rather unexciting in the first place, it can sometimes have an unfortunate effect." He continues, saying that "you are trying hard to use words with care and to present your material with real integrity and I certainly hope that you will continue writing, and that we will be given the opportunity to read some later stories of yours." Munro replies in a week, apologizing for not getting the manuscript back sooner and thanking Weaver for his "encouragement and criticism." She then details the changes she has made to reach the needed length: she "rewrote the first two pages entirely" and made more cuts later in the manuscript, but "in case the revision is not satisfactory I am sending also the original two pages" in case he would like to make alternative changes.[16]

This exchange of letters is interesting in itself, certainly, but it is most significant in the way it begins the Weaver-Munro relation: for his part, Weaver is supportive and interested, but he is also critical – there is no mistaking what he has to say about "The Widower." For hers, Munro shows herself understanding of his editorial needs, willing to make changes to "The Strangers" and, though she is just nineteen years old and this is her first such exchange, professional. Years later, in 1984 when Weaver was reaching retirement age and his program *Anthology* (successor to *Canadian Short Stories*) was celebrating its thirtieth anniversary, Munro wrote to Marian Engel seeking her support for a plan to have him made an honorary member of the Writers' Union of Canada. She says that she has "been thinking how a long . . . relationship can still be there, still sustaining, after other relationships so much more intimate & important have burned right out." Thus Weaver has been to Munro since she began her professional career in 1951. For her part, whenever Weaver has been singled out to be celebrated, Munro has been there. In a 1979 profile of Weaver in *Books in Canada*, Mark Abley wrote that "when Alice Munro is read and remembered, Weaver will be forgotten." Clearly, Abley was wrong.[17]

When he received the revision, Weaver wrote that Munro "had done an extremely good job on the re-write" of "The Strangers," and he was sorry that its broadcast on June 1 had to be postponed by their reporting on the Massey Commission. He had wired her with this news, but in his letter of June 1 he offered more information. Since they had arranged to do a series of half-hour stories until the program's summer break, "The Strangers" had to wait until October 5. He tells her that the cheque for the story will be arriving in three weeks, asks for clarification about her relationship with the Canadian Writers' Service, and solicits other stories. Munro wastes no time responding, since on June 8 she replies and submits "The Liberation" for Weaver's consideration. He replies about five weeks later, buying the story outright and saying that he sees no point in cutting it – they will pay her ninety dollars and save it until they have a half-hour slot available. Weaver continues, "I was very pleased to hear from you again, and I hope you will continue to send us fiction from time to time. 'The Liberation' is really a very nice story and it is fine to know that you are continuing to work in this field. Incidentally, it is a small point, but if you intend to do very much free lance writing I think you will soon discover that editors much prefer to receive manuscripts double-spaced. This makes it a good deal easier to tell at a glance [how] long a piece is." In and of itself, such a suggestion is of little import. But this letter shows Weaver adopting the role of advisor that he played crucially to Munro for the next twenty years, until she made other contacts in the literary world. Weaver was her literary lifeline: he encouraged, made practical suggestions, responded, and generally cared for Alice Munro the writer. And he did so for scores of other writers besides.[18]

By the time Alice and Jim Munro were married and heading for Vancouver, Weaver had considered and rejected two more stories, "The Unfortunate Lady" and "The Uncertain Spring." The latter, Weaver wrote, showed that Munro was "steadily improving as a writer." Weaver did not buy it only because he already had her long story, "The Liberation," on hand. During 1952 Munro submitted at least two more stories, "The Shivaree" and "The Man from Melberry"; these were also rejected.

For his part, Weaver compliments Munro on the descriptive sections and on character analysis, but "the three of us" who read the stories "were all agreed in feeling that [the stories] were not entirely successful." Weaver goes on to say he is sorry about this, and he hopes Munro will send him "more fiction quite soon." He adds, "I am sure that you realize that we are very much interested in the work you are doing and I hope that we are able to use one or two of your stories in the Canadian Short Stories series this winter." Weaver's concluding paragraph is as follows:

> Once or twice I have wondered whether you have ever sent any of your stories to one or two of the better Canadian magazines. While you wouldn't receive any payment from either *Northern Review* or the *Canadian Forum* it might be helpful to you if either magazine published one of your stories and the editors might also send you some useful comments. I mentioned your work to John Sutherland of *Northern Review* and I know that he would be most interested in hearing from you.[19]

Munro did not have another story broadcast on the CBC until "The Idyllic Summer" was used on *Anthology* in 1954. In August of the same year, that story appeared in the *Canadian Forum*. By then, Munro had already sold her first story for commercial publication – "A Basket of Strawberries" to *Mayfair*, which ran it in their November 1953 issue. She did sell a story, "Magdalene," to John Sutherland at the *Northern Review* during the 1950s, but it was never published. Also at Weaver's suggestion, during the mid-1950s Munro began sending stories to magazines in the United States – her first submissions to the *New Yorker* date from this time, and she recalls sending stories to little magazines listed in the back of a *Discovery* magazine.

Thus Munro apparently wasted no time responding to Weaver's suggestion that she submit to magazines. As "the only person" she knew "from the world of writing," Robert Weaver was critical to her evolving career. His letters, she has written, "didn't reprove me for not writing or exhort me to get busy. They reminded me that I was a writer. The most precious encouragement was not in what they said, but in what they took for granted." For his part, Weaver saw from the first that Alice Laidlaw Munro was "a real writer": "Alice knew early what she was trying to do – she had a strong will – and she wasn't to be deflected."[20]

"Three Dark Rooms in Kitsilano"

A fragment that is probably connected to "Chaddeleys and Flemings" – and thus a product of the late 1970s – begins "We were married during the Christmas holidays and went at once to Vancouver where we were going to live. As we walked through the Vancouver railway station workmen were taking the lights off a huge Christmas tree. Richard had been living in Vancouver since early summer, articling with a law firm, and writing letters to me describing the mountains, the ocean, the great ships that came into port and making confident promises concerning our love and future life." Obviously, Munro is drawing here, in her usual precise detail, on her own recollected experiences. Once she and Jim had married in December 1951, they took the train from Toronto directly to Vancouver. Another wedding announcement, cited by their daughter Sheila, mentions a wedding trip to Banff, but Munro recalls only that they may have merely stepped off the train and walked around there. The train trip, an adventure in itself, passed for a honeymoon, and they arrived in Vancouver on January 2, 1952. Having been working at Eaton's since the previous summer, Jim had found an apartment for them. Munro recalls,

The apartment he had found for us was on Arbutus Street, facing the park, the beach, the water[.] We had half the downstairs of a pink stucco house. Across the front of the house was a glassed in porch, which kept our living room quite dark. There was dark green linoleum on the floor, and a dark red chesterfield and chair, a fireplace with an electric heater and on either side of the fireplace a little window with a tulip of pink and green glass.

Behind the living room was our bedroom, and beyond that was the kitchen. We shared the bathroom with the people in the other downstairs apartment.

The house, at 1316 Arbutus, still looks across Kitsilano Beach Park to English Bay and Burrard Inlet beyond. The Munros lived there through the summer of 1952 but had to move in the fall owing to renovations, so they found a place on Argyle Street where they lived into 1953, until they bought their first house in North Vancouver.

Among the stories in *The Love of a Good Woman* is "Cortes Island," which begins: "Little bride. I was twenty years old, five feet seven inches tall, weighing between a hundred and thirty-five and a hundred and forty pounds." While this story's central incident is imaginary and some of the details of the protagonist and her husband differ from the Munros, she draws here upon the circumstances of her early months in Vancouver, recreating the atmosphere, tone, and circumstances of their experience. The narrator is of the same age and size, and has many of the attributes of Munro herself (she is a writer, is mechanically inept, and is drawn to libraries). More than this, though, the story concludes with finality – the narrator rejects Mrs. Gorrie, the mother of the landlord who lived upstairs and who had at first befriended her (and was among those calling her "little bride"), but who ultimately turned on her. "I didn't take a final look at the house, and I didn't walk down that street, that block of Arbutus Street that faces the park and the sea, ever again." Naming the actual street where she lived, Munro again harkens back to her arrival in Vancouver, revisiting the person she was then. As in "Home," where she wonders about her feelings for the family home in Wingham and writes, "It seems to me it was myself I loved here, some self I have finished with," in "Cortes Island" she revisits herself as a young bride.

"Running away to the West was an adventure," Munro once told a journalist. "We were very young; we had no idea what to expect." Settling in to her new role of wife and her new life was both exhilarating and daunting, as she and her husband both tried to conform to what was expected, both by the mores of the time and by one another. While Jim went off to work downtown every day, Alice read, and she wrote – in "Cortes Island," she refers to "filling page after page with failure" – and looked after their apartment, doing the domestic chores, adapting to her new role as housewife. As in her Wingham and university years, Munro was drawn to the library. The month after she arrived in Vancouver, she got a part-time job at the Kitsilano branch of the Vancouver Public Library. She worked part-time until the fall of 1952, full-time until June 1953 and, after Sheila was born in October of that year, part-time again until her next pregnancy in 1955. Looking back on her reasons for marrying, the years that followed, and what she did during those years, Munro has said,

> I got married because that was what you did. Actually, that was what you did to have a sex life, because there was absolutely no reliable birth control. So it was your next step into adulthood. So I was quite happy to leave and get married and go on. But then I didn't foresee at all that it would be such a long haul to get anything written that would be any good at all. Mostly, all through my twenties all I did was read. I read an awful lot. I read most of the writers of the twentieth century that you're supposed to have read.

In "Cortes Island," Munro's narrator mentions that "I read books I got from the Kitsilano Library a few blocks away. . . . I bolted them down one after the other without establishing any preferences, surrendering to each in turn just as I'd done to the books of my childhood. I was still in that stage of leaping appetite, of voracity close to anguish."[21]

Meanwhile, Jim continued to go downtown daily. Eaton's, the leading Canadian department store at the time, did not have a management training program – young men like Jim Munro were hired and assigned to a department to work and learn on the job. Although initially he indicated an interest in books, and Eaton's certainly had a book department, the personnel manager told him flatly that there was no money in books and assigned him to men's underwear. (Alice, for her part, says that Eaton's "would never let you do anything you were really good at.") After a stint in underwear, which left him itching to do something else, he wrote advertising copy for the bargain basement; this was an assignment he enjoyed, and a creative one, since he got to write all the advertising. Eaton's advertised in the Vancouver papers almost every day, so Jim got to use, he has said, "every cliché in the book." He then moved into drapery before becoming the assistant manager of household linens. After that, he moved on to the fabric department. Jim spent twelve years at Eaton's and, though he thought it a good place to work, he also never thought he was a good fit with the organization. His aesthetic and literary interests were at odds with the expected corporate norms; though he made money for Eaton's, his colleagues and superiors did not much care. It was his view that they preferred someone who played golf.[22]

The draft beginning "We were married during the Christmas vacation" describes the narrator and her new husband, the two just arrived in Vancouver, going to dinner at "the Kellands, who were friends of Richard's parents. . . . They were generous people and they wanted to be kind to us for Richard's parents' sake and also because the way in which we lived, in three dark rooms in Kitsilano, without a car, seemed amazing, foolhardy." Another draft story offers a similar situation, this one connected to "The Turkey Season"; it pauses after the turkey-gutters in that story sing "I'm Dreaming of a White Christmas":

> In Vancouver our Sundays stretched from Kitsilano to Kerrisdale. We lived in Kitsilano in three rooms in an old wooden house. On Sundays we got up late and [ate] pancakes with honey and [drank] a large pot of coffee and listened to the

radio which played baroque music and gave reviews of books and plays and serious analysis of what was going on in the world. I used to think of the poem "Sunday Morning" particularly if the sun was shining and there was a patch of sunlight on the faded rug in our living-room. Up until about noon I was always hopeful that some marvelous expedition would take place. I wanted to go on a boat or take the chair-lift up Grouse Mountain.

Munro then details the possibilities that attract the narrator, who recognizes that all the things she wants to do cost money and, besides, they may not really be all that enticing. In any case, after they discuss various possibilities, "what Andrew often said was, 'Well, could we get back in time.' He did not go on to say 'in time to get to Kerrisdale' or 'in time to get to the Adams.'" That assumption is implied, however, because

every Sunday we went to the Adams for dinner. Andrew liked to go early to play ping-pong or checkers with Graham Adams, his best friend. Going to the Adams' was a subject we were careful about. I never complained about going there but sometimes I would say, "Do you think they really want us there every Sunday?" I never made any criticism of Graham or of Mr. and Mrs. Adams who besides being Graham's parents were friends of Andrew's mother; but often I said sharp things about Susan Adams, Graham's sister, and Andrew hastened to agree with me that she was a very boring, annoying girl, a "sorority girl." Often Andrew would comment on something about the Adams that he thought I would approve of — "I see they take the Atlantic Monthly" — or he would say that he hoped I wasn't too tired (we had been married only a few months and I was already pregnant). And when I said that I wasn't tired or made some favorable remark about the Adams he would be relieved and grateful and I would feel generous.

Again, Munro was drawing from her memories of those early years in Vancouver. One of Jim's good friends from Oakville, Bill MacKendrick,

Boston Presbyterian Church, Halton, Esquesing Township, Ontario. Built on land sold by her Great-Great-Uncle Andrew in 1824, it figures in *The View from Castle Rock*. Many of Munro's Laidlaw ancestors are buried to the left of the church.

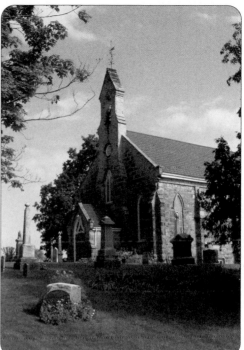

The Code sisters as young girls: Sadie (Alice's grandmother), Maud, Elsie, and May

Source: Arlyn Montgomery

The Code sisters as young women: Sadie, Maud, Elsie, and May. Sarah Jane "Sadie" Code Laidlaw (1876–1966), Anna "Maud" Code Porterfield (1878–1976), Laura "Elsie" Code Powell (1880–1934), Melissa "May" Code Kennedy (1882–?)

Source: Arlyn Montgomery

Sadie (Sarah Jane Code Laidlaw) and Maud Code Porterfield (Leopold Street, Wingham)

Insert: Thomas (1844–1927) and Annie (1841–1913) Code,
Alice's great-grandparents from the Ottawa Valley
A January 1879 map of Wingham, Ontario

Source: Eleanor Henderson

CHAMNEY FAMILY PORTRAIT:
Front: Bertha Ann Stanley Chamney (1867–1935),
Joseph Henry Chamney (1900–1970),
George Chamney (1853–1934);
Back: John Gillman Chamney (1894–1972),
Annie Clarke Chamney (1898–1959), Alice's mother
Edward Melbourne Chamney (1892–1951)

Annie Clarke Chamney, ca. 1913–14

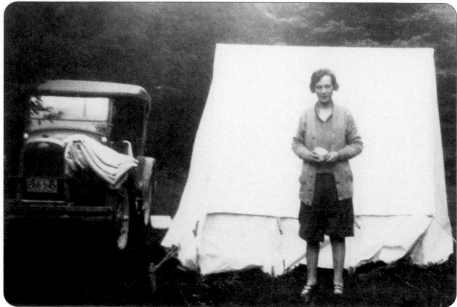

Anne Chamney Laidlaw, summer 1927, honeymoon, Christie Lake

Alice Laidlaw Munro's girlhood home

Baby Alice with
her grandfather
George Chamney
(ca. 1933)

Source: Eleanor Henderson

Alice Laidlaw with
her grandparents
Sadie and William
Code Laidlaw,
ca. 1935–36

Source: AM

Alice and Anne Laidlaw, fall 1931, Wingham

had moved to Vancouver and lived, as Munro writes here, in the Kerrisdale section of the city, a better part of town. Another family, the Careys, were friends of Jim's aunt and uncle from Winnipeg. Jim recalls that "we went there for dinner on Sunday afternoons. The Careys sort of adopted us; we went there more often than we didn't." For her part, Munro remembers these visits as "simply wonderful. We played word games after dinner and it was fun." Mary Carey became one of Alice's great friends, a person she visited regularly in Vancouver until the older woman's death. She is one of three departed friends to whom Munro dedicated *Runaway*.23

After she returned to Ontario in 1973, she frequently created characters with husbands who condescend to their wives' rural backgrounds: there is Patrick in "The Beggar Maid" saying "You were right," as he and Rose leave Hanratty on the bus after his first visit there. "It is a dump. You must be glad to get away." Or Richard the lawyer in "Chaddeleys and Flemings 1. Connection" pronouncing the narrator's visiting cousin Iris "a pathetic old tart" and "pointing out the grammatical mistakes she had made, of the would-be genteel variety"; for this outburst, he gets whacked by a piece of lemon meringue his wife throws at him. Or in "Miles City, Montana," the father of the narrator's two daughters is suddenly dismissed: "I haven't seen Andrew for years, don't know if he is still thin, has gone completely gray, insists on lettuce, tells the truth, or is hearty and disappointed."24 Without doubt, each of these husbands – all three are long divorced in each story's present – owes something to Jim Munro.

The class differences between Alice Laidlaw and Jim Munro – as she makes utterly clear in her commentary on the wedding photograph – were immense. The two were from very different worlds. Their Oakville-based connections in Vancouver were but one indication of differences lying submerged, unacknowledged but present, which Munro drew upon after their divorce. But during the 1950s and into the 1960s, the Munros were busy establishing themselves and their young family; hence these differences remained mostly unstated between them, rooted far away in Ontario, though sometimes evident in their personal life in Vancouver.

Those differences, while powerful enough and ultimately contributing to the end of the Munros' marriage by the early 1970s, should not obscure a key fact: throughout their marriage, Jim Munro supported and encouraged Alice's writing. Alice has said that Jim is one of the very few men she has known – apart from English teachers – who "really read fiction seriously." And Robert Weaver remarked that Alice was "lucky to have a husband who supported her writing" at a time when many husbands, given the mores of the time, had difficulty with the time spent and the achievements of a wife who wrote. Weaver was in a position to know, certainly. Emblematic of Jim's support was his gift of a typewriter to his wife on her twenty-first birthday on July 10, 1952.[25]

In tune with this, in "Cortes Island" Munro recreates a younger self, this time as a writer:

> But one complication had been added since childhood – it seemed that I had to be a writer as well as a reader. I bought a school notebook and tried to write – did write, pages that started off authoritatively and then went dry, so that I had to tear them out and twist them up in hard punishment and put them in the garbage can. I did this over and over again until I had only the notebook cover left. Then I bought another notebook and started the whole process once more. The same cycle – excitement and despair, excitement and despair. It was like having a secret pregnancy and miscarriage every week.
>
> Not entirely secret either. Chess knew that I read a lot and that I was trying to write. He didn't discourage it at all. He thought that it was something reasonable that I might quite possibly learn to do. It would take hard practice but could be mastered, like bridge or tennis. This generous faith I did not thank him for. It just added to the farce of my disasters.

Elsewhere in the story, once the narrator has fallen out with Mrs. Gorrie, it becomes clear that the older woman has been using a pass key to snoop around the young couple's apartment. Mrs. Gorrie says that the narrator would "sit down there and say she's writing letters and she writes the same thing over and over again – it's not letters, it's the same thing over and over." Hearing this, the narrator says, "Now I knew that she must have uncrumpled the pages in my wastebasket. I often tried to start the same story with the same words. As she said, over and over."

As with "Is She as Kind as She Is Fair?", Munro would follow the same practice herself – the Calgary archives are filled with hundreds of pages of fragments, many of them beginnings only, often with numerous repetitions of the same words in similar paragraphs. While Jim Munro learned quickly that the girl he "fell hard" for at Western was a writer, and once they were married knew she was always working on something, he seldom knew much more than that. He hardly ever saw anything in manuscript. "Her writing was very private," he remembers. "She was always changing and revising it. I didn't ever ask to see anything in manuscript. When they came out, I'd see them when they were published."

"Due to Things in My Life, and Writing Blocks, and So On"

When *Mayfair* published Munro's "A Basket of Strawberries" in its November 1953 issue, the editors concluded the "About Ourselves" column, which appeared on the masthead page, with the following paragraph:

> When we read "A Basket of Strawberries," this month's *Mayfair* short story, for the first time we assumed that the author Alice Munro was a mature woman who had spent years learning about life and mastering the writer's craft. We were astonished when we learned she's only twenty-one. She was born in Wingham, Ontario, spent two years at the University of Western Ontario, left to get married and is a housewife in Vancouver. This is the first story to be published professionally – it arrives in the world simultaneously with her first child and we congratulate her on both achievements.[26]

Like many of the stories Munro was writing during the 1950s, "A Basket of Strawberries" focuses on an older character, one not altogether outside her experience, but certainly not close to it – its protagonist is Mr. Torrance, a small-town high school Latin teacher who is cut off from all around him by his intellectualism and his aesthetic values. Because of a long-ago affair with a student whom he was forced to marry by the press of the town's proprieties, he remains disgraced and so can never become principal; his wife is a woman who now disgusts him and with whom he has little in common. The story focuses on a moment when Mr. Torrance loses his grip; he confesses his disgrace to one of his prize students, who reveals the lapse to her friends. Nothing good for Mr. Torrance will come of this; his situation is bleak – the basket of strawberries an emblem of things he will never have.

Interviewed by J.R. (Tim) Struthers of the University of Western Ontario in 1981, Munro spoke about the stories she was writing during the 1950s, some of which were later included in *Dance of the Happy Shades*, saying, "I think every young writer starts off this way, where at first the stories are exercises. They're necessary exercises, and I don't mean they aren't felt and imagined as well as you can do them." She then differentiates these stories from "The Peace of Utrecht," "the first story I absolutely had to write and wasn't writing to see if I could write that kind of story." Looking at the contents of *Dance* and thinking particularly of the stories from the 1950s, Munro recalls, "Well, you see, there were periods in here where I wrote hardly anything, due to things in my life, and writing blocks, and so on."[27] "Cortes Island" recreates the frenzied pace of Munro's writing, the repeated, rejected beginnings – "excitement and despair, excitement and despair" – and the *Mayfair* editorial note highlights one of the major "things" in Munro's life that competed with her writing: the publication of her first commercial story was concurrent with the birth of the Munros' first daughter. Combining marriage and family with "the black life of the artist" as she did from 1952 through the 1970s, this coincidence of births is a fitting one for Alice Munro. During that time, she was to outward appearances both wife and mother, but concurrently and somewhat secretly, she was also a deeply serious writer, writing on, draft after draft. This is the "double life" Catherine Ross sees in her biography, an apt characterization that well defines Munro's time in British Columbia.

ꙮ

The Munros lived in the apartment on Arbutus Street until the fall of 1952. One of the other tenants there, a woman who looked after an ancient and infirm woman, had been friendly to Alice initially but then turned on her. The summer was hot, and this woman took exception to Munro's walking to the beach in her bathing suit, carrying only a towel. Some of this is captured in Mrs. Gorrie in "Cortes Island." Working at the library, Munro made friends there with co-workers such as Mari Stainsby, who later was a neighbour in West Vancouver and who, in 1971, did one of the first published interviews with Munro. Through the library, too, Munro also met people who were students at the University of British Columbia – images of student housing in Quonset huts, later referred to in stories, come from these years. There were other associations too, and the regular visits to the Careys and MacKendricks. During fall 1952 they moved to another apartment on Argyle Street, where they lived into 1953, though for just six months. Early that year Alice became pregnant so, with financial help from Jim's father, they bought their first house at 445 West King's Road, North Vancouver. They were living there when Sheila Margaret Munro was born on October 5, 1953. Alice was just twenty-two at the time.

As anyone who has had children knows, a baby's arrival changes the life parents have had – utterly. During the 1950s most of those changes fell almost wholly on the mother. In just over a year after Sheila's birth Munro was pregnant again and, less than two years after that, she was pregnant a third time. Remembering this period, Munro has said, "I was reading all the time, things that I would never try to read now, and [I would] write, and of course keep house and have babies to look after and dodge the neighbours." (This dodging, she now says, happened when they lived on West King's Road, not on Lawson.) More than this, Vancouver was not a place Munro took to readily. The image of the narrator in "Material," pregnant and sulky in the midst of unceasing rains, captures her feeling of discomfort, but the best image of Alice Munro, as young mother in Vancouver during the fifties, is found in "The Moons of Jupiter." There, Janet, the narrator, says that she was offended when her father told her that the years she was growing up were a blur to him. She is offended because those same years are so vivid to her. Yet the years when her own children

> were little, when I lived with their father – yes, blur is the word for it. I remember hanging out diapers, bringing in and folding diapers; I can recall the kitchen counters of two houses and where the clothesbaskets sat. I remember the television programs – *Popeye the Sailor, The Three Stooges, Funorama.* When *Funorama* came on it was time to turn out the lights and cook supper. But I couldn't tell the years apart. We lived outside Vancouver in a dormitory suburb: Dormir, Dormer, Dormouse – something like that. I was sleepy all the time then; pregnancy made me sleepy, and the night feedings, and the West Coast rain falling. Dark dripping cedars, shiny dripping laurel; wives yawning, napping, visiting, drinking coffee, folding diapers; husbands coming home at night from the city across the water. Every night I kissed my homecoming husband in his wet Burberry and hoped he might wake me up; I served up meat and potatoes and one of the four vegetables he permitted. He ate with a violent appetite, then fell asleep on the living-room sofa. We had become a cartoon couple, more middle-aged in our twenties than we would be in middle age.

After this vignette, Munro writes a summary two-sentence paragraph that, along with the ending of "Miles City, Montana," stands out as a profound articulation of the child-parent relation: "Those bumbling years are the years our children will remember all their lives. Corners of the yards I never visited will stay in their heads."[28]

The two houses, with their separate kitchen counters and places for laundry baskets, correspond to the Munros' moves. They were in the house on West King's Road – a small, one-storey bungalow they moved into in 1953 – and lived there for just a few years before in 1956 they moved to 2749 Lawson Avenue, West Vancouver. It was a larger, grander house, ringed round by luxuriant hedges and bushes and with a view looking down over other residential streets and Marine Drive to Burrard Inlet with its ships at anchor west of the Lion's Gate Bridge and, more distant, Vancouver itself. There they lived until the family moved to Victoria during the summer of 1963 in order to open Munro's Bookstore. On Lawson Sheila and her younger sister, Jenny Alison, born June 4, 1957, grew, played, and went to school. The Munro family left that house on Lawson during the summer of 1961 to make a trip back home to Ontario, for a visit that became the basis of "Miles City, Montana," one of Munro's most autobiographical stories.

Between Sheila and Jenny, Alice and Jim had a second daughter. Catherine Alice Munro was born early on the morning of July 28, 1955. But before that day was through she was dead, having been born without functioning kidneys. Initially, it looked as if the Munros would face a long-term infirmity. The Munros opted to have Catherine buried without a funeral in an available grave – the body placed in a small box, a common practice in such situations – without any formal marker or service. In subsequent years, Munro was deeply affected by the memories of Catherine; she told Ross that she had recurrent dreams about Catherine until Jenny was born in 1957, dreams that involved a lost baby left outside. Another story in *The Love of a Good Woman*, "My Mother's Dream," connects with these dreams.

But more than that, Catherine Alice Munro – and a fictional figure named Elizabeth based on her – has been a presence in her mother's writings. When Munro was pregnant for the last time, with her daughter Andrea in 1966, she took to writing poetry. Many of these poems are signed – in Munro's hand – "Anne Chamney," and one appeared in the *Canadian Forum* so attributed. Among them is one contrasting Catherine, her "dark child," with her two daughters who lived: "Her face was long and dark / Pulled down by the harrowing effort / To live, to drive blood through her poisoned body. / In a few hours she died." She says that "it would be presumptuous to bring any word to her," since she does not even know where her "dark child" is buried. Addressing her directly, Munro sees her as a "child who went without comfort / Without a word to make you human / Helplessly poisoning yourself / Because my body made your body incomplete."

During the late 1970s, Munro worked on a story she called "Shoebox Babies." In a notebook version of this story, the focus is on Prue, the adult daughter to Bonnie, a famous poet. While Prue was still a child, Bonnie bore Elizabeth, a daughter who lived less than a day. The draft includes Bonnie's account of the shoebox burial, a meeting between Bonnie and an undertaker to make burial arrangements, and Prue's discovery, years later when she was an adult, that her mother had published a book of poems called "Shoebox Babies." Shocked by this discovery, Prue thinks, "I don't understand the function of art. Art."

In the same way and at about the same time, Munro wrote a notebook draft of "Miles City, Montana." It includes another baby Elizabeth, stillborn, buried in the same way. Her presence between the two living children – born fifteen months after the eldest, Cynthia – animates that story's meditation on the child-parent relation. Munro contrasts the personality of each parent as she dissects each person's reaction to the near drowning of their younger daughter, Meg, in the story's central episode. After four-year-old Meg is pulled from the pool, safe and alive, the narrator meditates on what would have occurred had she drowned; those thoughts are in the finished story. What is not there, however, is any mention of the dead baby Elizabeth. "Andrew believed in luck," Munro writes, "his luck, would celebrate it like a virtue. If something not lucky happened, he would shove that out of mind, ashamed. That was why he never mentioned the dead baby. And my mentioning it would seem a kind of sickening parade of misfortune, a dishonesty."[29] Having Catherine Alice buried so long without formal recognition wore on Munro; in 1990, she arranged to have a marker placed in the North Vancouver cemetery – it does not mark her grave, but it at least recognizes her being.

The 1961 Munro family car trip from which "Miles City, Montana" derives was not her first trip home to Ontario. When Sheila was still an infant, just nine months old, Munro flew with her baby back to visit the families. Her father-in-law, Arthur Munro, had made a business trip to Vancouver just before Sheila's birth and, afterwards, Margaret Munro had flown out to help after the baby arrived. So when she was back east during the summer of 1954 Munro visited her family in Wingham. Given Mrs. Laidlaw's illness and the expense involved, her parents could not travel.

During the summer of 1956, Munro took Sheila back to Ontario by train for a visit. That was the last time she saw her mother. Jenny was born the next year, so Munro was not able to make the trip again until 1959 after Anne Chamney Laidlaw's death. During these years, the years of her mother's last illness, Munro wrote to her parents ("Dad wrote *wonderful* letters" – he was the correspondent) and to her grandmother, Sadie Laidlaw – "I wrote to Grandma less often, because I had to be more circumspect." During her trips home, those of the 1960s as well as the 1950s, Alice and her daughters would also visit the Munros in Oakville. After her years at university and in Vancouver, she found she was more used to the middle-class life the Munros lived than she was to the circumscribed life at home. While it was clear that Arthur and Margaret Munro were initially bewildered by their son's choice of a girl to marry, there is no doubt that they came genuinely to like and value her as the years passed. However, when they visited his parents, things were more difficult for Jim than for Alice – in some ways his choice of a wife was indicative of his difference in his parents' eyes. As a child, Jim had felt closer to his paternal grandfather, a minister who had moved from a church in a very small town in Manitoba to Oakville, and spent considerable time with him. His aesthetic interests, too, were at variance with his accountant father's views. But throughout their relations, Alice says, Jim's family was very good to her: "Everything was amicable." Once she left British Columbia and moved back to Ontario, she continued to visit Margaret Munro and also saw a good deal of Jim's sister, also named Margaret.[30]

In "The Moons of Jupiter," Munro uses the phrase "bumbling years" to refer to the time when Sheila and Jenny were children, and that may well be an apt characterization of Munro's life as a housewife in North and West Vancouver from 1953 until the family moved to Victoria in 1963. Given Andrea's later arrival in 1966, Munro thinks of her role as a mother as falling into two periods, one in Vancouver, the other later in Victoria, after they established the bookstore and settled into a new place, one Munro found more comfortable than she had Vancouver. The neighbours that Munro had dodged in Vancouver were women, also housewives and mothers who, in seeking for connection, interfered with Munro's ongoing writing by inviting her to coffee or to engage in other neighbourhood activities when she might be writing. Not at all forthcoming about what she was actually doing, and too polite to rebuff people, Munro was drawn into more of these activities during the years on Lawson Avenue than she would have liked. Jim Munro remembers that when people would call while Alice was writing, she was loath to tell them that she was busy, that she was working, and certainly not that she was writing. As she would later write in "Material," "I never said the word *write*, Hugo had trained me not to, that word was like a bare wire to us." Although she was annoyed that she had been inter-rupted, she never let her friends know they had done so.[31]

In "The Moons of Jupiter," Munro offers a passage that, though ostensibly about Janet, her narrator, seems actually to derive from her own experiences as a young mother in Vancouver:

> When I was the age Nichola is now I had Nichola herself in a carry-cot or squirming in my lap, and I was drinking coffee all the rainy Vancouver afternoons with my neighbourhood friend, Ruth Boudreau, who read a lot and was bewildered by her situ-ation, as I was. We talked about our parents, our childhoods, though for some time we kept clear of our marriages. How thor-oughly we dealt with our fathers and mothers, deplored their marriages, their mistaken ambitions or fear of ambition, how competently we filed them away, defined them beyond any pos-sibility of change. What presumption.

Ruth Boudreau is based on Daphne Cue, who moved into a house across the laneway from the Munros in June 1959. She and her husband, Vic, then a commercial fisherman, were born and raised in West Vancouver. When they moved in across from the Munros, they had just had their first daughter, so the woman who was vacating the house thought to introduce her to Munro, who she knew had young daughters and also liked to read. The two became fast friends, and remain so today. They quickly saw that they were in danger of taking up too much of one another's time, so they decided to meet just one afternoon a week, and that afternoon became sacred, according to both. They met, laughed, told stories, drank coffee, and smoked – but above all they talked about what they were reading. Like Munro, Cue had attended university (taking commerce, which she loathed). They each remember reading and discussing a three-volume biography of D.H. Lawrence together – probably Edward Nehls's *D.H. Lawrence: A Composite Biography*, which was published between 1957 and 1959 – reading all of Katherine Mansfield, also Stendhal's *The Red and the Black*, and discussing Dickens, a particular favourite of Cue's. Daphne recalls Munro seeming to have already read everything. Indeed, by the late fifties, Munro's personal post-university reading of "most of the writers of the twentieth century you're supposed to have read" had been going on for some time. "She was just a walking library as far as I was concerned."

Munro describes these times as not "like literary conversation. It would be just like high-powered gossip. All we knew about these people," the authors and the characters they created, "and their books and their writing and everything. It was the most exciting talk I ever had; of course, it was the only time in our lives that we got to do this. We both read but we didn't know anybody who read like this." Beyond their shared reading, the women were personally compatible – they shared an irreverent sense of humour that allowed them to delight, when they were together, in making fun of the pretensions of their neighbours and acquaintances, giving them nicknames, making up funny stories about their lives. One such episode involved an affected and very British couple who lived in the neighbourhood. It had them naming the woman "Difficult Passage" because of a comment her husband made about his wife's difficulties in childbirth; Cue and Munro imagined the couple's sex life, told each other their versions of it, laughing so much that "we sat down on street benches and just broke up," Cue remembers. Although the two did sometimes see each other as couples – Cue recalls attending the Munros' parties with her husband –

the relationship was mainly between the two women. Recalling this time, Cue says that she "thinks Alice probably got a lot from women friends"; besides Cue, there were other friends, Mari Stainsby among them.

Although the two spoke most frequently about their daily lives, local matters, and reading, Cue was well aware Munro was writing – the bedroom at the back of the house Munro worked in was next to their shared lane. "She'd be typing away every day, in the afternoons, when Sheila was at school and Jenny was having a nap." Munro has frequently said that, during the time Sheila and Jenny were growing up, she was "very big on naps." Generally, she did not talk much about what she was writing, but in two instances Cue was her source for stories. Apart from the grafting on of a play from her own high school experience, and having the boyfriend become an undertaker, Munro took the whole of "An Ounce of Cure" from Cue's experience. When Munro sold the story to the *Montrealer,* she took Cue to dinner – there two sailors tried to pick them up. They were delighted by the impulse, but rebuffed the men. And while the circumstantial details are different, the hapless brother in "Forgiveness in Families" owes much to Cue's own brother.[32]

Munro's "double life" during the 1950s and early 1960s in West Vancouver involved, on the one hand, the day-to-day details of suburban living with a husband and a young family, and a disciplined writing schedule on the other. As she would write in "Miles City, Montana," her narrator's "real work" was "a sort of wooing of distant parts of myself." The children needed care, the house needed cleaning, there were meals to prepare. There were also regular local excursions – Jim Munro remembers trips with the children to the beach (one is detailed in "Shoebox Babies") and around Vancouver, as well as trips back home to Ontario.

There was adult society too. Daphne Cue recalls that the Munros would periodically have parties, often around holidays, as would other couples. This was a time of great drinking at parties – "We didn't fool around," Munro recalls. They did not keep liquor in the house normally, but when they had a party, she says, "everybody got plastered. . . . I can remember hanging out diapers with such a hangover, such a headache, every motion painful. We thought that's just what you did." There was then also, both at these parties and other social occasions, a fair amount of extramarital flirtation. Munro attributes this to the fact that most people were in their twenties or early thirties and had married young; hence, things happened. But the more dramatic incidents, of flirtation acted upon, lay ahead. What happened at a party during the 1950s didn't count. Munro offers a recreation of one of these West Vancouver parties, and one of these extramarital situations in "Jakarta," in *The Love of a Good Woman.* Cue recalls such parties then down on the beach at Oak Bay in West Vancouver, parties that included skinny-dipping, though she does not remember being at any with the Munros. Judging from "Jakarta," though, Munro must have found her way to one, since she offers a scene of "bare bodies splashing and running and falling into the dark water" and her character, Kath, talks to naked people emerging from the sea.[33]

"The Kind of Writer Who Won't Fold up Under Firm Criticism"

When Munro arrived in Vancouver in January 1952, she had written several stories in addition to those that had appeared in *Folio* or had been submitted to Robert Weaver at CBC. During the summer of 1951, she had produced two stories, "The Return of the Poet," which drew on her time at Western, and "The Yellow Afternoon," which looked back to her high school years. Much edited and Canadianized – references to *Maria Chapdelaine* were added at a later stage – it was broadcast on *Anthology,* Weaver's new program, in 1955. In conversation with Struthers in 1981, Munro characterized the 1950s – the time before she wrote "The Peace of Utrecht" – as the time when her attitude was "I will be a writer." After that story, which takes up the searing "personal material" surrounding her mother's death in 1959, her attitude became "some things have to be written by me."[34] Thus Munro sees the 1950s stories largely as exercises, or what she calls "holding-pattern stories." As with her subsequent characterization of her decision to leave her university studies behind, Munro is mostly persuasive here, but not completely. The stories Munro wrote, submitted, and published during the 1950s are more than exercises; they show her grappling with personal material early on – perhaps not with the deep feelings like those about her mother, but with the personal material derived from Wingham.

Talking about the way she has accommodated herself to her reputation, Munro said, "In a way, I pretend that I'm not that person," the writer, "and I go about my life as if I wasn't." Such an approach was easy to manage in the 1950s and into the 1960s – to all appearances Munro was just another suburban housewife and mother. Yet the connection she had made with Robert Weaver in 1951 was alive and the advice he offered, suggesting that she submit to "better Canadian magazines," the *Northern Review* and the *Canadian Forum,* was advice she followed. The two stories she published after "A Basket of Strawberries" appeared in the *Forum,* "The Idyllic Summer" (which Weaver broadcast on *Anthology* in March 1954) and "At the Other Place." These were followed, in 1955, with "The Edge of Town" in *Queen's Quarterly.* Each of these stories shares the same weaknesses and strengths of "A Basket of Strawberries": the descriptions of place are vivid, but the characters and situations are incompletely rendered.

Yet in "At the Other Place" Munro uses first-person narration for the first time in a published story and, although the story's action is melodramatic, the perspective she offers there is one that became characteristic. Signed Alice Laidlaw, the story begins: "On Sunday afternoons in the summer my father and Uncle Bert took turns going down to the other place to have a look at the sheep which were pastured there. Sometimes my father let us come with him. In July we all went down after church, and took a hamper of food with us and had a picnic. We did not go away – even five miles away – very often, and we did not have many picnics. We were excited." After describing the food, Munro offers more family detail before establishing the narrative perspective:

> We took our bathing suits, though the creek was hardly deep
> enough to wade in at this time of year; my mother took a library
> book, not her knitting – she did not knit on Sunday. She and

my father and Elinor, the youngest, got into the front of the milk-truck, and the rest of us sat in the back, as we liked to do, and watched the road unwind behind us, the hills rise up as we went down – riding backwards gave you a funny feeling and made you seem to be going much faster.

Characteristically, Munro follows this image – the children riding backwards – by then describing the country they saw, and with such detail that the reader sees it too: "It was a very hot day, but there had not been enough hot weather yet to burn the country up. The roadside bushes were still green and the money-musk was blooming unfaded in the long grass. Haying-time was almost over, but in some of the fields the coils were still standing."[35]

Apart from its first-person narration, "At the Other Place" is interesting because it draws on Munro's own experience of the land the family kept in Blyth – presumably the Laidlaws went on such excursions. Similarly, the other stories from the early 1950s may be seen touching on her experience – "The Idyllic Summer" is set in the Muskoka of Munro's summer spent waitressing, and "The Edge of Town" begins with a detailed description of Lower Wingham and the Lower Town Store. There Munro emphasizes the place's separateness: "The sidewalk does not go any further, there are no more street lamps, and the town policeman does not cross the bridge." The story is concerned with an outcast character, Harry Brooke, who is not introduced until the story's second page, once the setting is established: "Up here the soil is shallow and stony; the creeks dry up in summer, and a harsh wind from the west blows all year long." Harry, an ineffective storekeeper, is a person set apart from the town by his manner: "His expectancy, his seeking," made the townspeople "wary, uneasily mocking. In a poor town like this, in a poor country, facing the year-long winds and the hard winters, people expect and seek very little; a rooted pessimism is their final wisdom. Among the raw bony faces of the Scotch-Irish, with their unspeaking eyes, the face of Harry was a flickering light, an unsteady blade; his exaggerated, flowering talk ran riot among barren statements and silences." Like Mr.

Torrance in "A Basket of Strawberries," nothing good will come of this difference. But Munro is clearly back home in Wingham – this is personal material; when Jill Gardiner, of the University of New Brunswick, read it to her during an interview in June 1973, she commented, "And yet, you know, that was not an imagined setting. I actually lived [it] . . . it's all *real.* It's all there. I did not *make* it for its meaning. I was trying to find meaning."

During 1953 Munro worked on a story, never published, called "Pastime of a Saturday Night." Like "A Basket of Strawberries," it takes up the time she was studying for her exams toward the end of high school. She tried the material in both third and first person. She may have submitted the latter version to Weaver, since her name is written on the first page in his hand. Indeed, throughout her career, Munro has frequently sent stories off unsigned, "just to get rid of them," she has said. And while the story's plot is of little concern, there is no doubt that she was drawing upon her own and her family's circumstances. Thus, the grandmother here was influenced by Sadie Code Laidlaw:

> My grandmother was a big straight woman, with auburn-grey hair piled in a pyramid on top of her head. She had great strength, and she loved a job she could swing to with her whole body; she missed the farm work she had done as a girl and a young wife. In her dealings with town people, and her conduct of town life, she was timid, strict, and haughty. She was not at ease there and the care of my mother fretted her, as all womanly business did, that asked delicacy and patience more than strength. But she drove herself to do it, believing that all uncongenial duties were for the strengthening of the soul. She was a Presbyterian; her harsh and stirring voice rang out above all the others as they sang the Psalms.

In this story too Munro offers descriptions of the country, the town clock in its tower, and the activities on the town's main street (that is, on Josephine Street, Wingham) of a Saturday night that all turn up in later work.[36]

In January 1956 Weaver offered to buy "The Green April" for $125 for *Anthology*. Like "Pastime of a Saturday Night," some of its characters are based on Munro's aunt Maud and grandmother Laidlaw living in town, though Munro has invented a half-witted cousin. In the same letter, he returns "The Day of the Butterfly," a story published in the July 1956 issue of *Chatelaine* and later included in *Dance of the Happy Shades*. Weaver also comments on "The Edge of Town" in *Queen's Quarterly*, which he had seen, and reports that he had heard that *Chatelaine* had bought one of her stories – this one was probably "How Could I Do That?", a story Weaver had rejected (as "The Chesterfield Suite") but which appeared in the March 1956 issue of the magazine. He asks, "I wonder if you have tried to send any of your fiction to the United States? I have often thought that you might find it useful and interesting to have some comments from editors in the United States, and I am sure that some of the more serious magazines there would at least be interested in reading some of your stories."

This letter, written about five years after Munro first made contact with Weaver and more than two after they had met – Weaver had walked up to the North Vancouver house on a very hot day in 1953 – might well be seen as typifying his interest in and support of Munro's work: an acceptance, compliments, a useful suggestion, and a rejection – in that order. The year before he wrote this letter, Weaver had written a CBC memorandum to Robert Patchell, who worked on literary programs in Vancouver, regarding Munro. Weaver reports and details his Toronto group's negative readings of Munro's "Thanks for the Ride" and "The Chesterfield Suite," but in the final paragraph he addresses a disagreement between those in the CBC in Vancouver and those in Toronto:

> One reason I have been very slow to write you about the stories is that I admire Alice just about as much as you do – after all I did manage to buy what I suspect was the first short story she ever sold – but she also strikes me as the kind of writer who won't fold up under firm criticism, and I don't think we need to take stories from her because we are afraid she might otherwise stop writing all together.

Weaver recalls that there was a feeling among Patchell and others in Vancouver, who had come to know Munro there as something of a local talent, that if the CBC asked too much of her she might "be damaged," and "might stop writing." Weaver saw this, then and now, as having something to do with the relation between a regional office and the centre, Toronto – that is, as an instance of Canadian regionalism – but he also thinks it was a real fear about Munro in British Columbia. Obviously, Weaver did not think the caution was justified and, just as obviously, he was right.37

ᘒ

Throughout the 1950s, Munro kept writing stories, submitting them to Weaver for broadcast consideration and also sending them to magazines. In 1953 and 1954 a story was published each year and there were two in 1955. Weaver also broadcast two stories during 1954–55. Three Munro stories were published in both 1956 and 1957, and she had another, "The Green April," broadcast on *Anthology*. Of these latter seven stories, Munro excluded four from *Dance of the Happy Shades*, but the other three – "The Time of Death," "The Day of the Butterfly," and "Thanks for the Ride" – were included in that first book when it was published in 1968. During the mid-1950s Munro was producing her first mature work.

During 1956–57 Munro published three stories in *Chatelaine*. The first of these, "The Chesterfield Suite," was the one that Weaver rejected, writing to Patchell that though "it could be done quite successfully on radio," it is "not terribly exciting." The four people who read her work in Toronto agreed "Alice is a writer who should be encouraged in every possible way" but, for Weaver, "The Chesterfield Suite" and "Thanks for the Ride" were "not really successful." When he returned the second *Chatelaine* story, "The Day of the Butterfly," to Munro, Weaver said it was "a pleasant story, but not really as interesting as much of your other work." But he adds that "it is quite possible you might be able to interest a magazine in this story." The third story, "The Dangerous One," appeared in the July 1957 *Chatelaine*. In the March 1956 issue, which carried "The Chesterfield Suite" as "How

Could I Do That?", Munro is described, accompanied by a small pho-tograph, on the masthead page as "a prolific and successful writer. Since she began writing during her student days at the University of Western Ontario, twenty-four-year-old Mrs. Munro has had stories read over the CBC and published in magazines and university journals. Most of them have had a small-town background similar to her own that, until six years ago, was Wingham, Ont. Now she lives in North Vancouver, does part-time work in a library, and cares for a daughter, Sheila, who is, her mother says, 'wild and merry, contrary and delightful, as only a two-year-old can be.'"[38]

Since this brief biography notes that with "How Could I Do That?", Munro was making "her first appearance in Chatelaine," it is fair to surmise that editors at the magazine thought they had found a new talent appropriate to their readers' tastes. But as Weaver's faint praise of "Day of the Butterfly" implies, magazines like *Chatelaine* were looking for a certain sort of story – those centred on women's experi-ences – and the three stories of Munro's they published conformed to type: "How Could I Do That?" focuses on a teenaged daughter's cruel snub to her mother in front of her girlfriends; "The Day of the Butterfly" (published in the magazine as "Good-By, Myra"), on the nar-rator's memory of Myra Sayla, an outsider from her group of schoolgirl friends, who falls ill and dies; "The Dangerous One," about a cousin who comes to live with a protagonist's grandmother and who proves to be dangerous because she is both a liar and a thief.

That Weaver rejected such stories – and that *Chatelaine* bought them – is significant. Weaver and his colleagues at the CBC were pushing Munro away from conventional stories and toward her own material. In May of 1957, Weaver wrote Munro, rejecting a story called "The Cousins." After taking detailed issue with Munro's treatment of her material, Weaver summarized their reaction to the piece by describ-ing it bluntly as "a fairly disastrous failure." After such a categorical rejection, Weaver asks for a letter telling him what she is doing. "Have you begun work on a novel yet?" He says, "I may have given your name to Robert Fulford, Managing Editor of *Mayfair Magazine*" because that magazine "is once again buying short stories from time to time and might be worth trying." As it happened, Gladys Shenner, the *Chatelaine* editor who had bought Munro's stories, had left the magazine, so it is not altogether clear that Munro would have continued selling stories to them in any case. But here – and over the next three or four years especially, as Munro submitted and then sold stories to the *Montrealer* at Weaver's suggestion, and as the idea of a collection of stories became more possible – Weaver was consistently both critical and encouraging.[39]

A key instance of Weaver's ability to both support Munro and push her involves "Thanks for the Ride," a story she no longer admires but one that, when she wrote it in 1955, represented just the ambition Weaver was speaking about when he rejected "The Cousins." The story focuses on an adolescent pickup affair. Responding to the readings it received at the CBC, Munro kept revising and working on it.[40] Along with several other editors, Weaver was just then founding a new literary quarterly, the *Tamarack Review* (1956–1982), an important presence during this early and crucial time in Canadian literary history. Weaver was one of two editors of the quarterly; the other was William Toye, who worked at Oxford University Press in Toronto. Weaver ran *Tamarack* concurrent with his work at the CBC; at some point "Thanks for the Ride" left the CBC and went there. Munro recalls having to redo it once it was rejected by the *Tamarack Review*, since Jim, having read it, made some critical comments when it came back. She responded, in a rage, by taking the manuscript to the trash and throwing it out. Then Weaver wrote and asked to see it again, so she redid it yet again and "Thanks for the Ride" – the same version that was included in *Dance of the Happy Shades* – was the lead story in *Tamarack*'s second issue.

Throughout, Weaver was doubtless well aware that, given its risqué subject matter, he could not broadcast the story, but publishing it in a literary review was another matter. For him, that was not the point: he was prodding Munro to make this ambitious story a more accomplished one. Whether he knew it or not, Weaver was also pushing Munro to go deeper into her personal material: although Lois in "Thanks for the Ride" is not an explicitly autobiographical character, Munro doubtless knew girls like her who lived in Lower Town, girls who dropped out of school early and found work in the Wingham glove works, girls who were often viewed by boys as sexual objects rather than as persons. Dick, the narrator, is a middle-class boy who has his father's car for a weekend visit to his mother at a religious health camp; his background is thus somewhat analogous to Jim Munro's. By encouraging Munro to go deeper into these characters, Weaver was pressing her to sharpen her sense of the class differences that existed in her marriage, differences that, she has said, were always there during her time with Jim.

These contexts define "Thanks for the Ride" as an important transitional story. The first-person narrative, one that manages to reveal Lois's anguish by way of external description, shows a marked improvement in Munro's handling of character relative to setting, and the development in the story as revealed by the versions in the Calgary archive demonstrates that Munro did respond to Weaver's critique. Munro has said, speaking of the whole of her career, that "at a certain point I need somebody"; that is, she needs another set of eyes, another sensibility, another assessment. For her, the first such person was Robert Weaver, backed up by his primary reader, Joyce Marshall, and the other readers at the CBC: he supported and encouraged her, he criticized her work in a professional, positive way, he suggested other publishers, he kept up their literary and professional connection. As she was later to write: "Connection. That was what it was all about."[41] During the 1950s, Robert Weaver was Alice Munro's most important connection to the growing world of serious Canadian writing.

⟫

Yet but for the lifeline Weaver offered to Munro through his letters and his very occasional literary parties when he visited, Alice Munro had to persist alone as a writer. Jim was very supportive although, as his comments about "Thanks for the Ride" showed, like many spouses he was not always able to hit the right note; in any case, he saw little of his wife's work in progress. Through Weaver Munro had made some local literary contacts in Vancouver, but her personality and family situation did not incline her to encourage them. In 1955, just after Catherine's birth and death, Munro went out to the University of British Columbia to hear Ethel Wilson speak – Wilson was a writer whose work she admired and who, she knew, also lived in Vancouver. Munro later wrote to Mary McAlpine, a writer and early Wilson biographer, that her discovery of Wilson's work in the early 1950s made her go "out of my mind with delight. Real writing was being done right where I lived!"[42] But Munro did not speak to her. Through Weaver she had met some of the people at the university involved in creative writing – people like novelist Robert Harlow – but this, too, was not a connection Munro was prepared to follow up, aware as she was of her own lack of university credentials. During her years in Vancouver, Munro came to know Margaret Laurence, who had returned from Africa and settled there with her family in 1957. Munro met her in 1960 at a book launch for Laurence's first novel, *This Side Jordan*, and both Munros remember seeing the Laurences socially during the early 1960s. Particularly, Munro recalls being aware that Laurence was writing *The Stone Angel*.

But mainly it was a solitary business for Munro as she pressed on, writing and submitting her stories, having some broadcast and publishing an increasing number of them in a variety of venues as the decade passed. When she was profiled for the first time in the North Vancouver *Citizen* in August 1961 under the headline "Housewife Finds Time to Write Short Stories," the writer quoted Robert Fulford who described her as "the least praised good writer in Canada."[43]

"A Lump of Complicated Painful Truth Pushing at My Heart"

After Jenny Munro's birth in June 1957 and ongoing, ultimately fruitless attempts at novels – work that brought on depression and a period of writer's block – Munro had no publications or any stories broadcast until the early 1960s. Almost twenty years later she wrote about this period in what appears a draft connected to "The Moons of Jupiter." In a scene showing the narrator at home with her children in rainy Vancouver, Munro writes: "Yesterday I was sick and stayed in bed. I was not very sick, just wanted to shut things down and pull up the covers and have hot drinks and watch television." She continues, offering remembered details of *Funorama*, of her daughters' reactions to that program (it is 1959, they are six and two, just as Sheila and Jenny were that year), and of the time the program kept the girls occupied and so gave her time to think:

> I never thought a television program would make me nostalgic, if nostalgic is what I am. I spent a lot of time then being nostalgic for, or at least harking back to, something else. I wanted that fifteen minutes to myself for harking-back purposes. I was trying to be a writer but I seldom wrote anything. What I did was try to get clear my mind, and hold on to, something I meant to write about. It was the past, it wasn't yet my past. In my bedroom I had a print of Chagall's *I and the Village* which I looked to for help. I don't like admitting that – the moony white cow's head, the precious stones, the upside-down church, all seem rather stylish and cleaned-up, in relation to that real past I had to deal with, even as a dream that picture is a long way out – but it is true that when I lay on the bed and looked at it I could feel a lump of complicated painful truth pushing at my heart; I knew I wasn't empty, I knew that I had streets and houses and conversations inside; not much idea how to get them out and no time or way to get at them.[44]

The draft goes on to explain why this Chagall print hung where it did, and this in turn takes her into an analysis of her marriage, and her husband and men generally. This vignette captures Munro the writer in Vancouver in 1959 feeling "a lump of complicated painful truth pushing at" her heart, but knowing "she wasn't empty." It was about this time that in her reading Munro discovered Eudora Welty's *The Golden Apples*, a book that proved to be talismanic. Comparing her first reading of *Emily of New Moon* to Welty's 1949 collection of stories, Munro has said that she read Emily "when I was just touching on becoming a writer." Welty's book, by contrast, came to Munro when she *was* a writer: "It is so good, it is so good, and I read it over and over again. And not really to find out how she did it, just to let it sink in. It

was the kind of writing I most hoped to do. . . . I read it for just transcendence, almost to get into that world." "That world" is the creation
of Morgana, Mississippi – its people, its place, its ethos – so richly and
fully drawn that a reader participates in its very being, its essences. So
deep was the effect of *The Golden Apples* on Munro that as the years
passed she felt "that I shouldn't read it too often, because there are
writers who can absolutely mesmerize you so you're echoing things they
do without even knowing it, so you stay away from them when you're
writing." And at the time she discovered Welty's book, as her recollection of that time in the *Funorama* fragment shows, Munro was tentative, open to influence. Just after she spoke about Welty, Munro added
that during her early years as a writer she "felt so unsure of my voice. I
can still feel unsure of it." Being a writer is not like being a surgeon –
you learn an operation and then just go in there and do it, confident you
will do it right – "Writing isn't like this at all. It isn't like this at all. It's
just constant despair." Constant despair over the insufficiency of what
has actually been created. Or, as she wrote in her tribute essay "Golden
Apples," she was struck, reading Welty, "by the beauty of our lives
streaming by, in Morgana and elsewhere."45

Doubtless part of the appeal of *The Golden Apples*, for Munro, had
to do with its form: it is a collection of interconnected short stories,
with all its characters derived from the same Mississippi town. When
he had written to her about "The Cousins" in May 1957, Weaver had
also asked what was to be, for Munro during the late 1950s and into the
1960s, *the* vexed question: "Have you begun work on a novel yet?" At
this time in North American publishing in general, but in Canada especially, there was a widely held prejudice against collections of short
stories. It was a truism among publishers that such collections did not
sell, and that they should be attempted only once an author's reputation was already established through the prior publication of a novel.
Munro came up against this view early, and it hounded her well into
the 1970s – indeed, it is fair to see the almost twenty-year genesis of her
first book, *Dance of the Happy Shades*, as a direct result of this attitude.

So much of the "constant despair" Munro felt during the later
1950s and into the 1960s was brought on by her ongoing response to

Weaver's question. Her depression was not clinical, it was derived from her continuing failure during these year to write a novel, despite numerous attempts. The process proved counterproductive for her, but during this time she worked away at a projected novel, one variously entitled "The Death of the White Fox" or "The White Norwegian," or just "The Norwegian," which exists in manuscript in the Calgary archives. There is another, "The Boy Murderer," which features a character named Franklin coming home from the war and jumping off the train before it gets to his hometown, Goldenrod. Munro wrote this scene numerous times; some of Franklin's situation and some members of his family were the basis of Garnett French's in *Lives of Girls and Women*. And Munro has said that "The Found Boat," a story included in *Something I've Been Meaning to Tell You*, was salvaged from another attempt at a novel.

"The Death of a White Fox" is the most complete of these ventures. It is the story of two sisters – Angie, fifteen, and May, seven – who are sent to live with relatives in Jubilee during the summer of 1947 because their mother, a widow living in London, is either dead or going into a sanatorium for six months. (This is something of the same circumstance faced by her grandmother Bertha and aunt Blanche Stanley, who were each taken in as teenagers when their mother died.) One draft begins:

> On the bus all afternoon and all evening, from noon till dark. How far was it, then, from the city to Jubilee? Not that far. It was only that the bus did not travel very fast, that we stopped and had waits in all the little towns along the way. Towards evening we stopped in Dungannon, in St. Augustine, in Kincaid, Crosshill, and Black Horse. Names familiar to me from my mother's stories of her old life at home, little legendary towns of brick and wood and modern service stations; I had always wanted to see them. Why; what did I expect to find? Nothing, really; I knew they would not be very different from other places, I knew there would be nothing in particular to recognize. But my mother had been here, my mother had gone to

dances and taught school here before I was born, and so I saw these towns in a fabled light, an emanation, probably, of my own marvelous, mystical egoism.

In an interesting way, Munro is reversing geography here – she takes Angie and May to Huron County where they find their mother's personal history; this is what Alice Laidlaw, from Huron County, found in Scotch Corners when she visited there, both with her mother and sister in 1943 and later alone when she was herself sixteen. Equally, the geography Angie finds in Jubilee is reminiscent of Scotch Corners – a small lake formed by the widening of a river, as the Mississippi does there. And more than the setting is borrowed from life. Munro draws obliquely on her parents' history here; Chris, the stepson of Angie and May's remarried grandmother, returned home from the war to begin fox farming:

> And Chris spent his time making a special and elaborate kind of feeding-dish for each pen, making watering-dishes that could be tipped and emptied from the outside of the pen, so the water would always be fresh, building new, ventilated kennels and wooden runs along the wire. He was a slow worker, and all the things he made were ingenious and carefully finished. In the colony of pens where the foxes lived everything was of his own design. The foxes inhabited a world he had made for them; it was separate and complete. In the fall he would kill those he wanted to pelt, using chloroform, and a box he had invented for that purpose.

These details are taken from Bob Laidlaw's fox farm. Chris, who is something of a ne'er-do-well, is engaged to a nurse in Toronto, Alice Kelling, who provides him with the money to buy an expensive white fox, a Norwegian, to introduce into his breeding stock. While not exact, this relation is reminiscent of Annie Chamney's provision of money to begin the Laidlaw fox farm in Wingham. Though engaged, Chris is attracted to Angie, just as she is to him, and the two act on it –

stealing away several times to kiss and explore one another, not more than that – until Chris withdraws; in response, Angie releases his prized white fox and, as a consequence, the two sisters are sent away again.

Reasonably complete, "The Death of the White Fox" in its various guises and directions reads more like a long short story than it does a novel, although there are sections where a broader, novelistic, background is created. Remembering the progress of the writing, Munro said that she had it going for a while but then Jim's parents came to visit, keeping her from the novel. When she returned to it, she discovered it was not working. More than that, she sees this time as a "bleak period" in her life as a writer, noting that "you don't like to tell anybody about it."[46] Looking at "The Death of a White Fox" now, what is most interesting about this manuscript is the way Munro drew on its various details and motifs in her subsequent writing: elements of "Boys and Girls," "Images," *Lives of Girls and Women*, "Chaddeleys and Flemings," as well as others are readily visible here. And though intended as a novel, and pursued in just that way for some time, "The Death of the White Fox" demonstrates that Munro's imagination has long seemed most fixed on the story form, that the broader canvas and single narrative of the traditional novel have consistently eluded her. Rather, Munro has created novelistic effects in her use of shorter forms, a method that has become ever more pronounced as her career has progressed.

☙

Though the late 1950s was a frustrating time for Munro, she continued to pursue possibilities through Robert Weaver. In early 1958, for example, he wrote her about including one of her stories in an anthology he was editing for Oxford University Press and wondered about the progress of her novel. He had heard about her work on it from Robert Harlow in Vancouver and suggested that he might "broadcast or publish a chapter." He offers to suggest publishers for the novel and asks, "Did you have any luck with the English magazines I mentioned to you?" Late that year Weaver orchestrated Munro's first application for a grant from the newly formed Canada Council in support of her writing. She wanted to use the money to pay for babysitting. He arranged for application forms, suggested people who would be willing to write letters of recommendation, and then contacted them himself. At one point he writes Munro that he's "glad you don't mind my interfering" with this matter. At this time too Weaver was encouraging Munro to apply to another new body, the Humanities Research Council of Canada – something she apparently did, though there is no record of an application.

Although Munro's application to the Canada Council proved unsuccessful, this episode reveals Weaver's utter willingness to work on Munro's behalf and, as well, it reveals Munro herself in early 1959. In December 1958 Weaver telegraphs Munro that he has arranged letters of support for her application from Murdo MacKinnon (the Western English professor who recruited her for Honours English), Milton Wilson (literary editor, *Canadian Forum*), and Weaver himself. He also said that no one was available to write from *Chatelaine*, owing to staff changes, and he suggested that she approach George Woodcock, who "knows your work and would probably write from Vancouver if you wish." Just then, Woodcock was founding the magazine *Canadian Literature* – it began publication in 1959. A few days after the new year, Munro wrote back to Weaver:

> I got your telegram suggesting George Woodcock. Do you know I very carefully composed a letter, feeling that since I hadn't met him I couldn't really phone, and I put it in an envelope, sealed and addressed it, and then I simply couldn't send it. This is rather peculiar and hard to explain. In fact I can't explain it. I suppose I felt I had no right to ask him. Or I was afraid of being turned down, which would bother me a good deal because I respect his opinion. I felt I was weakening my chances by not asking him but I could not do it. The truth is I would probably have been unable to bring myself to ask anybody, when it came right down to it. This is pretty stupid, because basically I don't feel so worthless and undeserving as all that. But thanks anyway.

When he replies to this, Weaver says that he is "sorry you didn't approach Woodcock" since "there was no reason for you to be shy. I'm sure that he would have been quite prepared to write a letter for you; if I had thought that shyness might keep you from getting in touch with him I would have sent him a wire myself and I'm sorry now that I didn't do it." Weaver continues to say that "three letters should be sufficient if the Council feels any sympathy for your application." They apparently did not: she did not get the grant.

In the same letter in which she describes not approaching Woodcock, Munro remarks that she "had heard of The Montrealer but I had no idea they paid as well as that. If you have time someday I would be glad of the address. Though I don't seem to think along the short-story lines any more. Jim wishes I did. It was much nicer, financially." In his next letter, Weaver provides the address and tells her that they would probably consider stories that have been broadcast but not published. Munro's comments here – both with regard to Woodcock and concerning the *Montrealer* – reveal her in early 1959 as just the person, and just the writer, she remembered when she recreated herself over-hearing her daughters watching *Funorama*: Munro "knew she wasn't empty." At the same time, as she explained to Weaver, she was also shy and unable to ask anyone to write on her behalf. When she also says she is not thinking "along short-story lines any more," it suggests that Munro was trying to bolster her own feelings about her various attempts at a novel.47

⋙

Little more than a month after Munro wrote to Weaver, Anne Clarke Chamney Laidlaw reached the end of her almost twenty-year struggle with Parkinson's disease. She died on February 10, 1959, in the Wingham hospital. The *Advance-Times* ran the notice at the top of its first page:

> Friends in this community were saddened to learn of the passing of Mrs. Robert E. Laidlaw at the Wingham General Hospital on Tuesday of last week. Mrs. Laidlaw had suffered for over 20 years from a chronic illness, which, as it progressed, left her greatly handicapped. For the past two months she had been

a patient at the hospital and her gallant fight against heavy odds will long be remembered by family and friends. She never lost interest in community affairs and until the last tried to lead a useful life.

Munro did not attend her mother's funeral. Jenny was just twenty months old, it was winter. The trip back east would have been expensive and this was a death long anticipated. Remembering, Munro says, "So I didn't try very hard, but I always wished I had – I wish very much I had. I wish I had come to see her when she was dying. But at the time, I had a harder heart. . . . That was part of your intellectual pride. It was part of mine, to look at things very clearly, and it was part of my revolt against Mother, who was, in her talk to me, sentimental in a self-serving way." Munro had not seen her mother since she visited Ontario with Sheila during the summer of 1956.

After Alice married and moved to Vancouver, Bob Laidlaw had continued to work as the second-shift night watchman at the foundry, and during those years began raising turkeys. This combination brought improved finances for the family and some luxuries they had never had. Mr. Laidlaw and Bill – who was in high school, and then also went to Western on scholarship – worked outside most of the time, leaving Mrs. Laidlaw with Sheila, a year younger than Bill, in the house. Their friend and neighbour Julie Cruikshank recalls visiting Mrs. Laidlaw regularly as a child during the early 1950s; she "was alone much of the time, and she was very, very welcoming when I came." Mrs. Laidlaw gave Julie chocolates – a real treat – and they would talk. Mrs. Laidlaw shook, and she was somewhat difficult to understand, but these visits were part of Julie Cruikshank's childhood routine. "Mr. Laidlaw would come in, usually from the barn, and sit down and be very friendly." Mrs. Laidlaw was very slow, she also recalls, "sitting much of the time."[48]

During the late 1940s, when Alice was still at home and was looking after things, Mrs. Laidlaw acknowledged her daughter's contribution and was grateful. But during the years after Alice had married, her sister, Sheila – then also in high school – had to deal with Mrs.

Laidlaw, who had "gone right under with the disease," according to Munro. Sheila was able to finish high school and leave for art college, but there is no question in Munro's mind that her sister's circumstances were more difficult than her own. To help, the Laidlaws had a succession of women come in, but none worked out well. By the time of Mrs. Laidlaw's death in 1959, all the children were gone, and Bob Laidlaw was left to look after things himself, along with such assistance as his elderly mother and aunt in town and friends could provide.

On July 10, 2002, Munro's birthday, the Wingham Horticultural Society dedicated the Alice Munro Garden next to the North Huron Museum, the former post office, on Josephine Street in Wingham. It was a gala occasion and Munro was being celebrated by hundreds of people. As she said, "all was wonderful and happy." Then there was a surprise, a surprise worthy of an Alice Munro story. "I was signing books and a woman, an old woman, came up to me and said, did you know your mother got out of the hospital?

"She began to talk to me and then other people interrupted and she just stayed until she could get me, and she told me the whole story of how my mother got out in the snow barefoot, got out some back door." She had made her way to this woman's house. The woman, a nurse, had nursed her in the hospital, and Mrs. Laidlaw knew where she lived. "And she went and knocked on the door in her hospital gown and told her she had to get out of there and she had to go home."

As Munro wrote in "The Peace of Utrecht," the first of her stories to deal with the facts and memory of her mother, the one that uses Anne Chamney Laidlaw's flight, people emerge in life to make "sure the haunts we have contracted for are with us, not one gone without." When this woman approached her, Munro already knew about her mother's escape, as her story makes clear; Aunt Maud and her grandmother made sure to tell her, but she did not know the details, that her mother was barefoot in the snow. Bob Laidlaw had not told Alice, off in Vancouver, how bad things were with her mother – and he certainly did not tell her about the escape; "he didn't see why we had to know anything so harrowing."[49]

"I Felt As If My Old Life Was Lying Around Me, Waiting to Be Picked Up Again"

Anne Chamney Laidlaw's death led directly to "The Peace of Utrecht," which appeared in the spring 1960 issue of the *Tamarack Review*, little more than a year after her mother's death. Munro has called this story her "first really painful autobiographical story . . . the first time I wrote a story that tore me up"; it was one "I didn't even want to write." To another interviewer, she has commented that "Peace" "was the story where I first tackled personal material. It was the first story I absolutely had to write" and, because of this, there was nothing in it of the exercise Munro remembers in the stories she had written to this point.⁵⁰ And more than this, "The Peace of Utrecht" represents Munro's imaginative homecoming to Wingham after her years away in Vancouver, home to the personal material that would subsequently become her hallmark.

Set squarely in the centre of "The Peace of Utrecht" is the history of Anne Chamney Laidlaw's lingering imprisoning illness and death. There too are Maud Code Porterfield and Sadie Code Laidlaw, living together in Jubilee, though just as Helen and Maddy's aunts. It is the summer after their mother's death, their father is long dead, and Helen – who did not return home for the funeral – has driven across the country with her children for a long visit with her unmarried older sister, Maddy. Helen "had won a scholarship and gone off to university," as Munro writes in one draft, "and at the end of two years, to her own bewilderment, she was married, and going to live in Vancouver." She still lives there. She is the story's first-person narrator.

The core subject of the story and much of its detail are autobiographical. Having been home the summer after her mother's death, Munro had learned about her mother's "harrowing" escape from the hospital, and that is in the story. Much else is imagined: Maddy has elected for the past ten years, the years Helen has been away, to look after their mother, and many of Helen's circumstances do not correspond to Munro's. She draws on her own visit home, creating the homecoming she had experienced, but does so amid imagined family details – Helen drives herself across the continent, the home is more middle class, it is in the town, Maddy and Helen's father is dead.

> People ask me what it is like to be back in Jubilee. But I don't know, I'm still waiting for someone to tell me, to make me understand that I am back. The day I drove up from Toronto with my children in the back seat of the car I was very tired, on the last lap of a twenty-five-hundred-mile trip. I had to follow a complicated system of highways and sideroads, for there is no easy way to get to Jubilee from anywhere on earth. Then about two o'clock in the afternoon I saw ahead of me, so familiar and unexpected, the gaudy, peeling cupola of the town hall, which is no relation to any of the rest of the town's squarely-built, dingy grey-and-red-brick architecture. (Underneath it hangs a great bell, to be rung in the event of some mythical disaster.)

This is just how Wingham looks across the "prairie" river flats south of town as one drives north on Highway 4. The story is about the shared relation between sisters, one based on their mother's circumstances. Returning, discovering her own handwriting on some pages in a wash-stand, Helen "felt as if my old life was lying around me, waiting to be picked up again." When Munro first drafted the story it was called "Places at Home" – but the title, like Helen's life, is to be found in that washstand since her handwritten notes from years before read "The Peace of Utrecht, 1713, brought an end to the War of Spanish Succession."

"The problem, the only problem, is my mother," Munro would later write in the same manner in "The Ottawa Valley," produced after she had dealt more and more with personal material through the 1960s. "The Ottawa Valley" mother is more recognizably Anne Clarke Chamney Laidlaw. This one in "The Peace of Utrecht" is a more imaginative construction, more of a created character:

> "Everything has been taken away from me," she would say.
> To strangers, to friends of ours whom we tried always un-
> successfully to keep separate from her, to old friends of hers who

came guiltily infrequently to see her, she would speak like this, in the very slow and mournful voice that was not intelligible or quite human; we would have to interpret. Such theatricality humiliated us almost to death; yet now I think that without that egotism feeding stubbornly even on disaster she might have sunk rapidly into some dim vegetable life. She kept herself as much in the world as she could, not troubling about her welcome; restlessly she wandered through the house and into the streets of Jubilee. Oh, she was not resigned; she must have wept and struggled in that house of stone (as I can, but will not, imagine) until the very end.   .

At one point in the story Munro describes how the mother was seen by others in the town, and she has Helen conclude, "We should have let the town have her; it would have treated her better."[51] We cannot help thinking of Anne Chamney Laidlaw's obituary in the *Advance-Times* – its bereaved tone and genuine feeling, both born of the extended suffering involved, coming through strongly. While Munro was writing "The Peace of Utrecht" she tried to tell the story of the two sisters through a first-person narrator, Ruth, a neighbour and girlhood friend of Helen's, a person who stayed in Jubilee and so knew the family's history and each sister's relation to it. Though abandoned for Helen's narrative, this attempt is another indication of Munro's psychological return to Jubilee – that is, to Wingham – in order to write more personally this story that she had to write, one she did not much want to write. Ruth's narrative offers the town's point of view and she evidently was intended as the person who revealed to Helen the secret of her mother's flight from the hospital.

Some time in 1959 Munro sent "The Peace of Utrecht" to Weaver – her cover letter is undated but he has noted the story's title on it. Its text is indicative:

> I thought I'd send you these to hear what you thought of them – one is the old story I sent Mayfair & the other is the long one I mentioned[.] I have a couple of better ones – I hope – now

but I'm afraid the experience of feeling so fertile after the long drought has made me very uncertain of criticism – I mean I can't criticize myself very well. I hope I'm not taking up too much of your time.

"The Peace of Utrecht" is probably the long story Munro refers to here. As she first wrote it, the story was formally divided into three parts; published, it is in two. As she shaped the story, Munro appears to have purposely slowed its pace: the opening material about Maddy's relationship with Fred Powell that begins the story in the published version was moved there from a second section. Thus Munro consciously held off the revelation of the circumstances of the mother's death, and especially of her escape from the hospital. Following the undated letter dealing with "The Peace of Utrecht," there are two more letters to Weaver, dated but not explicitly mentioning the story, which probably chart her work on it. These were written in October, the first worrying about whether the story has arrived yet and the other enclosing a new version that Munro has done in the meantime because she "just wanted to get it out of the way. I was afraid that if I didn't do it I would just go stale on the whole thing." In December she writes that she "would like to do a little more work on the Tamarack story if it is not inconvenient though it is not really important." Munro also says that "I hope you will still write to me sometimes even if it isn't about stories. I am working again now after a period of considerable depression and uselessness this fall." Weaver notes on this letter that he wrote her on December 23 and enclosed a proof of the story.[52]

ꙮ

Self-deprecating as always ("I hope I'm not taking up too much of your time"), sounding unsure of herself still, Alice Munro nevertheless wrote to Weaver to make sure she was able to work further on "The Peace of Utrecht" before it appeared in the *Tamarack Review*. One draft version of the story called "Places at Home," a title she would later use again, contained the self-revelatory description of Helen as a person who "had won a scholarship and gone off to university, and at the end of two years, to her own bewilderment, she was married, and going to live in Vancouver." So it was with Alice Laidlaw Munro. But as her history reveals, and especially as her relationship with Robert Weaver confirms, her unwavering commitment to writing – though often occasioning feelings of frustration, isolation, and even depression – ultimately brought her back imaginatively to these same "Places at Home" during the 1950s. As Munro implies, no story demonstrates this better than "The Peace of Utrecht." And given Munro's own history, given Anne Clarke Chamney Laidlaw's long struggle and suffering, it was altogether fitting that when the editors of the *Tamarack Review* ran the story in their spring 1960 issue, they led with it and placed it right before five poems by Irving Layton. The first of these, "Keine Lazarovitch 1870–1959," was the first publication of Layton's later well-known elegy to his mother. It appears on the verso of the last page of "The Peace of Utrecht."53 Well it should, for Munro's story, the necessary return to her own "Places at Home," is an elegy too. And in the years to come, in the several more stories following this first one and the second, "The Ottawa Valley," this elegy continued as Munro probed ever more deeply and ever more consistently into her personal material, finding more stories she had to write. In 1960, a writer still named Alice Munro and still living in Vancouver had embarked on the material and trajectory that would make her Alice Munro.

"I Was Trying to Find a Meaning"

Victoria, *Munro's Bookstore*, Dance of the Happy Shades, *and* Lives of Girls and Women, *1960–1972*

You don't really think about why you write a story. You write it, you hope it works, it's finished. Somebody else can see far better than you can, what it is you're trying to say.
– Alice Munro to Audrey Coffin, April 3, 1968

In November 1960 Bob Laidlaw wrote a letter of condolence to his brother-in-law John Chamney in Scotch Corners – John and Ethel's daughter Lila, just nineteen, had died early that month, the result of a car accident. Once he had expressed his sympathy, Laidlaw reported on himself, Sheila, and Bill, and then added that "Alice & her two girls are well. She is doing well writing. Had a story in a book of Canadian Short Stories recently published. She writes as Alice Munro. It is queer stuff she writes at times but she seems to know what she is doing." Hearing for the first time of this unseen letter and especially its comment on her writing, Munro has said it typifies her father, and his use of the under-cut compliment. Laidlaw knew the details of his daughter's successes but implicitly apologized for them. Later in the letter, he wrote by way of shared grief, "It is now nearly two years since Anne died and I can think of her now as she was in early days. She was a good wife to me and she fought so hard to stay normal."[1]

The book that Laidlaw mentioned was Robert Weaver's *Canadian Short Stories*, published in London and New York by Oxford University Press in 1960 in its World's Classics series. It includes Munro's "The Time of Death," a story she wrote in 1953 and first published in the *Canadian Forum* in 1956. It is the earliest of her stories included in *Dance of the Happy Shades*. As Laidlaw wrote, it was to him "queer stuff." "The Time of Death" tells a stark story, one that begins "Afterwards the mother, Leona Parry, lay on the couch, with a quilt around her, and the women kept putting more wood on the fire although the kitchen was very hot, and no one turned the light on." This is Lower Town Wingham – or a place very like it – and the story takes place in very late, very grey, very stark autumn, as the first snow of winter impends. The whole of "The Time of Death" emerges from its first word: "Afterwards." Leona Parry's nine-year-old daughter, Patricia, whom her mother "had singing in public since she was three years old," was left to look after her younger sister and two brothers while her mother went to a neighbour's to sew her cowgirl outfit – Patricia was singing with the Maitland Valley entertainers. Once her mother is gone, Patricia looks around their slovenly house and says that "it never gets cleaned up like other places." Pronouncing further that she is "going to clean this place up," Patricia gets her brothers and sister to help her. She sets already hot water to boil on the stove to scrub the floor and in the central unseen accident, her youngest brother Benny, eighteen months old and "stupid," is scalded to death.

Though there is a glimpse of Benny's mortal injuries, Munro's focus is on the effects of the accident on others: on the women who have gathered to help and to mourn – Munro makes their personal distaste toward the Parrys, especially Leona, and their way of living, quite evident; on the men, largely unseen, staying outside, sharing a bottle as solace; and most especially on Leona, who has scorned Patricia for what she did, refusing to have anything to do with her. For her part, Patricia seems to have no reaction as she immerses herself in the social activities surrounding the funeral proceedings and ignores her mother and her censure. Once these rituals are over, November arrives, the first snow has still not fallen. Leona eventually reconciles with Patricia ("What's life? You gotta go on," she tells a friend), but still "Patricia did not cry." Benny had been "the only stupid thing [Patricia] did not hate."

Patricia's delayed reaction comes as the story ends with the reappearance of Old Brandon, the scissors-sharpener "who came along the road sometimes." Benny had had a special name for him, "Bram." "Benny remembered him, and ran out to meet him when he came." Seeing him again coming along the road while she is out playing during that first week of November, the snow still not there, Patricia begins screaming and cannot be controlled: "They thought she must be having some kind of fit . . . you'd think she'd gone off her head." The story ends: "The snow came, falling slowly, evenly, between the highway and the houses and the pine trees, falling in big flakes at first and in smaller and smaller flakes that did not melt on the hard furrows, the rock of earth."[2]

However "queer," "The Time of Death" is a powerful story, one rooted in Munro's home place. She told Jill Gardiner in June 1973, "When I first started writing, setting meant more to me than people. This was really what I was writing about. . . . At first I think I was just overwhelmed by a *place*, and the story was almost . . . a contrived illustration of whatever this meant to me." In "The Time of Death" the place, especially through the impending, delayed snow, confirms this comment. Yet Munro extends the characters in their setting to create what she told Boyle was the "positively Gothic" atmosphere of Lower Town Wingham, Huron County, Ontario. Munro also sees the story as "a kind of imitation Southern story . . . I was writing like the people I admired" – and though she does not name these admired writers here, leading candidates include Eudora Welty, Carson McCullers, and James Joyce in "The Dead."

Seen within the contexts of Munro's developing reputation, "The Time of Death" is a singular story. Although any casual scan of the *Wingham Advance-Times* during the 1930s and 1940s yields accounts of similar horrific accidents, one Lower Town family angrily identified its own history in Benny's death. One male member drunkenly threatened Bob Laidlaw because of the story, walking around his house, firing a shotgun into the air. No one was hurt. Known and liked by everyone there, Munro's father downplayed such acts; he knew the people in Lower Wingham, and so knew just who to worry about. But his daughter took them quite seriously and was wary of Wingham for some years after.

As such incidents illustrate, Munro's work was beginning to be noticed as the 1950s ended and the 1960s began. In early 1958, Weaver wrote to Munro asking her which story she preferred for his anthology and so "The Time of Death" became an early representation of Munro's work to a larger audience. In the mid-1960s the Ryerson Press put together another anthology, *Modern Canadian Stories*, and despite the press editor's preference for new stories, the volume editor selected "The Time of Death" as the Munro inclusion. In his introduction he wrote about Munro that "although she has written only short stories, she is highly respected by a good many critics" and that "'The Time of Death' is one of her best short stories."

There were others. "Sunday Afternoon," one of the stories derived from Munro's time as a maid during high school, was included in a revised edition of Desmond Pacey's *A Book of Canadian Stories* published in 1962. The year before, Weaver included Munro's "The Trip to the Coast" in *Ten for Wednesday Night*, a collection of stories first broadcast on the CBC program *Wednesday Night.* For this, "a small group of writers . . . were asked to submit new work for a series of radio readings" and first publication, Weaver wrote.[3]

As this suggests, by the early 1960s Weaver was no longer the lone literary person in Canada who saw Munro as a significant younger writer. Yet owing to her location, inclination, and situation, Munro was no more forthcoming in pressing her case than she had ever been. The word about her was out among people who paid attention to such things – Weaver had certainly succeeded that far – but her stories continued to appear as they had throughout the 1950s, here and there, one at a time. Owing to Weaver's efforts, in late 1961 there was a flurry of activity around the possibility of a collection of Munro's stories. Three publishers considered it, and the *Tamarack Review* did too, but no book emerged. The Ryerson Press, which was among the three publishers considering the idea in 1961 and the one to which Weaver had taken six of Munro's stories after the others had declined them, stuck with Munro. It encouraged her during the interim and eventually published *Dance of the Happy Shades* in the fall of 1968. Although sales were such that the first printing provided sufficient stock to hold the publisher well into the 1970s, Munro was launched. *Dance of the Happy Shades* won the Governor General's Award for Fiction in English. Robert Weaver, it should be noted, chaired the selection committee. In 1971 a putative novel, *Lives of Girls and Women,* followed that first book. It extended and confirmed Munro's growing reputation as one of Canada's leading writers, and it did so just as the nationalist fervour that characterized the late 1960s and early 1970s in Canada took firm hold.

"Sad, Sensitive, and Preoccupied with Detail": The *Montrealer*, a Possible First Book

In 1961, when "The Trip to the Coast" appeared in *Ten for Wednesday Night,* the biographical entry preceding the story ends "Mrs. Munro is now at work on a first novel." That year, too, in the first newspaper profile focused on her, the author wrote that since "her first success

Mrs. Munro has been selling stories to a variety of Canadian publications including 'Chatelaine' and 'Canadian Forum'. Her reputation as a writer of great talent and promise has grown with each story published. Possibly the most surprised, and certainly the most modest, about this success, is Mrs. Munro herself." Munro's modesty, during this time and throughout her career, was not based on any uncertainty about her identity as a writer – a writer was what she was, and what she was continuing to be. As she wrote to Weaver when she told him she had not approached George Woodcock for a reference letter to the Canada Council, "I don't feel so worthless and undeserving as all that." Her modesty has had more to do with her own shyness and, more pointedly, with her own high expectations for her work.

During the late 1950s and into the 1960s, the pressure to write a novel and the difficulties it occasioned vexed Munro; when she writes to Weaver in 1959 of "feeling so fertile after the long drought," or of "a period of considerable depression and uselessness this fall," Munro's drought and her depression were brought on by her dissatisfactions with her attempts at the novel form. A novel, long sought, continued as a major challenge during the 1960s. When one was finally published in 1971 as *Lives of Girls and Women*, that book certainly fulfilled the expectation, if not exactly the form. Throughout these years, as the author of that first profile maintained, Munro's "output has been very small because of the demands of home and family."4

While home and family certainly demanded much of her time – Munro's life at the time was that of any mother to young children, one of interruptions and other demands – it is equally clear that she was struggling with fictional form: "I was trying to find a meaning," she told Jill Gardiner in 1973. What this meant, practically, was that as a writer of fiction Munro was trying to write the novel that others were encouraging her to do. At the same time, as "The Peace of Utrecht" confirmed, Munro was beginning to discover material that was working at a deeper, more personal, level in her stories than she had previously. Thus as she tried to find her way into a novel that worked, Munro was also writing the stories that would prove to be the core of *Dance of the Happy Shades*.

The year 1959 is indicative of Munro's changing focus. When she was working on "The Peace of Utrecht" during that summer she was also at work on "A Trip to the Coast" and "Dance of the Happy Shades" – "feeling so fertile after [the] long drought," she told Weaver. Two of these stories – "Peace" and "Dance" – felt to Munro "like the first real stories" she had ever written. ("A Trip to the Coast," ironically given its connection with these two, is a story she now says she really does not like.) "Dance of the Happy Shades," in contrast to "Peace," does not much draw on personal material. It owes something to a music teacher named Miss McBain who taught Jim's aunt Ethel; it derives its setting from Munro's summer as a maid in Toronto and her visits to Oakville, and it gets its characters from there and from Munro's time in suburban Vancouver.[5]

But while "Dance of the Happy Shades" is a significant story because of Munro's view of it, and it is obviously prominent as the title story of her first book, the circumstances of its initial publication as her first contribution to the *Montrealer* bear comment.

The *Montrealer* (1924–1970) was a monthly magazine focused on the English-speaking society in the city that, certainly into the 1960s, was the cultural and business centre of Canada. English was its language. The *Montrealer* styled itself "the magazine for discriminating Canadians" and throughout its history it was characterized by good writing, though it was not especially literary until the late 1950s, when the editor, David Hackett, began publishing serious fiction. Hackett, an American, left the magazine to work on John Kennedy's presidential campaign and in May 1960 he was replaced by Gerald Taaffe. He also was an American who had emigrated to Canada in 1951 and had worked as a journalist in Quebec City; he wrote fiction as well. He found himself both editor and staff (though there was some help with layout and circulation) and with a budget of a thousand dollars per issue for all costs – journalism, fiction, cartoons, everything. During his time on the *Montrealer* – Taaffe was there until December 1965 – he had to do freelance journalism to support himself.

Taaffe took over the *Montrealer* intent on continuing Hackett's practice of publishing fiction, and as a writer of fiction himself, he wanted to get the best possible. On his arrival in 1960, he went through the slush pile of unsolicited manuscripts (it was over a foot high, he recalls) and found just one piece he wanted to publish – a story called "Dance of the Happy Shades." It was, unfortunately, unsigned. In order to identify its author Taaffe canvassed his Montreal contacts, to no avail. He also wrote with his inquiry to writing magazines in the United States; they published his letter and, after some months, he heard from an Alice Munro in Vancouver identifying herself as the story's author. Taaffe immediately bought it and published it in his February 1961 issue. Munro herself had not seen his letter. The Vancouver poet Elizabeth Gourlay saw it and, having heard the story broadcast on *Anthology* in October 1960, remembered it as one of Munro's. She contacted Munro, whom she did not know, and the two developed a friendship. When she sold "Dance" to the *Montrealer*, Munro took Gourlay to lunch.[6]

"Dance of the Happy Shades" proved to be the first of five Munro stories and one memoir ("Remember Roger Mortimer," February 1962) that Taaffe published in the *Montrealer* between 1961 and 1965. As such, only the *New Yorker* has exceeded this count; the *Tamarack Review* also saw six pieces by Munro, but it did so over a much longer period. "Dance" was followed in the *Montrealer* by "An Ounce of Cure" (May 1961), "The Office" (September 1962), "Boys and Girls" (December 1964), and "Red Dress – 1946" (May 1965). Except for the first, all are rooted in Munro's personal experience – what she calls in the Struthers interview "the real material." These five stories, along with the three that Munro wrote during 1967–68 to complete her book manuscript – "Images," "Postcard," and "Walker Brothers Cowboy" – are among the strongest stories in that book.

Once he found Munro, Taaffe was clearly taken by her work. After already publishing two stories in 1961, he wrote Munro in August. Noting that it "is a long time between your stories" he admitted that he wanted to encourage her, saying "I enjoyed the last two" stories and he is hoping to stimulate her to submit "more work to *The Montrealer.*" He also suggested that she might try "to write a good personal travel essay" but if "this doesn't work, perhaps you are experimenting with a new approach to fiction. . . . At any rate," he promised, "you can be sure of an appreciative reception of anything you send." Evidently, Munro responded quickly, since less than two months later Taaffe writes her apologizing for his "delay in reporting about your 'Remember Roger Mortimer', which I can use in February, and for which I can pay $75. . . . It was a very good personal essay, and I was particularly pleased to see that you have kept the same basic style as that you use in your fiction." In June 1962, Taaffe wrote to Munro about "The Office," telling her of its publication date and adding that he "liked the rewrite quite as much as I did the original version, which is a good deal."7 He had in fact received a revision he had not asked for, one Munro decided to do on her own. This pattern was often repeated in later years when she was publishing in the *New Yorker*. Although her editor might be satisfied, Munro was not.

Also during 1962, Taaffe did a freelance book review for the CBC program *Critically Speaking*, another of the group of programs produced by Weaver. The book under review was *The First Five Years: A Selection From "The Tamarack Review"* edited by Weaver and introduced by Robert Fulford. It was published by Oxford University Press. Taaffe asserts that

> somehow Alice Munro strikes me as the most typical of the *Tamarack* writers, although she would probably be the last to claim first place among them. Her story in this collection is "The Peace of Utrecht", and a single sentence, chosen more or less at random, should help situate it. I quote: "On the hall table was a bouquet of pink phlox, whose scent filled the hot dead air of a closed house on a summer afternoon". Miss Munro's sentence, like her story, is sad, sensitive, preoccupied with detail, as bleak as a ramshackle prairie town – it is written with painstaking perfection.8

Taaffe's enthusiasm for Munro's writing is another key to her growing reputation as the 1960s began. Equally, Munro's submission of an unsigned "Dance of the Happy Shades" is telling. Although Weaver remained her main literary contact, she was becoming known through the impressive qualities found in her prose rather than through personal connections or self-promotion. Taaffe was delighted to buy whatever writing he could get from Munro. He recalls her later stories commanded his top rate ($150 to $200), a sizable portion of his monthly editorial budget and a fee he also paid to such better-known writers as Norman Levine and Mordecai Richler. Thus the five Munro stories and personal essay that the *Montrealer* published between 1961 and 1965 are a reflection of Taaffe's enthusiasm. He paid Munro as much as he could and ran the stories as she sent them, without editing. Taaffe left the magazine at the end of 1965 and the *Montrealer* faded until it ceased publication in 1970.[9]

⤷

During the late summer and into the fall of 1961 the possibility of a book of Munro's stories was suggested for the first time. Three publishers – Appleton-Century-Crofts, McClelland & Stewart, and Ryerson Press – saw a proposed manuscript of five or six stories and Weaver, who of course helped to orchestrate the possibility, was prepared to do "a book through Tamarack Review if all else fails," as he wrote to Munro in August. While it is impossible to be certain, the manuscript likely comprised "The Time of Death," "Sunday Afternoon," "A Trip to the Coast," "The Peace of Utrecht," and "Dance of the Happy Shades." "An Ounce of Cure" was probably the sixth story. In his August letter to Munro, Weaver reported that "the stories have just gone to Jack McClelland" since "he says that he is at least interested in the idea of publishing perhaps half a dozen of the stories and I think he should be given a chance now to make a firm decision." Weaver then details the interest expressed by Appleton-Century-Crofts in New York. David Watmough, an English writer who had immigrated to Canada and settled in Vancouver in 1960, appears to have been an intermediary between Munro and the American publisher. A long paragraph by Weaver demonstrates his thoroughgoing attention to Munro's situation:

> Where does this leave you with Mr. Watmough and his firm in the United States? This sounds to me a little like a fishing expedition on his part since they would have a very tough time

introducing a completely unknown short story writer to an
American audience and in any case the firm isn't really all that
active in fiction. I think I also agree with you that a smaller book
might be a better idea for a beginning. I think perhaps you
should write to Watmough and tell him that six of the stories
have actually been submitted to McClelland and Stewart who
have shown at least some interest. You might offer to get in
touch with him as soon as you have heard from Jack or me, or
you might offer to send him a few of your stories just as long as
he keeps in mind that there is a formal investigation going on
somewhere else. If he really wants the book, who knows but that
he might then get in touch with McClelland and Stewart and
of course that would do you no harm. In any case, try to be a
little evasive right now and keep him on the string.

Following Weaver's suggestion, Munro apparently sent some stories to
Appleton-Century-Crofts since little more than a month later its
editor-in-chief, Theodore M. Purdy, wrote to express interest in
Munro's stories but to encourage her toward a novel as her first book.

Striking the same chord about two weeks later, Jack McClelland
wrote about her five stories: "We have read them here with interest
and appreciation but have some real doubt as to whether it makes sense
to issue them in book form at the present time." He then explains at
some length, providing examples from his own list including *Ten for
Wednesday Night,* just why he thinks story collections do not sell, and
so "don't make a very good start for a writer. . . . Thus our view would
be if there is any hope of your completing the novel in the next year or
so, let's leave the short stories and publish the novel first in book form.
By all means, publish the short stories in periodicals. Sell as many as
you can and as widely as you can. But what about the novel? How is it
progressing? Can we be of any help? Do bring me up to date on the situation." Deft publisher that he was, McClelland tempered this by
leaving the door open a bit: "If the novel is too far in the future and
you are very anxious to have the stories published in book form, just

say so and we will reconsider the matter." A month later Munro talked by phone to Hugh Kane, McClelland's second in command, who later wrote: "I was very glad to have the opportunity to talk to you this morning and happy to learn that you agree with us that publication of your short stories should follow rather than precede the novel on which you have been working."[10]

These publishers' letters – the assumptions they contain, the questions they ask – are worth pausing over as they relate to Munro's career as she moves toward *Dance of the Happy Shades.* Pronounced in her first newspaper profile "the least praised good writer in Canada" by one of the country's leading cultural journalists, championed by Robert Weaver of the CBC and the *Tamarack Review* (who was then broadcasting three more of her stories and seeking more for *Tamarack*), Munro in late 1961 *was* verging on a book. It was her logical next step. But though her stories were very well regarded, a novel and nothing but a novel was what was wanted by the public and by the publishing business. And from the late 1950s on through the 1960s, a novel was what Munro tried to produce, though she never could do so to her own satisfaction. While she had made various attempts at novels throughout this period, it is noteworthy that "The Death of a White Fox" – in its various guises, a long short story, really – is the only surviving narrative of any length in the papers at Calgary beyond preliminary material for *Lives of Girls and Women.* Some of the material from other attempted novels later emerged as stories – "Something I've Been Meaning to Tell You," or "The Found Boat," in her second collection – but much of this work was presumably abandoned or destroyed.

Just after Munro spoke to Kane in mid-November 1961, Weaver wrote her saying that "Ryerson Press wants to see the five short stories since they are trying to find some work by younger writers and obviously intend generally to improve their publishing program. I am going to assume that you won't mind and send the five stories to a friend of mine at Ryerson Press." In the same letter, Weaver also suggested that "if you get a story done which you feel is one of your better ones, why don't you make a concerted attempt to publish it in one of the better

U.S. magazines?" Munro had been doing this for several years, though without any success. Weaver offers to provide her with a list of magazines and adds both sympathetically and perceptively: "I don't know quite what to say to you at the moment about the novel problem, but if you don't feel anxious or even capable of writing a good novel right now and do feel ready to keep on with the short stories, I'd spend the winter on shorter fiction." Here is yet another example of Weaver's thoroughness in his support and advice to Munro – he is pressing on with the book possibility, and acting on it; he wants her to try new magazines for the exposure they might provide; and he is well aware of Munro's aesthetic predicament, balanced between her innate inclination to write short fiction while the market, and a part of herself, wants a novel. And in the earlier letter in which he advises Munro on how to respond to David Watmough, Weaver concludes by saying that "I'll see about an agent in October when I'm in New York."

What this last comment suggests is that during the fall of 1961 Munro and Weaver were investigating a variety of ways to advance Munro's career. This was a time when few Canadian writers had agents and, even in the United States, those who did had them just for book publication. Most short story writers still dealt directly with magazine editors, an arrangement that persisted into the 1970s. Yet here Munro is, implicitly at least, investigating that possibility through Weaver, one that continued to arise from time to time until she hired Virginia Barber as her agent in 1976. Here too Weaver is counselling her to nurture her talent for short fiction, sensing that Munro might not really want to write the novel everyone seemed to expect and, in any case, might not even be capable of it. As she has said of her writing generally, but of this period of her career in particular, and her various attempts at a novel, writing is "just constant despair."

Looking back on the whole of her career, Munro has also said that "at a certain point I need somebody" to respond to her writing. From the early 1950s through the 1960s, Weaver was most certainly that person, and Munro needed and valued his direct personal critique and support throughout these years. But as the 1960s passed, it is clear that Weaver's support involved his reaching outside his own sphere of control into book publishing as Munro's career developed with his careful and persistent help.

ஐ

Weaver's friend at the Ryerson Press was John Robert Colombo. Colombo was an editor there from 1960 to 1963 and had worked on *Tamarack*, where he first became aware of Munro's writing. He recalls receiving Munro's manuscript from Weaver and reading it with the sense "that here is writing of quality and character." As a result he urged the press's editor-in-chief, John Webster Grant, "to write to the author to offer to publish 1,000 copies of the work." Grant did this, but some time before the fall of 1962 Colombo followed up that letter by writing to Munro himself, saying, "We are eager to publish a collection of – say – ten stories, if you feel the time is ripe." He then names the six stories he has in mind – the full group – and notes also a recent "strong story in the Montrealer [that] would make a suitable introduction to the other stories"; that story was "The Office." Colombo also asks if there is unpublished material. As with her apparent reaction to McClelland, here too Munro did not press – in fact, Colombo recalls her "resisting Ryerson's offer to add 'Dance' to its next list" during 1962–63.

Yet Ryerson, owned by the United Church of Canada, was the publisher that eventually brought out *Dance of the Happy Shades*. Begun in 1829 as the Methodist Book and Publishing House, Ryerson had earned distinction for its publication of Canadian writing during the first decades of the century under, successively, E.S. Caswell and Lorne Pierce, who directed Ryerson from 1922 to 1960. John Webster Grant followed him and headed the firm for just three years, 1960 to 1963. He told Colombo after he hired him that he wanted to publish books good enough to receive Governor General's awards. That is, he wanted to publish books that would have both critical and commercial success. Munro was approached in just that spirit. But when Weaver delivered her manuscript of stories to the Ryerson Press, it ended up sitting in its vault for over five years. From time to time stories from the *Montrealer* – "The Office" then "Boys and Girls" (December 1964) and "Red Dress – 1946" (May 1965) – were added to the manuscript.[11]

This long delay is largely explained by working assumptions at the time, personnel changes at the press, and Munro's own hesitation. Many at Ryerson shared the general prejudice against collections of stories yet, as Colombo remembers and his own late-1962 letter to Munro indicates, the house was keen on the idea of a small book of stories from Munro. But by 1963 Colombo had left Ryerson to work on his own as an "editor-at-large," and Grant also left that year to take up a university post; there would not be a new editor-in-chief until Robin Farr joined Ryerson in early 1968. This left Earle Toppings responsible for trade and general books – that is, books that were neither educational nor religious. A graduate of the University of British Columbia and a native of Saskatchewan, Toppings was hired by John Webster Grant as a Ryerson editor in 1961. He recalls meeting Munro between 1962 and 1963 for lunch at the Georgia Hotel in Vancouver. She was "completely unprepossessing." More than that, during their lunch she was "obviously concerned about her children in a rather fidgety way" since "she got up from lunch at least three times to go and phone the sitter to make sure the children were all right." Beyond Munro's personal situation, Toppings "could tell that a book really was not a priority for her at that moment . . . but she still, I think, felt she was really an underground writer. Some of the stories were getting out and that was all right, but she was not at all promotional about it." Given her hesitant attitude and the industry prejudice against collections, given Munro's ongoing attempts at novels, and given the changes at Ryerson occasioned by Grant's departure in 1963, that no one pressed for a book until 1967 is probably not surprising. Yet Toppings remained in contact with Munro during the interim, and so the idea and Ryerson's commitment to the project remained real.[12]

"How Insistently I Am Warmed and Bound": Family, "The Office," and Leaving Vancouver

If during the early 1960s Munro was hesitant to press for book publication, she seems throughout these years rather to have been consumed by the tasks at hand: her family's needs, her own life, and the various stories that held her attention. Looking back at this time, Munro marvels still at how hesitant she was to make her own case then and, by contrast, how eager (and often successful) young writers are today to get that first book published. But during the early 1960s she was too busy. Her daughters were growing. Sheila, approaching the age of ten, was engaged in the myriad activities that she describes in *Lives of Mothers and Daughters* (though Jim was also involved in getting her to things). Her sister Jenny, three years younger, participating in those activities as the younger sister, was differentiated in age and also, as Munro makes clear when she thinks about her two daughters in "Miles City, Montana," in personality. Sheila Munro has registered her surprise at her mother's precise ability to capture her younger personality in that story. Jenny, the principal in that story's central episode – she did fall into the water in Miles City in 1961, a four-year-old who could not swim – remembers it happening. In a tribute to Marian Engel Munro published in 1984, she acknowledges Engel's use of her own experiences as a young mother, seeing in her a compatriot, "another who is just managing to keep afloat in the woozy world of maternity, with its shocks and confusions and fearful love and secret brutality."

Munro's writing, like Engel's, took place amid the demands of the circumstances of motherhood. And with the struggle to produce a novel during the late 1950s and early 1960s, that writing seldom seemed to go well. A fragment in Munro's papers captures this time, and Munro's situation, well:

> In the spring of 1963, in Vancouver, my husband was working in a department store, and I was staying at home looking after our two daughters – who, at six and nine, did not need so much looking-after as they used to – and trying to write. The typewriter was in our bedroom, by the window. I would sit down and type a few words on the yellow paper. A few sentences, maybe. Then I tried white paper. I never got halfway down the page. I went and made a cup of instant coffee and sat in the living-room, trying to see again the form of my lovely novel,

that big bright fish that slipped round and round in the depths of my mind, and would not be hauled into the daylight. I went into the bedroom and tried again. I thought about being over thirty. Nothing done.

I began to have trouble breathing. I was aware of each breath and couldn't be sure of the next. The air that was air to other people was to me a hostile jelly. But the children came in from the yard and my husband came home from work and I made dinner. I didn't tell anybody.

So it was with Munro in the early 1960s, as stories like "Miles City, Montana" make clear. The Munros' 1961 family trip across the continent back home to Ontario in their Morris Oxford – a car they did own – is deftly preserved in one of Munro's most autobiographical stories. While the drowning of Steve Gauley remembered from the narrator's childhood is imagined, and is an effective framing device, Jenny's near accident is not. What Munro describes is what happened; it was "one of the worst moments of my life," she recalls, saying she can still see "that pink frilly bottom" in the water. It lay in the Munros' memories until sometime during the 1970s when she chose to write about it; she tried to use it first in an earlier story connected with *Who Do You Think You Are?* "Miles City, Montana" represents an example of Munro's usual method, the use of an experience some years after it happened, recalled in tranquillity after some years of "teasing the mind."[13]

That was her normal method, but "The Office" was one story that grew directly from Munro's circumstances in 1960 or 1961 and so offers a precise sense of her situation then. The story focuses on the altercation Munro had with a difficult landlord, fairly immediately and without much rumination. In a 1978 essay, "On Writing 'The Office,'" Munro calls it "the most straightforward autobiographical story I have ever written." It details her relations with the landlord of an office she rented above a drugstore on the north side of the 2500 block of Marine Drive in Dundarave, a shopping area two blocks south of Lawson in West Vancouver, where the Munros lived. "The solution to my life occurred to me one evening while I was ironing a shirt," the story begins. The narrator then tells her husband, who is watching television, "I think I ought to have an office." Munro has said that "The Office" was the only thing she wrote during the time she occupied that office. What she was after was a novel: "I spent hours staring at the walls and the Venetian blinds, drinking cups of instant coffee with canned milk, believing that if I concentrated enough I could pull out of myself a novel that would be a full-blown miracle." But she had only this story: "I stayed in the office four months and never wrote another word, but I did get my first ulcer." These are clearly Munro's own comments on her creative anxiety.

The story speaks also to the circumstances of her life after about ten years of married life in Vancouver. Rhetorically, the narrator asks, "What do I want an office for? I have a house; it is pleasant and roomy and has a view of the sea . . . there is no lack of space." These details are true of the house on Lawson Avenue, encircled by hedges and vegetation, looking down on Burrard Inlet. Yet it was a house that Munro, after five years there, still did not care for very much. Like the even larger house they bought a few years later in Victoria, it was more to her husband's taste than her own. Shifting from the house in "The Office" to her self-image as a writer, and to her difficulty then in even telling anyone else that she writes, Munro explains that saying she writes humiliates her: "The words create their own space of silence, the delicate moment of exposure." The "delicate moment of exposure" Munro writes of here, the bedrock fact that lies at the core of her conflict with Mr. Malley in "The Office," is that she is a writer and a woman who at some level lives counter to the expectations of her social position. That is, she has an interest that takes her away – mentally if not physically – from the marriage and children women were supposed then to find made a sufficient life, completely satisfying. In her tribute to Engel, speaking of her situation, and especially of her women friends when she was a young mother in Vancouver, Munro wrote, "Our marriages were the unquestioned framework of our lives, our children were the content, our ties to each other were our lifelines to ourselves."

Though Munro does not dwell on conventional relations between the sexes here, she makes it clear how being a writer who is also a wife and mother is very different from the life of those men who write or work at home: "To write, as everyone knows, you need a typewriter, or at least a pencil, some paper, a table and chair; I have all these things in a corner of my bedroom. But now I want an office as well." Munro did have all these things in the house on Lawson, and she did write in her bedroom. Munro continues:

> A house is all right for a man to work in. He brings his work into the house, a place is cleared for it; the house rearranges as best it can around him. Everybody recognizes that his work *exists*. He is not expected to answer the telephone, to find things that are lost, to see why the children are crying, or feed the cat. He can shut his door. Imagine (I said) a mother shutting her door, and the children knowing she is behind it; why, the very thought is outrageous to them. A woman who sits staring into space, into a country that is not her husband's or her children's is likewise known to be an offense against nature. So a house is not the same for a woman. She is not someone who walks into the house, to make use of it, and will walk out again. She *is* the house; there is no separation possible.

As she often does, Munro offers this construction of things and then shifts direction; in a long parenthetical passage, she admits that on occasion she was able to get apart from her role of wife and mother, "feeling a fierce and lawless quiver of freedom, of loneliness too harsh and perfect for me now to bear." When this happened, she knew "how the rest of the time I am sheltered and encumbered, how insistently I am warmed and bound."

Both of the Munros' older daughters recall the times when their mother imaginatively went off "staring into space, into a country" not their father's, and not theirs. Sheila's recollections are recounted in *Lives of Mothers and Daughters*, and Jenny recalls knowing as a child when her mother was working intently on something, trying to finish it. At these times there would be a tension in the air, one created partly by the continuing sound of the typewriter's pounding reverberating throughout the house. Members of the family were all aware of what was happening. These recollections, connected to Munro's precise words in "The Office," combine to create the physical facts of Munro's "human position" – in Auden's phrase – as her children grew and her writing career slowly expanded during the family's last years in Vancouver.

Outwardly, the Munros were a typical suburban West Vancouver family: father working across the water in Vancouver, mother staying at home with the children; family outings to the beach, vacations back home in Ontario, dancing lessons, shows, and parties. Those who knew Munro then saw her as an encouraging mother, one who had realistic but keen expectations for her daughters. But inwardly at times, Munro was off staring into that other country. Here she spent her "real life," trying to fashion human constructions that always seemed to turn out to be so much less than she imagined when she first saw them in her mind's eye. So as the 1960s began for her in West Vancouver, Alice Munro was leading a double life, just as she had set out to do from Wingham – there was both a normal life and, behind it, "the black life of the artist."

The man from whom Munro rented her office, as it happened, was someone Daphne Cue's family had known about in West Vancouver, and Daphne herself had gone to school with his daughter. He had led, Cue recalls, "a very checkered life"; his first wife, the daughter's mother, "had run off on him and went with a number of other women to live with a hermit up the mountain" above West Vancouver. By the time Munro rented the office from him "he had another wife, that very pathetic creature" she depicts in the story. He did bring plants and other things she did not want, told her stories she had no interest in, and irritated her by interrupting her writing. Their relations worsened and Munro left. She was drawn to him as a character in her story, she recalled, because of his "clamorous humanity, his dreadful insistence, which had to get the better of that woman seeking isolation." He was in life as he is in her fiction, a man who, she concludes in the story, thought of her and arranged "in his mind the bizarre but somehow never quite satisfactory narrative of yet another betrayal of trust. While I arrange words, and think it is my right to be rid of him."[14]

Munro wrote about this period in her life, one she sees as its low point, in "On Writing 'The Office.'" The struggle for the novel she and everyone else seemed to be seeking continued, and it brought on physical side effects – she developed an ulcer and felt unable to write another word. As a writer, Munro was blocked; the numerous abandoned beginnings in her papers attest to this. Recalling this, Munro says, "I would start a story and then I would get totally discouraged with it and start another, so I would never finish anything. But in the last year I lived in Vancouver, I had a total blockage. I couldn't write a sentence. I couldn't. I could think of things but I couldn't write them." Confirming what she wrote about having difficulty breathing, Munro continues, "I would have fits where I couldn't breathe. And I went to a doctor and I guess I saw a psychiatrist a couple of times." Munro thinks now that these were panic attacks brought on by her anxieties over her writing.

ᐁ

A change was in the offing. By the early 1960s Jim Munro had become restive at Eaton's. He wanted to leave there in order to do something more to his interest and liking. And as he had told that personnel manager at Eaton's when he arrived, he was interested in books. With this in mind, Jim began working with Stephen Franklin, who was also a writer, in a small paperback bookstore called Pick-a-Pocket. It too was located in the Dundarave shopping area along Marine Drive. Initially the Munros thought about going into the business with Franklin and his wife, Elsa, but that plan did not work out. During their time in Vancouver, Munro recalls, "something would come up and we would get fired up about an idea" that would get Jim out of Eaton's, "but we didn't really get fired up until '63. Then we went on a holiday together without the kids; we had never done that before." Munro remembers being nervous over the girls – just as she had been at lunch with Earle Toppings – but during this "three- or four-day holiday," she says, "we solidified the idea of the bookstore." She recalls suggesting Victoria as a location.

During the 1950s, independent bookstores were few and far between in Canada. There were "thriving book sections in department stores such as Eaton's, Simpsons's, and Woodward's," Roy MacSkimming has written, "but publishers often decried the paucity of dedicated bookstores" that encouraged reading and celebrated books and authors by their very existence. "When the Canadian Retail Booksellers Association . . . started up in 1952, it had only thirty-five stores in its membership." Vancouver was out for the Munros, since Bill Duthie had started his first store there in 1957. Victoria, however, was possible: it had a university, a cultural community, and two bookstores (the Marionette and Ford's Bookstore) plus the book department at Eaton's as the main competition. The province had established its own scheduled car-carrying ferry service from the mainland only in 1960, so when the Munros decided to move there, Victoria was growing. And given his experience with Pick-a-Pocket in West Vancouver, Jim Munro knew that paperback books were changing the face of publishing. The Penguin line was established in Britain and in the United States, "quality paperbacks" (as opposed to cheap pocket books) were being marketed by the major publishers – Alfred A. Knopf, for example, had its Vintage editions. In Canada, MacSkimming has noted, there was a prejudice against paperbacks among the older generation of publishers, although in the late 1950s McClelland & Stewart had daringly launched its New Canadian Library reprint series.[15]

As is often the case, Alice Munro is the best source to account for what occurred once she and Jim had decided to take the plunge. The draft fragment describing the narrator's difficulties writing and her trouble breathing continues:

> Then at the beginning of summer my husband said that he couldn't stand working for the department store any longer. We sat on the steps in the summer twilight, talking about what we could do. We were young but we didn't know it. For more than ten years our lives had been dutiful, responsible, habitual. Buying the house, raising the children. Brief pinched holidays.
>
> Running a shop was what my husband knew about ("Merchandising" or "retailing" was the right thing to call that). I had worked in a library. So we said, why not a bookstore? We could sell our house, and move to some small city which had a

college, no good bookstores at present, and people who could
be persuaded to buy books.

We took the ferry to Victoria – not daring to tell our children what we were up to – and there was the store, empty and
waiting for us. A long, dark, dirty, low-rent store with an old-
fashioned entrance deep between two display windows. A tanner's
shed at the back. Once it had been a hat shop.

We had no money. My husband started in at once, cleaning and painting and putting up shelves. I packed and put the
house up for sale and moved the unenthusiastic children to a
little rented house across from Beacon Hill Park.

People told us you couldn't make a living selling books.

The fragment substantively captures just what the Munros did. They
found a storefront to rent at 753 Yates Street in downtown Victoria,
next to the Dominion Hotel, and set about during the summer of 1963
getting Munro's Bookstore ready for its fall opening. They rented a
house at 105 Cook Street across from Beacon Hill Park, within walking
distance to the store. Munro continues:

But we were released, energetic. Blue walls, pegboard and
shelves, black and white floor tiles. We made a plan that divided
the walls into sections. Philosophy, Poetry, Science Fiction,
History, Psychology, Drama, Cooking, Religion, War, Crime,
Erotica lumped in with Classics. We went through order lists. We
planned to open on the 19th of September. Boxes of books began
to arrive, which wouldn't have to be paid for till after Christmas.
The prim Penguins, orange-and-white and brown and white, the
Pelicans blue-and-white. This was to be a paperback store, with
the books temptingly face-out around the walls – a new idea at
the time. As soon as the varnish on the shelves was dry, we were
setting out the books, like separate prizes – salable books on sex
and cooking and flying saucers, and others I had ordered simply
because I loved the sound of their titles. In Praise of Folly. The
Cloud of Unknowing, the Book of the It, Love's Body, Seven

Types of Ambiguity. Beautiful rich covers some of them had, soft colours, designs of birds or unicorns or flowers, or a delicate script. Magical packages. That's what they seemed to me, and having them fill up the shelves produced an excitement that was giddy and childish and at times hardly bearable.

Turning back to herself and her situation, the narrator then says that "I had started breathing again, of course. The change saved me, the work, the risk and challenge. Other people's words, in wonderful profusion, rescued me, for a while, from the necessity of getting out my own."[16]

Just before Munro's Bookstore opened, a Help Wanted ad appeared on the book page of the Victoria *Daily Times*. Headed "Part Time Staff for New Book Store," it continued, "To open soon in downtown Victoria, pleasing personality and wide knowledge of literature absolutely essential, some university training preferable." The store opened on Thursday, September 19, and the Munros did $125 in business that day – Jim recalls it took them some time to get back to that figure again. During those early days, Jim got to use the ad-writing skills he had learned at Eaton's: one ad in the *Times* is headed "ATTENTION INSOMNIACS!" and continues "AT MUNRO'S BOOKSTORE We have books that will put you to sleep. . . . We also have books that will keep you awake." It concludes by asserting that Munro's has "Victoria's largest assortment of quality and non-quality paperbacks." A week later, their ad offers "A MEMO TO TIRED EXECUTIVES": "Stop Re-reading 'The Moon and Sixpence' and come down to Munro's Bookstore where you'll find plenty of books to give you a new lease on life. We have Victoria's largest assortment of quality paperbacks on all subjects and WE KNOW BOOKS."

Jim's differentiation between "quality and non-quality" paperbacks here suggests the changes occurring in the book trade just then, which he and Alice knew about and drew on when they opened the store. With justifiable pride he recalls that Munro's was the first store in Canada to stock City Lights Books from San Francisco, publishers of Lawrence Ferlinghetti, Allen Ginsberg, and their ilk. In 2004, having celebrated its fortieth anniversary in the massive former bank building on Government Street, Munro's Bookstore has certainly succeeded and flourished. Quite apart from the link with Alice, Jim Munro and Munro's Books have been a vibrant presence in Canadian letters in Victoria for four decades.

But the first few years were difficult ones. They brought Alice and Jim together in meeting the challenge of making a go of the store. Munro has described those first years, from 1963 to 1966, as the happiest years in their marriage: "We were very poor, but our aims were completely wound up with surviving in this place." The store was open from 9:30 to 5:30 daily, and then again from 7:00 to 9:00. Typically, Jim would be there all day, coming home after closing at 5:30 for dinner. Alice would stay at home in the morning and "do housework and think about writing" and, after she got lunch for the girls, go in for the afternoon, coming home at 4:30 to fix supper. She would always go back for the evening and would also fill in at other times whenever receipts were low to "save on the wage bill." Working in the bookstore brought Munro out of her natural shyness, and over the years she became quite popular with the regulars. And for their part some of her customers turn up in her stories – "Tell Me Yes or No," "Dulse," and "The Albanian Virgin" include a bookstore as part of the plot.

There was a memorable uniqueness about Munro's Bookstore, too. Craig Barrett, who represented McGraw-Hill during the late 1960s, remembers his surprise when he first visited the store. Jim was "quite an aesthetic-looking fellow" who made interesting conversation. Barrett had been on the road for about a month, visiting other bookstores most days, but his visit to Munro's "was the first time I actually sat down with a bookstore person and talked about literature." He also remembers Alice as "quite gracious." The three of them would sit down to tea in a back room and "talk about all kinds of things," though mostly literature. Nevertheless, Barrett acknowledges that to him there was nothing memorable about Alice at the time. As to what books Munro's Bookstore would buy, he recalled that Jim "made all the decisions." Alice "wasn't in on the buying process."

Another person who got to know the Munros through the bookstore during its early years was George Cuomo, a writer who taught English at the University of Victoria. He recalls Munro's as "the best bookstore in town at the time" and, through the store, he and his wife got to know Alice and Jim "quite well. I remember them as pleasant and friendly, and somewhat shy. Alice was lively and animated and full of laughter in small comfortable gatherings and while working in the bookstore." Cuomo particularly remembers what he calls Alice's "sweet kindness to our children." The Cuomos used to allow their two oldest children – then eight or nine – to take the bus downtown alone. If anything were to go wrong, though, or if they lost their return fare, they were to go straight to the bookstore and ask Alice for help. Cuomo thinks they did so once or twice, "and to this day they recall the Alice they knew then with warm good feelings."

In contrast to Vancouver, Victoria was much more to Munro's liking. Again, her notebook draft fragment about the move provides detail:

> Victoria, that summer, seemed to me a town out of the past. I don't mean that past the tourist parts of the town tried to evoke – an uncertain rather amazing discouraging hodge podge of Tudor and Victorian pretensions, but a past of settled neighbourhoods, shade trees, corner grocery-stores with striped awnings. In the mountainside suburb of Vancouver where we had lived there were no sidewalks, the trees were fir and cedar, behind the nine-foot laurel hedges there was a jungle splendor and the ditches ran full beside the road. Raw handsome houses, a rain-washed luxuriance. Victoria seemed, by contrast, dry and open and orderly and half-familiar, with a field of dry grass sloping up from the sea, the deep shade of the chestnut trees on the street where we lived[.] I could walk from our house to the store.[17]

"I've Almost Forgotten I Am a Writer":
Earle Toppings, Ryerson, and Making *Dance of the Happy Shades*

In November of 1964, writing on Munro's Bookstore stationery, Munro responded to a letter from Earle Toppings at Ryerson. She began by thanking him for his letter and ended by encouraging him to visit them, noting, "We're very proud of the store." In between she wrote, "I've almost forgotten I am a writer so it's nice to be reminded. I am still working at it though. I quit entirely the first year we had the store but I began again last September or October." Toppings replied immediately, "For some time I'd been afraid you weren't writing; it is great to know that you *are* again." He hoped to make the trip over to Victoria to see them and continues, "With a talent as genuine as yours you must not stop working; but then, a born writer never really ceases." He concludes, "You know how positively we have always felt about your manuscript of stories. I got it out of the vault again a few days ago and will reread it to touch up my original impressions. During the BC trip we can discuss the possibility of adding to the present MS."

This exchange of letters – Toppings was unable to get to Victoria as hoped – began a period during which he, as senior editor for trade books, tried to rekindle the project of publishing a collection of Munro's stories at Ryerson. The decision was a long time coming since the book was not agreed on until March 1967. In the meantime Toppings stayed in touch with Munro both about the collection and about Munro's contribution to the *Modern Canadian Stories* collection that he was working on at the time. The contact was sporadic. Toppings remembers that during this time "it was hard to get a letter from her," while Munro admits that she has never been much of a letter writer. The manuscript of the six stories Weaver had handed to Colombo in late 1961 thus remained in the Ryerson vault. It was augmented between 1961 and 1967 by new stories from the *Montrealer* and, in the case of "The Shining Houses," from CBC *Wednesday Night*. Two stories that had been omitted from the Colombo group, "The Day of the Butterfly" and "Thanks for the Ride," were also added. Toppings recalls that they would have a published story in hand and then write to Munro, who would send a typescript version. In this way, the original manuscript grew to twelve stories by the time Ryerson decided to go ahead with the collection.

During the three years Munro was on Cook Street – they bought the final house they lived in together, at 1648 Rockland Avenue, during the summer of 1966 when she was pregnant with Andrea – she completed just two stories, "Boys and Girls" and "Red Dress – 1946." Both were published in the *Montrealer*. Although the correspondence between Munro and Toppings during these years is not complete, surviving letters suggest what happened. In October 1965 Munro reports on a long-anticipated visit to their store by Ryerson sales representatives, writing that "The Men from Ryerson were in – Jim's feelings were considerably soothed – We just wanted somebody from Ryerson to know we're *here*." Turning to the *Modern Canadian Stories* anthology Toppings was working on, she hopes "it comes off." She agrees with Toppings that it would be better to include a story not already in an anthology, so she points to "Dance of the Happy Shades," "Boys and Girls," and "Red Dress – 1946." The latter story is one "which I like but everybody else thinks plain frivolous. . . . You – or somebody – must decide which to suggest. I sort of hate them all, once they're written, for being so much less than they were supposed to be." She signs off, "Yes, I'm still writing." Toppings replies at once with an explanation of how *Modern Canadian Stories* is coming together – the academic editor has the final say – and so while other stories have proponents, "in the end, . . . we may end up with *The Time of Death*. I think it is the strongest story you've written." As already noted, they made that choice.[18]

Ryerson's publication of *Dance of the Happy Shades* began to come together in early 1967. In February Munro replies to Toppings, "I'm so sorry – nothing new. Just those – Red Dress is the last story I've done." She notes that he hasn't mentioned "The Office" and offers to find it for him, something she subsequently did. "I had a baby last fall and with her and helping Jim in the store have been terribly busy, though I've started (again!) a novel, which is light & easy & may get finished if I ever get time."

‿

Andrea Sarah Munro was born on September 8, 1966. Her arrival coincided with changes in the Munro family's life in Victoria and occasioned some others as well – given the over nine-year age difference between Jenny and Andrea. The month before, the Munros had moved into their new house on Rockland Avenue, a twelve-room Tudor-style place that had been priced to sell. Munro has said that they were able to afford to buy it for a bargain price but could not afford to heat it. She hated it from the outset; it was a place that Jim and Sheila, then almost thirteen, wanted. She told Catherine Ross, "Once we moved to that house, which we did against my will when I was eight months pregnant, something happened right then. Something pulled apart." Sometime during the 1970s, Munro worked on a story that, clearly, drew on the acquisition of the house. Once they had some money, the narrator writes, her husband "bought the sort of house which apparently he had been seeking all along – a brick and Tudor-beamed affair set among great lawns and expansive trees, and this house had to be filled with sofas and chairs upholstered in crushed velvet, with a fake suit of armour for the hall, and pictures of stormy seas with little lights over them, and a chandelier which was a copy of one hanging in some castle in England, in some baronial dining hall I never want to see. When I was moved into that house I knew it was not to stay, though I stayed longer than I would have thought, and longer than I should have."[19]

Munro's letter to Toppings in February 1967 saying that she had again started a novel as he is rekindling the idea of a collection of Munro's stories both demonstrates her commitment to her writing and obscures the facts of her life just then. Munro ends by saying that "your letter has me very curious. I wish I'd done some stories." Toppings had obviously written asking after new material. When he replies on March 3 he emphasizes that he "is trying to rekindle a project here" and then asks for the copy of "The Office," "the one story we're missing." He is hopeful but unable to be specific. "Two other editors here, recent additions, have read your stories and are very high on them: joyously so."

Andrea's birth did allow Munro more time at home, but the years while Andrea was a baby were characterized by her mother's utter exhaustion. Munro had a new baby to care for, was working at the store, and now had a much larger house to tend to, with no help beyond Sheila's. She told Ross that during this time "nothing in life mattered to me as much as sleep, not sex, not anything. The marriage never regained anything after that."

In March 1967 when she sent Toppings a copy of "The Office," she commented that it "is an example of the Early-Awful period, and it is a good deal better than most. I went through them and was surprised how bad some were." A week later she wrote again, having heard in the meantime that Ryerson had decided to publish her collection; she is characteristically self-deprecating:

> Well I haven't got a telegram yet saying you've all changed your minds or you thought it was an April Fool's or anything like that so I guess you are going to publish those stories and I am of course delighted. Did you really mean fall of '68? I didn't know things were planned so far ahead and I thought it might be a mistake for fall '67. Anyway I'm glad its fall because anything can sell then, even a collection of unsexy short stories.

At the same time, Munro expresses concern about including "that old Chatelaine story," "Good-By, Myra," so she sends Toppings "a couple of other oldies to make a choice from, if you think either of them would do better." She tells him that her preferred choice for it is "The Day of the Butterfly." One of the other stories she sent for consideration was "The Shining Houses," which "was just broadcast on C.B.C.[,] never published, and I'd lost the last page of this manuscript but I found a rough copy and typed it up from that." Munro also characteristically notes that just "a few things have to be tidied up in the stories you have. For instance, in 'The Peace of Utrecht' the punctuation is awful – far too many brackets. I could fix that." She concludes, moving to her most pressing concern as a writer – the piece she is concentrating on now: "I am hopeful about the novel but get very little time. I think I might be able to do a Great Leap Forward this summer, when my teenage daughter is home to look after the baby, and we have some college girls in the store. . . . I hope to get a letter from you soon."

This period in March 1967 needs to be paused over. Largely through the advocacy of others – Robert Weaver, Earle Toppings, and, in the wings, Audrey Coffin, Munro's editor for her first three books –

Alice Munro's career as a writer was reaching a moment she had acknowledged as possible but had never much sought out: her first book. Because of its range, its detail, and its precision of emotion, *Dance of the Happy Shades* would launch Munro as a writer at a level she had not previously known; its immediate recognition through the Governor General's Award was an external sign of her writing's appeal, and of her presence as a Canadian writer to be noticed and watched closely. Yet owing to her shyness and uncertainty, this accomplishment was something that seemed to happen accidentally to her. Beyond responding to letters, putting stories in the mail, and following up suggestions, Munro did little to advocate her own cause. She concentrated on the work at hand and let things happen. More than that, in Victoria she was far from English-Canada's literary centre, Toronto. Thus in writing to Toppings in March 1967, she deprecates her past efforts while looking ahead to the work in progress, the novel.

Personally the spring of 1967 saw the beginnings of Munro's "long voyage from the house of marriage." As her 1970s draft fragment makes clear, the house on Rockland that Jim bought against his wife's will when she was pregnant was one to which she was never reconciled. Throughout their years together, Jim recalls, Alice was never assertive regarding decorating: "She never made a big fuss about decor; . . . it wasn't a big deal with her." Yet that new house – massive, calling out to be made a showcase home – reawakened the class differences between the Munros that had always been there but had remained mostly submerged in the daily lives. Away from Ontario, making their way, raising a family, the Munros did not have time to dwell on such differences until the late 1960s. By then, too, much of the world was in the midst of the public foment that characterized the decade: Vietnam, riots, feminism, free love, marriage breakdown. Looking back to that time after she left Jim in the Rockland house where he still lives, Munro has commented, "The things Jim and I fought about were often class things, and totally different ways of looking at things. I was not prepared to be at all a submissive wife. I think now, why did I – the fights we had about the Vietnam War! I could have let that go, I wasn't going to change his mind. But I was very much on the offensive. We didn't see things the same way." By the time *Dance of the Happy Shades* was published in September 1968, Munro's "long voyage" was well begun.[20]

෨

Once Earle Toppings had secured the firm's commitment to publish the stories, Ryerson Press had to assemble a manuscript and prepare it for publication. Toppings worked with Munro to add to what they had; once they had committed and the stories were arranged, Audrey Coffin was assigned to edit it. One of the new editors who was, as Toppings wrote, "joyously" enthusiastic about Munro's stories, Coffin got the job because of her keenness. She became the first of Munro's three impor tant book editors. A contract was drawn up sometime in 1967 – Munro was to deliver the manuscript to Ryerson by June 6 – but it was not executed until June 1968. Even then there was no title indicated for the book. In the clause stating that no part of the work has been published before, Munro wrote, "All of these stories have appeared in magazines."

Although she may have hoped that would be the case for all the inclusions, it was not for two of them – "Walker Brothers Cowboy," which opens the volume, and "Images," its third story. When she was assigned to edit the book at Ryerson, Coffin wrote to Munro "saying that they needed new stories. . . . I remember writing back to her saying, you know, I've got a five-month-old baby, do you expect me to write three new stories? And she wrote back and said, yes." Surprisingly, between the time Ryerson agreed to publish a collection and its publication, Munro wrote three new stories for the collection, "Postcard," "Walker Brothers Cowboy," and "Images." She wrote them, in that order, during 1967 and into the fall and winter of that year. "I remember Andrea was pretty small, because I used to wash the diapers every day and I would put them in the dryer and that would heat up the work room. That big house was terrible to heat, and [when] Jim and I moved in there, we didn't have any money. . . . That's why I worked in the laundry room, because the dryer would heat and that was when I was doing a daily wash." This laundry room, which seems to have entered legend as a symbol of Munro's feminist struggle, is a large room on the second floor of the Rockland house. It has ample windows; there is nothing basement-dank about it. Carole Sabiston, also an artist and Jim's second wife, has used it as a work room, too.[21]

Late in 1967, Earle Toppings left Ryerson for a freelance career, so Audrey Coffin became completely responsible within the house for Munro's book. But though he had left the press, Coffin consulted him as it progressed – on all of its details, really. Thus while he may have been gone, Toppings was still quite involved. Early in the new year he wrote to Munro offering to show her new stories – "Postcard" and "Walker Brothers Cowboy" – to editors in Toronto, not as an agent but as an intermediary, leaving her to negotiate fees herself. He also wanted to write a radio play based on "Walker Brothers Cowboy," and worked on it with Munro's acquiescence, though nothing came of it.

Toward the end of March, Munro sent Coffin "Images," saying, "I don't know if this will do. I intended typing a fair copy but find I must work the remainder of this week so I have just made a few corrections and send it as is." She says she has another story started but intends to "open it up and just let it develop the way it wants to and, who knows? I may get the novel I want out of it." Closing, Munro expresses her misgivings: "This story I'm sending may have been done too quickly & with too many distractions to have jelled properly but at least it's something." The next week, she sent Coffin some snapshots of herself ("They look a bit cheerful for a writer, that's all") and responds to Coffin's questions as to the book's title. *Walker Brothers Cowboy* and *Dance of the Happy Shades* were the house's main choices, although Munro also suggested "Trip to the Coast."[22]

About the same time, Coffin wrote to Hugh Garner, another Ryerson author of some reputation then, who had volunteered to write a preface to Munro's book because he knew her stories, liked them, and wanted to help. Given the general wariness about short story collections by little-known writers, Robin Farr, the new editor-in-chief, agreed to the idea. So did Munro. Coffin told Garner that she "was pleased to hear that you have very kindly offered to do a foreword to *Walker Brothers Cowboy*, stories by Alice Munro, which I am editing for

Ryerson's fall list." She expected "one or two more stories from Mrs. Munro at the end of March and shall then hope to go quickly into production." She hoped to receive his foreword in the near future. Coffin then provided Garner with the scant biographical information she had and copies of some manuscript stories. He had his foreword to her within a week's time and also voted for *Dance of the Happy Shades* as the better of the two titles. Coffin edited the foreword, excising two paragraphs on the market for short stories in Canada (which Garner suggested as a possible cut), and sent it to him for his approval. She also confirmed to him that she thought *Dance of the Happy Shades: Stories by Alice Munro* would be the title.[23]

In writing to Coffin in April, Munro offers something of a coda on her own approach to fiction: "I don't see the need for a preface. A foreword is plenty. What can you say about your own work? You don't really think about why you write a story. You write it, you hope it works, it's finished. Somebody else can see far better than you can, what it is you're trying to say." In the same letter, Munro returned Ryerson's standard author form and added "some autobiographical stuff on a separate page." It read:

> I was born and grew up in Wingham, Ontario, attended the University of Western Ontario, married and moved to British Columbia. I have three daughters, aged fifteen, eleven, and two (Sheila, Jenny, Andrea, respectively). My husband owns a bookstore in Victoria, where we live in a big old house with an antique furnace and a garden the tourist buses try not to notice.

Dance of the Happy Shades: Stories by Alice Munro with a foreword by Hugh Garner was published by the Ryerson Press in September 1968 in a first edition printing of 2,675. The book is dedicated to Robert E. Laidlaw. Robert Weaver wrote the jacket blurb. Besides the foreword, it contained fifteen stories written between 1953 and 1968. The managing editor sent Hugh Garner his copy on September 24. Alice Munro was launched.[24]

"The Wife of the Man Who Ran the Bookstore" Wins the Governor General's Award

After they opened the bookstore, the Munros naturally enough came into contact with people connected with the University of Victoria such as George Cuomo and his wife. At the time the city of Victoria was small and quiet; it had a distinctly English quality about it – more English than the English, some said. High tea at the Empress Hotel was a well-known ritual, as it still is. The old-country influence during the early 1960s was widespread. When Munro came to write about opening the bookstore, the paperback lines she remembers are Penguin and Pelican. At the university, and in the English department in particular, the British connection was amplified since many, if not most, of the faculty were Commonwealth or British types, people who had got seconds at Oxford or Cambridge and ended up in this desirable but backwater corner of the colonies. There were also a few Canadians and a few Americans, among the latter Cuomo. He taught American literature and was the first person to offer creative writing at Victoria; in 1963 he published his first novel, *Jack Be Nimble.* Alice and Jim, he recalls, knew "the writing types." Their bookstore, which Cuomo remembers as the only one in town, was "well-stocked and run in a friendly way by people who liked books." Alice was frequently there, but Jim was always on hand – he was clearly the dominant figure of the two, then, though both were shy. The Munros socialized with the Cuomos and with others from the university, mostly in dinner gatherings of about ten people, some held at the Munros'. Cuomo recalls that Alice was "somewhat in awe" of the people from the English department, owing to her own lack of a degree and the evident British mannerisms of many of them. At these events she was likely to sit quietly and listen while vigorous discussions were going on around her.

At some point Alice told Cuomo that she wrote, so he offered to look at something of her choice. He did, and though he does not remember that it was "Boys and Girls," one of the two stories she wrote during her time on Cook Street, he recalls liking it very much. So he "asked her if she would be interested in coming in as a guest and presenting it to the students" in his advanced creative writing course. (Cuomo has no recollection of Munro volunteering that she had published by then; when he was told, in 2004, of the extent of Munro's prior publication by 1964 he was astounded.) Cuomo had begun with an introductory course but then had arranged for the better students in the class to do a workshop. This was the class Munro visited, probably in late 1964 or early 1965. Cuomo recalls thinking that it would be good for his students "to be introduced to the work of a mature and significantly more advanced writer. I also felt that it would be encouraging for Alice to have these bright youngsters read and, as I innocently expected, be dutifully impressed by her work."

"It was a mistake," Cuomo now says. "For whatever reason they were highly critical of the story and not the least impressed." The students were "unduly harsh." He wonders if they resented an outsider, introduced to them with obvious enthusiasm by their teacher, but as the class progressed he found himself directing the discussion in a way he seldom did, trying to get the students to see what he valued in the story; by the end, he had brought most of them around. "Alice, though, was clearly hurt" despite Cuomo's attempts to cheer her up afterward. In a draft of an essay written over two decades later, Munro vividly recalled the incident, writing that up to that time, her "almost only contact with writers at the University of Victoria had been limited to a painful session with a man who told me my work reminded him of the kind of thing he himself had been writing when he was fifteen and had abandoned with the first glimmerings of maturity." This man was Lawrence Russell, one of the undergraduate members of Cuomo's workshop. Ultimately he became a creative writing professor at Victoria. While Cuomo does not remember Lawrence being especially harsh in that session, no more at least than others, he recalls him as "bright and sharp" and concedes he could be acerbic. When she recounted this incident in her memoir of her mother, Sheila Munro wrote that Lawrence "attacked the story savagely, saying it was something a typical housewife would write." She also maintains that her mother could not "write anything for about a year after this incident."

There is no doubt that her visit to Cuomo's workshop affected Munro deeply. To this day she recalls Russell's comments and scoffs at his claim that he has no recollection of it. In fact, remembering it, Munro used the words "savaged" and "destroyed" for what Russell did, but then added, "It was good for me. All those things are good for you. After that I really had great respect for people like Lawrence. But I always thought he might be wrong." Obviously, he was. For his part, Cuomo offers an explanation that seems to capture Munro's attitude toward the critical act in some fundamental ways. He called her reaction to his class "delicate" – that is, while she was able, in an impeccable way, to judge her own work – to know what she had done and where it was going, he could also see that at this point she had no experience listening to criticism. She was not used to it and she was not prepared for the give-and-take of a workshop. Munro lacked the "editorial mind" necessary to critique another person's work and improve it. Whether Cuomo is exactly right, and whether all this could have been seen in just that one session forty years ago, are open questions – perhaps even "open secrets." But there is no doubt that Munro's visit to Cuomo's workshop helped to confirm her lifelong scepticism about the putative teaching of writing. When, between 1973 and 1975 Munro found herself needing to undertake such work in order to finance her independence, and then again for other reasons in the late 1970s and 1980, she did so with considerable embarrassment, not at all believing in the process.[25]

ൠ

In the same essay in which she recounts her encounter with Lawrence Russell, Munro asserts that, in Victoria in the mid-1960s, "I had absolutely no status as a writer." While that was certainly true in Victoria at the time, Munro's name was becoming increasingly well known to the small coterie of people who watched alertly for emerging Canadian writers. When *Dance of the Happy Shades* appeared, many in this group acknowledged their prior awareness of her. Advertising in the Toronto *Globe and Mail*'s book section, the Ryerson Press ad asserts this prior status, describing Munro as "an author who is just beginning to reap the acclaim she has so long deserved." Dorothy Bishop in the Ottawa *Journal* wrote in December 1968 that "astute critics have for some time been placing [Munro] among the handful of our best younger writers of the short story," and Kent Thompson, reviewing the book on CBC radio in May 1969 after it had received the Governor General's Award, said that before the award "Mrs. Munro's work was known only to that Canadian literary community which reads the small literary magazines."

The public reception accorded *Dance of the Happy Shades* changed that unalterably. On the October 19 broadcast of the CBC's *Anthology*, writer Leo Simpson reviewed Munro's book along with Alden Nowlan's *Miracle at Indian River*, pronouncing himself to be "totally impressed by . . . her artistry." What struck him was "the breadth and depth of humanity in the woman herself, and the beauty – the almost terrifying beauty – she commands in expressing it." Looking back at this review now, Simpson's prescience is evident, for after noting Munro "came upon [him] unawares," leaving him "all the more astonished and delighted," he asserts that "she is already a writer of what I suppose can be called . . . an international interest. Her work is in basic humanity, and it makes seas and nationalities subordinate to her vision. She is of larger-than-Canadian interest too, in the nature of her talent itself, I believe. Her talent is immense, and disciplined." Simpson then goes on to declare Munro better than Irish writer Edna O'Brien without taking the comparison very far. In later years Munro's work shared the pages of the *New Yorker* with O'Brien's.[26]

Prescient and perceptive, Simpson's early review encapsulates the various newspaper reviews *Dance* received during the fall of 1968 and into 1969. Sheila Fischman, en route to a distinguished career as a translator of French literature, wrote in the *Globe and Mail* that "Munro's sensibility . . . makes common experiences become unique but universal expressions of something of what it means to be alive – children's parties, high school dances, traveling salesmen and the banal agonies of young love." Fischman sees Munro's use of her native Huron County as comparable to the invocation of the American South by such writers as Carson McCullers while, in the Regina *Leader-Post*, an anonymous reviewer sees parallels to James Reaney's writing. As these comments suggest, many reviewers paid special attention to Munro's evocation of her home. One of the Victoria reviewers addressed the importance of setting to Munro, "since very little happens in her stories," while the other is reminded of W. Somerset Maugham by Munro's "economy of style, observation, polish, and perception"; like him too, Munro "is a completely honest writer, neither adding nor subtracting for effect." But unlike Maugham's work, there is no cynicism in Munro's stories. Helen Tench in the *Ottawa Citizen* echoed one of Garner's phrasings ("ordinary people in ordinary situations, living ordinary lives") when she exclaims, "And what a collection it is – sparingly but superbly written, about ordinary things that happen to ordinary people." Jamie Portman, in the *Calgary Herald*, commented that "the Ryerson Press does not publish very much fiction these days, but what it does issue merits attention and respect." *Dance*, he noted, is "a sometimes brilliant and always impressive collection."27

The only Canadian review even remotely hesitant, let alone negative, was by Hilda Kirkwood in the *Canadian Forum*. She takes up Garner's assertion that Munro is one of "the real ones"; demurring, she details her preferred individual stories, leaving others alone. Apart from this review – which also considered two anthologies, one of them Weaver's second selection of Canadian stories in which Munro has two stories – the magazine and literary quarterlies were uniformly effusive. Writing the "Letters in Canada" essay in the *University of Toronto Quarterly*, Gordon Roper maintained that Munro's "sensitivity to a wide range of individuals, of feeling, and of situation and place is remarkable, and she conveys her awareness with a sure sense of touch that seems effortless." Kent Thompson, this time in the *Fiddlehead*, likened Munro's technique to James Agee's and noted that "she has a remarkable command of detail and nuance. She has an ability . . . to set details in tonal relationships to one another and thereby effect a mood out of a 'simple' description."

Toward the end of his foreword, Garner calls the book's contents "women's stories" and, relishing this in *Canadian Literature*, Audrey Thomas takes on this "fatuous conclusion." She writes that in Munro's stories "the *tone* of these stories is curiously detached and *un*-feminine, *un*-emotional and *un*-involved. And the work is never sentimental or sentimentalized." That, Thomas thinks, may even be a weakness: "One is almost aware, sometimes, of the writer consciously holding herself in, too much afraid that if her voice becomes passionate, even for a moment, she will be accused of writing 'women's stories' and told to get thee to *Chatelaine*, or the *Ladies' Home Journal*." Thomas also observes admiringly that "it might be possible to love Mrs. Munro for her sentences alone, they are so carefully considered and so beautifully in balance." John Peter, a South African who taught at the University of Victoria and was one of the founders of the *Malahat Review*, wrote there that Munro's prose "is a model of fastidiousness and precision. . . . Yet it is the human content of the stories that matters most," he continues, "and in many of them this is so sensitively handled that it beggars the imagination to try to suppose them in any way improved. . . . This is a book for the English-speaking world, and will hold its own against all comers, from anywhere." And in *Queen's Quarterly*, writer David Helwig comments that Munro's "art consists of an expansion inward, rather than outward, the discrimination of tone and language that makes a small event within a provincial society an important human matter."

Two critical notes often struck in these reviews had to do with the book's appearance and with the usefulness of Garner's foreword. Peter begins his review noting the "book's ugly jacket" and its "posturing introduction" and Joan Phillips in the St. Catharines *Standard* similarly begins by saying that "if ever there were a case for not judging a book by its cover" this is it, since "this outstanding collection" of stories is hidden behind "such an unappealing and uninspired, even downright ugly, dust jacket and binding." In the same vein, another commented that this book's designer must have previously done geometry textbooks. Beth Harvor, in an overview of Canada's women writers in *Saturday Night*, sees the foreword as unfortunate: Munro is "damned by extravagant praise" from Garner, who then "seizes the introduction and makes it into a soap-box from which to attack younger writers and other forms and styles they work in."[28]

In March 1969 Munro heard from Robin Farr at Ryerson that *Dance of the Happy Shades* was among the nominees for a Governor General's Award. Canada's leading literary award at the time, it had a mixed reputation. In his review of *Dance* John Peter expressed a commonly held view that, for a book to receive a Governor General's Award was "an artistic kiss of death." Munro recalls visiting a bookstore looking for *Dance* after it had won. When she asked for it, no doubt shyly, she was told by the owner that he did not keep those Governor General's books in his store – they did not sell. Originally an award without monetary prize, $1,000 was added to the honour some years before Munro's win. By the time of *Dance*'s nomination the prize was $2,500 and a specially bound copy of the book. In 1969, for the first time since the awards began in 1936, the names of all the nominees were announced by the Canada Council a month before the award ceremony. Moreover, when they were presented in May 1969 by the governor general at Rideau Hall, the prime minister of the day, Pierre Elliott Trudeau, attended for the first time. The English-language jury, which had to select 1968's three best books, irrespective of genre (a comment on how few Canadian books were published annually in those days), was made up of the novelist Henry Kreisel of the University of Alberta, critic and translator Philip Stratford of the University of Montreal, and Robert Weaver as its head. Just as he was going to withdraw from any discussion of *Dance of the Happy Shades* because of his long connection to Munro and to her book, Weaver was told by the other jurors that it had won.

"Literary Fame Catches City Mother Unprepared," the Victoria *Daily Times* wrote on receiving the news of the award. Playing the domestic theme to the hilt, the reporter began the piece with a scene of the Munro family at breakfast, the older girls getting off to school and Andrea sitting at the table, "crying because she isn't getting any attention." Munro then asked, "Have you got a camera that will hide circles under the eyes?" to which the unnamed reporter comments, "Life can be turmoil when one wins one of Canada's top literary awards." "I didn't think I had a chance," Munro told the reporter; "the award usually goes for a novel, not a collection of short stories." The article was accompanied by a picture of Munro holding the telephone to her ear and, in many ways, it well illustrated the amazed tone of much of the personalized reporting on the prize. The *Globe and Mail* said that she is "described as a 'shy housewife' with three daughters [who] helps her husband run a bookstore in Victoria." The *Vancouver Sun* offered "B.C. Mother of Three Wins Top Literary Award" while the other Victoria paper, the *Daily Colonist*, left the children out of it with "Victoria Woman's Book Wins Literary Award." In the smaller Ontario papers, local connections were noted: the *London Free Press* story was headlined "Ex-Wingham Resident Wins Literary Award" while a paper near Jim Munro's home preferred the headline "Oakville Man's Wife Wins Literary Award." Closer to home, the day after the award was announced, the secretary of Victoria's Bank Street PTA sent Munro, one of its members, a letter of congratulations.[29]

In what was probably an indication of the times – the turbulent 1960s, which, in Canada, saw the rise of separatism and "Trudeaumania" – Munro was the only Governor General's Award winner that year not from Quebec. Leonard Cohen, Munro, and Mordecai Richler were the winners in English while, on the French side, Hubert Aquin and Marie-Claire Blais each won for a novel and Fernand Dumont for a sociological study. Evidently, the juries were prepared to reward youth – only Dumont had turned forty. As the *Globe and Mail* headlined its story on the awards, "The Establishment Beware! These Awards Are With It." There was also controversy at the awards ceremony that year, since Aquin, former president of the RIN Québec indépendance party, refused his award on political grounds – the first Quebec writer to do so. So too Leonard Cohen for his *Collected Poems*. His reason was different, however: "The poems won't permit it," he said.

But Munro's stories certainly did permit the award, as well they ought, given all she had put into them, and into countless others over the years. Alice and Jim travelled to Ottawa to receive the prize. She is mentioned and pictured in the press coverage of the event, which was on May 13, but most of the journalistic attention is focused elsewhere: on the empty chairs reserved for Aquin and Cohen, on Richler (who won for two books and complained at receiving the same money as those who had written only one), and on Prime Minister Trudeau, who came to the celebration to the stunned pleasure of Munro's family. Bob Laidlaw and his new wife – he had married Mary Etta Charters Laidlaw, the widow of a cousin, earlier in 1969 – attended, as did Munro's sister Sheila and Jim's parents. Meeting Robert Weaver there, Alice's father was able to thank him for all he had done for her over the years. When asked years later about the effect of this first Governor General's Award, Munro laughed and said,

> It did a lot for my prestige in the family. I was living with my first husband when I won the first one and my being a writer had never been . . . well, I think to that point they were thinking of it as something I would get over. So my whole family was very proud. My parents-in-law were proud. My father was *astounded*. And so it did something for them, it did something for me. And it was after that I would tell people I was writing, and that it was a thing which I did, which occupied my time, and before that I would never mention it.
>
> So it does do a lot for you in that way, which is not to be sneezed at, because you have to survive in this world.[30]

"To Know You Have Gotten through to Somebody"

When Ryerson published *Dance of the Happy Shades*, one of its publicity announcements referred to Munro's book as a major "publishing event that will bring her national recognition." It certainly did. And the Governor General's Award it won, especially as a first book, and a collection of stories at that, crowned that attention. Her father may have been astounded, but so too were the people who knew Munro in Victoria, the people who came into the bookstore and the writers and professors at the university who knew her socially. Very few of these people were aware that she wrote. Once the award was announced and Munro went to Ottawa to receive it, though, newspaper profiles of her as a writer at work began; over the many years since, they have continued, waxing and waning according to publication, but never ceasing altogether.

One of the first profiles not connected to either *Dance* or the Governor General's Award appeared in the Victoria *Daily Times* in August 1969; after accounting for the book and its award, the writer turned to their effects:

> Then Alice Munro found she had become a celebrity being interviewed by established celebrities such as radio's Betty Kennedy, television's Elwood Glover and critic Robert Fulford. The Globe and Mail magazine discussed her; this month's Saturday Night magazine analyzes her work.
>
> It's not surprising that she says the last thing she wants is more publicity!
>
> Yet there is her growing readership and too many un-answered questions. People want to know in which magazines they will find her work. They ask why she writes and what she writes about, or how long she has lived in Victoria.

With her award money, the writer reports that Munro "indulged in the luxury of renting a fisherman's cottage on quiet Gabriola Island and has been spending some writing hours there. Currently she is taking a break from working part-time in her husband's bookstore on Yates Street." Even so, "Alice Munro says she leads a normal life."

Munro did rent an island cottage for a time, saying that she "had some things to work out" with her writing, although she recalls thinking that she did not get much done since she had her daughters with her. Less pressing, but implicit in Munro's decision to go to Gabriola, two hours north of Victoria, was a growing sense of dissatisfaction with her marriage.

Munro's "normal life" was changing. She offered an anecdote that has become well known, involving her reply to the person taking the 1971 Census of Canada. She says that when asked her occupation she replied "writer" instead of "housewife" for the first time. It was an exhilarating idea to her. While this most certainly happened and provided a moment of revelation for Munro herself, the transformation it embodies – from a little-known writer whose work was valued by a

coterie of literary types to public writer and celebrity – began with
Dance and its Governor General's Award. As she told Earle Toppings in
a 1969 interview after the award, once she published her book and it
garnered attention, she began receiving mail about her work for the first
time. That had not happened when her stories were only in magazines.
Munro found this to be "very encouraging and this is one of the best
things" about publishing a book, to hear from readers and "to know
that you've gotten through to somebody."[31]

In this same interview, Toppings asks Munro about her connections with other writers since she lives out there on the west coast, so
far away from Toronto, Canada's cultural and publishing centre. She
replies that she really is not connected to other writers and, anyway, "I
never want to talk about writing much when I'm doing it." While that
was certainly so to this point in Munro's career – Robert Weaver
remained her primary literary connection, although now she had the
people at Ryerson – all that also changed with *Dance* and the award.
Through it, Munro had "gotten through" to readers, to be sure, but she
had also reached other writers, and three of these connections had real
effects on Munro's subsequent career.

In September 1968, just as *Dance of the Happy Shades* was being
printed, *CBC Tuesday Night* broadcast the last story Munro wrote for
the book, "Images." Among its listeners was a young writer in Montreal
named John Metcalf. He was born in England in 1938 and after university studies there had emigrated to Canada in 1962, teaching first
high school and then at Loyola College, now part of Concordia
University. Impressed by the story, Metcalf decided to write Munro and
tell her so. He knew Earle Toppings and obtained her address from
him; in passing it on, Toppings warned Metcalf that he might not get
a reply, such were Munro's habits as a correspondent. When he wrote,
Metcalf promptly told Munro what Toppings had said.

In "Images," Metcalf recalls, he saw that Munro "had done exactly
what I was groping towards and she was there ahead of me. . . . But what
I was trying to do, what she did, you could sum up in the title she gave
to the story, 'Images.' Because this was what we were both trying to do
at the time, which was to lessen the intricacies of plot and move a story

forward by a succession of powerful images that had flowing in them, in common, a kind of common energy, but they would be extraordinary vivid." The story "moves forward in sort of nodules of picture or dialogue." "Images" and "Walker Brothers Cowboy" struck Metcalf as being technically radical, "extraordinary and demanding, very difficult. . . . It was such a technical feast for me, so when I read her I was thinking, ah, that's how you do that." Metcalf points as well to the narrator's account of the family's financial decline toward the beginning of "Walker Brothers Cowboy," calling it "the most incredible manipulation of voice I'd seen on a page in a very long time." Besides finding her address and writing to Munro, Metcalf says he bought an armload – seventeen, he remembers – of copies of *Dance of the Happy Shades* and gave them to friends saying, "Read this book."

Munro later called the letter she received from Metcalf in 1969 "a bouquet, a burst of handsome praise. He had taken the trouble to do this – to write so generously and thoughtfully, to a writer he didn't know, a writer of no importance, no connections. He didn't do it out of kindness alone, though it seemed to me so wonderfully kind. He did it because he believes writing is important."[32] Earle Toppings's comment notwithstanding, Munro replied to Metcalf and they began a correspondence that led to what Munro called a "literary friendship." Such a phrasing, which Munro comments "sounds to me too pretentious and genteel for the letters we wrote," does not really capture the importance of this connection for her. Over the next several years, owing to the extended dissolution and breakup of her marriage in 1973 and her return to Ontario, her friendship with Metcalf was something of a second literary lifeline for her. Coached by Metcalf, Munro spent a brief period – from 1972 through the fall of 1975 – supporting herself by way of her writing and by playing the public writer to a degree she had not before nor has since. During this time, Metcalf was an important literary friend.

At the time he first wrote to Munro, John Metcalf was himself freshly embarked on a career as a writer of short stories, novelist, editor, and anthologist. Later, especially as the 1970s gave way to the 1980s, he gained notoriety as a critical gadfly, waging a campaign aimed at academic critics of Canadian writing. He began publishing stories in the 1960s and had two stories in *Modern Canadian Stories* from Ryerson in 1966 – with Munro's "The Time of Death" – and five in *New Canadian Writing, 1969.* His own first collection, *The Lady Who Sold Furniture*, was published by Clarke, Irwin in 1970. Concurrently, he was assembling two anthologies of Canadian stories for Ryerson aimed at course adoption, *Sixteen by Twelve* (1970), for high school students, and *The Narrative Voice* (1972), for students in university. Given Metcalf's enthusiasm for her work, it is not surprising that he included two Munro stories in each anthology. And given his approach, she also had her first commissioned critical statements in those books, an "Author's Commentary" in the first and, in the second, one titled (by Metcalf as an acknowledged echo of the well-known essay by Mary McCarthy) "The Colonel's Hash Resettled."

Without detailing them, these pieces reveal Munro talking about her writing in her characteristic ways. She is sceptical of writing about writing, preferring that the story itself, rather than any commentary on it, be the real focus. In the first piece, she briefly addresses "An Ounce of Cure," a story in which a first-person narrator recalls an event when she was in high school. Spurned by a boy she liked, she decided to drown her sorrow by drinking one evening while babysitting. The story, an incident that happened to Daphne Cue as a girl, is mostly comical. Even so, in her essay Munro notes that its narrator "gets out of" what had happened to her "by changing from a participant to an observer" – this is what, as a writer, Munro does herself. Looking back at the story as she wrote her essay, Munro maintained that it accomplished what she sought for it. On the other hand, "Boys and Girls," a story she wrote "too purposely perhaps," uses her own history to analyze sex roles. She still wonders over it, and in doing so reveals herself an exacting artist: "When I read this story over I have a feeling of failure and despair; I feel that there's so much more that should be there, a whole world really, and I have strained it out into this little story and cannot tell if I got what matters." In "The Colonel's Hash Resettled," Munro first displays her fundamental scepticism over the ways of literary critics by undercutting someone's assertion that the house in

"Images" is symbolic, rather than just a description of a house Munro remembered from Lower Town; that is, nothing symbolic, a real house. Her doubts in this regard have never wavered, yet the best part of this essay is Munro's statement that as a writer she "feels like a juggler trying to describe exactly how he catches the balls . . . he still feels it may be luck, a good deal of the time, and luck is an unhappy thing to talk about, it is not reliable."33

However uncertain she may have been, Munro was writing stories that continued to attract attention and more unsought contacts with other writers. One day during the summer of 1969, Audrey Thomas, who in 1967 had published her own first collection of stories, *Ten Green Bottles*, went to Munro's Bookstore specifically to meet the author of *Dance of the Happy Shades*. George Woodcock had asked her to review it for *Canadian Literature* and, having done so, Thomas wanted to tell Munro personally how much she liked the book. Munro was not there, but Jim had Thomas call her up at home from the store. Alice invited her to come right over, and the two began a friendship that continues. Today Munro calls Thomas her best friend.

Also during the summer of 1969, Margaret Atwood, who was living in Edmonton at the time, came through Victoria with her husband James Polk. In response to Atwood's reading of Munro's stories in anthologies and *Dance of the Happy Shades*, they sought Munro out and ended up spending a weekend with Alice and Jim. That too was the beginning of a long and still ongoing friendship between the two women.

Recalling this first visit, Atwood said that "the world of Canadian writers was extremely small at that time. Anybody who had published a book of any kind" was sought out, for books were "like your calling card." An all-too common attitude toward Canadian writing at the time, suggesting something of the colonial assumptions still very much in play in Canadian culture, is offered in passing in Christopher Dafoe's May 1969 profile of Munro (whose picture there is captioned "a quiet Canadian"). Amazed as he seems to be at finding "a writer of exceptional gifts" in a Victoria bookstore, he casually writes that "it is easy enough to overlook Canadian writers. I first discovered Mordecai Richler in the pages of The Spectator, Ethel Wilson in The Reporter." Given such an inhospitable climate for their own writing and aware as they were of *Dance of the Happy Shades*, Atwood, Metcalf, and Thomas sought out Munro and long-standing personal connections were developed.

Thomas maintains that her friendship with Munro is not a literary one, that she does not think she has had any effect on Munro's career. While this is true, the same cannot be said for either Metcalf or Atwood. During the first half of the 1970s, Metcalf proved to be enormously important to Munro's career as she returned to Ontario and redirected her writing and career, finding her way eventually back to Clinton and Huron County. He was a critical connection for her – involving her in his editing projects, encouraging her as a public writer, and working with her in the creation of the Writers' Union of Canada. In doing so, Metcalf extended Munro's connections to other writers beyond the happenstance of people who took the initiative to write to her or to visit Munro's Bookstore in Victoria. Sometime in 1975, Munro talked about a literary agent with Atwood, who suggested her own New York agent, Phoebe Larmore. Though not then taking new clients, Larmore recommended Munro to an associate, Virginia Barber, an agent who was just starting out on her own. Barber followed this suggestion up and contacted Munro. So Munro's connection with Atwood, like those with Weaver and Metcalf, proved to be critical.[34]

Yet at the time *Dance of the Happy Shades* was being published, Alice Munro was just another of the very small band of Canadian writers of which Atwood speaks. Ryerson, the Canadian publisher most associated with Canadian writing, took several years to decide to do that book, felt compelled to offer Garner's foreword as imprimatur, and even considered a preface by Munro. She was herself hesitant about a book of stories, but this halting progress to first-book publication was mostly a reflection of the conditions affecting Canadian publishing at the time. Characterized as "the perilous trade" by Roy MacSkimming, Canadian publishing until the 1970s was historically an enterprise of, on the one hand, balancing the firm markets of textbooks and acting as agents for imported foreign writing with the trade publication of writing by Canadians for Canadians on Canadian subjects, a far weaker and so "perilous" market, on the other. Since the 1920s, Ryerson had published Canadian writing and continued to do so while most of its competitors contented themselves with the more lucrative textbook and foreign agency markets through the 1950s. Looking back from the mid-1960s, Macmillan of Canada's John Gray recalled stating during the 1950s that "the relationship of author and publisher in Canada [lacks] a rational economic basis; that the Canadian author who depended on books for money did not make it from sales in Canada; that the Canadian publisher made none of the net profit of his business from the overall result of his Canadian general publishing."

Yet this situation was changing. John G. "Jack" McClelland had returned from his war service and joined his father's firm, McClelland & Stewart. By the late 1950s, McClelland and Malcolm Ross, general editor of the series, had established the New Canadian Library reprint line of paperbacks and had embarked on the path that would make McClelland & Stewart the preeminent publisher of Canadian writing from the 1960s on. During this time, Macmillan of Canada and other publishers also commissioned and brought out Canadian books, as attitudes about Canadian writing began to change and nationalism rose. Yet as MacSkimming makes clear, the publishing of Canada's writers was quite economically perilous throughout the twentieth century. The economics of publishing in English to a potential audience of about two-thirds of Canada's small population at any given time (the other third expressing themselves in French), always in competition with a flood of imported books from British and American publishers, has always been one of balancing small sales against great critical successes, small margins against hesitant reprints and looming bookstore returns.

For a writer like Munro, with a book of fifteen stories and another fifteen either published or broadcast, 1968–69 was a propitious time. That decade had seen ferment throughout the world. In Canada, the country's centennial was embodied in Montreal's hosting of Expo '67 and was excitedly celebrated throughout the country; the next year, Pierre Elliott Trudeau emerged as leader of the Liberal Party and the new prime minister. Greeted by a widespread enthusiasm, dubbed Trudeaumania by the press, he was a federalist from Quebec intent on beating back the separatist threat there while assuring francophones of an equal status within the federal government. By virtue of the centennial celebrations and the dramatic advent of Trudeau and his federalist followers from Quebec, Canada seemed to be changing with the times, becoming less staid, less a colonial outpost, more a place where things happened.

This sense, along with a growing awareness of Canada's economic and military dependency on the United States, brought nationalism to the fore in English Canada to an extent not previously seen. With most of Canada's export trade going to the United States, and often through Canadian branch plants owned by U.S.-based multinationals, English-Canadian nationalists became deeply exercised. "So long as this country remains a small political satellite of the United States," the poet Earle Birney said when discussing Canadian publishing, "involved in the American economy of waste and war, our cultural future will be negligible." When Birney spoke, the Americans were just becoming mired in what would turn out to be a hopeless war in Vietnam that brought thousands of draft dodgers to Canada, many eager to pronounce its superiority as a more humane society. Coupled with this, some thought that Canadian universities had been taken over by American Ph.D.s and that Canadian culture was being strangled in those institutions as well.

These facts had the effect of enhancing the growing force of nationalism as the 1970s began and that, in turn, brought a new-found awareness of the importance of Canadian writing and culture to the life of the nation. "Read Canadian" was a frequent assertion that encouraged the rise during the 1960s and 1970s of an English-Canadian audience for literary works by Canadians that had been minor before. A major report on Canadian studies at the time was entitled *To Know Ourselves.* For Munro and for other writers as she came to know them then, this was a time of organization, of professionalization, and of expansion of interest in Canadian writing. It was a time for developing and nurturing a Canadian audience.[35]

In December 1970, just as she completed the manuscript of *Lives of Girls and Women,* Munro found herself caught up in one of the great nationalist *causes célèbres* of the era. On November 2 the United Church of Canada had announced that the Ryerson Press had been sold to

McGraw-Hill, an American firm "in the latest U.S. takeover to occur in this country," as a *Toronto Daily Star* columnist wrote. He also quoted Ryerson's manager, Gavin Clark, saying, "It's just another in a long line of Canadian sellouts." For 140 years a Canadian company, long associated with the publication of Canadian writing through its trade books, Ryerson was most attractive to McGraw-Hill for its $3-million-a-year textbook business. The reporter from the *Star* continued, "Jack McClelland called the 'decision to sell' to an American-controlled company 'absolutely appalling. The church should be severely criticized.' And that was the general consensus. The United Church was deluged with letters from across the country that lamented the sale to a foreign corporation." One person wrote that "if you sell Ryerson to foreigners my family and I will never set foot in the United Church again." "Amid more publicity than has ever before been attached to events in book publishing in this country," *Quill & Quire*, the book industry magazine, summarized just after the sale was concluded, "the deal was announced, discussed, quarreled with, and finally completed. As an outcome, the government of Ontario . . . appointed a royal commission" to look into book publishing in Canada.[36]

Munro became involved and closely watched the Ryerson sale because her contract for *Dance of the Happy Shades* contained the standard clause requiring her to submit her next manuscript to Ryerson. A few weeks after the sale was announced, she wrote to Earle Toppings seeking advice. She could not understand why Ryerson had not contacted the writers it had under contract. She asked him if the sale was going to happen and wondered if, should it occur, the next-book clause would be enforced. Munro also wondered if Toppings thought "McGraw-Hill is going to be interested in publishing Canadian fiction. . . . The reason for this," she continues, "is that I have another book finished which I was, naturally, going to send to Ryerson. Now I don't know what to do."

In mid-December, after the Ryerson sale had been finalized, Munro wrote again, thanking Toppings for "replying so fully to my bewildered bleatings." She explains that when she had not heard from him immediately, she had independently concluded what he later told her (the "next-book option never really holds up"). But the key for her was whether Audrey Coffin was moving to the new firm: "She is such a great person & editor." As it turned out, Coffin kept her job, so Munro sent the manuscript, then called *Real Life*, along to her. Concluding her letter to Toppings, Munro wrote, "Anyway, I have the most awful misgivings about the thing now. (I think I'll write Audrey a long letter about those & not bore you)." As her letters to Coffin about *Real Life* show, Munro's misgivings were doubtless as much about her manuscript as they were about the politics of the Ryerson sale. As someone who knew about selling books in Canada, she certainly shared the widespread dismay. But as she makes clear in her first letter to Toppings, Munro also knew that the change at Ryerson might affect the firm's attitude toward her kind of writing.

Munro's decision to send *Real Life* once she knew her editor was staying is indicative. Coffin's presence was key: it reveals both Munro's loyalty to someone she knows and feels comfortable with and, at the same time, suggests her need for such an editor as she shapes her writing for publication. While not a great deal of information is available about Coffin, it is clear that she and Munro were kindred spirits. Although she worked with other writers, Coffin once commented in a 1970 letter to Toppings that "my favourite reading is autobiography when done by the right person. Especially about his childhood – almost anyone who can write at all can do something exciting I believe. (Everyone has a romantic love for himself as a child?)." Given such preferences, Audrey Coffin was just the editor to receive Munro's manuscript, *Real Life*, in December 1970.[37]

By the time she did so, Munro's career was entering a new phase. Along with Atwood, she recalls the 1960s and 1970s as a period when writers in Canada supported one another freely, seeing common progress in an individual's success. In early 1969, Munro had herself been the recipient of such support from Margaret Laurence, her friend from Vancouver who had emerged during the 1960s as one of the leading Canadian novelists. Laurence was well known for calling writers a tribe. When *Dance of the Happy Shades* was published, Audrey Coffin sent Laurence a copy and, acknowledging it, she asked if Coffin had arranged American or English publication. If not,

Laurence volunteered to try to do so, though she did wonder if she was being presumptuous.

Coffin must have encouraged her, for in February 1969, just as *The Fire-Dwellers* was in press, Laurence wrote to Judith Jones, her editor at Alfred A. Knopf in New York. After dealing with her own business, Laurence mentions Munro's *Dance*, writing, "These stories seem so very good to me that I wonder if I might send you a copy?" The Canadian publisher, "it appears, [has] done nothing about submitting the book to any American publisher. Mrs. Munro does not have an agent, either." Jones immediately wrote away for a reading copy and inquired about American rights to the book. Very much liking what she found in *Dance*, Jones arranged its consideration by Knopf. However, the book was turned down since Munro's work was not known. There was the usual problem of selling collections of short stories by unknown writers and, besides, in Laurence, Knopf already had one woman writer from Canada. One was enough, apparently.

This brief episode suggests the underlying factors affecting Munro's career just after *Dance* was published: her stature as a writer in Canada was growing, owing to the quality of her work more than to her Governor General's Award; other writers were noticing and were making encouraging connections she had not much previously experienced, extending her reputation; and, as the episode of Knopf's consideration of *Dance* demonstrated, Munro faced real difficulties in taking the next step. Securing publication in the United States, despite the enthusiasm of an editor at a major publishing house, was not an easy thing. While Knopf eventually did publish Munro in 1979, that did not occur until her way had been prepared by McGraw-Hill, by the *New Yorker*, and especially by her agent, Virginia Barber. As she sent *Real Life* to Audrey Coffin at, now, McGraw-Hill Ryerson, Alice Munro was beginning another phase of her career. No longer Canada's "least-praised good writer," as Robert Fulford described her as the 1960s began, Alice Munro was on her way to becoming "world famous in Canada" as the decade ended. *Real Life*, retitled *Lives of Girls and Women* and advertised as a novel by McGraw-Hill Ryerson, would serve to accelerate that change.[38]

Lives of Girls and Women: "I Just Want to Keep Writing
Whatever I Can" – "And I'm Never Quite Sure Ahead
of Time What This Will Be"

Recalling the incidents that led to her story "The Office," Munro has
written, "And then it started to happen, the real small miracle, when
something, someone, starts to live and grow in your mind and the story
makes itself. I didn't even recognize this as anything to be grateful for,"
annoyed as she was at the landlord because he was "cutting into my
efforts to bring forth something important and beautiful, some real
writing." What she was after in her office above that drugstore in 1961
was a novel, the novel she had been after even then for some years and
would continue to pursue throughout the 1960s, trying repeatedly to
produce what she here calls "real writing." Munro then offers what
might now seem a shocking revelation: "I didn't want to write another
story. For years and years I didn't want to write more stories. I feel that
way yet some of the time, but am resigned." Even now, she says she
occasionally has this same feeling.

After years of these repeated attempts, *Lives of Girls and Women*
came together during 1970. She recalls beginning it on a Sunday in
January. Seeing that she was off ruminating in that other country of her
imagination, Jim told her to go down to the closed store to write, that
he would get supper for the family. She did, beginning with what she
calls "a regular novel" with the "Princess Ida" section of the finished
book. Munro kept at the material in this way until sometime in March
when, during a lunch with a group of other women, she realized that
the structure of a regular novel was "all wrong" for what she was doing,
so she went home and started to break the material into sections. By
late October Munro wrote to Coffin. After apologizing for being "such
an all-time record rotten correspondent," she reported that "I'm writing
very hard. Should be more or less finished in December, if I don't go
nuts trying to juggle kids, work, etc."

The manuscript was finished by then, and satisfied that Coffin
would remain at McGraw-Hill Ryerson, Munro sent *Real Life* to her on
December 10. She described the book as "partway between a novel and

series of long stories, all [a] 'growing up' sort of thing which I've at last, praise the Lord, worked out of my system." She adds that "the last, short, untitled section may not fit in perhaps could be dispensed with." Coffin wrote back on the fourteenth, acknowledging receipt and saying that she "is so happy that you have sent the MS to us" and that she has got "permission from the Authorities to read the manuscript first & am looking forward to doing it at home."

In her letter of the tenth, Munro was referring to "Epilogue: The Photographer," the then untitled portion of the text that would vex her – she alternated between keeping it and dropping it, continually rewriting it – well into 1971, even as the book went into production. Articulating these uncertainties to Coffin, on December 22 Munro sent her some revised pages for the "Baptizing" section and wrote: "The eighth section – those few pages at the end – isn't right and I suppose had better be scrapped. I wanted each section to cover an area of growing-up – Religion, Sex, etc – but creativity – how it starts & what happens to it – was beyond me. I thought of working it into section seven ['Baptizing'], but that would muddy the emphasis." It would have, indeed. For reasons biographical as well as aesthetic, Munro's struggle with the epilogue of *Lives of Girls and Women* is indicative, a key moment in her life, as well as in her career.[39]

As is well known, *Lives of Girls and Women* contains a signed author's disclaimer: "This novel is autobiographical in form but not in fact. My family, neighbours and friends did not serve as models. – A.M." Placed on the copyright page, this disclaimer appears just before the dedication: "For Jim." While just a passing comment, Munro has said that she worked on *Lives* that year ("I am writing very hard") in the knowledge that her marriage was coming to an end, so the book was done in a more determined and pressing way. When she talked to Thomas Tausky about *Lives* in 1984, Munro said she initially "saw the novel as a straight [story of a] girl growing up in Western Ontario. I saw it as being fairly comic, though how I could have got that notion I don't know. But I did. I saw set pieces. It was a very high-spirited novel to me. I enjoyed writing it." Seeing the story more effectively told through story-like "set pieces," Munro abandoned the initial "regular novel" form in March 1970; she had sought a continuous narrative, and evidence of this approach is in her papers. Once she had written the seven set pieces that make up most of *Lives,* though, she found herself struggling with the other implications of "Epilogue: The Photographer." It is no set piece.

In a December 1970 letter to Coffin, Munro continued: "I feel apologetic about turning out this sort of girl-growing-up thing, but I had to do it, it was there, I wanted to get it out. I've taken several vows now to get out of Jubilee forever. This has sort of wrapped it up for me. I hope you're not too disappointed." Alice Munro has never been able "to get out of Jubilee forever," and the reasons for her struggle with the epilogue to *Real Life* have everything to do with her own real life. Until she confronted the implications of that epilogue, Munro told Struthers, the book "was not the story of the artist as a young girl. It was just the story of a young girl. . . . And yet, I found eventually that the book didn't mean anything to me without it." To Tausky, she describes the transformation of Del from just a young girl into an artist as "all this stuff coming out – which I didn't really foresee or particularly want. I didn't know what to do with it." She spent about half as much time on the epilogue as she had, she told Struthers, "writing the whole book. And then I plucked it out and decided to publish the book without it . . . then I rewrote it and put it in."

The finished book's disclaimer notwithstanding, what was hap-pening in the composition of "Epilogue: The Photographer" was that Munro found herself being imaginatively pushed into a deeper, more essential, level of autobiography than the comic set pieces demanded. With its focus on Del as an artist and as a young woman, and on Del's own concomitant struggle with the life she finds herself living and the other world she imagines and is drawn to, the epilogue's few pages are infused with Alice Munro's own life history. Del, like her author, had to choose between the "real" Marion Sherriff and the imagined Caroline Halloway. In both renderings there is the matter of Huron County's factual detail, certainly, but more especially there is Munro's commit-ment to transform that detail into the exceptional writing she has long sought and always produced. Little wonder she struggled and worried over the epilogue, for in it she encapsulated not only her own life's detail – seen and imagined – but also the very sensibility that had made her the writer she had become.

The epilogue of *Lives of Girls and Women* returned Munro to her own beginnings by echoing the imitative Gothic novel she worked on, in her mind and on paper, when she was in high school. Called *Charlotte Muir* after the main character, a person who "lives in a lonely place off by herself," the working out of its plot over an extended time was what brought Munro to the realization of "the twin choices" of her life, "marriage and motherhood or the black life of the artist," as she told Tausky. In *Lives*, Munro put Del Jordan in much the same position as she had been herself. Writing her own novel with Gothic overtones, Del both rejects her uncle Craig's fact-based writing method and also knows that her romanticized story of Caroline Halloway, a story seen in the epilogue as contrasting with the bland reality of Bobby Sherriff, is not quite right either. Del is getting "an idea that all art is impossible." So was Munro herself at that time since, as Tausky has detailed in much the best article on the writing of *Lives*, this epilogue led directly to such stories as "Material," "The Ottawa Valley," and "Home" – that is, it led to stories that analyze a writer's relation to her material and, seemingly, offer a rejection of any fictional artifice.[40]

Munro's account of writing *Lives of Girls and Women* during 1970 makes a useful record but, at the same time, it needs qualification. The Sherriffs cum Halloways were a family that had existed as the Musgraves before she began *Lives*; in the Calgary archives there is considerable material concerning Miss Musgrave, an elderly spinster who inherited the family home from her staunchly Methodist father, who owned the local piano factory. Unlike her teetotalling father, Miss Musgrave drinks. She also has a boyfriend, Mr. Chamberlain, who visits her; she is a holdover from the 1920s, her best time. She had had the family house subdivided and had taken in tenants, among them Del and her family. Some of this material looks back to the circumstances of "Walker Brothers Cowboy," in that the fox-farm father had died of blood poisoning (common from fox bites, Munro says, something her father had suffered from) and his widow took to the road selling Walker Brothers goods south of Jubilee in places like "Sunshine" (which is south of Wingham) and "Scotch Corners" (which is not). Thus the material Munro was working on as she completed *Dance* combines with the material that becomes part of *Lives*. The "House of Musgrave" gives way to the "House of Sherriff" and each are Jubilee versions of Munro's reading and attraction to the Gothic element she detected in Wingham and its environs. These relocatings of her imaginings returned Munro to the abandoned house owned by the Cruikshanks where she went as an adolescent and where she found her first Tennyson. At the same time, Munro says she was writing a version of "The Photographer," a figure who takes revealing, and damning, photographs of people, well before *Lives*. These autobiographical and imaginative considerations combined and were brought into focus by "Epilogue: The Photographer."

Munro's uncertainties with, and difficulties over, the epilogue are evident in her letters to Audrey Coffin. After expressing her doubts in an earlier letter, on December 31 she sent a revision "which seems to me closer to what I want than the one I have, though maybe still not usable. I just had to do it once more and have taken a vow I'll leave the whole thing alone now." Then, in a postscript, she writes, "The other sections still seem to fit together better, in a way, without this." After she had received Coffin's positive reaction to the whole manuscript, Munro wrote on January 9 that the last revision of the epilogue

> *is* better in the last version (done during the indescribable chaos between Christmas & New Years, some of it in the middle of the night waiting for Andrea's next bout of throwing-up – we're all dragging around with flu) but it's not right yet. I don't like the way it sort of "distances" things. Writing about writing always runs into this problem.

She says further that the momentum "with regard to this work – sort of played out in early November. . . . What's to be done may come to me yet. I was so glad you like the work as a whole." Coffin was the only person who had read it apart from the typist who, Munro heard from a friend, reported to her husband that it was "a pretty kooky manuscript." Ten days later, on January 19, "with shamefaced apologies," Munro prepared to send the epilogue back. She had tried to make it a section about the same length as the others and it "didn't work." She was inclined to leave it out, but she decided to send it back to Coffin offering a postscript saying "REALLY, we better forget about Marion/ Caroline. It doesn't flow – it destroys credibility. I've started on a new thing." The next day she writes another letter to include with the one she wrote the day before, and here she has another plan: to take up some material "about the book" – Del's – now in "Baptizing," and use it at the end.

Recalling this flurry of revisions in 1984, Munro said she continued wavering about the epilogue until Bobby Sherriff's pirouette came to her ("he rose on his toes like a dancer, like a plump ballerina"; an act that "appeared to be a joke not shared with me so much as displayed for me"). The pirouette "turned it around. . . . When that came to me I knew I could leave it in."[41] This pirouette does capture, just as *Lives* ends, Munro's sense of the factual commonplace happily existing alongside the inexplicable – rather like Yeats's ending question in "Among School Children," "How can we know the dancer from the dance?" But Munro does not formulate her point as a portentous question, she lets the gesture speak enigmatically. Like Del, the reader is left with this Bobby Sherriff, an apparently harmless refugee from the madhouse, living and being. He feeds her cake and chats about diet one summer morning as she awaits her scholarship results. In her imaginings he embodies the tragic Sherriff family that has served as model for the Halloway family she had created before. Yet up close he seems, she realizes, to be so very ordinary, even pathetic.

Munro wrote another version of the epilogue right after she sent Coffin her letters of January 19 and 20. Uncharacteristically at that time, she dated it – January 24, 1971. It contains a notable description just after the photographer is described which, though later deleted, follows from Del's realization that she had not "worked out" just why Caroline's eyes were white in the class picture taken by the photographer. "I had not bothered to work out anything" in the novel, Munro wrote, "what I had were pictures, names, phrases. Sometimes I would try to write down bits of the story, a description or conversation, but this was always a mistake; what was so inadequately done marred the beauty and the wholeness of the novel in my mind." This was just what was happening as Munro struggled with finalizing the text of *Lives of Girls and Women* as the book was being prepared for publication. "Epilogue: The Photographer" was transforming Del's story in two important ways: the Sheriff/Halloway novel is another version of Munro's own *Charlotte Muir* composition. The book's story offers more than just a girl growing up; as Munro said, it became a portrait of an artist as a young woman, a fledgling artist just as Alice Laidlaw was herself in Lower Wingham and Wingham during the 1940s. Unlike Del, she then had no boyfriend and she did receive scholarships to carry her away from Wingham. But speaking directly to Munro's own demands of her fiction, this draft paragraph defines her sense that whatever is on the page never reaches the beauty and perfection she imagines for it. Thus changes must, always, be made to the manuscript at hand, as long as is possible. Munro has always done so, she does yet, to the dismay of her editors.

To be sure, changes continued to be made to the manuscript as *Real Life* moved toward publication by McGraw-Hill Ryerson in October 1971. While Audrey Coffin was still Munro's editor, the editor-in-chief of the trade department, Toivo Kiil, also became a presence in shaping Munro's career for both *Lives* and for her next collection, *Something I've Been Meaning to Tell You*. Born in Sweden and raised and educated in the United States, Kiil had come to Canada to do graduate work in English; he joined McGraw-Hill in 1968 in sales and, after the Ryerson takeover, was put in charge of the trade department. Given the public controversy surrounding the sale of Ryerson, the new company was understandably the focus of particular scrutiny from Canadian nationalists once the sale was completed and McGraw-Hill Ryerson was created. Primarily a publisher of textbooks, McGraw-Hill Canada had little reputation as a publisher of fiction or other creative work; taking over the new company's trade department, Kiil wanted to change that, and he saw Munro's work as having considerable sales potential both in Canada and, through McGraw-Hill in New York, in the United States and in the United Kingdom. Thus while Coffin remained Munro's manuscript editor, Kiil became very much involved in the marketing of her work. He handled contractual matters with Munro directly and worked with McGraw-Hill in New York in the hope of producing American editions of *Lives* and *Something*. As a way of enhancing her work's reputation in the United States, since she did not have an agent working on her behalf, Kiil sold first U.S. serial rights to some of Munro's stories to American magazines and looked after matters having to do with subsidiary rights (book clubs, film, large-print).

Kiil sent Munro a contract for *Real Life* on March 10, commenting that he considered "it a great privilege for our company to have this opportunity of working with an author of your standing." He summarized the contract and said that he "was almost certain that Audrey will be working with you on the copy editing of the manuscript" and that he was looking "forward to working with you on the preparation of *Real Life* in an advisory capacity." Munro replied with some questions on the sixteenth, and Kiil wrote again to her regarding American editions of both *Real Life* and *Dance of the Happy Shades* as well as a Canadian paperback edition of the latter, which was then still available only in the original Ryerson hardcover. Within two weeks he would be going to New York and would there discuss possibilities with his U.S. counterpart. Kiil thought that with *Dance* and the second manuscript in hand "we shall be able to reach a decision on the most effective strategy for guaranteeing you exposure in the U.S." Munro had asked, given her previous experience, about the standard "option on the next manuscript clause." Kiil assured her that they did not hold it as binding; in any case, he was "prepared to write an addendum or rider to the contract releasing" her from it. He continued, "As you requested, I am rushing your manuscript to you by registered mail in order that you may finalize it to your satisfaction. I am anxious to see the final form and present it to New York and to Simon & Schuster," a potential mass-market paperback publisher. It is notable that Munro was here negotiating on her own behalf and was, without an agent, largely dependent on Kiil as her publisher. His responsibility, clearly, was to McGraw-Hill Ryerson more than to his author. Just over ten years later, when a question arose over rights to *Lives of Girls and Women*, Virginia Barber wrote to the lawyer charged with sorting the matter out and mournfully commented that on the master contract under advance it read "none requested."

The evidence in the Alice Munro collection in Calgary allows a detailed examination of the textual progress of the manuscript Munro submitted to Audrey Coffin in December 1970. While this is not the place for a complete account, some details are notable. Munro's copy of her own typed version (which she probably gave to her typist) is there, as is the professionally typed and lightly copy-edited manuscript, which, smudged throughout, was used by the printer. There are inserts and other changes, some in Munro's hand, so it is likely that once Coffin had copy-edited the manuscript she sent it to Munro for her approval. That may indeed have been the version to which Kiil referred in late March. There are revised sections and other changes throughout the manuscript, but the epilogue – for a time Munro wanted it to be untitled and to use roman numerals as page numbers – continued to get the most attention. Munro held up production and was revising in proof. She remembers as much, as did Kiil. Bobby Sherriff's pirouette was inserted at this stage, since no manuscript version of it exists though the rest of the section is largely complete. Sometime between late March and the announcement of publication, the title was changed to *Lives of Girls and Women* since W.W. Norton in New York had recently announced a forthcoming novel by Deborah Pease titled *Real Life*. Kiil and Munro also agreed that the book would be called a novel. For his part, of course, a novel was what he wanted to sell. For hers, Munro knew that while it was not the conventional novel she had begun and later abandoned, the final result was in fact, as she wrote to Coffin, "part way between a novel and a series of long stories." Its epilogue finally completed, the Canadian edition of *Lives of Girls and Women* was published in October 1971.[42]

Positive responses were quick to appear. In the *Globe and Mail* in one of the earliest reviews to be published, Phyllis Grosskurth wrote that it is "a joy . . . to be able to proclaim that Lives of Girls and Women is a delight, a wonder, a blessing devoutly to be thankful for." "It's a familiar kind of book," Kildare Dobbs reported the same day in the *Toronto Star*, "the story of a girl growing up in small-town Canada, narrated with good humor in the first person." Dobbs, who misspells Munro's name "Monro" throughout, struck a note seen in other reviews by detecting apt parallels between *Lives* and Laurence's *A Bird in the House* published the year before. He also paid special attention to Del's mother, "a woman of tremendous energy and lively intelligence who goes out selling encyclopedias because she believes in them. It's her wish that Del make her own life and not wreck it for some man." Joan Coldwell in the *Victoria Daily Times* wrote that "what is extraordinary is the intensity of Del's awareness of people around her, of the fine lines of social distinction, the little self-deceptions, the ironical distance between one's own vision of oneself and that seen by others." E.D. Ward-Harris, in the Victoria *Daily Colonist*, held that Munro's "work is consistent, quietly brilliant. . . . I think it is fair to say that outside of Quebec, anyway, Alice Munro is the most skilled writer of fiction in Canada today." Christopher Dafoe, who met Munro after the publicity surrounding *Dance*, first wrote a personality column announcing the book's publication in the *Vancouver Sun* and then followed it up with a review. There he asserts that Munro's "literary talents have power to spare for the long haul" and concludes that *Lives* "is a work of art," a "deeply moving and splendidly fashioned novel."

Not surprisingly, one of the most thorough and compelling newspaper reviews was by John Metcalf in the *Montreal Star*. *Lives*, he wrote,

> is a disturbing book for a man to read; for most women perhaps
> even more uncomfortable, as they will recognise its horrible
> truth on page after page. It is, on one level, the doctrines of
> Women's Lib made, gloriously, flesh. Precisely because it is a
> novel and not a tract, it is full of delicate insights into the lives
> of girls and women – mothers, women of defeated ambition,
> schoolgirls – and, because it is real on every page, full of humour
> and splendid grossness.

Though "a sensitive girl," Del "is no drooping Pre-Raphaelite flower"; she "menstruates, and masturbates; she reads library books to find descriptions of people 'doing it'; and she encourages an exhibitionist in a scene which [exceeds in] humour and grotesquery." Taking note of such detail, Metcalf is at pains to say that there is nothing salacious here, that he does not wish to distort "the life and the truth of the book. . . . Lives of Girls and Women is also a loving and accurate portrait of a people and of a time and place. Growth, sexual or otherwise, does not take place in a vacuum. Del learns from and is formed by her mother and father, aunts, uncles, friends and lovers, by Jubilee itself." He then quotes the passage from the epilogue, one frequently cited since, where Del says that "no list could hold what I wanted"; seeing her words here as characteristic of Munro's writing, Metcalf asserts "you can touch and smell every word on every page."43

Some reviewers found fault, though. In Calgary Kevin Peterson, for instance, wanted Munro's strong descriptions to be shorter and called for "a tighter rein and better editing." More than a few pointed out that *Lives*, whatever its publisher asserted, is not really a novel. But Canadian newspaper reviews were generally very positive. As newspaper attention gave way to magazines and journals, the reviews became longer and more considered. Writing in a Vancouver monthly entitled *Monday Morning*, Irene Howard notices the subtlety with which Munro characterized Del's parents, her mother (in much the same way noticed by Dobbs) but also the father. He "remains in the background, generous, undemanding, accepting; another life to be explored, though not in this novel." That observation later proved to be true. Howard praises Munro "for the honesty she brings to her writing and for the respect and affection in which she holds her characters, men and women." Clara Thomas in the *Journal of Canadian Fiction* paid especial attention to the epilogue, seeing it as Munro's "statement of purpose" and asserting that through it she "has certainly succeeded in bringing and holding together the place, the time and the people."

Easily the best single notice *Lives of Girls and Women* received was James Polk's lead review in *Canadian Literature*. Taking up the book with a clear knowledge of *Dance of the Happy Shades*, Polk considered how *Lives* extends and amplifies the earlier work. Munro, he says, "hasn't forgotten a thing about lower-middle class life in the drab and frugal Forties." Unusually, given most writing from Ontario small towns, in her "work we see Ontario social myths from the bottom up; the poverty line runs smack through her part of town and her characters seem curiously estranged from their environment: the men struggle in silence to earn a living, the women – Munro's particular concern – are shown to be troubled by isolation and unfulfilled dreams." Polk also focuses on the epilogue, but he is more critical of its effect than most reviews. "By resisting" Garnet French, "Del loses the chance to become another forlorn Jubilee housewife, but salvages her soul, and in the novel's epilogue the dawn of her ambition to be a writer suggests another, better way she can 'have' her hometown without being trapped in it forever." But the "epilogue made me slightly uncomfortable, as if it were an advertisement for the writer's abilities rather than an afterword organically connected to the novel itself. . . . Del repeatedly wonders at the bizarre twists in people's lives, at the destinies that shape our ends. But somehow it's not good enough; the book, good as it is, never quite jells into the major piece of serious fiction I suspect the author intended it to be." Polk seeks the reasons for this, finding them in "the novel's loosely-woven, anecdotal structure" where "the chapters, basically unpruned short stories, are casually linked together by Del's consciousness." For Polk, while Munro's stories and this novel "are funny, well-written, and evocative, it seems the novel misses out on that black, brutal cutting edge that gives the stories their idiosyncratic power." But even if *Lives of Girls and Women* "falls short of its own ambitions, it is a remarkable book. . . . Reading Alice Munro's work is one of the joys of literacy," he concludes.[44]

Lives of Girls and Women was passed over for the 1971 Governor General's Award, which went again that year to Mordecai Richler, but it garnered new attentions and honours for Munro. It was named an Alternate Selection by the Literary Guild of America, a leading book club, and was the first Canadian work of fiction ever selected by the guild. It received the first Canadian Booksellers Association/International Book Year Award, intended by the booksellers "to focus attention on a

Canadian book which they feel has not generated the popular interest it merits." Munro travelled to Ottawa to collect the award in May 1972. Later that year she was named the Outstanding British Columbia Fiction Writer by the province's library association.

Meanwhile, Kiil pursued various publishing opportunities on Munro's and McGraw-Hill Ryerson's behalf. He arranged an American edition of *Lives* from McGraw-Hill scheduled for September 1972. Thus in the United States Munro did in fact have her first book publication as a novelist, since McGraw-Hill did not bring *Dance* out until fall 1973. He pursued publication for *Lives* in the United Kingdom and, in the United States, tried to interest the Book-of-the-Month Club, sought to place an excerpt from *Lives* in *Ms. Magazine*, and to get the book a film option; he worked also to arrange paperback versions of both books. He also kept pursuing U.S. magazine sales, with some success, selling "Red Dress – 1946" and "An Ounce of Cure" to *McCall's*. Each appeared there in 1973. By November 1972 Kiil was also asking Munro about her next book.[45]

☙

Less a matter of detail than one of trajectory, Munro's status as writer of note grew continually as the 1960s passed into the 1970s. When the decade began, "The Peace of Utrecht," which Munro saw as her first "real" story, was about to appear in the *Tamarack Review*. Its partner "real" story, "Dance of the Happy Shades," was one of a different sort, not personal material. That story was leading her, a bit haltingly to be sure, into the pages of the *Montrealer*. By 1960 Munro had published fewer than a dozen stories in magazines and Weaver had broadcast half that many. By 1972, she had two books to her credit, a Governor General's Award, among other awards, and her work was being published and noticed in the United States for the first time. Her career had gained momentum and was growing. Increasing attention was certainly being paid. That this had come about, mostly, through the qualities found in the writing itself is remarkable. Munro had been helped along by many people, foremost among them Robert Weaver – yet as the 1960s passed, Gerald Taaffe, John Robert Colombo, Earle

Toppings, Audrey Coffin, Toivo Kiil, and John Metcalf emerged also to play their respective roles in Munro's career. To a person, they saw in Munro's writing just what John Robert Colombo saw – "that here is writing of quality and character" – and each worked toward her success. Munro herself, dealing with all this, writing hard during 1970 to complete *Lives* and then gently pressing Kiil toward other opportunities, was getting ready for a trip she had long anticipated. Her "long voyage from the house of marriage" was reaching, in 1972 after *Lives* had been published, its point of embarkation.

5

Waiting Her Chance, Going "Home"
Who Do You Think You Are?, 1972–1975

We had seen in each other what we could not bear, and we had no idea that people do see that, and go on, and hate and try to kill each other, various ways, then love some more.
– *Lives of Girls and Women*

Oh, writing makes my life possible, it always has.
– Connolly, Freake, Sherman interview

In "Soon," the second story published in an Alice Munro triptych by the *New Yorker* in its 2004 summer fiction issue, Munro returns to Chagall's *I and the Village*. "Soon" opens with three paragraphs describing details of the image, a print found in the gift shop of the Vancouver Art Gallery. The first one reads:

> Two profiles face each other. One profile of a pure white heifer, with a particularly mild and tender expression, the other that of a green-faced man who is neither young nor old. He seems to be a minor official, maybe a postman – he wears that sort of cap. His lips are pale, the whites of his eyes shining. A hand that is probably his offers up, from the lower margin of the painting, a little tree or an exuberant branch, fruited with jewels.

After this description the story goes on: "Juliet decided at once to buy this print, as a Christmas present for her parents. 'Because it reminds me of them,'" she tells the friend who is with her there. "Soon" draws on the details and emotions of Munro's own visit home to Wingham during the summer of 1954, but the presence of *I and the Village* recalls Munro's fragment from "The Moons of Jupiter," where it also figures. There the narrator looks to the picture hanging on her daughters' bedroom wall "for help" with her writing: "When I lay on the bed and looked at it I could feel a lump of complicated painful truth pushing at my heart; I knew I wasn't empty, I knew I had streets and houses and conversations inside; not much idea how to get them out and no time or way to get at them." In this narrator Munro created a character analogous to herself in West Vancouver in 1959, a person stymied by her circumstances and mostly unable to write. Still, the "complicated painful truth" is pressing at this woman's heart; she knows she isn't "empty" because the Chagall print helps bring what she calls her "harking back" during the daily fifteen-minute respite created by *Funorama* on television. The show occupied her daughters, allowing her the daily contemplation she describes. "*Funorama*, I would think with relief, and know that I had fifteen minutes before I absolutely had to start supper." Starting supper was what she had to do as the mother, and as the wife too, since just after that her husband Andrew would arrive home from work in Vancouver across the water.

In 1959, Munro did have a print of Chagall's *I and the Village* hanging in her daughters' bedroom on Lawson because Jim did not like it and would not have it in the living room. Today, Munro does not know what became of it, but she remembers later hanging it in the children's section of the bookstore in Victoria. "Soon" shows *I and the Village* persisting still in Munro's imagination, its detail vivid yet, presumably, from those brief moments of respite in West Vancouver when she was in her late twenties, not writing much but longing to do so. After some success with stories that year, Munro went into the period of depression and writer's block described earlier.

In "The Moons of Jupiter" draft fragment, Munro continued to describe the print's personal contexts in a passage that bears attention:

> My husband wouldn't let me hang it in our room, let alone in the living room where anybody could see it. I deferred, of course, I said "Well, I like it, I really like it," but I said this in a childishly rebellious way almost with a Shirley Temple stamp. That was how I managed to hang onto something I really wanted. In the years since our marriage it seemed to me my husband had grown harder and darker and denser and I had dwindled, so that his presence was now like a block of something heavy in the house and I was whining and wheedling around it. He was on the lookout for subversion, treachery, which could appear to him in any form – rice instead of potatoes, a Chagall print, friends who voted NDP. And he was right. I was biding my time. He was not wrong to spot the danger signals, he was right. Many husbands were the same. These houses, lawns, children, cars, automatic washing-machines, which were supposed to [be] demanded by, created for, wives, seem to me, looking back, to have been more furiously created by husbands, by young men. Fortresses. Wives were pious or rebellious, in these situations. Pious women outdid each other.

I must get home and make the cabbage rolls they said. I must wash the cupboards. I was not allowed to make cabbage rolls. Andrew feared foreign food. He feared vulgarity.

Munro continued until the fragment breaks off: "Once at a party I heard a husband say he could never read any book written by a woman. He was a husband more belligerent than most, in his manliness, but nobody, no one of the women present, spoke seriously against him. We didn't hope to argue with men. At a gathering of men and women all under thirty-five in this time before first flirtations, invitations, adulteries, all began to erode and confuse things, I saw the men."

Written during the late 1970s when abandoned husbands – Patrick, Richard, Andrew – are characters frequently seen in Munro's stories, this autobiographical fragment offers a summary version of Alice and Jim Munro's marriage from her point of view in the late 1950s. In the final incomplete sentence it suggests something of what followed in the 1960s in their social group. As such, the fragment sets the stage for the breakup of their marriage. Alice's Chagall print was on the wall of their daughters' bedroom, her writing was a source of frustration and depression for her, and Jim took himself and his role as husband, father, and breadwinner seriously. After fifteen years of marriage, the fundamental class differences remained between them.

These differences became more pressing after the Munros had moved, just before Andrea was born, into the house on Rockland that Munro accepted but did not want. The size of the house, the image it projected, the requirements it seemed to demand – all underscored the class differences between them. While such differences existed throughout the marriage, they were often submerged below other needs – establishing themselves, raising a young family, opening Munro's Bookstore – but that house on Rockland was the undoing of the Munros' marriage.[1]

Alice Munro's personal situation was inextricably entwined with her developing career. As the breakup approached, it had given urgency to her writing throughout 1970 as she worked on *Lives of Girls and*

Women. After separating from Jim in fits and starts, Munro was finally able to leave Victoria for good in September 1973. Then, for the first time in her life, she needed to support herself – like Del, she expected to get a job wherever she decided to live. Even though *Lives* had been published in the United States in 1972 and *Dance* was scheduled for fall 1973, and she was well along on a third book, Munro doubted that she would be able to support herself as a writer.

Such doubts notwithstanding, she settled in London and began commuting weekly to Toronto to teach creative writing at York University. Through John Metcalf she became involved in the formation of the Writers' Union of Canada. She was writer-in-residence at the University of Western Ontario for 1974–75. In August 1974, promoting *Something I've Been Meaning to Tell You*, both Douglas Gibson of Macmillan of Canada and Gerald Fremlin heard her on the CBC talking to Harry Boyle. Each had his own designs on her, and each proved successful in time. A year later, by August 1975, Munro had fled the academy for Fremlin and was back where she never thought she would be again: in Huron County. Living in Clinton with Fremlin (and his mother, who was quite frail), trying to write in a new place that was also her old place, Munro confronted her material in a way she had not done before.

"So Shocking a Verdict in Real Life": "Work Is a Great Help, I Find"

When the Munros made the move into what Alice has called "the big house" on Rockland, she was thirty-five. She had been married for almost fifteen years and was going to have a baby in a few weeks' time. Sheila was about to turn thirteen, and Jenny was nine. Sheila has written, "I knew she did not want to live in such a house, but my father and I were so keen on having it that she did not protest very much. As a token of resistance, she said she would move to the house on one condition: I would have to do all the vacuuming." The Rockland house had five bedrooms, five fireplaces, twelve-foot ceilings with exposed beams, a maid's quarters, and two sets of stairs. Jim had his grandparents' "massive dining-room suite sent out from Ontario," lighting it with a large brass chandelier. Eventually Jim got a church organ and installed it in a hallway they called "the chapel," where the windows were painted to look like stained glass. James Polk, who visited the Munros with his wife Margaret Atwood in the summer of 1969, recalls Jim Munro's pride in the newly acquired instrument. A trained musician himself, Polk spent some time during their visit playing Handel on it. While Atwood and Munro talked writing and literary gossip, Jim showed Polk the organ as well as the house itself. Polk described Jim as "very present" during their visit.[2]

Andrea's birth, work in the bookstore, and the demands of a large house left Munro exhausted most of the time. She would often come home from the store and set about supper and other chores without taking off her coat. For his part, Jim "was already working incredibly hard six days a week at the store," Munro told Ross. "There was no way he could turn around and scrub the floors." While certainly Munro had thought of separation at other times in her marriage, she was all too aware of her financial dependence on him and her obligation to the children. Through the Vancouver years she had stayed and, in the years between the move to Victoria and Andrea's birth, she was fired up with helping to make the bookstore a success. But in the time after Andrea was born, she was transformed. As she told Ross, she then became "so tired and discouraged that when I came out of it I was on my own. Jim hadn't changed, but I had changed."

"Wives were pious or rebellious in these situations," Munro wrote in that *Funorama* fragment. She was a rebellious wife herself, and her rebellion was fuelled both by the times and by the class differences that had always separated her from Jim. People who knew the Munros socially saw them as very different people, with Jim tending to show a critical view of his wife to others in ways that might not have been unusual then but certainly were not kind. Sheila has written that while her mother "may have been above reproach as a writer in his eyes, there was an underlying rejection of her class and her background as something shameful. He corrected her Huron County accent and he treated the Wingham relatives who came to visit with scorn and even refused to speak to them on occasion." Writing this, Sheila cites a letter from Anne Laidlaw complaining of Jim's behaviour during a visit Alice's sister, Sheila, made to Vancouver. About her parents' arguments, Sheila continues,

> My father was on the side of conformity, conventional values, and conservative politics, and my mother was on the side of individualism, left-wing politics, and rebellion against conventional values. My mother thinks he did a very brave thing in marrying her and going against his parents, but that at some level what he wanted was for my mother to be the kind of conventional woman that his parents would have preferred him to marry – and he wanted the artist he did get.

These fights, Sheila recalls, were not over things immediate to the family, but rather were "philosophical and political, representing irreconcilable world views." Munro herself says that they ultimately realized their incompatibility, "not just with our opinions of things on the news but more with what we wanted life to be like, which became finally apparent when we moved to the big house."[3]

There were other contexts for the breakup as well. During the 1950s, in Vancouver, there was a fair amount of what Munro calls "extramarital flirtation" between individuals, each married to another. Describing one of her own, she said, "It was quite passionate and it was always unplanned. It was absolutely foolish." These attractions seldom led to breakups. During the 1960s in Victoria, owing to the temper of the times, among "people who had been married very young, there was an explosion of infidelity and of interest in affection, because none of us had had it in the normal period of life. So a lot of my friends got divorced then and had a lively time for maybe half a dozen years and then got married again. This was almost a pattern in our lives." Munro's "Jakarta" explores such a moment.

Sheila Munro details the ways of the Munro family, remembering her mother hating "the image of the mother who disapproved of everything, who had a different set of values, the mother who was at the ironing board." This sort of persona grew from Alice Munro's determination "to be as different from her own mother as possible." Sheila also makes it clear that her mother now has misgivings about this, thinking that she "didn't establish enough of a mother's authority, so that it left [Sheila] dangling without this natural reference point" in personally and culturally turbulent times. Sheila offers an extended quotation that speaks to Munro's sense of herself as a mother at that time and suggests how her attitudes might have accentuated her growing differences with Jim. Alice recalled, speaking to Sheila,

> I was into my own role but this had to be seen through the tremendous change of values that came in the late sixties and that split women of my age. Some women decided to go against it, some women decided to be like their mothers. I wanted to be as if I were ten years younger. With the women of thirty-five, women born in the early nineteen-thirties, there was a big problem about how to be an adult in this period, not only because prejudice against adults was so firm (Abbie Hoffman saying anyone over thirty couldn't be trusted) but also justified in my eyes. The times had a lot to do with the kind of mother I was to you and Jenny (then), but not earlier. There was more to let you be yourselves but it was also to let me be myself so I wasn't engaged in the terribly serious business of making you into the kind of people I thought you should be. I didn't have any notions about that. We were in this adventure.

Meanwhile Jim was a parent who did think that his daughters should be shaped. As Sheila makes clear, he was the one who arranged for and took her to lessons, who worried over clothes and friends, who had expectations of her. Given such views, the temper of the times, and his own conservative outlook, having a wife less than two years younger than he was who wanted to act considerably younger, who wanted to argue about Vietnam, who acquiesced to the counterculture then everywhere evident, must have flummoxed Jim Munro. Alice, a rebellious wife, one often "ready for battle" – a phrasing Jim used about her "when he found her moody and volatile," according to Sheila – continued to change, becoming increasingly dissatisfied with her situation. By the time she was at work on *Lives of Girls and Women* during 1970, she had decided that her only means of personal survival was to escape the bonds of her marriage.

That summer Alice, Jim, and Sheila toured Ireland for three weeks, leaving thirteen-year-old Jenny at home with a sitter and Andrea in a playschool. Sheila recounts returning to her parents' room unannounced during the trip and finding her mother weeping, obviously in the midst of a fight. At another point, she recalls an argument in which "my mother picks up a plate and flings it at my father, except she tosses the plate slowly and without conviction and he ducks from the path of its wobbly flight. It hits the wall behind him." Recalling these times years later, Munro stated that "when a marriage is breaking up . . . you use all kinds of things to mask what is the real problem. Lots of times you just try to deceive yourself to make a go of it. I still think it was a good thing it broke – it wasn't that good for the children, but it was good for me and for Jim."4

✤

Unlike most marriage breakups, the Munros' was rendered subsequently in a succession of Alice's stories. In "Material," the narrator at one point says she "was not able fully to protect or expose" her husband Hugo, "only to flog him with blame, desperate sometimes, feeling I would claw his head open to pour my vision into it, my notion of what had to be understood." Earlier she admits that when she was married to Hugo she never had confidence in him as a writer since she "believed that writers were calm, sad people, knowing too much. I believed that there was a difference about them, some hard and shining, rare intimidating quality they had from the beginning, and Hugo didn't have it." Munro wrote these lines just before she left Jim and Victoria behind, and well-positioned behind one of her characters' personae, "knowing too much" herself. Once she returned to Ontario, though, the versions of husband found in stories like "The Beggar Maid," "Chaddeleys and Flemings 1. Connection," "The Moons of Jupiter," and especially "Miles City, Montana" come closer and closer to Jim Munro, his likes and dislikes, his ways of behaving. Richard, the husband in the first

"Chaddeleys and Flemings" story, the husband who condescends to his wife's visiting Cousin Iris, is, like Jim, the target of a flung plate. Munro the artist has imagined a piece of lemon meringue pie on it, making the scene both humorous and sad, leaving the narrator amazed "that something people invariably thought funny in . . . old movies or an *I Love Lucy* show . . . should be so shocking a verdict in real life."

In "Miles City, Montana," the narrator abruptly dismisses her former husband Andrew, informing the reader that this man who is so very present in the story just then is actually long gone, his present circumstances unknown to her. It is a jarring revelation there at that point. Just before this, Munro writes that at "the bottom of their fights, we served up what we thought were the ugliest truths. . . . And finally – finally – racked and purged, we clasped hands and laughed, laughed at those two benighted people, ourselves. Their grudges, their grievances, their self-justification. We leap-frogged over them. We declared them liars. We would have wine with dinner, or decide to have a party." As she wrote in "Material," Munro's stories after she left her marriage were for her, ironically, just as she wrote about Hugo there, "ripe and useable, a paying investment."5

Jim Munro was not receptive to a separation. When it became clear that Alice was in earnest about leaving the marriage, things became very difficult. Each of the older girls was caught between her parents – Sheila has written of this time and Jenny also confirms its unpleasantness. Each parent represented a side. While the older girls were more able to understand, Andrea's situation was the more fraught; she was just five in 1971 and turning seven when Munro left finally in 1973. Given her age, throughout the breakup there was the question of where and with whom Andrea would live, what her contact with each parent would be, and how the break could best be effected. Because the decision to separate was taken between Alice and Jim before any physical break occurred, there was a protracted period of uncertainty for all the Munros.

During this time Alice's correspondence with John Metcalf, then living in Montreal, increased owing to her contributions to the anthologies he was editing and also to their shared interests. In one of her earliest letters to him, she says that it "is rather beastly of me never to answer letters especially since support such as yours means a great deal to me." That support continued and Metcalf's importance grew; over considerable distance and only by correspondence initially, their relationship developed. Once Alice had decided to leave her marriage but had not yet left, by 1971–72, Metcalf's own marriage had unexpectedly collapsed, his wife leaving him and taking their two-year-old daughter with her. As the breakups came, Munro and Metcalf were able to commiserate. In June 1971, while *Lives of Girls and Women* was going into production, she sent him a photograph for *The Narrative Voice* (she "came out looking untrustworthy and pregnant" though, she says, she is neither). "I have been in a black mood, too," she continues, "really bad, really the worst I've ever had, but for fairly specific reasons (is that a comfort?) and now things have brightened up. When I'm not writing (the last five months or so), I really mess up my life."

The undoubted cause of Munro's mood was her relationship with Jim. She comments later in the letter, after she expresses hope that his wife will stay with him, that "It is NOT EASY being married to a WRITER," that it is "worse being married to me when I'm not [writing]. I always have this idea about how I should live in a shack in the bush, but I'm dependent as hell too." This letter also shows her at this point still writing to Metcalf about their work, mainly, and it reveals her continued uncertainties about what she is doing. Thus she continues, "I have another idea working out. I wish now I had never written *Real Life*, because the *next* one might be good, and R. L. just seems in my way. But I won't do much till fall, because I'm taking my kids on the train to Ontario this summer." She ended by responding supportively to Metcalf's comments on the novel he was writing.

Munro is quite emphatic that she was the one who left the marriage and that Jim was much steadier than she was as they decided what to do. As this was happening, there were infidelities as each turned to others while they were nominally still together. Alice was first, and Jim reacted. Her attitude toward these new relationships is seen in a revelatory comment some years later when writing to Marian Engel; she offers a report on the circumstances of each of her daughters, contrasting their approaches to living, and says of Sheila, "Like me, she must figure getting burned is what it's all about."[6] Having decided as much for herself, Munro lived through a two-year period of turmoil when she was still in Victoria, initially in the house on Rockland. But, over time, through living elsewhere and through trips, she was able gradually to pull away.

In the summers of 1971 and 1972, before she finally left Victoria for good in 1973, Munro was able to leave with her children for long periods. During the summer of 1971 she took her daughters by train back to Ontario for a visit to Wingham and other places there; she recalls this trip especially because she and Andrea shared a room on the train while the older two daughters, then seventeen and fourteen, rode coach, ignoring their mother and sister and hanging out with the other teenagers on the train. While she was in Wingham, Munro read the proof of *Lives*. She returned to Victoria for the school year and did the publicity associated with her book from there. In June of 1972 she went with Andrea to Toronto, staying in Earle and Iris Toppings's house during July and August while they were in India. Besides visiting her father in Wingham, Munro wanted to be in Ontario because of a relationship with a man she had been seeing.

By then she had told Metcalf that she and Jim were separating and asked his advice as to how she might earn her living as a writer. Metcalf, who was about to head off to the University of New Brunswick as a writer-in-residence for a year, set about seeing if he might secure the same position for Munro for the subsequent year. He also visited Munro in Toronto in early August and, she later wrote to Toppings, "he looked bad enough" owing to his own marital problems. Metcalf was an important connection for Munro as she was making her break. Another writer and fellow sufferer, he shared her situation.[7]

When she returned to Victoria after her summer in Toronto, Munro took an apartment on Oak Bay Avenue not too far from the Rockland house and, after spending the morning writing, went over to be there when Andrea came home from school. She still did the cooking and the cleaning. Audrey Thomas recreates these circumstances in her story "Initram," first published in 1975. It is based in part on a visit she made to Munro when she was living between Rockland and her apartment. "When she came to see me that time, I nearly had a fit because I wasn't living at home," Munro told Ross, also noting that many details in the story were true to the visit, though others were not. In its background, the story recounts how the two women met and it offers a transparent version of details from Munro's biography – of Jim's family and her history as a writer. Once the narrator arrives to visit her friend and fellow writer, Lydia, the details of her living arrangements recreate Munro's just then. Since the story is a fiction, other details have been imagined or brought in from elsewhere, most especially the character of Lydia, whose personality and mannerisms are quite different from Munro's. Yet Thomas's editor at Oberon was sufficiently concerned about the likeness that, before the story was included in *Ladies and Escorts*, she checked with Munro to make sure she had no objection. "Initram" warrants mention here because it offers a glimpse into Munro's circumstances over the winter of 1972 – whatever else the story ultimately does, it had its beginnings in Thomas's visit to Munro at the time. The added material, however, means that it cannot really be said that Thomas's story is about the breakup of Munro's marriage; the circumstances are quite different from Munro's.[8]

✍

By the time Munro returned to Victoria from Toronto during the fall of 1972, she knew that a final break was coming soon. Consequently, she worked hard over that winter on the material that became *Something I've Been Meaning to Tell You*. In addition to the writing itself, Munro had begun a three-year period when she actively sought to promote herself as a writer, seeking grants and university appointments. The attention and awards *Lives* was bringing her in 1972 aided this plan, for it was adding significantly to her reputation as a Canadian writer to watch. This was the only time in her life when Munro actively did this. As her marriage ended and she prepared to strike out on her own, Munro did not have much expectation that she would be able to support herself by her writing. Thus while she tried to live this life for a time, she did so as a means to her particular ends – leaving Jim, their marriage, and Victoria – without any enthusiasm over what was to be required of her as she did so. Although she had never supported herself, her determination to leave her marriage saw her trying a variety of ways to be financially independent.

Sometime during the period of the breakup, Munro let Bob Weaver know what was happening, for on November 27 – either 1971 or 1972 is possible – he wrote a caring and very understanding letter to her in which he apologizes, saying, "I'm sorry I bothered you about the Canada Council when you were in a state," and continues, "I wasn't entirely surprised by your letter because I've sensed for a long time some kind of strain." He goes on to offer some of his own personal history; his father died when he was very young and he was raised wholly by and around women, making him "sensitive to the way women feel." Weaver commiserates and mentions some of his own family problems, adding, "It's sometimes grimly cheering to know that other people are in a mess." He ends, "I guess you know that I'm fond of you for yourself as well as because of your writing. Let me know if there's anything I can ever do (we'll try the Council again), and I hope things improve. Work is a great help, I find. Do I sound fatherly now?"

Munro had tried a second time for a Canada Council grant just before *Dance of the Happy Shades* came together at Ryerson, again unsuccessfully. Apparently Weaver was prodding her here to try again. Probably in response to this letter, she applied once more over the winter of 1972–73. In February 1973 she was writing to Metcalf, thanking him for what he did for her toward the writer-in-residence appointment at New Brunswick, saying that it was all right that she had not got it, but that "I'll probably get the grant." Munro did receive a $7,500 Canada Council Senior Arts Grant in 1973 – the only time she has received such support – but when it came it was mostly needed for the income tax she owed that year, for she had earned over $10,000 in royalties from McGraw-Hill Ryerson.

Munro's writing career was becoming more demanding as the marriage was ending and, through its various connections, she was looking to move from Victoria. In April of 1973 she called Weaver and asked him about a furnished apartment in Toronto as well as questions about income tax. Writing with suggestions a few days later, Weaver also put Munro in touch with George Jonas, a CBC television producer who was then arranging a series of original plays by Canadian writers. Munro's "How I Met My Husband," one of the stories about to appear in *Something* and probably her most successful dramatized piece, was included.9 Through Weaver as well, she had two of the stories forthcoming in *Something* broadcast on *Anthology*. In the fall of 1972 McGraw-Hill, New York, published *Lives of Girls and Women* in the United States and, based on its success, decided to bring out *Dance of the Happy Shades* there the next year. At the same time, Toivo Kiil at McGraw-Hill Ryerson was managing sales of Munro's subsidiary rights, bringing out a Canadian paperback of *Dance*, and beginning to anticipate Munro's next book. Her career was gaining a new level of momentum.

Early in 1973 Munro and Metcalf began correspondence as members of the selection committee of the incipient Writers' Union of Canada. As Metcalf wrote in a form letter intended to solicit members, an ad hoc group of writers met in Toronto in December 1972 to "lay the foundations" for a union. It would be "a truly professional organization which would help and protect us in relation to contracts, royalties, permissions, foreign rights, TV and film rights, and publicity." Munro attended this first meeting. She also went to another held in June 1973 in Toronto, as well as to the union's founding meeting in Ottawa in November. The Writers' Union was a necessary step in the professionalization of writing in Canada, one that grew directly out of the controversy over McGraw-Hill's purchase of Ryerson, the Ontario Royal Commission on Publishing in Canada, and the nationalist concerns of the early 1970s. The union was created, by coincidence, just as Munro was getting out of her marriage and was setting her energies more directly toward writing as a profession. It became very much a part of her identity as a writer then, and so it has remained. At the first meeting, she became a member of an eight-person membership committee. In her letters to Metcalf about it, she suggested possible writers from British Columbia, offering a list of about twenty. She advocated opening membership to anyone who had published a book. Metcalf was tentative on this point, as were others, trying apparently to differentiate between writers of quality and those whose work did not meet that stipulation. Throughout this debate, Munro thought the very notion of any such differentiation was impossible, if not ludicrous, although she continued to be interested in knowing what the arguments in favour of such elitism were.[10]

Seeing each other through their work together on the Writers' Union, sharing both interests and similar personal situations, and finding one another mutually attractive, Munro and Metcalf had a romantic relationship that began in mid-1973 and continued into 1974. Munro spent that summer in Montreal and, after that, they broke up. Her connections to Metcalf were most significant in relation to Munro's departure from married life but, even so, they continued and were maintained after they ended their romantic involvement. During the early 1970s Metcalf was a significant lifeline for Munro, connecting her to the world of writing in much the same way as Robert Weaver had during the 1950s and 1960s.

For his part, Metcalf was still very much involved in the making of Canadian writing during the early 1970s – Margaret Atwood remembers him as a delight, "the life of the party. . . . He was absolutely funny and very verbal and very there and very connected." A moving force behind "The Montreal Storytellers," an initiative to bring writing into schools and other public spaces; teacher; author of five books; writer-in-residence at New Brunswick, Ottawa, and Loyola universities; and recipient of two Canada Council Senior Arts Grants during the 1970s, Metcalf seemed senior to Munro during the time they were together. He was a person to both confide in and learn from. But owing to his penchant for polemic attacks on other Canadian writers and on the writing culture in Canada that began during the 1970s, he was also a writer whom she quickly surpassed – she did so with *Lives*.

While her relationship with Metcalf was developing, and while they worked with other writers in the union, Munro was still trying to leave Victoria for good. She needed something that would take her elsewhere. Over the winter of 1972–73, working on the stories that became *Something I've Been Meaning to Tell You*, she pursued an opportunity to teach a summer course in creative writing at Notre Dame University in Nelson, British Columbia. A small university in the Kootenay region in the southeastern portion of the province, Notre Dame was well away from Victoria and indeed from just about anyplace else. She accepted the job in March. It involved teaching the second half of an English class, the creative writing portion (the first half was taught by a visiting instructor from the University of British Columbia). The class met for two hours daily from July 23 to August 17. Her stipend was $425, and she was also given a three-room apartment from July 1 to August 18, plus a travel allowance of $70.[11]

In the Calgary archives there are numerous fragment versions of a story called "Creative Writing," which drew specifically on this experience and was probably written about the same time. Most versions are written from the point of view of a character in Munro's situation, though some feature the woman as wife to a husband who is teaching at a college in the mountains for the summer. This is an instance, one of several, in which Munro worked and reworked a situation, writing multiple versions, striving to find an effective way into the material. Here are two representative passages:

> Dorothy teaches creative writing. She is not qualified to teach anything else. This is the summer school session, at a little college in the Kootenay mountains. When Dorothy first arrived there, on the overnight bus from Vancouver, she was met by a boy, or a young man with a fuzzy beard, a fastidious voice, a cold serenity or contemptuous passivity of expression; whatever it was, she had seen it before and it made her nervous. Almost the first thing he said to her was, "We thought we were never going to get anybody for this job."

> Nellie had not realized the pay was poor. She was rather pleased at the prospect of being paid anything at all. For some reason she hadn't thought of being at the bottom of a list of people the college would have tried to get, she hadn't thought of so many people being able to turn down offers, to choose and reject. She

knew that she wasn't well-known. She had published one book of stories. She always spoke reluctantly and modestly about her work. Secretly she believed all the flattering things that had ever been said about it and thought the people who had said unflattering things were stupid and affected.

They [Nellie and Dahlia, the head of the English Department] were heading up a steep hill. The town was built around a mountain lake. "Why did you come?" said Dahlia. "Just out of curiosity?"

"My husband and I are splitting up," Nellie said. "I wanted to get away somewhere for a while and it seemed like – I remembered driving through here once and I thought it was a nice place, with the lake –"

While Munro changed the details of the marriage breakup, the elements of the writer/teacher's situation remain constant: the people at the college cannot believe anyone would come for the money they paid, she is working in "the smallest, dingiest, and – it is now July – the hottest university in the world," and she "is delighted" because she "has never had an office or a job before."

Munro writes that for Nellie, the first version of writer/teacher, this "was the first job she had held since waitressing in her college days. She was forty-three years old." While not quite true for Munro, who turned forty-two in Nelson and who had worked in the Vancouver library and in the bookstore since waitressing, it was pretty close. When she went to Nelson she had all three daughters with her, she had her own place, and she knew she was out of her marriage. No longer dependent, she was on her own. She found the teaching difficult because of her shyness but, more than that, as a person who has little belief in such programs Munro felt like a fraud as she was doing it. But there were things happening in Nelson, poetry readings and the like, Sheila worked construction and then on the roads, and Munro was meeting people through the college, which publicized her presence. She was happy that summer. Before going to Nelson, at the June meeting for the Writers' Union, she had started to break off one relationship with a man and, at that meeting and over the summer, she was developing another with Metcalf. So the summer she spent in Nelson proved to Munro that, like her narrator in "Red Dress – 1946," her new life was possible.

Once she finished teaching in Nelson on August 17, Munro set about organizing that new life quickly. She went to Toronto for a couple of weeks, staying in a friend's house and exploring possibilities there. Munro then saw Toronto as a city where she had good friends and felt comfortable, more alive. Nothing materialized, so she returned to Victoria, intending to pack up, find an apartment in Vancouver, and move back there – despite her dislike of that city. Its proximity to Victoria would allow her access to her daughters, especially Andrea. But while she was still in Victoria, packing, Munro received a call from the chair of the English Department at York University asking if she would be willing to take on a course in creative writing, needed on short notice because of overflow enrolment. Thinking it over, finding that Jenny – then sixteen –, was willing to come east with her, Munro accepted. The friend she had stayed with in Toronto taught at York and, knowing of Munro's situation, had suggested her as a possible teacher. So just a month after leaving Nelson, Munro was back in Ontario, looking to set up a household for herself and Jenny. Andrea would remain in Victoria with Jim, her school, and her friends. Instead of Toronto, however, Munro decided to return to London – it was a smaller city, a place she knew, closer to Wingham, and cheaper than Toronto – and commute to York once a week by train.[12]

Munro found a one-bedroom apartment at 383 Princess Avenue in London, settled into it with Jenny, and began her commute into York on Thursdays. While she enjoyed being in Toronto weekly and seeing friends there, Munro took an almost instant dislike to York and to her teaching assignment there. She found the university a frightful place and thought her work there ineffectual at best, fraudulent at worst. Within a month of beginning, and even having lost one class meeting to the Jewish holy days, she was thinking about quitting. Munro harboured that thought until she did quit early in 1974, citing her health as her primary reason; while she was treated for anemia in late 1973, her feelings over her own inability as a teacher and even the efficacy of the process itself were very important to her decision. During her time at York, though, Munro met and began mentoring Mary Swan, a young writer then in her final year. Swan sought Munro out to see whether she should keep at her writing and, at one point, asked if she should join Munro's class. Knowing that Swan had talent as a writer, Munro said "something like 'Not in a million years,'" Swan recalls, and told her to stay away from the class. (Munro's version: "I said, don't come into my class, they'll eat you alive, they're no good anyway.") Munro offered to continue to meet one-on-one. They did, and also kept meeting the next year in London when Munro was writer-in-residence at Western.[13]

Living in London, Munro was close enough to Wingham to continue seeing her father on a regular basis. She had begun to visit him during the summer of 1972 when she was living in Toronto. He was suffering from heart problems, so in addition to her concerns over Andrea in Victoria, Munro also had to cope with her father's declining health. Over Thanksgiving Bob Laidlaw became very sick and had to be hospitalized. There on the farm in Wingham, Munro found herself looking after things, coping with her stepmother, even spreading hay in the sheep yard, feeling that the life she had lived since leaving Wingham had all been something of a dream. This experience became the basis for "Home," a story she wrote immediately after Thanksgiving (October 8) as a birthday present for John Metcalf. She sent him the second draft, called "Notes for a Work"; it is dated October 30, 1973, and dedicated to him "with love."[14]

As she settled into London, a place she liked well enough but not one where she expected to stay long-term, Munro began to develop local connections and friends. She saw something of Margaret Laurence, who was writer-in-residence at Western during the fall 1973 term, connected with people in the English Department at Western, and also reconnected with her sister-in-law, Margaret Munro, who lived in London, had also divorced, and was going back to school. Through Margaret

Munro she later went to a party where she met people who were avowed Communists – they served as the basis of a story, "Gold," which is one of the few Munro finished to her own satisfaction and submitted but never sold. Andrea was her most pressing concern, though, so Munro went to Victoria in November to see her, and then went back again for Christmas. Earlier that month she had gone to Ottawa for the founding meeting of the Writers' Union and saw Metcalf there.

Throughout the fall of 1973 too, Munro was writing, worrying about the stories and the shape of *Something I've Been Meaning to Tell You*. She wrote "The Ottawa Valley," the last one written for the collection and something of a coda, a farewell to fiction, late that year. Owing to its depiction of her father's situation and precise, unflattering detail it contains about her stepmother, she kept "Home" out of the collection, placing it instead in *New Canadian Stories*, an annual anthology of new work published by Oberon. She thought there was little chance either would see it there. During the fall she had signed the contract for *Something* – after obtaining a higher advance than first offered and getting various assurances – with McGraw-Hill Ryerson and had accepted its $5,000 advance on royalties from Canadian sales.

Returning to London from her Christmas visit to Victoria utterly convinced that she had been justified in leaving Jim, she brought Andrea to live with her. On January 12 she resigned from York and shortly after moved from the apartment she and Jenny had been in to a house at 330 St. George Street across the street from a park. She was elated to have Andrea with her, delighted to have quit her job at York, and was starting in earnest on the work involved in getting *Something I've Been Meaning to Tell You* ready for publication. Just before Christmas Western offered her the writer-in-residence position for 1974–75 and she was again being considered for the same position at New Brunswick. By January 1974 Munro was well settled in London: she was out of her marriage, had two of her daughters with her and, while not satisfied with the public writer role she would continue to have to undertake nor pleased with McGraw-Hill Ryerson as her publisher, she was on her own and beginning to find her way.

"I Know We Can Sell Whatever You Produce":
U.S. Publication and *Something I've Been Meaning to Tell You*

In June 1973 William French, the *Globe and Mail*'s book editor, published a profile called "In Alice Land." It focuses on a visit French had made to Munro's Bookstore, transporting the reader to Victoria where *Dance* "is now in paperback, and it's displayed on the front counter, by the cash register, beside 'The Happy Hooker'. . . . Her second book, Lives of Girls and Women, is still available only in hardcover, but it sells steadily." The piece includes quotations from Jim Munro and recounts Alice's career and the bookstore's history. At one point French writes that "for a writer with only two books to her credit, Mrs. Munro has received a remarkable amount of attention and acclaim." He then ticks off some of the kudos *Lives* has received, anticipates its forthcoming paperback editions in Britain and the United States, and writes that "Dance of the Happy Shades will be published in the United States this fall, and American magazines like McCall's and Ms. have been publishing her short stories – stories, Jim Munro points out, once rejected by Chatelaine." Alice is nowhere to be seen. Clearly, she was not there the day French stopped by. Probably she had not been there lately, nor would she be there again any time soon.

Yet French's profile offers a snapshot of Munro's reputation at this key moment in her career. Having watched the encouraging performance of *Lives* in Canada after it had refused concurrent publication, McGraw-Hill New York published its own edition in fall 1972. When it was about to appear, *Publishers Weekly* called *Lives* a "remarkable novel in which peripheral characters and the landscape are made real and wondrously interesting by this gifted writer whose book merits major reviews." As French notes, *Dance* was recently published in paperback in Canada (in December 1972, so the original Ryerson hardback edition of 2,675 copies lasted over four years) and, after they were able to watch the performance of *Lives* in the United States, McGraw-Hill New York decided to bring the stories out there in 1973. Owing to Kiil's efforts as her agent, *McCall's* had already published "Red Dress –

1946" and was bringing out "An Ounce of Cure" that fall; it is doubtful that *Chatelaine* ever rejected those stories. *Ms.*, while considering some of Munro's stories then and later, did not publish anything of Munro's until 1978. Small barbs aside, Jim's point that Alice's work was catching on in the States is clear, and French's assertion that in Munro Canada had a writer whose work was causing excitement abroad is equally evident. Quite literally, a Canadian small-town girl was suddenly making good. Her own misgivings notwithstanding, Munro as writer was taking off.

But her career was taking off at a time when, as Munro had realized herself in 1970, publishing in Canada was changing. Here again, the circumstances surrounding the creation of the Writers' Union of Canada are relevant. In an editorial comment written just after the union's founding meeting and broadcast on CBC in November 1973, William French noted that "the union adopted a kind of charter which, in the current nationalist style, singled out as the enemy American books, American publishers, American distributors, and American-influenced bookstores. The charter committed the union to campaign against the dominance of American books in Canadian schools, libraries, and bookstores, without presenting specific proof of such dominance." Further, it "committed itself to press for legislation requiring Canadian ownership of publishing firms, distributors, bookstores and book clubs, to end what it called an 'essentially colonial system.' In other words it wants the McGraw-Hills, Prentice Halls and so on to be repatriated. That puts some of the union members in an odd position – Alice Munro, for example, is published by McGraw-Hill, and Harry Boyle's publisher is Doubleday. Now their union wants those publishers, in effect, to be dismantled."

Munro had begun with Ryerson, the most Canadian of publishers, and ended up through no fault of her own having her second and third books published by the "Canadian" house that in the minds of many writers most symbolized what was wrong with Canadian publishing. This anomalous position came about mostly because of Munro's loyalty to Audrey Coffin. When Toivo Kiil became editor-in-chief of the newly constituted trade department at McGraw-Hill Ryerson, he saw that Munro's writing had commercial potential both within Canada and

Alice Laidlaw, 1933–34

Fox farm building, Laidlaw's

Baby Alice
(ca. summer 1932)
with Reta Stapleton,
a neighbour

Alice Laidlaw,
ca. 1944–45

Alice and her sister,
Sheila Laidlaw,
on the Maitland River,
ca. 1946–47

Wingham Town Hall, Josephine Street

Wingham Hospital, where Alice Laidlaw was born and her mother was treated

Wingham High School

Maitland River flooding, Lower Town Wingham

WINGHAM PUBLIC SCHOOL, GRADE 6, 1941-42
Alice Ann Laidlaw is third from the right in the second row.

WINGHAM HIGH SCHOOL, GRADE 12, 1947
Last three girls on right at the front: Mary Allen, Donna Henry, Alice Laidlaw

Source: Robert Lawrence, courtesy Joan Lawrence

PROFESSOR ROBERT LAWRENCE'S ENGLISH 20 CLASS,
UNIVERSITY OF WESTERN ONTARIO, FEBRUARY 17, 1950
Woman in the front row: Joan Lawrence.
Alice Laidlaw is the woman turned away from the camera
while talking to another student, Diane Lane, on her right.

James and Alice Munro
with Robert and Anne Laidlaw,
December 29, 1951

without. Given the timing of *Real Life*, Munro seemed especially to demand his attention. Writing to Munro in November 1972, Kiil commented that the week before at a press reception McGraw-Hill Ryerson had held for two of their Canadian writers (Eric Nicol and Don Harron), he had spoken "to several of your colleagues. I must say, there is a lot of discontentment among Canadian writers – some of which I hope can be remedied by stronger pro-Cnd. Policy on our part. I think next year's list will reflect the outcome of a lot of pressuring of M-H, Int'l from here."

As the editor of the trade division of the American company that had swallowed Ryerson in 1970 – and that is really what happened, since McGraw-Hill primarily sought Ryerson's textbook business – and as a person from the United States himself, Kiil was certainly in a vulnerable position in relation to the nationalists. Given the times and his own position, there is little wonder that many writers expressed discontent to Kiil. Remembering this time in 2003, Kiil proudly noted the large number of Canadian writers he was able to publish at McGraw-Hill Ryerson before he left for McClelland & Stewart in 1975. Understandably, he was proud of the role he played in making Munro's career. In many ways, Kiil set the stage for Alice Munro as a writer with an international following. More than this, the years in which he was largely responsible for her business interests, 1971 to 1975, finally convinced her to hire a literary agent and, there again, he played a role.[15]

Once McGraw-Hill Ryerson had received *Real Life* from Munro and come to terms with her on a contract – one in which, as already noted, she asked for no advance against royalties – they were able to go into production for the Canadian edition. While Kiil and other editors at McGraw-Hill Ryerson knew and had working relationships with their counterparts at McGraw-Hill New York, editorial decisions regarding U.S. editions of titles acquired by McGraw-Hill Ryerson rested wholly with American editors. That is, the Canadian company had to stock books published in the U.S., but this arrangement was not reciprocal. Moreover, rights for any United Kingdom edition were sold by the New York office, as were first serial rights to American magazines. Thus when Kiil wrote to Munro that "next year's list will reflect the outcome of a lot of pressuring of M-H, Int'l from here" he was asserting his own efficacy in getting head-office editors to decide to publish Canadian writers in the United States, and to sell rights for these titles abroad. Put simply, Munro's *Lives* and, a few years later, *Something* found themselves in just the colonial relationship with McGraw-Hill New York that Canadian nationalists were decrying. As it happened, McGraw-Hill watched the sales of *Lives* in Canada and, based on them, decided on their own edition the next year, in fall 1972. Its real success – three U.S. printings by March 1973 and selection as an alternate by the Book-of-the-Month Club – led them to decide to bring out an American edition of *Dance* in 1973 while, concurrently, selling rights for both titles to Allen Lane in England, which published *Lives* in the fall of 1973 and *Dance* the next spring. They also arranged a mass-market paperback edition of *Lives* published by Signet/New American Library in 1974.

The reception of *Lives of Girls and Women* when it was published in the fall of 1972 in the United States and in Britain the next year was understandably different from its reaction at home. Reviewers saw its distinctive qualities clearly; most are characterized by forthright praise accompanied by a few hesitations or a quibble or two. *Lives* offers "some of the finest reading to reach us this year," Virginia Brasier wrote in the San Bernardino *Sun-Telegram,* asserting that "Alice Munro is a writer to watch." Janet Burroway in the *Tallahassee Democrat* held that "the pleasures of *Lives of Girls and Women* are those of skill rather than brilliance, recognition rather than revelation, flow rather than design." Like Canadian reviewers, many Americans focused on the book as a novel; Audrey C. Foote in the *Washington Post* notes that "it is designated a novel; it is not a finished novel but one in gestation, a series of expertly written short stories and memoirs which as the narrator develops from child to woman, mature into a novel." Mary Walfoort in the *Milwaukee Journal* sees the book as being "without a plot, with none of the tension that plot can generate," but "it manages nevertheless to spin a gauzy, strong and fascinating web, and the unwary reader is trapped tightly in it from the first page on." Something of the same note is struck by Barbara Rex in the *Philadelphia Inquirer*: "People, the seasons, time passing, the Wawanash River run through the book and hold it together. The episodes are tender, brutal, shocking, full of humor and also anguish."

Writing in *Time*, Geoffrey Wolff effused that though the "threads of this yarn are common enough stuff . . . what Alice Munro makes of it is rare. . . . By her tact, and power to recall, select and reduce, she has translated Jubilee into a birthplace, or something more than the name of a town. Call it fiction; praise it." An anonymous review in the *New Yorker* was more restrained when treating *Lives* in its "Briefly Noted" section, saying, "The straggling town of Jubilee becomes almost immediately familiar to us, and some of the characters," Del's mother and Fern Dogherty, "are given to us full size and with a touch of pity that makes them very real."

Given the times and Munro's subject and approach, many reviewers noted a relation between *Lives* and the women's liberation movement. Barbara Rex, the reviewer in the *Philadelphia Inquirer*, commented in passing that Del's mother Addie is "an early Women's Lib type" whom "Del regards with shame and pride." Margaret Ferrari, in *America*, writes that this "is not a strident novel, full of women's lib jargon and sentiments. Del's tone of voice is breezy and good-natured, closer to Huckleberry Finn's than to Betty Friedan's. The reader is made aware of her social conditioning, but obliquely and objectively." Mary Ellin Barrett, writing in *Cosmopolitan*, takes Ferrari's observation deeper since *Lives* "had me shivering from start to finish with what I call the 'recognition' goose bumps. You know the feeling, when you read something written out of another time, another land, an alien way of life, and suddenly you say to yourself, *Hey, how did she know that?*" She continued, "All sorts of women . . . are going to feel . . . close to Del Jordan and to Alice Munro, who, in a cool prose as brightly colored as a dime-store window, has put the awakening female under glass as Salinger once did the male. A lighter Sylvia Plath, a budding Jean Stafford – that's who this lovely writer is."

This last notice suggests a powerful reach for *Lives* among its American readers that was confirmed as the book's reputation grew. When the paperback edition was published, in January 1974, poet

Denise Levertov called it "an unclassifiable work"; noting Munro's disclaimer that *Lives* is "autobiographical in form but not in fact," she observed that if this "is true, I can think of no other work of fiction that appears so utterly nonfictional." Like Leo Simpson's review of *Dance* and Polk's of *Lives*, Levertov puts her finger on essential qualities in Munro's work:

> But having rejected both routine success and the trap of marriage to a boy whose mind is resolutely, even proudly, closed, she will have to find her own path out of Jubilee into the rest of her life.
>
> Because we cannot but believe Del and Alice Munro to be one and the same, we are assured that she did succeed in doing so. Munro's style – the quality of her language both in its precision of diction, which reflects her sharpness of observation, and its rhythms, which have the elegance and sense of expressive inevitability of a writer who loves and respects the art of syntax – is the style of a highly developed, mature artist. Despite Munro's disclaimer, one feels that is what Del becomes. . . . This short masterpiece of writing is open-ended; we walk out of it, like Del, into the rest of our lives, confirmed and changed.[16]

When *Lives* was published in Britain in fall 1973, the reviews were fewer; they were also shorter, given the British practice of taking up several books in a relatively short space. Julian Symons in the *Sunday Times* remarked that Munro "is one of two interesting new Canadian writers to have come my way recently, the other being Margaret Atwood, whose two remarkable novels are worth looking for." *Lives*, he maintained, "is a book of much charm and talent, and also one that is distinctly Canadian." Patrick Anderson in the *Sunday Telegraph* saw Munro as "emerging from the literary ferment which is a feature of contemporary Canada. . . . [She] is a writer of the greatest distinction – perceptive, amusing, richly detailed as to characters (credibly eccentric) and to place (scruffy farmland and claustrophobically parochial townships)." He saw her characters as representing a wide range of humanity, "all beautifully done." Ronald Blythe in *The Listener* maintained that

Munro treats an old theme with "distinction": "Del's affair with Garnet, the 'saved' boy, is a brilliant study of blind love." Claire Tomalin in *The Observer* also noted Del's relationship with Garnet as a convincing account "of that sort of short-lived but devastating obsession" and concludes, "There is not a dull or a false note in the book, which achieves exactly what it attempts." Summing the book up in the *New Statesman*, Marigold Johnson wrote, "Episodic and sometimes repetitive as this scrapbook of anecdotes appears, this is much more than local nostalgia – and much funnier, especially on the women's liberation front." When the Women's Press brought out a paperback edition of *Lives* in 1978, Patricia Beer in the *Times Literary Supplement* called *Lives* "an honest book" and went on to write that one "of the few criticisms that can be made of the book is that it often explains too much. The writing is in fact good enough to rely much more on implication than it allows itself to do."[17]

When *Dance of the Happy Shades* was published by McGraw-Hill New York in the fall and the next spring by Allen Lane in Britain, its reviews seem anticlimactic; yet, written as they were well after the book's first publication and after *Lives*, some of them also show Munro's growing reputation, while others notice elements not much remarked on previously. In this latter vein, Allison Engel, writing in the *Des Moines Register*, notes that Munro "manages to look backward without attaching adult significances to the events she recalls." A short notice in the *New York Times* mistitled the book "Dance of the Happy Hours" (the paper ran a correction); it summarized the stories and concluded that Munro "poses more questions than answers – a refreshing strategy." In the Nashville *Tennessean* Francis Neel Cheney put his finger on a salient connection, beginning "Not since I read Eudora Welty's 'A Worn Path' have I been as moved, as impressed, as I have by these fifteen stories, most of them set in Jubilee, patterned on Wingham, a small town in Western Ontario, where the author grew up, and which she knows so well. As she knew all its people." The anonymous review in the *New Yorker* praises the vivid strength of Munro's description but "personality and character" show her hand "weak and her work faint." Martha Byrd in the *Kingsport Times-News* (Tennessee) writes that Munro "has a knack for looking at ordinary people in ordinary situations and distilling the bonds that unite us as human beings. She paints vivid pictures without an excess of words; she draws distinct characters with the same admirable economy. Her stories do not have plots as much as they convey life, and the glimpses she provides into our universal experiences are alternately amusing, sad, and revealing."

In Britain, Peter Prince in the *New Statesman* writes that Munro, "the remarkable Canadian writer . . . offers an absolute object lesson" in restraint: "These tales of small-town Ontario life, mostly set in the Forties, are beautifully controlled and precise." Adrian Vale writes in the *Irish Times* that "Munro's selection of detail is so precise, she makes me see and feel it all"; compared to other writers at hand who also write about childhood, Munro is "a more experienced and accomplished writer, and the greater length and depth of her stories make them more satisfying." In the *Daily Telegraph* Tim Heald notes that Munro's stories are quiet, but she "is no worse for not shouting and her stories are full of deft observations and gentle profundities." Finally, in the *Birmingham Post* Jean Richardson sees Munro as "a writer who reveals a confident respect for the craft of writing and is concerned with expressing common, meaningful experiences. Her stories are not escapist. They deal with disillusion and betrayal with the gauche sorrows of youth, with the consciousness of failure and self-deception, but they do so with a perception that enriches the reader's experience."[18]

➥

Apart from the critical comment they offer, the bulk of these reviews confirm that with *Lives of Girls and Women* Munro's career began to take a much larger shape than it had after *Dance* won the Governor General's Award in 1969. With that award, her previously secret writer's life was exposed, lending her a minor celebrity status in Victoria and among those who knew the Canadian literary scene. But the attention *Lives* got was another thing altogether. It was just as genuine as that earned by the first book, but coming as it did shortly after *Dance*, and resonating with the feminist temper of the times, while reaching an international audience through successive Canadian, U.S., and British editions, *Lives* fundamentally altered Munro's status. With *Dance* Munro published a first book that showcased her abilities. *Lives* demonstrated that Munro was capable of, as no less a figure than Levertov had noticed, a "short masterpiece." It brought with it considerably more attention.

That happened just as Munro was leaving her marriage, returning to Ontario, and confronting the need to live on her own and support herself for the first time. Although Munro recalls that at the time she had no expectations that writing would be enough and that she expected to get a regular job, it is clear that she pursued her work with greater zeal and focus as the marriage ended. She spent 1970 writing *Lives* in part as a way out, plotting a drastic change. In much the same way, she concentrated on the stories that became *Something I've Been Meaning to Tell You* in the fifteen months that followed her return to Victoria in 1972. During this time she wrote new stories but, in ways unique to that collection, she returned to previous attempts at novels and salvaged individual stories from these manuscripts. Acutely concerned with the ethical position of the writer just then, wondering over her own work as her life was changing, Munro produced some of her most starkly introspective pieces regarding her craft: "Material," "Winter Wind," "The Ottawa Valley," and, though she kept it out of *Something*, "Home." With the exception of "Material," these are also among her most transparently autobiographical stories.

Just as Munro was getting into this work, Kiil wrote her the letter in which he mentions "discontentment among Canadian writers." With it he enclosed her money from *McCall's* purchase of first U.S. serial rights to "Red Dress – 1946," reporting also that the magazine wanted another from *Dance* but had not made a decision yet as to which one. After various other comments, he refers to a conversation Munro had with another person about "the work in progress" and comments, "Novels, of course, are more marketable but you must write what you do; and I know we can sell whatever you produce. If you think next fall is right for the new collection, I'd like to see the stories asap. because in this case I'd like to approximate simultaneous publication as closely as possible." When he had called her to tell her about the sale of "Red Dress – 1946" to *McCall's* – which paid in the thousands for the story, more than she had ever received for one story – Munro had expressed some dissatisfaction over this, saying "that she wasn't a supermarket kind of writer," that she wanted to be in the *New Yorker* or in the *Atlantic*. Kiil recalled that as he was trying to place her stories Munro was not especially encouraging.

This anecdote, amusing now, suggests something about Munro's own aspirations for her work – she did, as has often been remarked, lampoon supermarket publications aimed at women in *Lives*. But more than that, and more telling, is Kiil's comment, "I know we can sell whatever you produce." He had set about doing just that with *Lives*, using it as a property acquired by McGraw-Hill Ryerson to, as he says in the same letter, pressure McGraw-Hill International from Canada. Although it was never a matter of Munro making a conscious decision, Kiil's position as editor-in-chief of trade books at McGraw-Hill Ryerson in effect made him her agent, for he took charge of convincing McGraw-Hill New York to bring out *Lives*, *Dance*, and *Something I've Been Meaning to Tell You* in the United States and, through Beverly Loo in McGraw-Hill's subsidiary rights department in New York, arranged two British editions and sold serial rights to American magazines. Kiil did well enough, since *McCall's* bought four stories between 1972 and 1974 (two from *Dance* and another two from *Something* before it was published) and another was sold to *Chatelaine*. He knew Munro's career was rising and, as well, he knew that because of the marriage breakup and her return to Ontario she was largely without income but for her writing. Recalling this years later, he commented that he was a "bit pushy with Alice" – that is, as he told her, he knew he could sell what she was writing. Beyond her work's evident aesthetic appeal, Kiil saw its commercial possibility; at the time, others in publishing were noticing the same thing.

Kiil was able to act on Munro's behalf because the contracts she signed for her books with Ryerson and then McGraw-Hill Ryerson made them, in effect, company property. Clearly she needed guidance and perspective. Once again, the publishing conditions surrounding the forming of the Writers' Union of Canada are relevant. One of the group's initiating concerns was the availability of sample contracts. Many writers, happy to have their work appear in print, were willing to accept what publishers offered. Since there were few literary agents working in Canada then, not many writers had any intermediary to help them understand just what was being offered, how it compared to common practice, or what other strategies might be pursued. The union was being formed, in part, to address this need. Munro's experience was typical in that she dealt with Ryerson and McGraw-Hill Ryerson on her own, just as she had with various magazine editors and other literary types over the years. Robert Weaver had given her advice, but she wrote her own letters. Once *Lives* was accepted and Kiil began pushing McGraw-Hill New York on Munro's behalf, her business dealings – other editions, paperbacks, serial and other rights, licences – became much more complex. This would have been so anyway, but the breakup of her marriage and the need to secure an income from her writing gave these matters particular urgency.

While Munro was drawn to Ryerson initially by the people who worked there – she recalls Earle Toppings and Audrey Coffin, especially, as people who were working for her success because they believed in the quality of her writing – she lacked confidence in McGraw-Hill Ryerson throughout her connection with it. This was not only because of the Ryerson takeover, but also because of the nature of the company itself; the fact was that McGraw-Hill Ryerson was not so much interested in quality fiction as it was in textbooks, business books, nonfiction, and reference books. The Toronto executives, Kiil recalled, were hesitant about writers like Munro – since they had her work they had to do something with it, but they did so without much enthusiasm. At the same time, and without questioning anyone's good faith, having her publisher – really, her publisher's parent firm – negotiate subsidiary rights and foreign editions was not entirely in her best interest. While the publisher was keen to get her work out, the firm got a healthy share of whatever came in after their book version was in print; thus McGraw-Hill (both entities) had a vested interest in whatever deals were made. Taking a portion itself, McGraw-Hill could not look at any prospect strictly from the writer's point of view.[19]

Munro came to see this slowly, but by the time *Lives* had been published she knew this. After she submitted *Real Life* to Coffin in

1970, she watched what Kiil was doing with her work, asked specific questions, and was especially concerned about his plans for U.S. publication. At some point in 1973, she visited Kiil in Toronto to discuss the contractual terms for *Something I've Been Meaning to Tell You*. In August 1973 Kiil sent her the contract for the then-untitled collection. His letter begins with an apology for taking so long to get it to her and, throughout, he is at pains to detail the various things he is doing for her: he had "two firm offers for 'How I Met My Husband' and 'Forgiveness in Families'" (both appeared in *McCall's* before *Something* was published in May 1974). Munro's stories were then being considered by the *New Yorker, Ms., Redbook, Cosmopolitan, McCall's*, and *Penthouse*, he reports, and he names all the editors he was dealing with save the person from the *New Yorker*. Kiil also notes that Allen Lane had just bought the U.K. rights to *Dance*, that the New American Library (Signet) edition of *Lives* would be out "no earlier than January 1974," that the U.S. edition of *Dance* was due soon, and that he was working on "a complete resumé of the rights and royalties" of Munro's books and he promised "to have it to you shortly. I suspect such an accounting would place things into better perspective for you and all concerned." Kiil then mentioned the excellent reviews her books had been getting – the U.S. reviews of *Lives* – and the advertising planned in the United States for *Dance*. He ended, "I'm sure there is a lot more that needs discussing, but enough for now."

Judging from his rhetoric in this letter, Kiil was trying very hard to secure a contract from an important, and probably hesitant, author. It is both a firm accounting and a rhetorical shaping of the news. The advance against Canadian royalties he mentions in the letter is $2,500 but the advance McGraw-Hill actually paid was twice that, $5,000. More than that, on Munro's copy of the letter, written in another hand, is the following annotation:

> Before signing
> 1. Get *firm* committment for U.S. Edition
> 2. Also, *firm* committment for Cnd. Edition
> 3. Check out rights on English Edition

4. How many copies Dance printed in U.S.?
5. Is Lives still being flogged?
6. How many p.b. Dance sold in Can. – have they lots on hand?
7. Check the 7½ % for 1ˢᵗ 5,000
8. Get advance from U.S. edition
9. Want to approve jacket
10. When, how many, for Allan Lane Lives? – could you send copy where is the advance?
11. Where is money for U.S. edition?

Whoever wrote this – and Munro has no recollection herself, nor have other possibilities been confirmed – had a sound knowledge of publishing and certainly took Munro's point of view. All these questions were fair ones for Kiil. Once she satisfied herself on these points and doubled the advance, Munro signed another McGraw-Hill Ryerson contract. Yet, as this episode illustrates, her career was quickly moving to the point when she would need a skilled agent. Neither Kiil nor McGraw-Hill Ryerson would prove to be enough.[20]

"I Felt As If I Had Retrieved a Lost Part of Myself": "And So I Went Away and Wrote This Story"

In January 1974 Robert Fulford published a column in the *Toronto Star* noting the return of the *Tamarack Review* after a break in publication. Commenting initially about "a remarkably high proportion of rascals" among writers, Fulford connects his observation to Hugo Johnson, a writer and a rascal. "Hugo is the latest creation," he tells us, "of that remarkably talented writer, Alice Munro, and he appears in Material, a story in the new Tamarack Review." Focusing on Munro's story at some length, Fulford concludes his discussion by asserting that

Alice Munro's story is in itself a marvelously duplicitous and contradictory act. First, it expresses the view of someone who despises and rejects the literary world – and yet it is written from within that same world, the world of books, stories, prizes, grants that Alice Munro inhabits. It is, among other things, an attack on literary journals published in a literary journal. Second, Munro attacks through her narrator the idea of organizing life in print. Yet her story is itself superbly organized.

"Material" appeared as the lead story in the November 1973 issue of *Tamarack* and it is, as Fulford and others saw at once, a striking and contradictory piece of work. It was also the first story from *Something* to reach print, so it signalled the very different Munro readers would find when McGraw-Hill Ryerson published that collection in May 1974.

"Material" offers the first-person point of view of an unnamed narrator, the first wife of Hugo Johnson, who runs across a story he has published in a collection. Focusing on that story, which uses Dotty, a person they both knew when they were married, the narrator caustically dissects Hugo's pretensions, outrages, and, ultimately, his sustained power as a writer. Ironically, Munro's dissection of the writer's world came just at the moment when she was herself most clearly entering into it. Now involved with another proactive and aggressive writer, John Metcalf, Munro was well placed to both observe and live the writer's life. "Material" was very much a product of her observations and its appearance in the *Tamarack Review* in November 1973 signalled her sharp, self-reflective analysis of the writer's function.

"Material" is a story replete with aphoristic turns of phrase and, for that, as well as for its subject, it is one of Munro's most-quoted and -discussed stories. Though not as prominent as others found there, one quotation captures just what was happening as Munro was composing *Something I've Been Meaning to Tell You.* Having read Hugo's story, the narrator says, "The story is about Dotty. Of course, she has been changed in some unimportant ways and the main incident concerning her has been invented, or grafted on from some other reality." This is true of "Material," and also of most of the other stories in *Something*: they have been "grafted on from some other reality." Dotty, the woman who lived downstairs from Hugo and the narrator when they lived on

Argyle Street in Vancouver, was "grafted on" to "Material" from a largely finished but unpublished story called "Real People." There the Dotty character, Ruth, is the central focus but the details of her life are close to those found in "Material." The narrator and her husband, who look very much like Alice and Jim starting out in Vancouver, merely live upstairs; she is not a writer, only a pregnant young wife struggling with her circumstances.[21]

The relation of "Real People" to "Material" illustrates Munro's method as she shaped the stories in *Something*. That book's stories are unique within Munro's *oeuvre* in that they were mostly refashioned from earlier work, taken from the novels and stories she had struggled with in Vancouver and Victoria but never published. As such, its stories represent a moment in Munro's writing life when she looked back more than she looked forward. Given the changes in her life and in her ways of writing, this is hardly surprising. Munro needed to publish so as to kick-start her new life; heading back and returned to Ontario, she was in a new relation to her material. "Something I've Been Meaning to Tell You," the story, began in an attempted novel, as did "How I Met My Husband" and "The Found Boat." The fiancé in "How I Met," Alice Kelling, was in "Death of a White Fox." "Walking on Water," "Executioners," and, again, "The Found Boat" use material and characters Munro had originally used in *Lives* – that book had had a much broader scope, with more characters and incidents, when Munro began it. The origins of other stories were found in Munro's own experiences or in the anecdotes of others – "Forgiveness in Families" had its beginnings with Daphne Cue's brother, "Tell Me Yes or No" derives from Munro's work in the bookstore and the circumstances surrounding the breakup of her marriage, and "The Spanish Lady" uses material from Munro's experience as well – and not only the breakup; she did see a man collapse and die in the Vancouver train station when she was returning to Victoria with her daughters in 1971. On that trip back too, she met a man who claimed to have known her in another life, though he said he was an Arab. "Marrakesh" was called "A Blue-Eyed Arab" when the manuscript was first submitted. "Grafted on from some other reality," in fact.[22]

Two other stories in *Something*, "Winter Wind" and "The Ottawa Valley," warrant especial attention. The latter, Munro's second focusing sharply on her mother, has received considerable attention for that and, as well, for the way in which it meditates on just what a writer does – what critics call its metafictional qualities. It was the last story written for the book, probably during November 1973; along with "Home" and "Winter Wind" (also written about that time) it is one of a trio of stories that reveal the initial imaginative impact of Munro's return to Ontario.

For several reasons, "Winter Wind" seems to bring these considerations into focus. As a story, it is in an anomalous position among the *Something* stories in that it is the only one of them that left absolutely no trace in the Munro collection in Calgary. When asked about this absence, Munro was uncertain as to what might have happened to its first draft, but then commented that it "is from a true incident. So maybe it was very easy to write." When she is working with something that actually happened, Munro says, she does not "have to go through as much" in the writing. More than that, too, she said that "Winter Wind" offers a very precise characterization of her grandmother and aunt, sisters Sadie Code Laidlaw and Maud Code Porterfield, living together on Leopold Street in Wingham when she was in high school. A final point about the story is that, when the book manuscript was initially assembled, "Winter Wind" was to be the last story, placed immediately after "The Ottawa Valley." Had it been so, the effect created by the stories in succession would have been one of a narrator first discovering her mother's Parkinson's disease and then, years later and with the disease's effects well established, living with it as an adolescent. *Something* was eventually structured so that no such effect is created; with "Memorial," a very different story set on the west coast well away from Munro's childhood home, placed between the two, the effect is to mute "Winter Wind" and enhance "The Ottawa Valley."

Yet "Winter Wind" and its contexts bear examination as a story reflecting Munro's concerns in 1973 and in *Something* generally. It is one of several stories that take up the point of view of elderly people and, as Munro said, it explicitly derives from her grandmother and aunt, from a time when she went to stay with them in Wingham because of a blizzard.

Sadie Code Laidlaw had died in January 1966 as she was approaching her ninetieth birthday, and Maud had gone into the Huron View nursing home where she would live until her death at ninety-seven in 1976. Then living in Clinton, her niece Alice was one of the last family members to visit her there.

"Winter Wind" tells the personal and marital histories of the Code sisters, details their attitude toward and relations with the narrator's sickly mother, and accounts for the narrator's enforced visit to them because of the storm. It also offers the grandmother's pained reaction when, after two nights, the narrator announces that she plans to go home that evening. "I had never heard my grandmother lose control before. I had never imagined that she could. It seems strange to me now, but the fact is that I had never heard anything like plain hurt or anger in her voice, or seen it on her face. . . . The abdication here was what amazed me." A friend of the sisters, Susie Heferman, had just been found frozen to death in the storm, and the narrator's grandmother fears as much for her granddaughter should she try to make it home in such conditions. After her grandmother's singular outburst, the narrator does not attempt it. The story ends:

> I understand that my grandmother wept angrily for Susie Heferman and also for herself, that she knew how I longed for home, and why. She knew and did not understand how this had happened or how it could have been different or how she herself, once so baffled and struggling, had become another old woman whom people deceived and placated and were anxious to get away from.

Munro's first portrait of Sadie Code Laidlaw after Sadie's death (there would be another in the late 1970s in "Working for a Living") captures the woman's person and what the narrator feels about her person. Yet, probing artist that she is, Munro offers two paragraphs earlier in "Winter Wind" that vie in their importance with the evocative final paragraph in "The Ottawa Valley" ("The problem, the only problem, is my mother"). What she offers is a summary assessment of what she had herself written and published out of her own experience, what she has just been reviewing and reshaping for the stories to be offered in *Something*, and especially what she has just been doing with her aunt and grandmother and the "true incident" in "Winter Wind." She asks, "How does a writer know?" and her meditation is worth considering:

> And how is anybody to know, I think as I put this down, how am I to know what I claim to know? I have used these people, not all of them, but some of them, before. I have tricked them out and altered them and shaped them any way at all, to suit my purposes. I am not doing that now, I am being as careful as I can, but I stop and wonder, I feel compunction. Though I am only doing in a large and public way what has always been done, what my mother did, and other people did, who mentioned to me my grandmother's story. Even in that closed-mouth place, stories were being made. People carried their stories around with them. My grandmother carried hers, and nobody ever spoke of it to her face.
>
> But that only takes care of the facts. I have said other things. I have said that my grandmother would choose a certain kind of love. I have implied that she would be stubbornly, secretly, destructively romantic. Nothing she ever said to me, or in my hearing, would bear this out. Yet I have not invented it, I really believe it. Without any proof I believe it, and so I must believe that we get messages another way, that we have connections that cannot be investigated, but have to be relied on.[23]

"But that only takes care of the facts." What seems to have happened here, and in "Home" and in "The Ottawa Valley," is that Munro returned to Huron County and confronted memories that, as she worked on the stories that became *Something*, led her to question her very practice as an artist during the years since she left in 1951. Given the autobiographical cast of much of her work, such questions doubtless occurred to her previously but here such questions come into the fiction in a way they had not previously. Munro had come home and found it much the same yet different, its facts lying about, teasing her mind, urgent.

In "The Ottawa Valley" Munro's fascinations with her craft also emerge, and there the focus is once again on her mother. There too the question she raises is epistemological – she says she wants "to find out more, remember more" so as to "mark her [mother] off, to describe, to illumine, to celebrate, to *get rid* of her." But Munro also speaks of the insufficiency of her technical practices ("applying what skills I have, using what tricks I know") in trying to create the version of her mother, and the memory of this visit to the Ottawa Valley, that she seeks. Munro begins her final paragraph by asserting that what she has done does not meet an accepted criteria for a story: "If I had been making a proper story out of this, I would have ended it, I think, with my mother not answering and going ahead of me across the pasture. That would have done."

But needing to know more, to remember more herself, Munro pressed on beyond the imagined mother-daughter confrontation scene, a scene that would have ended the story with suitable literary mystery but insufficient memory, insufficient "real life." So briefly, between the confrontation scene and Munro's comment on what she has done, there appears another scene, this one a remembered image of her mother, her brother James, and their cousin Dodie reciting poetry from their school readers. As it ends "they were all reciting together, and laughing at each other: *Now by great marshes wrapped in mist, / Or past some river's mouth, / Throughout the long still autumn day / Wild birds are flying south.* 'Though when you come to think of it, even that has kind of a sad ring,' Aunt Dodie said."

Such a scene is needed, sandwiched between the story's crucial moment and Munro's own assessment of what she has done, because of what she was doing with "real people" in "real life." The literary artifice of the daughter confronting her mother ("Is your arm going to stop shaking?") is mitigated, and made more authentic, by the much less dramatic though utterly poignant image of the three older people sharing a recitation of a poem from their shared childhood. The family connection, just as "the path that [her mother] and Aunt Dodie had made when they were girls running back and forth to see each other . . . was still there." Like the central episode in "Winter Wind," the visit to the Ottawa Valley was based on a true incident, and the path existed. When Anne Chamney Laidlaw had taken her daughters to the Ottawa Valley in the summer of 1943, between the farms once owned by George and Edward Chamney, the paths made by their children going back and forth were still there. Munro remembered them thirty years later when she wrote "The Ottawa Valley."

Moving back to Ontario from British Columbia in September 1973, Munro again confronted the real place that had held her imagination, and had informed her writing, during her twenty-plus years on the west coast. Remembering her feelings, she once wrote: "When I lived in British Columbia, I longed for the sight of Ontario landscape – the big solitary oaks and beeches and maples looming in summer haze in the open fields, the carpet of leeks and trilliums and bloodroot in the sunny woods before the leaves come out, the unexpected little rough hills with hawthorns and tough daisies, the creeks and bogs and the long smooth grassy slopes." Once, on "a motor-trip home via the state of Washington, we came" upon a change of landscape "and I felt as if I had retrieved a lost part of myself, because it was something 'like home.'"

Although Munro's final return to Ontario came in 1973, the imaginative return was a process she had begun, really, two years before on the train trip home with her daughters. During the intervening year, she spent July and August in Ontario. And beyond Ontario as a place, Munro also imaginatively confronted people there. She returned to an Ontario with her grandmother Sadie gone and Maud still there, though diminished and living in Huron View. We see her memories of these two women in "Winter Wind" and other elderly characters in "Something I've Been Meaning to Tell You" and "Walking on Water." The title story draws indirectly on Sadie and Maud's living arrangement and in that story Et, like Maud before she was married, is a dressmaker.

But the most pressing imaginative confrontation for Munro was, quite literally, "Home," the Laidlaw farm in Lower Town along the Maitland, a place still embodying Anne Chamney Laidlaw though now lived in by Bob Laidlaw and his second wife. The story "Home," written quickly between October 8 (Thanksgiving weekend, when its events happened) and October 30 (when Munro sent it to John Metcalf as a present), is a textual rendering of Munro's imaginative reaction to her return home. Especially through what critics call its metafictional technique, in which Munro comments directly on what she has written, that story records its author's state of mind as she confronts, no longer a visitor from away, her most essential material, her home place. "*I don't want any more effects, I tell you, lying. I don't know what I want. I want to do this with honour, if I possibly can.*" This desire, to accomplish her writing "*with honour,*" continued to be Munro's ambition, but in her return to Ontario she was confronted with memories that presented themselves differently as subject to her imagination. It was no longer the place she left but still the home she remembered, and Munro may be seen reshaping her subject in 1973. Her three metafictional stories – each deeply autobiographical – and "Material" as well, confirm as much.[24]

Writer Jack Hodgins recalls visiting Munro for tea in 1974 when he was in London to receive an award and, during the conversation, she told him she did not think she would write any more. That was the first time he had heard her say this and, though he has heard Munro say as much since, Hodgins took her quite seriously that first time. Speaking of this feeling herself, Munro has said she was quite serious when she told Hodgins that, and added that though she has often felt this way, the feeling was especially strong during the time after her return to Ontario. "Maybe it's because I write stories and between every story there's a kind of break before the next one."

As Fulford had commented on "Material," it is possible to see Munro's technique here as "a marvelously duplicitous and contradictory act." Although it is offered as a story, the author nevertheless keeps stepping onto the page to comment on what she has just written, thus breaking the illusion that this is fiction. All these stories – "Material,"

"Winter Wind," "Home," and "The Ottawa Valley" – show Munro analyzing both the morality and the efficacy of what she was doing as a writer of fiction. As she wrote in "Winter Wind," "I feel compunction." While "Material" offers a more detached analysis of the writer's position, one written from behind the guise of the persona of Hugo Johnson's first wife, the other three are about as close to the bone as a writer might get. Each of them is patently autobiographical, drawing on verifiable family relations, and poised on the dotted line between imaginative fiction and what Munro called "true incident." Understood within Munro's own life experience, these stories detail the artistic crisis her return to Ontario brought her: read along with these other stories, the endings of "Home" and "The Ottawa Valley" sound like farewells to fiction because that might well have been what they were intended to be.

While critics have analyzed Munro's 1973 metafictional stories largely in technical terms, a more compelling rationale for her narrative experimentation lies in her biography: as the writing of "Home" in little more than three weeks demonstrates, Munro returned to Ontario to find it a place she could no longer imagine from far away in distance and time. It was real and immediate, both the place she remembered from her childhood and adolescence and alive in the present moment. Looking at Wingham as she travelled to the hospital with her sick father over the 1973 Thanksgiving weekend, Munro comments in "Home" that the town "has faded, for me. I have written about it and used it up. The same banks and barber shops and town hall tower, but all their secret, plentiful messages drained away." The messages Munro had imagined from Wingham when she was writing in British Columbia were borne of memory and distance.

By the end of 1973, when she completed the stories that were to make up her third book, Munro had in a significant way written herself out. She had returned to material she had set aside or long thought about and salvaged what she could as stories. This process had the effect of a reminiscence, since Munro looked again at things she had written years previously, or had been mulling over for some time, and had taken from them what she could. This doubtless took her back to her years of frustration and depression over the numerous stories begun with hope and expectation but then abandoned. Other stories, inspired by more recent personal circumstances and incidents like "Tell Me Yes or No," "The Spanish Lady," "Memorial," or "Forgiveness in Families," were, like those salvaged from her attempts at novels, essentially exercises and not, in the language Munro later used to characterize her more valued stories, "the real material." Speaking to Tim Struthers in 1981, Munro saw "The Ottawa Valley" and "Material" as the best stories in the book, "And 'Winter Wind' isn't too bad either." In the same interview, she mentioned "Home" as "sort of a final statement . . . about dissatisfaction with art" and said also that with *Something* she "was certainly trying hard with this book," she "*was* trying something very new" but had since become dissatisfied with what she did there.

Munro's dissatisfaction with the stories that were in *Something* was not altogether retrospective, however. Just before she wrote "Winter Wind," "The Ottawa Valley," and "Home," Munro commented to Metcalf that she was dissatisfied with what she had finished for the book, and through January 1974 she reiterated this feeling, complaining that she did not feel connected to that material. Yet despite her misgivings about her right to do what she was doing with the autobiographical material in the three stories she wrote toward the end of 1973, Munro had through them embarked on a new direction. Wingham remembered from British Columbia was, in fact, "used up" but, as "Winter Wind," "The Ottawa Valley," and especially "Home" demonstrate, Munro's return there to stay had brought about a new and sharper quality to her reminiscence: quite literally as 1974 began, Munro was home as she wrote "Home." Having the experiences she described there over the Thanksgiving weekend in 1973, going back to London after spreading hay for the sheep at her home in Wingham, Munro wrote what she thought would be the last sentence in "Home": "And so I went away and wrote this story." In October 1973 as she wrote "Home" for John Metcalf as a birthday present, she did not have to go very far away from Wingham in order to write that sentence, only to London. As 1974 opened and passed into 1975, Alice Munro was moving much closer to her home place in Huron County.[25]

Something I've Been Meaning to Tell You, John Metcalf,
and a Changed Career

After Munro came to terms with McGraw-Hill Ryerson during the fall
of 1973, Kiil went to London to discuss his plans for the book and pick
up the manuscript. The two had a genial lunch and discussion but,
when Kiil rose to leave and asked to carry the manuscript away with
him, she said no, it was not ready yet, there were more revisions she
wanted to do. She brought it into Toronto herself a few weeks later. It
was originally a group of ten stories before "Winter Wind," "The
Ottawa Valley," and a third story were added. The book went into production for spring publication, but all was not smooth sailing. When
Munro got the manuscript back from McGraw-Hill Ryerson, she took
exception to the editing. For both *Dance* and *Lives*, Audrey Coffin had
been her manuscript editor. She had not been intrusive; during the
making of each book she let Munro fashion it as she saw fit, supporting and understanding as the process evolved. With *Something*, either
Kiil or another editor made syntactical changes that Munro found to
be unacceptable; Coffin knew about the changes and fought them
before the manuscript went back to Munro, but was overruled. *Lives of
Girls and Women* had demonstrated to McGraw-Hill that Munro was a
writer on the rise – she was seen as valuable property – so her work was
now receiving additional attention. Unwelcome attention. Through
retyping parts of the manuscript and by rejecting most of the proposed
changes, Munro eventually came to terms with her publisher. Coffin
was then nearing retirement age; she was also the only person at
McGraw-Hill Ryerson in whom Munro had any real confidence. As a
writer who needs and values her editor's response when she knows and
respects that person, Munro was not impressed by this incident. It did
nothing for her confidence in McGraw-Hill Ryerson, all the more so
since she was not herself confident in the strengths of this collection.[26]

    Something I've Been Meaning to Tell You: Thirteen Stories was pub-
lished by McGraw-Hill Ryerson in May 1974. McGraw-Hill New York
brought out its edition in September (they used the Canadian printing
with their own title and copyright pages, binding theirs in the United

States). Significantly, there was no British hardcover edition. In Canada, reviews began appearing in late May. They were quite positive overall, although it is possible to see a thread of tentative reservation running through them, reservations over the settings, the age of the characters, or the variety of incident. Robert Fulford, writing in the *Toronto Star* (a review republished in the *Montreal Star* and the *Ottawa Citizen* as well), began, "You can't ever really understand anyone, you can only nibble at the edges of comprehension. This is a truth Alice Munro has been telling us, in one way or another, for two decades." Her new collection "justifies once again all the praise that has been showered on her in the last six years. Her beautifully solemn style now seems, if anything, even better; and her perceptions seem, if anything, more acute." William French in the *Globe and Mail* refers to "a nagging feeling, . . . despite Mrs. Munro's undeniable skill, . . . about her talent. How long could she continue to exploit the same themes? Was she trapped, creatively speaking, in rural Ontario, or could she break out and write about other aspects of Canadian life?" Answering his own questions he notes that while some of the stories derive from "typical Munro territory, . . . seven have contemporary urban settings, a new landscape for her. And the good news is that she has made the transition successfully; her talent is transportable." For her part, Munro saw these two reviews and was not convinced by this praise; her misgivings over the book continued.

Closer to this apprehension, Chaviva Hosek wrote in *Quill & Quire* that the "collection is clearly a point of transition for Munro, and is somewhat uneven for that." Munro does strike chords reminiscent of her earlier work, and "the strengths of her earlier style" are merged "with her newer concerns" in "The Found Boat" and "Material." Even so, there are places "where the new direction has not yet reached the poise and subtlety of Munro at her best." And given Munro's own reaction on hearing that one of her stories had been sold to *McCall's*, Kildare Dobbs in *Saturday Night* ironically observed that a "friend once complained to me that Alice Munro's stories were dangerously close to the style of the fiction in women's magazines." Dobbs concedes that similarities are real, but sides ultimately with Munro's own view, "There are far too many troubling undertones in her prose to make it suitable for slick women's magazines." Highlighting Munro's new direction in his review's title, Dobbs concludes, "It may well be that stories like 'Tell Me Yes or No' are pointers in this new direction. Alice Munro has it in her to become one of the best story tellers now writing." Reviewing the book in the Canadian edition of *Time* under the title "Moving Miniaturist," Geoffrey James asserts that Munro often "achieves a kind of subcutaneous empathy with her subjects. The revelations she provides may be small ones, but they are no less moving for that." Referring to Munro's earlier work, James celebrated this collection's wider range with another ironic allusion to another publication: "As any constant reader of *The New Yorker* can attest, the childhood reminiscence has a certain limited fascination. Now, in her third book, Munro shows welcome signs of growth, though half a dozen stories still retain their rural, childhood roots. Some of these are not much more than intensely experienced, vividly recollected incidents, skilled acts of ventriloquism." And the stories set in cities are "more pointed and more ambiguous than her rural pieces," he asserted, and he illustrated this by citing "Material."

Two things about the Canadian reviews of *Something* are worth noting. By the time Munro's third book appeared, the consensus on the quality of her work in the short newspaper reviews, those by and large in regional papers, was well established. This sense was shared in magazines as well. There is a homogeneous quality to the reception the book received, quite positive overall with the occasional idiosyncratic comment or objection, such as Dorothy Powell's order in the *Canadian Author and Bookman*, "Buy this book. Don't borrow it. It is worth reading and re-reading." The summaries and analyses echo the sense of Munro's work already seen, and they are written with confidence that Munro has ascended to the level of established Canadian writer – that is, she has joined the pantheon of "real writers." Thus Hilda Kirkwood, a long-time reviewer at the *Canadian Forum*, ends her review with a curious paragraph, one indicative of the times: "No doubt these stories will be grist for the Canadian Literature mills. But perhaps we could stop bleating about Canadian Women Writers and admit that these stories are literature and as such are of lasting interest anywhere, aside from the fact that the ladies they are 'about' live in Vancouver, Wiarton or Ottawa."

Kirkwood's comment leads directly to the second notable aspect of the reception of *Something* in Canada: with it, discussion of Munro's work by academics seemed to begin in earnest. The first academic article, by Hallvard Dahlie of the University of Calgary, had appeared in 1972, and the reviews of *Something* followed suit in that they were more numerous and more emphatic than they had been for either of Munro's first two books. Without question, this academic attention both recognized and advanced Munro's reputation since it brings additional authority to the judgements being offered. Although reviewing the book in the *London Free Press*, Struthers, then a graduate student at Western, adopted a professorial air and asserts at the beginning of his review that Munro's "achievement has been partially misunderstood and therefore underrated." Her real interest, he tells his reader, is in "ordering": "This awareness of how we all constantly order and re-create the lives of others and ourselves is what is most exciting about the fiction of Alice Munro." David Stouck of Simon Fraser University, writing in the *West Coast Review*, focused on Munro's style, "where the sentences are each carefully crafted, polished units and their effects carefully weighed and balanced. Like Flaubert, her prose has the authority of finished product, painstakingly executed and flawless in design." Also focusing on Munro's style, E.D. Blodgett (of the University of Alberta, a scholar who went on to write an important critical overview) wrote that "some poets – Rilke, Keats – fear to utter the most beautiful line. Munro, however, has created a style in which revelation would be a kind of cover-up." He also wrote that "the story dwells and lives darkly and erratically within the narrator. It is *her* story, and not *about* her."27

Such academic reviews were not so much validation of Munro's writing as they were an important next step in her growing reputation. All three reviewers were at pains to assert the complexity of Munro's work, and the latter two proposed lofty figures for comparison. Kirkwood's final paragraph suggests, too, that this was happening just at the time when English-Canadian nationalism, which held sway among intellectuals and, most especially, in the universities, was fostering Canadian literature as a field of academic study. Kirkwood, not an academic herself, also reflects Munro's status after *Lives* as a writer whose work was seen in an especial Canadian feminist context. Margaret Laurence, Margaret Atwood, and Munro formed a trinity of Canadian women writers. (During the 1970s academics in Canadian literature began to joke about "the three Margarets": Laurence, Atwood, and Alice Munro.)

But that was in Canada. When *Something* was published by McGraw-Hill in fall 1974, discussions of prior reputation and the development of Canadian literature were muted. Overall, the book got positive reviews in the United States. Three of the more considered ones, though, each a review appearing in major newspapers, were acerbic, even caustic. Bette Howland begins her review in the *Chicago Tribune* noting the praise and award Munro got for her first books, and continuing, "That's gratifying; she's talented and well worth the attention." But *Something* "is not so good as her earlier work; the stories are less than the talent they display. 'This is a message; I really believe it is,' she writes at the end of one, 'but I don't see how I can deliver it.' She might have been reviewing her own book." Howland sees two types of stories here. First, what she calls "'good ideas for a short story' – well made, carefully plotted, essentially contrived, and lacking in feeling." These are the stories Munro got from her earlier attempts. The other "kind of writing is flailing, experimental. The stories have less clearly defined plots, maybe none at all, and come to no conclusions. . . . Often their subject is the writer's relation to her material," and they are filled with disclaimers that emphasize the writer's position. They "are uttered so often that they become in themselves a 'trick.' They mar the ending of 'Ottawa Valley,' which contains by far the best and truest writing in the book." Howland's review deserves to be noted, for the flaws she saw in *Something* are those Munro came to see there herself, flaws she saw as she was making the book. Although still publishable, she thought, these stories were fundamentally flawed.

A similar review by Frederick Busch appeared in the *New York Times*. More negative though less considered and not as precisely argued as Howland's, Busch's review takes up the narrative reversal in "Tell Me Yes or No" and asserts that these stories "are journeyman's work. But they are no more than that, and by now – 'In Our Time' was published in 1925 – we ought to demand that a volume of stories delivers thrilling economy, the poetry which makes the form so valuable." Busch sees lots of information here, "but there is little emotional tension arising from the events." As with Howland, Munro's revelations about authorship seem to have irritated him. After discussing the ending of "How I Met My Husband," where the narrator is disingenuous about her reasons for letting her husband tell their courtship story the way he does, the reviewer writes, "That the author can provoke anger by betraying her character is evidence that she can *make* characters. The reason given (and there are too many reasons given in this book, too few admissions that a character may be reined in close to the page, yet dance beyond the author's logic) is an effort on the part of the narrative voice to be well-liked; the tone is sycophantic." In "most of these stories, there is the kind of innocence of tone that can make you grin, but the way you grin at someone else's charming child: already forgetting." Striking many of the same notes in the *Minneapolis Star*, Susan Cushman wonders about comparing Munro to Laurence and Atwood, though she thinks Munro "probably will prove that she deserves this status" eventually and continues, "This collection unfortunately lacks the generous sparkle that graced Ms. Munro's earlier work. Part of the problem seems to be a new ambivalence toward her craft," which Cushman calls "writerly guilt." Thus although Munro's "strong talent still shows through," *Something* "must be considered the weakest of her books so far."[28]

However mixed the message Munro received from American reviewers of *Something*, there was no question that it marked her ascent among Canadian writers. A June 1974 profile written for the *London Free Press* to accompany Struthers's review of *Something* captures Munro at that time, and it warrants attention for the detailed snapshot it provides. Her third book just published, her separation from Jim a fact, her position as Western's 1974–75 writer-in-residence confirmed, Munro had returned home. Speaking to the paper's reporter, Joanna Beyersbergen, Munro looks back as well as forward. The profile opens "She doesn't speak of leaving a husband of 20 years and 12-room house in Victoria, B.C., as though it was a cataclysmic experience." Nor, Beyersbergen writes, does Munro present herself as a "newly-liberated woman. She talks about it as though she has done nothing very remarkable at all. . . . Her separation is 'friendly,' Mrs. Munro says. 'We're not even legally separated.'" However Munro then wanted to present the breakup of her marriage, most of this profile is concerned with other parts of her life. Growing up in Wingham ("I had to learn to piece a quilt when I was eight, that was to make my first quilt for my hope chest"; her mother had her "wear blue tunics, which middle-class girls wore, but not girls of Wingham"); conforming to accepted views of marriage ("I felt it was my responsibility to pick up my husband's socks. I felt like that for 20 years"); motherhood ("I'm just so terribly glad I had my children when I did"); and career (she always wanted to "have the children and write"). Looking back is one thing, looking forward another. Beyersbergen writes that "it was the freedom which accompanies being unattached which was so inviting." Munro said she likes to cook, but she does not "like having to do things like that all the time. That's why I think I'll never live with anyone again."

Turning to the way she had been seen in Wingham since she began publishing, and especially since *Lives*, Munro commented that "I tried so hard to be like everyone else. I desperately wanted to be asked to a dance." But "I wasn't really so unconventional, just by Wingham's standards." She "expected people" in Wingham "to be more put off by the book than they were. Maybe they're not telling me. I think they react positively to success. Didn't Elizabeth Taylor say, 'Success is a great deodorant?'" Beyersbergen continues, "When Lives came out in England, Mrs. Munro says, she told her father who is still on the farm that she received good reviews in the London Times and the Manchester Guardian. Her father replied, she says with rumbles of belly laughter, 'Well, you'll never get one in the Wingham Advance-Times.'"

Again, this is Munro once she had completed the shift from Victoria to London, once Andrea's situation was stabilized, once *Something* was out, once Munro had the next year or so planned by way of her appointment at Western. Bob Laidlaw remained ill, so she was travelling to Wingham regularly. The month before this profile appeared, Munro had published in the syndicated *Weekend Magazine* "Everything Here Is Touchable and Mysterious," her brief affecting essay about her home place that she wrote with her father's help. Beyersbergen goes on,

> Her laughter is not mockery; there is unconcealed gratitude that she can go back, and she does. "I love that countryside more than any other. I love Wingham. I love the look of small towns, even the shabbiness. After all, most people who write about small towns are practically tarred and feathered. Apparently Thomas Wolfe could never go home again at all."
>
> It is the truthfulness of her perceptions which must make her writings disturbing to small town citizens.

Beyersbergen then turns to *Something*, citing a passage about these people's "simple, natural, poverty-bred materialism," and continues to assert that "as a writer, [Munro] is no longer primarily a girl or a young woman in Wingham, but a wife and mother in British Columbia." This is an arguable assertion about *Something*, but Munro's response to it is the more interesting, for it is the same one she wrote looking at Wingham in "Home": "'You use it up,' Mrs. Munro says of her Wingham writings. But later, she thinks she will write about this area again. 'There are stories about people there just crying out to be used.'"29

Here Beyersbergen has detailed Munro as she was during the spring of 1974: free, looking back, looking forward. There is prescience here, since Munro did indeed return to Wingham as subject, but there is also the unforeseen: Munro did go back to Huron County to live with another person. Less happily, the "deodorant" of her success was not sufficiently strong to keep the enmity of some of the people who lived there from being focused on her work, and on Munro herself, during the late 1970s and early 1980s.

In the way of such constructions, written for the moment and the particular occasion of *Something*'s publication, this profile simplifies what was really happening in Munro's life. When she had moved into the house on London's St. George Street in January 1974, Munro was delighted to have Andrea with her after their being separated during the fall. She was relieved to have got out of her teaching job at York for the balance of the year, but the writer-in-residence position she had been offered at Western would require some of the same duties that had made her uncomfortable at York. Her relationship with Metcalf was ongoing, but they saw each other infrequently, there was a tentativeness on both sides for fear of losing their friendship, and much of the relationship was maintained through letters and telephone calls. Munro was seeing other men, Metcalf other women. She was also continuing contacts with the literary people at Western, increasingly so after she accepted the writer-in-residence position for the fall. Her writing – how it was going, what she was doing, and what to do in relation to it – was another prime concern.

As the negotiations surrounding the contract for *Something* suggest, Munro had become increasingly aware of the intricacies involved in publishing throughout her relations with McGraw-Hill Ryerson. Needing income, Munro had agreed to have Kiil try to sell serial rights for her stories to American magazines, and he had some success in that regard. Any income from the stories in *Something* prior to the book's publication in May went completely to Munro; once the book had appeared, though, she had to share it with McGraw-Hill Ryerson. This never happened since the two stories from the book he sold to *McCall's* were published before *Something*, but this arrangement was but one indication of Munro's position. She wrote to Metcalf asking advice about this arrangement and, after he responded, indicated that she had been approached by an agent during the spring of 1973. During the summer of 1972 Munro had discussed the possibility of an agent with the man she was seeing there then; he had had some experience along this line himself and volunteered to represent her.

Munro continued to talk to Metcalf about her relations with McGraw-Hill Ryerson into 1974 and throughout that year kept looking into the matter of an agent. In October she received a letter from the Toronto-based writer Fred Bodsworth in response to her inquiry about agents. He gave her his New York agent's name, told her how things worked, and volunteered to write the agent on Munro's behalf if she

wanted. Munro continued in this vein, quite slowly, until she received
an inquiry in March 1976 from American agent Virginia Barber; after
some correspondence and a meeting, Munro hired her later that year.
Recalling her hesitancy to take the next step and hire an agent, particularly when Barber first approached her, Munro has said that she thought
"I may never write another thing and what I do write will never sell. I
just was almost fending off her enthusiasm. I felt so low in hope, and it
wasn't that I was low-spirited, I was fine, I wasn't depressed, but I just
had these ideas." Such feelings, though seemingly hard to understand in
light of what has happened to her since, are utterly consistent with her
misgivings about her work over the years, misgivings that were aggra-
vated by her changed living circumstance and reflected in the stories
she had written since returning to Ontario.[30]

No longer commuting to Toronto, Munro spent the first months
of 1974 attending to the various requirements of her craft. Thanks to
Lives (which had gone through four printings of the American edition
by then) and the forthcoming new book, Munro was receiving pro-
gressively more attention. Despite her own misgivings about the stories
it contained, *Something* went into production and Munro dealt with
the proposed changes to her manuscript. She was still writing things
for the book, she told a reporter, through February. In January, the
dramatic adaptation of Munro's "How I Met My Husband" had inaugurated CBC television's *The Play's the Thing* series, composed of four
commissioned plays by Canadian writers. When he came to review
Something in May in the *Globe and Mail*, William French commented
that it "was one of the most successful of the CBC's television plays last
winter." Munro had worked on another adaptation of "A Trip to the
Coast" for the CBC the year before, and she wrote another, "1847: The
Irish" specifically for the CBC a few years later. Munro accepted these
projects as further income, but they had the effect of extending her reputation beyond her readership. There was also a television adaptation
of "Baptizing" from *Lives*. Beyond visual adaptations of her work,
which continued throughout the 1970s, the CBC continued to broadcast her stories on radio. "The Found Boat" was read on *Anthology* in
April just before *Something* was published and, during fall 1974, Munro

worked with people from the CBC on a thirty-part radio adaptation of *Lives* that was used to inaugurate its new national morning program, "Judy," with Judy LaMarsh in fall 1975.

In May 1974 Munro learned that the U.S. edition of *Dance* had won the Great Lakes College Association's New Writer Award, an honour that involved a tour of the participating colleges. She also accepted invitations for what she certainly saw as literary chores – for example, she participated in a discussion at a local high school English teachers' banquet in February and, in May, attended a similar dinner in Toronto for the heads of English departments at Canadian universities. At Western, she spoke to a faculty wives luncheon. Because of *Something*, too, there were interviews and profiles.

Once school was over in June, Jenny and Andrea returned to Victoria to spend the summer with Jim, leaving Munro free of parental responsibilities. She thought for a time of going to England – McGraw-Hill Ryerson was telling inquiring journalists as much – but Munro ended up spending the summer in Montreal, she recalls, breaking up with John Metcalf. She stayed in Hugh and Nora Hood's house there, wrote, and saw John and his friends. Having lived in Montreal since he came to Canada in the early 1960s, apart from brief stints elsewhere, and having founded along with Hugh Hood a group calling itself the Montreal Storytellers, Metcalf was well connected in the literary community there. In October, after Munro returned to London to get Andrea back in school and begin her duties as writer-in-residence at Western, Audrey Coffin wrote returning the manuscript of *Something*. She hoped Munro had a good summer in Montreal and mentioned that she had heard that "you're now working (writing) and carousing (the job)" at Western.[31]

Munro's relationship with John Metcalf had begun with his fan letter to her after he heard "Images" broadcast on the CBC in September 1968 and continued, a regular connection, throughout the 1980s. There has been less contact in recent years and, in 2000, Munro took public exception to things Metcalf published – especially about Robert Weaver – in a critical piece on her work and reputation in the *National Post*. Yet during the early 1970s, and especially during the two years

Munro was completely on her own, mid-1973 through August 1975, Metcalf was a key connection for her. That they engaged in a brief romance is of less interest here than their continuing connection as two writers who shared many of the same concerns as artists. Each read the other's work as it was published and passed on their comments. Metcalf kept Munro up on literary gossip (especially after she moved to Clinton in August 1975) and each, throughout the correspondence, was quite candid with the other. Theirs was then a special relation, one based on long connection and, as the years passed, a certain outsider status each had. Metcalf was seen standing apart from the Canadian literary establishment as an "immigrant" (a reviewer on CBC once complained that it was too bad Metcalf had no Canadian childhood memories) and, as the years passed, he became better known for his contentious comments on Canadian literary matters. Munro, as the years passed and her career took off, was outside the Canadian literary scene in a very different way by virtue of her talent and success – by the end of the 1970s her standing at the *New Yorker* and Alfred A. Knopf said it all. Besides, she lived in Clinton and hardly ever came to Toronto.

In 1974, though, during her summer in Montreal, most of that lay ahead. Metcalf knew people, Munro met them, and they spent time together as they were breaking up. Before she went to Montreal, Munro was the person more invested in the relationship, Metcalf the person backing off, withdrawing. He wanted to marry again and he was looking elsewhere. Over her summer there, they reached a rapprochement and she returned to London still connected to Metcalf, still writing and speaking, but each person was getting on with a separate personal life, even while they were still gossiping and working together on various projects. Before Munro went back to London, she agreed to a joint reading with Metcalf in February 1975 at Loyola College in Montreal. That reading was taped and deposited in the John Metcalf Fonds at the University of Calgary along with a tape, made prior to the reading, of Metcalf coaching Munro as she prepared to read from the story she had sent him as a birthday present, "Home." She did need coaching, and Metcalf was helpful – just as he was throughout this key juncture of Munro's life and career.[32]

"In Her Mortal Anxiety": Western, Suitors, and "Places at Home"

Once *Something* was done in early 1974 and as it was going through the press and attracting review attention, Munro did what she had always done: she wrote. What she produced dissatisfied her mostly, so the manuscript stories that date to the year after her return to Ontario – beyond those already discussed – are hard to specify. One from this period is called "Married People." Munro dated it "Oct. 10/ 74" and offered it as a birthday present to another man in her life, Jim, since its dedication reads "For My Husband Jim" and that date was his fifty-fifth birthday. An apparently finished typescript copy exists in the John Metcalf Fonds – Metcalf thinks she probably sent it to him as a submission for one of his anthologies – and there is draft material in Munro's papers. Like the stories that ended *Something* and "Home," "Married People" anticipates the succession of the former-husband stories Munro wrote beginning with "The Beggar Maid" and continuing into the 1980s. The story is also ironically reminiscent of her dedication of *Lives* to Jim Munro: though the marriage was ending or had ended, it is a visible acknowledgement of both his unflagging support of her writing and of their time together.

"Married People" takes its point of departure from a coincidence that occurred to Munro when she was living in London. There she and a man she had known in Victoria recognized one another on the street, stopped, and talked. His marriage had broken up and he had moved east also. In the story, Munro focuses on Norah, a person recognizably in the same situation as her own since leaving the west coast ("She mentioned the university where she had been employed last summer. Her jobs were short-term, peripheral, she drifted from one campus to another."). Norah, who had been married to Andrew, recognizes and then goes and sits down to talk with Bob Johnson, who had been married to Mary – the four had been friends in Vancouver. Bob worked for an insurance company then, Andrew was in "retailing." As a story that Munro never published, "Married People" cannot be advanced as any type of key text, but it is indicative of her focus during 1974. Two passages, especially, seem worth looking at. The first, derived from

Norah's contemplation of the physical changes she notes in Johnson from her memories of him in the late 1950s, turns back on Norah herself:

> When she looked in the mirror she would sometimes see, with deep respectful feeling, almost of awe, almost of approval, how all that ordinary prettiness, roundness, readiness was melting and slipping away, and what looked out was the broad, deep eye-socketed, final face of her grandmother, her greatgran[d]mother, women who had been photographed on a farm porch, in front of a whitewashed cottage in Ireland, looking as if they had never asked anybody for anything in their lives.

Such a passage is cousin to some of those found in "Winter Wind," which also recreate Munro's grandmother. It might also be seen as a usual contemplation of a forty-four-year-old person looking in the mirror. Yet placed in the trajectory of Munro's life and, more pointedly, placed in relation to the writing she subsequently did after returning to Ontario, such a passage is resonant in that it reveals her meditating on the living family connections she found awaiting her there.

So too is the moment on which "Married People" ends, one Norah recalls from their time together one summer when the families shared a rented cottage on an island off the coast. Andrew and pregnant Mary had rowed off on an errand to the mainland. They are considerably overdue. Norah and Bob, worried, watch the horizon. The story ends:

> Norah, objecting to the possibility that Andrew might never come face to face with her, or speak to her, or lie beside her again, was arguing in her mind that there had not been enough time. She did not seem to mean by this that there had not been enough time for ordinary living together or raising their children or any of those things, but not enough time for delivery of some large and particularly urgent message, which was straining in her now, which she would shout at him, throw at him, dazzle and utterly change and save him with, the moment she saw his face, if she was lucky enough to see his face, which was the one face

she could not do without, not yet, not yet – again. The giving
and accepting of any such message was to prove impossible. But
it did not seem so to her when she was sitting on the beach,
vowing and waiting, in her mortal anxiety, that day.[33]

The whole of "Married People" builds to this moment, likely a moment
remembered from the summer of 1957 (the detail places the Munros
just after Jenny's birth), a moment when Munro probably also found
herself "in her mortal anxiety." The story shows Munro looking back
in ways different from her recollection of her childhood – now away
from her marriage, she is beginning to use its remembered images too.

Munro's phrase "mortal anxiety" might well be seen as apt for just
where she herself was as an artist when she walked into a CBC studio to
talk to Harry Boyle during the summer of 1974. Thinking that she had
"written out" the Wingham girlhood-to-young-adult material recalled
from British Columbia, having mined her manuscripts of earlier
attempts to produce about half the stories in *Something*, Munro was
looking not so much for new materials as she was for new ways of
seeing, of understanding her "old" material, her home place. Munro
herself knew that the mined stories in *Something* were exercises, proficient enough to publish but ultimately dissatisfying, just as some of
Something's keener reviewers observed. But that book also contained
the new style of autobiographical metafictional stories (and she had
done "Home" too), and it also had "Tell Me Yes or No" and "The
Spanish Lady," precursors of what Munro has come to call her "passion"
stories. When Munro talked to Joanna Beyersbergen late in spring 1974
and said of Huron County that there were "stories about people there
just crying out to be used" she doubtless knew that she might well use
them herself. But for a time, it seems, Munro was not yet in any position to do so.

That "Married People" builds to an ending focused on a remembered moment, long ago and far away, during which Norah saw herself
"vowing and waiting, in her mortal anxiety" is indicative of the imaginative change Munro was undergoing. This story was an early attempt
to reverse her usual technique and literally marry her former married

life in B.C. with her new life back in Ontario; dedicated to Jim and offered as a present, the story shows Munro beginning to scrutinize her marriage for meaning in the same way she had long examined her childhood and adolescence. More than this – and the technique would become increasingly evident as *Who Do You Think You Are?* gave way to *The Moons of Jupiter* – Munro accomplished her fictive effects by focusing on such moments as Norah experiences and remembers them years later. Home in Ontario a middle-aged woman (an adult, mother, much-praised writer, her position as daughter still intact at home with her father), Munro, like Norah, looked into the mirror and saw her grandmother's and her great-grandmother's faces staring back at her. Being Alice Munro, she also saw her mother's face and, going home to Wingham from London with some regularity, she saw her father still there. By August 1974 when she talked to Boyle, Munro was emphatically home. In "her mortal anxiety" – and Munro really did believe she might never write another thing – the question was what to do with this home now that she was there.

ꙮ

Listening to the leisurely talk Boyle had with Munro on *Sunday Supplement* were Munro's current and future editors – Audrey Coffin and Douglas M. Gibson. Coffin mentioned it in her letter returning the manuscript of *Something*, asking, "Have you noticed how your name keeps cropping up in Canadian book reviews and the like? And always now acknowledged as tops. Tomorrow the world! (Gratifying!!?)." When Gibson wrote, he acknowledged Munro's rising reputation as well. Citing a detail from the Boyle interview, Gibson agreed with a remark Munro had made about small towns; in his own in Scotland, too, "'even the town loonie' had his role and was recognized as a character," as she had said to Boyle.

After taking a bachelor's degree at St. Andrew's University in his native Scotland, Gibson came to North America in 1966 and took a master's degree at Yale. Then he embarked on a trip throughout the United States and Canada that saw him ending up in Toronto and, after a few months in the administration at McMaster University, answering an ad for editorial trainees at Doubleday Canada and being hired. Gibson worked there for six years before moving on to Macmillan to be editorial director of its trade division. Writing to Munro, Gibson probably knew that she was not happy at McGraw-Hill Ryerson and in his letter encouraged her to stop by his office if she was in Toronto. Such wooing was very much a part of the trade, both on the part of publishers and authors. Sometime in the fall Gibson travelled to London and met Munro for dinner. By January 1975 Gibson was writing her, "We at Macmillan would like to offer you a contract for your next book of fiction" and, as well, reported in the same letter that "on the other book, I have called Peter D'Angelo and he is sending along a lot of sample material for our perusal."34

Macmillan did not actually succeed in contracting for Munro's next book until spring 1978 when *Who Do You Think You Are?* was going into production. But as this second letter suggests, Gibson and Munro set to work immediately after their first meeting on a book of photographs, with a text by Munro, focused on Ontario and to be called "Places at Home." Peter D'Angelo, a medical student at Western and a photographer, had brought the idea to Munro when she was writer-in-residence there and she, in turn, took it to Gibson when they met. He was quite encouraging, so Munro and D'Angelo worked on the project throughout 1975, Munro producing a manuscript of about ten thousand words and D'Angelo spending that summer, supported by the advance he got from Macmillan, driving about southern Ontario taking photographs. The book was never published, but the work Munro did on it was important to her imaginative return to Huron County and much was later incorporated into *Who Do You Think You Are?*

After this book was abandoned in late 1975, Munro's relationship with Gibson, and so with Macmillan, continued through other connections. Munro wrote a blurb for Jack Hodgins's first book, *Spit Delaney's Island,* and she took the manuscript of her father's novel, completed just before his death in August 1976, to Macmillan. It published Laidlaw's *The McGregors* in 1979. She was nominally still connected to McGraw-Hill Ryerson after *Something* – there was a next-manuscript clause in her contract that McGraw-Hill wanted to hold her to. In

March 1975, just before he left the company, Kiil had written Munro about her next book, offering a $10,000 advance, better royalty terms, and promises of publicity in New York.[35] But with Audrey Coffin retired and the experience of *Something* behind her, there was little chance of Munro accepting the offer. By the end of 1975 she was a writer heading toward another publisher, most probably to Macmillan to work with Gibson.

By that time too Munro was focused on being a full-time writer. She had returned to London to take up the writer-in-residence position at Western for 1974–75. Andrea and Jenny were with her, and they moved again, into an apartment at 300 Oxford East. Munro was the university's third writer-in-residence, having been preceded by the poet Margaret Avison and by Margaret Laurence. She was expected to visit classes, keep office hours to meet with student and faculty writers, and give a public reading each term. Munro returned to Western at a time when Canadian literature was overwhelming the resistance it had traditionally faced within the English department from those on the faculty who taught British or American writing. Stan Dragland, whose field was Canadian literature and who had joined the English faculty in 1970, remembers Munro's year at Western. He recalls that resistance "was still in the air, though seldom spoken aloud to Canadianists, because it was there in the culture." It was spoken of to Munro, though, since she reported to Metcalf that at an academic dinner party in September it was made clear to her that Canadian literature was being forced on them, and that one member of the department had commented that she had met Munro but did not intend to read her. Meeting her, apparently, was enough.

Along with Dragland, D.M.R. Bentley and Catherine Ross also taught Canadian literature. Senior among them too was the poet and dramatist James Reaney, who had met Munro when she was still in Victoria and they had enjoyed social contacts there. Her time at Western allowed them to see a good deal of each other. Reaney, a native of Stratford and a person who had long taught a course on Ontario culture, recalls having fun with her sharing both remembered stories from childhood ("I had a stepfather who left dead animals lying about the barnyard") and an enthusiasm for *The Physiography of Southern Ontario*, a geographical text both knew. Reaney recalls that when Munro read in his Canadian literature class, "huge crowds came." Remembering one of these class visits also, Dragland said that in these Munro "could do no wrong" and he especially recalls her reading of "Postcard" to a class. When she read it to his class, though, she left off the last paragraph of the published version, the summary in which the narrator overtly addresses her pain at rejection. Dragland saw that act as an indication of Munro's direction then: "Less explicit means more involving," he recalls.

Typically Munro would read a story and then take questions. As Dragland and Reaney both recall, she was quite successful with audiences when she did this. She was not so sure herself, however. Although it was much less taxing than the regular classroom teaching she had done before, the requirements of the writer-in-residence position at Western still made Munro uncomfortable, just as most of the activities required of a public writer long have. Probably owing still to her experience in George Cuomo's writing workshop in Victoria ten years before, along with her shyness, Munro found such occasions difficult. As she made patently clear in "Material," much of what she saw as the academic adulation of the writer as truth-teller was essentially phony. While for her own purposes she saw it as necessary to accept such work and to display herself in this way, she never reconciled herself to it. No matter how well others thought she did, no matter what they took away from it, Munro herself found such occasions to be wearing, draining.

The social aspects of being in the university, however, were another matter. During her year at Western Munro attended and gave parties. These she enjoyed and, though such was not her intention, she was also able to use these parties as a means of gathering material for future writing. One party Rose attends in *Who Do You Think You Are?*, for instance, was derived from some Munro attended and one she herself gave during her time in London. Much of Simon's personal history in "Simon's Luck," for instance, came to Munro from a faculty member recounting his own history at one of these parties. Even so, by the time her year was ending Munro had had enough of the academy since she wrote to Metcalf that she was not able to go to a party without being accosted by people who wanted something from her. In March 1975 she wrote to Audrey Thomas that she had not got any work done because the "job is exhausting and unreal. I've read so much stuff now I couldn't tell Rod McKuen from Rilke. A terrible way to make a dollar. But it's soon over." She concluded from her year's return to Western that being a writer-in-residence was not for her.

Quite apart from the public occasions such a position demanded, Munro was ill suited as a writer-in-residence for a far more fundamental reason: she has never believed in the process of formally teaching so-called creative writing within the academy. More than belief, though, Munro seems unprepared to exercise what critical facility she has on other people's writing. There is no question but that her eye for what she is herself trying to do in her own work is sharp, acute; but there is also no evidence that she has been willing to apply that sensibility elsewhere. Leo Simpson, another writer who got to know Munro when she was in London and who was writer-in-residence after her, recalls Munro as one who had a clear sense of "what a writer's duties are," and that sense was to focus on her own work and make it as good as she possibly could. She would never be enthusiastic about reading student work, he recalls. Both Mary Swan – who continued to meet with Munro when she was at Western – and Stan Dragland – who took sections of his then-unpublished novel *Peckertracks* to her – agree as to Munro's methods. Swan wrote that "she didn't dissect things or offer specific advice or suggestions, [but] was always encouraging and supportive as she has continued to be all these years." Dragland is more analytical, writing that she offered "plenty of encouragement, but no direction." He notes, "On the wide gamut of possible responses to the writing of others, from dismissal to rave, undiscriminating praise has the advantage of leaving no scars."

Dragland, who confesses to being a bit disappointed by Munro's approach to his work and to that of students, has made some further comments that bear repeating. He remembers once hearing Munro say that "she never showed her writing to anyone before it went to her editor. She was the only writer I knew at the time who was so thoroughly professional in that regard." As he concludes his reminiscence of Munro at Western during 1974–75, Dragland maintains that "what was far more important about Alice than this cavilling" about her approach to others' writing "is that she was accessible as writer-in-residence. She was very friendly, highly sociable, anything but distant. She lived in London during her tenure; she was *in* residence and she hosted a variety of people and could talk about anything, even writing if it came to that. Many of Western's writers-in-residence preferred to commute from Toronto and thus established nothing like Alice's presence in the community."[36]

ꙮ

The third notable person who heard Munro's conversation with Harry Boyle was Gerald Fremlin. Driving between Ottawa and Clinton that afternoon, he did not miss Munro saying "Even since I've come back the past year to live here. . . ." Fremlin was returning to his hometown, Clinton, to help his mother. He did not intend to stay. Having learned that Alice was back in London, where he had first met and liked her, he called her up that fall. They met in London, and Munro took him to the Faculty Club, where they each had three martinis – Munro said they both must have been interested to have had so many drinks. By the middle of November, Munro told Metcalf about Fremlin and was clearly deeply attracted to him, though still a bit wary. She was happy he was not a writer, a bit amazed that he was an academic, and noted that he was Irish. As the winter passed, Munro began to cross-country ski with Fremlin, to be companionable, and she remarked to Metcalf that she was learning all about drumlins and eskers and moraines in what she thought were just innocent landscapes.

Munro went to Victoria for Christmas 1974 with the family. Although there were no scenes, she returned to London determined not to go again. By early January 1975 she mentioned "Places at Home" to Metcalf as something she was working on, and that she was intent on making it a sharp text rather than something bland. She knew and admired James Agee and Walker Evans's *Let Us Now Praise Famous Men* and Wright Morris's *The Home Place*, and her idea was to write a text made up of a series of vignettes to complement D'Angelo's photographs. These were descriptive of "Places at Home," but they also included characters. Munro worked on the text throughout 1975, first doing random vignettes and then trying to organize the material around a seasonal theme, what she called "a sort of Ontario Book of Days" in a letter she wrote to Gibson from Clinton on September 16. The Calgary archive contains over 150 pages of manuscript from "Places at Home," and in it Munro can be seen shaping this material, but she ultimately decided that she was unable to write the text that she imagined. Gibson agreed. Even so, the process of working on the photo-album text, begun in London, worked on while her relationship with Fremlin was growing, and carried back to Huron County when Munro moved to Clinton that fall was significant to her return home and, as will be seen, to *Who Do You Think You Are?* That book began with a working title of "Places at Home."

Once Munro completed her work at Western, she intended to find a place to rent for the summer near Lake Huron in Bayfield or Goderich. But as her letter to Gibson indicates, by mid-September she had moved to Clinton to live with Fremlin and his mother in the family home. When she wrote to Audrey Thomas in March, Munro told her that "my life has gone rosy, again. *This* time its real. I'm almost ashamed to tell you, after my crazy behavior in lost causes. He's 50, free, a good man if I ever saw one, tough and gentle like in the old tire ads, and this is the big thing – grown-up. Which is not the same as being middle-aged. . . . Luck exists, so does love, and I was right to go after it." Given this, and given Mrs. Fremlin's frailty – and that was the issue, since she was not then ill – if Munro and Fremlin were to have a relationship she had to go there, or at least move nearby.

So in August 1975 Alice Munro left London and moved north to Clinton, back to Huron County, just thirty-five kilometres south of Wingham, the place she had started out from and where her father still lived. She came back a much-praised and greatly valued writer, but she was coming back a grown-up who was moving into a new relationship. Fremlin also knew things about their shared home place that Munro did not know – innocent landscapes revealed as eskers, drumlins, and moraines, as she had commented – and he had his own Huron County history besides, a history he told her about. Having been back in Ontario for two years, Munro had been working on, and publishing, pieces that demonstrated some of the imaginative effects of her return. *Something* included them, but also revealed her as a writer poised between her past remembered Ontario and a new view of that place, one with the longer view, the deeper realizations, found in "Home," "Winter Wind," and "The Ottawa Valley." An Ontario whose images and associations demanded sharper renderings. When she went to Clinton, Munro returned to scrutinize her home place in ways she had never done before, and with a person who had things to tell her about this place she did not know.[37]

6

"Other Stories Are Wonderful and Also Read Like the Truth"

Virginia Barber, the **New Yorker,** *Macmillan, and Knopf, 1975–1980*

I was not very comfortable about being identified as a writer in the midst of what was, so to speak, my material. I was aware of having done things that must seem high-handed, pulling fictions up like rabbits out of hats; skinned rabbits, raw and startling, out of such familiar old hats. I knew that some of my inventions must seem puzzling and indecent.

– "Who Do You Think You Are?" (Proof of Supplanted Version)

I am somewhat crazed with admiration for these stories.

– Daniel Menaker, *New Yorker*, February 1977

A t the end of "Privilege," the second story in *Who Do You Think You Are?* and one that explicitly renders her two years at Wingham's Lower Town school, Munro wrote that "when Rose thought of West Hanratty during the war years, and during the years before, the two times were so separate it was as if an entirely different lighting had been used, or as if it was all on film and the film had been printed in a different way, so that on the one hand things looked clean-edged and decent and limited and ordinary, and on the other, dark, grainy, jumbled, and disturbing." In the collection's first story, "Royal Beatings," she had called this effect "a cloudy, interesting, problematical light on the world." These phrasings describe the imaginative effect of Munro's return in August 1975 to Huron County and to Clinton, very near Wingham. As has often been noticed, Munro concluded *Lives of Girls and Women* and *Something* with precise references to photography. (In *Lives* the Epilogue is entitled "The Photographer" while "The Ottawa Valley" includes the line "It is like a series of snapshots.") When she has described her method in such essays as "The Colonel's Hash Resettled" or in her introduction to *Selected Stories*, Munro has focused on the imaginative effects of specific recalled images. In the latter she wrote of the "scene which is the secret of the story" and described an image she once saw when she was about fifteen: it was then "like a blow to the chest." Confronting her imaginative relation to "the country to the east of Lake Huron," Munro asserts her love for it, details its components ("the almost flat fields, the swamps, the hardwood bush lots . . . the continental climate with its extravagant winters"), and goes on to express her hope "to be writing about and *through*" the life she knew there.[1]

The great fact of Alice Munro's writing career was her return to Huron County in 1975. Unplanned as it was, that move brought her back into the very midst of her material: feeling its life, knowing its sights, understanding its ways, speaking its language. And for the first time, in Gerald Fremlin, she was living with a man who shared much the same point of view, the same understandings. When she moved to Clinton, Munro was uncertain about whether, or just what, she would be able to write. With its looking back and its return to early writing attempts, *Something* had in some significant ways brought Munro to the end of her material; she was clearly uncertain about her future writing at that time. She was working on "Places at Home," the Peter D'Angelo project that had her focused on Wingham in ways immediate and sharp. Though it ultimately proved an intractable text, this work was crucial nevertheless. A succession of images drawn from the Ontario life she knew as a child, adolescent, and young woman but had not lived (but for visits) for more than twenty years, "Places at Home" was an imaginative return to Huron County concurrent to her literal return. Much of its material was incorporated into *Who Do You Think You Are?*, which was *the* critical book of Munro's career. *Who* was Munro's first book with Douglas Gibson and with Macmillan; it was the first book negotiated by her agent, Virginia Barber; the first with an altogether separate New York publisher, Alfred A. Knopf; and, famously, it was the book that she dramatically had pulled from the press the month before its publication so that she could reorganize it. All these facts resulted in various ways from Munro's return to Ontario.

But the great fact was the return itself. Munro returned well aware of what she remembered from her youth, knowing that she had already used such recollections from British Columbia, thinking that she may have "used it up," looking for a new relation to her material while living in its midst. As Munro returned to Huron to live instead of continuing as the public writer she had been in Toronto and London, and settled into a new relationship with a man who shared her passionate interest in Huron County landscapes, her life was completely changed. Her own close relatives gone or near gone, she was able from August 1975 on to create in her fiction a new imaginative relation with Huron County.

"Radiant, Everlasting": "Places at Home"

There is considerable evidence of the D'Angelo photo text in the Calgary archive, including one manuscript of almost fifty pages that has the appearance of being complete. That version has three renderings of an opening page-long descriptive vignette entitled "Places at Home," and twenty other pieces; some of these are descriptive while others feature characters and actions. Here is the first paragraph of "Places at Home":

> This country doesn't arrange itself into scenery very readily. Sometimes it will. Sometimes a river valley, everything melodious, the hills and willows and water and the dark cedar bush so cunningly fitted together, no drab edges or dead elms or gravel pits to be seen. But usually not. There is not much call for those places on the highway, where people can step out and give their attention to the view. Some of the country is flat, not plate-flat, not stunningly flat, to show off the sky. No sweeping horizons. Some of it is hilly; but as soon as it starts to get dramatic, with long bold sweeps and rugged knobs, it forgets what it was doing, dwindles into rubbly fields, bumps and bogs. You have to take it as it you find it. Fields and bush and swamps and stones. Rail fences, wire fences, electric fences. Log barns, weathered frame barns, new shiny barns with silos like big deodorant cans. Blooming hawthorn and rusting cars, pick-up trucks with the insides torn out, junk and wildflowers. Open and hidden country, fertile and scrubby. Cleared and tilled for a long time now, wasted and possessed. People who have lived away can complain here that they miss the mountains, miss the seashore, miss the calm distances, the space. But if you leave here and live away, what can you say you miss? Hard to describe.

The next paragraph summarizes the look of the towns, noting especially the post offices ("The old Post Offices had towers, though no Post Office needs one"). At a page long, this piece is representative of what Munro was doing in "Places at Home."

It is followed by "Pleistocene," which concerns a scene in a school classroom where "On an ordinary chalked map of Southern Ontario" a teacher named Mr. Cleaver "drew the lakes of former times, the old abandoned shores. Lake Iroquois and Lake Arkora. The Champlain Sea. The Tara Sands. Names [the students] had never heard before, and were not likely to remember." Introducing the students at this point, Munro uses them subsequently. They are resistant to this teacher's demands, concerned with more pressing things, as Munro makes clear when she concludes: "Winter afternoons swollen with boredom, secrecy, schemes, expectations, and unfocused fearfulness, messages of sex. Spreading, flattening." "Pleistocene" is followed by a short vignette called "Little Hill" in which, out for a drive years later with her husband, brother, and sister-in-law, Shirley Pickering "did remember one thing that Mr. Cleaver had told them. It was about the drumlins, left by the retreating ice like pebble tracks, to show the way it had gone. She remembered what it meant: *little hill.*" When she remarks this while on the drive, her relatives are taken aback: "Convicted of showing-off," displaying this useless bit of knowledge, Shirley "turned her face to the window," holds on to her thoughts, which sustain, cherish, and expand these meanings, and keeps her mouth shut. "She was not so far gone as to make mention" of her other thoughts.

"Little Hill" is followed by another half-page vignette called "Airship Over Michigan," which concerns some old men, "sitting on the bench in front of the Town Hall, [who were] receptive to the idea that what looked like a star in the western sky . . . was in reality an airship hovering over Bay City, Michigan, lit up by ten thousand electric light bulbs." This view became so widespread that the editor of the paper felt compelled to assert that "this brightest decoration of the western sky was no airship, or any man-made wonder, but the planet Venus. . . . Not everyone was persuaded."

When Munro came to publish *Who Do You Think You Are?* in 1978, some reviewers complained that she had returned to much the same material seen in *Lives.* That complaint misses the essence of what Munro did in *Who,* but there is no question that the text of "Places at Home" recollects Del's realization in "Epilogue: The Photographer": "No list could hold what I wanted, for what I wanted was every last thing, every layer of speech and thought, stroke of light on bark or walls, every smell, pothole, pain, crack, delusion, held still and held together – radiant, everlasting." Rather like Uncle Craig – whom Del is reacting against here – Munro includes lists in "Places at Home":

a list of nicknames in one vignette ("Moon-eyes," "Shot-a-Rat," "Horse," "Runt," "Half-a-Grapefruit," and others: "Those are names that will last a lifetime, unless you can move away") and a list of churches and lodges in another ("There is no reason for anybody not to belong to something. If they don't make you welcome in one place, you can keep on going until you find some place where they do."). There is also a brief description beginning "Flo knew the best way to kill a chicken, and it was this."[2]

These lists complement her brief fictional renderings of character and incident in "Places at Home." Following on "Pleistocene" and "Hill," she has, among others, "Poison Cake," about a "woman living on the Huron road [who] had second sight"; "Digging for Gold," about a treasure believed to have been buried by Jesse James; "Currant Bushes," about a father who buried his money in jars so as to stymie his children after his death; "June," about three boys who coerce a country girl into having sex with them under a porch; "Nosebleed," about a girl whose father gave her away to work for a rich family; "Hearse," about the "most successful seducer of women that there ever was in that country"; "Suicide Corners," about "Shepherd Street and Alma Street," where two men who committed suicide lived; and "The Boy Murderer," about a man named Franklin who returns home from the war unscathed only to be shot by his brother playing with a loaded gun at Franklin's welcome-home party. In one of the last pieces, "History," Munro offers lists of potatoes, roses, and names of streets (grouped thematically) before commenting "Too much altogether. The chronicler's job becomes depressing" and concluding that "history seems a gentle avocation, orderly and consoling, until you get into it. Then you see the shambles, the prodigal, dizzying, discouraging confusion. Just here, just on this one patch of the earth's surface where things have not been piling up for very long, or so we think; what must it be like in other places? Nevertheless some people will continue; some people are fired with the lasting hope of getting things straight."[3]

Reading through the lengthy unpublished manuscripts of "Places at Home" now, one is impressed by the synthesis of Munro's writing they reveal. Some small proportion of the writing looks back to things she had written previously, the echoes of *Lives* seen in the approach and in "The Boy Murderer," which reminds us of her depiction of Garnet French's family. Yet more interesting is how "Places at Home" shows Munro rediscovering her home place and its detail anew in ways appropriate to her own situation in 1975–76. Geographical considerations (the Pleistocene era, pre-glacial lakes, drumlins) reveal Munro's time and talks with Fremlin, who also provided the story of one of the suicides in "Suicide Corners," which his father had told him. That incident – a person threatening suicide with a rope not tied to a beam – appears here for the first time; Munro tried several times to place it until she finally got it into "The Progress of Love." Fremlin also provided her with the details for the girl's circumstances in "Nosebleed" – his notes about a twelve-year-old girl whose father "gave" her away to work for another family are in Munro's papers. That same history became Flo's in "Half a Grapefruit." Once she had written the text of "Places at Home" and it became clear that the book would not be published, Munro kept it and has used much of it since. "Pleistocene" became the uncollected story "Characters" and was considered for inclusion in *Who*. "June" and several other vignettes were used in *Who Do You Think You Are?*, the apparent shooting in "The Boy Murderer" became part of "Monsieur les Deux Chapeaux," and the phrasing at the end of "History" ("the lasting hope of getting things straight") would inform the conclusion of "Meneseteung." The seducer in "Hearse" reappears in *Who* and, though no longer an undertaker, again as D.M. Willens in "The Love of a Good Woman." Munro wrote to Gibson when she was struggling with the form of this manuscript; she was apologetic about the time she was taking to realize its best form but, even so, "I don't feel the effort to be wasted – in this game, eventually, nothing is wasted."[4]

That certainly proved to be the case, but the importance of "Places at Home" has to do with its role in bringing Munro imaginatively back to her home place just as she was literally returning to live there. Peter D'Angelo had approached her with the idea late in 1974; by January 1975 Gibson had contacted him and was expecting sample photographs; by April Fremlin was writing notes for Munro's use in "Nosebleed" and, toward the end of July, Gibson writes about various matters, commenting that "Peter D'Angelo tells me that you are hard at work on the prose sketches for that book" and asking to see sample text. Munro responded by sending Gibson her manuscript, writing in an undated cover letter that it is "in small and medium-sized segments which could, except for the first and last, be arranged every which way, or cut" and estimating the length at ten thousand words. Throughout, Gibson was acting as an effective editor, responding, making suggestions, and letting both Munro and D'Angelo work toward their text. He was also building his relationship with Munro.

When she wrote again from Clinton in mid-September, Munro had seen D'Angelo's pictures and said she liked them ("like some of them very much"). At the same time, she rejects the approach they have been taking, an "impressionistic book, done at random. . . . I don't think we can use the text I've written – after all, there has to be some theme, some connection," she continues, and suggests using additional pictures from the 1930s and 1940s. "One idea I have is – a sort of Ontario Book of Days, a seasonal book using (or appearing to use) the changes in one community over one year – work, play, a wedding, funeral, etc. The stores, the school, the churches, people. I could do a tight, factual text." Munro wanted to talk to Gibson about this, and she feared undercutting D'Angelo since she had not talked to him about it yet. Having not heard from Gibson, she wrote again eleven days later. When he responds on October 9, Gibson apologizes for his delay and writes that he had already imposed "a fairly strict seasonal division" and "have been driving the poor lad out to get more photos of fall fairs and so on," so Munro's "'Book of Days' idea" works well with that direction.

Such optimism was misplaced. By the end of December Gibson wrote to Munro that "after midnight on December 24 you must stop racking your brain to find a text for Peter D'Angelo's photographs." She responded on December 30 thanking him for "the letting-off-the-hook" and, picking up a reference made in his last letter, wrote that "one Calvinist conscience can always tell what ails another." She admitted that she could not do it but felt she had to make the effort – Munro felt especially bad for D'Angelo, "whose work I like a lot." While

neither Gibson nor Munro have particular memories of the progress of
"Places at Home," Peter D'Angelo recalls that at some point it became
clear that the book was not going to happen; he never saw any of
Munro's text.[5]

Looking at the manuscript remains of "Places at Home," it is easy
to see why Munro and Gibson decided that the text she wrote could not
be properly linked to a series of attractive photographs. Munro really
needed the sort of photographer she had imagined in *Lives*: "The pictures he took turned out to be unusual, even frightening. People saw that
in his pictures they had aged twenty or thirty years. Middle-aged people
saw in their own features the terrible, growing, inescapable likeness of
their dead parents; young fresh girls and men showed what gaunt or
dulled or stupid faces they would have when they were fifty. Brides
looked pregnant, children adenoidal." Important to this connection is
"Clues," the final vignette in the manuscript and one which – along with
the first, "Places at Home" – Munro saw as having an absolute position.
There she describes what one sees in a "little glassed-in porch":

> A calendar picture of a kitten and a puppy, faces turned
> toward each other so the noses touched, and the space between
> them formed a heart. The dates were not current, the calendar
> was eleven years old.
>
> A photograph, in colour, of Princess Anne as a child.
>
> A blue mountain pottery vase with three yellow plastic
> roses in it, both vase and roses bearing a soft film of dust.
>
> Six shells from the Pacific coast.
>
> *The Lord is My Shepherd*, in black cut-out scroll sprinkled
> with glitter.
>
> An amber glass cream jug, from Woolworth's probably,
> a bunch of flowers in it that a child might have brought –
> roadside weeds, buttercups, big coarse daisies, white and purple
> money-musk, even a couple of dandelions. . . .
>
> Newspaper photograph of seven coffins in a row. Two
> large, five small. Father, mother, five little children. All shot by
> the father in the middle of the night a few years ago in a house

about five miles out of town. That house is hard to find but many people have persisted, asking directions at a gas station on the highway and then at a crossroads store[.] Many people have driven past. . . .

Some blue and yellow paper birds, that look as if they were cut by the wobbly hand of a six-year-old child, but were cut out in fact by Ella herself, with her curled arthritic hands, and strung on little sticks the way it said to do, in the paper. A *mobile*. She made it to have something moving to look at it . . . and sure enough the birds are bobbing encouragingly, even on so close a day, riding on undetectable currents of air[.][6]

Munro's awareness (and perhaps emulation) of Wright Morris's *The Home Place* is readily apparent here. Following him, she is focusing on materials that, separate and stark, stand out in her mind, each an image embodying a story. But unlike Morris, who took his own photographs depicting such images from his own rural Nebraska childhood, Munro was working with a photographer who, however he might try, did not share her stark vision or her sense of personal story of Huron County. When in January 1975 Munro wrote to Metcalf that she might be doing the book with D'Angelo, she recounted a conversation with the photographer in which she said the text would neither be bland nor suitable for *Reader's Digest*. It certainly is not: "Places at Home" is both starkly Munro's own response to her home place, as well as a harbinger of what she would be writing in the years immediately to come. It points the way toward a new-found, sharply defined, and precise use of her material – no longer away from Huron County, Munro began in 1975 to write there with a longer, deeper perspective, one rooted in its soil, expansive, and bent on discovering "the rest of the story" in such images as are found in "Clues" and throughout "Places at Home."

ꙮ

When Munro wrote to Gibson at the end of 1975 acknowledging the decision to abandon "Places at Home," she also said that she was "into a new book, just shaping. I think it will work." Gibson circulated this letter to his colleagues with the annotation "I shall write soon with a formal offer to publish." Since he had met Munro in late 1974, Gibson kept at his suit. He sent her another formal offer for a contract in early February 1976. Meanwhile, he kept in touch, sending her books, asking her to blurb one by Harry Boyle and another by Jack Hodgins. His letters continued through 1976 and, during the spring of 1977, he told her that Macmillan was willing to publish Robert Laidlaw's novel *The McGregors*. By then *Who Do You Think You Are?* was emerging as a collection. Macmillan, however, still had no contract with her. Having received Gibson's second "formal offer to publish" in February 1976, Munro wrote back about a month later asking Gibson to send back the manuscript of "Places at Home," "that unusable text for the photographs." It was "the only complete ms. of that I've got, and I'm thinking of doing something with it," she told him. Regarding Gibson's offer to publish, she thanks him for his "kind words" and leaves it at that. He returned the manuscript a few days later, commenting that "there's a lot of good stuff in there" that he hopes she can put "to good use."7

While it might be possible to see Munro's behaviour as coy in the face of Gibson's protracted wooing, such an interpretation assumes a certainty about her ongoing writing that, though quite clear in retrospect, was by no means clear to Munro herself at the time. Gibson's continuing suit between late 1974 and spring 1978 – when he finally secured a contract with Munro for Macmillan – served as foundation for the working relationship that was formalized then and has been sustained ever since.

In March 1976 a second wooing began, that pressed by Virginia Barber. In each instance, though, editor and agent were after an author who, because of the changes in her life since 1973 and especially since moving to Clinton, was not at all sure that she would have material for the one to publish and the other to sell. Recalling this time, and Barber's offer in particular, Munro has said that

> I was terribly frightened that I was going to be a total disappointment, because at that time I thought I . . . may never write

another thing and what I do write will never sell. I just was almost fending off her enthusiasm. I felt so low in hope, and it wasn't that I was low-spirited, I was fine, I wasn't depressed, but I just had these ideas. Maybe it's because I write stories and between every story there's a kind of break before the next one. That isn't always true, but that's the way it was then. And I had entered into this new relationship that had taken a lot of my energy.

Among Munro's papers is a single sheet, a list of titles called "Places at Home," that lists "Pleistocene," "Airship," "The Boy Murderer," and others. In addition, it lists titles later used in *Who Do You Think You Are?* – "Half-a-Grapefruit," "Privilege," and "Providence." There are also other titles that probably represent working titles for stories that ultimately were published in *Who* or had been written by then: "Father" may have been "Royal Beatings"; "Norwegian Lover" may have been "Accident"; and "Simon and Children" may be connected to "Simon's Luck." Munro also listed "Married People," a story that was never published. Though just a single, undated sheet in her hand, it nonetheless confirms the emergence of *Who Do You Think You Are?* from "Places at Home." Given the imaginative adjustments brought about by her return, Munro took some time finding her way into her next book as she settled in with Fremlin and his mother in Huron County.[8]

When Munro moved to Clinton in August 1975, she and Gerry Fremlin did not see it as a permanent arrangement. She joined in with his plan to look after his mother, hoping to get her situated at home and the house fixed up, before moving elsewhere. Munro remembers saying, on a walk with Fremlin during the summer of 1975, that she did not think she was going to write any more, that she would "find something else to do." So initially she was not especially concerned with establishing a regular writing routine in Clinton. Such feelings aside, during that autumn Munro struggled with "Places at Home" and, despite her misgivings, found herself beginning a new story that became "Privilege," the second story in *Who*. Remembering this moment and the uncertainties she then felt, she has mentioned that when I came home that time I was interested in something different about the county. When I was in British Columbia, writing about home, it was just like an enchanted land of your childhood. It was very odd to say that Lower Town was the enchanted land, but it was. It was sort of out of time and place. And then when I came back I saw this was all happening in a sociological way, and I saw the memories I had as being, in a way, much harsher, though they were never very gentle, actually.

She was stirred by a "new interest in [these] harsher" memories, and that interest led to the stories she wrote during 1976, among them "Privilege" and "Royal Beatings."

During 1976 Munro also worked on a television script, for CBC, entitled "1847: The Irish," for a series called *The Newcomers/Les arrivants*. She wrote the screenplay, which was revised, and the episode was shot during the summer of 1977. It was broadcast in January 1978. Munro later returned to the material and changed the screenplay into a story, "A Better Place Than Home," which was published in 1979 in a volume drawn from the entire series. Focusing on an Irish family's story of emigration to Canada during the Potato Famine exodus, her story was based on research rather than personal materials (her own Irish ancestors having emigrated to Canada well before 1847). A comment she makes in draft notes about the piece catches the effect, and certainty, of her knowledge once she had finished her work for the script: "There can't be any spectacular 'Making it' in the new land because they usually didn't get that far; they remained mostly working-class, lower middle-class, or proud poor farmers. (Never mind Timothy Eaton)." But her protagonist, who remembers her own difficulties in emigrating to Canada, "speaking in 1900, would see her family's survival, their modest occupations, as a source of great pride and satisfaction. (I'm sorry, but I think it inevitable with a family of this size, at that time, that some would have gone to the United States and 'done well': but one of them is seeking his fortune in the opening of the Canadian West.)" Like "Places at Home," this writing proved to be useful later, since some of her later writing from the 1980s on has been based on such research.

ࣷ

During 1975–76 there was much more to Munro's life than writing. As her recollection suggests, she faced considerable imaginative change in returning to Huron County, to the people and culture she had been born into and still very much knew as her own. She was concentrating on developing her new relationship with Fremlin, but there were many other connections as well. They were living with his mother, so Munro had to deal once again with familiar gender-based cultural assumptions – as a woman she was expected to look after the housework, despite Fremlin's willingness to participate, and all the more so since she was not "working." There was also the fact that she and Fremlin were not married but living together, something that did not sit well with either person's parent. Munro was seeing her stepmother and father in Wingham then too, and Bob Laidlaw's heart problems were persisting. His health was in decline.

Then there was the place itself. Maud Code Porterfield's funeral in January 1976 was held during a major blizzard. It created considerable difficulty for the family as they returned from the cemetery, reminding Munro of the physical struggle that was part of winter in Huron. But winter had its consolations. She and Fremlin often cross-country skied, and did so at night. On one such occasion Munro remembers coming upon a group of indefinable shapes covered with snow. What were the shapes under the covering? They strained to make out the reality. Ultimately, they realized that they were looking at wrecked cars strewn about a field. That haunted moment later became the basis for the same realization in her story "Fits," a story rejected by the *New Yorker* (three times), but first published in *Grand Street*, and ultimately included in *The Progress of Love*. This rooting of "Fits" – a story that is primarily about the imaginative effects of a proximate murder-suicide – in an evening cross-country outing with Fremlin suggests the progress at work in Munro after she moved back to Huron County: once the "enchanted place of her childhood," Munro now found in Clinton a place equal to her mature imagination, a place familiar yet mysterious. Seeing it anew upon her return she found in its mysteries and suggestions the very stuff of life itself. Despite her characteristic uncertainties, new stories soon emerged.9

"I Wonder If You've Considered a Literary Agent?": Virginia Barber

The foreword Hugh Garner had submitted to Ryerson for *Dance of the Happy Shades* in 1968 included two paragraphs describing the market for short stories in Canada during the late 1960s. Though Audrey Coffin excised them from the published version, they reveal what Munro confronted as a short story writer in Canada:

> The commercial magazine used to be the natural home of the short story, but today only one national consumer magazine, *Chatelaine*, remains as a market for classic short fiction. *Canadian Home Journal, Liberty, National Home Monthly*, and *Mayfair* died, *The Star Weekly, Maclean's*, and *The Montreal Standard's* successor *Weekend* gave up short fiction. Only one, *Saturday Night*, publishes a couple of short stories a year, as part of a commercial deal with a tobacco company. Today's apprentice short story writer must rely on the quarterlies such as *Tamarack Review*, the college quarterlies, *Canadian Forum*, and other low- and non-paying publications.

Munro knew this market vividly from her experiences throughout the 1950s and 1960s and, as Kiil's placement of four of her stories in *McCall's* (plus another in *Chatelaine*) during 1973–74 demonstrated, she also knew that her work appealed to well-paying consumer magazines in the United States. But despite submitting stories to these magazines since the late 1950s, and having Kiil do so during the time she was successful with *McCall's*, Munro had not been able to succeed with the *New Yorker*, the premier venue for short fiction in North America, nor with its competitors there.

All that changed in 1976. Munro had been approached by literary agents before and, especially after the complexities surrounding *Something*, she had made inquiries regarding their utility. Still, she had taken no action, characteristically hesitant about such major shifts. Few Canadian writers had agents and, conversely, there were not many Canadian agents. Margaret Atwood hired hers, Phoebe Larmore, after being pressed to get one by Peter Davison, her editor at Little, Brown – he thought she needed one. Larmore has represented her since. Probably sometime in late 1975 Atwood told her that Munro was a writer who might be interested in an agent and she may also have mentioned Larmore to Munro. In New York, Larmore had friends who were also agents, among them Virginia Barber, who since 1974 had run her own agency. A similar sort of discussion took place between Larmore and Toivo Kiil in Toronto in 1975. In December she wrote to him recommending Barber as a possible agent for Munro as one of three writers he had suggested who needed agents (Harry Pollock and Carol Shields were the others). Her associate had been reading Munro's work and had recommended that Barber write to Kiil directly and introduce herself. Though Kiil was no longer at McGraw-Hill Ryerson, he continued to play a role in Munro's career.

Barber wrote to Kiil introducing herself in January, indicating that her main interest was "good fiction." "I have a Ph.D. in American Literature (Duke Univ.) and was teaching literature before becoming an agent. It is very difficult, as you well know, to find quality fiction that is also commercial enough to attract a publisher, but that is indeed what I'm looking for." She had read Munro's work and would be "very pleased to work with her." Barber then listed several recent books she had represented and concluded, "I'm being highly selective at this point about taking on new clients, but I'll always find room for someone of the caliber of Alice Munro. Therefore, I hope you will think of me if you know of good Canadian writers who are seeking American representation." In a postscript, she added that even though she had had her own agency for less than two years she had good co-agents abroad and lists them.[10]

Characteristically, Virginia Barber was forthright in presenting herself. Born and raised Virginia Price in Galax, Virginia, a small town about twice the size of Wingham in the Blue Ridge region, her family was socially prominent and Presbyterian when most others there were Baptists. Segregation was still a fact then. Her father was a retired federal civil servant and they belonged to the country club. Like Munro, she was academically accomplished and also was encouraged by the people of Galax who recognized her accomplishments. After high school she attended Randolph-Macon College for Women and then Duke University where she earned a Ph.D. in English with a dissertation on William Carlos Williams's poetics. At Duke she met and married Edwin Barber, a Mississippian, and the couple moved to New York in 1959, where he worked as an editor in publishing, first at Harcourt, Brace and then at W.W. Norton. They had two daughters and, after some time spent teaching at Columbia University Teachers College, Barber became an agent through her friend Helen Merrill. Initially she worked with Merrill in the theatre, but, given its "weekend meetings, midnight decisions, and wild temperaments," she decided to set up her own agency and concentrate on prose writers.

At the time she wrote to Kiil, Barber's agency shared office space with Larmore on Greenwich Avenue in New York. Although Munro emerged as an especially attractive prospect for Barber, she was interested in other Canadian writers as well, for her agency was relatively new and growing. The first writer Barber wrote a scouting letter to when she became an agent was Clark Blaise, who already had an agent; but at one time or another she has represented Marian Engel, John Metcalf, Carol Shields, Aritha van Herk, Rudy Wiebe, L.R. Wright, and others. Barber and Munro met at a gathering of the Writers' Union of Canada in Toronto in 1976.

Barber first wrote to Munro in March 1976: "Dear Alice Munro, I wonder if you've considered a literary agent?", she began and, even before introducing herself, continued to assert that "I believe your work should be represented by someone, and I would very much like to be that someone. I've been thinking about this for some time and have talked with Robert Stewart, Joyce Johnson, Phoebe Larmore, Alma Lee, and I wrote Toivo Kiil, telling him of my admiration of your writing. It's time I wrote you." Barber's letter is itself a tempting text, since she presents herself precisely, carefully, and effectively. The people she names here – two New York editors, Atwood's agent, a person involved in the Writers' Union, and Munro's nominal editor – were all known to Munro. Barber had done her homework. Her primary interest was "good fiction" and she sketched her background in much the same way she had to Kiil although, tellingly, she added, "I'm married (my husband has been an editor for 17 years, so I was around the business before I was in it) and have two children."

After a paragraph expressing her admiration for "Material," Barber describes the resonance of Munro's work within her own life. Looking back to the time she was studying "fiction about the artist or the making of fiction" in graduate school, Barber offers an image of herself "changing diapers or scraping egg off plates," wondering

> if Henry James would have changed places with me, allowing me to tell him that it's "art which *makes* life" while I dined out the 355 evenings a year in his place. So, I had an occasional sense of "It's not enough" in my own terms. "Material" put the subject in a perspective I hadn't seen but which has meant a great deal to me – the one word "authority" calls to mind the whole story for me.

Barber concludes by asking Munro to not "be shy about answering this letter. Let's begin talking through the mails. And if you have any questions about my agency or background or whatever, ask." Her final sentences get right to the point: "I'm convinced that there are many people who would value your writing and who don't know your work – I believe I can help. It would give me much pleasure if you should decide so too."

Barber's approach to Munro was apt. Writing from the centre of American publishing, the market Munro needed to get into (since Kiil's success at *McCall's* had shown as much), Barber here is thorough, professional, and knowledgeable. Even more importantly, she is also wry and a bit self-deprecating, revealing herself as a woman with a point of view and sense of humour similar to Munro's own. With children and years spent scraping egg off plates, Munro could readily relate to Barber's experiences.

She responded to this letter quickly. Less than two weeks after her first letter, Barber wrote again, addressing her this time as just Alice and beginning, "I'm sending you noisy greetings and the word that I've never trusted rumors anyway." Munro must have raised a question about agents, or about the way they work, since the balance of this letter specifically explains an agent's standard charges (10 per cent for domestic sales, 20 per cent for foreign) and, in much greater detail, what an agent does and how she could help an author's career. Barber itemized such duties as matching manuscripts with publishers, negotiating the contract, looking after production, and helping with publicity. "Very often, problems come up along the way – again, the agent helps resolve them." The agent also handles subsidiary rights, which are often a difficult matter. In addition, the agent acts as "first reader" for the author should she wish. "I know it's to your advantage to have an agent," Barber wrote toward the end of the letter, "but before you accept such an arrangement, you should be convinced. No good agent would want a reluctant client. Why don't you talk with some of your friends who have agents?" Munro had been doing just that for some time; so it is probable that her response to Barber's first letter was a request to know more about this agent's sense of her own methods.

Characteristically, Munro was slow to respond. Barber recalls that she sent back a very nice letter thanking her but maintained that she did not need an agent. Responding to this, Barber sent Munro a copy of a just-published first novel by one of the authors she represented, Rosellen Brown's *The Autobiography of My Mother*. Munro read the book and eventually decided that anyone who handled such writing was a person she wanted to work with too. Meanwhile, she had doubtless been doing her own homework on Barber. The two women confirmed their arrangement in Toronto that summer, first meeting at a raucous writers' party at Pierre Berton's house in Kleinburg. Barber

Photo by and courtesy of James Munro

Alice Munro in front of the B.C. legislature, Victoria,
early 1952. Alice is wearing her "honeymoon suit."

Courtesy Jenny Munro

Alice and Jim Munro, Grouse Mountain, B.C.,
summer 1953. Alice is pregnant with Sheila.

Source: Author photo, April 2002

Left: 1316 Arbutus Street, Vancouver

Centre: The first house Alice and Jim Munro owned, 445 West King's Road, North Vancouver. (The house has since been altered.)

Bottom: View from 2749 Lawson Avenue, West Vancouver

Source: Author photo, April 2002

Source: Author photo, April 2002

Alice Munro, West Vancouver, 1957

Alice Munro, ca.
1958 – 60,
West Vancouver

Alice and Jim Munro at home in West Vancouver

Arthur Munro,
Robert Laidlaw,
Margaret Munro,
Jenny, Sheila, and Alice Munro,
West Vancouver,
May 1963

Robert Laidlaw and Jenny Munro, Vancouver 1961

Jenny,
Andrea,
and
Margaret Munro,
Victoria,
April 1968

Jenny, Alice, and Sheila Munro, Vancouver, July 1961,
the summer of the "Miles City, Montana" trip

1648 Rockland Avenue, Victoria

Munro's Books of Victoria today

remembers arriving in Toronto and calling Munro to confirm their meeting arrangements from a payphone at the Windsor Arms Hotel. They had their chat, and when Barber hung up change came cascading out of the phone, "just like at the end of 'Providence' when the little girl is filled with wonder . . . life in its potential for largesse and the wonder at the good luck. . . . But I had to call Alice [back] and tell her – it literally went to the floor, came out of the box and spilled onto the floor. . . . It was like some slot machine."

At that point Barber had not read "Providence" – Munro wrote the story in October 1976 – but in calling the author and telling her what had happened, she may well have contributed an incident to that story's making. By that summer, Munro was working on the *Who* stories, and "Providence" was among the first seven she sent to New York. Whether the cascading change was a propitious sign or not, the events of that weekend confirmed Munro's hiring of Barber as her agent. This proved to be a critical decision, for it had almost immediate effects.

Barber's work on Munro's behalf began in earnest early in November 1976, once Munro had sent Barber seven stories that were to be the core of *Who*. Looking back, Barber has commented that by that time Alice "had already done such wonderful work that it didn't take much of a brain to recognize that this was a great writer." She set about introducing Munro to New York publishing in a way she had never been presented previously. Having an agent on the ground there was a very different thing from having a publisher, McGraw-Hill, which received her work from its Canadian subsidiary. An agent "has to have faith in her own opinion," Barber has said, "because she is the front line." Still in the process of starting out herself, but armed with a writer who had already proved her mettle in Canada, where she was "world famous," Virginia Barber hit the ground running once she had material to sell. It was more than business; in Barber Munro had found a friend, a person of integrity, experience, and knowledge commensurate with her own. As she asserted when she dedicated her *Selected Stories*, Munro saw Barber as an "essential support" in fact.[11]

When Barber first wrote Munro early in 1976, she had little new material on hand beyond "Places at Home." She had only just retrieved that manuscript from Gibson when Barber's initial letter arrived. Munro felt that she was "almost fending off her enthusiasm," because she was worried that she might not write anything else. Still, she was working steadily, and on one level at least, things were coming together. She reported as much to Metcalf just after her great-aunt's funeral in January. These projects were probably extensions of materials from "Places at Home" (like "Pleistocene," which she expanded from the initial sketch) or "Privilege," which Munro recalls as the first of the *Who Do You Think You Are?* stories to emerge. Despite misgivings, and despite the busy new life she was leading, 1976 proved a busy writing year for Munro. By the end of October she was able to send seven new stories to Barber in New York.

✏

Quite apart from her writing, Munro spent the fall of 1975 settling back once again into the life of Huron County. She and Gerry went on long walks, she canned quarts and quarts of ginger pears, harvested the garden (the tomatoes were a disappointment), went often to the library for Mrs. Fremlin, and generally realigned herself to the rhythms of small-town rural life. There were periodic forays to London, just over an hour away, for readings and parties connected with the university, and they once went to a party given by her sister-in-law Margaret Munro, who had joined a Communist cell. She did not miss the city in any way – there were no Communists in Clinton (though there were Orangemen, who still hated the French Canadians and were opposed to Catholicism in general), and no one there approached her with a manuscript to read. Although she knew that her growing status as a writer made her seem an odd fit with Clinton, no one was fawning over her or making anything of her celebrity, as some people in London had. Even so, back home, she knew that she was thought of as lazy, with no proper work to do, and so something of a family embarrassment, but Munro also knew that such a status in a place she was comfortable in was better for her work.

Fearing boredom for Alice in Clinton, Gerry encouraged her to accept invitations to read and to present herself as a writer. Munro read at Western that fall and in February she went on a Canada Council reading tour through the prairies to British Columbia. (Her reading at Simon Fraser University garnered one of the few really grumpy reviews Munro has ever received, in the Vancouver *Sun*, from a reporter dismayed that she had nothing new to read and gave no interviews.) The tour was followed by a visit to Victoria to see Andrea, who was approaching her tenth birthday. Jim was in a new relationship with Carole Sabiston, an artist, who had a son about Andrea's age. Later that year, when the divorce was final, Jim and Carole married at the house on Rockland. Andrea came to Clinton for the summer, as did Jenny, who found a waitressing job nearby.

The tension and trouble leading to the breakup of her marriage was now well behind. By the summer of 1976, Munro had settled comfortably into life in Clinton. Walking, gardening, looking after Mrs. Fremlin, Gerry working on renovations to the house, both of them cross-country skiing in winter: "Real life." Munro was happy with this routine; it felt normal. In April, she and Fremlin told their parents that they had married while on a trip to Ottawa. The story was a saving fiction: the marriage never took place, but it satisfied their parents. By June she was telling Metcalf that the new book was started, though typically she wondered when she would ever get it done.[12]

On June 9, 1976, Munro was in London to receive an honorary degree from her alma mater, the University of Western Ontario. Numerous others have been offered over the years – from such other universities as Manitoba, Queen's, and Toronto – but Western's was the only one she has accepted. She became a Doctor of Letters, *honoris causa*: "Here," its citation ends, "is an Alice who, from everyday experience, has created her own Wonderland, making of it a looking glass through which we begin to identify vital aspects of our world and of ourselves." The singularity of Munro's acceptance here illustrates her attitude toward such awards. In 1983, for example, she declined an appointment as an Officer of the Order of Canada. Asked about it, she explained that while she had no problem with awards received for particular books or for her body of work, she was uncomfortable with awards recognizing a person by virtue of celebrity. Having studied and

excelled for two years at Western as an undergraduate, and having
served a year as its writer-in-residence, Munro probably felt that its
degree was not as honorific as all that, that she had earned it.[13]

Late in June Bob Laidlaw's heart took a turn for the worse. He was
admitted to Victoria hospital in London, where tests were done to see
if he was well enough to withstand open-heart surgery. If he had the
operation and survived it, his circumstances would have been considerably improved; if not, he would be confined to bed for the rest of his
life – the prognosis expected just a few months to a year. He passed the
tests and decided to have the operation, but because of the surgeon's
schedule he had to return home for three weeks to await the surgery. It
was performed in late July but, right after the operation, he suffered a
massive coronary; though he was revived, he never regained consciousness. Alice and her sister, Sheila, were at the hospital throughout
the ordeal. Finally, on August 2, at the age of seventy-four, Robert
Eric Laidlaw passed away. The funeral was somewhat controversial
since Laidlaw had specified that there was to be no minister present;
instead, his son, William, read a statement his father had written. In it
Laidlaw offered goodbyes and thanks, and politely said how he had
always thought Christianity was rather silly. He did not want to give
offence, but that was just how it struck him. This was news to many
who knew him, and some took it badly.

Munro had been scheduled to teach at the Banff Centre for the
Arts that summer but, owing to her father's illness and death, went there
a week late. Throughout her growing career, Bob Laidlaw had watched
her reach new levels of accomplishment, knew the details of her publication, and felt the brunt of whatever local reaction there was to his
daughter's writing. He celebrated the news of her first published story,
"The Dimensions of a Shadow," yet he recognized the inadvisability of
her use of "Jesus Christ" there, given his wife's and mother's feelings. He
dealt with the gun-toting man who saw his own family's history in "The
Time of Death" and so threatened him because he was Alice's father.
And on reading the copy of Lives she sent to him, pronounced it "a powerful book and very strong medicine indeed. I sometimes wished that
you had not been quite so explicit in the matter of sex but then you have

set out to write of a young girl's growing up, her reaction to that very important part of life, sex." As Munro has said, her father never offered a word of criticism, for he understood the artist in her.

Well he might. Always a reader, always a thoughtful man, during the last years of his life he had become a writer himself. After a lifetime of hard, physical labour in the bush, on his fur farm, at the foundry, and in the turkey barns, he took up writing, and succeeded well. Between 1974 and 1976 he published six pieces, five memoirs, and a short story, in the *Village Squire*, an Ontario magazine published in Blyth. At the same time he was working on his historical novel, *The McGregors*, set between the 1850s (when the Laidlaws first came to Huron) and 1925 (when the county could be seen as settled). In 1974, he told his daughter that he wanted "to bring out the tragedy of reticent people."

Among Munro's papers is a brief unpublished manuscript intended as a separate commentary on "Working for a Living." Munro wrote there that "this story, or memoir, is about [my father's] working life, and to some extent about my mother's. But I took him only up to his middle years, when his fox farm had failed and [he] was working in the Wingham Foundry." She then describes his subsequent work as a turkey farmer and writes that "in the last years – really in the very last months – of his life, he became a writer. He had been working on the first draft of a novel about Ontario pioneer life when he went into the hospital for a check on his worsening heart condition. . . . When I visited him in the hospital all he wanted to talk about was his characters, and the ways he had thought of strengthening his book." This was the last conversation the two had. "During the three weeks he had left he produced a second draft that I read with astonishment after his death. He had made a wonderful leap, in organization, in grasp, in love, of his material. His book *The McGregors* was published in 1979."

Munro then wonders whether Laidlaw should have been a writer. Such a decision, she realized, "would have been unthinkable, in his family, his community, his time. It would have seemed unmanly, impractical, indecently presumptuous. (It was possible for me because I was a girl and a girl's choice was not so important, it would all be forgotten when she married and had children[.])" The real significance of these facts for Munro is her realization that "he had at any rate the moments of greatest pleasure in a writer's life, which come long before publication, vindication, or even completion. I mean those moments when he . . . caught hold of his story, his creation, with such effort and determination and flashes of power and delight." Her "memoir" – as she calls "Working for a Living" – was about her father's working life. Yet, as her commentary confirms, when she wrote of her father's working life she knew of his writing and, indeed, knew that *The McGregors* would be published. That is, the communion between writer-daughter and writer-father existed – its feeling is present on each page of "Working for a Living" though emerging first in "Royal Beatings" and "The Moons of Jupiter."[14]

Laidlaw's death became part of his daughter's own perspective as "Places at Home" was passing into *Who Do You Think You Are?* Just as her loss of her mother had allowed her to soon take up the "personal material" surrounding her mother's death in "The Peace of Utrecht," so too her father's passing allowed a similar, though much less literal, use of autobiographical materials in "Royal Beatings." And like "Peace," "Royal Beatings" proved to be "a *big* breakthrough story" for her, the "kind of story that I didn't intend to write at all. That led on to most of the stories" in *Who Do You Think You Are?* "Royal Beatings" proved to be the first story Munro sold to the *New Yorker* and the lead story in *Who*. "The Moons of Jupiter," a lyric memorial to Robert Laidlaw, grew directly from Laidlaw's death. Always an interested observer of his daughter's success, after his death he became an intimate presence in the fabric of her breakthrough stories of the late 1970s and into the 1980s.

A little-remarked scene featuring a character based on her father appears in "Miles City, Montana." Contrasting her background with her husband Andrew's, the narrator writes that "my home was a turkey farm, where my father lived as a widower, and though it was the same house my mother had lived in, had papered, painted, cleaned, furnished, it showed the effects now of neglect and of some wild socia-bility." She also recalls a visit when, home alone with her father just after her mother died and, newly married, just before she was to join her husband in Vancouver, she and her father used a rowboat to rescue turkeys that had been trapped by rising waters from a sudden rainstorm. "The job was difficult and absurd and very uncomfortable. We were laughing. I was happy to be working with my father. I felt close to all hard, repetitive, appalling work, in which the body is finally worn out, the mind sunk (though sometimes the spirit can stay marvelously light), and I was homesick in advance for this life and this place." That is, she was there at home knowing she would miss that place and her father in the years to come.

"A Cloudy, Interesting, Problematical Light on the World": "Royal Beatings," Virginia Barber, and the *New Yorker*

In late 1984 Munro's first editor at the *New Yorker*, Charles McGrath, wrote to Barber renewing her first-reading agreement with the magazine. He did so "with particular pleasure after the Munro bonanza we've had these last few months. She is simply one of the finest short story writers alive, and it's a great honor and privilege for us to be able to publish her."[15] By this time Munro was well established among the *New Yorker's* "stable" of writers. Between April 1980 and December 1984, she had nine stories accepted by the *New Yorker*. She also had ten others that the editors there considered and rejected – in one case, "Fits," they saw it three times before finally letting it go. By June 2004 forty-seven Munro stories had first appeared in the *New Yorker*, under four different editors-in-chief – William Shawn, Robert Gottlieb, Tina Brown, and David Remnick – and the numerous changes their goings and comings occasioned. Recalling Munro's position with the magazine, McGrath has observed that she has been among "the sinews that held the *New Yorker* together" throughout its many changes. "It's sort of odd and ironic that this Canadian writer would become a *New Yorker* mainstay."

The inclination today is to take Munro's connection to the *New Yorker* as an inevitable component of her career. Perhaps it was. But her inclusion in the magazine's august stable was the result of several factors: the quality of her work, Virginia Barber's abilities, good timing, and a bit of luck. She had been submitting stories herself to the *New Yorker* since at least the late 1950s – Jim Munro recalls that they were convinced the magazine must have had a special mailing point near the west coast, so quickly did stories come back. Alice herself recalls *New Yorker* rejection slips, sometimes with handwritten comments. And in August 1973 when Kiil was trying to place Munro's stories from *Dance* and those forthcoming in *Something*, the *New Yorker* was the first magazine he mentioned. Yet Munro had no success there until she placed her work in Virginia "Ginger" Barber's hands.

By early October 1976, their agreement confirmed, Barber wrote then that "of course I want to see some stories. Send them as soon as you can. I'll read them, send them out, and share my thoughts briefly with you. Then you can say whether or not you'd like to hear more than the brief comments. Never mind about the typing." Moving past business, she continued, "Share or spare the domestic life, as you will. But if you have any whimsically ironic comments, send them – they're the get-through-the-day boost that I like." Two weeks later, Barber wrote again. Not yet having any new stories to consider, she worked in a different direction. She was trying to understand the nature and scope of Munro's past book contracts and wanted to contact Marilyn Gray, the person who handled rights at McGraw-Hill Ryerson. Her hope was to get access to the rights to Munro's past work so she could resell them; she wanted "to absorb the facts and figures from your past contracts so that I'll have done my homework when the future project comes into my present."

On November 1, a Monday, Barber reported that "the stories arrived, finally" the previous Thursday and that she "carried them home like a treasure, which they are" to read over the weekend. She had already submitted four of the seven stories to the *New Yorker* – "Honeyman's Granddaughter" (later titled "Privilege"), "Providence," "Royal Beatings," and "Spelling." Barber was planning to send "some of the others" to Lisel Eisenheimer at *McCall's* the next day. Beyond the stories, she also told Munro that she had just met, in New York, with John Savage and Robin Brass from McGraw-Hill Ryerson. They brought "the contracts and other relevant information. We had a good talk." Barber concluded this letter by offering an indicative hope that proved prescient: "I'm delighted to have the stories, Alice, and I hope this is the real beginning of a fine working relationship. I'm already waving banners for you down here, and that means you can roll your eyes heavenward in mild protest but no more. You also don't have to look. I feel you've turned me loose at last, and I'm ever so ready to go! Write well, enjoy, and I'll be sending these stories to all decent magazines."

Barber's timing with the *New Yorker*, the first among these magazines, proved excellent. She approached Charles McGrath, a new fiction editor there, and submitted Munro's stories to him over lunch. At the time, the two did not know each other. McGrath was one of two young editors – the other was Daniel Menaker – who had joined the fiction department earlier that same year as a result of the forced retirements of Robert Henderson and William Maxwell. Both McGrath and Menaker had graduated from university in the 1960s and, after some graduate work, had each joined the magazine in entry-level editorial positions, Menaker as a fact-checker in 1969 and McGrath as a copy editor in 1973. When the retirements were looming, each spent a period of time apprenticing with Maxwell, sitting at a desk opposite his in order to learn just what a fiction editor did.[16]

At the *New Yorker* it is customary to speak of "the fiction department," an entity made up of a head editor and several other editors. When Munro's stories came in, the *New Yorker* was still being edited by its second and longest-serving editor, William Shawn. He had been with the magazine since 1933 and had been editor since 1952, when he took over after the death of its founding editor, Harold W. Ross. A native of Colorado, a reporter, and a veteran who had edited *Stars and Stripes* as a private in France during the war, Ross founded the *New Yorker* in 1925 with the financial backing of Raoul Fleischmann, whose family made its money in baking. It sought an audience that was both urban and urbane. Almost weekly for over eighty years now, the *New Yorker* has published as broad a range of comment, humour, essays, politics, analysis, cartoons, fiction, poetry, oddities, and silly pieces as might be imagined. While fiction was not of particular moment during the magazine's early years, it rose to prominence under Katherine

White and expanded further under Shawn's editorship. By the time Munro was submitting stories to the *New Yorker* the size of its "slush pile" was famous, and there was no doubt that the magazine was regarded as the leading venue for short fiction in the United States.[17]

When McGrath and Menaker were brought in, the fiction department was headed by Roger Angell; the other editors were Frances Kiernan, Rachel MacKenzie, and Derrick Morgan. There were also young people whose job it was to sift through the slush pile and forward stories with potential to one of the editors. The department operated by consensus. Each editor would read those stories that came directly to them and then write an opinion of the piece – strengths, weaknesses, needed revisions, and a conclusion whether to buy it or not. Through this process a decision gradually emerged, although most of the time one or another editor was on the other side of the decision. Stories recommended for purchase were sent on to Shawn, who had the final say. According to McGrath, Shawn was a very good reader of fiction, though by no means expert. He had suggestions of his own, but he usually went along with the department's recommendation. The head of the fiction department – which McGrath was for many years after Angell – managed the paper flow and had a larger vote in the group discussions.

When Barber invited "Chip" McGrath to lunch at the University Club on Fifth Avenue, he knew she wanted something. At the time, it was unusual for short story writers to have agents and, as McGrath knew, Shawn was leery of agents, preferring to deal with authors directly. Still, as new fiction editors at the *New Yorker*, McGrath and Menaker were eager to find new writers for its pages. As McGrath recalled, "I felt that was my mission in life at that point." Barber came to lunch with Phyllis Seidel, a friend, and at the end of it she told McGrath that she had "this Canadian writer that I think is great, and gave [him] a bunch of stories in an envelope." "To be honest," he recalled, "I had no expectations. I went back and read them and the rest is history."

Yet it was not quite that simple. McGrath and Menaker were completely enthusiastic about the four Munro stories they had read. Their older colleagues in the department were also impressed. Weighing one story against another, it became clear that of the four the group was most interested in "Royal Beatings." That story incorporates three vignettes from "Places at Home" including this schoolyard rhyme:

> Two Vancouvers fried in snot!
> Two pickled arseholes in a knot!

McGrath recalls that the very things he and Menaker liked about Munro's writing – such as this rhyme – "made it a slight bit of a hurdle to get it into the magazine." Part of the problem was the magazine's "Naughty Words Policy." It was real enough: William Shawn did insist that coarse language had no place in the *New Yorker*. Reconsidering this in 2003, McGrath felt that it was "roughness" that most bothered Shawn, "the violence, the intensity of emotion, the rawness of the setting and of what people do." "Shawn had probably never seen [this] before in fiction of this quality and I think he was a little nonplussed." These same issues, again, were "the very things that recommended the story to those of us who were younger. We thought this was great."

By November 17 McGrath had informed Barber that the magazine would buy "Royal Beatings" but he returned the other stories to her. He also told her about the excitement that Munro's stories had occasioned among its readers at the *New Yorker*, for Barber added a postscript to a letter to Munro: "Chip says, judging by the excitement, that he's sure you're going to be one of the New Yorker's authors – they want to see all your new stories. So far, it's a rainbow. We shall see if there's a treasure at its end." The next day McGrath wrote Munro directly for the first time:

> Your story "Royal Beatings" has occasioned as much excitement around here as any story I can remember. It's an extraordinary, original piece of writing, and we very much want to publish it. Everyone who has read it has been moved by the story's intelligence and sensitivity, and has marveled at its emotional range.

In this, his first letter to Munro as her *New Yorker* editor, McGrath was at pains to explain the magazine's editorial procedures. "What I propose to do – with your permission, of course – is to undertake some preliminary editing." This would involve points where alternative expressions might be used and others where additional information would be helpful. "One of the story's strengths is the way it moves so easily back and forth in time – in fact, it seems to work as memory works – but, even so, I think there are a few places where events tend to run together." The "only possible difficulty" he foresaw was that "Mr. Shawn, the editor-in-chief – who, by the way, likes 'Royal Beatings' a great deal – has questioned, on the ground of 'earthiness,' both the paragraph on toilet noises on page 3 and the rhyme about pickled arseholes." For his part, McGrath did not think "the toilet-noise passage is absolutely essential to the story" but conceded that the "pickled arsehole" rhyme might be. He says he is prepared to argue her case with Shawn, "though I can't guarantee that I will win. I do think we can reach some compromise, however, and troublesome as it may be, I hope you will try to understand our position in this regard."

In closing, McGrath details the various steps on the way to publication, including payment once the story is set in type. The *New Yorker* pays on a word rate, so the author cannot be paid until a story is set in type and the word count is established: "We never pay less than a thousand dollars, though, and my guess is that 'Royal Beatings' would bring at least two and probably three times that much." After encouraging Munro to call him ("collect, of course") to let him "know whether or not to go ahead," he concluded that "Royal Beatings" is a rare and wonderful piece of work, and "we will be honored if you will let us publish it." For her part, Munro says that she had never heard of Shawn and thought that people in New York might be making him up. Such a view is not far-fetched: despite his long association with the magazine, Shawn's name had never been published in its pages to that point.[18]

"Royal Beatings" appeared in the March 14, 1977, issue of the *New Yorker*. McGrath lost the battle about bathroom noises (Munro reinstated the paragraph in *Who*) but he "was able to win the point about 'arsehole.'" By that time the magazine had bought another story,

"The Beggar Maid," and had considered eight more, ten if one counts revisions of "Pleistocene" and "Spelling." Barber now feels that it took her too long to learn not to send the *New Yorker* Munro's stories in groups. While Munro has for many years written in spurts and sent her stories in clusters, the act of submitting more than one at a time seemed reasonable at first. However, editors naturally enough pitted the stories against one another, choosing what seemed to them the strongest one. Given its status and the many submissions it received, the *New Yorker*'s editors could afford to be choosy. There was also the matter of the magazine's appetite: under Shawn it published upwards of a hundred stories annually.

Yet while they rejected far more of Munro's stories in the first years than they took, McGrath and his colleagues knew that in Munro they had a real find. Rejections were always tempered by compliments and encouragements. Sending "Mischief" back to Barber, McGrath wrote that they hoped to see another story soon since "we value Alice Munro's writing very highly here: one editor [Daniel Menaker] has said, 'I am somewhat crazed with admiration for these stories.'" Menaker's unabashed enthusiasm for Munro's stories was evident from the first. Closing his December 21 letter to Barber, McGrath wrote, "I hope this is just the beginning of a long relationship between Alice Munro and The New Yorker, and I thank you for helping to make it possible."[19]

Throughout 1977 Barber and her assistant, Mary Evans, continued to stoke the flames of Munro's growing reputation in New York. A real buzz was developing, and they worked to keep it buzzing even louder. Just as she promised Munro, she sorted through Munro's previous book contracts and prepared for the next negotiation, familiarizing herself with Canadian publishers and scouting possibilities among U.S. houses, looking for the right in-house editor for Munro's next book.

Kate Medina, a senior editor at Doubleday, had heard of Munro from Clark Blaise. She called McGrath, who referred her to Barber. She wanted to borrow a copy of *Lives* and to see copies of Munro's manuscript stories. Barber reported this to Munro and commented, "I'm not at all concerned about *finding* you a publisher here, for I think we'll be able to pick and choose." When Medina returned the book to Barber, she began her letter by writing, "I have fallen in love with Alice Munro," expressing her unwillingness to give up the book – "it's the sort of book one wants to keep *handy*." Medina was keen on bringing Munro to Doubleday, promising to "lobby zealously for her work here." The making of such connections would continue into 1978, when most of the stories to be included in the next book had been sold to magazines.

As most of those stories were turned down by the *New Yorker* during 1977, Barber and Evans, whose primary responsibility was serial placement, sent them to other magazines. They began with other commercial publications in New York before trying Canadian magazines or literary quarterlies. In February, when the *New Yorker* rejected "Mischief" "very reluctantly," Barber sent it to Gordon Lish at *Esquire*. Lish wrote a long letter to Evans detailing his response and wondering whether Munro would be willing to address his concerns. She did revise the story, but he did not take it, backing off once he saw "The Beggar Maid" in the June 27 issue of the *New Yorker*. It was bought by *Viva* for its April 1978 issue. *Redbook* took "Providence" for August 1977 and then had "Half a Grapefruit" under consideration. Its fiction editor, Anne Mollegen Smith, wrote Barber asking for revisions. Munro made them, and it was published in May 1978. As such instances suggest, Barber's agency was energetic and persistent. At one point in summer 1977 she mentions that she has tried "Spelling" at ten magazines, "including *Mother Jones* where the fiction editor is a client of mine." After the *New Yorker*, "Wild Swans" went to *McCall's* and *Cosmopolitan* before being bought by *Toronto Life*, which had also taken "Accident." *Ms.* bought "The Honeyman's Granddaughter," also known and published in the *Tamarack Review* as "Privilege." Of the stories in *Who*, only one had not been previously published in a serial.[20]

When she wrote to Munro reporting on Gordon Lish's decision to reject the revision of "Mischief" after reading "The Beggar Maid," which he thought a much better story, Barber wryly observed that we "think the seductiveness of the New Yorker's printed page has temporarily deranged editors. We find Mischief a very strong story indeed and will continue to knock at every conceivable door." Barber's comment here – though admittedly written by an agent who was still

in the process of winning her author's confidence in her own abilities —
captures the key qualities of her stewardship throughout her work with
Munro: her reaction is wry, humorous; her determination is dogged;
and her faith in the quality of Munro's writing unwavering. Munro had
found an agent who did indeed "wave banners" for her throughout the
publishing world.

The reason for such rising interest throughout literary New York
was, as McGrath and Menaker saw, the strong qualities in Munro's
stories that set her work apart. The spirit of the reaction it caused
throughout New York during 1977 was captured by Alice Quinn, who
in the future became Munro's third editor at the *New Yorker*. Then an
editor at Knopf, Quinn wrote to Barber expressing her pleasure (and
Knopf's implicit interest) in "The Beggar Maid" on its publication in
the magazine: "Some stories are wonderful stories and other stories are
wonderful and also read like the truth. It certainly is a provocative piece
of writing." There really was a Munro buzz in New York. Despite
numerous rejections of her stories, the *New Yorker* was feeling the buzz
too. In December 1977 they sent Munro a "first-reading agreement" for
1978. Shortly thereafter, they bought "The Moons of Jupiter," their
third Munro story. Munro has had the same agreement with the magazine ever since.[21]

Sending this agreement to Munro for her signature, Barber wrote
that this "is very, very good news . . . which I decided to keep to myself
until I was certain of its reality." These agreements, which reflected
what Barber called the *New Yorker*'s "amusing hauteur," were offered,
in McGrath's words, "to a very few writers whose work we especially
admire, and the general idea is that in return for your giving us a first
look at your stories we will pay you a higher rate for those stories we do
take." Under these terms, if a writer sold four stories within a twelve-
month period, she received an additional 20 per cent for all four stories;
should she sell six, an additional 15 per cent for all six, or a total 35 per
cent bonus. At the time, as McGrath said when he first wrote Munro
regarding "Royal Beatings," the *New Yorker*'s word rate worked out to a
payment of between two and three thousand dollars, so the advantage
of this arrangement to Munro was clear. By contrast, during 1977

Munro received in the range of fifteen hundred dollars from other U.S. magazines buying stories the *New Yorker* had declined.

Barber is amused because the payment schedule "listed is *less* than you received previously. However, for the next story *The New Yorker* buys, they will pay you *more* than you received previously." Signing the first-reading agreement brought a payment of just one hundred dollars. Although the money involved from the *New Yorker* was very real, much more than writers could obtain elsewhere, the importance of the contract to Munro and her career is found in McGrath's penultimate sentence: "The point of all this is simply that we feel your writing is very special, and we want to express our gratitude to you for letting us see it." Recalling this decision early in 2003, McGrath indicated that a first-reading agreement made little more than a year after he and his colleagues first took up Munro's stories made her work special indeed, quite exceptional. It normally took a person considerably more time to get to that point.[22]

What Barber called the *New Yorker*'s "amusing hauteur" under William Shawn bears comment since similar formalities may be inferred in McGrath's constructions ("we want to express our gratitude" or, when he first wrote, "we would be honored if you will let us publish" "Royal Beatings"). Writing Munro then, McGrath was establishing a relationship with her that he already had with other writers, relationships enacted largely through the mails and over the telephone, in which he had to both explain the *New Yorker*'s ways and maintain the writer's control and cooperation as the process moved toward publication. Given the magazine's prominence – especially since the 1970s was one of its most prosperous decades – it could well afford to buy the best. At the same time, and this was a peculiarity that began under Harold Ross but was enshrined under Shawn, the writer's agreement to whatever changes were proposed was paramount. Thus authors could, and occasionally did, refuse to go along with changes and pull their work. So McGrath's formalities were not nearly the pose they might sound, nor were they disingenuous. McGrath knew he had the power brought by a big cheque and he wielded it carefully.

The results for Alice Munro herself were enormous, certainly. Without question, getting into the *New Yorker*, causing a buzz in New York publishing circles, and receiving a first-reading agreement within just a year's time, all moved her career to another level. However, the real effect of the new arrangement was on her work itself. During the 1950s and 1960s Robert Weaver and his colleagues at the CBC and at the *Tamarack Review* responded to, and appreciated, the stories she sent. In Earle Toppings and Audrey Coffin at Ryerson she had sympathetic editors who responded to, encouraged, and to some degree prodded her. With John Metcalf it was mostly commiseration, although his frequent comments on her published work were a real tonic. But in Barber and, by extension, McGrath and the rest of the fiction editors at the *New Yorker*, and editors at other magazines too, Munro had a group of people who were responding to, encouraging her and, often, pushing toward a revision. Barber, of course, had a vested interest in Munro's success; as her author succeeded, so did she. But in reading the correspondence, weighing the questions and answers it contains, and inferring the telephone conversations that accompanied those letters, one sees that it is clear that Barber and Munro formed a partnership very quickly. Both of them were engaged in and stimulated by the contacts Barber had made in New York.

⌘

Yet for Munro's art and the growth of her career, these new arrangements were much more than publication by the continent's leading venue for short fiction. Her return to Huron County and the renewal of her imaginative connections there meant that the stories Munro wrote during 1976 were imbued with a more immediate sensibility and also a different imaginative relation to her subject matter than she had previously displayed. In the stories she intended for *Who Do You Think You Are?* (including those ultimately held out of that volume to await the next collection, *The Moons of Jupiter*), Munro can be seen to be looking back to childhood, but reconnecting to the continuity of life itself in Huron County from her middle-aged perspective. She still remembered her discovery of the complexities of her home ("Connection. That was what it was all about") but those memories were now more distant. While this balancing of a child's perspective with the narrating adult's sensibility is also evident in many of the stories in *Dance* and *Lives*, there is a qualitative difference, a new-found complexity, in the stories Munro wrote after she returned to Huron County. The home she wrote about from British Columbia, she recalled, "was just like an enchanted land of your childhood." But the Huron County she had returned to and began seeing anew in 1975 was harsher and a place she saw in a more sociological way. With Huron's people, Huron's culture, Huron's life staring her full in the face – no longer being remembered over time and distance – Munro saw social differences even more clearly, resulting in greater complexity from *Who* on. That book felt in some ways like *Lives*, but its longer perspective and its much more complex composition suggest a writer finding a new relation to her material. Back in Huron County, Munro was literally "a writer in the midst of what was, so to speak, [her] material," as she wrote in the unpublished proof version of "Who Do You Think You Are?" Munro had never really been in that position before. Thus there is both a perceptual shift and a greater social complexity in the stories Munro wrote from 1976 on. As McGrath commented when he first wrote her regarding "Royal Beatings," the narrative "seems to work the way that memory works."

Always an intuitive writer, Munro proceeded as she always had in Clinton. She tried things; sometimes they worked, sometimes they did not. The Rose and Janet stories worked. She attempted stories focused on a middle-aged couple living in the house the man grew up in with the man's mother. ("Sounds like Mrs. Fremlin, doesn't it?" Munro commented, hearing of these, having forgotten them.) They did not work. Once she sent stories off to Barber the response was real, and relatively fast; Barber would comment but promptly got them off to the *New Yorker*, which, for its part, also responded with dispatch. At times too, when it was judicious to wait before submitting a story, Barber did. Thus as she worked on the stories that became *Who* and, as well, four of the stories in *Moons*, Munro was receiving more professional response to her work than she ever had before. And because she was also trying old material in new ways, undertaking new subjects, and revelling in the fact of a new, yet renewed, relation to her home, the period 1976 through the mid-1980s is an especially rich one in her career.

When McGrath returned a story, he never did so without summarizing the discussion it had occasioned among the editors. The importance of this relation to Munro's art may be seen in the case of "Simon's Luck," a story that she wrote initially as a larger, more complicated narrative than the version eventually published. She continued to wonder over, revise, and tinker with it. A new version of this story helped spark her decision to pull *Who* from the presses and reorganize it, and she was considering a new version for the American edition even after *Who* had been published in Canada. It deals with Simon, an inscrutable character whose personal history Munro had heard from a faculty member at Western, and focuses on his relations with three different women. In August 1977 McGrath had returned a long version of "Simon's Luck" with a rejection letter. He reported that it "had many readings here, and while we all thought it was brilliantly written, and full of life and intelligence, in the end we agreed that somehow it didn't quite work." After commenting on the story's focus, Simon himself, his attractiveness to women, McGrath concluded:

> I'm sorry to go on so long, and if I sound critical I don't mean to. The truth is that we all greatly admired this story, and feel very unhappy about sending it back. In fact, we would be more than happy to reconsider it if you decided to revise it. It's only fair for me to say, though, that for some reason (maybe that editors never really know what they want) resubmissions rarely work out here, and I also think that if you fixed the beginning a little you could sell this in a minute somewhere else. This is all up to you and Ginger, and whatever you decide is fine with us. I really am sorry, and one thing that makes me feel better is knowing that you're working on another story.

Despite the warning here – Munro had revised two stories and resubmitted them (unsuccessfully) before this – she revised the story, giving a separate section to each woman. A manuscript of this sectioned version is in Calgary (thirty-three legal typescript pages, double-spaced). Here the women are Emily, Sheila, and Angela, each of whom breaks with Simon. Angela does so most dramatically – she runs an errand to the store but decides to drive Simon's car to a train station, where she buys a ticket and boards the transcontinental train, returning the keys by mail. The Emily section was the section published in *Who*, with Emily's name changed to Rose; relocated, some of Sheila's and Angela's situations and actions inform the character of Lydia in "Dulse." As Munro reported to Gibson, she did not waste much of her writing.

McGrath and his colleagues at the *New Yorker* came to the same conclusion about the revised "Simon's Luck," for he wrote to Barber in December with the comment that "the three sections do stand by themselves, I guess, but they seem skimpy somehow – compared with the fullness of the first version, anyway – and in these separate stories Simon seems as enigmatic as ever; at times he hardly seems to be there at all." He added, "What I do know is that there's a lot of wonderful writing here, and I hate to lose it. We all do." Even in the face of this second rejection, Barber and Munro continued to press the story since the *New Yorker* saw, and again rejected, the Sheila section as a separate story. "Emily," which became "Simon's Luck" in *Who* (after Munro tried shifting it to first person), appeared in *Viva* in 1978.[23]

When "Royal Beatings" appeared in the *New Yorker* in March 1977, John Metcalf wrote Munro congratulating her on its appearance. In her return letter Munro told him about the magazine's back-and-forth editing process, its pickiness, and especially its prudery, which surprised her. "Everyone at the *New Yorker* is in thrall to some deity upstairs called Mr. Shawn. 'We doubt very much if this will get by Mr. Shawn,' they say sadly. They have not been so hard on 'The Beggar Maid,' the second story they took." Munro then moves on to other topics.

However long she may have tried to get her stories into the *New Yorker*, like most people Munro was unaware of Mr. Shawn's position atop the magazine until she had to deal with his policies through McGrath. His task was to carry the discussion to Shawn, to win the point over pickled arseholes and snot but lose over the bathroom noises, which were duly reinstated in the book. Her job, as Barber would continue to tell Munro, was to "write well." So Munro did. And through the offices of Ginger Barber and Chip McGrath – for so they were to one another very quickly, despite initial formalities – the literary world outside of Canada began to take notice.

"Huron County Blues"

Canada certainly noticed Munro being noticed. In a March 1977 piece on Munro and Richler in the *Globe and Mail*, William French called attention to "Royal Beatings" in the previous week's *New Yorker*, offering a progress report on her current writing. Like Richler, whose novel-in-progress had been excerpted in *Saturday Night*, Munro was still "on good terms" with her typewriter. Since her last book, French reports, Munro "has remarried – her new husband is Gerald Fremlin – and settled down in the small town of Clinton, Ont., about 60 miles north of London. 'I like small town life,' she explained when I called her the other day. 'We go for long walks and do a lot of cross-country skiing.' Clinton is in the snowbelt, but Munro is accustomed to rigorous winters. Wingham, where she grew up and which has provided the setting for many of her stories – the fictional version is called Jubilee – is only 20 miles from Clinton."[24]

Munro was settling back into life in Huron County, Ontario, and through such published pieces as this, people who knew and admired her work became aware of her return. Munro and Fremlin gradually began to recognize that their life together would be in Clinton, a shared life in a small town where they both felt comfortable. She wrote, her already major reputation in Canada grew through her *New Yorker* appearances, and life settled into a regular seasonal pattern. Andrea came east for summers, her older sisters visited as they could, Munro and Fremlin skied in winter, walked in the spring, summer, and fall, and drove about the countryside exploring and rediscovering – it is not by chance that both "Working for a Living" and "What Do You Want to Know For?" begin with images of Munro and Fremlin on the road, driving about, noticing something. As Munro has said, such drives have long been one of their recreations.

Munro was not able to settle back into Huron County anonymously nor, given her reputation and the increasing number of requests that reputation brought, was she able to stay in Clinton as much as she would have preferred. By 1977 her career had begun its transformation from famous Canadian writer to much-admired international writer to watch. She accepted occasional invitations to participate in public events of one sort or another, and during 1977 she continued to work on the stories that went into *Who* and some into *The Moons of Jupiter*. At the same time, she was involved in other activities. In the spring Munro served, along with Margaret Laurence and Mordecai Richler, on the committee that selected the 1976 Governor General's Award for Fiction. The award went to Marian Engel's *Bear*, a controversial choice and one in which Munro differed from the committee's other members. Their discussions led to some friction with Laurence, who wanted the decision to be unanimous; as a result, Munro withdrew from the committee for the next year's award. Other recognitions came her way as well. Her story "Accident," which was first published in *Toronto Life*, received the National Magazine Gold Medal; she received a Silver Jubilee Medal from the Queen commemorating the anniversary of the coronation; and early in January 1978 it was announced that Munro had won the 1977 Canada-Australia Literary Prize. She was its second winner, the first Canadian. Intended to make writers from one country better known in the other, it involved a tour of Australia that Munro undertook during the spring of 1979.[25]

Munro's move back to Huron County came with a price. In 1978 she spoke out against attempts to ban three books from the grade thirteen English curriculum in Huron County high schools. They were Laurence's *The Diviners*, John Steinbeck's *Of Mice and Men*, and J.D. Salinger's *The Catcher in the Rye*. She was publicly outspoken and drew considerable press attention to herself as she helped lead the opposition of the Writers' Union against this attempt. Speaking in London in late May to the Association of Canadian University Teachers of English, she argued, according to a news report in the *Montreal Star*, that "Canadian writers must fight a conservative backlash that has forced some books from high school reading lists [as] obscene or pornographic." At the annual Writers' Union meeting, she was appointed to its committee charged with fighting "this strong uprising of people who feel there has been too much permissiveness." Though such advocacy was uncharacteristic, Munro's belief in the need to undertake this work was deep and unwavering. She knew of it first-hand.

In early 1976, *Lives of Girls and Women* had been singled out for banning on "moral" grounds by the principal of a Peterborough, Ontario, high school at the same time as *The Diviners* was removed from the Grade 13 curriculum by the Lakefield school board just north of Peterborough. (Laurence lived in Lakefield then.) The two writers were linked by these actions, and they commiserated by mail, Munro addressing Laurence as "F.F.P.," "that's *famous* fellow pornographer." In the same letter Munro added that she had been "getting the blast in Wingham for ages" and, though she was used to it, she regretted it for her father's and stepmother's sakes. Hence when *The Diviners* was attacked again in spring 1978, Munro was in no joking mood. Throughout, she was an outspoken defender of the targeted novels and, more particularly, of the integrity of teenagers as thinking persons, and of their right to read what they chose to read, just as she had done herself. She understood that there are always plenty of people made uncomfortable by the literary depiction of life as it is and by the fact that literature both communicates ideas and makes people think.

Munro's position in this debate was especially precarious since she was living among the very people who were bent on banning the three books. A motion to that effect had come before the Huron County school board. Votes had been taken in the townships, and Munro's native Turnberry Township had voted 35–1 in favour of the ban. A public meeting organized by opponents to the ban was held in Clinton on June 13. In support of the local English teachers, the Writers' Union sent along three representatives, William French reported in the *Globe and Mail,* "vice-president June Callwood, children's writer Janet Lunn, and Alice Munro, who lives in the eye of the storm in Clinton." Almost five hundred people attended. French, who reported on the meeting, also noted that "the five people on the platform made some low-key remarks in defence of freedom and the three books specifically, trying not to offend or inflame." Munro asserted that "the tradition of pro-priety in literature is not an ancient one but a fairly recent one" and then went on to illustrate this "from a book" she valued very much. "In a fairly short space this tells about 1) an incestuous rape 2) a case of extreme drunken-ness and double incest, 3) a daughter-in-law who dis-guises herself as a prostitute to trick her father-in-law, and finally, about a king who falls in love with a beautiful married woman he sees bathing on the roof-top, seduces her, tries to trick her husband into thinking he – the husband – is the father of her expected child, then when this fails sends the husband back into the thick of the battle to be killed." Reporting on this part of her speech, the reporter from the *Clinton News-Record* wrote that "Munro's comparison of the alleged porno-graphic materials in the novels to material in The Bible sparked an audience reaction that began to resemble a faith healing session." Once she was finished with King David and Bathsheba, Munro continued:

> Writers do have responsibilities – all serious writers make a con-tinual, and painful, and developing effort, to get as close as they can to what they see as reality – the shifting complex reality of human experience. A serious writer is always doing that, not attempting to please people, or flatter them, *or* offend them. The three books under consideration are all by serious writers. They are also moral books in that they deal with the question of how to live – what makes life not only bearable but what makes it honourable, how can people care for each other, how can we deal with hypocrisy and self-deception, how can we grow and learn and survive?

Ultimately, the board voted to remove *The Diviners* from the high school but compromised on the other two books.

After the meeting Munro received an encouraging letter from Laurence, who had written in response to the press coverage. Some of Munro's comments in her reply are revelatory: "In a personal way this is all good for me – I have a problem wanting people to like me and it's high time I got over it. I think it's harder because I'm *not* an outsider living here, I have relatives[.] G.[erry] grew up here. *Good* people who were kind and friendly are now distant and disappointed." And beyond her personal revelation about the pain she felt as an insider, a person from Huron County, she also writes that "a man came up to me after the meeting and said, 'Your mother taught me in Sunday School. She would be ashamed of you.' And it's *true*. My mother burned *Grapes of Wrath* in the kitchen stove." Recounting the same incident to another friend, Munro recognized that her writing reflected her own preference – that she rejected her mother's piety and conventional notions, and she knew that she had become someone her mother would have been ashamed of.

William French described Munro as one who "had the uncomfortable feeling of looking out at the somewhat hostile faces she usually encounters in more genial circumstances in the grocery store and on Clinton's neighborly streets."[26] While there is no question but that Munro's return to Huron County to live had a positive effect on her writing, it is evident equally that proximity to the people of the area exacted a personal price. Along with the evident slights of the people she knew, Munro received anonymous letters full of righteous indignation over her stand in defence of *The Diviners* and the other books. She had no illusions about how she was seen and, especially, how her work was viewed by many there. Her outspoken actions during the book-banning controversy embody the uneasy relationship. Into the 1980s, that relationship was particularly fraught. Munro's luminous question, one she mentioned in her 1974 interview with Boyle and was just then making famous – Who do you think you are? – became a fact of her own daily life in Clinton. The low point occurred, certainly, in December 1981 when Barry Wenger, president and publisher of the *Wingham Advance-Times*, published an anti-Munro editorial entitled "A Genius of Sour Grapes." He was expressing the indignation felt by many in Wingham over a newspaper piece syndicated across Canada by Wayne Grady called "Story Tellers to the World." It seemed to attribute Grady's sneering and condescending descriptions of Wingham and Lower Town to Munro herself. Given what had happened in public since her return, and given their reading of her fiction, many in the community were prepared to believe the characterizations as Munro's. Looking back on these years in a 1982 profile in *Books in Canada*, Joyce Wayne entitled her piece "Huron County Blues." Referring to Munro's recent relations with Huron County generally and Wingham particularly, Wayne offers an apt summary, calling them "both the heartbreak and strength of her writer's life."[27]

Canada's *Who Do You Think You Are?*, America's *The Beggar Maid*

When she wrote Munro in December 1977 enclosing the *New Yorker's* first-reading contract, Barber called it "a rare and lovely item" and chortled a bit, continuing, "Can't wait to sound the news all over town, and drive book editors even more to distraction since they haven't been able to get me to send them your manuscript." Having had real success in selling Munro's stories throughout 1977, Barber's attentions gradually shifted to Munro's next book. During that year, too, Barber sorted through her author's existing book contracts, both so that she understood them herself and also in order to investigate new paperback possibilities. She needed to understand Canadian publishing better, its shape and detail, and to establish contacts there. Concurrent with those first stories Barber had met with John Savage and Robin Brass from McGraw-Hill Ryerson and, in May 1977, she made a trip to Canada, coming back "with a much clearer sense of houses and editors" than she had had before. She wrote this to Bella Pomer, one of Gibson's colleagues at Macmillan, who had given her "helpful information . . . about who's who and what's what in Canadian publishing." Barber knew that there was an editor at Macmillan whom Munro liked, though she did not then know his name, and she also knew that the house had promised her that it would publish Robert Laidlaw's novel. During that summer, too, Barber heard from John Pearce, senior editor at Clarke, Irwin in Toronto, who called her "to ask about Alice Munro's publishing future and to express [his] considerable enthusiasm for her work." He came to see her in November (she thought he might be the Canadian editor Munro liked), and Robin Brass also wrote saying that McGraw-Hill Ryerson was "as keen as ever."[28]

While Canadian houses were showing great eagerness about Munro, her next book was taking shape. By early October 1977 Barber wrote Munro formulating a sort of plan:

> Let's think of a title for the short story collection. And don't you think the book should have two sections – the first section 5 Flo and Rose stories ("Royal Beatings" Privilege, Half a G., Wild Swans and Spelling) and then, Accident, Beggar Maid, Mischief, Providence and Simon's Luck? Mr. Black too? How would you like the stories ordered. Give this a little time, and then you may put this out of your mind for a while, if that pleases you. If Simon's Luck is now three stories, you have more than enough for a collection, and could remove some. Or we could enlist the aid of an editor.

Barber was, as usual, on top of things; she had taken a considered look at both the body of Munro's work and her more recent stories. As good as her word, Barber was nudging Munro to the next step and was doing so in a supportive and direct way: indeed, her suggestion of a two-part structure for *Who Do You Think You Are?* was the direction Munro initially followed.

For his part, Douglas Gibson at Macmillan had not slackened in his pursuit of Munro. After apparently considering her father's manuscript for some time, he told her in April 1977 that Macmillan had decided to publish it. He was not sure just when they would bring it out, since that was dependent on his own busy schedule and he wanted to edit it himself. "I know how much the publication of this book means to you, and as you and I agree, you ought not to spend time revising it, but should be working on your short stories." Arrangements regarding *The McGregors* remained in limbo until January 1978, when Munro wrote to Gibson asking for a progress report. Her stepmother, Mary Etta Laidlaw, was quite ill and had been asking her about it.

Munro hoped "to give her some news, even if she may not get to see it." Gibson replied that he would work to get the book out that fall, promising a contract for it soon. He then continued: "I have been deliberately staying out of your way for some time, since I don't want to pester you with repeated offers of a contract. In the meantime, of course, I've been keeping an approving eye on your work: in 'The New Yorker', on 'The Immigrants' [on CBC-TV], and most recently in connection with the Australian prize." Congratulating her, he then wondered if she is "now close to having a book-length collection and therefore to drawing up a contract with us. I can think of no other author I would rather have on Macmillan's list." Gibson also sent her a copy of a book they had just published called *Remembering the Farm* because it contained a story that "instantly struck me as an Alice Munro story in miniature." Though he did not say so, that book also contains photographs by Peter D'Angelo.

Gibson's wooing strategy was not without critique within Macmillan. A few days after Gibson wrote this letter to Munro, Robert J. Stuart, vice-president of trade books, wrote him an internal memo critical of the decision to publish *The McGregors*, one he himself had acquiesced to. His memo is within a particular context that Stuart is quite explicit about: "I know how badly you want Alice Munro on the Macmillan list, as do all of us in the division." He allows that the publication of the book might "make some difference to Alice although, in retrospect, we are going about getting her in the wrong way. We should attract her to this house by our ability to edit *her* work, and sell and promote her books, not that of her father." Stuart is disgruntled over the time Gibson would need to edit the Laidlaw book, its dim prospect for sales, and what he saw as a breakdown in Macmillan's internal procedures for having manuscripts evaluated by persons other than the sponsoring editor.[29]

Whatever Stuart's misgivings, Gibson's approach worked. When she replied to his letter about placing *The McGregors* on the Macmillan fall list, Munro told him that she "had a bunch of stories on hand now, though I would still like a couple more for a collection." She reiterated that McGraw-Hill Ryerson wanted to hold her to the next-manuscript clause in her contract for *Something*, but added, "I don't think they should publish me and my agent knows this. I have told her that I would like Macmillan for my Canadian publisher, and that I have talked to you informally about this." For her part, Barber sent Gibson Munro's manuscript, entitled *The Beggar Maid*, on March 8. It contained a section of five "Rose" stories – "Royal Beatings," "Privilege," "Half a Grapefruit," "Wild Swans," and "Spelling." "Characters," the new title of "Pleistocene," was there too, but Barber indicated that it might be dropped. This section was followed by "Accident" and "Simon's Luck" (each of these titles was struck out, Barber promising a revision of the latter "which pulls the three parts together with a new ending"); then "Chaddeleys and Flemings," "The Moons of Jupiter," "Mischief," "Providence," and "The Beggar Maid." The last three were then about three different characters rather than a single person. In keeping with Stuart's preferred practice, the manuscript was read at Macmillan by Charlotte Weiss, who agreed with Gibson that it was excellent. By April 10 Gibson was formally authorized to make an offer for the book. He did, and it was accepted. Munro received a $25,000 advance against royalties on Canadian sales, with royalties at 10 per cent for the first 5,000 copies, 12.5 per cent up to 10,000, and 15 per cent after that. There was a straight 10 per cent on the Macmillan-New American Library paperback that would follow the hardcover edition. Macmillan's share of the advance was $15,000, NAL's $10,000.

By the end of April Gibson wrote Munro a three-page "Welcome to Macmillan" letter. "I know that you will be happy here, and promise that any disappointments that may be in the future will not be for a lack of care." Responding to the manuscript as a whole, he called it "marvelous," and predicted that "its publication will be without question the major literary event in Canada this year." He then suggests a new title taken from something one of the characters says in "Providence"; they might call the book *True Lies*. He also suggests that the Rose stories not be grouped together but rather arranged throughout the volume; and he wonders whether Munro would consider breaking "Chaddeleys and Flemings" in two, just at the point where the narrator throws the plate with lemon meringue pie at her husband.

Having read the manuscript and orally agreed on a contract for it, Gibson was brimming with its possibilities. He was looking to a chance to sit down with Munro and go over it, knowing that she was "still hard at work, obsessively polishing away." That was indeed her habit, but with this book Munro would make changes continually during its march toward publication, seemingly unable to leave it alone. Writing Gibson little more than a week after his welcoming letter to Munro, Barber told him that "Alice has now put the whole book in first person, removed three stories (Chaddeleys and Flemings, Moons of Jupiter and Accident) and rewritten Simon's Luck as the last of the adult Rose stories (only one woman, Rose, and Simon)." But for the first person and the addition of "Who Do You Think You Are?" the book as Barber described here is close to the one published, but there were many more changes to consider yet. Within the month, for instance, "The Moons of Jupiter" was back in. She closed her letter with an enticement: "If you'll call me one day next week, I'll tell you about the U.S. situation; it's looking extremely good."[30]

With Macmillan settled as her Canadian publisher, focus shifted to the American scene. And having prepared the ground, Barber was ready for serious negotiations with interested houses. Barber was keen on finding the right publisher and particularly the right editor, one who would work toward establishing Munro's reputation in ways compatible with what she herself had already accomplished through magazines. While numerous editors (including Kate Medina at Doubleday) and several publishers were interested in the book, Knopf, Norton, and Viking emerged as the leading bidders. Munro went down to New York to meet them. She and Barber accepted a bid from Norton of a fifteen-thousand-dollar advance. Barber has said that there is "a lot of work for an editor to do in house. They have to work with the marketing department, with publicity and promotion, and they have to be the in-house advocate of the book." This, she knew, was especially necessary with a collection of stories, one she was seeing as a first collection in the United States, McGraw-Hill's *Dance* notwithstanding. Sherry Huber, an editor at Norton, was keen on Munro's work; she seemed to fill the bill. The contract with Norton signed by mid-May, Munro sent Huber the manuscript as it was then.

Having looked at the manuscript during the bidding process, Huber had already talked to Munro about the Norton book's organization. Munro wrote Huber two letters on May 19 as she was sending the manuscript. The longer one, probably written first, outlines the organizational possibilities as Munro saw them. She had done all the stories in the first person and, reading them over after getting them back from her typist, she concluded that "the idea of connections did not work. It would make the book seem like a failed, fallen-apart novel. It has to stand as separate stories."

Who Do You Think You Are?/The Beggar Maid unquestionably has the most complex, and fraught, publication history of any of Munro's books. At the heart of the matter was the tension between a novel and a collection of stories, and then over the exact shape of the collection. Throughout this shaping – which continued throughout 1978 – a group of six stories the book ultimately contained were consistently seen as being about a single character, Rose, who emerged as the focus of the finished book. (These were "Royal Beatings," "Privilege," "Half a Grapefruit," "Wild Swans," "The Beggar Maid," and "Spelling.") Another story, "Characters," was about Rose but dropped. Six other stories (or seven since "Chaddeleys and Flemings" was, as Gibson had suggested, divided into two) were in play. As Munro indicated to Huber, she experimented in them with first- and third-person voice, trying each at various times, but the real question regarding these latter stories was whether they were about Rose or some other character, usually Janet, a writer (though at the suggestion of the *New Yorker* when "The Moons of Jupiter" was published there, she also appeared as a painter). Writing to Huber in her first May 19 letter, Munro further weighed various means of arranging the stories and arrived at "a solution very close to what you suggested in the first place. That is, a *Rose* section with all the stories that go so well together about Rose: Royal Beatings, Privilege, Grapefruit, Swans, Spelling, Beggar Maid (the position of *Spelling* is a bit of a problem). Then, a *Janet* section, with

Chaddeleys & Flemings, Mischief, Providence, Moons of Jupiter and a story I'm just finishing now, called 'Who Do You Think You Are?' This makes two almost equal parts." Macmillan wanted to use "Accident" set between the two sections and leave out "Simon's Luck."

When she wrote Huber again on May 19 she sets the Macmillan "Rose and Janet" structure out on a page, schematically indicating arrangement: first Rose stories in third person (arranged as above the first time), "Accident" in the middle, then the first-person Janet stories ("Chaddeleys and Flemings," "Who Do You Think You Are?" "Mischief," "Providence," "Moons of Jupiter"). Munro also tells her that she has sent her a revised version of "Simon's Luck," now in the first person but, after she had sent it, she decided to redo it as a Rose story in third person and so encloses it, asking Huber to copy it and send a copy to Gibson, giving her his address. At that point she saw it as replacing "Accident."[31]

Apart from Munro's inborn striving to achieve a satisfactory form for each of her stories, what all these changes indicate is a writer unusually willing to experiment with the shape her book is taking. She was also listening and responding to her editors' reactions. Because she was dealing with two editors, each of whom was responding differently to the book's various possibilities, Munro was moving throughout 1978 toward two very different books.

For its part, Macmillan pressed ahead. At Munro's suggestion, Gibson had arranged for Audrey Coffin, by then retired from McGraw-Hill Ryerson but still living near Toronto, to copy-edit Munro's book. Gibson's suggestion of "True Lies" as a title to replace "The Beggar Maid" did not succeed with Munro; for a time it looked as if the book would be called "Rose and Janet." That title was met within Macmillan by general "disgust and dismay"; one person there called it "about as exciting as toad shit on a warm rock." Following Munro's own suggestion, they decided on *Who Do You Think You Are?* She characterized that story, which she had just completed, as "slight but important" and suggested further that, as the title story, it "could come at the very end." Coffin delivered the copy-edited manuscript at the end of the first week of June. Within a week *Who Do You Think You Are?* went into Canadian production.

Just as that happened, Gibson was writing a letter to Virginia Barber – his first, actually – that began "Mea culpa." On June 9 a concerned Barber had written to him,

> I'm extremely unhappy with you and Macmillan. We are hearing from U.S. scouts about a book by Alice Munro called *Who Do You Think You Are?* which is to be published in the fall. We do not have a contract with you, and neither the American publisher nor I has heard that title. I'm sure you've discussed this with Alice, but she has an agent for good reasons. One of them is to have a central place where all the information about her work is collected. That's this office, and never do I want a repetition of the past where her works were sold abroad without her knowledge or consent, where different houses were working at cross purposes for the same volume, and so on. Please send us the contract and some information.

In his reply, Gibson was at pains to satisfy Barber on every point she raised and to describe in some detail just how he and Alice had been working together on the shape of *Who Do You Think You Are?* He wrote that the contract should be arriving momentarily if it had not already, that he and Alice had been on the phone a great deal, and that having weighed the various possible titles, they had decided on *Who*, the title Alice most wanted. He outlined the collection's structure – it is just as Munro described in her second letter of May 19, save that "Accident" has been dropped – and he indicated that in "Who Do You Think You Are?" it is revealed, in "a coup de theatre," that Janet is the author of the Rose stories. Thus for the dust jacket he and Alice had been "studying dozens of magic realist paintings in the hope of finding just the right one" to capture the Rose-Janet relation. Gibson ends, "I'm awfully sorry about my past sins of omission. Let's be friends."

This incident is important less for the specifics of what happened than for what it portended. In writing Gibson as directly as she did and by the manner in which she presented herself, Barber was asserting her necessary presence in Munro's affairs. Gibson readily acknowledged his understanding of her presence and indicated his willingness to establish an ongoing professional relation with her that respected her role. In retrospect, this exchange proved a formative moment in Munro's career. Through the making of *Who Do You Think You Are?/The Beggar Maid*, Barber, Gibson, and Munro were establishing for the first time the professional relations that have served Munro's work well in the succession of books she has published since, from *The Moons of Jupiter* in 1982 through *Runaway* in 2004. Gibson's comment that he and Munro had been looking for "just the right" magic realist painting is indicative, too, since as her Canadian editor he has justifiably prided himself on the choice of appropriate artworks for her dust jackets. Given the initial Rose-Janet relation in *Who*, they first settled on a detail from Christopher Pratt's *Young Woman in a Slip*, where the young woman is looking into a mirror. Rejecting it (though it was later used on the dust jacket of the Canadian edition of *Moons*), they ultimately opted for a detail of Ken Danby's *The Sunbather*. Gibson's covers, from this one to the painting of a dishevelled bed by Mary Pratt on the dust jacket of *Runaway*, have been capsule symbols of the elegant everyday found in Munro's writing.

ᴐᴑ

In his mea-culpa letter, Gibson also remarks that "Alice, as you perhaps know, is a little worried about what she hears of Norton's plans, and it would obviously be ideal for Norton and Macmillan to publish the same book. My hope is that when they see our galleys they will be immensely impressed and will wish to publish it."[32] Nothing of the kind happened, however. As Helen Hoy has written in the best account of the making of *Who Do You Think You Are?/The Beggar Maid*, "Norton was moving in another direction, making earnest attempts to turn the same material into a novel. As early as 20 June 1978 . . . the editors were assuming the publication of two quite different collections, with Sherry Huber resolute about excluding material extraneous to Rose's story." The difference between the two publishers, as Hoy details, was that Macmillan, unlike Norton, "was scrupulous not to pressure [Munro] to produce that more marketable commodity, a novel." While true enough with regard to the structure, Macmillan's deadline in late spring 1978 had pressed Munro into coming up with the two-part arrangement of Rose and Janet stories. With the book in production by mid-June, Munro's work with Huber – separate, through the mails and the phone, extending over the summer – involved what Hoy called "her more leisurely mulling over of the single-heroine version she was working on for Norton."

Recalling that work when she was interviewed by Hoy in 1988, Huber said that she had seen Munro's manuscript as connected short stories all along, that the other heroines – those who became Janet in the first Macmillan *Who* – were clearly Rose. She saw the question of whether the book was called a novel or short stories to be one of marketing. A book marketed as a novel in those days always sold considerably more than one presented as short stories. In notes dated June 11, 1978, Huber can be seen differentiating the Rose material ("Royal Beatings," "Privilege," "Half a Grapefruit," "Characters," "Wild Swans," "Spelling," and "The Beggar Maid") from the way Macmillan was structuring those stories and the others. She set "Mischief" and "Providence" apart, as Janet stories, and then "Simon's Luck" further apart with the notation that Munro thinks it is better in three sections. Huber was working on the manuscript over the summer, although her plan was to concentrate on it in September with the intention of getting it into production by the end of the month. After Munro reported that she was about to send another version of "Simon's Luck" along, Huber responded that they would begin connecting the stories through their details when Munro was ready. She had not received galleys from Gibson, but she did not see that as relevant to the book they were working on. In fact, Huber saw her project as a wholly separate book.

That separateness is borne out by the materials connected to it in the Calgary archives. On September 12 Huber wrote a long letter to Munro outlining her proposed organization, one she saw as a novel, she wrote, at least as much as *Lives*. The arrangement she envisioned corresponds to a manuscript table of contents of *The Beggar Maid* – that is its title there – with "chapters" listed as follows:

One: Royal Beatings
Two: Privilege
Three: Half a Grapefruit
Four: Characters
Five: Nerve
Six: The Beggar Maid
Seven: Mischief
Eight: Providence
Nine: True Enemies
Ten: Simon's Luck
Eleven: Spelling

But for the exclusion of "Characters," the addition of "Who Do You Think You Are?" and the reposition of "Spelling," this arrangement anticipates the final book. ("Nerve" was Huber's preferred title for "Wild Swans.") In its final guise, *The Beggar Maid* had stories, of course, not "chapters."

The Norton version of *The Beggar Maid* was written in the first person and, as Huber edited the manuscript, that did not change. She did propose, and Munro accepted, large-scale shifts from present tense to past, and Huber paid particular attention to the endings of each story. The chapter listed as "True Enemies," for instance, is actually the final scene of "The Beggar Maid" – when Rose happens upon Patrick in the Toronto airport years after their marriage ended and he makes a horrid face at her – moved back and treated as a separate unit. In another instance, Huber proposed the deletion of the last section of "Privilege," the part beginning "The school changed with the war." Throughout, she pressed to lessen the sense of stories ending so that the reader moved smoothly into the next chapter. To Hoy, Huber commented that Munro was easy about the changes to the ending. When she came to draft descriptive copy for the book's dust jacket flap, Huber used language that made clear her novelistic strategy:

> *The Beggar Maid* is the story of Rose, in her journey from childhood to womanhood, a trip that takes her from an

ingrown, rude life in a small town, to college, marriage, motherhood, and later a separate peace as an actress. It is an *immense*
journey, a painful journey, which Rose makes alone, armed with
an unwavering, penetrating sense of other people's foibles and
sins. She is shy but ambitious, and gifted with a ribald, humorous sense of appreciation for the "luck" in her life.

When Munro wrote to Gibson with the suggestion of "Who Do
You Think You Are?" as a better title for the book, she also asked him,
"What do you think of its revelation that Janet has written the Rose
stories?" To Barber, he reported that he was quite happy with this revelation. But as the book proceeded through production over the
summer and as Huber reshaped the Rose material she envisioned, it
turned out that Munro was not satisfied with the revelation herself. After
hearing that Huber liked the new "Simon's Luck," which she had sent in
August, Munro wrote to her on September 16 that she "was in a frenzied
state here, trying to get" Macmillan to pull *Who* "and print a Rose book
with the new *Simon's Luck.*" Writing to Huber again on the nineteenth,
this time from the Macmillan offices in Toronto, Munro explained what
she realized and what she did about it:

> After you said you liked *Simon's Luck* I got more and more
> convinced that the series of Rose stories was the only way to do
> this book and that the Macmillan book was a dreadful awkward
> waste of good material and I *couldn't* let them do it. (I couldn't
> have reached this decision any earlier because I didn't have
> *Simon's Luck.*) Upshot of this was that I came down here and
> made my case. The book is already at the printers pub date Nov.
> 18th and they daren't get it out any later. So, I said, what about
> leaving the first half – Royal Beatings to the Beggar Maid,
> intact, and reprinting the second half, as follows: Mischief,
> Providence, Simon's Luck, Spelling, all in *third person* (Rose) to
> jibe with the first half. They said they could only do it with the
> same title (*Who Do You Think You Are?*) because the cover is
> designed and in production. Okay, I said, I'll re-write *Who Do*

You Think? as a Rose story, and I did, and its good. So here's the book I asked them to do.

Munro then listed the contents as subsequently published, with the notation "All Rose and in third person," and continued, "This is like your book except that it omits *Characters* and adds *Who Do You Think*, and is in 3rd person."[33]

Munro's admission to being in "a frenzied state" was probably written on the same afternoon, a Saturday, she called Gibson at home. He recalls returning from the store, bags in hand, and setting them on the counter to answer the phone. Munro announced herself, asked after him, and inquired as to the progress of *Who Do You Think You Are?* He replied, "It's at the printer, it's all done. You and I don't have to do another thing, we should have finished copies before very long." He recalls her replying, "'Oh dear, because I've been looking at it and I think I want to change'" the Janet section. Then Gibson got into a "frenzied state" himself. Before they got off the phone, though, they agreed that on Monday morning he would stop the presses and Munro would come into the office to explain what she had in mind. Gibson recalled that those in charge at Macmillan "were very scared . . . because this was our main title for fall, and a huge part of our budget was based on that book getting out and selling," so the prospect of a delay caused by pulling it off the presses was nothing they relished, especially since it was already coming out, in November, dangerously late in the season.

As she makes clear in her second September 19 letter to Huber, Munro knew just what she was doing and was quite prepared to pay the costs involved. When she got into Toronto on the morning of the eighteenth, she met with Macmillan staff and explained what she wanted to do. The reorganization involved the omission of three stories ("Chaddeleys and Flemings: Connection," "The Stone in the Field," and "The Moons of Jupiter"), the revision of "Mischief," "Providence," and "Who Do You Think You Are?" into Rose stories, the moving of "Spelling" to a new position, and the addition of the new "Simon's Luck," a revised Rose story that was the cause of all the commotion after Munro had heard from Huber. At the meeting on the eighteenth it was decided that Gibson would read the new manuscript that morning and, at two o'clock, he would tell his colleagues "whether or not [he] thought it was worth going through all the trouble and expense." While he was at work, the people in production would investigate the exact costs. He read the new manuscript – as far as it was, since there was further work to do – and decided that the changes were worth their trouble. So Macmillan set about the work involved to make, in effect, a new book. Reporting on these changes to his colleagues at Macmillan, knowing full well that what they were doing would cause a stir, Gibson wrote that "a very good manuscript" had been made a "very very good" manuscript.

Continuing her explanation of all this to Huber, Munro wrote:

> As is, the cost of re-setting, with continual overtime to meet the same pub. date, is nearly $2500, which I have to pay. I am naturally unhappy about this but there was no other way I could get them to do it and I knew the book they were going to get out would do me harm. They said it would sell on my name (true) and they would not gain or make back their costs by making it a better book artistically. So if I wanted it, I had to pay. All this had to be decided at once because we had to get the altered mss. to the printers *today* if the schedule even with overtime is going to work. So I didn't even call Ginger. I felt we had to go ahead. Worked all night and in an hour or two the new one will be ready to go.
>
> Very tough decision but I am relieved – They have a very handsome cover.

Munro also mentions to Huber that at one point in the negotiations with Macmillan

> Norton's doing the same book would virtually be a condition of their giving in to me – even at my expense, but I of course have nothing to do with that. I do like having *Characters* out and *Who Do You Think* in, otherwise I have no preference. . . .

> Anyway we've now got two books that are very close and I am immensely happier though poorer.

Munro's final sentence, doubtless quite heartfelt at the time, proved in later years to carry an ironic burden: "Never again will I write two versions of anything."

Munro's estimate on the cost was high. The production person at Macmillan told Gibson the cost would be $2,210, but in the end they needed just 99 reset pages, not the 120 originally estimated, so the cost to Munro was $1,864.08. Macmillan was careful to take this from the second half of Munro's advance, due on publication, rather than send her a bill. Internally, Gibson pointed out that the three omitted stories, already in type, amounted to a subsidy of Munro's next book, something they should remember when they contracted for it. Macmillan published *Who Do You Think You Are?* on November 11. And on the Friday of the week that saw all the flurry of changes undertaken, Macmillan sent Munro a contract for Robert Laidlaw's *The McGregors* for 1979 publication. Macmillan clearly knew what they had in Munro and, despite the hard-edged economic realities of publishing in Canada, acted in ways intended to make her welcome and happy.

Looking back at this episode, Gibson put a positive spin on that process – "The printers were quite thrilled to be involved. This had never happened, and they realized they were part of literary history. Because they knew this was an important book they did amazing things. In the end we only lost about ten days in the whole process." A good book, he added, "is going to be around for a long, long time."34

The large wrinkles in this book's publication history were not yet over. Sometime in late September or early October Huber had left Norton. In October Gibson commented to Barber that he was "sorry to hear about Sherry's departure, since 'orphaned' authors are so vulnerable to being over-looked." Barber, for her part, was not prepared to have Munro's book left adrift without an advocating editor at Norton. She approached Robert Gottlieb, the head editor at Alfred A. Knopf, who was among those in the original bidding. Given a fresh opportunity, he took it. Barber withdrew the book from Norton.

By early November Barber was sending Munro the Knopf contract and, at the same time, soliciting her comments on Huber's work with her at Norton, since the editor was then looking for another job. Barber reminded Munro that she had told her Huber had made a "substantial contribution" to the book. As Huber was the person whose reaction to the revised "Simon's Luck" prompted Munro to pull *Who Do You Think You Are?* from the press and reorganize it, that assessment might qualify as a radical understatement.

At Knopf, Munro's new editor was Ann Close. In her first letter to Munro, written two days after *Who Do You Think You Are?* was published, she announced that she herself might be leaving Knopf ("You seem to have run into a batch of peripatetic editors") and addressed what they would do if she did. Close never did leave Knopf, though. With her arrival, the third member of Munro's editorial book team was in place. Along with Barber and Gibson, Close has been overseeing the publication of Munro's books ever since – the ninth such shared volume being *Runaway.* The Knopf contract for the book completed (and that with Norton cancelled), Close set out to see Munro's first separate book publication in the United States on booksellers' shelves. Gibson still hoped that Munro's American publisher would use Macmillan's version and sent Close and Gottlieb copies of *Who* to that end, offering to assist Knopf should they decide to offset from Macmillan's book. Close was able to choose between it and the Norton first-person version (she also had Norton's plans for the cover) and she also had at hand yet another rewrite of "Simon's Luck." By early December she and Gottlieb had decided to print for themselves, wanting a larger typeface than Macmillan's and a more appealing overall design. By mid-January they, with Barber, had decided that *The Beggar Maid* was their preferred title; informing Munro about their thinking, Close wrote that "if you feel strongly (or even mildly) in favor of [the Canadian title], that is what we'll use." As she was deciding what to do with Munro, Close watched the book's progress in Canada by means of the reviews Gibson provided.

Acknowledging the books he sent and the help he offered in his first letter to her, Close commented that Munro "seems very happy with the success of the book in Canada. I only hope we can do as well for her next fall."[35]

❧

Who Do You Think You Are? was certainly doing *very* well in Canada. In a talk he gave to Macmillan's sales people as *Who* was imminent, Gibson maintained that "every Canadian critic asked to name Canada's best writers invariably includes Alice Munro on the list." He concluded that "this is a very, very big book – we're lucky to have it, and we're going to see it high on the best-seller list." The book's reviews verified this prediction. They were quite positive overall, and sales were brisk; the initial printing of 8,500 copies was exhausted by early January so Macmillan arranged a second one of 2,500. *Who* was initially announced at $9.95 but, just after Munro's changes were made and the book was back in production, Macmillan hedged its bet and raised the price to $10.95.

For her part, Munro embarked on a cross-country tour that took her to Toronto, Winnipeg, Edmonton, Calgary, Vancouver, and Ottawa by the end of the month. She also visited one or two other smaller Ontario cities. Gibson reported to Close, "Even her shyness about promoting the books seems to be wearing off." Munro had specifically asked not to do readings or bookstore signings, limiting herself to interviews. Always one to husband her energies, Munro did no more than four a day. Arranging this schedule, she avoided Victoria altogether, although she did break the tour while in British Columbia to visit with Andrea and friends. At her suggestion, this publicity tour emphasized her involvement in the anti-censorship dispute. As Gibson wrote to his colleagues when the publicity for *Who* was being planned, "In the course of promoting this book, she would be glad to become a spokesman for the anti-censorship forces." They would, of course, "want to carefully consider the implications of identifying Alice and this book with the cause of anti-censorship."[36]

The first reviews appeared in October. Two of these – in *Books in Canada* and *Quill & Quire* – were based on the advance proof of the "Rose and Janet" version of the book. In the former, Wayne Grady noted that, compared to Munro's earlier work, she "still works the same raw material, but she writes now in a minor, sadder key, and the result is a novel of literary as well as nostalgic value." After he describes Rose and Janet, he writes that "there is a peculiar two-way mirror effect at the end of the book, a faint Nabokian twist, when a Dalgleish woman asks Janet: 'That Rose you write about. Is she supposed to be you?'" The reviewer in *Quill & Quire* wished that Munro would "expand her horizons" by taking up different material and moving "on to somewhere else." The Janet stories "are not, on the whole, as engaging as the Rose collection," a small confirmation of Munro's decision to rearrange the book.

Widely reported, Munro's changes were mentioned in passing but most reviewers focused on the book itself. William French in the *Globe and Mail* observes that some of these individual stories, appearing as they did "isolated and out of context" in magazines, "raised doubts about where [Munro] was going, after the great artistic success of her first three books. They seemed to lack the cohesion and vision of her earlier work." The book, however, makes clear that "there was no need to worry": "arranged in chronological order," the stories "come together beautifully, with unexpected unity." This book "is stamped with the same seal of quality as Munro's earlier books." There is, he added, no other "contemporary Canadian writer as good as Munro in conveying the mood and texture of Ontario's small towns in the three decades to the end of the fifties." Gina Mallet in the *Toronto Star* focuses on the payphone windfall in "Providence," writing that "the lucky strike briefly releases" Rose, who "'wasn't at the mercy of past or future, or love, or anybody.'" In the stories Munro "continually surprises. The drifting nostalgia, the exquisitely turned phrases do not produce a jeweled façade, they are inextricably part of a commentary on a rough, crude, earthy evocation of Ontario. It's like seeing a perfectly manicured hand with mud under the fingernails." In the *Ottawa Journal* Claire Harrison wrote that "these stories are stripped of the romanticism that characterized Munro's earlier works. They display control and polish along with a gripping sense of immediacy – an outstanding collection by one of Canada's outstanding writers." Tim Struthers in the *London Free Press* saw *Who* as "much more complex and mature than Munro's *Lives of Girls and Women* (1971), despite a superficial resemblance between the two books." "Simon's Luck," he added, is "possibly Munro's most overpowering story to date."37

There is a sense that the reviewers of *Who* felt the heft of Munro's work as a body. Summary comments strove to offer deeper and more literary judgements. In *Maclean's*, Mark Abley wrote, "The humor in Alice Munro's new collection of fiction has a trenchant, bittersweet edge. Good times don't last long. Love is always tangled up with competing emotions: loneliness, pity, lust. Fun is usually had at the expense of somebody else. Munro is a master of mixed feelings." *Who* "is deeper, wiser, more plaintive"; its very title proclaims that "even the fact of identity must be probed, tested, thought over." In her work "nothing, including the truth, can make us free. The only triumph is the blessing of understanding, a mixed blessing, like them all." Describing the author herself, Brian Bartlett in the Montreal *Gazette* saw *Who* as "further proof of her lavish talent, but it also raises questions about a severity in her vision." Citing what he calls her "fierce humor," he points out a description of the student who "attacks Rose" at a party "with obscene insults: 'He was white and brittle-looking, desperately drunk. He had probably been brought up in a gentle home, where people talked about answering Nature's call and blessed each other for sneezing.' The brilliant sharpness of that sarcasm has seldom been seen in Munro." Linda Leitch, in the University of Guelph *Ontarian*, offered an encompassing assessment that still holds; she notes "a deliberation and calculation . . . that is often overlooked in the critical praise of her particular brand of kitchen-sink realism. Beneath the deceptive simplicity of her immensely readable prose lie the marks of a conscientious craftsman; beyond the astonishing precision of detail with which Munro presents the 'true lies' of her fiction is a vision and scope that transcends regionalism, feminism and nationalism." Recalling that

Munro won a Governor General's Award for *Dance*, Leitch concluded: "I think there's little doubt that she'll be receiving another." Writing in the Newfoundland *Evening Telegram*, Helen Porter maintained that Munro "is at least as unsparing of her leading character as she is anyone else in the book." Noting the growth of Munro's reputation in the United States, Porter asserted that "Alice Munro is one of the best writers of fiction in the world."

There were a few dissenters. Some reviewers found West Hanratty to be an unattractive place populated by grotesque characters. Writing in the annual "Letters in Canada" feature of the *University of Toronto Quarterly*, Sam Solecki placed the book in the context of "feminist fiction of the last two decades" but regretted Munro's "failure to go much beyond what she had already achieved in that mode in *Lives of Girls and Women* and in her earlier stories." He took issue with Munro's characterization of Rose's husband, Patrick Blatchford, and related this to a "failure to create fully realized central characters – and her emphasis has always been on character above all other aspects of the story – [which] prevents the book from [being] a worthy successor to *Lives of Girls and Women*."

Reviews of *Who* are also characterized by comments on specific stylistic matters. Gerald Noonan in the *Canadian Book Review Annual* takes up Munro's "most flamboyant phrasing," what he calls "the excrement vision in winter," pointing to an image in "Privilege" where the reader finds "framed by the hole of the outdoor toilet; the residual deposits lie glazed with ice, 'preserved as if under glass, bright as mustard or grimy as charcoal.'" Gordon Powers in the *Ottawa Revue* notes that most of the stories in *Who* have appeared in U.S. magazines "and a number of Munro's fans have found this worrisome, as if there is something unseemly about fiction in publications with a larger circulation than Tamarack Review." Michael Taylor, in *The Fiddlehead*, uses his review as an occasion to address the growing, progressive wider appeal such magazine publication implies: "What we have in Alice Munro is a fine, serious writer who attracts readers and publishers from a wide spectrum without her having to do anything drastic either to her style or to her seriousness in the process. She neither writes down for *Toronto Life* nor up for *The New Yorker*." Taylor takes up a key instance, Munro's use of the phrase "royal beating," and after quoting it, writes, "This, it seems to me, is Alice Munro writing at her best and most distinctive, seizing upon the buried richness of the literal rendering of a dead metaphor, bringing it to vivid life, modulating beautifully between its incipient imaginative royalty ('and the blood came leaping out like banners') and its crassly ordinary immediacy ('You take that look off your face')."38

Here was an author, reviewers and readers were realizing, whose writing would endure for a long, long time. In *Saturday Night*, Urjo Kareda commented that Munro "has the ability to isolate the one detail that will evoke the rest of the landscape," and that the collection builds "a rueful understanding of how hard we must struggle, and against what odds, for the little that is actually *possible*." This is because "Alice Munro has Chekhov's eye – and there is no higher praise – for the way in which we ourselves provide the blade which slits the thin, protective partition between what we think we would like to be and what in fact we are capable of being." In conclusion, Kareda wrote, "Alice Munro's instinct about the way in which we translate ourselves, the routes of fear or vanity or self-deception by which we allow ourselves to be deflected from the road we long ago mapped out, is what gives her writing its urgency and heartbeat. Her stories are the subtlest summonings to reconsider our lives. Their effect reminded me of Gorky's description of Chekhov's presence: 'Everyone unwittingly felt an inner longing to be simpler, more truthful, to be more himself.'" In much the same vein, in the *Winnipeg Free Press* David Williamson asked whether Munro was "the best Canadian writer." "It is difficult to say how very good these stories are without becoming repetitious," he wrote. "Perhaps I had best put it this way: my last reviewing assignment was *The Stories of John Cheever*. I found that book excellent and said that it confirmed Mr. Cheever's place as the best American short story writer. Immediately afterward, I have turned to this new group of stories by Alice Munro without feeling any let-down in quality – much of the same shrewd insight and sheer story-telling ability is there. Her stories are just as good as John Cheever's."

♪

When Gibson wrote to Barber telling her he had sent copies of *Who Do You Think You Are?* to Close and Gottlieb at Knopf, he was already envisioning Munro's second Governor General's Award. His hope proved true in March 1979. Margaret Laurence chaired the selection committee. When he wrote congratulating Munro on this award, Robert J. Stuart at Macmillan commented, "You were absolutely right in making the changes you did in your manuscript! Although we had to do some handsprings in order to bring the book out in the fall, the efforts were certainly worth it." Stuart also noted the reviews *Who* had received, writing, "Few of our books have been praised so highly." *Who* was selected Book of the Year by the Canadian Booksellers Association, and the Book-of-the-Month Club in Canada selected it as well. Having done so, they bought a thousand copies to distribute to their members at the standard – and very deep – discount customary at the time. Learning of this, Barber questioned Macmillan's action ("Book-of-the-Month Club isn't any poor relation") and, while she was not happy about this since it was an exception to Munro's contract, she went along with the arrangement. This incident illustrates that Barber was looking out for her author's financial well-being. Because the U.S. book club did not get equivalent discounts, Macmillan was led to rethink these arrangements in the future.

In mid-February 1979, Barber told Gibson she was pleased to learn that he was considering work by another of her authors, John Metcalf, and asked for reviews of *Who* ("Knopf wants them; England wants them; I want them") and more copies of the Canadian edition of the book. "And there's Alice, about to be swept away by a prize to Australia. She needs time to *write*. Tell people to leave her alone." Barber here is characteristically both light-hearted and serious. *Who* had created a notable fuss around Munro in Canada that was quite evidently growing, something Barber could only delight in; at the same time, she realized that such activities were keeping her writer from the writing time she needed. Munro's trip to Australia – arranged as part of the Canada-Australia prize she had won the year before – took her away from March 5 to 30, 1979, for a round of meetings, discussions, dinners, and interviews. She was, however, back home in time to accept the Governor General's Award in Ottawa on April 4 from Governor General Edward Schreyer. During April Robert Laidlaw's *The McGregors: A Novel of an Ontario Pioneer Family*, with an introduction by Harry Boyle, was published by Macmillan. Too late, though, for Mary Etta Laidlaw, who died in February. Although there was no author to promote it, Laidlaw's book was widely reviewed and praised. Munro's "The Stone in the Field" appeared in the April 1979 issue of *Saturday Night*; after it did, that story won the McClelland & Stewart Award for Fiction, a National Magazine Award. As 1979 progressed and Alfred A. Knopf prepared to publish its *The Beggar Maid* that September, and Allen Lane its edition in the United Kingdom the following April, Munro's writing was reaching out to an ever-widening audience.[39]

When Close wrote to Munro explaining her preference for *The Beggar Maid* title over *Who Do You Think You Are?* she noted the difference between the two national markets. She wrote that Macmillan's choice with its recognizable image on the jacket is "a little sassy," that "it hit just the right note of national pride and recognition. Here we need to establish you as a Canadian, yes, but mainly as a writer of distinction." Establishing writers in just this way was what Alfred A. Knopf – the publisher who had founded the company in 1915 – was about, the literary trade publishing of well-made books by distinctive writers. He had done as much with numerous writers himself, among them one of Munro's admitted influences, Willa Cather, and the house still saw this project as its mandate. Not surprisingly, then, *The Stories of John Cheever* was a Knopf book, and Close sent Munro a copy of it when she sent this letter. Thanking Close and agreeing to *The Beggar Maid* as her title in the United States, Munro called the Cheever book "the very thing I most wanted." David Williamson was right to connect Cheever's book with Munro's in his *Winnipeg Free Press* review: writers of distinction, and writers from the *New Yorker*.

Part of Knopf's introductory strategy involved manufacturing and producing its own version of Munro's text, making a book in keeping with the firm's historically meticulous methods. Hence, Gibson's hope that Knopf's book be the same as Macmillan's went nowhere. Knopf did, though, cut up a copy of *Who* to use for typesetting. While such matters lie mainly within the realm of editorial scholarship, such a fact is significant in that, along with the work done on the book by Norton, Knopf's decision to reset the book allowed Munro a chance to revisit her material one more time. While most of the textual differences between *Who* and *The Beggar Maid* are syntactical and stylistic, there are some that go further. "Providence," for example, has a different ending in each book.

Knopf had inherited the preliminary work on the cover that Norton had done with the Edward Burne-Jones painting mentioned by Patrick to Rose in "The Beggar Maid" (there the girl was "meek and voluptuous, with her shy white feet. The milky surrender of her, the helplessness and gratitude"). They decided to use it, *King Cophetua and the Beggar Maid*, on the jacket, giving the book a subdued, medieval look, implying a chivalrous romance. One American reviewer confessed to being misled by this cover; seeking "a lurid bodice-ripper or two," she rummaged through the paper's rejected review copies looking for "a deliberate retreat from reality." With *The Beggar Maid*, though "prepared for blood-and-thunder romance," she found herself reading "a marvelous book that had been wrongly rejected – victimized by its hopelessly romantic-looking cover." A source of differentiation throughout Munro's career has been the look of Knopf's books as opposed to Gibson's; it began with this first shared project and has continued since, though only on that first occasion did Munro's American publishers opt for a different title.[40]

The Beggar Maid was published by Knopf on September 28, 1979, with advance praise from John Gardner, Margaret Laurence, Ross Macdonald, and Joyce Carol Oates. In August, the *Kirkus Reviews* had pronounced it a "bountifully compassionate and moving book," noting that some of its stories had been in the *New Yorker*. Julia O'Faolain, whose novel *No Country for Young Men* would be competing against *The*

Beggar Maid as finalist for the Booker Prize, wrote an advance review for the *New York Times Book Review*. She began with the Burne-Jones cover image, writing that Patrick is attracted to Rose as a romantic ideal, that as in the painting he sees in her "qualities she hasn't got." She also noted too that Munro's "humor here is under restraint. . . . Deft with social detail, she anchors her people firmly to class and place and commands the classic realist's strengths: moral seriousness, compassion, a sense of the particular." In this book, Munro offered "the two great, mutually enhancing pleasures of fiction. The first is the sense that a writer has seen through the muddle of experience to an imminent significance and presented us with it: a conviction that things must be thus and not otherwise." The second is that "an apparently conclusive truth may not be true after all."

Other reviews followed suit. In the *New Republic*, Jack Beatty wrote that "the impressive Canadian writer Alice Munro has combined the form of the short story with the narrative interest of the novel to provide an unusual kind of literary pleasure." Like Noonan, he also wrote that "the look of turds frozen in piles of snow in the crumbling lavatory of Rose's school" is one he will not forget. Beatty maintained that "everything in these stories is a mix of better and worse, of gain and loss, of misery and happiness. Moving, hard, lucid, they throw a 'cloudy, interesting, problematical light on the world.'" Oates, whose review for *Mademoiselle* was published before the book's appearance, calls it "a considerable accomplishment" and writes that its "technique is sometimes jarring, but often dramatically powerful. . . . [Rose] is drawn back obsessively to Hanratty, as if in pursuit of her own soul. But she doesn't find it – the question once posed to her by an officious teacher, 'who do you think you are?' has no answer."

As it happened, Munro's collection was published concurrently with Mavis Gallant's *From the Fifteenth District* from Random House. As a result, the two Canadians were sometimes yoked together in reviews. Munro had blurbed Gallant's book for Macmillan when it was published in Canada. Yet since American reviewers were scarcely able to say anything sensible about Canadian contexts, they usually looked to other matters. Ted Morgan, writing in the *Saturday Review*, differentiated in a review essay between "women writers" and "Writers Who Happen to Be Women," as his title has it. Critiquing the feminism then current, he saw more in Gallant's accomplishment, but of Munro's Rose he wrote, aptly, "She is immensely likable, and there is gallantry in her willingness to take risks, open herself to the chance of love, and measure herself against what she was and fled from." For Morgan, "Munro is as good as John Updike in chronicling the hesitations and sidesteps of adultery, its secret rules and regulations, its Geneva conventions, and the dozens of practical details that must be dealt with to make the grand passion possible." Also noting Munro's relation to ideological feminism, Thomas R. Edwards in the *New York Review of Books* writes that Rose's "experiences are her own and no one else's. For this, as well as for its quiet refusal ever to say more than is needed, Munro's book seems to me very fine."

The stories in *The Beggar Maid*, Paul Wilner wrote in the *Village Voice*, "take on the deliberate air of fairy tales" and, like several other reviewers, he was drawn to a particular line from "Half a Grapefruit": "We sweat for our pretensions." Drawn particularly to "the incidental revelations of character and setting along the way," Wilner concluded that in Munro's work "the princess steps forth epiphanized in the mundane garb of everyday life, no less beautiful for showing her sweat." Beginning her review by noting the "small but growing cult of admirers" Munro has attracted, Dorothy Rabinowitz in the *Wall Street Journal* focused most sharply on "Simon's Luck," "which may well be the finest story in the collection. In that story, Munro shows that she knows 'that the rest of life is not incidental to, but competitive with, love.'" Rose's actions in "Simon's Luck," and in other stories too, demonstrate that. Munro offers "the world as one recognizes it: One in which hope, however absurd and frequently disappointed, is always resurgent. It is, moreover, a world brought to life in thick, sensual detail":

> The way things look, Mrs. Munro knows, is the way things are; she knows that surfaces speak for reality as much as do the hidden depths of things, and she puts that knowledge to better use than any writer of fiction working today.

How does one know when one is in the grip of art – of a major talent? One feels it in the assurance, the sensibility behind every line of a work; one knows its presence as much from what is withheld as from what is given, or explained.

Seeing Rose's life as "one long attempt to belong, to make connections, to bridge gulfs," Johanna Higgins in the *Lone Star Book Review* paid especial attention to Flo, Rose's stepmother, noting that whenever Rose "thinks of Flo or recalls her stories, the language evokes Flo's country dignity, strong idiom, and enviable certainties. . . . Such prose reflects Flo's secure, nailed-down life. Economically and culturally deprived, she nevertheless is not burdened by anxiety or ambiguity. When she finishes a story, there is no more to be said or thought." As these comments suggest, Higgins was particularly attuned to Munro's treatment of class, and especially the differences between places like West Hanratty and Hanratty. Other reviewers took up the more evident contrast between Rose and Patrick Blatchford, a department store heir and Rose's husband for a time, but Higgins sharply analyzed the deeper relation between Rose's class and her character.[41]

Reading these reviews in their order of appearance, one is struck by their difference in tone and focus from Canadian reviews. While Rabinowitz articulated most clearly the case for Munro as a major talent, the American reviews consistently show that reviewers saw her as "a writer of distinction." And while they noted Munro's reputation in Canada, the American (and the next spring, the British) reviewers of *The Beggar Maid* focused on the range of imaginative effects in the text they read. The reviewer in the *Washington Post* called it "a civilized pleasure," *Nation* saw in it "the best stories of the year," and the reviewer in the *New York Times* wrote that "there's hardly a story in this volume that doesn't glow." *Ms.* reminded its readers that "Privilege" first appeared in its pages and called the lot "beautifully written stories." Virtually alone in her slightly negative assessment, Nancy Gail Reed in the *Christian Science Monitor* notes that some of the stories do not stand up well alone and "vast jumps in space and time often leave the reader with a kind of literary jet-lag."[42]

Writing to Munro in June 1980, Close sent her some late reviews and commented that "although, as always, we would have been happy with more sales, etc., we are all extremely pleased with the reception of *The Beggar Maid*. People still approach me about it, always with great praise." Knopf had every reason to be pleased since they certainly had accomplished their aim: Munro had been introduced to the American market as "a writer of distinction." The reviews attested as much. The book was selected as an alternate by the Book-of-the-Month Club in the United States, and the American Library Association chose it as a notable book of the year. But as Close indicated, its sales were disappointing. By March 1981, *The Beggar Maid* had sold just under four thousand copies, earning back about a third of the advance Knopf had paid.

In London, Allen Lane published its edition of *The Beggar Maid* in the spring of 1980. As in the United States, reviews were mostly direct and positive. Alan Hollinghurst in the *New Statesman* begins with the book's Governor General's Award and its title in Canada, saying that it "appears here under the less happy title of *The Beggar Maid* and in a vulgar pictorial wrapper. But it is important not to be put off: it is a work of great brilliance and depth." For him, "Munro's power of analysis, of sensations and thoughts, is almost Proustian in its sureness, and though her forms are scrupulously small, she accumulates an extremely moving sense of the *length* of life." He noted also that "the fragmented structure of the book offers a sophisticated metaphor for the mind's preferred habit of seeing life in fictionally distinct episodes." Another reviewer called *The Beggar Maid* a "gentle, observant book – we should hear a lot more from Alice Munro in the future." Marsaili Cameron, in the *Gay News*, wrote that "tales of past and present are interwoven with immense skill in this book; it combines literary virtuosity, wit and searing insights." In *Blackwood's Magazine*, Andrew Lothian wrote that Munro "tells her story vividly and economically, subtly varying her style of narrative to suit her characters' changing circumstances. This is a work of sharply accurate observation, often funny, always affecting – in the end a convincing portrait of a contemporary woman."

About the only negative voice was that of Eva Tucker in the *Hampstead and Highgate Express*, who wrote that it was a surprise to her that *The Beggar Maid* "has got on to the short list" for the Booker-McConnell prize for the best novel of the year. Tucker summarizes the book and concludes, "When Rose makes it to college and attracts the attentions of a well-heeled young man, the novel deteriorates into provincial dreariness." Tucker's condescending view notwithstanding, the Booker nomination was probably the best indication of how the book really did in Great Britain. Judges for the prize were charged to come up with a list of five finalists but they were unable to agree, so they accepted a list with seven titles – *The Beggar Maid* was one of those contending for the final spots on the list. The real competition that year was between Anthony Burgess's *Early Powers* and William Golding's *Rites of Passage*. Golding's book won, but Munro's having been a finalist at all was tribute enough – *The Beggar Maid*, as it turned out, came in fourth. As story collections, none of her subsequent books has been eligible for the Booker Prize since then. Notwithstanding the nomination, sales of the Allen Lane hardback were disappointing (1,300) though the paperback did well enough (11,000 – both by April 1982).

ॐ

When *The McGregors* by Robert Laidlaw was published it was reviewed by Timothy Findley, another Ontarian whose writing sharply defined his own deeply felt cultural inheritances. Offering an appreciative analysis of Laidlaw's book, he begins his concluding paragraph writing,

> In one of Alice Munro's best stories, Home, there is, I think, the most graceful and tactful evocation ever put on paper of how the generations part from one another. Sadly, ineluctably, with all the knives "so carefully applied" but so incisively wielded, a daughter deserts her ailing father and his second wife and the scene of her childhood. She abandons all three – even the place – to their integrity and goes away to claim her own. As an elegy in prose, it is beyond compare. I do hope Robert Laidlaw, now dead, had lived to read that story; in it, through fiction, his daughter makes her break with the past that is implicit in her father's book without destroying that past.

Writing in 1979, Findley had no way of knowing what Munro would produce in the years to come. "Home," it turned out, is really more of a preamble to her actual incomparable "elegy in prose" for her father, "Working for a Living." She was working on that elegy herself just as Findley was reviewing her father's novel. And though "Home" may have looked to Findley as if Munro was engaging in some act of desertion or rejection, nothing could be further from the truth. "Home" was not desertion, "Home" was an affirmation of the complex personal and cultural connections embodied by that word. In October 1973, when its events occurred, "Home" was staring Munro full in the face with a power really only felt by a returned native. Writing "Home" that month, Alice Munro embarked on an imaginative journey that took her ever more deeply into the cultural inheritances of her home place. When she returned to Huron County, she began the imaginative and textual progression that proved the great fact of her career. Back in Ontario, she moved from "Home" to "Places at Home" to *Who Do You Think You Are?* to *The Beggar Maid* toward *The Moons of Jupiter.* Returning home, she became Alice Munro.[43]

PART THREE

Being Alice Munro

7

Feeling Like Rilke's Editor

Making **The Moons of Jupiter, The Progress of Love, Friend of My Youth,** *1980–1990*

Connection. That was what it was all about. The cousins were a show in themselves, but they also provided a connection. A connection with the real, and prodigal, and dangerous, world. They knew how to get on in it, they had made it take notice.
– "Chaddeleys and Flemings: 1. Connection"

What are those times that stand out, clear patches in your life – what do they have to do with it? They aren't exactly promises. Breathing spaces. Is that all?
– "Circle of Prayer"

All this acceptance comes as rather a shock to someone so well schooled in surviving without it.
– Alice Munro, 1986

In September 1980 Douglas Gibson wrote to Munro, who was then in Australia as a visiting writer at the University of Queensland. "Brisbane, for crying out loud," he wrote, "well, stone the bleeding crows, as your students no doubt say. . . . Ginger delighted me by mentioning the five stories just sold to the New Yorker [and] the exciting idea of a book fictionally based around your parents." This letter's real significance lay in Gibson's subsequent words: "But keep in mind the assurance that I gave you some years ago. I'm not going to pester you to write novels. I'm perfectly pleased to go on publishing collections of Alice Munro stories – related or unrelated – as long as you keep writing them." This assurance, first offered to Munro when he began wooing her to Macmillan, is one he has maintained throughout their relationship.

Replying from Australia with a jovial apology – "Didn't I tell you I was going into exile?" – Munro reported that she did "have enough stories for a book now," and that she was working on the first draft of something that might prove "a more held-together piece of work (I avoid saying 'novel')." This may well have been what an Australian journalist described a few months later as "a novel tracing three generations of women"; it evolved, probably, into "The Progress of Love." In addition to the *New Yorker* stories, she also mentioned "a long Memoir I wrote about my father, which I think is pretty good, but I think it should be kept out for a kind of family book I want to do someday – maybe about the Laidlaws in Huron County and in Ettrick and James Hogg whose mother was a Laidlaw." Munro has indeed gone on to write about the Laidlaws in Huron County, in "Working for a Living," the piece mentioned here, "Changing Places," and "A Wilderness Station," and she has written about James Hogg and the Laidlaws in Ettrick in "Changing Places" too. So while she was writing Gibson from Australia, Alice Munro's imagination in September 1980 was focused on home.

The kind of "family book" she described here, as it turned out, waited another twenty-five years and saw Munro publish seven more new collections before it appeared in 2006 as *The View from Castle Rock*, a hybrid of family history, fiction, memoir, and closely made autobiographical stories. So long a preliminary, involving such deep and considered rumination, enhances the longstanding presence of

"Home," "Everything Here Is Touchable and Mysterious," "Working for a Living," and "Changing Places," among others, within Munro's work. Her return brought on an enriched awareness of her home, its culture, and her relation to it. Examples of this process are evident throughout her writing then. Between the first appearance of "Royal Beatings" in the *New Yorker*, for instance, and its inclusion in *Who Do You Think You Are?* Munro revised her description of West Hanratty and its relation to Hanratty so that it is much expanded into the long paragraph ending "and a cloudy, interesting, problematical light on the world." That paragraph begins,

> They lived in a poor part of town. There was Hanratty and West Hanratty, with the river flowing between them. This was West Hanratty. In Hanratty the social structure ran from doctors and dentists and lawyers down to foundry workers and factory workers and draymen; in West Hanratty it ran from factory workers and foundry workers down to large improvident families of casual bootleggers and prostitutes and unsuccessful thieves. Rose thought of her own family as straddling the river, belonging nowhere, but that was not true. West Hanratty was where the store was and they were, on the straggling tail end of the main street.

Such added details confirm that Rose's West Hanratty is based on the facts of Alice Munro's Lower Wingham, remembered. So too other pieces written at the time. In fall 1977, just under a year after he first wrote Munro accepting "Royal Beatings" and just before the *New Yorker* offered her an initial first-reading agreement, McGrath wrote her rejecting the long version of "Chaddeleys and Flemings." Mr. Shawn, he explained, "felt it read more like straight reminiscence than a story," so for the first (and probably only) time, Shawn overruled the fiction department's recommendation regarding a Munro story. McGrath continued, saying he was "not sure" he agreed and, while he did think that the magazine had published too much reminiscence and auto-biographical fiction in the past, he did not think "Chaddeleys and

Flemings" was "that kind of piece. I don't know whether it's autobiographical or not, but it's my feeling that you've taken the material of reminiscence and turned it into something much stronger – a moving, complicated work of fiction."

McGrath was sensing the shift that was still taking place in Munro's writing since returning to Huron County. This succession – "Royal Beatings" to "Chaddeleys and Flemings" to "Working for a Living" – reveals the rising autobiographical impulse in Munro's work. In "Royal Beatings," the detail of West Hanratty just over the bridge from Hanratty and Rose's family store there replicates the geography of the Lower Town of Munro's childhood. Remembered, fictionalized, it is consistent with Rose's sense of her family's status. With "Chaddeleys and Flemings," there are also points of autobiographical correspondence: the cousins in "Connection" existed, even if their exact visit did not take place; so too Mr. Black in "The Stone in the Field," and the father's sisters were there though they have been moved up a generation from Munro's experience. "Working for a Living" was a story begun with autobiographical underpinnings that became, upon revision, a beautiful memoir. It was one that Munro herself thought good and that McGrath, when he rejected it as a memoir after rejecting it the year before as a story, called "a considerable achievement." He continued: "It's lively, touching, and beautifully written. But the trouble – for us, I mean – is that not only is this a memoir, but in tone and form and style it's a kind of *classic*, or completely traditional, one: exactly the kind of piece, that is, that we did so much of in the past and are now overcompensating for." McGrath rejected "Working for a Living" just at the beginning of the magazine's first "Munro bonanza" (as he would later describe another run of stories).[1] Between April 1 and early September 1980 McGrath accepted five Munro stories ("Dulse," "Wood," "The Turkey Season," "Labor Day Dinner," and "Prue") while rejecting two others ("Mrs. Cross and Mrs. Kidd" and "Visitors") in addition to "Working." Bonanza indeed: Munro qualified for the *New Yorker* first-reading bonus of an extra 20 per cent for all five stories. Enough stories for another collection in fact.

After she had read the first of these stories and just as she was devising a submission strategy for them, Barber sent Munro her enthusiastic response:

> I sense a new style in this "stuff" you've sent – plainer, bare of metaphor, but with rhythms so strong that I feel safer than I've felt in years. Your sentences always treat the reader so well – no manhandling, no tricks, no dead falls. Not that there's anything placid or safe about the stories. There's that grief in "Dulse" which suddenly springs out and bowls you over. Or [from "Working"] "was his life now something that only other people had a use for." I hadn't thought about that. I'm not going to go on except to say what fun, and thanks. They're wonderful stories.

These stories became the core of *The Moons of Jupiter*. The next run, those that became *The Progress of Love*, had McGrath reeling: "You're sending in these stories faster than I can edit them," he wrote to Munro, "and each one is more dazzling than the last. I feel the way Rilke's editor must have felt – if he had one." When *Progress* appeared in 1986, David Macfarlane asserted in *Saturday Night* that it "is probably the best collection of short stories – the most confident and, at the same time, the most adventurous – ever written by a Canadian."[2] By then, such a view had become truism, certainly in Canada and rapidly elsewhere too: like the cousins in "Connection," Alice Munro had made the world take notice. When *Friend of My Youth* was published in spring 1990, eight of its ten stories having already been in the *New Yorker*, that notice was continual.

Both Reader and Writer: Memory and Perception and Self-Understanding

What McGrath saw in "Chaddeleys and Flemings" and in the memoir version of "Working for a Living," what Barber sensed as she first read the stories in that first bonanza, what Gibson had seen all along, were qualities that emerged from Munro's return to Huron County. Probably, too, the compositional difficulties linked with "Places at Home" and *Who Do You Think You Are?/The Beggar Maid* played some role in this too. Whatever the reason, there is no question but that Munro burst forth in the late 1970s and into the 1980s with successive stories that create the feelings of being alive, that replicate for their readers the very sense of being itself. Those stories offer Munro's readers moments of insight equal to the events each story creates.

While other examples might be chosen, the concluding section of "Chaddeleys and Flemings: 1. Connection" seems best to illustrate this sense. Originally it appeared after the final line in "Chaddeleys and Flemings: 2. The Stone in the Field," "the life buried here is one you have to think twice about regretting." Sometime between its first publication in *Chatelaine* and its appearance as the first story in *The Moons of Jupiter*, Munro moved it up to conclude "Connection" when the two parts were separated at Gibson's suggestion. Just after the narrator – then named Janet – "threw the Pyrex plate" at her husband Richard's head, an act that was "so shocking a verdict in real life," there is a break and Munro harkens back to an image from the cousins' visit to the narrator's girlhood town Dalgleish:

> *Row, row, row your boat*
> *Gently down the stream.*
> *Merrily, merrily, merrily, merrily,*
> *Life is but a dream.*

> I lie in bed beside my little sister, listening to the singing in the yard. Life is transformed, by these voices, by these presences, by their high spirits and grand esteem, for themselves and each other. My parents, all of us, are on holiday. The mixture of voices and words is so complicated and varied it seems that such confusion, such jolly rivalry, will go on forever, and to my surprise – for I am surprised, even though I know the pattern of the rounds – the song is thinning out, you can hear the two voices striving.

> *Merrily, merrily, merrily merrily,*

> *Life is but a dream.*
>
> Then the one voice alone, one of them singing on, gamely,
> to the finish. One voice in which there is an unexpected note of
> entreaty, of warning, as it hangs the five separate words on the
> air. *Life is.* Wait. *But a.* Now, wait. *Dream.*

This placement creates a very powerful effect. It is an apt embodiment
of the narrator's own sense of her own time, both in sweet childhood
memory and sour adulthood present, feeling like a passing dream.
Munro infuses the cliché lyrics of the child's song with new meaning, a
"warning," and this use is rooted in the facts of the cousins' remembered
visit. When he wrote an introductory piece to the first publication of
"The Stone in the Field" in *Saturday Night*, editor Robert Fulford commented of Munro that "to suggest that she conveys . . . her own
background with lucidity and honesty is to hint at only a part of her
talent. What happens in a Munro story is vastly more complicated than
that, a process involving memory and perception and self-understanding
on the part of both reader and writer."[3] Exactly so.

Later in 1979, Fulford followed this first publication of "The
Stone in the Field" by commissioning a major profile of Munro by
Martin Knelman, one that begins with her own version of events surrounding the reorganization of *Who Do You Think You Are?* It also
captures Munro just at the moment when she was becoming a
celebrity of a different kind. When Munro met with Knelman, *The
Beggar Maid* was just about to appear in the States. Its publication in
Britain and the Booker nomination there were still a way off. Yet in
tone and substance, the piece makes it clear that much was afoot.
Knelman mentions the first-reading contract at the *New Yorker* (then
in its second year), the sale of her papers to the University of Calgary
(she confided, "They'll take *anything*"), and the offers she had received
to be a writer-in-residence. Though she was about to take up that kind
of work again, both at the University of British Columbia and, later
the same year, at Queensland, she made her hesitations clear: "You
have an Alice Munro character that you play, and you've found out
that people accept it. I wind up feeling like a total fraud. I like the

students, but I think that if I had to work regularly I would rather get a job in a store."

If the critical success and Booker nomination of *The Beggar Maid* ended the 1970s, the 1980s opened with the "Munro bonanza" of more deeply affecting stories in the *New Yorker*. The five they bought in just five months in 1980 eclipsed the total of three bought since 1976 and confirmed the promise of the first-reading contract. Joyce Carol Oates had selected "Spelling" for *Best American Stories 1979* and that inaugurated Munro's frequent inclusion (and more frequent mention) in that annual ever since. Both in Canada and abroad – through the dutiful, precise, and constant attentions of Virginia Barber – her work was appearing in mass-market paperbacks that, as the 1980s passed into the 1990s, gave way to quality trade paperbacks of all of her works from Penguin in Canada and from Vintage in the United States and eventually in Great Britain as well. Translations of Munro's works into other languages also began during the 1980s.

Personally, in the 1980s, the opportunities she received increased. She had long since been receiving the offers attendant to well-known writers – requests for contributions of writing, invitations to speak, read, or apply for some visiting-writer position or teaching post at a university. Libraries were after her as well. Editors wanted her to read and blurb books, provide reviews, contribute to anthologies, write screenplays, or to adapt a story for the stage. Writer friends asked for letters of support for grant applications. Aspiring writers sought guidance and, seeing some quality of note in one or the other of these, she would sometimes respond. During the 1980s all these supplications increased in frequency and urgency owing to Munro's growing reputation, and increasingly they came from outside Canada as her reputation grew through the *New Yorker* and Knopf. Just as the 1970s saw Munro emerge as one of Canada's leading authors, the 1980s saw the same thing happen abroad. By December 1984, McGrath wrote to Barber that "she is simply one of the finest short story writers alive, and it's a great honor and privilege for us to be able to publish her."

Munro dealt with all this as best she could. Other writers whom she knew often found her willing to do what was needed. The same was true with editors though, at times, Munro would be signally unresponsive – she says she has no ability to review books and has carefully avoided such requests. One in particular, a review of *The Collected Stories of Eudora Welty* sent to her by the *Canadian Forum* in 1981, would have been well worth reading, but it was never done. Munro did correspond with Elizabeth Spenser about it, apparently having suggested that Spenser might review it in her place. From the American South herself, Spenser encouraged Munro to undertake the review since she had been impressed with Munro's knowledge of Southern writing when they met in Montreal in 1974. What is more, Spenser knew that readers would be interested in what Munro had to say about Welty. Still, no review was written.4

During the early 1980s Munro was responsive to some of the invitations that involved travel to places she wanted to visit. She spent from January to April 1980 as Distinguished Visiting Artist in the Department of Creative Writing at the University of British Columbia; she was the program's first writer-in-residence and had no teaching duties; the only requirement was that she should be there. That was an opportunity for her to take a break from looking after Mrs. Fremlin (who was in Huron View nursing home) and also a chance to see Andrea, then a teenager, on the weekends. Her time in Australia, that fall and into the new year, allowed her and Fremlin the opportunity to drive around the country, exploring its hidden places, and seeing its landscapes. To John Metcalf, she recounted that in Sydney they

> went to the King's Domain on a Sunday afternoon. People bring a step ladder and get up and talk. Christians and Commies and plain loonies yelling but there were two special hecklers. One was a happy drunk who said to the Christians – looking at the sky – "I don't see no heaven" and the other was a serious Syrian or Lebanese well-dressed gent who interrupted every speaker with "And what about Her Majesty the Queen?" It threw every one of them.

In the same letter, Munro vowed that she would never be a writer-in-residence again, and for much the same reasons she had expressed to Knelman. She never has felt comfortable in the role, feeling that "the actual 'work' is useless and dishonest." Even though such posts allowed her to see places she wanted to see – in the midst of this she mentioned being tempted by a similar job in Scotland – she vowed to resist the temptation. She has resisted ever since.

During the summer of 1981, Munro joined a group of other Canadian writers on a tour of China. In fact, she celebrated her fiftieth birthday there. Along with her were Gary Geddes, Geoffrey Hancock, Robert Kroetsch, Patrick Lane, Suzanne Paradis, and Adele Wiseman. They were hosted by the Chinese Writers Association. Writing about the trip to Metcalf, Munro characterized the trip as "hot and intensive"; the Chinese were "friendly and polite" but, to them, "irony is unknown." The Chinese writers they met gave them "a chilling discourse on art in the service of socialism." Reminiscing about the trip in an interview with Hancock, she commented that though she liked travelling, she "was not enthusiastic about going to China at first. It's the sort of thing you don't turn down, but I felt overwhelmed by the idea, that nothing would be familiar enough to touch me at any point." She also said "the people [were] the thing I came back with most of all. It kept occurring to me that there probably were lots of people there who'd never been alone in a room in their lives. There is no *alone* in China." The group itself was comradely, and Munro's birthday contributed to their conviviality: "A fiftieth birthday in China? I thought it was gorgeous. . . . Fifty, to me, always sounds a little grey – something kind of withered about it. And there I was having this wonderful banquet in Guangzhou. And then my birthday went on in Hong Kong and across the Pacific and finally it sort of petered out as we approached Vancouver. [It] went on for days. . . . It was the greatest birthday of my life."[5]

While Munro's reputation continued to grow internationally, there was a backlash in her hometown. The December 5, 1981, issue of *Today*, a weekly magazine supplement to many Canadian newspapers, carried an article by Wayne Grady entitled "Story Tellers to the World."

It focused on Munro and four other Canadian writers, arguing that the short story form is "uniquely suited to the Canadian experience" and detailing the attentions Canadian short story writers had been getting outside the country. Alongside the main story, the five writers were briefly profiled. Hers began with a quotation from Munro's description of Lower Town in her interview with Alan Twigg; it was followed by this paragraph:

> Wingham, where Alice Munro was born Alice Laidlaw in 1931, is a small but stately town in Huron County, an area of Ontario not known for its progressive views. Fictionalized as Jubilee in Munro's second book, *Lives of Girls and Women* (1971), and as Hanratty in her most recent book, *Who Do You Think You Are?* (1980) [sic], the town is stultifyingly provincial and only occasionally reaches the comic heights of Stephen Leacock's Mariposa.

The next paragraph noted that Munro "escaped" Wingham by going to university.

This article is notable less for what it said than for the reaction it received. The December 16 issue of the Wingham *Advance-Times* carried an editorial entitled "A Genius of Sour Grapes." Written by Barry Wenger, president and publisher of the paper, it began with the *Today* article and then turned its attention to Munro herself: "Sadly enough Wingham people have never had much chance to enjoy the excellence of her writing ability because we have repeatedly been made the butt of soured and cruel introspection on the part of a gifted author." Wenger took exception to Munro's presentation of Lower Town as "this kind of ghetto where all the bootleggers and prostitutes and hangers-on lived," but he saved his real ire for the characterization of Wingham as "stultifyingly provincial." While he left open the possibility that this characterization might be Grady's, not Munro's, he tended to connect the opinion to her: "But it seems that something less than greatness impels her to return again and again to a time and place in her life where bitterness warped her personality." The next week's *Advance-Times* ran a letter from Joyce McDougall, a former neighbour of the Laidlaws ("We were friends, then – I'm almost ashamed to admit") who, agreeing with the editorial, claimed to "know the truth behind most of the stories she has written – in fact, I and my family were cruelly depicted in one of them." According to her, Lower Town "was truly a town of hardworking, moral and respectable people."

Responding to the *Advance-Times*, Munro wrote that Grady was "a journalist who never interviewed me, to whom I have not said one word about Wingham, or writing, or anything else of importance." She talked to him once about something else. Munro also disputes "the supposition made by you and this journalist that I have created my fictional towns out of Wingham, which is not true. . . . Far from being bitter," she ended, "I have always had a certain affection for Wingham, though I can see from your editorial the feeling is not mutual." Munro wrote also to *Today*, maintaining that her fictional towns were "created out of bits of Wingham and many other towns, and quite a bit out of my own head, and that Jubilee is not Wingham, Hanratty is not Wingham. I am not writing autobiography. If I ever do, it will be time to talk about Wingham."

While Grady's article was certainly the catalyst for this spate of criticisms, the hostile reactions toward Munro and her writing probably sprang from a range of factors. First among these, and most especially among people in Huron County who shared Munro's pioneer Scots-Irish Protestant background while having little appreciation for fiction, was that deep-seated distrust of noticeable individuality encapsulated in the question "Who Do You Think You Are?" There was a clear preference for people who stayed in line, always doing the so-called normal, so some combination of envy or jealousy, with little appreciation of Munro's talent, marked the general local reaction. No doubt, too, there were residual feelings over Munro's defence, as a representative of the Writers' Union, of *The Diviners* and the other targeted books. Last, some people around Wingham took exception to Munro's depiction of a character they saw as based on her father – probably the father in "Royal Beatings."

As it happened, about a year later Munro took exception herself to a description of her father in the *Globe and Mail*'s profile of her, "Writing's Something I Did, Like the Ironing." There, Laidlaw was referred to as a "failed fox-farmer, a failed turkey farmer." She sent a letter to the *Globe* defending him and evidently submitted it to the *Advance-Times* as well, although it was not published there. Writing to her about her letter, Wenger began, "There is no need to fear my sharp pencil. I knew your father personally and always respected him as a man of great courage who faced life's difficulties with dignity." Responding to what Munro had said about journalistic practice – the need to clearly differentiate their subject's views from their own – Wenger wrote that in Grady's article "it was the author's remarks about Wingham, rather than your own which enraged so many here." Wenger also wrote that he was "personally glad to know that in both cases the observations about Wingham and your father were not your own."

These responses reveal a deeper aspect to Munro's return to Huron County. While journalists came, saw, and characterized the area (Grady finding it "stultifyingly provincial," Wayne writing her "Huron County Blues," and French giving the memorable image of Munro meeting people from the book-banning meeting in the grocery), Munro was living in the midst of her material, as she wrote about Janet. She lived there knowing what some people around her – not necessarily people she much worried about – thought of her, and of the level of celebrity she had achieved. This awareness cut, most probably, two ways: it both spurred Munro on, and it served as a caution. Or, put another way, it kept her writing and also kept her grounded. Even before her return to Huron County in 1975 to begin her work on "Who Do You Think You Are?" that local voice may be heard in Dotty's transformation in "Material": "Dotty was a lucky person, people who understand and value this act might say (not everybody, of course, does understand and value this act)." Munro knew that some people in Huron County very much valued what she was writing; others did not. On balance, though, back there in Clinton she was much more comfortable among such people and amid its landscapes, which, as she looked on them, still moved and fascinated her. Besides, as she told the journalist who wrote "Writing's Something I Did," "Oh, I'm very stubborn. . . . We've created this nice life for ourselves, and nobody's going to run me out of town."[6]

During the early 1980s too, Munro's correspondence with Metcalf continued, and her letters to him are revelatory. While he kept writing fiction, Metcalf was becoming known for his editorial work. Usually working with others, he continued to edit anthologies of Canadian writing. And more notoriously, Metcalf's voice was increasingly heard in the land critiquing the practice and accomplishment of Canadian literature generally. Owing to their friendship and her success, Metcalf regularly solicited Munro for stories for his various projects, while they kept each other abreast of their doings. Responding to one of Metcalf's requests just after her return from another trip to Australia in 1983, this one a vacation, Munro commented that she hoped Metcalf "found out I was in Australia and not just churlishly avoiding requests to do literary chores." She then offers an explanation that very much contextualizes just why, as her reputation has soared, she has often seemed aloof from her own accomplishment. She wrote that she "would have tried to avoid" Metcalf's request, and continued:

> Why? It's not so simple as laziness. I don't think so. It's that after every book, after practically every story, I'm "trying to get back to" writing. I always have to get back, I'm never safely "in" it – as I imagine other writers are. I'm always frantically trying to protect myself and draw back and clear my time and husband my energies and half the time that doesn't work, anyway. That, and having almost *no* intellectual grasp – I hope you believe that, a lot of people think it's an affectation – well, you can see the problem.
>
> Australia was really very good. There is *no* Canlit in Australia. Also no Barbara Frum, no Barbara Amiel, etc. etc. What's going on is – football (footies), cricket, races – the Melbourne Cup is a huge event for which the whole country comes to a halt – and a lot of bashing.

Munro's explanation rings utterly true here – there is no affectation involved. She is, and always has been, an intuitive writer. She finds the stories and the forms she seeks by writing, not planning, so the key for her is time left alone to write. Apart from the activities of her daily life with Fremlin in Clinton, everything else is interruption. Thus Barbara Frum and Barbara Amiel – two journalists, the first on television, the second in newspapers and *Maclean's* – embody those who wish to speak to Munro about her fiction.

As she ended this letter Munro commented that Metcalf was "*good* in the Globe, and I hope I'd say so even if you weren't good to me. About stories vs. novel. About the whole Canlit business." Throughout their friendship and their correspondence, they shared a certain scepticism toward the nationalistic impulse then ongoing in English-Canadian literary circles. Munro's views were private (though, in truth, not very different from those held by her old friend Robert Weaver). Metcalf's views, by contrast, were *very* public, thanks to his repeated attacks through various polemic publications, on the quality and mores of writing in English Canada. In her letter, Munro was referring to one of these, "What Happened to CanLit," just published in the *Globe and Mail*: "Think of Canlit as a pyramid. Inverted. And kept upright by the power of subsidy," it begins. Metcalf objected to fiction being praised because it is "about" Canada, and he argued that too much was being published without ever being read, as a result of subsidies to writer and publisher alike.

Here and elsewhere, Metcalf attracted the ire of other writers. Responding to this article, W.P. Kinsella wrote, "Mr. Metcalf – an immigrant – continually and in the most galling manner has the temerity to preach to Canadians about their own literature." Metcalf became a Canadian in 1970, so Kinsella's attack on him here is gratuitous, nasty; he also called attention in particular to Metcalf's special view of Munro:

> The majority of the authors he gushes over, and continu-
> ally reprints in his seldom-read anthologies, are minor talents,
> rightfully neglected by Canadian readers. A major exception is

Alice Munro who is, I believe, Canada's finest writer, and who surely must be embarrassed to be included constantly in Mr. Metcalf's incestuous little clique.

However Kinsella viewed Metcalf's opinions, for him Munro's work set her apart from such spats. While certainly a political person and quite able to take stands on issues of concern, Munro had deliberately remained a sideline observer of the politics of "CanLit." She saw the long-term utility of government subsidy for writers (and had accepted some herself, as Metcalf most certainly did); a few years later, Munro responded to another polemical piece by Metcalf, writing, "God knows you may be right about subsidizing but how otherwise could we have published anything? Ryerson Press, Tamarack, etc." Even so, this debate was one that she avoided – she rose above it, as her material, talent, and accomplishment allowed her to do.7

"Feeling My Own Powers": *The Moons of Jupiter* through the *New Yorker*

For all his polemics, Metcalf was not blind to talent: "About some of our writers there is widespread agreement: Alice Munro, Michael Ondaatje and, belatedly, Mavis Gallant." His point, as Kinsella concedes regarding Munro, is that these writers had made excellent reputations based on achievement. While in 1983 it was certainly possible to question this as regards the others, by then there was no doubt about Munro. Evidence of this is not hard to find just before and after *The Moons of Jupiter* was published in 1982. "Working for a Living," the memoir, after being rejected at the *New Yorker* was eventually bought (for $5,000) and published as the first piece in the first issue of *Grand Street*, a literary review just founded in New York. Besides Munro, contributors to that issue included Northrop Frye, Ted Hughes, W.S. Merwin, and Glenway Wescott. Edited by Ben Sonnenberg, *Grand Street* went on to publish three more Munro pieces, including "The Ferguson Girls Must Never Marry," a story Munro has never included in a book and is still working on. Two of the *New Yorker* stories, "Wood" and "Prue," went immediately into Metcalf anthologies, *Best Canadian Stories* for 1981 and 1982. In Britain, Penguin published *The Beggar Maid* as a King Penguin text before publishing Munro's earlier books in the same format. In November 1981 the first accession of Munro's papers were formally received by the University of Calgary and, in March 1982, an academic conference on Munro and her work, where she spoke and saw a one-person production of "Forgiveness in Families," was held at the University of St. Jerome's College, University of Waterloo. Reviews and theses had given way to academic articles, and in 1983 *Probable Fictions*, the first book devoted to Munro's work, was published by ECW Press. Munro accepted some invitations during this time. After returning from China in 1981 she appeared in Toronto at Harbourfront International Festival of Authors in October, reading "The Moons of Jupiter." Early in 1982 she and Fremlin were in Europe, visiting Norway for the February 16 launch of the Norwegian translation of *Who Do You Think You Are?*, *Tiggerpiken*, and travelling also to Denmark and Scotland, where she did public readings.

Once he had re-established contact with Munro in Australia in September 1980, Gibson stayed in touch, enquiring each time he wrote about possibilities for the next book. Not surprisingly, given the attention Munro had received for *Who Do You Think You Are?*, other Canadian publishers were interested in wooing her away from Macmillan; Jack McClelland wrote her during the summer of 1980 claiming he had heard that either Munro or her agent was planning to move her to a new publisher. Even when Gibson, having discussed matters with Munro herself, wrote Virginia Barber about the next book and initiated contract discussions, Barber first asked Munro directly whether she wanted to remain with Macmillan; Barber was thinking specifically of McClelland & Stewart (and its paperback line, Seal), but also knew that other major Canadian publishers would be delighted too. "Tell me which house you want. I'll let the lucky devils know, and then create a glorious contract," she wrote.

Munro must have immediately told her that she wanted to stay with Gibson and Macmillan, since Barber wrote him with an initial table of contents within a week. She proposed the three stories held out of *Who* plus "Accident," another one from that time, and a selection of four more recent stories: "Labor Day Dinner," "Prue," "The Turkey Season," and "Bardon Bus." Gibson annotated this letter with page lengths for the stories and, having conversed with Munro himself, he also listed other stories that might be added: "Visitors," "Mrs. Cross and Mrs. Kidd," "The Ferguson Girls Must Never Marry," and "Dulse."[8] He did not include "Wood," which had appeared in the *New Yorker* in November 1980, feeling that it did not belong with the other stories. Clearly there was no shortage of material.

The making of *The Moons of Jupiter* represented another significant step for Munro. Once *Who/The Beggar Maid* was done, her new editorial and managerial relations were firmly in place: Barber handled all business matters, McGrath oversaw the *New Yorker's* first serial consideration, Gibson at Macmillan looked to her Canadian audience, and Close at Knopf saw to American book publication. Once Munro had confidence in someone, that was it. While Barber might have been able to negotiate better book contracts elsewhere, whether in Canada or New York, her author was loyal and supportive. Besides, she had taken her own time finding Gibson, the diligent editor who never pushed her toward a novel, in the first place. Likewise, Munro and Close hit it off from the first and have maintained their excellent working relation since.

Then there was the *New Yorker*. Until 1994 Munro was edited there by either McGrath or Daniel Menaker. Both were highly enthusiastic and encouraging, and had been since 1976. So too when Menaker left the magazine, Alice Quinn, who had known Munro's work in the magazine from its first publication there, brought a similar spirit to her editing. During the 1980s the magazine went through considerable internal vicissitudes as its owner and chief editors changed, but its commitment to Munro and to her writing has never wavered. What is more, from the stories included in *The Moons of Jupiter* on, the magazine's editorial methods and tastes have had some role in shaping Munro's stories; responding to her *New Yorker* editors' critiques and the magazine's famed editorial idiosyncrasies, Munro moved them farther in the direction she saw them taking.

Most of the stories that went into *Moons* were considered by the *New Yorker* after Munro was under a first-reading contract. As early as April 1978 in turning down "Joanne," a never-published story that exists now only in manuscript, McGrath wrote to Barber, "I hate turning down Alice Munro stories, because even when they're not completely successful, the writing is always first-rate – just as it is here." He took solace on this occasion from the fact that he had three more stories on his desk, but those were turned down as well. The first bonanza did not begin until early 1980, just at the point when Barber sensed "a new style" in the stories she was seeing. By the time Barber and Gibson were beginning to shape *Moons* in early 1982, the *New Yorker* had seen all twelve stories and published five of them (plus "Wood"); five of the other seven had been published elsewhere (*Atlantic Monthly, Chatelaine, Saturday Night, Tamarack Review,* and *Toronto Life*). Two – "Bardon Bus" and "Hard Luck Stories" – first appeared in *The Moons of Jupiter* collection.

In a draft version of "Working for a Living" as a memoir, Munro wrote passages about herself that seem to demonstrate the new qualities Barber felt – that is, a deeper and richer meditation on her home place. Thinking of herself at eighteen, her mother stricken by Parkinson's and her father working in the foundry after his fox farm failed, she wrote:

> In spite of all the defeats of the grown-ups around me, the incursions of poverty and sickness, my spirits didn't need much lightening. I was often happy to the point of dizziness, contemplating the world, feeling my own powers, which seemed enormous but hard to get at, anticipating love and victory. . . . I mourned the passing of the fox-farm, in a rather pleasurable way. I was just discovering nostalgia. And I did truly see that though it might never have made us rich it had made us unique and independent.

The stories that made up both Munro bonanzas – the five that went into *Moons* and, after, another five for *The Progress of Love* – reveal a writer who had certainly discovered nostalgia. But what Munro did with it, in company with the *New Yorker*'s editors and fact-checkers, bears attention as the stories passed through the magazine on the way to her books. The first of the *Moons* stories McGrath saw was "Accident," which he thought good but not as good as "The Beggar Maid," which he bought. After that, they rejected the long "Chaddeleys and Flemings" over McGrath's objection because Shawn thought it a reminiscence rather than a story. As McGrath makes clear, it was fiction to him. He was right. They then bought a third Munro story, "The Moons of Jupiter," a piece connected to "Chaddeleys and Flemings" and so one that might also be seen as reminiscence. Certainly the death of the father in the story bears a strong resemblance to the circumstances of Robert Laidlaw's death. Certainly some of the story's other details happened – they are close to what occurred. Thus the connections in these stories to Munro's own life – connections from which she herself derived considerable imaginative power, adding to her fictional magic – are of real consequence to a reader's experience of them.

Tracing the stories' progress, this consequence is twofold: the form the story takes and the work Munro did preparing her stories for the *New Yorker*'s first publication. When Barber submitted "The Moons of Jupiter" to McGrath in late 1977 it was written in the third person; the *New Yorker* accepted it that way, perhaps under its initial title, "Taking Chances." Early in January, however, McGrath wrote acknowledging that the new version of the story, which Munro had done on her own, had arrived: "The first-person seems more intimate, somehow, and more affecting. . . . Already I have trouble imagining this as a third-person story." McGrath continued to ask about Janet's profession – they had had too many stories about writers, so they wanted her to be something else – and concluded: "You've made a fine story even better, and we're doubly glad to have it now."

With "Dulse," the process of authorial revision between its *New Yorker* appearance in July 1980 and book publication was stark. In writing it, Munro had combined aspects of characters from Sheila and Angela, two of the women in the three-part "Simon's Luck," in order to create Lydia. Her boyfriend, named Alex in the *New Yorker* and Duncan in the book, also draws on the earlier Simon. But the story's central episode – the visit to Grand Manan Island and the meeting of the prototype for Mr. Stanley, the "Willa Cather fanatic" as Munro once called him – draws on Munro's own visit there and her own meeting of that person in 1979. While there, Munro also met the woman who ran the inn where she was staying and, as writers do, she integrated her into "Dulse." Meeting Munro at an unhappy moment in her life, that woman later recognized herself as she was then; she had "passed into art," and was not entirely happy about it. Talking about the incident years later, she only wished she could remember what Munro had looked like.

These matters led to the writing of "Dulse" and, once the story got to the *New Yorker* and beyond, Munro characteristically kept shaping and changing it. The *New Yorker* version is in the first person, the book version in the third; hence, with this story Munro reversed the change she had made in revising "The Moons of Jupiter," deliberately distancing Lydia and her circumstances from the reader. Also, Lydia's former boyfriend becomes a less interesting and more negative character with the changes. But the most compelling changes between the two published versions lie in Munro's depiction of Willa Cather – this story offers a beautiful analysis of a writer's self-absorption, and of Cather's in particular. In her revisions, Munro makes her Cather more inscrutable and much more compelling. For some readers the story is a dig at Cather's putative homosexuality; as McGrath commented in a letter to Munro referring to that reading, "People who are looking for a slight can find one almost anywhere. It's a humane and compassionate story, and you ought to feel nothing but pride in it." McGrath is right. While Lydia's anxieties in the story have much to do with her relations with men, and she does use the fact that Cather lived with another woman against Mr. Stanley, these details sharpen and deepen Munro's "human and compassionate" depiction of her characters and of Cather herself.[9]

Yet the changes in "Dulse" do not really address the various ways that the *New Yorker* itself furthered Munro's fiction. "The Turkey Season" offers a particular instance of both what Munro was doing in her stories in 1980 and just how McGrath and the other editors at the *New Yorker* were responding. She explained the story's beginnings in an interview she gave on the book tour for *Moons*; asked about it, Munro replied, "Why is it interesting to me to make turkey-gutting vivid? It just is." She also explained the story's contexts, and some of her comments speak to "Working for a Living" as well:

> A few years ago when I was going through my father's effects, I saw a picture of the workers at the turkey barn. My father had a turkey barn: it was a very small business, but he would have a half a dozen people at Christmas. My brother and sister worked there, too, although I didn't. I was in college by that time. What I wanted to do was to portray all this complicated social life that goes on in work places, in jobs that most people think are hideous and boring. And also the work itself – there's some kind of enormous satisfaction in jobs like that, in doing them well. I wrote a memoir about my father and the kinds of work he did. . . .

Thus Munro began with a literal picture – her father's photograph became the photograph of the turkey crew taken just as "The Turkey Season" ends – and she set to work imagining her story. Having never worked as a turkey-gutter herself, she got expert advice from her brother-in-law, Joe Radford, who had. (Thus the story's dedication in book form. She had availed herself of Fremlin's knowledge of wood-cutting, in the same way, for "Wood.")

Once the story was submitted and accepted, Munro sent McGrath another version, as is her frequent practice. Most of the time when this happened, as with "The Moons of Jupiter," McGrath thought the second version an improvement; here he did not. He told Munro – on the phone, he recalled, since at this point they still had not met – that "the best story here is a combination," so he set about combining the two versions before the story was set. In sending her the proofs of the combined version, he characterized the result as "a kind of composite made up from your two versions. I didn't keep track, exactly, but I would guess that it's about 50–50, new and old. In general, whenever it was a question of a word or a line, the second version almost always seemed to me finer or sharper, but in the case of some of the longer

additions I sometimes felt that some of the spareness and understatement of the first version was preferable."

Munro liked what he had done. McGrath recalls this time period
as one when Munro "started really experimenting with form and with
the notion of what a story was." Her stories "stopped being so linear
and she brought them into this whole thing of taking these long
temporal detours and then coming back." Not too far into their writer-
editor relationship, McGrath recalls, "the trust kicked in." They sensed
that they were both working in the same direction.

At the same time, "The Turkey Season" had language ("'shit' and
'fuck'") in it that violated the *New Yorker*'s "Naughty Words Policy."
Regarding such words, McGrath told her that "Mr. Shawn remains
unyielding." One set of galleys illustrates the ways of the *New Yorker* at
the time. Writing about "Lily and Marjorie, two middle-aged sisters,"
Munro characterized them as "very fast and thorough and competitive
gutters. They sang at their work and talked abusively and intimately
to the turkey carcasses. 'Don't you nick me, you old bugger!' 'Aren't you
the old shit factory!'" Munro had inserted "shit factory" on the proof
and McGrath commented, "I'm still negotiating this!" He lost, since
the phrase ran (and was retained in the book) as "crap factory."

The *New Yorker*'s famous checking department is in evidence here
also. At the point when the narrator is describing herself gutting a
turkey, someone from checking commented, "Normally most of the
connecting tissues are pulled out of the rear end of the turkey, not by
the neck route." Equally, the proof has numerous suggested changes,
mostly punctuational or grammatical, from Shawn. Each one is initialled. When, at one point, Munro was pushing to have a character,
Brian, say "Fuckin' boats, I got outa that," Shawn has placed a question mark and initialled it. As McGrath said, he was unyielding. Munro
had her own way in the book version. On this galley too, there is a
request from the legal department first for Munro's assurances that
none of these characters resembles "actual people still living" and sec-
ondly if the town in the story is recognizable. Because of legal problems
the magazine was then having, before the story ran, Munro had to telegraph the legal department other assurances from Australia. McGrath

was quite apologetic about this and undertook to pay the costs involved.

Ending his final letter about "The Turkey Season," McGrath effused, "I *really* love this story, and I'm extremely proud of how it turned out. I'm also delighted that it's running in the Christmas issue, because I think of it as a present to our readers."[10] He now recalls this collaboration as one of *the* moments in his work with Munro, and he concedes that his own combination of the two versions of the story fuels his pleasure. Even though most of Munro's stories have scarcely needed such extensive reorganization, what McGrath did with "The Turkey Season" should be seen as indicative of the role of the *New Yorker* in Munro's development. This arrangement not only continued but it increased. Both *Moons* and *The Progress of Love* included five stories that had been first published in the magazine, and those that were not had been considered under the first-reading agreement. In *Friend of My Youth*, eight of ten had appeared in the *New Yorker*, in *Open Secrets* seven of eight. Not all the stories in the last three collections were published previously, but in each case five stories, or most, first saw print in the *New Yorker*. Thus from *The Moons of Jupiter* on, the editors at the magazine have played an important role in Munro's career, serving along with Virginia Barber as her first response: questioning, pressing, suggesting so as to improve her stories and showcase them in the *New Yorker*'s pages. There have been some difficulties along the way, to be sure, but there is no question as to the magazine's importance to Munro's career.

❧

The Moons of Jupiter, meanwhile, was taking shape. An undated list in Munro's hand of fourteen titles, the bulk of those in the volume, shows her attempting to pull the collection together: "Dulse" and "Bardon Bus" are marked "rewrite"; "Labor Day Dinner," "Wood," "The Turkey Season," and "Ferguson Girls" are satisfactory (though the latter turned out not to be and still is not); and the others need only "slight" revision. "Working for a Living" is listed but gets no comment. The rewrite of "Dulse" has been described, but that of "Bardon Bus" is notable in that Munro's incessant revision resulted in a second separate version of the story, one that jockeyed with the earlier version to be the one printed. Munro seems to have been inclined all along to exclude "The Ferguson Girls," her decision to allow it to be published in *Grand Street* notwithstanding. In addition to the *New Yorker, Redbook, McCall's*, and *Harper's* each passed on it. Since she did not think that it fit with the other stories, "Wood" was also out. Once she had done her revising – Munro delivered the new "Dulse" to Gibson herself – and having agreed on a lineup with her agent, Barber submitted *The Moons of Jupiter and Other Stories* to Macmillan in mid-March 1982 and sent it to England – to Allen Lane and Penguin, which were coordinating editions there – at the same time. Knopf took a bit longer, for Munro did not hear from Close until April 23.

By then Gibson and Munro had begun to work out an order for the stories at Macmillan. In early April he wrote Munro offering two suggested arrangements. In putting them together, Gibson was trying to space "out the *really* strong stories," and trying even more to have them "follow a logical life-flow pattern," childhood to old age. So he offered an arrangement that after some adjustment became the final order. Once Close joined the discussion, she successfully pushed for placing "Accident" ahead of "Bardon Bus." When he first wrote Munro about this change, Gibson also suggested grouping the first- and third-person stories together but, given Munro's experience with the first version of *Who*, that predictably went nowhere. By mid-May they had agreed on the final order, and Close and Gibson were working on their respective covers, the book's design, and a possible co-printing arrangement. Since Macmillan was publishing in fall 1982 and Knopf in spring 1983, Gibson was again in the position of trying to induce Close into sharing overhead (and lowering costs) by using the same design. He had more success with *Moons* since Knopf elected to use Macmillan's typesetting, though, because Knopf published a physically smaller book, they redesigned the look of the page. As for the dust jacket, Gibson initially intended to use Christopher Pratt's *Woman at a Dresser* but ultimately decided on a detail from his *Young Woman in a Slip*. He offered this design to Close, who opted for a drawing of a hospital room with a window opening to a night sky. Even so, *Moons* began a collaboration on Munro's book production that has continued since.[11]

At the same time, Barber was working on the contracts. While they had doubtless discussed terms before the manuscript was sent, Barber sent Gibson a list of changes to the contract that were duly made. It called for a $20,000 advance against Canadian sales and a graduated royalty to 15 per cent after 10,000 copies sold. As these increasing numbers suggest, Munro's reputation in Canada warranted higher payments. True enough, but it was Macmillan's sale of the paperback rights (something controlled by the publisher with a straight 10 per cent royalty to the author once the advance had been earned back) for *The Moons of Jupiter* that garnered Barber's special attention. Early on the bidding between interested firms was at $20,000 but when the dust settled Penguin Canada got them for a record-breaking $45,000.[12]

The Canadian edition was published by Macmillan on October 16, 1982. That day Munro was interviewed on *Anthology* by William French, and "The Turkey Season" was read to listeners. She then embarked on a cross-country publicity tour, as she had with *Who*, visiting Windsor, London, Waterloo, and Guelph between October 13 and 20 and, after a few days off, heading west to Winnipeg, Edmonton, Vancouver, and Victoria, stopping in Calgary on the way home. In Victoria, she stayed at the Empress Hotel but this time autographed books at Munro's. Back home for a week, she headed east to Burlington, Toronto, Kingston, Ottawa, and Halifax. Along the way she garnered considerable publicity for both herself and for the book, and the headlines of some of the profiles that appeared indicate just how Munro, and her new book, were then being seen: "She's a Person First" (*Windsor Star*), "Munro Says Artistic Backwater Was Boon to Early Endeavors" (*London Free Press*), "Alice Munro Takes Her Success in Stride" (*Kitchener-Waterloo Record*), "Munro Battles Huron County" (*Winnipeg Free Press*), "Age Brings Urge 'To Do Something Great'" (*Edmonton Journal*), "Alice Doesn't Live There Anymore" (*Vancouver* magazine), "Alice Munro Prefers the Risk of a Life Filled with Choice" (*Burlington Post*), and "The Enigmatic Alice Munro: Literary Paradox with a Purpose" (*Ottawa Citizen*). The

Globe and Mail's "Writing's Something I Did, Like the Ironing" was among these profiles.

Such headlines and the profiles themselves confirm that, with *The Moons of Jupiter*, Munro's status as a major Canadian talent was acknowledged across the country. The book was published by Knopf on February 28, 1983, in the United States and just after that by Allen Lane in Great Britain. The reviews it received – in Canada, the United States, and Britain – vary by the position Munro then had in each audience's literary pantheon, but there was almost no variance from the view that her writing is an accomplished delight, work to be savoured. Nuala O'Faolain, writing in the Dublin *Sunday Tribune* in a 1984 review focused on the Penguin paperbacks of *Moons* and *The Beggar Maid*, captures just how *Moons* was received overall. O'Faolain recalls being surprised that Munro's earlier book was a Booker finalist, but "now I'm amazed that she didn't win it. Not for years have I come across a writer so congenial. She seems to see how life is and to be serene in her own priorities that she can effortlessly shape experience so as to make it resonate colour in its significances. Not that you feel her shaping hand at work." Her stories "leave one wondering not how does a person get to write like that, but how does a person get to be like that." O'Faolain's review is called "Alice Munro: Soaring Clear," and the allusion is to Munro's superiority over Anne Hébert (also under review) and Barbara Pym, a writer of "infinitesimal talent."

Canadian reviewers of *Moons* realized that mere superlatives would not do, that they needed to analyze just why Munro's writing is so affecting. Bharati Mukherjee, in *Quill & Quire*, wrote that Munro's "lyrical eye is more perceptive and intense than ever, but now it is augmented with psychological density." In *Books in Canada*, Wayne Grady wrote that Munro's stories do not offer the "searing vision" he finds in Gallant, but though Munro's "stories are not intellectual at all . . . they are full of intelligence and an emotional intensity camouflaged by deliberate naivety." William French in the *Globe and Mail* wrote that Munro's "ability to convey nuances and imply the ambiguities inherent in human relationships has never been greater. She can describe a character so deftly in a phrase or two that you know exactly what she means." Munro is, he concluded, "one of the great short-story writers of our time." At the same time, French wondered if Munro was becoming a "minimalist" since "there's an occasional hermetic sense of being too closely involved with people who aren't all that interesting." Ken Adachi in the *Toronto Star* noted Munro's "mastery of tone and mood," and Sam Solecki, writing this time in the *Canadian Forum* rather than an academic review, still found much to be picky about, although he sees that in *Moons* the "only ironies or twists of the plot that interest Munro are those that are inevitable in, and therefore common to most of our lives." She offers "ordinary lives and mundane events described realistically in everyday diction, imagery, and syntax, yet one leaves the story feeling as if one had just encountered something unusual."[13]

Urjo Kareda described *Moons* as "a transitional volume: thrilling, mysterious, astonishing." Munro, he wrote, "seems to be shedding her skin. Half the stories show the author at her most familiarly assured, but there is something unexpected and disruptive in the others. The prose reveals a new edge of tension, as if previously protected nerve-ends had suddenly been exposed." Kareda saw Munro making new demands on her readers, writing that her "great achievement is to make us accept our inability to know." Larry Scanlan in the *Kingston Whig-Standard* saw in Munro's work what Atwood has called "the complex truth," and notes her "reliance on the present tense, as if the action were unfolding before our eyes, and we, its witnesses, had only to absorb it."

Reviewers in Canada sought to define the essence of Munro's powerful effects. In a Vancouver paper, Alan Twigg described Munro as "painstakingly perfect" while, in *Western Living*, John Faustman asserted that reading Munro "is an unalloyed pleasure." A reader can feel her "warmth right through the pages." Conceding all this and setting it aside, David Williamson again wrote one of the best Canadian reviews of Munro in the *Winnipeg Free Press*. He posed two questions: What makes her stories so good and, second, Are there no flaws? The first answer is longer, and it follows Williamson's view that her "people are not symbols or props, they are individuals, each and every one of them." For flaws, he manages a paragraph on the "flatness" of ordinary people as characters and on Huron County as setting, and he concedes that some "readers may wish for a stronger narrative pull, less meandering in and out of the past."

Though there are many more Canadian reviews than these, fulsome praise was their overall response. Leo Simpson began his review in the *Hamilton Spectator* with an august assertion: "This is probably as good a short story collection as James Joyce's *Dubliners*." Joyce's book may be the weaker of the two, he continued, noting "relatively light-weight pieces as Araby." Since no stories in *Moons* are notably weak, "the Munro book seems to me stronger." However one sees the comparison, this is heady stuff.

The Joyce-Munro parallel had been well known among critics since the mid-1970s, but Simpson (originally from Ireland himself) was pressing the matter further. Thus not only were Canadian reviewers dissecting their superlatives, they were seeking superlative comparison. Kareda's review of *Who* made and detailed the comparison with Chekhov. As both these reviews suggest, readers were beginning to see and understand the enduring quality of Munro's work. Tom Crerar, in his review of *Moons* in *Brick* saw these same qualities in probably the most succinct summary of the book's effect: "In these stories, no future escapes its past." He continued, "For the real subject of these stories is not everyday people in everyday places. The real subject is time. Not time in the sense of a chronicle or a history. But time as a condition, a sentence to life."14

ᗡᕽ

As *Moons* was being reviewed and Munro was seeing to her authorial duties across the country, Ann Close was moving the Knopf edition toward its February 28 publication in the United States. Munro had agreed to do publicity for the Knopf edition, including a trip to New York just as *Moons* was published there, and later visits to Boston and Washington. Hoping for usable comments, Close made sure the book went out to a select group of American writers, among them Shirley Hazzard, Alice McDermott, Bobbie Ann Mason, and Tim O'Brien. All responded and Mason, for instance, wrote back to say that she "would have bought it anyway" since Munro is one of her "favorite writers."

Indeed, she had wanted to write her a fan letter for some time. When Munro came to New York, she read at the YMHA Poetry Center (with Marilyn Robinson) on February 28 and attended a reception for both writers afterwards; the next night, she read with Cynthia Ozick at Books & Company and at another bookstore on March 3. During the New York visit she did interviews, met people (including, finally, Charles McGrath and other *New Yorker* editors), and attended luncheons.

Meanwhile, the American edition was beginning to gather attention. The advance review in *Publishers Weekly* began, "These painfully honest stories . . . are as hard, clear and mysterious as a cold winter morning." Paying particular attention to "Labor Day Dinner," "The Stone in the Field," and "The Turkey Season," it asserted that "this moving, finely written volume leaves the reader facing up to life." In February the large newspapers began weighing in. Anatole Broyard concentrated on descriptions of characters and actions in his review in the *New York Times*, seeing the situation in "The Turkey Season" as an instance of Munro's "genius for homely images." "The Moons of Jupiter" he regarded as "particularly good" and most of the other stories are as intriguing; picking up a description from "Visitors," Broyard saw the book "filled with squawks, calls, screeches and cries of a human nature." In the *Philadelphia Inquirer*, Lisa Zeidner commented that Munro's stories "have the deceptive simplicity of Edward Hopper's paintings," and that in them she "records not only grief and longing, but happiness as potent as it is fragile – almost pantheistic moments that pass as quickly as gorgeous dusks." Among other major papers reviewing *Moons* were the *Boston Globe* and the *Los Angeles Times* while, in the *Miami Herald*, book editor William Robertson observed that "there is nothing flashy about Munro's writing. It is absolutely precise in observed detail. . . . An unsentimental view of the heart is what Munro is after and most of the time she finds it." He concluded: "That's good for her. But it's better for us."

The reviewer in *Time*, Patricia Blake, wrote that Munro's stories possess "a melodic line that catches at the heart with its freshness," and that her "originality is all the more striking because her subject is ordinariness." Noting "Accident" and "Bardon Bus" particularly, Blake also introduced the Chekhov comparison, concluding that writing "about ordinary life is hazardous; it may induce the boredom that is its subject. Munro defies the danger, and triumphs." Gardner McFall, the reviewer in *Newsday*, called *Moons* "dazzling" and asserted that Munro "writes with such acuity that description becomes perception" – he pointed to the gift of seaweed at the end of "Dulse," calling it a crystallization of such a moment. Taking up the opening paragraph of the first story, "Chaddeleys and Flemings: 1. Connection," Ann Hulbert in the *New Republic* focused on Munro's style: "With a sure rhythmic sense, she builds from the clipped first sentences to the long last sentence, its clauses as firmly balanced as the ladies themselves. Her words, too, are carefully weighed, yet her tone throughout is disarmingly colloquial. Boldly drawn, Munro's stories are like busy scenes in a larger novelistic landscape." Despite such consensus, there was the odd negative response. Arthur Evenchik in the Baltimore *Sun* was looking for "a greater store of discoveries – an enlightened perception of character and place, which Alice Munro cannot afford to have momentarily lost." Putting it in perspective, he sees "a new doubtfulness in this book, a loss of incisiveness and spirit, that causes most of the stories to fall below her usual standard."

On March 20 the *New York Times Book Review* ran its notice of *Moons* on the front page. There Benjamin DeMott saw *Moons* as stronger than *The Beggar Maid*, calling it "witty, subtle, passionate. . . . It's exceptionally knowledgeable about the content and movement – the entanglements and entailments – of individual human feeling. And the knowledge it offers can't be looked up elsewhere." Munro's "sense of style and craft is impeccable," and she is especially impressive "when she takes us inside the experience of letting go – accepting the end of a human connection." When she does this, DeMott wrote in a line that is impressively accurate, Munro is "seldom sentimental yet never mean." Others made the same point: few writers at work today, David Lehman wrote in *Newsweek*, "can move us as deeply as Alice Munro." *Moons* "is a triumph of sentiment over sentimentality." Gail Cooper in the *Los Angeles Herald Examiner* noted that the "deftness and accuracy of her portrayal of characters is founded . . . on sensitivity to the nuances, the strangeness of life. A seemingly atypical or inconse-quential event will adumbrate a life's significance." Cooper also paid close attention to Munro's use of point of view in "The Turkey Season" and in "Mrs. Cross and Mrs. Kidd": "their lives are an extrapolation of the girls they once were."[15]

Late in April 1983 the reviews of *Moons* in England began to appear and, as was to continue to be the norm, the British notices tended to remark on different things in the book. Nina Bawsen in the *Daily Telegraph* wrote that Munro's stories are distinguished not "by resigna-tion but a wise and perceptive acceptance" of the way life is. In *City Limits*, Gillian Allnutt saw Munro's writing as "matter-of-fact, almost laconic," writing that seems poetic: "in its choice of detail, of incident and conversation, the suggestive juxtapositions, the often surprising ending, that give these stories their power. So much is left to silence that each story, once settled in the imagination, begins to grow into a novel." Writing in *The Observer*, Peter Kemp saw Munro's strength in her ability to establish "the characters' inner and outer lives – and the connections between them – these are sparely written, richly resonant pieces." Kemp reviewed *Moons* alongside William Trevor's *Fools of Fortune*, and he treated them as equals despite Trevor's larger reputa-tion. Reviewing Munro a second time, Alan Hollinghurst in the *Times Literary Supplement* saw "a deep ambiguity about this book – though one felt on the pulses rather than in an intellectually playful way: her writing has a penetrating concision, at once watchfully spare and lyrically intense, which contradicts or refuses the too facile satisfaction of accounting for everything." Illustrating this significant point, Hollinghurst wrote that Munro "seems fastidiously to question the very trust she inspires, like Lydia in the story 'Dulse', constantly fabricating explanations which she does not believe herself." Christopher Wordsworth in the *Financial Guardian* called *Moons* a "wise and impressive collection." Noting her command of "the art which conceals art," he pronounced Munro "a writer who can mix with the very highest company." Summarizing Munro's career, Isabel Quigly in the *Financial Times* pronounced her a "real writer" and continued,

Alice Munro has been compared with Proust (also, most unsuitably, with Joyce Carol Oates, Hemingway, and John Cheever), short-listed for the Booker prize and remains (though dazzling) quite unperturbed and unaffected, her writing smooth and supple, reticent in expressing feeling yet filled to the brim with exactly the right emotional quantity; never a false one, so never a jarring emotional note.

Other reviewers dealt with Munro's sense of reality. Paul Bailey in the *Standard* noted that reality "is of the essence in Alice Munro's art — reality of a peculiarly raw kind," especially in "The Turkey Season." Bailey calls "Dulse" delicate, and he saw "Chaddeleys and Flemings: 2. The Stone in the Field" as a story "worthy of Willa Cather herself." Taking up the scene between Janet and her father in the hospital in "The Moons of Jupiter" when she notices the read-out from the heart monitor, Dorothy Porter in the Glasgow *Herald* sees in it an equivalent of "Munro's technique: she looks almost scientifically at the human heart, and then tactfully withdraws, respecting the essential privacy of the individual." Finally, John Mellors in the *Listener* began by asserting "Alice Munro, like O'Faolain and Chekhov and, indeed, all the best short-story writers, leaves you with the feeling of having known real people with lives of their own before and after the events described. Nothing seems made up or embroidered." He also notes that the stories "are all set in Canada, and Munro, while waving no maple leaves, has a strong sense of place and history."

"Have you thought about what a terrible threat to illiteracy you are?"

Throughout the reviews of *Moons*, several readers commented that Munro tended, in moments of especial insight, to compose epigrams. Frequently cited was one from "Accident" when Frances describes her correspondence with "old friends from the conservatory": "They were all in their early thirties. An age at which it is sometimes hard to admit that what you are living is your life." For Munro, her thirties were those "bumbling years" when her older daughters were growing up in West Vancouver and the bookstore had been launched in Victoria. There was Andrea's arrival. Her marriage's decline. A first book, finally. A nascent reputation. Leaving Victoria, out on her own. London, Metcalf, Western, Fremlin. Clinton. "Real Life."

Another moment that attracted reviewers appears in "Hard-Luck Stories," a story from *Moons* that also used some of the material left over from the extended "Simon's Luck." Derived therefore from the story that might reasonably be characterized as Munro's first real "passion" story, "Hard-Luck Stories," like "Simon's Luck" and "Dulse," meditates on female-male relations. Like them, it captures a moment in a life when the main character, imperceptibly but unmistakably, shifts into another way of seeing. In such a moment there is a sense of groping toward realization that is never completely grasped nor understood. In draft, "Hard-Luck Stories" was at one point called "A Perfect Story." The passage that attracted special notice was one that described the narrator's reaction to a surprise touch she received from Douglas, a man she scarcely knows, as they tour a church with another woman:

> I felt that I had been overtaken – stumped by a truth about myself, or at least a fact, that I couldn't do anything about. A pressure of the hand, with no promise about it, could admonish and comfort me. Something unresolved could become permanent. I could be always bent on knowing, and always in the dark, about what was important to him, and what was not.

In closing, the narrator envisions the three of them leaving Toronto and running away to Nova Scotia: "Julie and I would work as barmaids. Douglas could set traps for lobsters. Then we could all be happy."

One of the British reviewers of *Moons* noticed that ten of its twelve stories look "through the eyes of someone at the halfway mark." True enough. The somewhat rueful, middle-aged perspective presented in *Moons*, with apt phrasings like "what you are living is your life" and the wise, wondering, feeling concentration on moments of transformation, revealed Munro creating her most wrenching and evocative stories yet. Each of the two bonanzas McGrath enjoyed at the *New Yorker* resulted in an especially strong collection and touched off something of a Munro renaissance. The *Moons* stories gave way to those that made up *The Progress of Love*, certainly her best collection thus far and, perhaps, her best collection overall. Reading one of its stories one night during the summer of 1984, Virginia Barber made her husband put down his own manuscript and read Munro's story. They both agreed on its beauty, and as she closed her letter Barber asked, "Have you thought about what a terrible threat to illiteracy you are?"

The reception *Moons* got outside of Canada confirmed that by 1983 Munro's reputation abroad was reaching a level equivalent to that she had enjoyed at home since the early 1970s. A Canadian Press story that followed her visit to Boston to read at Bentley College in May showed the folks at home noticing how she was doing. Beginning "Alice Munro's mind flutters freely, remembering odd places and people – especially bigots and the not-so-good old days," the story captures Munro and her career just then and here, her subject and problems in Huron County. Nonetheless, it continues, "Peers have ranked her among the finest short-story writers in the English language. But writing is a never-ending struggle, the Canadian author says. Her latest book, The Moons of Jupiter, has won exceptional praise from book reviewers in the United States since it was published in February." Later, before quoting from several U.S. reviews by "heavy hitters," it reported that *Moons* "has sold well in the U.S., considering that the market for short stories is gener-ally limited, a spokesman for Knopf said. Sales have passed the 10,000 mark. 'For short stories, that is absolutely wonderful,' the spokesman added." Knopf has by then taken the book into a fourth printing. Another profile, originally in the *Boston Globe* but reprinted in Canada, has Munro saying that she is "'surprised to be on the front page of the New York Times' and that 'Everyone has been incredibly kind.'" Summing her up, the reporter asserts that "she's no longer obsessed with being a writer of the first rank. She continues to produce stories, writing with many false starts, trashing a great deal of what she's produced before she gets what she wants."

Knopf had indeed done much better with *Moons* than they had with *The Beggar Maid*. In mid-October Close wrote Munro that she did not think sales would drop below 10,000: "Really in sales and certainly in reviews [it is] a major success. I can hardly wait for the next go round." By the time *Moons* went into paperback, Close recalls, sales of the hardback had almost reached 11,000 (of the 12,500 printed). But because Knopf's intention, with Munro, had been to introduce her work to a U.S. audience as a "writer of distinction," sales were not their prime concern with either book. Knopf had long been, and continued to be, a literary house committed to her as an author who should be respected and allowed as much as possible to write and publish the way she wanted to. Knopf was, in effect, a book-publishing equivalent of the *New Yorker*. When *The Beggar Maid* sold just under 4,000 copies, Close recalls, no one at Knopf was "upset by that sale, or disappointed." Even though Munro's $15,000 advance was thought at the time to be quite high for a book of stories, its sale was considered good for a first try. But when *Moons* sold almost three times as many copies, Close and her colleagues could see that Munro was finding an audience in the United States, one that could certainly grow.[16]

Virginia Barber's reaction to the sales of *The Beggar Maid* is another matter. "Enclosed is the unappetizing royalty statement from Knopf," she wrote to Munro as she passed it on in August 1980. "Hard to believe how few people read good books." The March 1981 statement showed royalties earned against the advance of just over $4,000, probably in the range of what Munro was then getting for a single story in the *New Yorker*. Barber added, "However, do not worry. Your audience here will grow, and you're getting some offers from paperback houses. We'll know tomorrow, I expect, whether or not Bantam, Penguin or Pocket Books is the winner. There's no money for us, alas, as the top offer is $3,500. Still, I want the U.S. paperback, and I've worked hard for this. You'll notice I just sounded my own horn, but it's more out of frustration than pride."

Frustrated or not, still worried about various markets, Barber had every reason to "sound her own horn" regarding Munro's career just then. Whether or not she feared pride, she equally had every reason to be proud of what she done over the previous four years to ensure its progress. From the time she became Munro's agent, Barber engaged in building Munro's career in all possible ways. She attracted the attention of the *New Yorker* and other magazine editors; she arranged book contracts, first with Macmillan and then with Norton and Knopf, and pursued the paperback prospects. She tracked and verified rights questions with an eye always to having them revert to Munro so she could resell them, she kept an eye on royalties, and she fielded whatever offers came in for film rights, translations, or anthologies. These activities came, of course, after she had read Munro's stories, responded to them, and kept encouraging her author to "Write, girl!", as she suggested more than once. Tracing Barber's activities as Munro's agent – and she was following this same path for several other writers concurrently – one can readily see just why Munro would call Barber her "essential support" in the dedication to the *Selected Stories*. As a friendship blossomed from their initial business relation, Munro and Barber formed a real partnership.

Bantam was the publisher that won the rights for a mass-market paperback of *The Beggar Maid* in the United States. Such rights questions are indicative of how publishers work; they contract for the original book and then are able to sell the paperback rights and, under certain circumstances, those rights can in turn be licensed to another publisher for another paperback edition. With books in English, rights are usually for the United Kingdom or North America – Canadian rights either subsumed or excluded depending on point of view or predilection. (During the time of Munro's first books this was a point of contention between McGraw-Hill New York and McGraw-Hill Ryerson.) Such concerns are a necessary preliminary to an incident that suggests just what Barber was able to do for Munro as her career grew. They confirm just why she needed an agent in the first place.

In September 1982, Barber wrote Munro just after she received Penguin Canada's paperback offer for *Moons*:

> We are still dancing over Penguin's offer. Peter Waldock [at Penguin] called to say he was "on Cloud 9" and wanted to buy

"all Alice Munro's books." He wants to publish a boxed set in Fall, 1984. We're still trying to straighten out the highly confused rights situation on *Lives* and on *Something*. Somebody has licensed U.K. rights on *Lives* to Penguin and so far, nobody I've talked to has been willing to confess. We reverted the rights, you remember. I've talked with Ryerson, McGraw N.Y., Penguin, NAL [New American Library] here, Macmillan, the Ryerson agent in Toronto and my English agent – and with some of these, there have been several talks. Just don't want you to think agents sit back twiddling thumbs. I'll untangle this knot or else! So far it's been both infuriating and amusing.

Barber was concerned here for several reasons. The licensing of *Lives* to Penguin in Great Britain effectively meant that any income from it would flow to the British licence holder, then to McGraw-Hill Ryerson, and only then to Munro, each company taking a portion. The fact was that neither Barber nor Munro had granted permission for the licence. When Barber got farther into it, she discovered that neither had McGraw-Hill Ryerson granted permission. With regard to *Lives* and *Something* in the United States, Barber wanted to terminate any connection between those titles and McGraw-Hill, New York and, also, to terminate licences held on them for mass-market paperbacks by NAL.

Barber's work reveals something of the network of issues handled by an agent. What she was undoing was a set of arrangements that had failed to address the author's long-term prospects. Intent on ensuring that Munro's work stayed in print in Canada, the United States, and Great Britain, and was available to other markets in translation, Barber needed to undo arrangements that impeded a single paperback publisher from obtaining rights to the whole of the work. She was successful in this – Penguin now publishes Munro in Canada, Vintage in the United States and Great Britain.

It took Barber a year to sort this out. She had to hire a lawyer on Munro's behalf, John Diamond, who had worked in publishing and was keen to go after NAL; he ultimately accomplished what Barber asked him to do for less than two thousand dollars. Sending him the relevant materials, Barber summarized her understanding of the situation in a five-page letter supported by two appendices and sixty-four pages of documents. Writing to Munro after she had heard Diamond's positive assessment of the situation, Barber maintained that his fee constituted "a valid investment for you – it's hell to spend money to get back your own work, but I believe your books will be in print for many generations to come and the present license situation assures you the smallest possible piece of the financial pie." As Barber pointed out, Penguin – in both Canada and Great Britain – wanted the titles in question, but she could not sell them the rights as things stood. "You would recoup the two thousand dollars – and more – from those sales alone."

Throughout the correspondence surviving from this episode there are frequent examples of Barber's assiduous advocacy of Munro's position and her desire to do what was right. Pushing McGraw-Hill Ryerson, which was also wronged by the licence that the Women's Press had granted without permission to Penguin U.K., Barber wrote:

> I hope you will change your mind about not wanting to "rock the boat." This contract is highly unfavorable to Alice Munro's interests. Further, it is not even a contract you yourselves thought adequate. I've done business with Women's Press successfully in the past and hope to do so in the future. But I don't think that should stop me from trying to right what I see as a wrong. Why was their contract still in effect anyway? The original purchaser of U.K. rights was Allen Lane. I assume somebody at McGraw terminated the Lane contract when their edition went out-of-print. Why wasn't the Women's Press contract terminated when their edition went out-of-print? At any rate, so far as we know now, Women's Press did not receive "prior written permission from the Proprietor" before licensing rights to Penguin. You have no copy of that license and have received none of the money due.

In September 1983, when Barber was able to send Munro her copy of the termination agreement with "the McGraws," she wrote, "I consider this document a golden one." She reported also that the contract from the Women's Press was coming and that NAL's was in process (it would yield Munro another $15,000), and she asked Munro to send Diamond a thank-you note. "He really did a splendid job. Of course," she added wryly, "so did I." She most certainly did.[17]

Another particular concern for Barber were Munro's royalty statements. Macmillan had been taken over by Gage, which now produced its royalty statements. In December 1983, after Gibson had written her asking for permission to include a Munro story in an anthology called *Illuminations*, Barber declined his proposal and offered a counter-proposal with better terms for Munro. She also wrote, "I'm very sorry if we've made your anthology impossible: on the other hand, I can't in good conscience give away Alice Munro's work." She continued: "I must tell you, too, Doug, that the royalty statements we receive from Gage are unacceptable in their lack of information and their incomprehensibility. We have now spent many hours as a result of the latest *Who Do You Think You Are* statement, trying without success to make sense of it. We are continuing our efforts, but I'll probably have to write for clarification." In a postscript note sent just to Munro, Barber wrote that the royalty statements were so confusing that she would "go after them. It's ridiculous not to send an author a legitimate accounting."

This letter set Gibson to work and early in January 1984 he was writing Barber to report on the royalty situation of *Who*, to send her copies of missing statements, and to try to clarify things generally. In the process he turned up an anomaly that Macmillan saw in its favour – a supposed three thousand dollars' worth of advance that had not yet been earned by the book. When Barber replied, it was clear that she knew her facts, that she knew her (and Munro's) position in relation to Macmillan on *Who*, and that on the question of its royalties she had been made to do the publisher's work. "It's a cruel blow to have no royalties," she concluded. Gibson replied gratefully and amiably, offering to put some money in Munro's hands by contracting for the next collection then and there. Passing this on to Munro, Barber wrote that she did not yet want a contract, but that Alice should indicate if she did. She continued, "Do you realize that if all goes well, all of your books will be in print in the

U.S. next year. What a splendid endorsement of your work! Cheers to you." Shortly thereafter she wrote again, noting that on a new royalty statement they had just received from Gage there was a mistake in their favour; she had decided to deposit the small cheque "as payment for work on their royalty statements. Send in the cops."

In hiring Barber as her agent, Munro found a person much more than equal to her tasks: as these exchanges (and numerous others in the Alice Munro archives) show, she was professional, knowledgeable, persistent, ethical, and very witty. Barber's reputation as an agent grew in step with Munro's as an author, so the two careers proved symbiotic, personally edifying, and utterly complementary. Very early on in the relation Barber began signing her letters "Love, Ginger," and that emotion is palpable in every letter that has survived. When the Alice Munro Garden was dedicated in Wingham in July 2002 Virginia Barber was among those who were there, and among those who spoke. Taking Munro's own question, "Who do you think you are?", as her motif, Barber described her as being among "the talented few [who] stick their heads up above the rules and take a fresh look around." She also reminded her audience that Munro's writing had not always been appreciated in Wingham, that "it's not necessarily comfortable up there, outside the box, being stared at and talked about. . . . I love the irony, the humor, with which Alice Munro often deals with the conflict." As one of Munro's best and most enthusiastic readers, Barber certainly knows this well.[18]

✥

When Gibson wrote to Barber in January 1984 he also offered "congratulations all round for Alice's *New York Times* best book listing." *Moons* had been chosen for the paper's list of the ten best books published in 1983. Its singular success in the United States, complementing as it did Munro's established reputation in Canada, brought about a marked increase in the number of invitations she received. Munro disregarded university positions; these, however, were increasingly coming from U.S. schools, although Canadian offers still arrived. During the early 1980s she still accepted some reading engagements. She appeared, for example, in Ottawa in February 1983 at a benefit for Interval House, a local community service centre; in March 1984 she read at the David Thompson Centre in Nelson, British Columbia – where she had taught in 1973 – and also at the University of Houston, where Rosellen Brown, another of Barber's clients, taught; Barber attended. And in September 1984 she participated in a program on censorship at Harbourfront in Toronto called "Freedom to Read." Offers to contribute specified pieces to various publication projects were continual (for example, *Canadian Literature, Chatelaine, Mosaic, Saturday Night,* a book on hometowns, another on women and sex), as were requests to blurb books by others. Although Munro was by then well known for her avoidance of such literary chores in favour of her own writing (a CBC radio profile broadcast as she set out on her Canadian *Moons* publicity tour in October 1982 made a special point of this), such requests continued. She did support writers she knew and whose work she read and respected. She blurbed books by Clark Blaise, Janette Turner Hospital, and Edna O'Brien ("There are only two or three writers in the world who mean as much to me as Edna O'Brien does") and was offered others; she wrote recommendations for grant support for Metcalf, Carol Shields, and Leo Simpson, among others. Particularly, she helped emerging Canadian writers whose work she liked: just as she championed Jack Hodgins in the 1970s, in the 1980s she did the same for Guy Vanderhaeghe and Jane Urquhart. Occasionally she tried to help an aspiring writer directly, as when she submitted a collection of poems directly to a publisher on the writer's behalf.

Prizes of various sorts also came Munro's way. In 1983 Munro was being considered for the Order of Canada (and Gibson provided background materials on her behalf), the next year Queen's University offered an honorary doctorate; in each case Munro declined. She won another Gold Award from the National Magazine Foundation for "Mrs. Cross and Mrs. Kidd," but a special highlight was the Academy Award won by the Atlantis Films production of her story "Boys and Girls," as best short-live-action film. It was an early success for Atlantis, a small company made up of three recent Queen's graduates. This award was suggestive of a growing interest in the cinematic possibilities of Munro's work. The CBC had done "Postcard," "How I Met My Husband," and "Baptizing" previously, but during the 1980s inquiries came in for films based on *Lives of Girls and Women*, "An Ounce of Cure," "Simon's Luck," "Tell Me Yes or No," and "Thanks for the Ride." Films of *Lives* and "Thanks" were eventually made.

Munro and Fremlin returned to Australia for a holiday between June and October 1983, but for the most part Munro remained in Clinton, dodging as many of these chores as possible in order to guard her time to write. Between her *New Yorker* bonanzas, 1982 through early 1984 were largely given over to writing. No stories were considered by the magazine between December 1981 and July 1984, but they looked at seven (plus the first revision of "Fits") between July and the end of the year. These were the stories that so impressed McGrath and became the core of *The Progress of Love*, her next book.

One chore Munro did not dodge but rather ᵥolunteered for and embraced was the writing of the foreword for a book edited by Robert Weaver and co-published by the CBC and Macmillan. *The Anthology Anthology* was published to celebrate the thirtieth anniversary of the radio program. Anne Holloway and Gibson at Macmillan knew that Weaver would do nothing to showcase his own work. So Munro was asked to do it and she readily accepted – her own "The Shining Houses," read on the CBC in 1962, was the lead story in the collection. An early draft of the foreword begins its closing paragraph with these words: "My personal debt to Robert Weaver is simply beyond measure." In the published version, Munro describes the bases for this recognition from her first contact with Weaver in 1951 through their first meeting in 1953 and their many contacts since, but she does not detail her own perpetual acknowledgement of Weaver throughout her career.

This is the other side of the view of Munro as recluse. She seems to have mentioned him in every interview she ever gave, certainly in any that touched on her first publication. While Munro has become famous (or infamous) for avoiding the limelight herself (you have to be "selfish, self-protective" to be a writer, she told Patrick Watson in 1976), she has never hesitated from doing chores involving people who matter to her and to whom she is grateful. Foremost among these people is Robert

Weaver. Munro wrote the book's foreword, was interviewed along with Morley Callaghan by Weaver for the anniversary *Anthology* program and on CBC-TV's *The Journal,* and participated in the tribute to Weaver at Harbourfront. All of this followed her dedication of *Moons* to him. Self-protecting when it came to her writing, Munro has not stinted those to whom she feels grateful. At just about the same time, when the *Malahat Review* was putting together a tribute volume for John Metcalf, Munro wrote something for him as well.[19]

"I want some kind of purity": *The Progress of Love* and Its Progress from Macmillan to McClelland & Stewart

When the *New Yorker* editors received three new Munro stories to consider in July 1984, it had been well over two years since they had seen "Bardon Bus." The new stories were "Gold," "Monsieur les Deux Chapeaux," and "The Moon in the Orange Street Skating Rink." As they tended to do (despite Barber's best efforts), McGrath and his colleagues set one Munro story against another, buying "Skating Rink" and rejecting the others. "Gold," a story that recreates the scene of people giving impromptu speeches that Munro and Fremlin saw at the King's Domain in Sydney, is one of only a few completed Munro stories Barber has not managed to sell. "Monsieur" was bought and published by *Grand Street* after which it was selected by Raymond Carver for *Best American Stories 1986* (he wrote that "for some years, [Munro's] been quietly writing some of the best short fiction in the world"). The *New Yorker* editors did pretty much the same thing with the next three stories that they received late in the summer – "Eskimo," "Fits," and "Lichen" – rejecting "Eskimo" ("it seems somewhat cryptic and inaccessible") and encouraging a revision of "Fits." ("Eskimo" went to *GQ-Gentleman's Quarterly* – while Munro revised "Fits" twice to no avail. It also went into *Grand Street* after other magazines had passed.)

Just after he sent these back, McGrath received and immediately bought "Miles City, Montana." It caused a stir at the magazine, as Barber reported to Munro, apparently paraphrasing what McGrath had said to her: "The *New Yorker* is beside itself over 'Miles City.' One of the best you've ever written. Wonderful to see your experiments with technique, form – you're pushing the traditional limits of the short story. No one else is writing stories like yours."

It was this run of stories – seven since July – that prompted McGrath's remark about feeling like Rilke's editor. In that October 15 letter, he enclosed his edited manuscript of "Lichen." He was "querying or toning down some of the crotch imagery" and asking for a specific change: "The real magic of this story, it seems to me, is the way it earns and then miraculously effects that transformation of pubic hair into lichen, but I think it should happen effortlessly and almost invisibly – as it does in the photograph – and without the additional reference to the rat between Dina's legs." McGrath did not win this point – the rat stayed – but he recognized that with these descriptions Munro "had broken new ground at the *New Yorker* which has never before referred or alluded to crotch shots. Mr. Shawn said, 'The central image gave me misgivings, but the writer has earned the right to use it.'" Laughing about this exchange, Barber wrote to Munro, "So, you've a dirty mind, Alice Munro, but it's a *talented* dirty mind and that's O.K."[20]

When she wrote Munro describing the *New Yorker* reaction to "Miles City, Montana," Barber noted that they were just one story away from the magazine's bonus. Her strategy was to hold back "'Progress of Love' until they cool off up there. They're so dazzled by 'Miles City' that they can't be trusted to read for awhile." Her instincts were right. Just after Christmas McGrath wrote to Munro that "Ginger doesn't seem to be in the office today, so for once I get to pass along the good news: Everyone here was just delighted with *The Progress of Love*. It's a wonderful, brilliant story, and we're pleased to have it." This was less than two weeks after he wrote to Barber that Munro "is simply one of the finest short story writers alive and it's a great honor and privilege for us to be able to publish her." The word about "The Progress of Love" was spreading farther afield, since Close reported a conversation she had had with *New Yorker* fiction editor Fran Kiernan who was "just ecstatic about" it. These two stories, particularly, garnered the strongest reaction at the *New Yorker*. Before he had seen "Progress," McGrath wrote to Munro that "Miles City" was his favourite of the group "because the writing is impeccable." For her part, Munro told Barber that it was her favourite too, though doubtless she would not have described it as "impeccable" writing. Munro probably would have said that it was "all right."

After "Progress" Munro's success rate with the *New Yorker* dropped off since the magazine saw four more stories plus two revisions (a second of "Fits" and one of "Circle of Prayer") but bought only one, "White Dump." Rejecting "Jesse and Meribeth" in February 1985, McGrath explained to Barber their specific problems with the story: "Though it's all handled with subtlety and dispatch, we couldn't help feeling that the substance of the story never really measured up to her skill in presenting it. Or perhaps another, simpler way to put it all is that we've just been spoiled by her recent stories. It's a very high standard we're holding her to – there is no question about that." These comments point up sentiments similar to Munro's own. Just over two years later, when she was working on the stories that became a third "Munro bonanza" for the *New Yorker* and the core of *Friend of My Youth*, she wrote to Metcalf about the stories she was working on: "There is an attenuated bleak feeling about the one long story and an untrustworthy *facility* about two chunky ones. They are not *bad*. I am feeling rather happy – or content – about my life but doubtful about my writing. I want some kind of purity. Instead I've got a lot of technique." One should not look askance at Munro's comments here – the *New Yorker* published five of eleven stories in *Progress* and eight of ten in *Friend* – but, that notwithstanding, the 1980s reveal her still as a writer who despite past success viewed each story as a new beginning, a desperate struggle.

"Jesse and Meribeth" went on to the *Atlantic Monthly* before ending up in *Mademoiselle* as "Secrets Between Friends." The other stories the *New Yorker* passed on followed the same path: "Eskimo" in *GQ-Gentleman's Quarterly*, "Deux Chapeaux" and "Fits" in *Grand Street*, "Circle of Prayer" in the *Paris Review*, and "A Queer Streak" (published in two parts) in *Granta*. Barber's strategy was to try mass-market magazines and only then let stories go to more literary publications that paid.

Owing to internal changes, *Grand Street* paid less than the $5,000 they paid for "Working for a Living" ("Deux Chapeaux," for example, brought $1,200), but at least these magazines still paid for contributions. With "A Queer Streak" in *Granta*, too, Munro had her direct first contact with Bill Buford who, under Tina Brown's editorship, headed the fiction department at the *New Yorker* during the 1990s. The year 1985 proved, though, to be the last time many of Munro's stories went elsewhere. Barber recalls that once during the 1980s she was almost pleased to have the *New Yorker* turn down a story so that she could send it to Michael Curtis at the *Atlantic Monthly*. He published the two stories in *Friend of My Youth* that the *New Yorker* did not.[21]

ꚛ

In 1985 Penguin Canada prevailed upon Munro to write an introduction for its second edition of *Moons*. There she begins, "I find it very hard to talk about, or look at – let alone read – any work of mine, after it is published, shut away in its book. Part of this is simple misgiving. Couldn't I have done it better, make the words serve me better?" There is a sense of separation from published work, she continues: "It's a queasiness, an unwillingness to look or examine. I try to master this, feeling that it's primitive and childish. . . . Some of these stories are closer to my own life than others are, but not one of them is as close as people seem to think." She then writes about the relation between "The Moons of Jupiter" and her father's death, explaining the gestation of "The Turkey Season" (which grew out of her early attempts to use her own summer 1950 experience as a waitress at Milford Manor, previously attempted in "Is She as Kind as She Is Fair?", connected to her father's experience running a turkey barn), and tells when some of the others were written. Munro concludes saying that she has "to make an effort, now, to remember what's in these stories. . . . I make them with such energy and devotion and secret pains, and then I wiggle out and leave them, to harden and settle in their place[.] I feel free."

Like the stories in *Moons*, those destined for *Progress* seemed to have a different, deeper quality. This same sense pervaded each successive collection, but it might be noted especially in *The Progress of Love, Open*

Secrets, and *Runaway*. Each stands apart as a transforming collection – one in which it feels that the work has become deeper and denser – although the title story of *The Love of a Good Woman* and its "My Mother's Dream" probably ought to be added to any such list. While other stories in *Progress* certainly might be taken up to illustrate the quality here, such as "Lichen" or "White Dump," the two stories that seem to best exemplify just how Munro was writing during her second bonanza are "Miles City, Montana" and "The Progress of Love." The reaction they got, certainly, was most immediate and effusive.

Both "Miles City, Montana" and "Progress of Love," each drafted in the same notebook and finished about this same time, are stories close to Munro's own life. The near-drowning incident at the centre of the first is virtually memoir, the four family members who were there remembering it as narrated. Munro and her father rescuing turkeys from drowning is a memory too, but Steve Gauley, his drowning, and his funeral were imagined, though Munro recalls knowing boys who later drowned. "The Progress of Love" draws on the lives of her great-grandmother, her grandmother, and her mother while Phemie (or Fame), its narrator, includes elements of Munro herself. She is given some of Munro's own memories, certainly, but Fame is also a character offering what might have become of Munro herself had she never got away from Wingham. The narrator's perspective, like Munro's, is that of a middle-aged native. All this admitted, Munro is nevertheless right about these two stories: "not one is as close [to her life] as people seem to think." This is so because of Munro's "energy and devotion and secret pains" – they transform whatever had been remembered, whatever is "real," into the different reality that is the story's world. The story, an artifice, is able to affect its readers on its own terms by way of the words she arranges, those words that she thinks never serve her well enough.

"Miles City, Montana" and "The Progress of Love" demonstrate just how Munro's writing during this time began in actual experiences but then, through her art, became something considerably more than experience transcribed. "Miles City" seems to have begun when Munro was working on "The Beggar Maid" during 1976–77; a draft of the Miles City incident includes a courtship for the narrator and her husband Hugh similar to Rose and Patrick's. About this time too there was also the draft story, "Shoebox Babies," which Munro worked on during the late 1970s but never published and which drew from the circumstances of Catherine Munro's birth and death in July 1955. It moved into a notebook draft called just "Miles City," which contains a fairly complete rendering of the near-drowning episode and the family's trip; but rather than just the recollected dead deer the family saw when playing "I Spy" in the finished story, the older daughter recalls Elizabeth, the baby who died. This draft also includes the image of the drowned Steve Gauley being carried by the narrator's father, although it appears just at the story's end where it is connected to the narrator's misgivings about their vulnerability. Its narrator is explicitly Munro herself in 1961: "During those years I was trying to be a writer. I could say that I was trying to write – short stories, and, once, a novel – but it would be more accurate to say that I was trying to be a writer, because I felt as if I had to assemble distant parts of myself and hold them together, before I could start the actual writing. This was my job – this assembling – and it was a tricky business." Neither version includes the narrator and her father saving turkeys from drowning, an experience in the finished story that confirms the narrator's role as daughter and allows her to appreciate his hard-working way of life.

Munro's own "assembling" of "Miles City, Montana" was indeed a tricky business. It takes her memoir – the near-drowning and its circumstances – and marries it to the imagined drowning and funeral of Steve Gauley. Human helplessness in the face of death, and her parents' attitudes toward it, are felt as the narrator and Andrew talk in the aftermath. It is then she imagines what it would have been like if Meg had not been saved. "Who is ready to be a father, a mother, who is fit?" the narrator asks in the draft, just before she shifts back to Steve Gauley's drowning and his funeral, asking the central unanswerable question of "Miles City, Montana." And though Munro omitted any direct reference to Catherine Munro's death in the final version, it is felt on the page, created there in Munro's sensed and mediated human vulnerability.

So while it is possible to see Jenny Munro's near-drowning in 1961 in Miles City, Montana, at the centre of the story, to insist on that incident's recounting as the story's core misses the point of any fiction, and of Munro's in particular. What she creates on the page is the feeling of being, the feeling of authentic experience captured through words. This writing has a kind of purity when it works – as it most certainly does in "Miles City, Montana" and in "The Progress of Love." Yet any created purity is not just in the story's details, since those may be grafted on from anywhere (the swimming pool in Miles City, Montana, for example, was not a swimming pool but a man-made body called Scanlon Lake). Their connection to Munro's own life, while real, is secondary to anyone reading a story that emerges from such connections. For Munro, and for her readers too, the significance of any autobiographical connection comes back to the image of Cynthia and Meg, still in their back seat, still headed to Ontario, still expecting to return home to Vancouver: "So we went on, with the two in the back seat trusting us, because of no choice, and we ourselves trusting to be forgiven, in time, for everything that had first to be seen and condemned by those children: whatever was flippant, arbitrary, careless, callous – all our natural, and particular, mistakes."

There is a deeply felt but unarticulated wisdom in this ending, just as there is at the end of "The Progress of Love" where Munro invokes the circumstances of "those old marriages, where love and grudges could be growing underground, so confused and stubborn, it must have seemed they had forever." This story, probably the one Munro described to an Australian journalist as a novel-in-progress "tracing three generations of women," did grow from the circumstances of her maternal ancestors, but it is much less overtly autobiographical than "Miles City." Essentially, Phemie's recollection that is the story examines the way her mother and her grandmother lived their lives, a recollection brought on by the news of her mother's death. In the wake of "Working for a Living," a memoir that is in some ways an analysis of her parents' marriage, "The Progress of Love" fictionalizes the same sort of analysis and pushes it back another generation through Phemie's grandmother's threatened hanging. That act, while a real one, did not happen in Munro's family, nor did the other central event, the mother's burning of the money inherited from her father. Yet Bertha Stanley Chamney's religiosity was real, as her resentment toward her own father likely was. Thus here Munro may again be seen "assembling" materials, some that happened, some that she knows from her own experience, some that she has read or heard about, and some that she imagined. "I make them with such energy and devotion and secret pains," Munro wrote. Once they are published, "I wiggle out and leave them, to harden and settle in their place." There they are, asking crucial questions such as what is true about the image Phemie holds in her mind of her mother burning the inherited money as rejection of her father ("That's a lot of hate," Phemie's friend Bob Marks comments). Imagining that scene, Phemie describes it: "And my father, standing by, seems not just to be permitting her to do this but to be protecting her. A solemn scene, but not crazy." Even though Phemie realizes, once the story's action is over, that this scene could never have happened, she still sees it as true and emblematic of her parents' relation. Munro phrased this same mystery in "Chaddeleys and Flemings: 2. The Stone in the Field": "Taking the mystery of his life with him." So Munro knows, and so she writes: "some kind of purity" indeed.[22]

"The Progress of Love," like "Miles City, Montana" and many of Munro's most successful stories, had a long gestation; elements of the story connect to pre-*Lives* material and to "Places at Home." As was her practice, Munro kept revising it. She sent Gibson a second "final" version, which she called "a new, *finally final*, third person version." McGrath expressed surprise at receiving a new version (probably the same one she sent Gibson) in September 1985 since "it seemed just about perfect to me the way it was – but the new version is even better." She had shifted it into the third person, which was the way it appeared in the *New Yorker*, but she then returned it to the first person in the book version. Looking at the third-person version for the first time, Close could not decide on a preference since first she "felt that you had lost an emotional edge" through the shift, but "putting Phemie in the third person places the mother's story in greater relief." She continued,

"Ginger hasn't read the third person version yet. What does Chip McGrath think? Or Doug Gibson? Or, most important, you?" In this letter, too, Close expressed her hope that Munro comes around to the view (held by Gibson and Close) that the book should be called *The Progress of Love*. What such a response confirms is that by the mid-1980s Munro's editors and agent were all of a single mind, responding, encouraging, and working in the same direction. An apt illustration of their attitudes was Barber's when she reported to Alice the reaction at the *New Yorker* to "Miles City, Montana": "What a book these stories are going to make!" she exclaimed. "Sending out your stories gives us so much pleasure that I feel like sending thank you notes."

In July 1985 Barber sent the still-untitled collection to Gibson at Macmillan, noting that they would not be able to publish before August 1986 because the *New Yorker* still had to publish four stories. She sent it to Knopf at the same time. Once her boss Robert Gottlieb returned from a trip, Close wrote, "we can try to put a price on the priceless." This manuscript included ten of the eleven stories in *Progress* ("Circle of Prayer" was not finished, but was added in late August). As the book was proceeding toward publication, revisions of "The Moon in the Orange Street Skating Rink," "Circle of Prayer," and "Jessie and Meribeth" were added.

By early August Gibson had drafted a contract for "*The Progress of Love* (and other stories)" and was getting the approvals necessary to send it to Barber. They needed to negotiate various points – and Gibson had to satisfy her on various royalty-reporting questions – before it went in mid-September. After further negotiations and another draft, the contract was completed by December 2. Munro was to receive a $25,000 advance and royalties beginning at 10 per cent and increasing to 15 per cent after 10,000 copies; on the paperback, she got 8 per cent until 40,000 copies, 10 per cent thereafter. Macmillan then set to work designing the book. Both the Canadian firm and Knopf wanted an internal design they both could use without adaptation, and Gibson wanted to continue the magic realism look of the previous two dust jackets. Munro was doubtful about this latter point; her daughter Jenny, an artist, was to make an attempt at an image of an old barn with a rainbow on it as one possibility, and Gibson envisioned a similar sort of photographic image.[23]

Ironically, Macmillan never published the book. When Munro sent along a "final, final page" for "Circle of Prayer" in late November, she wrote expressing sympathy for Gibson's situation at Macmillan, indicating she knew that there were problems. There had been changes at the top, and as a result Gibson decided to look elsewhere. In February he resigned in order to move to McClelland & Stewart, where he been promised his own imprint, Douglas Gibson Books. Learning of this, Munro indicated her desire to move *The Progress of Love* from Macmillan to McClelland & Stewart as the first book published under the new imprint.

So *Progress* proved to be. Understandably Macmillan took a *very* dim view of this prospect since they had a contract, the book was in production (both in Toronto and New York), and especially since it involved a very valuable author. The dispute and the resultant negotiations lasted from February to April; the Macmillan executives well knew that Munro had sold over 12,000 copies of *Moons* and had brought the firm a record $45,000 from Penguin for the Canadian paperback rights. Early on, Linda McKnight, the new executive vice-president and publisher, wrote a detailed memo to the file assessing the situation at each level (production, marketing and sales, damage to Macmillan) and concluded that Gibson was not needed to produce a quality book and that the repayment of the $12,500 advance already received would in no way adequately compensate the firm for the loss of Munro and her book. If Macmillan were to accede to the request, more compensation would be needed. In any case, McKnight was not prepared to agree to it.

On February 28, McKnight met with Barber in New York to discuss the situation. McKnight wrote a summary of the meeting, beginning with Barber's explicit support of Gibson, whom Munro saw as "the best editor in the world," and continuing: "You stated your client's position very firmly, and suggested that while there were no legal grounds for contract termination, you felt moral-suasion held great force in this situation, and that no publisher should force an author unhappy with a contract." McKnight's argument was as follows: Macmillan understood that Gibson would publish Munro's subsequent books, but as for *Progress*, Macmillan had performed well in the past and was concerned about the effect of Munro's move on its reputation; the book was in production in New York (where most of the editorial work had been done) so Gibson was not needed in that regard. In effect, the financial blow to Macmillan would be great. McKnight closed by suggesting that they travel to Clinton to meet with Munro. Replying to McKnight on March 14, Barber said her memory of their meeting differed a bit but, in any case, McKnight should have received Munro's letter by then, and "I don't see how you can deny her after you've read it, and I'm hoping you will then agree to promptly put through termination papers. Because Alice's request to be released is based on her desire to continue her successful partnership with Doug Gibson, you know surely that we will express openly and privately our gratitude to Macmillan and our satisfaction with your publishing program."

Munro's letter clearly states her wish to be let out of the contract with Macmillan, but it is more interesting for the view it offers of her own career:

> Doug first talked to me about publishing with Macmillan in the mid-seventies. I was very discouraged at that time. Ryerson had done nothing to promote or even distribute my first book. McGraw-Hill Ryerson had published the second with expressed reluctance and the third without enthusiasm – merely, I believe, to keep a Canadian fiction writer on their list. Every publisher I had met had assured me that I would have to grow up and write novels before I could be taken seriously as a writer. No one in Canada had shown the least interest in taking on a writer who was going to turn out book after book of short stories. The result of this is that I wasted much time and effort trying to turn myself into a novelist, and had become so depressed that I was unable to write at all. Doug changed that. He was absolutely the first person in Canadian publishing who made me feel that there was no need to apologize for being a short story writer, and

that a book of short stories could be published and promoted as major fiction. This was a fairly revolutionary notion, at the time. It was this support that enabled me to go on working, when I had been totally uncertain about my future.

I came to Macmillan because of Doug, and his respect for my work changed me from a minor, "literary" writer who sold poorly into a major writer who sold well. I hope that you will understand how I have felt, from that time on, that I owe him a great deal, and that I want him to have charge of any book I publish. I am not making a judgement against Macmillan – my relations in the house have always been good – but for Doug Gibson.

I realize that I do not have a legal right to move this book, but I hope that my very strong feelings about publishing with Doug will influence you to let me go.

They did not. On April 2 McKnight wrote again to Barber announcing Macmillan's decision not to let Munro and *The Progress of Love* go.

Viewed as a minor episode in publishing history, things got really interesting at this point. Barber called McKnight and asked what it would take to buy Macmillan out. Macmillan replied that it wanted the $12,500 advance, $80,000, and half of the publisher's share of the paperback. Armed with this offer, Gibson wrote Avie Bennett and Peter Waldock, his colleagues at McClelland & Stewart, that his "inclination here is to make a good offer that makes sense from our point of view, and ask Ginger to make it clear that if they turn it down, the fact that they did so is likely to come out." Then Macmillan would be seen holding Munro against her will and having turned down an offer that would have been straight profit to them. They would look bad, even silly.

On April 11 McClelland & Stewart agreed to return the advance and split the publisher's share of the paperback contract, but refused the $80,000 payment, offering $32,150 instead and outlining how they came up with that figure. (Throughout, each side was estimating its real cost for the book versus their assumptions about those of the other; Macmillan assumed a sale of 10,000, while McClelland & Stewart thought 15,000 more realistic.) McKnight found this offer offensive and advocated going to arbitration. In the end Barber, who was handling the negotiations, persuaded Macmillan to accept a $40,000 payment, the return of the advance, and the 50–50 split of paperback monies contingent on Macmillan issuing all press releases. This was agreed to on April 16. There were details to work out, mostly connected to the publication of the paperback, but the agreement was signed and a public announcement made on April 29. The parties did not announce the amount Macmillan received but did say in the press release that it "was arrived at after extensive negotiation"; McKnight was quoted saying "The figure agreed to, plus the return of our advance and a share of the paperback income, made the settlement viable." Barber was named as the initiator of the deal, and she "stated how delighted Alice Munro was with the professional manner of Macmillan in considering the sale of her contract." Munro's reasons for requesting the sale had "nothing to do with Macmillan's performance as her publisher."[24]

Munro's and Barber's comments notwithstanding, the immediate public reaction to the news of Munro's move seemed to confirm McKnight's concerns regarding Macmillan's reputation. Writing in the *Toronto Star* Ken Adachi began his story by asserting that Gibson had "scored a coup by acquiring Canadian publishing rights to the work of Alice Munro from Macmillan." *The Progress of Love* would inaugurate Douglas Gibson Books, a personal imprint of about ten books a year published by McClelland & Stewart, and Munro was quoted as saying she was following Gibson "because I have respect for his editorial abilities. But I'm glad there is someone like Doug in Canada. . . . He cares about books." Adachi also reported that Hugh MacLennan and W.O. Mitchell, two other authors published by Macmillan, had signed with him. Macmillan, and McKnight's comments on the sale, were relegated to the end of the story. The *Globe and Mail*, reporting the same information, did so under the headline "CanLit Luminaries Stick with Gibson."

Years before Munro encountered this situation, when *Moons* was just coming together and she needed to start looking for a Canadian publisher, Barber had expressed doubts about trade publishing at

Macmillan. Gibson's own move to McClelland & Stewart, and the decisions of Munro and other well-known authors to follow him, certainly did nothing to help Macmillan's position. But for Munro, as she eloquently wrote in her letter to McKnight and said to Adachi, it was not about publishing; it was about the making of her books and the preservation of the ongoing relation she had established with Gibson. That she is still with him, five books later, confirms that mutual commitment. Such relations have been a hallmark of Munro's career.

"I began to be almost a popular writer": The Progress of Love

Even before the agreement between the publishers was finalized, McClelland & Stewart had set to work producing their edition of *The Progress of Love*. With Knopf handling the typesetting, the book was already in production in New York. Gibson and his colleagues had to confirm their contract with Munro, coordinate production with Knopf, and plan publicity. The contract was essentially the same one Munro had had with Macmillan (as regards advance and royalties), and McClelland & Stewart was able to offset from the Knopf typesetting, printing in Canada. For the first time, the U.S. and Canadian editions of Munro's book would be published at effectively the same time, September 15 in the United States and September 20 in Canada – and Munro's publicity tours dovetailed in September and October. British publication, this time by Chatto & Windus, followed in January 1987.

As the first Douglas Gibson Book and one that came at a propitious moment in its author's career, *The Progress of Love* received a considerable publicity push from McClelland & Stewart. Even before its acquisition was announced, in late April, they had arranged for 160 sets of bound galley proofs from Knopf's printer. These were sent out well in advance of publication and made available to their salespeople. Meanwhile, Gibson had continued with his jacket design, settling on Alex Colville's *Elm Tree at Horton Landing*, a recognizable Canadian image (an example of "hyper-realism") from the collection of the Art Gallery of Ontario. McClelland & Stewart had arranged an initial press run of 15,000 copies (consistent with the negotiations with Macmillan). In August Penguin bought the paperback rights (for mass market and trade editions) for $50,000. By the end of August Gibson sent finished copies of *The Progress of Love* to both Munro and Barber. To the author he wrote, "I hope that you are very proud of it. I know that I am." To her agent, he expressed gratitude for what she did with Macmillan: "I hope that the arrival of the finished book will convince you that all of the hard and imaginative work you did to bring *The Progress of Love* to Douglas Gibson Books was worthwhile." McClelland & Stewart launched the book – and so the Douglas Gibson Books imprint – on the evening of September 18 at its new offices on University Avenue in Toronto.

Munro's publicity tour began on September 16 in Toronto, continued to Montreal and Ottawa through the twenty-fifth, broke for three days, and then continued in Victoria, Vancouver, Edmonton, and Calgary through October 3. She then got ten days off, before starting again in Windsor and at the International Festival of Authors at Harbourfront. There she read "The Progress of Love" and, also, was the recipient of the first Marian Engel Award, a $10,000 award given to a female writer by the Writers' Development Trust for "a distinguished and continuing body of work." Engel, a friend of Munro's and in her later years one of Barber's writers, had died in 1985. Then came the U.S. tour – New York and Washington – before another stint in Ontario, followed by a trip to Halifax. After well over two months of meeting and greeting, the last publicity event on the tour was a reading in Toronto on December 8.

Munro had not lost her aversion to such activity. As preparation for such an extended tour, she and Fremlin took a holiday of their own into the United States, where, among other things, they visited Barber's hometown in the Blue Ridge region of Virginia. Even so, before the tour was finished, she wrote Metcalf acknowledging the copy of his *Adult Entertainment* (Macmillan) that she had received: "Awful tour," she told him. "I won't do this again even if I have to publish with some little outfit like Laprang-Oolong Press." Metcalf replied asking for an inscribed copy of *Progress*. The day after she got home from her third swing through Ontario and the trip to Halifax, Munro sent him a copy and commented, "There is something really sickening about this selling yourself, so why am I doing it? Because it seems so precious and rarified *not* to?" In the same letter, she added, "I never give away my give-away copies – too scared people won't like the book, won't know what to say, etc." This is a revelatory comment regarding Munro's own view of her accomplishment. It is one reminiscent of the last glimpse of Frances in "Accident": "But inside she's ticking away, all by herself, the same Frances who was there before any of it."[25] Well-established as Alice Munro, Writer, she was still wondering about all the fuss: Who Do You Think You Are? was a question she continued to ask even then.

Because the Canadian and U.S. editions of *Progress* were published within a week of one another, the attention the book received was concurrent and mutually affirming. In keeping with the longstanding intimacy of Canada-U.S. cultural relations, the attention Munro got in the United States was watched closely back home. Beverly Slopen, a Toronto-based literary journalist and agent, prepared an advance profile of Munro for *Publishers Weekly*. While she was doing so, she also wrote in the *Toronto Star* over a month before the book's publication, "There are signs that Alice Munro's sixth collection of short stories . . . will be her most successful book to date in the U.S." Similarly, when the *Vancouver Sun* wanted an advance review of *Progress* it ran the one that had just been published in the *New York Times*. Overall, reviews of *Progress*, especially those published in the United States and Britain, reveal a level of care and consideration befitting a major author of considerable gifts and power.

In a prepublication feature review in *Quill & Quire*, Patricia Bradbury wrote that "more than ever before, Munro is a social historian, thinking nothing of placing three generations in a tale and removing, like tissued layers, the deep strata in people's lives. Old houses, like relationships, are sky-lighted or ruined, and underlying every story is a bedrock of stubbornness, a dark lump in the gut, which Munro circles calmly, giving us all we might know while saying it's never enough." Most major Canadian papers offered their assessments on the day *Progress* was published. Robert Stewart, in the *Montreal Gazette*, oddly condescends to the small towns of southern Ontario, calling Munro's territory a "sterile landscape." But when he asks rhetorically why a reader should care about Munro's "buttoned-up" WASPs, he answered his question with another: "Who cared about the drab existence of the Russian serfs in the works of Chekhov and Turgenev?" In the *Globe and Mail*, William French savoured the book, noting that Munro – with the exception of "Eskimo," a story seen by many as below her usual standard – stays in her familiar territory, Huron County, Ontario. He also notes her "dextrous handling of time. . . . Munro has become even more adept at intercutting past, present, and future." As had been the case before among Canadian newspaper reviews, the single best one was David Williamson's in the *Winnipeg Free Press*. He cited a passage from the American writer Kay Boyle, "a short story should 'invest a brief sequence of events with reverberating human significance by means of style, selection and ordering of detail,'" and agreed with her too that a story should be "at once a parable and a slice of life, at once symbolic and real." Addressing this conception, Williamson compared Munro to other short story luminaries like Donald Barthelme, Raymond Carver, Ann Beattie, and Peter Taylor, and sounded a note that became a frequent clarion call for *Progress*: that Munro's stories seem more like "compressed novels." *Progress* is Munro's "best work yet," he concluded.

Munro's handling of time comes in for especial attention, with Heather Henderson in *Maclean's* concluding that in her work "the past is not a better place – but is a part of everyone, demanding acknowledgement." Even though there is evidence of the beginning of another angle of criticism of her work – one reviewer refers to her somewhat snidely as "the darling of Canadian literature" and a CBC panel of literary types discussing the book on *Morningside*, ignoring her innovative treatment of time, complained that Munro was not doing anything new – the Canadian reviews of *Progress* are largely summarized by Audrey Andrews's assertion in the *Calgary Herald*: "Munro lifts out the essence of reality. That is her art. Reading her work, we recognize ourselves."[26]

If Canadian reviewers, who had been responding to Munro's books for almost twenty years, were by now understandably reaching for other ways to assess her work ("of course her stories are brilliant, but . . ."), reviewers in the United States and Britain were just hitting their stride with *Progress*. The *Publishers Weekly* advance review on July 4 set the tone: Munro "brings to each story a freshness of vision, a breadth of sympathy and a wide-ranging imagination that makes her work both unpredictable and scrupulously true. . . . One senses Munro's conviction that human nature is mysterious and wonderful. Her stories are magically captivating. They will stand the test of time." Slopen's *Publishers Weekly* profile appeared in August. She asserted of Munro that "few people writing today can bring a character, a mood or a scene to life with such economy. And she has an exhilarating ability to make the reader see the familiar and ordinary with fresh insight and compassion." Slopen also quoted Munro on her preferred form: "I no longer feel attracted to the well-made novel. I want to write the story that will zero in and give you intense, but not connected, moments of experience. I guess that's the way I see life. People remake themselves bit by bit and do things they don't understand. The novel has to have a coherence which I don't see any more in the lives around me."

Michiko Kakutani, in the *New York Times*, offered this conclusion: "Drawing upon her seemingly infinite reserves of sympathy," Munro offers "pictures of life, of relationships, of love, glimpsed from a succession of mirrors and frames – pictures that possess both the pain and immediacy of life and the clear, hard radiance of art." Paul Gray, in *Time*, began his notice by asserting that Munro "continues to buck the genre's fashionable trend toward miniaturization and microplots. Her characters stubbornly refuse to trudge through brief but nonetheless tedious interludes." Gray was one of a number of careful, thoughtful reviewers who sought to get at just why Munro's stories have the effects they have, why her vision is both different, and better, from that of other writers. Citing "White Dump" as an example, Gray wrote that "the major event" in the story's action, "the decision years earlier of the first wife to run away, evolves almost glancingly into a stunning finale."

Following this same line, two reviews of *Progress* by other writers are among the sharpest, most considered, and persuasive. Joyce Carol Oates, writing in the *New York Times Book Review*, began by comparing Munro to Peter Taylor, William Trevor, and Edna O'Brien and holds that, like them, she "writes stories that have the density – moral, emotional, sometimes historical – of other writers' novels." Oates got to the heart of just what Munro has been working toward throughout her entire career:

> As remote from the techniques and ambitions of what is currently known as "minimalist" fiction as it is possible to get and still inhabit the same genre, these writers give us fictitious worlds that are mimetic paradigms of utterly real worlds yet are fictions, composed with so assured an art that it might be mistaken for artlessness. They give voice to the voices of their regions, filtering the natural rhythms of speech through a more refined (but not obtrusively refined) writerly speech. They are faithful to the contours of local legend, tall tales, anecdotes, family reminiscences; their material is nearly always realistic – "Realism" being that convention among competing others that swept all before it in the mid and late 19th century – and their characters behave, generally, like real people. That is, they surprise us at every turn, without violating probability. They so resemble ourselves that reading about them, at times, is emotionally risky. Esthetically experimental literature, while evoking our admiration, rarely moves us in the way this sort of literature moves us.

Oates placed Munro's writing generally, and *Progress* specifically, in this intellectual and aesthetic context. She "has concentrated on short fiction that explores the lives of fairly undistinguished men and women – but particularly women – who live in rural Ontario. . . . The most powerful of the 11 stories collected in 'The Progress of Love' take on bluntly and without sentiment the themes of mortality, self-delusion, puzzlement over the inexplicable ways of fate." Oates cited "A Queer Streak," "White Dump," and especially "The Progress of Love" as the volume's strongest stories but, sharp critic that she is, also argued that more than the two collections preceding it, *The Progress of Love* "does contain less fully realized stories." She cites "Eskimo" as one that "reads like an early draft of a typically rich, layered, provocative Munro story," and sees the two parts of "Miles City, Montana" as insufficiently integrated, connected by their "rather forced epiphany." But even the weaker stories offer "passages of genuinely inspired prose and yield the solid pleasures of a three-dimensional world that has been respectfully, if not always lovingly, recorded." Thematically, Oates summarizes *The Progress of Love* as "a volume of unflinching honesty, uncompromising in its dissection of the ways we deceive ourselves in the name of love; the bleakness of its vision is enriched by the author's exquisite eye and ear for detail. Life is heartbreak, but it is also uncharted moments of kindness and reconciliation."

Novelist Anne Tyler, writing in the *New Republic*, offered another thorough and resonant assessment. "Once in these stories," she wrote, "you really are inside them; you have a vivid sense of the world that's being described." Tyler also sought to place *The Progress of Love* within the context of Munro's evolving art: "The characters in the earlier collections were traveling along the distinct, deeply grooved tracks of their life stories, and it was the tracks themselves that provided the focus." She cited Rose's story in *Who* as an instance of this, and maintained that "in *The Progress of Love*, the focus has changed. The characters in these 11 stories are concerned not so much with the journey as with the journey's hidden meaning – how to view the journey, how to make sense of it." Tyler also notes Munro's method in "Miles City, Montana," but she praises Munro's handling of Steve Gauley's drowning, "the juxtaposed event . . . dealt out to the reader so artfully." Holding the anger the narrator felt years ago – stemming from Gauley's funeral and focused on all adults, including her parents, though excluding the boy's father – until the story's end after her own child's near drowning, Munro achieves much more: "This narrative restraint sets up a tension beyond anything the plot alone could evoke. We're pulled along not just by What happened? But also by Why did she feel that way? And What is the significance?" Tyler then examines "The Progress of Love," "which may be the richest in the collection," to demonstrate just what she means.

This same sort of considered analysis characterized the best of the British reviews. Claire Tomalin, in the *Observer* (she had also reviewed *Lives* there), offers a detailed perspective on Munro and her work.

Reviewing the ending of "Walker Brothers Cowboy," Tomalin commented that as Munro "has grown older, her power to unravel a whole tangle of family history has grown stronger and surer, and this latest collection her best yet. Munro is as much a regional writer as Walter Scott or Mauriac, which is to say she broods closely over her chosen territory, discovering richness in what many would be tempted to dismiss as dull and barren." Like most critics, Tomalin singles out the title story asserting that "when critics call Munro Proustian (as they do) they may be pointing to this virtuoso grasp of a time-span as well as her skill in deploying single physical details – a scrap of wallpaper, a blurred snapshot – as emblems of feeling." Munro, Tomalin concluded, "is never going to write a blockbuster, thank goodness. Read not more than one of her stories a day, and allow them to work their spell slowly: they are made to last."

Also taking a long view was Patricia Craig in the *Sunday Times.* Craig began by quoting from "An Ounce of Cure" from *Dance* and also by applying Munro's words to "Material" and "The Ottawa Valley" in *Something*: "The snapshot method, in the hands of an author like Alice Munro, is among the subtlest and most illuminating of techniques." Describing the new collection and seeing it as a more complex extension of what Munro has already done, Craig concluded: "Alice Munro's imagination is set going by the particulars of local life – gossip, reminiscence, family landmarks. There's a phrase in the current collection which describes the concerns of all of them: 'the stories, and griefs, the old puzzles you can't resist or solve.'" In the *Times Literary Supplement*, Anne Duchêne reflected on Munro's still-growing reputation in Great Britain: "No newcomer, then; yet this accomplished writer – so serious, careful and full of sardonic good humour – remains curiously under-celebrated."[27]

Beyond reviews, there were numerous other signs of the large success of *The Progress of Love.* It was named the main selection for November by the Book-of-the-Month Club in Canada (Mordecai Richler wrote its description for club members) and, in the United States, Knopf was giving it a quite visible push: they ran a three-column ad placed next to the table of contents in the October 19 *New York Times*

Book Review and also advertised in the *New Yorker*. Munro's U.S. publicity tour the next week attracted considerable media attention and, in December, *The Progress of Love* was selected by the *New York Times* as one of the best works of fiction for 1986 (books by Margaret Atwood, John le Carré, and John Updike were also chosen). McClelland & Stewart went through another printing after the initial run proved insufficient; by the spring they were reporting sales (and royalties) to Munro based on 19,690 copies sold (its total sales in Canada, including the book club, would be almost 32,000). By then, too, the book was announced as being a finalist for the 1986 Governor General's Award for fiction. Among the other finalists, ironically, was John Metcalf's *Adult Entertainment*. But *Progress* won; Munro received her third Governor General's Award on May 27.

While all this was in process David Macfarlane met with Munro for his December 1986 profile for *Saturday Night*. There he asserted that *Progress* was the "best collection of short stories – the most confident and, at the same time, the most adventurous – ever written by a Canadian." Here is his final image of the author:

> In a few weeks' time she will be interviewed by *The Paris Review*, placing her among many of the writers – Hemingway, Faulkner, Forster, Welty – that she read so avidly when she was a young girl growing up, as someone once put it, on the wrong side of the tracks in Wingham. Now, at a point in time called middle age, she wonders if any of this is relevant to her and to her work. "I was terribly surprised when I began to be almost a popular writer," she says. "Because I never thought that this would happen. All this acceptance comes as rather a shock to someone so well schooled in surviving without it."

To "be almost a popular writer." Once *The Progress of Love* was published, there was nothing tentative about Munro's situation, not in Canada certainly and, with that book, nowhere else in the English-reading world either. As Tomalin wrote in the *Observer*, Munro was never going to write a blockbuster, but with *The Progress of Love* she had garnered readers and respect much more than sufficient.[28]

The level of acceptance that surprised Munro had been growing through the 1980s. For example, in January 1986 and even before *Progress* hit the bookstores, Munro was an "honored guest," along with Robertson Davies and Mavis Gallant, at the 48th Congress of PEN International in New York. Like the Writers' Union, PEN is an organization Munro has supported throughout her career, contributing to it personally and reading at its fundraisers. But during the latter half of the 1980s Munro's reputation and position achieved a level that it has sustained since. If Richler's sardonic phrase "World Famous in Canada" had been applied to Munro when she was being interviewed by Harry Boyle in August 1974, it would have been accurate; by the late 1980s it was no longer valid. Judging by the success of *Progress* and the ongoing translation of Munro's works into other languages, "world famous" worked just fine, at least in literary circles.[29]

"Countless, Vivid Shocks of Recognition Between Reader and Writer": *Friend of My Youth*

While all this was happening, Munro wrote on quietly in Clinton. "I write as I always have," she told a journalist doing a profile for *Maclean's* at the time of *Friend of My Youth*. "I sit in a corner of the chesterfield and stare at the wall, and I keep getting it, and *getting* it, and when I've got it enough in my mind, I start to write. And then, of course, I don't really have it at all." About this time, too, Munro was quoted saying, "I write about where I am in life." Just where she was continued changing as Munro herself grew older. Changes in perspective, the ability to encompass shifts in time, the capturing of a whole sense of a long life could come alive in a very few pages. And she did write as she always had, spending long periods of time thinking before writing in longhand, and after that moving to the typewriter or, since the late 1990s, the word processor.

In March 1985 Munro sent a remarkable letter to John Metcalf – remarkable for its reflection of herself and the way her mind works. She was writing while travelling "On-the-Bus-Between-Mitchell-and-Stratford . . . to Toronto to do a Journal interview about Bob Weaver. . . . Will I wear earrings? I don't know yet." She then wrote that she would look around for some nice ones, which will have to be "screw-on or clip-on because I once had my ears pierced but they aren't anymore. . . . Do you have to know all this? I guess not. Earrings will keep me from thinking what twaddle I'm going to say."

Bob Weaver had been asked to take early retirement, so the CBC news magazine, *The Journal*, was interviewing her for that occasion. The image of Munro on the bus is interesting. Not mechanically inclined, she has never learned to drive, despite attempts by her father, Jim Munro, and Gerry Fremlin to teach her. So the bus and the train have been her usual conveyances about Ontario. Later in the letter, Munro updates Metcalf on two of her daughters. "I think my kids are in a time warp," she reported.

> There's a lovely new lot of snow here. (This is between Stratford and Kitchener.) I met a woman I used to go to school with in the Stratford Depot. She looked like a nice, brisk, grandmother. Grey coat, little hat, United Church Woman. I thought, I bet she has a nice life. I really did think that. I thought about what she'd have in her overnight bag (blue flowered nightie, *The Far Pavilions*). I am getting an awful interest in that kind of thing. I bet you think this is a bad sign.

Three years later Munro wrote Metcalf again, this time commenting that she had "been reading a lot about Albania and all the countries that went into Yugoslavia, because there is a story of a Clinton librarian being captured – c. 1900 – by 'bandits in Albania'." These two letters, in effect, bookend *The Progress of Love*. Each looks to changes in Munro's writing already evident in that book – where a middle-aged point of view has come to dominate. It would become clearer still in *Friend of My Youth* and *Open Secrets*. The second letter reveals the bases of the research Munro did for "The Albanian Virgin" and, perhaps too in the librarian's situation in Clinton, for the story "Carried Away."

The same *Maclean's* profile in which Munro's writing methods are described quoted Daniel Menaker at the *New Yorker*, who characterized her as "a kind of trailblazer, structurally and aesthetically. . . . Along with her characters, [Munro] has gone through a very painful and disciplined examination of self." By that time Menaker had been Munro's *New Yorker* editor for two years. At the end of 1987, after McGrath had handled the submission of Munro's first four post-*Progress* stories to the magazine, Menaker had taken her over as one of his authors; as deputy editor, McGrath had taken on other responsibilities. Amid some controversy, Robert Gottlieb had left Knopf in February 1987 to become editor of the *New Yorker*. During 1987 McGrath bought "Oh, What Avails" and "Meneseteung" while returning "Pictures of the Ice" and "Five Points." A revised version of the latter story, bought early in 1988, was the first Munro story Menaker edited. By the summer of 1989, Menaker had handled his own Munro "bonanza," her third at the magazine. They had seen seven more stories and bought all but one.

Friend of My Youth, made up of these stories, was published in spring 1990. Menaker's phrasing, "a very painful and disciplined examination of the self," captures just what Munro was still undertaking in that collection. Two stories in particular, "Meneseteung" and "Friend of My Youth," have drawn the greatest attention. For good reason. *Friend of My Youth* is dedicated "To the Memory of My Mother" and, as in most of Munro's previous books, Anne Clarke Chamney Laidlaw is a presence in one story and so in the collection as a whole. Unlike "The Ottawa Valley," which closes *Something* on the note of Munro's inability to fictionalize and so "*get rid*" of her very real historical mother, *Friend of My Youth* opens with the title story examining, in a "painful and disciplined" way, what Munro calls the mother's "welcome turnaround, this reprieve." This is the image of the still-living mother, often dreamed by her daughter, which opens the story. There, the narrator would dream of her mother "looking quite well – not entirely untouched by the paralyzing disease that held her in its grip for a decade or more before her death, but so much better than I remembered that I would be astonished." This transformation effects a change as the story nears its end. Her mother, transformed in her dream, "changes the bitter lump of love I have carried all this time into a phantom – something useless and uncalled for, like a phantom pregnancy." Still working with the memory of her mother, in "Friend of My Youth" Munro moves well beyond the transcription of facts recalled. The story is based on her mother, and presumably on her own dreams, yet there is much more there besides. Munro had Chamney relatives who divided their house in ways similar to Flora and to Robert and Ellie, but the information about the Cameronians she got from a friend, who had known some of this sect in the Ottawa Valley. Using this information, grafting it on to her own mother's story to make "Friend of My Youth," the logic is the story's own. Like Frost's description of a poem, it rides on its own melting.[30]

"Meneseteung" does the same thing. Historical prototypes for nineteenth-century small-town southwestern Ontario poets existed, and Munro acknowledged her awareness of the two most likely ones when her story was reprinted in *Best American Short Stories 1989*. These were Clinton's Clara Mountcastle and Goderich's Eloise A. Skimings, who was known as "The Poetess of Lake Huron." Of the two, Mountcastle is the better known, having published books of verse and other material in the 1880s and 1890s; in 1904, Skimings published a collection of poems entitled *Golden Leaves*. Even so, Almeda Joynt Roth is Munro's own creation. Characteristically, she roots the poet's circumstances in Wingham and so in details close to her own history: one of the predecessors of the *Advance-Times* was the Gorrie *Vidette*, the name used in the story. When Munro was a child, there was a schoolteacher in Wingham named Joynt. She also creates a first-person narrator analogous to herself as the author of Roth's story. This narra-tor, for reasons of her own, is attempting to understand the record left by Roth, "just in the hope of seeing this trickle in time, rescuing one thing from the rubbish." When Munro submitted "Meneseteung" to the *New Yorker*, the ending after "rubbish" read: "I don't know if she ever took laudanum. Many ladies did. I don't know if she ever made grape jelly." This was cut for magazine publication but, characteristi-cally, Munro considered restoring the original ending. She asked Close what she thought, and revised it so it became "And they may get it wrong, after all. I may have got it wrong. I don't know if she ever took laudanum. Many ladies did. I don't know if she ever made grape jelly."

In some ways a classic short story – focused on a key moment in Roth's life, contextualized in terms of that life – "Meneseteung" offers Huron County as home place within a longer, and through the first-person narrator more deeply considered, historical perspective. But the remarkable part of the story occurs after the "dead body" that Almeda finds outside her house on a Sunday morning proves merely to be a dishevelled woman, drunk, sleeping it off on the ground. Jarvis Poulter, her neighbour, the person she calls upon to investigate the "body," and a possible husband for her, goes home afterwards having announced his intention to walk her to church, a sign of serious wooing. Still disoriented from the "nerve medicine" (laudanum) she had taken the night before, Almeda makes tea and takes "more medicine," even though she knows it is affecting her perceptions. The grape jelly she had begun making the day before is overflowing ("*Plop, plup*, into the basin beneath"); feeling hot from both the summer weather and from her impending menstrual flow, Almeda is presented in a rapt, though disoriented, state of mind. Then Munro focuses on her character's art: "Almeda in her observations cannot escape words." Poems. "Isn't that the idea one very great poem that will contain everything and, oh, that will make all the other poems she has written, inconsequential, mere trial and error, mere rags?" She "has to think of so many things at once":

> All this can be borne only if it is channelled into a poem, and the word "channelled" is appropriate, because the name of the poem will be – it *is* – "The Meneseteung." The name of the poem is the name of the river. No, in fact it is the river, the Meneseteung, that is the poem – with its deep holes and rapids and blissful pools under the summer trees and its grinding blocks of ice thrown up at the end of winter and its desolating spring floods. Almeda looks deep, deep into the river of her mind and into the tablecloth, and she sees the crocheted roses floating. They look bunchy and foolish, her mother's crocheted

roses – they don't look much like real flowers. But their effort, their floating independence, their pleasure in their silly selves do seem to her so admirable. A hopeful sign. *Meneseteung.*

Munro's creation of Almeda's medicated state of mind here could bear extended analysis, but precise as they are, her literary effects are of less interest in a biography than her method. She has gone back here to "Everything Here Is Touchable and Mysterious," having Almeda Joynt Roth peering deep into the Meneseteung/Maitland River flowing by Munro's own home place – literally and imaginatively. Like her author, the character is peering deep into the river seeking greater clarity, understanding. For Roth, this is such a moment imagined: "A hopeful sign." Or, as Munro phrased it in "Circle of Prayer," "What are those times that stand out, clear patches in your life – what do they have to do with it? They aren't exactly promises. Breathing spaces. Is that all?" In both stories, but especially in "Meneseteung" and in ways new to her work, she was pushing deeper, deeper in time, and deeper into the accumulated detail of history, of her own cultural inheritance: "just in the hope of seeing this trickle in time, rescuing one thing from the rubbish."[31]

With *Friend of My Youth* Munro finally renounced book tours for good. Informing his colleagues at McClelland & Stewart of her resolve, Gibson wrote that she "sturdily repeats her refusal to tour to promote this book," but she had agreed to do four or five engagements "that will be of greatest benefit to the book." He reminded them that "despite being a reluctant promoter, [Munro] is a very good interviewee, and an excellent reader." In making publicity plans, he continued, they needed to accommodate her schedule since she planned to spend the first three months of 1990 living in Melrose, Scotland, just south of Edinburgh. She had visited there before, but this time she wanted a longer stay at a time "when it wouldn't be so touristy," she explained to a reporter, "to get a chance to know the place, settle down in it a bit." Late in March she flew to Boston for a reading and the Knopf launch. She followed up with appearances in Seattle, San Francisco, and New York. In Canada, the strategy was to have some of the events in the spring near to the book's publication. Thus Munro read at Harbourfront on May 3 with Irving Layton, W.O. Mitchell, Al Purdy, and Veronica Tennant. During the crucial fall season, she read at a similar event to encourage sales.

Gibson and Munro agreed on another realist cover image, Mary Pratt's *Wedding Dress*, for the book's dust jacket. He had to scramble a bit to secure it, since it had been promised to Magdalene Redekop, who had written a critical study on Alice Munro. Generously, Redekop was more than willing to forfeit her claim in favour of Munro. Having secured book-club orders of 13,000 copies, McClelland & Stewart had over 36,000 copies printed. *Friend of My Youth* was published in late March in the United States and April 21 in Canada. Though of different sizes, both were set and printed in the United States. Chatto & Windus brought out the British edition on October 15. Sales in Canada were immediately strong; indeed, on June 6 Gibson reported to an editor at Chatto & Windus that, including book clubs, they had sold almost 27,000 copies; ultimately sales in Canada settled at about 34,000 copies.[32]

By this point promotional efforts aided sales but were not driving them. McClelland & Stewart's initial ad in the *Globe and Mail* quoted from Bharati Mukherjee's front-page review from the March 18 *New York Times Books Review*: "I want to list every story in this collection as my favorite." They might also have quoted her assertion that Munro is "fast becoming – like Raymond Carver – one of the world's great totemic writers, able to excite recognition even among readers who grew up in times and societies very different from hers." Each of Munro's stories, Mukherjee also wrote, "is a marvel of construction, containing within it parallel narratives of inquiry and retrospection." Malcolm Jones, Jr., the reviewer in *Newsweek*, observed that it is easy "to make Alice Munro's stories sound as interesting as a trip to the dentist," but what they are about misses the point. They are "quiet, complicated, revealing themselves" slowly. Munro herself is "wickedly funny," and her sentences "are always perfectly cadenced, and almost epigrammatically beautiful." She is a "rarity, an author unafraid to write about people as intelligent as she is" – these people, like their creator, are truly interested in "the interior, speculative life."

In each country the reviews are characterized by a ready acknowledgement of Munro's accomplishment and genius, but this sense as usual was most pointed in Canada. William French revisited Hugh Garner's foreword to *Dance* in order to say that what Garner saw then is emphatically still true in Munro's stories: she continues to endow "the lives of ordinary people in ordinary places with extra-ordinary interest." In an extended and thorough reading, Philip Marchand in the *Toronto Star* asked parenthetically while discussing Munro's description of kitchen walls, "Is there another contemporary writer who has dwelt, in her fiction, so lovingly on trim?" He might have also said wallpaper, or types of cloth, or the appearance of dishes on a counter, or a multitude of other things. He then continued to assert quite correctly that in Munro's fiction "people remain the same fools they always were."

Like Marchand, reviewers of *Friend of My Youth* were keen to refer to some of Munro's earlier work as a way into the present book. Mary Jo Salter's offering in the *New Republic* began with a detailed reading of "Accident" from *Moons*, which concludes with Frances's realization that "people don't matter, [they] are not terribly distinctive or important; and we all end up," like the two characters who die in the story, "in a casket." Salter wrote that "what moves and unnerves me each time I look at 'Accident' is the simultaneous impression Munro gives that we are both irreplaceable and dispensable." Moving from "Accident" to "Miles City, Montana," Salter referred to the narrator's dismissal of her former husband Andrew as a "single-sentence, lacerating paragraph." Moving finally into the new book, she noted that Munro is a writer who "respects our intelligence, our right to sift on our own the cruel world she shows us. . . . Cruel and bizarre things do happen in this book," and there's "a tonal harshness, too, which we welcome."

The balanced thoroughness of Salter's review of *Friend of My Youth* is most evident when she takes up the question of authorial range:

Nearly every major character in this book, as in Munro's others, is a woman; most are adulterers; most are seen over a span of some years; most are perceptive and articulate about their own longings and failings; and every story but 'Friend of My Youth' is recounted in the third person. Such a clustering of similarities is often the sign of a limited writer, and probably an auto-biographical writer (not necessarily, of course, the same thing).

Yet although Munro strikes me as exactly the sort of person I would care to know, I don't at all have the feeling that I do. Like the machinery of her sentences, she is in some important way admirably invisible. Munro writes of certain attributes – selfishness or carelessness, for example – with the authority of one who has 'been there'; but she is remarkably selfless in her presentation of material that may, in this way or that, be auto-biographical. And given other similarities among her stories – their rueful but not lugubrious tone, the acute sense her charac-ters suffer of the ineffability of life's lessons – the mutations Munro achieves in characterization and plotting are even more impressive. Finally, though, it is the largeness of Munro's wisdom that confirms her range.

Robert Towers in the *New York Review of Books* also treated *Friend* at some length and on an elevated plane: taking the book up with William Trevor's *Family Sins and Other Stories*, he likened Munro's work to Hardy's and asserted that she is an expert at what James called foreshortening – "the art of creating an illusion of depth by bringing certain details forward for emphasis while allowing others to recede into the background." The title story is a fine example of Munro's use of this technique.

Among the British reviews, Patricia Craig's in the *Times Literary Supplement* also pointed sharply at particularly effective techniques. Munro is "a specialist in odd-angled observation, telling detail, and the striking ways in which past and present slot into one another." *Friend* "testifies to the supreme effectiveness of her search for connections –

between one generation and its predecessors, between different modes of behaviour, or just between one thing and another." She cited the beginning of "Pictures of the Ice" as an example of Munro's audacity, of her invention. There we learn of Austin's death in the first sentence, "Arresting, astringent, deft, idiosyncratic . . . you can't avoid these adjectives while trying to characterize her work."

Along with Salter's, Carol Shields's review of *Friend* in the *London Review of Books* stands out as one that brings a long perspective to the task. More than that, Shields writes with the perspective of one who has attempted, and succeeded at, much the same art as has Munro herself. In her case too, she writes with real knowledge of Munro as a person. The two had met in the 1970s and, though Shields was only a few years younger, her fiction is usually seen as coming after, and being influenced by, Munro's. Recalling her first reading of Shields's *Small Ceremonies*, Munro commented, "You just get that shiver when you come across a real writer, and I had that with [this book]." Throughout, Munro was supportive of Shields's work and career, writing references for her and providing quotations about her work. When Shields died after a long illness, Munro was among those quoted.

Not surprisingly, in her review of *Friend* Shields offered a detailed overview of Munro's career, one that is confirmed further by the pleasures of the book at hand. The reader finds "on every page the particular satisfactions of prose that is supple, tart and spare, yet elegant and complex." In the midst of this writing, Shields sees Munro "guarding, by means of her unpredictable cadences and spirited vocabulary, the particular salt and twang of rural Ontario – the corner of the universe that Munro calls home. Her voice is unmistakably her own. Artlessness collides with erudition in almost every paragraph, but in Munro's hands these contradictions seem natural, just one more manifestation of a planet whose parts are unbalanced, mismatched, puzzling and random." Like several other reviewers, Shields notices that in *Friend* the "time line moves all over the place. . . . Munro is good at handling long windy stretches of time, whole lifetimes or generations, and the stories here seem even bolder in this respect. . . . Many of the stories are cunningly hinged to moments in time: these stories draw breath from narrowly avoided accidents, the mock suicide, the almost tragedy, the near brush with happiness." Working through her material, Munro "is careful about leaving keys. A reader can almost always find in the closing pages of a Munro piece a little silver ingot of compaction, an insight that throws light on the story. These sentences are often her most graceful, and they are skillfully embedded in the text, cushioned by the colloquialism and ease that define her writing." Summing up Munro's work, though not the book itself, Shields writes with precision that the "enchantment to be found in Munro's books lies in the countless, vivid shocks of recognition between reader and writer."

Such vivid shocks of recognition might be seen to characterize *Friend of My Youth*, certainly, but they also encompass the whole of Munro's work during the 1980s. Like her narrator in "Meneseteung," Munro may be seen focused on the day-to-day, wondering, seeing "this trickle in time, making a connection, rescuing one thing from the rubbish."[33] Alice Munro's progress continued, but with *Friend of My Youth* she most emphatically was Alice Munro.

8

"She's Our Chekhov"

**Open Secrets, Selected Stories,
The Love of a Good Woman,** *1990–1998*

It was anarchy she was up against – a devouring muddle. Sudden
holes and impromptu tricks and radiant vanishing consolations.
– "Carried Away"

The corn in tassel, the height of summer passing, time opening out
with room for ordinary anxieties, weariness, tiffs, triviality. No more
hard edges, or blamelessness, or fate buzzing around in your veins
like a swarm of bees. Back where nothing seems to be happening,
beyond the change of seasons.
– "What Do You Want to Know For?"

But Chekhov's art is more than merely Chekhovian. It is dedicated
to explicit and definitive portraiture and the muscular trajectory of
whole lives. Each story, however elusive or broken off, is nevertheless
exhaustive – like the curve of a shard that implies not simply the form
of the pitcher entire, but also the thirsts of its shattered civilization.
– Cynthia Ozick, "A Short Note on 'Chekhovian'"

Munro's most ubiquitous publisher's blurb is one Cynthia Ozick made available to Ann Close some time in the late 1980s: "She is our Chekhov, and is going to outlast most of her contemporaries." It first appeared above the flap copy in the Knopf *Friend of My Youth*; the first phrase ran on the back of the Canadian edition's dust jacket; and it has been used to describe Munro's reputation repeatedly since, quoted almost always with warm agreement. It was the only quotation Knopf used on the jacket of its *Open Secrets* and was the lead quotation on McClelland & Stewart's. Ozick, who had met Munro and read with her in New York when *Moons* was published by Knopf in 1983, had contributed "A Short Note on 'Chekhovian'" to a volume of *The Tales of Chekhov* in 1985. A wide-ranging novelist, essayist, and reviewer, she had been thinking about the Russian master's stories, his work: "We feel Chekhov's patience, his clarity – his meticulous humanity, lacking so much as a grain of malevolence or spite," she wrote. "He is an interpreter of the underneath life, even when his characters appear to be cut off from inwardness." Ozick concludes that "he teaches us us." So too Munro, the late-twentieth-century Chekhov.

Throughout the 1990s the object of this consistent and unstinting adulation mostly just kept doing what she had always done: she wrote, she lived her life. Apart from occasional appearances in print in the *New Yorker* (and very occasionally elsewhere), and in person at a few public events, Munro kept pretty much to herself. During the late 1980s she and Fremlin had begun dividing their time between Clinton and Comox, British Columbia, on Vancouver Island. They were attracted to Comox for its ironic combination of good skiing and milder winters, eventually buying a condominium and spending some portion of the year there ever since. Reaching Comox and then returning home has allowed Munro and Fremlin to indulge one of their great shared pleasures, driving and investigating, back and forth across the continent. They have taken numerous routes for variety and interest's sake.

Another pleasure Munro pursued during the 1990s was acting in theatrical fundraisers for the nearby Blyth Festival Theatre. A journalist quoted her speaking of the two productions she had been in: "'In one play – both of them were murder mysteries – I was an aging but still sexually voracious professor of English,' she says with a laugh. 'And in another, I played a lady writer who comes into the library and demands to know if any of her books are available. I *loved* it.'" When the journalist asked her why she would do this since she was well known for avoiding publicity connected with her writing, Munro's response was interesting: "'Well, that's because I have to be me,' she says to explain her dislike of such self-promotion. 'With acting, I love the mask.'"

Daniel Menaker at the *New Yorker*, the Mysteries of *Open Secrets*

Munro's life changed in other ways, too, as the 1990s began and she moved into another phase. As she approached her sixtieth year, her health became more of an issue – just after *Friend* was published, Munro went into hospital for an operation, and during the decade other medical concerns, including some heart problems, were treated. In August 1990 her daughter Sheila married, and in July of 1991 Jenny did as well. Munro became a grandmother when Sheila and her husband had their first son, James, in 1991, and he was followed in 1995 by his brother, Thomas. As it happened, Sheila and her family settled in Powell River, British Columbia – on the mainland just across from Comox, with a ferry route connecting the two – so for part of each year Munro was able to see her grandsons regularly and to watch them grow.

In the literary world, Munro's career seemed also to enter a new phase after *Friend* was published. In the fall of 1990 Munro won the $10,000 Trillium Award from the Province of Ontario for that book and, at the same time, Munro and *Friend* were shortlisted for the $40,000 Aer Lingus Irish Times Literary Award; the other nominees were Russell Banks, A.S. Byatt, and John Mickelhern. She did not win that one, but she did win the $50,000 1990 Canada Council Molson Prize for "outstanding lifetime contributions to the cultural and intellectual life of Canada." In August 1991 Munro was named a regional winner for Canada and the Caribbean of the Commonwealth Writers Prize for *Friend of My Youth*. In May 1994 she received the Order of

Ontario and, in 1995, the £10,000 W.H. Smith Award for the best book in the United Kingdom for *Open Secrets.* In September 1995 she received a $50,000 Lannan Foundation Literary Prize, given since 1989 to writers "whose work is of exceptional quality." While some of these awards were for particular books, there was also the evident sense that they were being made as much for the body of Munro's work as for any individual book. In the same 1994 profile in which Munro talks about her acting for the Blyth Festival, Diane Turbide wrote, " 'The incomparable Alice Munro,' as a *New York Times* critic recently described her, 'is not just a good writer but a great one, the first Canada has produced.' "

In the same piece Turbide quotes Menaker on Munro: "She's a distinctive, original and complex voice. . . . And the things she says with that voice – her stories – are vastly interesting and complicated, and work on every single level that you would ask a piece of writing to work on. She has very few equals in the entire history of short fiction – I feel very sure about that."[1] When he said that, Menaker had just left the *New Yorker* to work at Random House. Having been completely enthusiastic about Munro's stories from the time McGrath got them from Barber and brought them to the magazine, Menaker had been the logical replacement editor once McGrath took up other work there. Menaker was her editor from 1988 through most of 1994; he handled five of the seven stories first published in the *New Yorker* from *Friend of My Youth* and all seven of those in *Open Secrets.*

The last Munro story Menaker edited was "The Albanian Virgin." It grew out of Munro's pursuit of the circumstances of a Clinton librarian named Minnie Rudd, who had been "captured – c. 1900 – by 'bandits in Albania,' " as she wrote to Metcalf in early 1988. In some significant ways that story encapsulates what might be seen as Munro's second phase as a *New Yorker* writer, a time when she was well established there while changes occurred within the magazine itself. McGrath shifted to other responsibilities as the new editor Gottlieb's deputy, and Menaker became Munro's editor as 1988 began; he finally met her in New York about that time, despite their decade-old connection. Menaker continued as her editor – and that of numerous other authors besides – through the transition from Gottlieb to Tina Brown, the young Englishwoman who had previously transformed *Vanity Fair*, and who was made editor of the *New Yorker* in 1992 to effect the same transformation there. As editor, she set about changing the magazine in myriad ways, striving to make it more topical, cutting the space devoted to fiction by half, introducing photography, creating what was always called "buzz" around the magazine. Radically, too, she began running stories signed on the first page rather than the last, long the magazine's custom.

"The Albanian Virgin" ran as the centrepiece of a "buzz" double issue called "The *New Yorker* Celebrates Fiction," one that included five other stories, a piece by Roger Angell on what makes a *New Yorker* story, selections from past *New Yorker* stories, and various other fiction-connected items. Most strikingly, there was a "portfolio" of photographs of fourteen *New Yorker* authors by staff photographer Richard Avedon; in May 1994 most of them had come to New York for a party and to be photographed, Munro among them. There their images are, standing side-by-side with varying expressions of seriousness and rapt delight, spread across seven pages. Describing the circumstances producing the images, Menaker wrote that "Bobbie Ann Mason was startled and flattered to learn that Alice Munro and her husband had travelled through western Kentucky because they admired her work and wanted to see the region her stories describe. Tom Drury – along with nearly everyone else, it seemed – was delighted to meet Alice Munro at last; they had been carrying on a lively correspondence for months." The shared delight at meeting Munro stemmed, probably, from her own buzz. Because she avoided the literary limelight in favour of Clinton, Comox, and driving with Fremlin, she was seen as something of a literary enigma.

While she had little specific sense of the magazine's relations with its writers, and perhaps did not know much about Munro, Tina Brown saw the June 27 and July 4 1994 all-fiction issue as a chance to draw attention to the *New Yorker's* distinguished record as a publisher of fiction. With its party and pictures, and a hyperbolic cover showing the figure of Liberty, fireworks behind, extending her arms over a group of famed American writers each holding her or his major book, the issue really was a celebration of fiction. Ironically, given this patriotic imagery, Munro's "The Albanian Virgin" served as the issue's centrepiece, and the portfolio of pictures is followed immediately by her Canadian story.

Menaker recalls his work as Munro's editor as "the high point of my editorial work – at once the greatest fun and the greatest privilege of my career." His work is not now so well documented as McGrath's, but Menaker's recollections suggest just how her work was handled. "Since Alice's stories are often a-chronological, there were one or two occasions, as with 'Vandals' in particular, when I would suggest taking a whole section and putting it elsewhere." On another occasion, Menaker noticed the phrase "a real life" in the story they were working on and suggested it to Munro on the phone as a better title – it was then being called "A Form of Marriage." Munro agreed. Particularly, too, Menaker recalls "punctuation issues, especially with comma splices – two independent clauses that Alice had a fondness for hooking together with a measly comma – forget the conjunction and hold the semicolon. At first these constructions troubled me, but after a while I saw that she used them only in selected places, and I began to leave them alone and defend them from the invading hordes of copy editors and proofreaders indignant over this punctuation transgression. . . . I had a name for this unruly device of hers – I started calling it 'The Munro Splice' to myself." Throughout Munro's papers there are numerous instances of this splice, where it is indeed a characteristic device of hers. They frequently reached print, and just as Menaker said, she uses them at key junctures in her stories.

Menaker never edited Munro for style, "because her style was her voice, her natural way of speaking at its very best (I found this out when I met her)." He saw his work with her to be equivalent to his editing of Pauline Kael, who would "read her sentences out loud to see if, as she put it, 'they sound like me.'" Munro, he remembers, "knew when an idea I had for changing a word or syntax or sentence structure of hers sounded like her or didn't. As with Kael, I think I got better at hearing sentences as Alice would write them." Menaker sees working with Munro and Kael as instrumental in his development of his own voice as a fiction writer. Summarizing their working relation, Menaker wrote that "Munro was always very cooperative and courteous – if anything, I think she was a little too easy about accepting suggestions, but after having worked with more than a few real doozy narcissists, I realized then and appreciate even more now what a joy she was to work with."

For her part, Munro found Menaker to be a congenial partner as they worked together on her stories. Writing him about "A Real Life" in November 1991, she asks him what he thinks of "Around the Horn" as a title and continues, "I know Wilkie is a kind of a prince in a fairy tale. I guess the whole problem is – I'm really interested in Millicent, in seeing everything through her eyes. Her emotional attachment to women, aversion to sex, something submerged and confused. (She's based a lot on my mother) so it's mostly what she'd understand. But I agree it may not be enough. I've added a piece to make it a bit stronger. What do you think? And I thought the dog bit was O.K. It's not Dorrie he sniffs but the idea of her life – the trapping and gutting, etc. Is that clear? *All suggestions welcome.*" In its indications of their shared shaping of her work, the questions and implied responses it contains, this passage reveals Munro's own sense of the story as she works in partnership with Menaker. Throughout such letters, Munro may be seen reaching toward the form she seeks; in another, this one regarding "The Albanian Virgin," she begins, "I've taken my new scissors to Lottar (or the A.V.) with drastic results. Not enough to make it publishable, maybe – it's still long and weird – but enough to cure, I think, the imbalance, leaving the 'frame' around the Albanian stuff as a definite, though fairly heavy frame, cutting all the Donald and Nelson and concentrating mostly on Charlotte through the narrator's eyes surrounding Charlotte's story." Amid the serious work they did together, Munro also often jokes, writing at the end of a note regarding some changes to "The Albanian Virgin," for instance, "Isn't this a dandy for the checkers? Albania! Montenegro! Joe Hill! *Perkin Warbeck!*"

Munro's letters to Menaker reveal her a person out on a high wire, intuitively feeling what she is after in a story but needing her editor's response as she works toward it. A letter she wrote to him in July 1993 encapsulates her need; given its timing, it may be referring to "The Jack Randa Hotel," just published by the *New Yorker*, or "Vandals," which was to appear in the magazine that fall. In any case, Munro's sentiment is notable:

> I was so encouraged by your letter and very grateful that you took time to write it in the middle of a holiday when you'd surely want to be free of all thoughts of – etc. etc.
>
> You have enormous generosity and a great understanding of how shaky I (and I suppose most writers) often feel. Also you're a terrific editor and a fine writer – I guess I'm always a little surprised that such a good writer can be so generous – it doesn't always go together.

Munro signs herself "With thanks" here, with genuine thanks for help and response that Menaker has just given her so freely. Such gratitude has characterized Munro's relations with her editors, and with her agent, throughout her career.[2]

The stories Menaker was editing, especially those that were gathered in *Open Secrets*, had qualities that displayed Munro's further movement away from the linear and the realistic. He and his colleagues at the *New Yorker* followed her along this path, since they rejected only one of the eight, "Spaceships Have Landed" – Munro said that they thought it was "too far out." (George Plimpton bought it for the *Paris Review* and he cut the opening detailed scene in the bootlegger's house; Munro went along then, but reinstated the passage in the book.) What she was trying to do in these stories, she told Peter Gzowski on CBC radio's *Morningside* when the book was published, was "to move away from what happened," hoping to create a sense of the character's fantasy life, to suggest what might have happened. Munro knew this was risky, since the various elements that suggest possibility "have to work pretty well or the whole story doesn't hold at all." Louisa in "Carried Away," for example, is shown at the end in the 1950s having a conversation with Jack Agnew, a man she never knew but had exchanged letters with during World War I while he was overseas; the two are developing a romance through their letters, their passion is felt, but it is quashed by Agnew's prior (and unmentioned) engagement to another girl in Carstairs. The literal problem with Louisa's 1950s conversation with Agnew, though, is the fact that he had been dead since the early 1920s. He is horribly killed, decapitated, in an industrial accident at Douds piano factory that is described in the story, his head "carried away."

Recounting how this story had taken shape, Munro told Gzowski that she thought it was complete when Louisa met her husband, the owner of Douds, through the agency of Agnew's accidental death. But that ending did not satisfy her, so she wrote the present ending, in which Louisa and Agnew meet – perhaps fantasy, perhaps real – the reader does not know. When speaking of one such ending in *Open Secrets*, Gzowski said that he was not sure he wanted to know just what happened. Replying, Munro said, "That's good. That's really the response I want to get. I want to move away from what happened, to the possibility of this happening, or that happening, and a kind of idea that life is not just made up of the facts, the things that happened. . . . But all the things that happen in fantasy, the things that might have happened, the kind of alternate life that can almost seem to be accompanying what we call our real lives. I wanted to get all that, sort of, working together."

Munro also comments to Gzowski that "a story doesn't have a single thread to me." Through *Open Secrets*, she interweaves plot lines and, as in "Carried Away," uses letters as a complicating, distancing technique. Letters figure also in "The Jack Randa Hotel," "Vandals," and "A Wilderness Station," a story inspired by Munro's Laidlaw ancestors homesteading in Morris township from November 1851 on, when one of them was killed by a falling tree during their second winter. There are other storytelling devices; the title story "Open Secrets" includes a ballad about the girl who was lost. Stories take readers off to Albania and to Australia, as if Munro was defiantly thumbing her nose at those critics who complained that her stories always had a drab, predictable setting. Even so, she remains rooted in Huron County and in her own experience. Minnie Rudd was from Clinton, which had a piano factory like Douds, and Gail in "The Jack Randa Hotel" goes to Brisbane, where Munro had lived for an extended period. At one point in "The Albanian Virgin" these sentences appear, describing some of Lottar's work with the Albanian women before she becomes a virgin: "In the tobacco fields they took off their jerkins and blouses and worked half naked in the sun, hidden between the rows of the tall plants. The tobacco juice was black and sticky, like molasses, and it ran down their arms and was smeared over their breasts." Imagining this experience in an Albanian setting, Munro was recalling her own work in the tobacco fields of Ontario with Diane Lane back in 1951. In "A Real Life," "a man in the area had named a horse after" Dorrie, just as had happened with Sarah Jane Code Laidlaw. And Lower Wingham's geography is evident in "Spaceships Have Landed." As she told Harry Boyle in 1974, there is always some basis in reality.

Throughout the stories in *Open Secrets* there are occasional casual references to the piano factory in Carstairs where Jack Agnew is decapitated in "Carried Away"; through them the reader can chart the factory's rise and decline. With six of the eight stories set in Carstairs, too, Munro creates another larger sense of shared community, connection, and culture; people in these stories are known to one another, in the way of the small town. Here she renamed the Maitland River the Peregrine, an Ontario historical joke, given that the lieutenant governor in the 1830s was Sir Peregrine Maitland. The Peregrine would flow on into "The Love of a Good Woman."

Munro's use of her friend Reg Thompson's research is evident in *Open Secrets* too. Thompson, who works in the library in Goderich, has provided Munro with material she has used in some of her stories. Drawing from his own relatives and his knowledge of the Ottawa Valley, he supplied Munro with the material on the Cameronians she used in "Friend of My Youth" – he is the person acknowledged in the book version of that story. With "Carried Away," for which Munro asked for an industrial accident, the two ended up creating something of a mystery. Munro's decapitation incident was inspired by a newspaper account of the death of Mazo de la Roche's uncle Frank Lundy published in the Newmarket, Ontario, *Era* in 1886. Thompson had found the account of the accident not in the newspaper but rather in an early biography of the once-celebrated Ontario writer. Thus when Joan Givner, a subsequent de la Roche biographer, wrote to Munro about the correspondences she saw between the two writers, she was disappointed to find that Munro had not read de la Roche. In a lecture she gave about the correspondences, "The Mysteries of the Severed Head," Givner sees parallels between the two writers but does not address just how she thinks the newspaper description got into Munro's story. Reg Thompson brought it to her, as he has other facts that Munro, through her stories, has transformed into truths.[3]

᎓

A week after *Open Secrets* was published in the fall of 1994, a profile appeared in the *Globe and Mail* that began by recounting a story of Munro's – an anecdote, not a short story. As a volunteer supporting the Blyth Festival, Munro was waiting table at a supper in the Blyth Hall during summer 1993. She was summoned by a man who asked if the woman across the room, who looked "artistic and dramatic," might be the "famous lady writer who lives near here." " 'I'm not sure,' admitted the waitress. She sized up the woman and then, encouragingly, whispered back, 'Yes, I think that might be her.' " Telling this story to Val Ross, the reporter, Munro gave "a guilty laugh. . . . 'I wanted that man to have this vision of a writer with beautiful red hair. I did it because she was so beautiful.' " True enough, but for Munro herself and with her wry sense of celebrity and humour, the chance was too good to miss. Later in the profile, Ross describes Munro "dressed in the same flowing, patterned pants she wore for a multi-page photograph Richard Avedon took of the giants of modern fiction" earlier that year for the *New Yorker* and writes that Munro is "still puzzling over why she gave up perfectly good housekeeping and writing time to go to New York in May for that Avedon photo. 'The next day I met John Updike on the street outside the Algonquin Hotel. He said, "Why did we *do* that?" Neither of us knew.' "

Perhaps not, but Tina Brown's *New Yorker* photo party, in conjunction with the story of the beautiful red-haired "writer" in the Blyth Hall, captures Alice Munro very well just as *Open Secrets* was going to press. Her stories were compelling in just the ways Menaker and other literary types knew, and in the ways she explained to Gzowski. Munro was well aware of this and, at home in Clinton, still quite grounded: she did rue "housekeeping and writing time." But equally, too, the sociable and very well-read Munro did not want to miss a party with such an invitation list. Besides, the trip also gave her a chance to see

Barber and Close, and to be in New York. In the course of his description of the *New Yorker* party, Menaker wrote, "Alice Munro felt at home enough to take off her shoes. 'They hurt,' she said, 'so I just took them off.' She explained that she had worn those particular shoes 'so I would look taller in the pictures.'" The *New York Review of Books* gave David Levine the *New Yorker* picture as the basis of its drawing for its review of *Open Secrets*: there she is, staring right back at the viewer just as she is in the Avedon photograph, making eye contact – they have used that drawing in their subsequent reviews of Munro's books. In the course of her profile, Ross calls the collection Munro's "most romantic, and riskiest book yet." "Risky" was the word Munro used for it herself.

Barber sent *Open Secrets* to Gibson and Close in November 1993 and, early in 1994 after Munro had stopped to see Gibson in Toronto, they had an order for the stories. The first three – "Carried Away," "A Real Life," and "The Albanian Virgin" – had all grown from Munro's researches into Minnie Rudd and Albania so she saw them as a group. As was usual in the making of Munro's books, changes were made between the magazine and book publication versions. In one instance, Gibson pointed out that "some of our readers had found the story 'Open Secrets' a little too opaque for their taste." Having heard this from others, Munro responded with this new paragraph characterizing Marian's relation with her husband just after they have left their interview with Lawyer Stephens: "But Marian stopped him, she clamped a hand down on his. The way a mother might interrupt the carrying on of a simple-minded child – with a burst of abhorrence, a moment's break in her tired-out love." In "The Albanian Virgin" – a story that had been tentatively titled "Lottar" by the *New Yorker* and might have also been called "An Albanian Virgin" – Munro reinstated to the book a long passage about Nelson dropped from the serial, telling Close, "I want this 'life with Nelson' inserted here, as a present-tense forecast, before he actually appears. (It was this way originally, curse me)." She then wrote the insertion on the proof sheet. And she had the opening scene in the bootlegger's restored to "Spaceships Have Landed." The book was designed and set by Knopf but printed separately in Canada and the United States, McClelland & Stewart printing in its larger format, and, as usual, each publisher used separate dust jackets. Gibson and Munro departed from magic realism with this book's dust jacket, opting for *Colette*, a "risky" original painting by Jenny Munro. Knopf chose a distant view of Niagara Falls with the book's title interceding. McClelland & Stewart published its initial printing of 30,000 copies on September 24, Knopf its edition in September, too.

As with "The Ferguson Girls Must Never Marry," held out of any collection, here too Munro kept a recent story, "Hired Girl," out of *Open Secrets*. It did not fit in with the rest. Published in the *New Yorker* in April 1994, the story is indeed quite different from those in the collection. Rather than being expansive and indeterminate, "Hired Girl" is reminiscent of Munro's earlier work; it is based on her experience as a serving girl at a summer home on Georgian Bay when she was in high school. There, the first-person narrator realizes she "didn't have the grace or fortitude to be a servant" and her reading made her feel as if she "had just been rescued from my life. Words could become a burning-glass for me in those days, and no shame of my nature or condition could hold out among the flares of pleasure." There is a certainty in this story's epiphany, and in the narrator's realization of her embarked self, that Munro apparently could no longer countenance; "Hired Girl" remained consigned to its single appearance in the *New Yorker* until it was included in *The View from Castle Rock* in 2006.

What Munro wanted in all of the eight stories she included in *Open Secrets* were new qualities of suggestion, deliberate suggestion without certainty. The risks she took and the effects she achieved were noticed at once. Characterizing *Open Secrets* for the *New York Times* bestseller list, an anonymous editor wrote that the book contains "bold, ambitious, risky short stories that never stop where stopping would be easy but go on to reach for the most expensive and difficult truths." Always among the first to appear, the review in *Publishers Weekly* asserted that even though all the stories had appeared in serials, "to read them here is in many ways to read each anew. The careful ordering of these works, the casual reappearances of characters in various entries, the layering of time, the unity of place – all expand the depth of each entry, heightening the illusion that Munro's fiction is as infinitely startling as life itself."

David Helwig in the Montreal *Gazette* wrote, "You never know, the stories keep saying, you just never know, and what you come to suspect might be almost unbearable. This is gossip informed by genius."4

Writing in *Quill & Quire*, George Woodcock's review put Munro's career in long perspective; he remembers that Munro "was already much talked about in literary circles" when he met her during the 1950s, so much so that when it was published, *Dance* "seemed almost like a summing-up." It was nothing of the sort, of course, since her books have continued to appear, he conceded. *Open Secrets* offers eight stories that are "close to novellas. . . . For what she is doing is taking the world of experience and discovering its inner light, so that, however mundane the situation, however tedious and sometimes repellent the characters, life stands before us, rendered into perfectly pitched prose, into preternatural observation, into some splendid creative synthesis, the product of a life of writing both modest and wholly exemplary." In the *New York Times*, Michiko Kakutani notes that many of these stories "are set in the distant past" and so "the volume as a whole feels somewhat more detached than earlier Munro collections." Kakutani also notes the numerous abrupt shifts in characters' lives here: "Given Ms. Munro's consummate control of her craft, these often startling developments never come across as mere plot twists or gratuitous displays of authorial invention. Rather, they feel like wholly organic developments in her characters' lives." In her hands, "the 'swift decision' and 'unforeseen intervention' become metaphors for the unpredictability of life, the incalculable imagination of fate."

Josephine Humphreys, in the *New York Times Book Review*'s lead review, begins with "Carried Away" and asserts that all the stories in Munro's book "are lessons. Ms. Munro's work has always been ambitious and risky precisely because it dares to teach, and by the hardest, best method: without giving answers." Continuing with "Carried Away," Humphreys writes of Jack Agnew's decapitation at Douds that "few writers would dare such a move, and fewer still could make it work. But Ms. Munro does. The narrative fabric into which this horrible event is woven is tight with a sense of time and place, a solid realism that allows even the bizarre to appear normal." In the world of these stories, though, "some parts of life aren't quickly apprehendable through language" so that "the open secrets, near-at-hand mysteries that can't readily be talked or written into clarity" abound. Munro focuses on such secrets, weaving their meaning into her characters' lives, with audacious technique: "Every story in the collection contains some sort of startling leap, whether it's a huge jump forward in time (more than 100 years in 'A Wilderness Station'), a geographical change (as in 'The Jack Randa Hotel' . . .) or a sudden switch in viewpoint that changes the whole nature of the story. . . . By thus expanding – you might even say *exploding* – the fictional context, Ms. Munro reaches toward difficult truths." She is able to do so because of her acute sensibility: "It's no coincidence that almost every story in 'Open Secrets' has as its time frame the span of an entire life, for these stories draw upon the complexity of a mature, long-vigilant sensibility." Maintaining that "fiction is the telling that startles, the telling that teaches," Humphreys concludes: "Heedless of convention, hazarding everything, firmly convincing us of the unseen good despite acknowledging our fears and harrowing experiences, 'Open Secrets' is a book that dazzles with its faith in language and in life."

As with Woodcock's review, Canadian critics assumed longstanding familiarity with Munro and with her work, a familiarity leading to a certain daunted quality in their assessments. Sharon Butala, in the *Globe and Mail*, begins by asking "Can Alice Munro fail?" and continues to write that when she read "The Albanian Virgin" in the *New Yorker* she thought Munro had, "but when I read it as one of eight stories in her new collection, *Open Secrets*, I realized it as necessary, even inevitable and in a sense the keystone of the collection." Having established her own writing from the mid-1980s on, Butala adopts a mystified tone toward Munro's work: "With each of her eight books I've grown more fascinated and more puzzled by her stories. They seem to me not written by a living human hand, more like the words carved on an ancient tomb, hidden for centuries from human eyes, till an archeologist unearths it, brushes away the dirt, and reveals the words that have always been there." With this collection, Butala claims, she "saw at last how to read" Munro's work: "In story after story she has given us glimpses of what lies buried beneath the façade of respectability and 'normal' lives." Many reviewers, Butala among them, paid especial attention to "The Albanian Virgin" because of its apparent singularity within Munro's work, set so far away from Huron County. Yet the story's exotic locale and Hollywood-style plot are entwined with the quotidian details of a "normal" not disconnected from Munro's own history: the narrator, left by her husband in London, Ontario, over her adulterous transgressions, moves to Victoria in the 1960s and opens a bookstore. She longs for Nelson, the lover she has herself left behind in London, hearing the story of the Albanian Virgin from Charlotte, a woman she has come to know through the store. As Munro told a reporter for the *New York Times*, "The two stories combined there are a romantic fairy tale and a sort of romance worked out in real life." Acknowledging this, Butala calls *Open Secrets* "too good to be called merely brilliant: It is a marvel. . . . Munro treats the women of these stories with tenderness and honesty while she shines a merciless light on their (and our) pasts, to make us see what we forgot when we chose real lives."

Reaching much the same conclusion ("Munro reveals the exhilarating character of life itself") in *Books in Canada*, Tim Struthers notices the reference to Thomas Hardy in "Carried Away" and writes that "like Hardy, in one magnificent volume of fiction after another, Munro is able to explore with increasing graveness and love, with increasing precision and wonder, the complexities of the human condition." Without the literary antecedent, most reviewers in the popular press struck similar chords. Munro's work, David Holmstrom wrote in the *Christian Science Monitor*, has "the hallmark of surprise, of creating such sharp twists in the lives of seemingly ordinary women and men that her fiction comes loaded with important, timeless questions hiding in the narrative." In *Time*, R.Z. Sheppard quotes Louisa's apprehension at the end of the story of life as "a devouring muddle," in Munro's phrase, and continues, "It takes some living to get to this insight. Other than Munro's considerable talent, the only constants in these stories are remorseless time and blind fate." Malcolm Jones, Jr., holds in *Newsweek* that "Munro's wonderfully compressed tales are not easily summarized" since each of them "contains enough Dickensian detail to flesh out a lesser writer's novel." Citing instances and details, Jones comments too that "the bold assurance with which Munro works carries with it an implied sense of risk. It is a challenge so seductive, with everything on the line, that you can't help but take her up on it. So every time you egg her on. And every time she pulls it off, leaving us slack-jawed with wonder and filled with delight."

Beyond the superlatives of the response to *Open Secrets*, there is also the sense that in Munro her readers have a writer who transcends the narrowly provincial, ironically, by knowing her home place so well and focusing so unerringly on its details, its textures. Thus Ann Hurlbert in the *New York Review of Books*:

> In Carstairs – more joltingly than in its predecessors Jubilee, Hanratty, Dalgleish – Munro is preoccupied with disconnections and unpredictable, implausible reconnections between then and now, between here in town and there beyond it. In turn, the jaggedness of the juxtaposition doesn't feel predictably postmodern: more than a sense of relativist muddle, there is a sense of miracle in the transformations that have taken place. . . .
>
> She betrays no sense of the defensive insecurity about her region's place on the map that Margaret Atwood has called the "the great Canadian victim complex." On the contrary, the particular, peripheral sense of place that inspires her fiction gives her the assurance to matter-of-factly take up an especially large theme, the disorienting power of time.

Defining Munro as "a regional writer without borders," Hurlbert sees this quality most especially in "The Albanian Virgin," which she regards as "a kind of symbolic culmination. In venturing so far from her traditional landscape, Munro has stumbled on a place in which her peculiar and powerful version of the provincial story meets a ritualized version of itself." Following Lottar's transformation from inopportune captive to Albanian virgin, Hurlbert acknowledges her escape but recognizes that it will lead to yet another: "As so often in Munro, the search for a new balance almost always means the discovery of new ambivalence." For

Munro, the intertwining of Lottar's Hollywood-like story with the nar-rator's more usual longing for Nelson is a way of achieving "jolts of recognition amid strangeness." Hurlbert is mistaken in characterizing Munro's choice of Albania as a "stumble," however: as Munro made clear when speaking to Gzowski, she saw the parallel between the Albanians' acceptance of virgins in their midst and her own society's view of "old maids." Both were set apart by their disavowal of sex.

Just as Munro foresaw, too, reviewers of *Open Secrets* paid partic-ular attention to the ways she tells the stories it contains; many saw its stories as a new direction for her. In a long and careful review in the *Nation,* Ted Solotaroff comments that "both Munro and Carver have the authority of seeming to write directly from personal experience without the blind spots and obtrusiveness of the ego one finds in Hemingway or Cheever or Mary McCarthy." He also writes that "Munro's imagination is constitutionally dialectical"; that is, each observation seems to imply its opposite. He observes further that "it's remarkable how many times Munro can place a woman in a man's shadow or have it cross her life at its dividing line without seeming to limit or repeat herself." Sensing her own history from her writing, Solotaroff continues, "She taps a rich vein in the broken marriages of the sixties era (one survivor looks back at it 'as though she had once gone in for skydiving'), but the madness they are escaping from or into comes in various shapes and depths." (He might have quoted this ques-tion from "Vandals," "But what was living with a man if it wasn't living inside his insanity?")

In her review in the *New Republic,* Wendy Lesser has much posi-tive to say about the book but is also critical at various points. She says, for example, that "A Real Life" and "Spaceships Have Landed" are "like outtakes from an earlier Munro." Lesser also takes exception to Munro's description, in a *Paris Review* interview, of "The Jack Randa Hotel" as a story she wrote as "an entertainment." Lesser quotes Munro's remarks in that interview: in contrast to a story like "Friend of My Youth," which "'works at my deepest level,'" Munro said, "The Jack Randa Hotel" feels "'lighter to me. . . . I don't feel a big commitment to'" these stories. This comparison is problematic, Lesser says, because in *Open Secrets* "Munro is venturing into new terrain: the terrain of the fantastical, the psycho-logically introverted, the purely suppositional." She continues in a passage that gets right to the heart of Munro's transformation:

> No story in *Open Secrets* has the intense visceral solidity of most of Munro's earlier work, the feel and texture of experienced reality evident in her partly autobiographical novel, *Lives of Girls and Women,* and in collections such as *The Progress of Love* and *The Moons of Jupiter.* These days she is no longer remembering, but guessing or imagining; and her material tends now to be the history of others – researched or overheard, contemplated, explored, added to – rather than her own immediate personal history.

Lesser is overstating her case, but she has apprehended just the shift Munro spoke of to Gzowski and which is apparent in *Open Secrets.* Writing these stories, Munro was still very much remembering, but those memories come largely in the details. The cores of these stories lie, as Lesser rightly asserts, in the guessing and the remembering. Lesser also notices a telling incidental appearance of Louisa's daughter, Bea Doud – the central character in "Vandals" – in "Carried Away." Quoting the passages in question, she asks what amounts to a crucial succession of questions about Munro's narrative technique: "Who is telling us this, and what is her relation either to us (the audience) or Bea (the actor)? Can we trust her on things? Is something being kept from us? Is there a verifiable truth here, or is someone just imagining it all?" All fair questions, though largely unanswerable ones. As Marlene Goldman and Teresa Heffernan wrote in "Letters in Canada 1994" in the *University of Toronto Quarterly,* "Often just as the narrative reaches its climax, promising to explain the life of the character or the logic of a dramatic event, it quickly recedes, retracting its promise; the event quietly fades, swept up in a blur of new events and buried by the future."

Julia O'Faolain in the *Times Literary Supplement* also notes that several of Munro's "new stories here pivot on reality's slipperiness – in the light of which, realism can only be a convention and a willed distortion. All the better, we may feel, since it is by distorting that writers share their vision. It is for the distortion that we read. Besides, Alice Munro does not impose her views, but leaves us wondering." Closing her review in the *Canadian Forum*, Myrna Summers surveyed *Open Secrets* and Munro's work more generally and wrote that "we read her with exhilaration, whatever her subject, and a hundred years from now, I believe that there will be every bit as much reason to read her work as there is to read Chekhov today."⁵

The focus of all this, the writer herself, missed most of these kudos since, for the first time, she decided not to read the book's reviews. She told Gzowski that she had heard that Doris Lessing never saw her reviews and decided "to try it this time. . . . I thought I'd experiment to see what it did for my mental health." However busy and otherwise directed she was, seeing and hearing about her reviews worried her and put her off her day. So while others told her about some of the reviews of *Open Secrets*, Munro ignored them and went on living her life.

As had then become her custom, Munro limited her engagements to three or four events surrounding the book's publication. She went on *Morningside* on September 30 and, on October 7, read along with Robertson Davies at a gala celebration of the two pre-eminent writers published by Douglas Gibson Books. The reading was sponsored by the Harbourfront Reading Series and McClelland & Stewart and was held in a thousand-seat auditorium at the North York Performing Arts Centre. A press announcement from the reading series asserted that this "historic literary event . . . marks Alice Munro's first public reading in Toronto in five years, and her only Toronto appearance this year." The *Toronto Star* ran a story on the reading calling Munro and Davies "two of the country's most beloved authors" and noting that they were reading together "for the first time in their careers." While regular tickets were $20 and $15, for $100 seventy-five people got a preferred seat and signed copies of *Open Secrets* and Davies's novel, *The Cunning Man*, in a Harbourfront Reading Series canvas book bag. Munro was to follow this up with two other events in Toronto at the end of October and early November and, once she was in Comox, read as part of the Vancouver International Writers Festival on February 5.

On November 2 Munro was scheduled to attend the first presentation of the Giller Prize, a $25,000 prize for Canadian fiction established in 1995 by Jack Rabinovitch to honour his late wife, Doris Giller. Along with Mordecai Richler and University of Ottawa professor David Staines, Munro served as a juror to choose the first recipient. Munro credited Staines's powers of persuasion (once saying it was a good thing he did not want her to be a drug runner) but it was widely thought she agreed so that *Open Secrets* would not be eligible, and so was not the first winner. M.G. Vassanji's *The Book of Secrets* won, but Munro, who served only on the inaugural jury, went on to win the prize in 1998 for *The Love of a Good Woman* and, in 2004, for *Runaway*. That Munro was sought out for the first jury is an apt illustration of just how she was seen as Canada's major author. Along with Richler's, her presence on the jury gave the Giller Prize immediate prominence.

Owing to illness, Munro was not able to attend the first Giller presentation – though in January 1994 she had attended the gathering for the prize's public announcement where, Staines recalls, she was the only person the press wanted to speak to. On that same trip, she met with Gibson and they agreed on the ordering of the stories in *Open Secrets*. By the time the prize was awarded, her book was in the bookstores and selling extremely well. In January 1995 Gibson wrote Munro that "by the end of the year" *Open Secrets* had "'sold' 33,000 copies in the bookstores, with a further 3,500 going to the Book of the Month Club." Gibson put "sold" in quotation marks because he knew there would be some returns, "but our sense is that by the end of the day *Open Secrets* is going to have sold over 30,000 copies in Canadian bookstores, which is an astonishing achievement for such a fine literary work that contains not one single car chase or attempt to over-throw the U.S. Presidency." (The final sales figure in Canada was much better than he expected: 38,530 with another 7,070 through the Book-of-the-Month Club.) *Open Secrets* was moving well in the United States too, given its presence on the *New York Times* bestseller list and, in the same letter, Gibson congratulates Munro on the W.H. Smith Award in Britain "given to the best book of the year, fiction, non-fiction or poetry, so the honour is all the greater for that." Beyond prizes, it is worth noting, too,

Alice Munro,
Montreal, 1974

Alice and Andrea Munro, ca. 1976–77

Alice Munro and Morley Callaghan
(Geraldine Fulford, Bob Weaver in background), 1980s

Alice Munro and Robertson Davies, Massey College, June 8, 1984

Alice Munro and Patrick Lane,
summer 1981, China

Alice Munro and Robert Kroetsch,
summer 1981, Great Wall of China

Source: Author photo

"And this was the road where I went on my walks. I loved this road.
This is my favourite road in the world." – Alice Munro, Wingham, June 19, 2003

Source: Audrey Boe Tiffin Marples

Alice Munro and Gerry Fremlin, 1993

The Alice Munro Literary Garden, Wingham

Alice Munro and Audrey Boe Tiffin Marples, Wingham

Taken in the early 1980s, this favourite photograph was chosen by
Alice Munro to appear on the back of *Too Much Happiness* in 2009.

Alice Munro, Dublin, 1996

that as it was published in English *Open Secrets* had been or was being translated for publication into French, German, Italian, Norwegian, and Spanish. Most of her previous books offered a similar list of translations; *Friend of My Youth* was not in Norwegian, but it was in Danish, Dutch, Japanese, and Swedish. By 1996 Munro's work had been translated into thirteen different languages.[6]

Making *Selected Stories*

In its May 1994 issue *Books in Canada* published an article, "In Search of Alice Munro" by David Creighton, which suggests how Munro was being seen in Canadian letters just before *Open Secrets* was published. Neither a profile nor a review, the piece is based on Creighton's excursion to Wingham, Clinton, and Blyth to look at Munro's home place for himself, to identify the places she had described, to make contact with some people in Wingham who remembered her living there. The article is illustrated with photographs: Wingham's town hall, the family home, the Maitland River, the Lyceum theatre, a monument to the Huron Tract pioneers, a coffee shop, the former post office now the museum, the Wingham branch of the Royal Canadian Legion. By the 1990s literary types were talking about something called "Munroviana" (in Creighton's article it is "Munrovia") and, more widely, people were beginning to refer to Huron County as "Alice Munro Country." Like Hardy's Wessex, Cather's Nebraska, Faulkner's Mississippi, or Laurence's Neepawa, Munro's Huron County was being seen as a mythic place, a literal place made magical by its rendering in Alice Munro's fiction. Creighton's article is indicative of as much. Its impulse was furthered in 2000 by the creation of a self-guided "Alice Munro Tour" of Wingham available at the North Huron District Museum. In 2002, the Alice Munro Literary Garden was dedicated beside that museum.[7]

In keeping with such recognition of stature, in early 1995 work began on a volume of *Selected Stories*. The desirability of such a book had been growing for some time and was, as well, indicative of Munro's differing levels of reputation in Canada, the United States, and Great

Britain. Barber had been approached with the same idea in 1984 by Penguin Canada but, passing it along to Munro, commented that she expected Knopf would think it too soon. They apparently did. But by March 1995 the idea was being pressed from outside Canada. Writing to Gibson then, Barber reported to him on Munro's trip to London to receive the W.H. Smith Award and went on to tell him that she had received an offer for the *Selected Stories* from Knopf and so was "ready to go ahead in Canada." Given Munro's publishing history in Canada, she and Barber needed to get permission to reprint – and so pay fees for – stories originally published by McGraw-Hill Ryerson and by Macmillan, so a selected volume was a bit more complicated there.

At the same time and also because of Munro's longer history, the selected volume that Barber, Close, and Alison Samuel, the British editor at Chatto & Windus, were working toward was not exactly suited to the Canadian market. While it was certainly of great appeal to Gibson as a trade book, he knew it might not yield the paperback version of Munro's stories he and his house wanted. Since he joined McClelland & Stewart Gibson had wanted to see a selected Munro in its New Canadian Library paperback series aimed at high school and university classes. Once he had come to terms on the *Selected Stories* with Barber, Gibson wrote Munro, "What delights us especially here is that this book affords us the prospect of being able to bring it, in two volumes, into the New Canadian Library." Although that was his hope, Munro's reputation both at home and abroad – and so her most suitable form for paperback publication once the trade version of *Selected Stories* had run its course – dictated otherwise, and in due course the large trade paperback *Selected Stories* was published in Canada by Penguin. No selected Munro would join the New Canadian Library until 2003 when an entirely different selection, still large but not of the extent of *Selected Stories*, was published for Canada only under the title *No Love Lost*. This particular need in the Canadian market, a niche, is indicative of the *Selected Stories'* larger context: the need for a large selection of Munro's stories was far greater in the United States and, perhaps especially, in Great Britain. These places had effectively missed Munro's first book publication, so the reprise *Selected Stories* would appeal to readers who had discovered her work during the 1980s or early 1990s. Given Munro's longer-running reputation in Canada, that need was less pressing at home.

While Munro was willing to have a volume of stories selected, she was not especially keen on doing the selecting herself. After talking the matter over with her, Gibson wrote to Barber that "she has been convinced that it is a good idea but welcomes assistance in selecting the best stories." He continued to express his willingness to help in the selection, and that of David Staines, general editor of the New Canadian Library. A list of thirty-one possible stories was drawn up at Chatto & Windus and, in early December 1995, everyone (Munro, her three editors plus Barber and Staines) had their say. Staines, writing to Gibson, argued in favour of including something from *Lives* so as to not give the impression that it is a novel and, in much the same fashion, he also argued against including all the title stories, since that would seem to lend to them an extra importance. The first argument was unsuccessful and the second only barely persuasive: "Who Do You Think You Are?" and "Open Secrets" were the last stories omitted, and then mostly for reasons of space. "The Beggar Maid" was included.

While Munro had the final say, her participation in the decisions was limited. She left home in September for six months in Ireland – she planned to live in a cottage, Carrigrise, "on the edge of a village called Carrigadrohid, on the River Lee, in County Cork," as she later wrote. The group did not want *Open Secrets* to be overrepresented, in view of its recent publication, so Close, who took the lead as the book went into the initial stages of production, talked to Munro about dropping both "Open Secrets" and "A Wilderness Station." By mid-February she was reporting to the others that Munro had agreed to cut the first but wanted to keep the second, suggesting dropping either "Something I've Been Meaning to Tell You" or "Who Do You Think You Are?" instead. She and Close ultimately decided on the latter. This left them with a collection of twenty-nine stories (though "Chaddeleys and Flemings" was treated as one story, so it looks like twenty-eight) that ran to 560 pages. *Selected Stories* was published in a larger 6.25" by 9.25" format by both McClelland & Stewart and Knopf; they both used the

Knopf setting but printed separately. Chatto & Windus produced their own version of just twenty-three stories, but published on November 7, virtually the same time as McClelland & Stewart (October 19) and Knopf (October also, with 40,000 as a first printing). In addition to its regular trade edition, Knopf produced a number signed by Munro and packaged in a slipcase.[8]

Munro's out-of-the-way location during the book's manufacture handicapped her involvement, but there is no evidence that she was much involved beyond the selection of stories and approval of the photographs used in connection with the book. It was set from photo-copied pages of first publication and, while copy-editing and other textual changes were kept to a minimum, it is probably not surprising that there were more changes – beyond the wholesale shift to American spellings throughout – in the earlier stories. Some changes were sub-stantive, though most were not; some, too, were dictated by the demands of design (some of the "silent" space breaks were omitted, for example). Munro did not read galleys of the book and, throughout the material in the Calgary archives there is no evidence her direct involve-ment. Of the twenty-nine stories *Selected Stories* includes, four are from *Dance*, three from *Something*, four from *Who / Beggar Maid*, six (though it looks like five) from *Moons*, five from *Progress*, three from *Friend*, and four from *Open Secrets*. Some of the ordering is changed from the first publication. Finally, and tellingly, the *Selected Stories* was published without any explanation of the basis of selection, any identification of who made the selection. Neither was there an author's introduction.

The copy Gibson wrote for the McClelland & Stewart catalogue defines just how Munro's *Selected Stories* was offered: "A literary event. A generous selection of stories drawn from Alice Munro's seven collec-tions spanning almost 30 years. A volume that will give enormous pleasure while it confirms Munro's place in the very front ranks of today's writers of fiction." In his Editor's Note used inside the publish-ing house to describe the book, Gibson also wrote that "this volume is both a tribute to [Munro] and a demonstration how richly that tribute is deserved." Contextually, too, Munro's *Selected Stories* was being published as a Douglas Gibson Book on the same fall 1996 list as Mavis Gallant's *Selected Stories* – they were added to that list through the same memorandum. This coincidence led to inevitable comparisons of Canada's two leading practitioners of the short story, both of whom had made much of their reputation through the pages of the *New Yorker*.

Each writer was seen differently at home, however. Writing one of the first reviews to appear in Canada in *Quill & Quire*, Bert Archer treated the two books together and clearly preferred Gallant's stories. Of Munro, he wrote that in Canada she "is the better known and more widely read, concentrating as she does on our own stories, on characters and situations often so familiar that our lives and her stories mesh, her writing becomes part of the fabric of our memories." Writing that Gallant's "prose makes us forget that a misstep is even possible, Munro, from time to time, stumbles. Her sentences are written, rather than crafted, are often a little rough, probably intentionally, like her characters, like her world." Although he admits that there is "a simplicity, an honesty [in this,] what there is not is transcendence" as there is in Gallant's stories. He concludes "that there is likely no reading person in this country who would like neither. These two careers spread out before us like monuments." The co-publication of these two books "is the biggest publishing event we're likely to see for decades."

Archer's point that these two careers are "monuments in the making" was reinforced by most of the reviews, which focused on the shape of her career, the qualities of her prose, the ways her stories have attracted and kept readers. The review in *Newsweek* by Malcolm Jones, Jr. – his third there – is more profile than review since he had recently met Munro in Toronto; still, assessing her as a great writer who "just keeps getting better," Jones makes the case that, as the piece's subtitle declares, the "unassuming Alice Munro has quietly emerged as one of our greatest living writers."

Two reviews in particular, A.S. Byatt's in the *Globe and Mail* and John Updike's in the *New York Times Book Review*, are of special interest both because of who wrote them and because of what they have to say. Byatt's opening paragraphs grab her reader sharply:

Alice Munro is a great short story writer. She is the equal of Chekhov and de Maupassant and the Flaubert of the *Trois Contes*, as innovatory and illuminating as they are. My discovery of her work has changed the way I think about short fiction, and the way I write, over the last decade or so.

Her stories are Canadian, rooted in a particular part of the earth and a particular society, full of precise details that make her world so lively that the foreign reader has the illusion of knowing exactly how those people and places were and are. (There are many good local writers who cannot perform this transfiguration.) She is a writer's writer – I come back again and again to the felicity of particular sentences, particular narrative twists – but anyone could read her and recognize something, and then be shocked by the unexpected.

Byatt's sense of Munro's work and its details of method, technique, and effect make her review singular among those Munro has ever received. The author of *Possession* continues, asserting that "even at the beginning of her career she almost never wrote a conventional 'well-made story'; her tales concern episodes, reversals, revelations, but they are always concerned to contain *everything*, a whole life and quite a lot of what is behind it, in the short space." Noting changes over time, the "increasing versatility" with which Munro handles "point of view and the eyes from which the story looks out," Byatt ends by focusing on Munro's passing mention of Cather in "Carried Away" and her treatment of the other writer as "a riddling object of contemplation in 'Dulse'": "I would guess that Munro has learned something about the shocking, the paradox of the formed in the formless, from that other local writer who transcended her local preoccupations without betraying them. But she really is unique; there is no one quite like her."

Updike offers much the same sort of review: summarizing Munro's "recognizable heroine" through the stories read chronologically in the *Selected Stories*, he writes that she is likeable but "neither virtuous nor a victim; what she is is vital." Stepping back from the stories themselves, Updike maintains that they "in their freedom of range, their intricately

arranged surprises and their historical imagination, are like few others."
He sends readers back to pieces by Tolstoy and Chekhov; of contemporaries, "only the Mark Helprin of 'A Dove of the East' comes to
mind." As he might, Updike noted delicious bits along the way, writing
at one point that "in one of the sternest of many stern asides, she has a
character reflect that 'love is not kind or honest and does not contribute
to happiness in any reliable way.'" Summing Munro up, he asserts that
she "is an implacable destiny spinner, whose authorial voice breaks into
her fiction like that of a God who can no longer bear to keep quiet."

But if Byatt's review is singular by its first paragraph's, Updike's is
made so by its last:

> While not every story brought me equal illumination and
> delight, my main reservation about *Selected Stories* is the book
> itself. No preface or foreword offers to tell us who selected these
> stories, or why. All of them have been published in handier,
> pleasanter formats in previous collections, of which the most
> recent, *Open Secrets*, came out just two years ago. The purpose of
> *Selected Stories*, one can only surmise, is to elicit homage such as
> I have just rendered; the book may widen Ms. Munro's admiring
> American audience, but to her *oeuvre* it adds precisely nothing.

While Byatt's and Updike's reviews stand out among those the
Selected Stories received, other reviewers made comments well worth
noting too. Dennis Duffy in *Books in Canada* sidesteps Updike's com-
plaints as to the authority of selection and maintains that Munro was
here "offering her readers a cyclical way of reading her work" and in
"her selections [she] has pruned . . . a suite from each of her collections.
Each successive suite builds upon what has gone before, as subjects,
themes, and stylistic motifs recur, often in a more complex fashion."
The effect of this, Duffy writes, is that the *Selected Stories* "takes on that
monumentality that we have always sensed in Munro's fiction, but
which is now unmistakably apparent." He then continues to demonstrate his meaning by comparing the selections from *Who* and *Open
Secrets*; while the comparison is a bit forced at times, there is no

questioning that this volume puts stories in new relation to one another, creating new meanings.

Writing in the *Times Literary Supplement*, Adam Mars-Jones saw Munro's *Selected Stories* as perhaps a book to "re-establish the reputation of a writer whose time has been felt to have come and gone," citing Cheever's collected stories as such an instance and writing that Munro "has never been in fashion. . . . Is she doomed to remain (terrible accolade) a writer's writer?" Mars-Jones notes in an apt phrase that "there are signs from some of her most characteristic sentences that she actively chooses not to be a comic writer." This is true enough, but his best observation comes in response to a passage in "Lichen": "In passages like this, Munro's eye and ear, her heart and mind, move beyond the categories of forgiving and unforgiving. The tides of richness and bleakness in her writing pass through each other without making a ripple." James Wood, another British reviewer writing in the *London Review of Books*, sees Munro as being like V.S. Pritchett, writing that like him, "Alice Munro is such a good writer that nobody bothers anymore to judge her goodness. . . . Her reputation is like a good address." Like Pritchett's stories too, "Munro's are fat with community: her characters steal their lean solitude from the thickness that surrounds them." He also notes that "tiny seeds of comedy lie hidden in the folds of every story in this collection." Noting the ill mother in "Images," unaware of the specifics of Munro's own mother or of Munro's own history, Woods nevertheless infers just what she creates in those stories connected to Anne Chamney Laidlaw: "This mother, who recurs throughout the book, may not be an autobiographical ghost. Seen so tenderly yet so comically, betraying herself in the act of protecting herself, she can, however, be seen as the spirit of these stories."

As with the comparison to Gallant, John Banville in the *New York Review of Books* treats *Selected Stories* alongside William Trevor's *After Rain*. He sees the two together in producing short stories "subtle and rich," "heartening and heart-rending." More largely, Banville sees the survival of the short story as a form – one "largely untouched by modernism" – as demonstrating "the tenacity of its practitioners." Connecting both writers to the *New Yorker* (since half of Trevor's stories first appeared there and just over half of Munro's), he sees that magazine as playing a crucial role in keeping the short story alive and well. When looking at the ending of "Friend of My Youth" and connecting it to Trevor's title story, "After Rain," Banville maintains that in each the knowledge the writer achieves, the sense the reader gets, is "delicate, luminous, and moving."9

↪

Updike's caustic comments at the end of his otherwise laudatory review seem to have had a telling effect, and rather quickly. In early January 1997 Gibson reported to his colleagues that he had "just learned that in the U.S. they plan to launch a Vintage paperback edition – complete with an all-new Introduction by Alice – in November 1997."

This offered McClelland & Stewart both a problem and an opportunity as they sold their *Selected Stories*. Details of their own paperback, ultimately licensed to Penguin Canada for five years, had not yet been worked out. They hoped to hold off that paperback so as to get a second Christmas season for Munro's book, so the publication of the Vintage edition in the United States before then was a problem. McClelland & Stewart took the steps necessary to keep copies of the Vintage edition out of Canada, avoiding what is called a "buy around," whereby Canadian bookstores damage the sales of a Canadian hardcover by smuggling in a foreign (usually U.S.) paperback edition of the same book despite the fact that it is not licensed for sale in Canada.

Munro's forthcoming introduction for the Vintage paperback offered an opportunity because, as Gibson wrote in the same memorandum, they could use it for marketing the *Selected Stories*, "perhaps as an eight-page handout for stores to give away with the book." As he had expected, the book had done well enough in Canada but, owing to Munro's longer history of reputation there, its sales were not overwhelming; by the end of 1997 the publisher still had almost 10,000 of its original 25,440 print run on hand. In view of these circumstances, they took two steps. First, in their negotiations with Penguin Canada over the subsidiary rights, McClelland & Stewart insisted that the Canadian paperback edition would not be shipped to stores before

January 1, 1998, ensuring a second Christmas sale of the hardcover *Selected Stories*. Second, they decided to offer a nine-dollar rebate on the book from December 10 to January 2 and, in concert with this, Gibson set about producing "Alice Munro: A Tribute," a "sixteen-page pre-Christmas 'Tribute' to accompany *Selected Stories* as a free hand-out."

Gibson had 5,000 copies of the tribute printed. It contained Munro's Vintage introduction, retitled "About This Book" and signed by Munro, Gibson's "Alice Munro's *Selected Stories* – A Publisher's View," a biographical note, selections of reviews of *Selected Stories* in three sections (Britain, the United States, Canada), an excerpt from a Gzowski interview, and a "Garland of Praise for Alice Munro's Previous Work." When Gibson sent Munro copies of the tribute, he explained that the "plan is [that booksellers] will display them on the counters and give them to local book clubs – and that everyone who has not yet bought the *Selected Stories* (which includes quite a fair share of Canada's population) will feel ashamed of themselves and rush out and buy the book." Quite clearly a publisher making a case to his author about sales efforts ("So we are doing all we can," he writes), Gibson also reminds her (and Barber too, since she got a copy) that McClelland & Stewart was "right to be concerned . . . that the book would do better in the U.S. and the U.K., since your Canadian followers were so loyal that most of them already had all of your work."

Gibson also comments here that he would be unable to attend the upcoming award ceremony in Washington but that Avie Bennett would be there to represent McClelland & Stewart at the major event where Munro was the first non-American to receive the PEN-Malamud Award for Excellence in Short Fiction. This prize had already been given to Saul Bellow, Joyce Carol Oates, and John Updike, among others, in each case celebrating a body of work. The PEN-Malamud was presented to Munro in Washington at the Folger Shakespeare Library on December 12, where she also read. Speaking at the presentation ceremony, Canadian broadcaster Robert MacNeil offered this evaluation:

> Her stories *feel* like novels. You come away knowing as much
> about her people as you might in a novel, more than many

novels, after just twenty-five pages. . . . Her observation of
human nature, first practiced so tellingly on her home ground,
but refined over four decades, has reached levels of universal
application, in which understanding of the human heart is more
important than any geographical peculiarities.

As such an award and such public assessments suggest, Munro's work
continued to attract even more adulation. At home, she had opted not
to enter the *Selected Stories* for consideration for the Governor General's
Award just as, by serving on its first selection committee, she had
avoided the first Giller for *Open Secrets*, to Gibson's dismay. But that
book received the W.H. Smith Award in Britain as the best book of the
year and, in Washington, the PEN-Malamud came for the whole of her
work. As the 1990s passed, such foreign awards from abroad were starting to become a regular feature of Munro's career.

PEN figured in Munro's writing at about this time, too, in that she
contributed two essays, "What Do You Want to Know For?" and
"Changing Places," to PEN Canada volumes published in support of
the Canadian Centre of International PEN. Each essay is revelatory: the
latter is an investigation of the Laidlaws' pioneering history. The
former, in effect, is an elaboration of something the narrator in "Walker
Brothers Cowboy" says after she hears her father's explanation of "how
the Great Lakes came to be": "The tiny share we have of time appalls
me, though my father seems to regard it with tranquility." In it, Munro
reveals her knowledge of glacial deposition and geological time in
concert with a sense of the time passed since Huron County's first settlement and a sense of her own time. Recounting an investigation she
and Fremlin undertook to learn about a crypt they spotted in a cemetery on one of their drives to explore their area, Munro interweaves it
with the account of her own brush with a possible cancer in her breast.
Contemplating this possibility, at one point she writes, "I am over sixty.
My death would not be a calamity. Not in comparison with the death
of a young mother, a family wage-earner, a child."

Though very real at the time – in 1993 – this possibility proved
groundless. But the essay proved prescient: the later 1990s saw Munro

increasingly dealing with other health problems, with her heart in particular. These personal contexts make "What Do You Want to Know For?" all the more revealing, but it is the essay's final paragraph that captures Munro's sense of life ongoing: "The corn in tassel, the height of summer passing, time opening out with room for ordinary anxieties, weariness, tiffs, triviality. No more hard edges, or blamelessness, or fate buzzing around in your veins like a swarm of bees. Back where nothing seems to be happening, beyond the change of seasons."[10]

"And there is the boat, still, waiting by the bank of Maitland River": New Editors at the *New Yorker*, *The Love of a Good Woman*

Just after "The Albanian Virgin" had appeared in the *New Yorker* in July 1994, Daniel Menaker left the magazine to become senior editor at Random House. (One of the first projects he edited was the runaway political bestseller *Primary Colors*, by "Anonymous," a book that features a character who loves Alice Munro's writing.) Menaker's departure was followed in November with the announcement that Charles McGrath would also leave in March 1995 to become editor of the *New York Times Book Review*. Since she had replaced Robert Gottlieb as editor in 1992, Tina Brown had effected wholesale changes at the *New Yorker* – the authors' party, with its glitz, its buzz, and its stylish photographs typified Brown's approach. But beyond such events, there were more fundamental changes. One of the most-remarked was her decision to change the magazine's approach to fiction: she cut the number of stories published by about half, moved them back in the presentation (toward what staffers call "the back of the book"), and made fiction compete with non-fiction in a way it had not previously.

McGrath was deputy editor and had been head of the fiction department for many years before that. When he left, Brown decided to replace him with Bill Buford, an American who had lived in England and edited *Granta* since 1978. Under his direction, it had changed from a small, nondescript publication into a respected quarterly of fiction and non-fiction. Brown gave Buford the new title of fiction and literary editor, one that defined a new relation between writer and editor at the magazine. No longer would individual editors directly acquire and then edit the stories of the writers they dealt with. Buford handled the acquiring and oversaw the work of other editors while they worked directly with authors; that is, Brown had Buford supervise the fiction department in a way that had not been done before. His approach was to put his own stamp on the magazine's fiction rather than proceed by consensus; Buford was to be more than first among equals. After Buford arrived, Brown in typical fashion arranged a luncheon to present him to the New York literary establishment. In June 1995 Buford addressed a room at a trendy restaurant filled with "writers, publishers, agents and editors," as one account described the scene, naming some of the famed literati present that day. Buford, so presented, was offered by Brown as one who, in fact, had been made "suddenly one of the most important tastemakers in the country."

Much of this happened at the *New Yorker* during Munro's writing time – that is, after she had completed *Open Secrets* and before the stories that became *The Love of a Good Woman* were ready for consideration. While Buford acquired Munro's stories for the magazine between 1996 and 2002, and certainly helped shape her stories for publication while he headed the fiction department, her primary editors at the *New Yorker* were Alice Quinn from 1996 to 2000 and, since then, Deborah Treisman. Quinn, who was an editor at Knopf when she first ran across Munro's work in 1977, joined the *New Yorker* in 1987 and later succeeded Howard Moss as its poetry editor. The first Munro story Quinn handled was "The Love of a Good Woman," one Barber submitted during the spring of 1996 just after Munro had returned from Ireland and had rewritten the story.

Buford may have seen the story before Barber wrote him in early May telling him that Munro had not been able to turn the three-part "Love" into stories. She enclosed a copy of it in any case, and also passed along Munro's apology that the story is so "old-fashioned." By the end of May Barber reported to Gibson that the *New Yorker* did want to buy "Love," but the cuts they had proposed would change the story considerably. So Alice and she were talking. In August Buford wrote

Munro directly, indicating his admiration for the story, explaining that at first he thought "a single, substantial cut" would work, but indicating that even with it the story would still be seventeen thousand words long. His preference was to run it in a single issue, but the difficulty was finding the space. He also suggested running the story in two instalments, as they had when "A Queer Streak" was published in *Granta*. Responding, Munro, Barber, and Close had discussions about ways to handle the story, but ultimately they decided that it needed to go into one issue. Barber wrote to Buford on September 18, telling him of the decision and asking to be released. He replied the next week saying that he had concluded as much himself but, regretfully, he knew he could not get the pages needed. The next day, Barber confirmed the situation and asked to be set free as soon as possible since she wanted the story to run before the end of the year. Buford wrote a letter of release September 25, asking Barber to encourage Munro to send them another story soon. The release of "The Love of a Good Woman" was duly secured. Even so, the story did first appear in the *New Yorker* – it ran in the December 1996 "Special Fiction Issue." Ironically, after he had released the story, Buford was able to get the pages so he reclaimed "The Love of a Good Woman."[11]

In many ways, its appearance in that special fiction issue of the *New Yorker* encapsulates the magazine under Tina Brown's editorship. Munro's story was the third of three, the first two by Richard Russo and Don DeLillo; there are pieces on food by Salman Rushdie and Anton Chekhov (the latter, obviously, not new but a new translation), and Buford asks in his "Comment," "Can fiction be nourishing?" His comment tries to tie the pieces on food to the stories. On the contents page along with the title, each story is offered with a rhetorical cutline. Under "The Love of a Good Woman," the editors have asked and asserted "How much is too much? A story of murder, an appalling secret, and a perversion of the romantic." The *New Yorker* subtitle as Munro's text begins is "A murder, a mystery, a romance" and throughout the text there are quotations used as running heads referring to the story's incidents or lifted from its language. Carol Beran has analyzed the presentation of "The Love of a Good Woman" here within a discussion of Munro's fiction in the *New Yorker* since 1977. She comments that the running heads focus attention "on how the story touches on popular media images," notes 122 interruptions in the text of "Love," and sees Munro's treatment of adultery as flourishing under Brown's editorship. Such shapings – typographical illustrations of Brown and Buford's attempts to make the fiction in the *New Yorker* topical, "cutting edge" – are of less moment than the author's note Munro decided to insert at the beginning of *The Love of a Good Woman* when the book appeared in September 1998: "Stories included in this collection that were previously published in *The New Yorker* appeared there in very different form."

When the book version appeared, Tina Brown was no longer editor of the *New Yorker* – in July 1998 she became the first editor to resign. Buford remained head of fiction through October 2002. Nonetheless, Munro felt sufficiently strongly enough on the point to call attention to the handling of some of the stories included in the volume. In two or three stories "the cuts were really more drastic than I thought they should be." She understood the necessity and was certainly used to the usual cutting, but in these cases the cuts made the story "not the same story I wanted to publish." Changes to "The Love of a Good Woman" were actually very few, but those to "The Children Stay" were a different matter. Munro said that "I cut quite a bit out of that and I felt the cuts were not good for [it]." As she had done before, Munro restored this material to the book publication, but here she felt the need to call attention publicly to what had happened. Alice Quinn, whose job it was to effect the changes asked of her by Buford, concedes that at the time she thought some of the cuts were a bit arbitrary, that his style of editing "was a little more aggressive." She recalls being told to "cut a column and a half," for instance, and knows that Munro was well aware that such cuts were being made for reasons of space rather than for any justifiable editorial purpose. Quinn explained further that under Brown competition for space in the magazine between various types of writing was keen and that long stories, already long and getting longer like Munro's, were especially vulnerable. Whether these space problems were driven by display advertising, as has often been asserted, there is no question but that they affected Munro's stories. (Under Brown, circulation went up but advertising dropped and the *New Yorker* remained in the red, losing money throughout her tenure.)

Though clearly affected by space constraints brought on by new editors bent on remaking the *New Yorker*, Munro was by the late 1990s still a very respected presence in its pages. Recalling these times, McGrath commented that she just sailed on during the years after he left: "By then she was Alice Munro." Quinn has said in an interview on other matters that "to read a story by Alice Munro is to be swept away." Interviewing Munro herself in "Go Ask Alice," Quinn asked her about her first sale to the *New Yorker* in 1976, and Munro replied, "Selling to *The New Yorker* made the whole business of being a short-story writer valid in a way, because I still have these recurring fits of I must give this up and write a novel." More than this, Munro continued, the *New Yorker* "came along at absolutely the right time" in her career. "And it also got me the readership that I needed to feel encouraged, because in Canada I was for a long time seen as a slightly outmoded writer." Drawing on the magazine's internal files for a talk she gave on Munro at a short story conference in Stratford in 2000, Quinn quoted editor Rachel MacKenzie's critique of "Royal Beatings" and, from her own time there, one from long-time editor and writer Roger Angell's first assessment of "The Children Stay": "This is prime Munro – a strongly written, absorbing, wholly original story, with a startling turn of events in the middle. One great source of power in her work that you notice over and over again is the way her characters accept the bizarre, the out-landish, with so little protest, they're saying, OK, this is the way life is, nothing can be done about it. She's onto truth, I think, and that's why she can write this way, with daring and calm, and absolute pitch."

"The Children Stay" came into the *New Yorker* in October 1997 and, given such a reading by such a person as Angell and despite difficulties with its cuts, found its way into print before the end of the year. Other stories were not so fortunate. In the same letter in which she sent "The Children Stay," Barber asked to "trade" Buford it for

"Queenie" – she had another outlet for it and comments that the latter "is getting old there." Since it later appeared in the *London Review of Books*, Buford must have taken the trade. Another story from this time, "Jakarta," was published in *Saturday Night* and drew press attention in Canada since it was Munro's first appearance in a Canadian magazine since 1982. A reviewer for the *Globe and Mail* wrote that "it's awfully nice to see Munro's mild-mannered Canadian misfits in *The New Yorker*. But it's even better to read a Munro story, with characters one can relate to, set against a Canadian background, in a Canadian magazine." Nationalist celebrating aside, the availability of "Jakarta" to *Saturday Night* meant that the *New Yorker* had passed on it. Still, despite the problems Munro experienced under Brown's editorship, the magazine published five of the eight stories included in *Love*. One, "Cortes Island," varied from longstanding *New Yorker* practice by appearing after the book had been published while another, "Before the Change," barely preceded it. Two stories, "Rich as Stink" and "My Mother's Dream," had their first publication in the book.[12]

Probably more than any other single story Munro had written, "The Love of a Good Woman" had an almost immediate effect. That the *New Yorker* found the pages necessary for a story of its length – over seventy pages in straight type, often called a novella – was worth remarking, but beyond that, readers and critics immediately saw it as a *tour de force*. It was selected for an O. Henry Prize (the first year Canadians were eligible), and critical articles on the story began appearing almost immediately. When it appeared in the O. Henry Prize volume, Munro described its beginnings:

> What did I know about this story? A man and woman dis-
> posing of her lover's body. This happened on an island off the
> B.C. coast – they put him in his own boat and towed him out
> into open water (into Desolation Sound, actually, which is a bit
> too much for a story). The sudden switch from sex to murder
> to marital cooperation seemed to me one of those marvelous,
> unlikely, acrobatic pieces of human behavior. The lover got
> transferred into a car, and it all went on in Huron County, and

the boys got into it, and their families, and Enid, who took over the story as insistently as she took over a sickroom. And there is the boat, still, waiting by the bank of Maitland River.

Tellingly, Munro makes no effort here to disguise the identity of her home place. In the story, too, details resonate wonderfully without achieving clear meaning: The murdered man, Mr. Willens, bears the same name as the lothario in Alice Laidlaw's second published story, "Story for Sunday"; "Love" takes place during the same spring and summer that Alice Laidlaw left university, worked in the tobacco fields, and prepared to marry James Munro; and finally, its putative adulterer, Jeannette Quinn, dies on Alice Laidlaw's twentieth birthday.

More than this, "Love" is connected to "Cortes Island," the third story in the collection, which begins "Little bride. I was twenty years old, five feet seven inches tall, weighing between a hundred and thirty-five and a hundred and forty pounds, but some people – Chess's boss's wife, and the older secretary in his office, and Mrs. Gorrie upstairs, referred to me as a little bride. Our little bride, sometimes. Chess and I made a joke of it, but his public reaction was a look fond and cherishing. Mine was a pouty smile – bashful, acquiescent." Here, Munro was describing herself and her own situation in 1952 – this "little bride" writes ("filling page after page with failure") while her husband is at work, and lives on Arbutus Street in Vancouver looking out at English Bay. Autobiographical connections abound throughout the stories in *The Love of a Good Woman*, though, as Munro casually said in her contributor's note about "Love," "it all went on in Huron County" – she marshalled the facts and situations she needed to create the image and action she was after, and used them to great effect.

As usual, McClelland & Stewart and Knopf each printed its own edition of *The Love of a Good Woman* from the Knopf typesetting. The book was set during May and, judging by the proofs available in the Calgary archives, Munro made a considerable number of changes throughout the first pass. (Although some stories were set from *New Yorker* pages, "The Children Stay" was set from a typescript dated

"February 21/98" by Munro – after the story had been in the magazine, restoring its cuts.)

The Canadian edition of *Love* was published in late September, the U.S. in November. Gibson was especially keen to ensure exact timing on a late September publication date to meet the deadlines for the Giller Prize and the Governor General's prize – he wrote to Close in mid-May about this, saying that he was "confident that Alice will win this year – perhaps even be a double winner. So the stakes are high here for our getting the book out in September." This was true enough but, beyond prizes, Gibson expected *Love* to take a large step up in Canadian sales – it did, for by June 1999 there had been five printings of about 60,000 copies. Munro's advance on Canadian earnings for the book had gone to $70,000. The book's Canadian dust jacket illustration was Paul Peel's *Le repos* while Knopf used a vintage photograph (1920s or 1930s) of a man paddling a woman in a canoe.

While the book was in production during the spring and into the summer, Munro was feeling poorly – heart problems were vexing her by this point. Both in 1997 and again in 1998, Greg Gatenby, director of the Harbourfront writers series, sought to arrange a tribute to Munro as Harbourfront Author of the Year. She turned it down the first time. Early the next year Gibson raised the possibility once more with Barber, who reported back in early March that Munro had again refused, this time explicitly for health reasons since the nervousness brought on by such events took a real toll. As things turned out, though, Munro agreed to a dual reading with Jack Hodgins (who also had a Gibson book that fall) to cap the Harbourfront series on October 31. It was the second time Hodgins had read with her in this way and, once again, she upstaged him – not by anything she did but by simply being the person and writer she is. "Last night," a newspaper account reported, "1,200 people rose to their feet in a standing ovation for what Alice Munro says will be her final literary public appearance. 'Absolutely my last reading,' she had said earlier over dinner. . . ." Munro said she had told Gerry Fremlin as much when he drove her to the train that morning, and he claimed to have "heard that before." The reporter set

Hodgins's work and his reading early in her article but admitted that "Munro, three-time Governor-General's Award winner and the front-runner for the Giller prize" to be announced that week "was the big draw." Not exempted by sitting on its jury this time, Munro and her book did win the Giller but, amid some controversy, *The Love of a Good Woman* was not even shortlisted for the Governor General's Award. Munro and *Love* did, however, win the National Book Critics Circle Award for Fiction in the United States, making her the first native-born Canadian to do so. (Illinois-born Carol Shields had won the award previously, as had Toni Morrison, Jane Smiley, and Frank McCourt, among others.)[13]

McClelland & Stewart published a poster promoting *The Love of a Good Woman*, which included this quotation from "The Children Stay" under a picture of Munro: "So her life was falling forward, she was becoming one of those people who ran away. A woman who shockingly and incomprehensibly gave everything up. For love, observers would say wryly. Meaning, for sex. None of this would happen if it weren't for sex." Pauline's moment here, her life-changing decision to leave her husband, Brian, and their children for what turns out to be a short-term fling, does embody the sorts of moments Munro creates and contextualizes in *Love*. Returning for a second Munro review in the *Globe and Mail*, A.S. Byatt begins by asking, "Do we experience life as a continuum or as a series of disconnected shocks and accidents?" She then writes briefly of Munro's early work, noting that in *Love* Munro "seems to be looking" at her characters' lives "from further away. The lovingly described human lives come and go in flashes, punctuated by disaster." Byatt then methodically works her way through some of the stories, noting that in both titles "Rich as Stink" and "The Children Stay," "the phrase is brisk, colloquial and perfectly natural. In both cases, as part of Alice Munro's precise and subtle writing, the phrase resonates, morally and esthetically, throughout its story." "The children stay," Byatt wrote, "is a perfect example of ambiguity." As it embodies what happened to Pauline, as it embodies the whole of her characters' lives in the story – the staying of children who never do stay but also do stay, in various ways, as they go – Munro's phrase captures her effect.

Byatt's review of *Love* is one of three appearing in Canada, each by another woman writer, that bear special notice. Addressing "Save the Reaper," one of Munro's strangest and most telescopic stories, ever, Byatt describes Munro's complex handling of time and suggests that "only another writer, perhaps, could know how difficult that pace was to direct and control." Concluding, Byatt draws attention to one of the stories first published in *Love*, "My Mother's Dream," and seems almost to exclaim: "Consider the effect, as you read this comic, moving, and wild tale, of the choice of the baby herself as the narrator, describing the dead show-off and obsessed artist stopped in her tracks. Who but Alice Munro could have turned the moral and drama of a tale on the choice made by a speechless infant lost under a sofa, and made the reader feel that something had been achieved and understood, against the odds?" As here, Byatt noticed particular details and described just how she saw them as effective. By contrast, Jane Urquhart in the *Ottawa Citizen* does something of the same but mostly just describes the stories and gushes her admiration ("And what rich canvases they are!"). *Love*, she concludes, is an "extraordinary achievement which, while it in no way diminishes her earlier work, takes the genius of her insight to yet another level."

The third review of *Love* by another woman writer in a Canadian publication was Aritha van Herk's "Between the Stirrup and the Ground" in the *Canadian Forum*. It, along with Michael Gorra's in the *New York Times Book Review*, concedes Munro's accomplishment and genius but then sharply analyzes this writer's relation to her audience – together, these two brief reviews capture her position in fall 1998. Van Herk begins by writing that "readers approach a new volume of stories by Alice Munro with an awe that arguably no other writer in Canada inspires." A bit snidely, van Herk has critics on their knees, editors genuflecting, and readers clutching the new Munro book; with more than a hint of a sneer, she notes that many of its stories "have already appeared in *The New Yorker*, that arbiter of excellence for all Canadian writing." The reasons for such reactions are complex, van Herk knows, but she wonders if "a Munro story rehearses the suspicion that everything we value in Canadian culture is inherited from the

1950s. . . . Certainly, a volume by Munro offers none of the zesty spike of the unknown, none of the crisp window of the previously un-encountered. Hers is a territory we recognize, a space we are complicit with." Concluding her preamble, van Herk asks if Munro's fiction is "a yardstick for Canada's sense of self?"

To answer this question, in stark contrast to Urquhart's gushings about Munro as a "national treasure," she probes the world Munro delimits with a sharp critical eye. "Reading Munro is akin to opening an album of black and white photographs and remembering the names of maiden aunts and lecherous cousins otherwise forgotten." Though she notes the feeling of the 1950s running through these stories, van Herk is at her best in describing atmosphere and character: "Munro evokes intensely claustrophobic atmospheres with tonal precision. A sinister stone of judgement weighs heavily on these stories and their characters. The world portrayed is hypocritical; every ordinary face masks a monster." True enough, but van Herk also makes an essential point about Munro, and about her work, that is too seldom made: "Snide class judgements are frequent." Although Munro early achieved a middle-class way of living through family aspiration, study, and mar-riage, her Lower Town Wingham upbringing has never left her – it echoes throughout her work.

While it is possible to read van Herk's review as one writer dis-daining the subject and method of another more successful one, that is giving it too short a shrift. Placing Munro's later work within a defined context of Canadian culture, not giving in to the dominant gush, is a fair approach for any reviewer, but especially one writing in the nation-alist *Canadian Forum.* Yet even though van Herk announces such matters in her preamble, she ultimately reviews the vision of humanity Munro herself offers rather than any nationalist concerns. She writes at one point, "There is a surface, and then there is the nether world below. And in Munro's world that substratum inevitably collaborates with all that is 'deliberately vile.'" Given this, "perhaps our fascination with Munro's fiction is that she is really a virtuoso of domestic horror." So van Herk concludes:

These characters discover that they know more than they believe they know, and that knowledge, with its hungers and satisfactions, will enable them to survive every crucible. The hallucinatory extravagance that infects these stories is indeed akin to love of a good woman. Such a love goes beyond the gothic, to a grotesque realm that is almost hilarious – if it were not so horribly horrible.

If van Herk's precise review places and examines *Love* in an explicitly Canadian context, then Michael Gorra's does the same thing in an explicitly American one. Like her, too, Gorra writes with a discerning critical sharpness that illumines the artist and art at hand in ways compelling and complete. Beginning, Gorra notes that Munro "most always presents her men as seen by women, [but] though she is no more interested in the lives of men than Conrad was in those of women, I would hesitate to call her a feminist writer." Citing Woolf's "A Room of One's Own," he comments that Munro's "work never feels as though it has had the question of gender thrust upon it," and in this it differs from Lessing, or Morrison, or Woolf. More than this, Gorra likens Munro to Flannery O'Connor as a regionalist, a writer "whose achievement she may now have outstripped." This comparison ultimately collapses for him, though, since Munro writes from "a radically different formal imperative" than O'Connor: "Munro's feel for her own characters is, in contrast, as pure as Chekhov's and as unviolated by any appeal to an external system of thought."

Like that sense in Munro's work, Gorra feels a very great deal of accurate biographical information about this author by reading these stories well and by knowing the work of other writers. Commenting that there is no new territory in *Love* – "the moral geography of her fiction remains as familiar as its physical one" – he notes that "only one of these stories is rooted in the present, and though an element of retrospection has always been prominent in her work, never before has she seemed so autumnal, so concerned with mediating between the way we live now and the way we lived then." Noting that most of the stories take place around 1960 so that, read together, "they so reinforce one another as to amount to the portrait of a generation: a generation that came to adulthood with one set of rules and then found it could live with another; a generation of women through whom the great turn of our times first quickened into life." Continuing, in prescient though quite accurate fashion, Gorra writes before fastening on to "Cortes Island":

> The dates tell me that this is Munro's own generation. But her stories never feel autobiographical. And yet nothing here looks like a performance, either, a voice put on or ventriloquized. Her work has a motion that seems as natural as walking. As natural? Better say as complicated, and then add that these stories walk not only forward but backward and sideways as well. They are never just about one character, one situation. They open out, always, into other lives and other moments.

Summarizing details from Munro's story narrated by the "Little Bride," Gorra notes that there the narrator "casually and briefly evokes her own later married life – 'the first house we owned, the second house . . . Until the last which I entered with inklings of disaster and the faintest premonitions of escape.'" There is no reason for Gorra to know it as he reads this passage, it is impressive enough that he senses it, but we know that this narrator's words here were born in Munro's own move into the house on Rockland in Victoria, her third daughter Andrea about to be born, she herself not much liking the place, not wanting to live there. Focused on this moment, not knowing but apprehending its autobiographical beginning, Gorra writes that at such moments "Munro's work has the dazzling but utter simplicity of Wordsworth who, in lyrics like 'The Two April Mornings' and 'I Wandered Lonely as a Cloud,' could collapse one moment, one memory, into another with an unrivaled combination of clarity and subtlety."

Two more points in Gorra's excellent review are worth noting. To end it he writes that "nothing in this volume is finer than its long title story." Contrasting its structure to what he calls "the formal balance" of "Jakarta," Gorra describes the circumstances of the three boys who discover Mr. Willens's body submerged in his little blue Austin (the Munros owned an Austin in the 1960s) and writes: "We never make it back to the boys on whom Munro spent the story's first 30 pages. But that structural dissonance, that enormous loose end, is precisely what makes the story's conclusion seem so large and enigmatic." Second, Gorra writes that "long ago, Woolf described George Eliot as one of the few writers 'for grown-up people.' The same might today, and with equal justice, be said of Alice Munro."

Given the precision and thought with which van Herk and Gorra analyzed *The Love of a Good Woman*, their reviews certainly warrant the detailed attention featured here, but the book consistently drew excellent analysis wherever one looks. In *Time*, R.Z. Sheppard maintained that "it's Munro's quality, not her quantity, that puts her in the company of today's most accomplished writers" and he likens her "balance of compassion and detachment [to] Minerva, the goddess of wisdom." In the *Yale Review* Michael Frank, reviewing the book along with Lorrie Moore's *Birds of America*, discusses Enid's nursing of Mrs. Quinn in the title story, writing, "It is all so authentic, so subtle, so *felt* – the woman, the house, the children, the smell. Past and present join in a slow summery swirl of heat and dying. The reader has forgotten all about the opening – until, quite casually, Mrs. Quinn one day asks Enid if she went to Mr. Willens funeral when he drowned." Focusing on the boy in "Save the Reaper" – a character, one notes, who reprises in age and perspective the narrator in "Images" – Frank discusses Munro's concern for the "private work of storing and secreting, deciding on the meaning of one's own experience: this young boy is at the beginning of the journey Munro sends all her characters on, in all her stories. . . . She believes in the revelation of meaning," Frank concludes, and so her stories stay with a reader who has scrutinized them: "So powerful an afterlife is central to the sustaining magic of Alice Munro."

Barbara Croft, in the *Women's Review of Books*, focuses sharply on the book at hand, writing that "Munro permits herself the latitude of a novelist, and the resulting stories achieve an extraordinary depth and range." Croft offers a metaphor that, while a bit hackneyed, still applies:

These stories are like a flock of birds in flight. Separate, often disparate-seeming, elements are swept along by the energy of the narrator's voice. We *feel* a kind of magnetic force holding the characters and incidents together, but it's never clear, until the very end, just how these elements are linked. The moment of revelation is achieved quietly, often with an image from nature or a short, simple line of exposition.

Croft concludes, "These are amazing stories. . . . On the surface, they seem almost artless, meandering and random, cluttered with detail. But they will haunt you."

In Britain, reviews were of much the same cast though, as usual, a bit more distant. Referring to Munro's women, an unnamed reviewer in the *Economist* notes that "accidental revelations, nightmares . . . barge into their lives – parodic, unbidden, unwanted reflections of the everyday. . . . The cost, of course, is an inner loneliness." Elizabeth Lowry, writing in the *Times Literary Supplement*, sees Munro's talent as extremely fine but ultimately limited – she does not buy comparisons to Proust and Chekhov, although she feels Munro's abilities in writing "Canadian Gothic" are unique. Noting that "the dazzlingly exact specificity of the prose is deceptive, promising a solid world that is in fact highly unstable," Lowry disputes with Munro who, she says, "remains uneasily convinced that love – the getting of love, the keeping of love, the loss of love, the getting over the loss of love – is the central fact of female experience." This, effectively, is Munro's limitation. Tamsin Todd in the *New Statesman* wonders about Munro's reputation: "There are a good many slice-of-life writers out there, [but] this isn't enough to explain why Munro is anthologized, collected, offered up in classrooms as a master of the short story. So what's the big deal about Alice Munro?" Todd sees the answer in the details: "Part of the experience in reading the eight stories here is to be overwhelmed by detail. . . . Hers are more than slice-of-life stories, concerned not only with depicting life, but with the possible paths a life (and a story) can take. . . . Like the teller of medieval morality tales, Munro leads readers along a winding path to those moments when the moral decisions that determine a shape of a life are made."[14] Like the other reviewers of *Love*, Todd certainly does come to see in these details the big deal about Munro.

ॐ

When he wanted to know just how Munro's *Selected Stories* came together, John Updike in the *New York Times Book Review* made a fair point. Judging by Vintage's swift addition of an Introduction to the paperback, others found it compelling too. One wonders if Munro herself did, though. Once, when granting Helen Hoy permission to quote from her letters, Munro wrote, "I wish I could tell you that more goes into the work than the flippant and casual or serious and evasive, explanations and dodges that the author voices in letters and interviews, and I wish with all my heart the finished work could be let alone, to stand by itself, but I know this is not possible. So you have my permission." Munro certainly has been consistent to this credo. While she has agreed to be interviewed numerous times, talking amiably, volubly, and thoughtfully about pretty much whatever an interviewer chooses to ask, she has never written a critical explanation of her work as a writer on her own. Such pieces have always been at another's request.

Introducing her *Selected Stories*, Munro's piece is revelatory, precise, and, given its subject and the timing, summative. She seems to bridle a bit at what has been asked of her, beginning her second paragraph with "Some clarifying statements about my work are requested by others" and later, "I am forced, in writing this introduction. . . ." As she told Hoy, such statements do not interest her, she does not believe them, she has little faith in their utility. Even so, as she makes clear in the introduction, what does interest her are images that she understands as "beginnings or essentials" to her work. Munro highlights one such image, one she saw from the window of the Wingham library when she was about fifteen: "Snow falling straight down. . . . A team of horses, pulling a sleigh, was moving onto the scales. The sleigh was piled high with sacks of grain." This image, one she "never wrote a story about," is one she tried to use in "Spaceships Have Landed" – it appeared in the *Paris Review* version of the story as something Rhea remembered seeing but was taken out of the *Open Secrets* version. And in that earlier guise Rhea's recollection of the image is connected to Janet's vision of her hometown in the fictional version of "Working for a Living." That is, when her college-educated imagination recasts the town into a version of *Winesburg, Ohio* or something from the stories of Chekhov. None of this – Munro makes clear in her somewhat truculent introduction – is a matter of conscious planning for her:

> The only choice I make is to write about what interests me in a way that interests me, that gives me pleasure. It may not look like pleasure, because the difficulties can make me morose and distracted, but that's what it is – the pleasure of telling the story I mean to tell as wholly as I can tell it, of finding out in fact what that story is, by working around the different ways of telling it.

Looking back at the image of the man, horses, and sleigh she saw in 1946 or 1947, Munro wrote that she saw the image as "alive and potent, and it gave me something like a blow to the chest. What does this mean, what can be discovered about it, what is the rest of the story? The man and the horse are not symbolic or picturesque, they are moving through a story which is hidden, and now, for a moment, carelessly revealed. How can you get your finger on it, feel that life beating? It was more a torment than a comfort to think about this, because I couldn't get hold of it at all."

What these descriptions suggest about their author's intuitive aesthetic is that, for her, a story is and always has been an organic, living thing. Thus after she recounts the "beginnings or essentials" in some of the stories included in her *Selected Stories*, Munro speaks of the time when a story exists in first draft, "has put on rough but adequate clothes" and may need nothing more than "tightening here and expanding there," or other such adjustment. "It's then, in fact, that the story is in greatest danger of losing its life, of appearing so hopelessly misbegotten that my only relief comes from abandoning it." She does still give up, though not so often as she did in her early days – her papers in Calgary testify to this with abandonment after abandonment, page after page, start after start. As she concludes her introduction, Munro seems to be fulfilling her own assessment of her working methods by avoiding an ending here, shifting uncharacteristically to a quotation from Sterne's *Tristram Shandy* in which he writes, "The most obvious things, which come in our way, have dark sides, which the quickest sight cannot penetrate into." This continues on and on until, finally, we reach an ending to the quotation, and so to her introduction, after a suitably extended eighteenth-century sentence. But the wondering continues: What is the rest of the story?

The boat still floating on the Maitland/Peregrine River in 1951 closes "The Love of a Good Woman" but remains there, beckoning to the reader certainly, but most especially to its author herself. What is "the rest of the story" along the Maitland River, that place where "everything is touchable and mysterious." Still both touchable and most emphatically very mysterious, the landscapes of Alice Munro's stories from the 1990s are quite recognizable but also frightening. As Lesser said in her review of *Open Secrets*, Munro was not primarily "remembering, but guessing or imagining." The stories she produced during the decade were at once risky, strange, and familiarly rooted in Huron County. Roger Angell wrote after he had just read "The Children Stay" in manuscript: "She's onto truth, I think, and that's why she can write this way, with daring and calm, and absolute pitch."[15]

9

"But She's Not in a Class with Most Other People"

Hateship, Friendship, Courtship, Loveship, Marriage, *the* New Yorker's *Munro Triptych,* Runaway

I chart a course which is called a career and expect to make progress in it. I know what I am up to. Short stories, yes. Novels, no. I accept that rural folk are never sophisticated and sophisticates are never rural, and I make my choice. Also I keep an eye on feminism and Canada and try to figure out my duty to both.
– "Introduction," *Selected Stories*

And it has worked out in some way.
– Peter Gzowski Interview, 2001

Writing "Home" in 1973 Alice Munro concluded on this brief paragraph: "*I don't want any more effects, I tell you, lying. I don't know what I want. I want to do this with honour, if I possibly can.*" As with the wry caricature of herself as a writer she offered at the beginning of the introduction to *Selected Stories*, here too Munro was concerned about the difference between the ways others see her writing and how that same work feels to her, how she sees it. Munro's desire to write in a way that both honours her subject and treats it honestly ("*I don't want any more effects, I tell you, lying*") has been a constant throughout her life and work. In "Home," describing her father and stepmother living in the home she grew up in, Munro's desire for an honest balance in that deeply autobiographical narrative was especially acute. (Tellingly, Munro omitted almost all of these analytical comments when she revised "Home" for *The View from Castle Rock*; she was seeking a less strained honesty.) Writing honestly and with honour without effects was then, has been, and remains Alice Munro's intention, and she has achieved it beyond any argument. Acknowledging just this quality in Munro's work after her reviews of *Selected Stories* and *The Love of a Good Woman*, A.S. Byatt dropped Munro's name into another book review in 2000: "One of the best tributes I know to the art of Willa Cather is the work of Alice Munro, who has learned to depict whole lives from a distance in the same strangely unworked-up and unaccented way, while also making it entirely new, as her landscape and *moeurs* are new."

When Munro accepted her first Giller Prize in 1998 – on television, since the award ceremony was on the Bravo cable network – she made special mention of Robert Weaver, who was "the reason I kept writing all those years." "The Giller caps a distinguished career in Canadian letters," the reporter for the *Toronto Star* opined, continuing that the award "has quickly become the country's pre-eminent fiction prize." Certainly that was true about the prize then, and now, but the notion of that first Giller "capping" Munro's career proved delightfully wrong. When *The Love of a Good Woman* appeared in fall 1998, Munro read that October and claimed it would be her last public reading, indicating she was winding down. But she collected her first Giller and just

kept right on writing. Six years later the same reporter, writing about
Munro's appearance as one of the six 2004 Giller nominees closing the
twenty-fifth Harbourfront International Festival of Authors, began by
reminding readers that Munro had said that 1998 appearance would be
her last. Ten days later, Munro made another appearance in Toronto
and accepted her second Giller for *Runaway*, the second book since her
"last" last public reading in 1998. Receiving the award, Munro told the
audience – which now included a national CBC-TV audience – about
selling books in Victoria in the 1960s.[1]

Here is Alice Munro in November 2004: harkening back amid
the Giller gala to the years when only Robert Weaver and her family
knew she was a writer. The years she spent sitting alone in the
evenings at Munro's Books on Yates Street, looking out, thinking
about "the rest of the story" when she was not talking to people who
had ventured into the store. People who would tell her that they made
a point of never reading a Canadian book. Or people, as Munro wrote
in "The Albanian Virgin," who "would browse for half an hour, an
hour, before spending seventy-five cents." Talking to Peter Gzowski
in September 2001 about her treatment of sexual attraction in
Hateship, Friendship, Courtship, Loveship, Marriage – in the stories
"Nettles" and "What Is Remembered" – Munro spoke of

> fantasies that never come true, but do come true in a way and
> are misrepresented, and how we need those dreams to live by.
> So I'm still very interested in that sort of thing. I say "still" in
> that way because I'm very aware of my advanced age and the
> propriety it should bring or the calm it should bring and I'm
> always surprised that I don't feel very different. Ever. You're the
> same person at nineteen that you are at thirty-nine that you are
> at sixty that you go on being in a way.

They continued to talk, and Gzowski asked Munro about her
thinking on death. She replied that she thought of death with more fear
when she was forty than she does now. "I don't have that feeling any
more that death will snatch me off before I've done what I could do."

In the midst of this answer, Munro offers what amounts to something of a personal summary:

> And also, I think in some ways – not in all ways but in some ways – I'm very satisfied and grateful for my life because I've done the work I've wanted to do. Not that I've done all of it or that I've done it as well as I would have liked to have done, but I've done what I could do. It was hard for me to see in the beginning how I would ever do that. In fact, I thought it more or less impossible. And this wasn't just because I was a woman of a certain generation, and a certain form of life to fulfill, it was just that I thought it's too hard and it will never work out in any way at all. And it has worked out in some way. And for that I am so astonished and pleased.

After Munro received her first Giller Prize for *The Love of a Good Woman* in 1998, awards and award nominations kept up their steady pace. In early 2001, she received the $30,000 Rea Award for Lifetime Achievement (among previous winners were Richard Ford and, appropriately, Cynthia Ozick and Eudora Welty). *Hateship* was named a finalist for the National Book Critics Award, it was selected one of the best books of the year by the *New York Times Book Review*, it was nominated for the *Los Angeles Times* Book Prize and the 2002 Torgi Literary Award in the category of CNIB-Produced Fiction, and it won the third Upper Canada Brewing Company Writers' Craft Award and was the winner in the Caribbean-Canada region for the 2002 Commonwealth Writers' Prize. In November 2001, just as *Hateship* was being published, Munro was feted at the 92nd Street Y in New York City, where she received the O. Henry Award for Continuing Achievement in Short Fiction. There, Munro gave a talk, "Stories," which was still on the Knopf website. On Munro's seventh-first birthday the Alice Munro Literary Garden was dedicated in Wingham. Her name has been mentioned in connection with the Nobel Prize.

Enjoying all of this to some real extent, though not exactly revelling in it, Munro kept living the life she has lived, back and forth from

Clinton to Comox. In March 2001 Munro had to miss a planned dinner with Gibson in Comox to talk about the publishing details of *Hateship* because she ended up in the local emergency room, where they had a brief meeting. A heart problem for which she had been operated on previously flared up again, so she required further surgery in Toronto in October. While she was waiting, Munro worked on older pieces, such as "Home," "Working for a Living," and "The Ferguson Girls Must Never Marry" – they yet may reappear in print. Her author's copies of *Hateship, Friendship, Courtship, Loveship, Marriage* arrived in Clinton on August 21 but, as of the next day, she had not opened the parcel. ("I was just terribly lacking in confidence. I still am. My new book came yesterday and I hid it.") One of her daughters, visiting, threatened to stage a public reading unless her mother had a look.[2]

The *New Yorker* and *Hateship, Friendship, Loveship, Courtship, Marriage*

Once *The Love of a Good Woman* was completed Munro kept writing, producing stories at a regular rate, sending them on to Barber, who sent them on to the *New Yorker*, which usually bought them. "The Bear Came Over the Mountain," the second story destined for *Hateship* ("Queenie" having been held out of *Love*), appeared in the *New Yorker* in December 1999, "Nettles" in February 2000. Alice Quinn was Munro's editor for these, as she had been since Buford had found the space for "The Love of a Good Woman." After "Nettles," Quinn continued to edit Munro through "Floating Bridge," "Post and Beam," "What Is Remembered," and "Family Furnishings." At that point, also the magazine's poetry editor and having other work to do, Quinn cut back on her editing of fiction. Deborah Treisman, who had joined the *New Yorker* as deputy editor of fiction in 1997, became Munro's editor for "Comfort" and has been since. When Buford left the fiction department in October 2002, Treisman succeeded him as fiction editor. Born in England of academic parents, Treisman grew up in Vancouver and attended the University of California at Berkeley; before joining the magazine, she worked in publishing in Vancouver and New York, where she was managing editor of *Grand Street*.

Little archival evidence has been found revealing Menaker's and Quinn's approaches to Munro's stories as they moved from manuscript to publication, but those that reveal Treisman's work show it as quite consistent with McGrath's during the late 1970s and into the 1980s. Like his, her comments are always couched as suggestions and, throughout the proofs and letters she wrote to Munro, Treisman explains her rationale in each instance. While they worked together, initially, Buford was a superior presence in the process. Just as Quinn said, his proofs show him to be more intrusively directing. In his set of proofs for "Post and Beam," for example, Buford writes a message directly to Munro, telling her the story is great but that the fix she had done for the beginning has not worked. Also, he did not like using two names beginning with "l," Lionel and Lorna. Throughout, he points out issues and probes weak spots, asking questions about characters and their actions. As the *New Yorker* has always done, Buford combines many of Munro's short paragraphs into longer ones. It fell to Treisman to handle all this, working with Munro to incorporate changes – in her letters, she indicates that they are almost done, although more suggestions from Buford might still appear and need to be dealt with. Getting ready to close "Family Furnishings" in early July 2001, for example, Treisman reports that she has not got Buford's comments; writing on the ninth, she jokes that he may let Munro be, since it is her birthday. Her proof shows that she has gone over the story with Munro on the telephone; most of her proposed changes are checked as agreeable to Munro, others crossed out as not.

While some cuts remained a fact of life at the *New Yorker*, there is no evidence of difficulties of the sort surrounding "The Children Stay." That acknowledged, Treisman knows she has a particular problem with Munro, who is now writing stories that are quite long. Any story is competing against all the non-fiction for space in the magazine, and since most writers working there write non-fiction, Treisman essentially has to negotiate space for longer stories; she has said that after she runs one of Munro's stories she has to "atone" by following it with a succession of shorter ones. Even so, there are exceptions. The *New Yorker* looked at "Hateship, Friendship, Courtship, Loveship, Marriage" but passed on it largely because of its length; it first appeared in the book. So too "Powers" in *Runaway*. "Hateship" is over fifty pages, "Powers" over sixty. There was just no way, Treisman said about "Powers."

When Treisman was appointed fiction editor she was quoted as saying her goal was "to publish the best fiction out there" and as she has done that Munro's has loomed large, perhaps even the largest. In June 2004 Treisman and her colleagues took the radical step of running three Munro stories – "Chance," "Soon," and "Silence," over thirty thousand words in all – in their summer fiction issue. This just after they had run "Passion" in March and "Runaway" the previous August. The magazine had run more than one story by the same author in a single issue before, but only once or twice. What this confirms, and in a way far more compelling than Tina Brown's glitzy "buzz"-fiction party in 1994, is Munro's position as a *New Yorker* writer. Speaking of Munro since she herself arrived at the magazine in 1997, Treisman has said that "the understanding has always been that we're going to take the story," although they always ask for changes toward improvement. "But she's not in a class with most other people." Recognizing this, Treisman continued: "But it's not about political stature in the literary world, it's about the quality of the writing. I didn't appreciate until I started editing her just how intricately she constructs a story. Reading them, something from page three will come and hit you on page thirty, but you had not registered the matter when you first read page three. When you're editing, and you might think, 'Oh that line is sort of odd there; maybe it doesn't need to be there.' But you get five pages on and you realize exactly why that line is there. Then you appreciate it."

Working closely with Munro on a story, Treisman sees her in the same way her predecessors did: She is a writer who understands the process, knows an editorial improvement when she sees it, and works with her editor. Treisman said that, when going over a proof, Munro will go for pages agreeing to suggestions until, knowing just what she wants, she will refuse one, saying, "Well, I think I want to keep that." Consistent with the example of the brief addition to "Open Secrets"

Munro provided to Gibson, Treisman has said that "if you ask her for something, and you might be imagining something quite – not radical – but you might be thinking of a different ending. In fact, she'll come back with just three lines, but she will have thought about them so carefully that those three lines will make the difference." And finally Treisman, given her own Canadian experience, has tended to value Munro's local resonances: "She is, in the best sense, a regional writer. She's very, very grounded in the landscape, and in social mores, social exchanges which are vocal. She's writing about very specific small-town life, which is similar to American small-town life, but it's not the same." In passing, too, Treisman commented that she "loves the fact" that Munro and Fremlin do "this drive back and forth every year wandering randomly through different small towns."3

⁕

Hateship, Friendship, Courtship, Loveship, Marriage went into production early in 2001. There was little discussion of the ordering of the stories, although "Queenie" and "What Is Remembered" were reversed during the process; the two publishers produced books in their usual fashion, sharing typesetting but printing separately with different dust jackets. For this book's jacket, Munro and Gibson decided to use *Eve's Delight*, a colour etching by Sheila Laidlaw-Radford, Munro's sister. Given the length of the book's title, Knopf decided to forgo an image and just use type. As the book was being set and was well in to the process heading toward the printer, Munro once again called Gibson with a specific request about its production, though what she wanted was not so dramatic as it had been when she called about *Who*: "Doug, I understand that there's a new recycled, environmentally friendly type of paper that can be used for books," Gibson recalled Munro saying. "I'd like my book to be printed on it." Although it took considerable doing, McClelland & Stewart gave Munro what she wanted, just as Macmillan had: the Canadian edition of *Hateship* bears the note "Forest Friendly" on its dust jacket. (Munro's decision had a widespread impact on the Canadian book trade; many other authors and publishers have followed suit, and now a much higher proportion of books are being printed on recycled stock.) McClelland & Stewart published in October and by January had got 43,000 copies out. By mid-October the book was atop the *Globe and Mail*'s bestseller list. Knopf's edition appeared in November; Chatto & Windus also published in November in Great Britain. The Knopf edition was anticipated the previous month in *Publishers Weekly* with this forecast: "Munro's collections are true modern classics, as the 75,000 first printing of her latest attests. Expect vigorous sales."

Just before that forecast *Publishers Weekly* concluded its brief but categorical review, "The stories share Munro's characteristic style, looping gracefully from the present to the past, interpolating vignettes that seem extraneous and bringing the strands together in a deceptively gentle windup whose impact takes the breath away. Munro has few peers in her understanding of the bargains women make with life and the measureless price they pay." As with her books from the 1990s, Munro received a remarkable range of reviews for *Hateship* – broad in numbers and types of publications – and like those focused on the books of the previous decade, its reviews spend considerable effort trying to define just how her work is so very good, so very affecting.

Singular among such reviews is Mona Simpson's "A Quiet Genius" in the *Atlantic Monthly*, an extended personal meditation on what Munro's work means to one reader and a somewhat grumpy assertion that it still needs to be better known. A writer herself, Simpson had met Munro when she came to New York for the U.S. launch of *The Moons of Jupiter* in 1983 and had interviewed her for *The Paris Review*. Simpson's review of *Hateship* is published beneath a singular, now often quoted, cutline: "Alice Munro is the living writer most likely to be read in a hundred years." Beginning by looking back on herself when she discovered Munro's writing, in her twenties working in publishing in New York, Simpson wrote that she "read Alice Munro's stories of adulterous wives, and country girls gutting turkeys, with the page-turning avidity of someone discovering her own true future." She and a friend read them together, they "read them deeply personally, to learn how to live." Thus in reviewing *Hateship* Simpson writes as a person who has been reading Munro for over twenty years, a person who has long seen her work as resonant, a person who has met Munro (twice, at least) and wants to differentiate between the person and the genius. "A Quiet Genius" is an indicative review: in it, Simpson more than persuades her readers of the importance of Munro's work – to her personally and when compared to both Munro's contemporaries and past masters of fiction. Simpson quotes Richard Ford, who says that he is "in awe of how she operates in the third person. . . . She manages to make that third person *do* more than anybody I've ever seen in my life." For Simpson in *Hateship*, Munro's "men and women . . . are now seen from the perspective of an adult watching the doings of kindergarten children. She is far beyond taking sides." Like many reviewers, Simpson is drawn to "Family Furnishings," a writer's story that both echoes Munro autobiographically and is also quite fictional, and like other reviewers she fastens on a final image of the narrator, completely apart, not connected to anyone else, watching: "such happiness, to be alone."

Bronwyn Drainie, the first Canadian reviewer to weigh in, was also attracted to this story, writing in *Quill & Quire* that it "could be subtitled 'Portrait of the Artist as a Cool Young Bitch.'" It is "the most disturbing story in the collection" and represents "the writer's dilemma and the writer's curse. The selfishness is necessary to the creativity, but it distances the writer from the very people she most wants and needs to impress." Recalling the 1974 essay in which everything is "touchable and mysterious," Drainie concludes that Munro "remains faithful to these two literary beacons, giving her readers clear, sensual realities to experience and then leaving them to wonder and ponder."

Toronto's *Globe and Mail* again called on a well-known writer, in this case Ann Beattie, who steps back from *Hateship* and asks, "Who among us understands the way things are?" and continues, "The boy from the past may reappear, rendered unobtainable by fate (*Nettles*); one may search for a missing person only to realize that the person is a sort of escape artist from her own life, eluding herself as well as the pursuer (*Queenie*). Even furniture seems to have great mobility and to serve the same function as a character in many of these stories (the wonderful title story; *Family Furnishings, Queenie*). Furniture, for heaven's sake: It's larger than life and can't be cast off! It would be funny, except that it carries the weight – is the weight – of the present-determining past." Munro, she maintains in a passage that unknowingly picks up some of Ozick's comments on Chekhov, "orients the reader toward realizing that a story is composed of pieces and shows us that shards, as well as neat slices, are necessary to complete the puzzle."

Not to be outdone, Toronto's other national paper, the *National Post*, also commissioned a well-known writer, Anne Enright, to review *Hateship*. She begins by deprecating a view of Munro's writing that holds it "wants to be liked." That is, the writing is accessible. "The democratic ease with which she tells her stories and the transparent quality of her prose mean you can love her work without realizing quite how good it is. Once this simple and singular fact clicks – that she is a brilliant writer – you can never read her with the same relaxed companionship again." Acknowledging the truth of this, Enright reviews *Hateship* and concludes, "She has gotten better. The vultures who circle over literary reputations must be getting pretty fed up with Alice Munro." While Enright has several perceptive things to say about individual stories, her sharpest point is a generalization about Munro's art: "Sometimes it seems as though her work is all insight, but its greatness comes not just from letting us see inside a character. It comes from allowing us a larger view. Time and again, we pull back to see the image of a woman in a landscape, alone."

Merilyn Simonds, in the Montreal *Gazette*, contrasted *Hateship* to *Love* where she saw "a certain sadness, a despair" weigh its stories, "making them almost unbearable to read. . . . Her redeeming vision seemed to cloud." Here "the tone is tougher, as if she's rediscovered the fibre that gives resilience to the human heart." Philip Marchand, in the *Toronto Star*, made something of the same point when he wrote that "some of Munro's recent stories have been marked by so much withheld information that the effect has been a certain frustration for readers, as if the point of the story is known only to the angels and to Munro herself." Like other reviewers, Marchand calls special attention to the last story in the collection, "The Bear Came Over the Mountain." There Grant, a retired professor and longtime rué, ironically has to contend with his wife's romance with another patient in the nursing home where she lives because of Alzheimer's – in getting on, seemingly, with a new life, she has forgotten who Grant is.

The novelist Thomas Wharton, in a fine review in the *Edmonton Journal* syndicated to other papers, begins by recalling a student of his in a writing class who argued that Munro's stories were "too slow. 'Why doesn't she just get on with it?' he wanted to know." Disagreeing, Wharton argues that the stories in *Hateship* do " 'get on with it,' but they do it in the way our lives do: with stops and starts and backtrackings and revelations, surprises that divert us from our intended path along unexpected branchings." Wharton feels that, with Munro, it is important "not to read too much, too fast." Central incidents in her stories are key, but beyond them "the stories trace the shape of a life. . . . Reading Alice Munro," he concludes, "is a quiet reminder that, amid the big ideas, the big important books always in a rush to sum up 'society as a whole,' it is always the solitary, observing, ultimately unknowable self to whom life, and death, happen." Striking a similar note in the *Ottawa Citizen*, the Scottish critic Catherine Lockerbie calls the stories in *Hateship* "wise and wry, true and endlessly moving," writing also that they "achieve the only proper purpose of literature and art: to touch us more deeply and teach us more fully what it means to be human."

Not all Canadian reviewers were prepared to revel in *Hateship*. Candace Fertile in the *Vancouver Sun* argues that, "after dozens of stories, the style gets predictable and verges on self-parody." There is also the question of audience: "Munro's stories have increasingly become meaningful to a smaller group – generally, older women who grew up at a time when women's options were severely limited." And though Munro handles her material with real dexterity, "the 'stifled woman' theme and the generally negative view of men get a bit tiresome." Fertile seems intent on spotting and poking at weaknesses, and like several other reviewers she is not taken by the title story. (Roughly the same number, though, see it as one of the best.)

By the time of *Hateship*, Simpson's assertions notwithstanding, there is little discernible material difference between Munro's reviews in Canada, the United States, and Great Britain to see real differences in reputation in each country. True, in Canada there remains the matter of Munro as a "national treasure," but in the United States and Great Britain her reputation was established sufficiently among critics so that reviewers are by and large focused on the same elements and show an equal deep appreciation. What is evident, and this is what makes Simpson's piece so interesting, is that with this book foreign critics took the long view of Munro's art that was already so familiar in Canada. Thus Jeff Giles in *Newsweek* begins by writing that *Hateship* "isn't as good as her best work, but virtually nothing is." Noting an unevenness, he maintains that the "best stories here resonate so deeply that the rest feel drab." Michiko Kakutani in the *New York Times* begins by seeing Munro's women as equivalent to Updike's men, writing that she "has created tales that limn entire lifetimes in a handful of pages, tales whose emotional amplitude and keen sense of the mundane muddles of ordinary life have established her over the last three decades as one of the foremost practitioners of the short story." Like other reviewers who have written on Munro's previous books, Kakutani notices that the "people in this volume tend to be somewhat older versions of people we met in Ms. Munro's earliest stories." Noting especially "Nettles," "Family Furnishings," and "Post and Beam," Kakutani asserts that "these tales have the intimacy of a family photo album and the organic feel of real life, and they give us portraits created not through willful artifice, but through imaginative sympathy and virtuosic craft." The *New York Times Book Review*'s notice, by William H. Pritchard, does not especially stand out – uncharacteristically, in view of the prominence of his previous reviews there. Pritchard summarizes the stories well enough, and like many others he lingers on "Family Furnishings," but Pritchard offers very little by way of differentiated insight.

That certainly cannot be said of Lorrie Moore's review in the *New York Review of Books*. Likening Munro's insights into domesticity to those of Henry James, Moore offers this telling assessment:

> Unlike James, a permanent tourist in the land of marriage and romantic union – a subject endlessly suited to the short-story genre – Alice Munro is intimately informed about what actually goes on there, and it is but one of the many reasons she is (to

speak historically, and to speak even, say, in a Russian or French or even Irish saloon, loudly and unarmed) one of the world's greatest short story writers. As the writer Ethan Canin once said, "The stories of Alice Munro make everyone else's look like the work of babies."

She is also interested in social class. And there is not one of her stories in this new book that does not put together characters with real if subtle class divisions between them. This Munro does with a neutral, unsentimental eye and limber sympathies.

Moore anticipates disputation over which stories are the strongest and, quite rightly, she expects that "Hateship, Friendship, Courtship, Loveship, Marriage" "may come under the most fire." Yet she sees the title story as embarked on one of Munro's "signature themes – the random, permanent fate brought about by an illusion of love." Luxuriating in Munro's style, Moore writes that the ending of "Nettles" with its "swift and economical use of the word 'dwindling,' thriftily closing two stories at once, is Munro at her stunning best."

Like many other writer-reviewers, Moore also sees "Family Furnishings" as arguably "the finest story in *Hateship, Friendship, Courtship, Loveship, Marriage,* and surely one of several here that are among the most powerful she has written." So impressed is Moore by the story ("There is not a more moving piece by anyone that I can think of") that she devotes over a third of her space to its analysis. "Family Furnishings" is, as Moore asserts, an "exploration of the spiritual escape and emotional cost of becoming a writer." Like other reviewers who note this story, Moore is aware of Del Jordan and some other would-be writers elsewhere in Munro's work; like them, too, she makes no mention of either "Material" or of "Dulse," two earlier protracted analyses of the writer's self-absorption. Quite rightly, Moore sees "Family Furnishings" "as an acknowledgement of [the literary life's] emotional distances and thefts and its willing trade of the human for art. It is a song of relief alloyed with shame. Munro has beautifully registered the ambivalent conscience of the writer – not judgmentally but helplessly, as before love and the life story love brings before dying."

The intellectual magazines in the United States offered good reviews of *Hateship*, too. In *Commonweal*, Tom Deignan begins by noting that "National Book Award-winner Jonathan Franzen made a fascinating admission" to the *New York Times Magazine*, that after DeLillo, the living author he most admired was Alice Munro. (This had been noticed as well by K. Gordon Neufeld when he reviewed *Hateship* in the *Calgary Herald*, and ever since Franzen reviewed *Runaway* in a famously enthusiastic way for the *New York Times Book Review*, it was recalled elsewhere too.) Contrasting DiLillo's "sweeping intercontinental tomes with Munro's exquisite portraits of confused Canadiana," Deignan opts for Munro. "Take the endlessly plundered topic of gender," he writes, "on which no author is quite as illuminating." Citing "Family Furnishings," he maintains that Munro's "deft manipulation of past and present tense, of narrative voice, as well as her exploration of the writer's role in society, put her postmodern credentials on display. But inevitably, the drama of love, mortality, and human entanglement trump such formal matters." Deignan moves through the stories, noting in passing that Munro's "stories sprawl, lacking a central focus. This is mostly a good thing, giving her stories a unique depth." Ultimately, he concludes that "nobody ever has written stories quite like Alice Munro's."

In the *New Republic* Ruth Franklin begins wondering just why Munro is undervalued. She cites a reviewer who "just came out and said what we were all thinking: 'Alice Munro should write a novel.'" Franklin then takes up Munro's introduction to her *Selected Stories* and examines the rationale Munro offers there for why she writes short stories – that when she was a young mother in Vancouver and Victoria, extended blocks of time were just not possible. Franklin is sceptical, and she remains so throughout her review, in which she moves carefully and precisely through the stories in *Hateship*. At one point, just before she takes up "Family Furnishings," Franklin writes, "I hope that this will not be true, but there is an elegiac mood to this book that makes it feel as if it might be Munro's last." The reviewer notices how Munro's characters have aged with her and that, as well, "several of the stories [here] read as answers to stories that Munro has written before." "Family Furnishings" is just such a story, looking at "the purpose of her art, the justification for it." Working her way through the narrator's story, her history and her relations with Alfrida both as a child and later, when she saw her one time when she lived in the same town while attending university, Franklin focuses on the narrator's key realization: "'More like grabbing something out of the air than constructing stories' – we are back with the teenaged Munro, looking out the window at the horses on the scale, at the image that reveals the story that falls into place around it. And here it is not something to be fit in between diaper changes, but 'the work I wanted to do.' The short story has been chosen after all."

It is probably worth noting that the *Yale Review* allowed Michael Ravitch ten pages to consider *Hateship* at considerable length. There he begins, "The modest airs of Alice Munro's short stories slyly conceal their extraordinary amplitude." Placing her work within the contexts of the twentieth-century short story, citing Hemingway, noting realism and other trends, Ravitch asserts that Munro "embraces all that her contemporaries repudiated: exposition and analysis, plot and character. She writes about very specific places . . . and invites history back into fiction, with all its messy complications. Her characters are far from rootless; in fact, they tend to feel burdened by attachments they cannot easily shed. They live in an old world, a world in which memory is still more powerful than forgetting, a world full of unusual and vivid stories." Ravitch continues to make specific points within his generalities, including "Leaving home, in one form or another, is the perpetual drama for Munro" and "no matter how far they travel, [her characters] can never free themselves of the spell of family." Citing "What Is Remembered," Ravitch asserts that "Munro writes about sexuality with more lyrical intensity than any writer since D.H. Lawrence." He ultimately concludes that "Munro is ironic to the point of nihilism. No rapture survives her scrutiny, no certainty earns her confidence," and she has an "almost inhuman acceptance [which] may be key to her immense imaginative powers: armed with her wise humor, she is equal to whatever shall happen."

Reviews from Great Britain offer many of the same judgements though, again, less extensively. The anonymous reviewer in the *Economist* maintains that the "greatest pleasure of reading Ms Munro, though, is the prose itself: unaffected, modest, quietly elegant. . . . She is one of the most accomplished and downright exhilarating writers working today. Her human understanding is acute." Lisa Allardice in the *New Statesman* notes that although "Munro flirts with melodrama, the undertone of grim humour is unmistakable: an atheist's long-suffering widow finds comfort in the arms of an undertaker; the terminally ill wife of a sanctimonious social worker kisses a young thug, and a woman with Alzheimer's rekindles romance with an old flame. . . . There is nothing ordinary about Alice Munro's writing." Writing in the *London Review of Books*, Benjamin Markovits notes that *Hateship* "reads like a book, which is all the more remarkable given the variety of narrators, and narrative styles, it employs: from the traditional device of the title-story . . . to the seemingly undoctored memories of 'Family Furnishings.'" John McGahern in the *Times Literary Supplement* asserts that Munro "has an imaginative boldness." He too takes up "the rich and surefooted 'Family Furnishings'" and concludes with this estimation: "Everything is true and breathtakingly sure and is as good as Alice Munro has ever written, which is to say that it is written as well as anybody who has written in her time, and with her own uniqueness."4

"The Most Wonderful Walks You Can Imagine": The Alice Munro Literary Garden, *No Love Lost*

Following her first Giller Prize in November 1998, Munro continued to receive public attention. Some of this was caused by the success of *Love*, some by the Giller (and Gibson's ongoing public irritation with the Governor General's Award committee for failing to even shortlist the book), but most was just in genuine recognition of the power and reach of her writing. At home, *Maclean's* included her in its Honour Roll for 1998 with a brief profile featuring a photo of Munro standing by the shore of Lake Huron: "'I love the landscape here,' she says. 'We go for long walks; they're the most wonderful walks you can imagine.'" She is also quoted as remembering someone in her family, not her husband, who supported her writing, saying when she was about thirty-one, "It's time you recognized your limitations and quit this," her writing. "But somehow I just had to ignore that and go on."

Another article that appeared in December 1998 was a long reminiscent piece in the *Wingham Advance-Times* by Margaret Stapleton called "Alice Munro – Friend of Our Youth." Drawing on the memories and photographs of people who remembered Alice Laidlaw growing up in Wingham, Stapleton offers a hometown view of the town's now most famous native. As this suggests too, Stapleton's article reveals a considerable contrast in attitude from the early 1980s, when Munro, and her depiction of Wingham with its Lower Town section, met with public disapproval by many there. With the passing of time, far fewer Wingham-based references in the writing, and Munro's vastly increased reputation in the literary world at home and abroad, things had changed between Munro and her hometown. The time was ripe for Wingham to more formally recognize Munro's importance. As Ross and Carol Hamilton wrote to the *Advance-Times* in response to Stapleton's article, "We who knew her and all those who live in her hometown cannot but feel a glow of pride in her accomplishments." Very clearly a consensus was growing.

The North Huron District Museum, along with the *Advance-Times*, began to work at collecting Munro-connected items for display. At the same time, the Wingham and District Horticultural Society, which was planning on erecting new signs along the roads leading into Wingham, was encouraged to add "Proud Hometown of Alice Munro" to the signs. This culminated after some time in the creation of the Alice Munro Literary Garden. The project was spearheaded by Verna Steffler, chair of the horticultural society, and Ross Procter, a local farmer, who served as the financial chair of the project; he had attended school with Munro. Steffler and Procter raised considerable funds for the garden locally, holding occasions referred to as "A.M. in the P.M." These were get-togethers at Procter's house. Munro would attend and give a little talk, and Procter would make a quiet pitch. With local support and a grant from the Ontario Trillium Foundation, work on the garden began in April 2002 and was completed for the dedication on July 10, Munro's seventy-first birthday.

Since he had seen Stapleton's article in late 1998, Gibson had been aware that things were happening in Wingham. Once the garden materialized, he was keen to help by inviting appropriate literary people to the dedication and by attending himself. Almost five hundred people were there on a beautiful summer day, Munro was resplendent in a hat given her by daughter Jenny and goddaughter Rebecca, and the press was out in force. Munro's picture was on the front page the next day of both the *Globe and Mail* and the *National Post*, and the *Star* ran its story on the dedication under the witty, and apt, headline "Jubilation in Jubilee." Gibson and Barber spoke, as did David Staines, editor of the New Canadian Library, and Jane Urquhart, novelist and friend. At the local theatre each read from a favourite Munro story and talked about their associations with Alice, after which Munro read from one of her stories. A garden luncheon followed on the lawn. Among the contributors listed in the program was Munro's Books.

Avie Bennett, chairman and publisher of McClelland & Stewart and a good friend of Munro's, spoke at the earlier dedication at the sunlit garden and was quoted saying "Alice is one of the finest writers this country has ever known. She is also notorious for saying no to public attention. It is a frustrating business trying to give Alice Munro the attention she deserves. . . . How did Wingham manage to succeed where so many have failed?" Barber, who made her first trip to Wingham for the occasion, said this in her remarks:

> I've known Alice Munro for many years and have seen her hesitations about her own work, her many revisions, her modesty and humility if you wish. She works on several stories at once, maybe putting two aside to look at later and grappling with the third on a particular day. She often sends me three stories at once, and on one occasion she called me in advance to say, "I'm giving a dinner party tonight, and I'm more nervous about that than I am the three stories I'm working on, so I just put them in an envelope and sent them to you." As you can imagine, I've used this story against her, calling her from time to time to say, when we haven't received stories in many weeks,

"Alice it's time to give another dinner party." The stories arrive with no name on them, no date, just typed manuscripts, as if she isn't ready to own them yet, and sure enough, she sometimes continues to make revisions, even after the stories have been accepted. It takes a great deal of courage to publish your work, thereby asking all the world to read it, and I know how many times Alice has heard "Who Do You Think You Are?" echoing in her head.

It was on this day of celebration too, this day of "Jubilation in Jubilee," that Alice Munro found a woman waiting to tell her the details of Anne Clarke Chamney Laidlaw's winter 1959 escape from the Wingham hospital.[5]

In one of the stories written about the dedication, Virginia Barber was quoted regarding Munro's most recent publication in the *New Yorker*, "Lying Under the Apple Tree." It "chronicles the daily struggles of an adolescent girl, 'secretly devoted to nature' and echoes Ms. Munro's life,'" Barber said, continuing, "'Alice's stories deal with her conflict – the comfort of being part of a family, versus the need to stand outside, alone,' she said." "Lying Under the Apple Tree," published the previous month, does just that – it is a story of adolescent first love and wondering, and it does echo Alice Laidlaw's circumstances in 1944. Invited to her boyfriend's house for supper and not willing to tell her mother, who is ill, the narrator lies and says she is going to a girlfriend's house. A passage excised from the *New Yorker* shows that the narrator's situation was very close to Alice Laidlaw's:

> Now that my father had to be at the foundry by five o'clock and my mother was so often not feeling well, our suppers had become rather haphazard. If I cooked, there were things that I liked. One was sliced bread and cheese with milk and beaten eggs poured over it, baked in the oven. Another, also oven-baked, was a loaf of tinned meat coated with brown sugar. Or heaps of slices of raw potatoes, fried to a crisp. Left to themselves, my brother and sister would make themselves something like sardines on

soda crackers or peanut butter on graham wafer. This erosion of regular custom seemed to make my deception easier.

Preparing "Lying Under the Apple Tree" for publication, Treisman chose to present it as a memoir, and at one point thought of running a picture of a teenaged Alice Laidlaw sitting beside her sister, Sheila, on the bank of the Maitland, circa 1946, which Munro sent at her request. As this excised passage confirms, the story certainly echoed Munro's life and included biographically correct details. But as they were going through the editing process, it became clear to Treisman that while the core of the story was memoir – Munro has said that this is an account of her first infatuation – there was also invention involved. Talking it over with Buford and the fact-checker (who, in famed *New Yorker* fashion, had doubtless turned up some questions), they elected to insert a disclaimer into the end of the first paragraph: "(To disguise some people and events, I have allowed myself a certain amount of invention with names and details.)" And they decided not to use the picture.

What was happening here, probably, is just what has been happening in Munro's work throughout her career. In "Lying Under the Apple Tree" Munro does recreate a sense of her younger self – "Sunday afternoons in 1944," the magazine's cutline reads – but whether this is memoir as "Working for a Living" is memoir is doubtful. It reads much like other first-person reminiscent stories – "Nettles," or "Family Furnishings." It further confirms, as if any further confirmation were needed, that some major portion of Alice Munro's core material is made up of her memories, just as Barber said, of being a member of that family in their brick house by the Maitland in Lower Wingham. In "What Do You Want to Know For?" Munro meets a man, through her investigations of the crypt she and Fremlin are discovering, who had known her father when he was in the turkey business. They talk about those days, and she concludes the matter, writing, "I was happy to find somebody who could see me still in my family, who could remember my father and the place where my parents lived and worked all their lives, first in hope and then in honourable persistence. A place astonishingly changed now, though the house is still there." When she talked to Mona Simpson and

Jeanne McCulloch in Clinton in 1993, at a second meeting to complete the interview they began in 1983, Munro remarked, "The material about my mother is my central material in life . . . and it always comes the most readily to me. If I just relax, that's what will come up." In keeping with this, in "Fathers" Munro explicitly uses an autobiographical incident – her father's 1943 near-electrocution in a neighbour's barn – as the basis of a fiction. Yet "Fathers" is a fiction, for the father in the story is nothing like Robert Laidlaw and, besides, he is electrocuted.

Neither "Lying Under the Apple Tree" nor "Fathers" was included in *Runaway*. They were passed over because, as Munro would explain in the foreword to the volume which did include them, *The View from Castle Rock*, she judged them "closer to my own life than the other stories" she had to consider for *Runaway*. Having long contemplated what she had once called "a family book," the one that she was now to take up as both a project of new composition and long-considered revisions, Munro ultimately saw these stories as better placed there – *Castle Rock*, as well, was one she was then calling "my last book."[6]

Before *Runaway*, published in the fall of 2004, there was in fact another book: *No Love Lost*. It is a collection of Munro's stories on a theme selected by Jane Urquhart and published by the New Canadian Library in Canada only, aimed at school adoption as well as bookstore sales. It was published in 2003 and, through it, Gibson and Staines were able finally to get Munro into the firm's paperback line. Gibson made his formal proposal in August 2000 – the proposed title was "Falling in Love: Stories on a Theme" – and Munro accepted it immediately. Urquhart was to select the stories; the original plan was seven stories, a book of about 250 pages priced at $9.95. This size and price addressed Barber's concern that the existence of a smaller, cheaper selection of Munro's stories should not compete directly with Penguin's large paperback *Selected Stories*.

Once terms were settled and Urquhart set to work, she found that she was unable to get the collection down even close to the intended size. Urquhart and Staines worked together on the selections but, after considerable effort, Urquhart concluded with a selection of ten stories, and some long ones at that, so the finished book is over four hundred pages. Given this, Gibson had to go back to Barber for her approval, and Barber in turn talked to Munro about it. Munro wanted to include all the stories selected, saying, according to Barber, "that if she was going to do this volume, she wanted the subject covered correctly." Barber, who probably still had misgivings about the book's effect on Canadian sales of the *Selected Stories*, conceded. *No Love Lost* was published in spring 2003 with a stunning painting by Mary Pratt, *Barby in the Dress She Made Herself*, on the cover. The initial run was 10,000 copies and, at 430 pages, the book retailed for $12.95.

Urquhart's selection of stories is both unusual and affecting. It is unusual because it is does not follow chronology. She begins with "Bardon Bus" (1982), follows it with "Carried Away" (1991), and then "Mischief" (1978); this mixed pattern is followed throughout. The selection is affecting because, as Urquhart writes of "the state commonly referred to as 'falling in love'" in her afterword, "Munro is more interested in the singularity of the experience, in the days and months or years that precede or follow acts of communion, or in long, inward-looking periods of reflection that are born of a love that is either unrequited, difficult, or impossible."7 By making and arranging her selections to display the various ways Munro has made these times the core of her stories, Urquhart contributes through *No Love Lost* to the now unquestionable realization that Alice Munro's art creates what might be called the feelings of being, just being a human being. *No Love Lost* in its focus anticipates a concluding comment made by Claire Messud in a review of *Runaway*: "That which each of us holds to be unique – our pain, our joy – is as common as dirt. To be made aware of each soul's isolation, and of our vast human indifference (in all senses of that word), is at once glorious and appalling. It is the stuff of great art."

"Our Chekhov, Our Flaubert": The *New Yorker's* Munro Triptych, *Runaway*

Munro's vaunted ability to encapsulate whole lives in a single story – the by now clichéd view that each of her stories contains material sufficient for a novel – may have reached its apogee with the triptych of Juliet stories the *New Yorker* published in June 2004 as most of its summer fiction issue. Its three stories – "Chance," "Soon," and "Silence" – treat Juliet in the three phases of human life that are Munro hallmarks: as a young woman setting out, finding her own way in "Chance," leaving Ontario for British Columbia; as an adult, a young mother though still very much a daughter, returned home to visit her aged parents, her mother dying, in "Soon"; in "Silence," as the middle-aged mother of the adult Penelope who has elected to have no contact with her. That story ends with Juliet's thoughts described: "She keeps on hoping for a word from Penelope, but not in any strenuous way. She hopes as people who know better hope for undeserved blessings, spontaneous remissions, things of that sort." In her unceasing search for perfection – just the right cadence, the rhythm that captures the story's and the triptych's end moment and emotion – Munro has continued to edit: the *New Yorker*'s final sentence included a comma after "hopes" and "or" before the final phrase. Alice Munro, writing on.

That Treisman and the other editors at the *New Yorker* were willing to commit so much of the fiction issue to Munro – some were almost giddy at the prospect as they planned it – says just what might be said as to how her work is valued there today. The triptych is over thirty thousand words, leaving room for just one other story. (They had show-cased Munro before: the length of "The Love of a Good Woman" alone warrants such a designation, and the seventy-fifth anniversary issue – February 21 and 28, 2000 – contains just one other story, by Woody Allen, along with "Nettles.") Still, the *New Yorker* had only once or twice run more than one story by a single author in the same issue before.

McClelland & Stewart and Knopf, as had long been their prac-tice, each printed its own edition of *Runaway* from the same Knopf setting, each with its own dust jacket. Munro and Gibson opted for another painting by Mary Pratt, this one an image of a four-poster bed with the top cover thrown back, with part of the cutline from Simpson's review of *Hateship* ("the living writer most likely to be read in a hundred years") included below the title. Munro and Close covered the Knopf edition with a drawing of stately blades of grass. McClelland & Stewart published on September 25, printing 40,000 initial copies as the book went to the stores. Knopf's edition was published on November 14 with a first printing of 100,000.

Faced with an eleventh book from a writer whose work has been praised for well over thirty years, a writer who was reaching her mid-seventies, reviewers of *Runaway* understandably took the long view of Munro's career. In Canada, that view was especially long. Claire Messud, in the *Globe and Mail*, especially noted "Powers" and the Juliet triptych, and commented, "Both undertakings are extraordinary, the former as a departure for Munro, in its final entwining of Gothic personal histories and imaginings; the latter as an example of the author in full and glorious literary force." Messud concluded with a correction to Ozick's ubiquitous assertion that Munro is "our Chekhov," writing that "but like the character Juliet, Munro does always choose to show compassion. Like life itself, she remains neutral. So she is our Flaubert, too." Philip Marchand in the *Toronto Star* maintained that Munro's "powers of verbal precision are undiminished," that her "trademark techniques" of creating utterly precise settings and "note-perfect dialogue" are unwavering, but above all she knows that "to engage the heart of the reader, it is also necessary to show these characters in desperate circumstances."

Jane Urquhart, in the *National Post*, like Marchand, writes from long familiarity: "Munro never lets us walk away without knowing that some other narrative was possible, and she has always been a master at showing us how missed cues and misperceptions can alter the course of an entire life. And an entire life is what we get in each of these stories, the full canvas. One of the great mysteries of Alice Munro's genius as a writer of short stories is just how she manages to cause her readers to feel closer to the characters she creates than they do to certain members of their own family." Judith Timson, reviewing *Runaway* in *Maclean's*, maintained that "in Alice Munro's hands, the smallest moments contain the central truths of a lifetime, in which disaster, honesty and hope are teased out as if indeed there was not a minute to lose." These stories, Bruce Erskine in the Halifax *Chronicle-Herald* asserted, "demonstrate how random, arbitrary and false life can be, and how little we truly know about what we experience."

In the United States, such ready familiarity with Munro's work as that found in Canada was evident too. A. Alvarez, in the *New York Review of Books*, begins an extended review by focusing on the three characters in the title story, writing that they "are held tight together by a net of erotic tension." Like many reviewers, Alvarez found "Passion" to be the volume's singular story and used it to generalize about Munro's women, who "assume from the start that love doesn't last, marriages go sour, and people generally are unfaithful. . . . Her pessimism in these new stories is relentless." That this review beat the *Publishers Weekly* notice for *Runaway* to press was an indication of Munro's still-growing status. "One never knows quite where a Munro story will end," the anonymous *PW* reviewer asserted, "only that it will leave an incandescent trail of psychological insight."

These reviews began a progress in the United States that is remarkable both for its range of publication and the unanimity of its verdict. From one end of the country to the other – the *Hartford Courant* to the *Seattle Times* – *Runaway* was seen as yet another offering from an accomplished, known, and well-appreciated author. The two reviews produced by the *New York Times* were at something of cross purposes, however: Michiko Kakutani, who has been reviewing Munro since *Progress*, wrote in "Books of the *Times*" that the triptych of Juliet stories offers "an affecting portrait [and] the harrowing trajectory of her life, but most of the entries in this volume are more stilted affairs." Kakutani feels that unlike Munro's previous work, these stories seemed forced, "relying on awkwardly withheld secrets and O'Henryesque twists to create narrative suspense." Other reviewers, including Mary Hawthorne in the *London Review of Books*, also felt that some of these structural shifts failed to convince.

At the *New York Times Book Review*, the editor apparently followed up on Jonathan Franzen's admiring comment in the *New York Times Magazine* profile of Munro on October 24 and commissioned a four-page lead review of *Runaway* by Franzen. His review is singular in that it reviews *Runaway* without telling the reader anything about any of the stories in the book.

Franzen began: "Alice Munro has a strong claim to being the best fiction writer now working in North America, but outside of Canada, where her books are No. 1 best sellers, she has never had a large readership." Franzen meant large by U.S. standards. Working against recent books that have had "large readerships" – Bill Clinton's autobiography and Philip Roth's *The Plot Against America* – Franzen wrote that "I want to circle around Munro's latest marvel of a book, *Runaway*, by taking some guesses at why her excellence so dismayingly exceeds her fame." He then continued to offer eight guesses, most of which are utterly accurate ("Munro's work is all about storytelling pleasure," "Because, worse yet, Munro is a pure short-story writer"). Franzen considers the perennial question of short story writers versus novelists, asserting that beyond "the Great One herself" – Munro – "the most exciting fiction written in the last 25 years – the stuff I immediately mention if somebody asks me what's terrific – has been short fiction." He then offered a long list of names. He also conjectured that because reviewing fiction is harder than non-fiction, and stories harder than novels, Munro has got short shrift. Throughout, probably demonstrating that very point, he made no mention of any story in *Runaway*, preferring to discuss "The Bear Came Over the Mountain" from *Hateship* as his example of Munro's art. In writing this quirky and well-informed review, Franzen used the bully pulpit of the lead feature review in the *New York Times Book Review* to make just one crucial point: "Read Munro! Read Munro!" Franzen called this a "simple instruction." It is, and in a singular way, it must have had some effect.

Of the wide range of detailed notices *Runaway* received in the United States, Lorrie Moore's in the *Atlantic Monthly*, "Leave Them and Love Them," is among the most considered. Beginning with Munro's perpetual concern with daughters, mothers, and families, Moore wrote:

> Great literature of the past two centuries has sentimental-
> ized politics, crime, nature, and madness, but seldom the family,

and the wrenching incompatibility of a woman's professional or artistic expression with her familial commitments has made its way into the most undidactic of literary minds. It has appeared, to powerful and unexpected effect, in much of Munro's work, especially her most recent collection, *Runaway*.

Moore detailed just how Munro accomplishes this throughout, paying special attention to "Passion" and to the Juliet triptych, and continued, saying of these stories that

> they are constructions of calm perplexity, coolly observed human mysteries. One can feel the suspense, poolside, as well as any reader of *The Da Vinci Code*; one can cast a quick eye toward one's nine-year-old son on the high dive and get back to the exact sentence where one left off. The thrilling unexpectedness of real life, which Munro rightly insists on, will in her hands keep a reader glued — even if that reader is torn by the very conflicts (work to do, kid on the high dive) dramatized therein.

For Moore, Munro is a writer whose "writing never loses its juice, never goes brittle; it also never equivocates or blinks, but simply lets observations speak for themselves. In fiction real turmoil is made artificial turmoil, only to seem real again; this is literary realism's wish, and one of Munro's compelling accomplishments." Toward the end of this thorough review, Moore noted the absence of "Hired Girl" and "Fathers" from this, or any collection, though they have each appeared in the *New Yorker*. "Maybe even more stories are lying in wait," she hoped. "Someone writing at this level well into her seventies, outliving the female friends to whose memory the book is dedicated and who must have been part of its inspiration, is a literary inspiration herself."

Major daily newspapers and national magazines to one side, *Runaway* showed every sign of reaching into publications with different audiences. On *Identity Theory* – identitytheory.com, which calls itself "a literary Web site, sort of" – for example, Angie Kritenbrink wrote that she wanted to "thank Whoever Is Listening that Alice

Munro never went through an MFA program; instead, she has been able to craft her very own unique voice, in postmodern literature. Instead of being self-consciously avant garde or, well, postmodern, Munro's stories have an organic feel – the way stories feel when they are being told by real women, with stops and starts, bends and turns, and going back for explanations, focusing more on feelings and reactions than twists of plot. There have been many times I have been reading Munro stories waiting for a question to be answered, a plot point to be revealed, only to realize that she wasn't going to do it, and anyway that wasn't the point of the story at all."

Besides on Web publications, *Runaway* was reviewed in popular national publications in the United States. Lee Aitken in *People* writes that "Munro is wise in the ways of human emotion, and her stories are so rich in subplots, asides and ancillary characters that even a tale of less than 50 pages feels as rounded as a novel." In the same vein, in *USA Today* Maria Fish wrote that *Runaway* "may very well be the synthesizing work of literature's keenest investigators into the human soul. It will, in any case, reach far beyond its time." Franzen wrote that "Oprah Winfrey will not touch short story collections," but *People* and *USA Today* certainly deal with the same mass market as Oprah Winfrey.[8]

Taking up the Chatto & Windus *Runaway*, editors in the United Kingdom clearly saw it as something of an inspiration too, since the book received extensive and detailed notice. In the *Economist*, the reviewer held that these "plots ring true but never feel trite. Ms. Munro's prose is translucent, never intruding. Indeed, her whole approach is a humble one, focused on the stories themselves. It is easy to overlook how skilfully they are told." In the *Spectator*, Sebastian Smee confessed that "it is difficult, I find, to go from reading Munro's work to reading almost any other contemporary fiction (I tend to stick to non-fiction for a while). By comparison, other authors' voices seem naïve, histrionic or absurdly style-conscious." Smee calls Munro's "almost melodramatic congestion of coincidence, tragedy and death" in the Juliet triptych especially, but throughout, "a kind of aesthetic brinkmanship." He continued:

Munro will stretch the credibility of her plot to breaking point; yet somehow, in pointing to the very real limits of empathy, she elicits a nod of hard-hearted recognition more powerful and seductive than even the most compassionate and all-encompassing prose.

The key to it all is the quality that is easiest to pinpoint but hardest to achieve; Munro's characters never breathe the thin, tangy air of melodrama. They move in the richer, more oxidised atmosphere of great fiction.

Paul Bailey, in the *Independent*, asserted that the art of Alice Munro is rightly called "incomparable," that Munro's great gift "is to pull the rug out from beneath the reader's feet at the very point when he or she feels secure. These reminders of the haphazard nature of human relationships are delivered to chilling effect, frequently in one well-placed sentence." Bailey says further that this is "the moment when her pen becomes a scalpel, cutting away at the certainties that have sustained her characters." Unlike other critics, though, Bailey found to his dismay that the third story in the Juliet triptych, "Silence," falters – there Juliet "has outstayed her welcome. She is no longer interesting." In the same vein, he found "Tricks" dissatisfying as well and in "Powers," "potentially the most resonant story" in the collection, Munro "becomes diffuse, wayward and unsure of where she is going."

Writing in the *Irish Times*, Éilís Ní Dhubhne called *Runaway* a treasure and, although the book would probably not be the best book to begin reading Munro's writing, "for those familiar with her work . . . the collection is a precious gem." She is a writer who "has lived and written on, and changed. Yeats, I think, said that hard thinking was the basis of good art. Alice Munro is lyrical, painterly, comic, but she is a thinker. Her ideas mature with every book. This is a real cause for literary celebration." In the *Times* of London, Tom Gatti wrote that *Runaway* is "an echo-chamber of a book" since, like Faulkner, "Munro is aware of the impossibility of ever truly 'starting over'" despite her characters' attempts to run away. "Millions of words have been spilt in attempts to tell us exactly what it means to be human. In eight short stories . . . Munro performs that very miracle."

Alan Hollinghurst, who reviewed Munro's work in the 1970s and 1980s, brought that perspective to his review of *Runaway* in the *Guardian*. He likened the Juliet triptych to *The Beggar Maid* and commented on Munro's ability to manipulate "gaps and jumps in time" by which she creates "the effect in each case of a life revealed, not a life explained, and certainly not a life explained away. [Munro] knows that life in the past was unhampered by any sense of its future quaintness, so she doesn't explain. She gives us a past as unselfconscious as today." Concluding, Hollinghurst focused on a passage from "Passion" – which he called "among the finest things she has ever done" – and wrote that "Munro has never made a fuss about sex, but a deep understanding of it is integral, in different ways, to each of these stories."

A similar extended and thoughtful treatment was offered by Mary Hawthorne in the *London Review of Books*. She began with an extended biographical overview of Munro and, before she took up *Runaway*, offered this reminiscence of her own:

> Years ago, I came across a note written by Munro in the margin of the last galley of "Oranges and Apples" (a story that ran in the *New Yorker*, where I was working), which documents the insane things that a character has done in his life in the hope of somehow crashing out of it. He does not know that he is doing these things, and does not ever manage to get out, because when it comes down to it he never really wants to. "I see this as a fairly normal state of mind," her note read.

Hawthorne paid special attention to the Juliet triptych, finding fault both with Juliet's exchange with Don, the minister who visits her dying mother, and with the woman from the commune who gleefully informs Juliet that her daughter Penelope would not be contacting her. These scenes, Hawthorne wrote, "are so uncharacteristic of Munro as to make for almost painful reading." Another such instance is the scene in which Eric's body, found on a beach after he drowned in a storm, is ritualistically burned by those who knew him. Juliet, Hawthorne concluded, "is always less than candid, but perhaps that's the point: like all of us, she's stuck with who she is."

Other reviewers of *Runaway* in Great Britain offered assessments that ring true. Mary Blanche Ridge in the *Tablet* commented that "some of the stories are almost unbearable to read. But all are redeemed by the wonderful writing: by the humour (even when it is black) with which many of them are imbued, and most of all by Munro's own vigorous belief in the resilience of the human spirit." Citing the passage describing Robin's anticipation of her yearly trip to Stratford to see a Shakespearian play in "Tricks," Oliver Herford in the *Times Literary Supplement* described it as being about "the value of art within a life." This, he wrote, "is the best and most lasting reason to read Alice Munro: she can accommodate the reader's desire temporarily to inhabit the world of the fiction and to feel that there is room to turn around there." In the *Scottish Review of Books*, Karl Miller began his review by asserting that "two of Scotland's most gifted writers, of all time, are born-and-bred Canadians – Alice Munro and Alistair MacLeod, now in their seventies." In a thorough review that takes up Munro's Scots heritage – and details her connections to James Hogg while tracing Scottish material in various stories – Miller treats *Runaway* within the contexts of the whole of her work. He notes too that Munro's "complete stories are the one long story of her life, the one work of art."

Beyond reviews, there are the many ongoing recognitions that *Runaway* has brought Munro. She was named the Arts Person of the Year by the *Globe and Mail*. Besides another Giller Prize and a near-miss on a fourth Governor General's Award, *Runaway* won the 2004 Rogers Writers' Trust Fiction Prize. Its citation, in part, summarized the effect *Runaway* has had: "Writing at the height of her powers, Alice Munro continues to define the short story for an international audience. Through her mastery, she creates fully realized worlds with astonishing economy. Hers is an art visible only in its effects, her prose never postures, her characters never speak for anyone but themselves." In May 2005 Munro was recipient of the Terasen Lifetime Achievement Award for an Outstanding Literary Career in British Columbia. In the

United States, *Runaway* was among the Ten Best Books of 2004 selected by the *New York Times*, and there was even talk in *New York* magazine about "Alice Munro Mania" in New York. In Great Britain, renewed hope for a Booker was evident throughout the reviews of *Runaway*. In April 2005, Munro was among those *Time* magazine named to "The *Time* 100: The World's Most Influential People." Writing once again in the vein that characterized her review of *Hateship* in the *Atlantic Monthly*, Mona Simpson held there that Munro's "fiction admits readers to a more intimate knowledge and respect for what they already possess. [It] takes on huge swaths of time, with breathtaking skips and breaks and vision, while still writing about women, about Canadians, about the extraordinary nature of ordinary love."

ॐ

For readers who have followed Munro through her career, *Runaway* offers special pleasures. "Soon," the middle story in the *New Yorker*'s triptych, offers Juliet at her most assured, her most certain. In "Chance," she had gone off on her own to British Columbia and, after her youthful chance meeting on the transcontinental train with Eric, a fisherman from Whale Bay, B.C., she sought him out. They formed a relationship. They had a daughter, Penelope. "Soon" begins with Munro's detailed description of a print of Chagall's *I and the Village*, which she fictionalizes and has Juliet buy for her mother, Sara. On a trip home with Penelope in 1969 – the details of which Munro has said were taken from the one she herself made to Wingham with the baby Sheila in 1954 – Juliet visits her parents. Her father, Sam, is much the same, but Sara is dying. In her old home Juliet discovers the Chagall print off in the attic. "Soon" deals most urgently with Juliet's presence in her parents' house, with her interest in Irene, a brisk young woman hired to help them out, and with an argument over belief in God that Juliet has with a visiting minister in front of her mother. This causes a small scene. Defending her own faith to Juliet after Don, the minister, has gone, Sara says, "It's a – wonderful – *something*. When it gets really bad for me – when it gets so bad I – you know what I think then? I think – Soon. *Soon I'll see Juliet.*" Originally Munro followed this with the paragraph that now ends the story, but she later moved it so that after these lines the story moves to the text of a letter Juliet wrote to "Dreaded (Dearest) Eric" and sent to him during that visit.

Then "Soon" telescopes, for Juliet finds this letter years later — presumably after Eric is dead, for so it feels — and she thinks that he "must have saved it by accident – it had no particular importance in their lives." Munro then offers us the ensuing years in a paragraph: Sara's death, Sam's remarrying, visits made by them to Juliet and Eric, Eric taking Sam out on his boat. "He and Sam got along well. As Sam said, like a house afire." Then, in the three paragraphs that remain in "Soon," Alice Munro once again goes home. She does it with honour, as only she can. It is just a moment in the story, but what a moment, encapsulating as it does Juliet's life. But stepping back from Juliet and her circumstances, these paragraphs may also be seen as encapsulating Alice Munro's life and art:

> When she read the letter, Juliet winced, as anybody does on discovering the preserved and disconcerting voice of some past fabricated self. She wondered at the sprightly cover-up, contrasting with the pain of her memories. Then she thought that some shift must have taken place, at that time, which she had not remembered. Some shift concerning where home was. Not at Whale Bay with Eric but back where it had been before, all her life before.
>
> Because it's what happens at home that you try to protect, as best you can, for as long as you can.
>
> But she had not protected Sara. When Sara had said, *soon I'll see Juliet*, Juliet had found no reply. Could it not have been managed? Why should it have been so difficult? Just to say *Yes*. To Sara it would have meant so much – to herself, surely, so little. But she had turned away, she had carried the tray to the kitchen, and there she washed and dried the cups and also the glass that had held the grape soda. She had put everything away.[9]

10

"So This Is How It Should Be Done"

The View from Castle Rock, *the Man Booker*
***International Prize, and* Too Much Happiness**

Writing [*The View from Castle Rock*] was very important to me. . . .
I felt it wouldn't be popular but at my age you don't care. You do
what you need to do. I was encouraged by reading William Maxwell.
– AM to Judy Stoffman, October 28, 2006

This story is told again and again in Maxwell's fiction, in stories that
seem autobiographical but may not be as autobiographical as they
seem – and there is something new with each telling, some new
action at the periphery or revelation near the centre, a different light
or shading, a discovery, as there must be in the stories at the heart of
our lives, stories that grow and change as we do and never go away.
– "Maxwell" (2004)

Isn't the really good time when you are getting the idea, or rather
when you encounter the idea, bump into it, as if it has already been
wandering around in your head? There it is, still fairly featureless, but

shapely and glowing. It's not the story – it's more like the spirit, the centre, of the story, something there's no word for, that can only come into life, a public sort of a life, when words are wrapped around it.

– "Writing. Or, Giving Up Writing" (2006)

I n 1988 Alice Munro published an appreciation, "The Novels of William Maxwell," in the literary magazine *Brick*. Maxwell was a writer whose influence she has long and gratefully acknowledged, so much so that she once characterized that influence as "especially and forever." He was also, not incidentally, one of the longtime editors at the *New Yorker*, whose 1976 retirement brought Charles McGrath and Daniel Menaker to its fiction department where they, in turn, advocated Munro's stories and brought about her first publication there. After Maxwell died in the summer of 2000, *Brick* republished her essay as its tribute to his passing. Later, when a volume of essays in his honour was being assembled, its editors approached Munro to see if she might expand her essay for the book. Doubtful over her abilities as a critic, she hesitated; but bowing to what one of those editors has called "her love for the man and his work," Munro took it up again and reshaped it. The original version is matter-of-fact, relying overly on long quotations from Maxwell's fiction. Concluding with a long passage from Maxwell's great novel, *So Long, See You Tomorrow* (1980), Munro steps back and writes: "There you are. The simple, banal, terrible story and its mysterious heart." The revised version is both more considered and articulate, sharper and deeper. There Munro still quotes at some length – "I know it," she writes, acknowledging this – but then excuses herself by saying in the essay's final words that the experience "has been such a joy, and something like a renewal of hope, to let the words and sentences of this writer flow through my mind and my fingertips." Her return to this essay after Maxwell's death was prompted by a desire to improve it, certainly, but also by a desire to return to the feelings his work occasioned in her, just as she says. And that the essay's ending brought the most telling revisions is wholly consistent with Munro's own practice and art: revision is perpetual with her. This ending, like those in all of her stories, always seems to call to her for improving, refining, revisiting, reshaping.[1]

In both versions of the essay Munro recounts her reaction to *So Long, See You Tomorrow*: "I went back and reread the novels I had read before, together with *Time Will Darken It* and all the short stories I could find. And I thought: So this is how it should be done. I thought: If only I could go back and write again every single thing that I have written. Not that my writing would, or should, imitate his, but that it might be informed by his spirit." In one of the newspaper profiles that appeared concurrently with *The View from Castle Rock* in the autumn of 2006, Munro mentioned the whole of Maxwell's work as encouragement toward that book and, more recently, pointed to his *Ancestors* (1971) as an explicit model for what she was trying out in *Castle Rock*. "So this is how it should be done."[2]

Seeing Munro's work since 2005 – when this biography was first published – in relation to her acknowledgement of Maxwell's influence is important in a variety of ways, but especially through the image she offers of herself, after reading Maxwell, wanting to go back to "write again every single thing" that she had written. From the outset, here in this book, fugitive pieces within Munro's *oeuvre* – most particularly the deeply autobiographical "Home" (1974) and "Working for a Living" (1981), but also "What Do You Want to Know For?" (1994) and "Changing Places" (1997) – have been emphasized as key texts, because of the autobiographical detail they offer, explaining both Munro's life and career.

It is significant too that other autobiographical pieces, more explicitly stories, were held back from publication in book form, since Munro saw them as not fitting the collection then at hand. Some readers noticed these missing stories. For example, Lorrie Moore, concluding her 2004 review of *Runaway* in the *Atlantic Monthly*, noted the absence from any collection of "Hired Girl" (1994) and "Fathers" (2002), but she might then have also noted "Wood" (1980), "The Ferguson Girls Must Never Marry" (1982), or "Lying Under the Apple Tree" (2002).[3]

Now, in late 2010, we can see that Munro has effectively done what she envisioned after reading *So Long, See You Tomorrow*: she returned to these earlier autobiographical writings and produced *The View from Castle Rock* – a book she says she knew would not be popular, but one she needed to do. The idea of it dated from the 1970s, from the time of her return to Ontario and to Huron County from British Columbia; she and Virginia Barber referred to it occasionally during the intervening years. Thanks to her perfectionist penchant for revision and reshaping, the versions of the previously published pieces found in the 2006 book emerge as parts of a coherent whole – the ancestry and life of Alice Munro, shaped and reshaped, as she has written her lives. To accomplish this, Munro revised ("Home" and "Working for a Living"), she reshaped and expanded ("Changing Places"), she wrote new material as needed elements to fill in gaps in her own life story ("The Ticket," "Messenger"), and she brought in stories little changed from their first *New Yorker* appearances ("Hired Girl," "Lying Under the Apple Tree," and "Fathers"). Making *Castle Rock,* she once more passed over "Wood," leaving it (as well as the more recent "Wenlock Edge" [2005]) for *Too Much Happiness* (2009).

Given its long provenance, its ancestral and personal subjects, and its inclusion of finally reshaped versions of Munro's most revealing autobiographical writings, *The View from Castle Rock* might well have been – and quite fittingly – Munro's last book. She publicly said it would be in June 2006, causing a small flap. Yet other stories and *Too Much Happiness* have followed. (Incidentally, that book's title story – called a novella by *Harper's* on its first publication – yet again reveals Munro's penchant for historical writing, although there she writes on a subject wholly apart from anything personal, since it is focused on the life of a nineteenth-century Russian mathematician.) And now, in the winter of 2010–11, Munro has had two new stories published in the *New Yorker* – "Corrie" in October and "Axis" in January – while two more, "Train" and "Pride," are forthcoming from *Harper's*. These stories reveal her writing out of the 1950s and '60s, which, like her return to her long-published pieces, is wholly consistent with her method and vision. Thus in 2010, and to the utter delight of her legions of readers – their numbers still growing through the acclaim her work continues to draw – Alice Munro continues to write on as she nears the beginning of her ninth decade.

"*Maybe* I Can Do Something Unexpected with It": The Long Approach to *The View from Castle Rock*

By the time she published *Runaway* in 2004 to its excellent reviews and sales – British hardback sales were 7,200 with over 70,000 for the paperback, Canadian were 72,000 in hardback and 60,000 for the paperback, and Knopf sold over 100,000 hardbacks and Vintage twice that in paper – Munro's daily life had long followed its regular pattern: most of her time was spent in Clinton; she travelled in winter to British Columbia; she saw family and friends. She wrote. Her literary celebrity was something held at arm's length but was nonetheless a fact of her life – journalists, critics, and others from outside Huron County were met at Bailey's restaurant in Goderich; she talked to people on the telephone and, occasionally, for one attracting reason or another, Munro went somewhere to make an appearance or give a reading. But today, in the fall of 2010, she recognizes that both she and Gerry Fremlin are older; daily activities take longer, she has said; health issues have been, and remain, a concern. Their cross-country drives – though not the more local ones – have ceased.

During the two years between *Runaway* and *The View from Castle Rock* Munro continued to appear in the *New Yorker,* with "The View from Castle Rock" and "Wenlock Edge" published in 2005, and "Dimensions" in 2006. Thus material that would appear in her next two books was published while, at the same time, she was also republishing in the United States some of the revised autobiographical pieces that had first appeared in Canada. "Home: A Story" was in the summer 2006 issue of *Virginia Quarterly Review* as part of "Ordinary Outsiders: A Symposium on Alice Munro."4 (Besides Munro's contribution, it included a biographical overview, and appreciations by other writers, Munro's editors, and others.) "What Do You Want to Know For?" appeared that summer in the *American Scholar* and, just as *The View from Castle Rock* was being prepared throughout 2006, Knopf was also assembling *Carried Away: A Selection of Stories* (2006), with a detailed and precise introduction by Margaret Atwood, as a volume in its Everyman's Library series. The two books were published concurrently in September.[5]

Apart from all the ongoing publication, there was a major change in Munro's career: Virginia Barber had retired from the William Morris Agency at the end of 2003 – Munro went to New York for the party in November – and Barber's longtime associate Jennifer Rudolph Walsh became her agent. While Barber is no longer responsible for placing Munro's work, she is still an early reader of new stories, as is Ann Close at Knopf. Her agent may have changed, but Munro continued to receive awards, both abroad and at home. She was named a "Woman of Achievement" by the Edith Wharton Society and in May 2003 travelled to New York to receive the award – Barber was a bit mystified at this acceptance, since Munro had passed on others her agent thought to be equally or more significant. In May 2005, Munro received the Terasen Lifetime Achievement Award, given to a senior British Columbia writer and sponsored by the Terasen Gas Company, *B.C. BookWorld,* and the Vancouver Public Library. Accepting this award, Munro recalled her time working as a clerk in Vancouver's Hastings and Main library – there was a rule, she said, that only librarians could direct patrons to books, that she was not allowed to and, in fact, had been reprimanded for doing so. She would still like to be allowed to do this, she said: "That would be a treat." She also recalled writing in the library when she lived there, avoiding the landlady who wanted to talk to her, the person she later used in her story "Cortes Island."

There were other sorts of notice confirming Munro's reputation too: in October 2005 *Harper's* ran a long essay by Ben Marcus taking extended issue with Jonathan Franzen's writings on contemporary fiction and the market – Marcus cites Franzen's handling of Munro and *Runaway* in his 2004 review in *New York Times Book Review* as a central instance of Franzen's self-indulgent errors. And in June 2006, tracing the whole of Munro's Vancouver experiences and using her renderings of the city as a kind of literary guided tour, travel writer David Laskin published a piece on Alice Munro's Vancouver in the *New York Times*.[6]

When she received the lifetime achievement award in Vancouver in May 2005, Munro remarked of her next book that "It's not a book of complete fiction like I've always written before," referring to its historical cast. After making this comment, she added that she intended to retire after it was completed. Two months later Munro published an essay as her contribution to a volume aimed at raising money for PEN Canada, *Writing Life*. It is called "Writing. Or, Giving Up Writing," and it does suggest that she may stop writing, although its meaning is equivocal. When the book containing this essay was about to be launched at a Toronto gala on June 20, 2006, where Munro was scheduled to read, a syndicated story appeared throughout Canada with headlines like "Literary Icon Alice Munro Expected to Retire Tonight." At the event, Munro closed her presentation by telling the audience that "I wrote this essay about six months ago. At the time, I thought it to be true." Her editor, Douglas Gibson, insisted that this forthcoming book would not be Munro's last.[7]

Well he might insist, since Gibson had been working with Munro and her intuitive methods since the mid-1970s – he had seen her uncertainties before and had even, famously, and at a critical point in Munro's career in 1978, pulled *Who Do You Think You Are?* from the press for restructuring according to her wishes. Two years after that episode, as she was envisioning the contents of what would be *The Moons of Jupiter*, Munro wrote to Gibson from Australia summarizing her available stories, concluding: "so these ten stories quite definitely have enough length for a book." Complicating her situation just then, Munro continues, is another finished piece she has at hand, as she explains:

> There is also a long Memoir I wrote about my father, which I think is pretty good, but I think it should be kept out for a kind of family book I want to do someday – maybe about the Laidlaws in Huron County and in Ettrick & James Hogg whose mother was Laidlaw. There's a whole lot of interesting stuff about the family, who seem to have been story-tellers since the

Middle Ages. I know people going on about their families can be very tiresome but maybe I can do something unexpected with it.

Faced with these musings from Munro, it makes sense to take her back again to the 1970s, to the productive decade that began in Victoria with the rapid composition of *Lives of Girls and Women* and ended with her back living in Huron County and writing – among other things – "Working for a Living," the long memoir she refers to here. That decade saw her returning to, reshaping, and revising some of her writings from the 1950s and '60s to help make *Something I've Been Meaning to Tell You*. Then too she took up once more – but now that she was back in Ontario, differently – the remnants of her family inheritances she found there in such pieces as "Home," "Winter Wind," and most especially and significantly, "The Ottawa Valley," for that 1974 collection as well. Just as that book was published, in an essay she effectively co-wrote with her father (who had given her most of the factual information it contains), Munro proclaimed that the stretch of the Maitland River flowing by their farm in Lower Wingham is for her a place where "everything is touchable and mysterious." This rediscovery of Huron County as her home place led to Munro's abandoned 1974–75 photo-text, "Places at Home," and it led ultimately to what remains the single most important book in her *oeuvre* – at least as regards her development as a writer – *Who Do You Think You Are? / The Beggar Maid*. After 1973 as well Munro was a daughter returned home who was able to talk over, read, and appreciate her father's own emerging gifts as a writer during his last years after a lifetime of hard physical labour. All of this sets the stage for Munro's shaping of *The View from Castle Rock*.

Every August, on "Medal Day," the famed MacDowell artists' colony outside Peterborough, New Hampshire throws open its grounds to the public – the only day in the year it does so – in order to present the Edward MacDowell Medal for an outstanding contribution to the arts. On August 13, 2006, its forty-seventh recipient was Alice Munro. Receiving the award, Munro offered gracious and detailed thanks to Robert Weaver and to Virginia Barber, to her editors, and to both of her husbands, "men who believed that a woman doing really serious work, not just amusing herself, was possible. In my generation those men were not that easy to find, and the fact that I nabbed two of them is certainly lucky." But while the centrepiece of the day's program was Munro herself, the most extended presentation was by Virginia Barber, who offered a warm, detailed, and heartfelt reminiscence of her relations with Alice Munro alongside a clear-sighted and sharp analysis of the intimacies Munro's stories offer readers, "the stuff of a magical alchemy." Barber also said this:

> I've also learned that nearly every time Alice completes a book she opines that it will be her last. She used up all of her materials; she has nothing to say. After the publication of *Runaway* in 2004, she said the same sort of thing, and this time I suggested she write a non-fiction book about her Laidlaw ancestors – material she's been interested in since we met. But in spite of the extraordinary number of letters, diaries, journals, printed material reaching back to the 1700s in Scotland, non-fiction wasn't satisfying. How could she fill the historical gaps? But even more, what did they look like? What did they say to one another? What were they feeling? So, we quickly agree: Turn it into stories. And that material is the first hundred or so pages in her new book, *The View from Castle Rock*, which will be out in November.

Here Barber confirms Munro's "family book" as dating back to the critical 1974–76 period of her career (the two met in mid-1976 at a Writers' Union of Canada meeting in Toronto); here too she also reconfirms Munro's habit of predicting that her latest book will be her last.[8]

While modest uncertainty over her work – irrespective of what her readers said and wrote – has characterized Munro's own sense of her trajectory as a writer, this public airing of such misgivings should be seen as an appropriate preliminary to *The View from Castle Rock*. Even though inspired by Maxwell's *Ancestors* and by the whole of his *oeuvre*, and having for well over twenty years contemplated what she called the "family book," with *The View from Castle Rock* Munro showed herself well aware that she was producing a book that was both unlike any other she had previously published and – given age, the fullness of time, and very close proximity of its subject and characters (her own ancestors, her immediate family, herself) – it was a book that seemed to complete the life-circle Munro had begun through her stories since she began publishing them in the early 1950s.

"Calamity Had Arrived with the End of Childhood": Writing *Her* Life: *The View from Castle Rock*

"Working for a Living," which Munro mentions in her 1980 letter to Gibson, is a piece that began as a story. Through repeated revision (at the hands of the *New Yorker* editors) it became a memoir – only to be rejected by them in that form. It was finally published in 1981 as the first piece of the inaugural issue of *Grand Street,* alongside contributions by Northrop Frye, Ted Hughes, W.S. Merwin, and Glenway Wescott, among others. Reshaped and expanded, it is in *Castle Rock* as the conclusion to the first section, "No Advantages." Given its history, its subject, and Munro's placement of it – conversations with her editors, both Gibson and Close, confirm that the book's structure was largely Munro's own – "Working for a Living" plays a central role in *The View from Castle Rock.* Other "family" pieces – all of which Munro insists in her foreword to that book need to be called "*stories*" – appear there in revised form. Begun, as she announces in the first sentence of a notebook draft, on "the twenty-fourth of October, 1979," the memoir version may be readily seen as growing from both Munro's return to Ontario and her reaction to the death of her father in August 1976.

The revised version in *Castle Rock* bears the marks of sustained rewriting (Munro has acknowledged working on it at least since 2001), although the most substantial revision is the addition of the last two pages or so of meditation on her father's late writing career. "Working" is a distilled and poignant rendering of her parents as individuals and, more than that, it defines Munro's own relation to each of them at two critical moments in her childhood: First, when she travelled in 1943 as a nine- or ten-year-old with her father to the Muskoka hotel where

Anne Chamney Laidlaw, blooming in her new role, had been successfully selling fox furs directly to American tourists. And second, some
years later when the family fox farm had failed, when her mother's
health had taken an irrefutable turn for the worse, and when Munro
was sufficiently inured to the family's situation that she looked to
protect herself imaginatively while still living at home and was working
toward a scholarship to university as a way out. Thus "Working" bal-
ances her mother's real self – before she fell ill with Parkinson's – with
her struggles and eventual death. So too her father is shown as an
unusually independent adolescent with his own trap line, then as a fox
farmer who shared his fortunes with his wife and young family, and
finally as a foundry night watchman and caretaker who worked to
support that same family and look after his sick wife. Throughout,
Munro contrasts her family's circumstances with those of her grandparents – Sadie Code Laidlaw and her husband William. She meditates
on their relationship, on their marriage and their rearing of her father,
and on her grandmother's presence in Wingham as Anne Chamney
Laidlaw struggled with Parkinson's and died.

Munro has repeatedly seen her mother's circumstances, once she
had fallen ill and was in decline, as her default material, her central
subject – pivotal stories like "The Peace of Utrecht," "The Ottawa
Valley," and "Soon" suggest as much. In another notebook draft version
of "Working" Munro confirms this when she writes:

> I was just starting high school when this happened. At the same
> time that it became clear that we were poor, and could not hope
> as we had once, for a dazzling change of fortune[,] it became
> clear that my mother was sick for good, not plagued by passing
> ailments. Calamity had arrived with the end of childhood[.] I
> pretended not to notice, living in fantasy in books, in private
> expectation of some vaunting success.

The presence of long-published but never collected fugitive pieces like
"Working" and the even older "Home," the ongoing creation and publication of other stories which spring from Munro's own experience and

history and her return to Ontario in 1973, plus the standing idea of the "family book" that she wanted to do someday – these facts all combine to make *The View from Castle Rock* almost an inevitability. Just as Munro re-imagines her young self "living in fantasy in books," ignoring the family's calamity, in this volume (like William Maxwell before her in *Ancestors*) she takes an even longer view back in time to reach her ancestral Laidlaws, shepherds in the Ettrick Valley in Scotland. She reaches back into the seventeenth century to detail these people, who were related to James Hogg, the Ettrick Shepherd, who himself had associations with such figures as Sir Walter Scott. Ultimately, of course, she follows them to Canada in 1818 as emigrants, to begin her family story here.

In doing so, Munro sets herself at the forefront of her project. "No Advantages," the book's opening section, almost immediately offers her reader an image of Munro herself in the Ettrick Valley, a restless and solitary seeker: "Nevertheless," she writes, "the valley disappointed me the first time I saw it. Places are apt to do that when you've set them up in your imagination. The time of year was very early spring, and the hills were brown, or a kind of lilac brown, reminding me of the hills around Calgary. Ettrick Water was running fast and clear, but it was hardly as wide as the Maitland River, which flows past the farm where I grew up, in Ontario." Just after this, and with an explanation of her travel to the Ettrick Church and its graveyard, in the rain, Munro writes: "I felt conspicuous, out of place, and cold. I huddled by the wall till the rain let up for a bit, then I explored the churchyard, with the long wet grass soaking my legs." There she finds the gravestone of William Laidlaw, her "direct ancestor, born at the end of the seventeenth century, and known as Will O'Phaup. This was a man who took on, at least locally, something of the radiance of myth, and he managed that at the very last time in history – that is, in the history of the British Isles – when a man could do so." There too she also finds, "among various Laidlaws, a stone bearing the name of Robert Laidlaw, who died at Hopehouse on January 29th 1800 aged seventy-two years. Son of Will, brother of Margaret, uncle of James, who probably never knew he would be remembered by his link to these others, any more than he would know the date of his own death. My great-great-great-great-grandfather."

Munro realizes that she needs to move on so as to catch the bus to return – still in the rain – to Selkirk where she is staying, and so concludes: "I was struck with a feeling familiar, I suppose, to many people whose long history goes back to a country far away from the place where they grew up. I was a naïve North American, in spite of my stored knowledge. Past and present lumped together here made a reality that was commonplace yet disturbing beyond anything I had imagined."[9]

Quite apart from "Home" and "Working for a Living," Munro has long tended toward the genealogical. In the late 1970s she took up the subject of Irish emigration to Canada – linked with her mother's side of her family, though historically rather than personally – with "1847: The Irish" (1978), a CBC television script, and then its prose version, "A Better Place than Home" (1979). As for more recent generations, speaking of the Wingham cemetery where her parents are buried, Munro has said that she takes Fremlin there "and I tell him stories about every tombstone." "It's just like walking down Main Street in 1940. All the people you meet, they're all together, people who died around Dad's age." During a 2003 visit there, she said, "I just saw somebody I went to school with, I saw their grave. I come here and people I didn't know were dead are here."

Such interests and investigations continued beyond the personal to her writing, since they are at the root of "What Do You Want to Know For?," eventually (although not initially) included in *Castle Rock.* So here at the outset of "No Advantages," Munro offers her readers the image of herself in Ettrick Churchyard reading gravestones. This should be seen as a typical position for her, one she herself has described in her probing story, "Menesetung": "People are curious. A few people are. They will put things together. You see them going around with notebooks, scraping the dirt off gravestones, reading microfilm, just in the hope of seeing this trickle in time, making a connection, rescuing one thing from the rubbish." The *New Yorker* version of this story ended with these words, but Munro restored her originally submitted ending when she published the story in *Friend of My Youth* and, doing so, revised it further, with these words about the limitations of fiction: "And they may get it wrong, after all. I may have got it wrong. I don't know if [the protagonist, Almeda Joynt Roth] took laudanum. Many ladies did. I don't know if she ever made grape jelly."

In *Castle Rock* too, Munro ends the long title story, "The View from Castle Rock," with another personal tour of the family gravestones found in the Boston Presbyterian Church (named after the Ettrick minister she writes about) graveyard in Halton, Esquesing Township, Ontario – built, largely with volunteer labour, on land sold to the church by Andrew Laidlaw, Munro's great-great-uncle, in 1824. And still seeking another graveyard – one that might reveal the grave of her great-great-grandfather, William Laidlaw, who died of cholera in Joliet, Illinois in early 1839 or '40 – Munro ends *Castle Rock* in an epilogue entitled "Messenger" with the image of herself in yet another cemetery.

This one is in Blyth, Ontario – a place midway between Clinton and Wingham, the place where her father was a boy, and the place where she and Gerry Fremlin have bought plots for themselves. There she finds, among those of her relatives, the grave of William's wife, Mary Scott, who after his death in a foreign country was brought with their children to Canada by William's brother Andrew and a team of oxen. "Mary who wrote the letter from Ettrick to lure the man she wanted to come and marry her. On her stone is the name of that man, *William Laidlaw. Died in Illinois.* And buried God knows where."

Just after this, having made more connections in her mind and memory with others memorialized in the Blyth cemetery, Munro steps back and synthesizes what she's been doing throughout the whole of *The View from Castle Rock,* writing: "Now all these names I have been recording are joined to the living people in my mind, and to the lost kitchens, the polished nickel trim on the commodious presiding black stoves, the sour wooden drainboards that never quite dried, the yellow light of the coal-oil lamps." Continuing in this vein to her conclusion, Munro recalls "a magic doorstop, a big mother-of-pearl seashell that I recognized as a messenger from near and far" that she could hold to her ear "and discover the tremendous pounding of my own blood, and of the sea."[10]

If, as Munro wrote toward the beginning of one of the stories she mentions to Gibson from Australia in 1980, "Chaddeleys and Flemings: 1. Connection," connection "was what it was all about," then the whole of *The View from Castle Rock* shows Munro pursuing a complex web of connections – personal, cultural, and historical – with the single-minded determination of someone who has been meditating the prospect for some time. When she submitted "The View from Castle Rock" to the *New Yorker* in March 2005, it was in the form of a 140-page manuscript that, seen now against the finished book, was made up of the whole of the first part, "No Advantages," including parts of "Messenger," subsequently moved to end of the book. Tellingly, it bore the title "Laidlaws II: The View from Castle Rock." The editors there were immediately drawn to the manuscript and – characteristically, though in this instance quite practically – set about finding ways to shorten it effectively for their needs. Deborah Treisman, who had written to Munro that her 2004 Juliet triptych was "the longest manuscript I've sat down to edit in my history at this magazine, or any other!", had to tackle an even longer one in "The View from Castle Rock." Recognizing that in it they had, as she wrote to editor David Remnick, a "combination of family history and fiction," she proposed for his approval ways to both shorten it and sharpen it, for "it has some real Munrovian highlights" in it.

As Barber described Munro's method in *Castle Rock* on Medal Day at the MacDowell Colony, Munro draws explicitly on family letters and other archival materials surrounding her ancestors' emigration, and on published materials regarding them that had appeared in *Blackwood's Magazine,* but much of the "No Advantages" section of the book is imagined, created within the text. As has long been the case, Munro's work with the *New Yorker* played a role in this larger process. Agreeing to publish only a portion of the submitted manuscript, Treisman and her colleagues shaped the story of the Laidlaws' passage from Scotland to Canada into the twelve magazine pages they published in August 2005. When the book version was published, the effects of this process were evident, since the story published in the magazine (itself an expansion of the earlier "Changing Places") is retained, with the rest of the long submitted manuscript shaped into the full separate pieces that make up the book's first section, "No Advantages."

Such details of composition, admittedly of keen interest only to Munro's most devoted readers, nevertheless point to the unique process she undertook in the making and shaping of *The View from Castle Rock*: given its long gestation dating back to the 1970s, *Castle Rock* is a sustained instance of Munro's writing *her* own life as the book's central fact. With the "No Advantages" section of *Castle Rock,* Munro creates an ancestral context, in which she places herself in the second section, "Home." In both sections, her treatment is anchored by pieces she had long meditated and had already written – "Working for a Living" and "Home" – freeing her to imagine, realign, and shape the rest of the book, using many of her fugitive pieces. As she explains in her foreword to *Castle Rock* – which Munro, urged by Gibson, agreed was necessary to explain the book to the reader (but which had some unintended consequences when connected to her several announcements that it would be her last book) – in these stories she "was doing something closer to what memoir does – exploring a life, my own life, but not in an austere or rigorously factual way. I put myself in the center and wrote about that self, as searchingly as I could."[11]

While it is possible here to point to several instances in which Munro may be seen imagining further, making new connections, bridging gaps in her ancestral story, an entirely new and first-published story, "The Ticket," is the best illustration of what Munro's made reshapings in *Castle Rock* reveal about her own life. Structurally, it is a needed story, for it bridges the gap between the revised "Hired Girl" (1994), which treats Munro's high school summer spent working for a family at a cottage on Georgian Bay, and "Home," which has Munro returned home to Ontario in 1973, visiting her father and his second wife in Wingham. "The Ticket" returns to Wingham just before Alice Laidlaw's marriage to James Munro in 1951 and, in so doing, it recreates her circumstances as she awaits that marriage – her mother ill, her brother and sister much younger, the anticipation, the wedding itself. But most especially it meditates on her relations with her grandmother and aunt – the Code sisters, each a widow helping her prepare for her wedding – and muses over each older woman's marriage along with, once again, that of her parents.

At the centre of the story are Munro's own desires, the feelings that led her to accept the proposal of a young man she here calls Michael: "He had bought me a diamond ring. He had found a job in Vancouver that was certain to lead to better things, and had bound himself to support me and our children, for the rest of his life. Nothing would make him happier. He said so, and I believed it was true." This established, the story shifts to Munro's feelings, to details of her grandmother and aunt's lives, their loves, their marriages – and to their actions as they helped Munro prepare. Eventually, as she usually does, Munro returns to the core of her story, to the central image that carries the most pressing insight she offers: her own, retrospectively seen, lack of faith in what she was doing then, crucially, her own lack of commitment: "And I thought I loved him. Love and marriage. That was a lighted and agreeable room you went into, where you were safe. The lovers I had imagined, the bold-plumed predators, had not appeared, perhaps did not exist, and I could hardly think myself a match for them anyway. He deserved better than me, Michael did. He deserved a whole heart."

Although it is possible to say that Munro has described these relations before – in "The Peace of Utrecht," in "Winter Wind," in *Who Do You Think You Are?*, in "Chaddeleys and Flemings: Connection" and elsewhere – "The Ticket" is both precise as to actual biographical detail and, in this quotation and its title image, is explicitly confessional. The ticket referred to in the title is her Aunt Charley's secret gift of two hundred dollars in cash in case the young bride decided, at the last moment, to flee the marriage. Should she not, though, her aunt tells her, then "'you must be – you must promise – *you must be a good wife.*' 'Naturally,' I said, as if there was no need to whisper." Writing here with long retrospection – over fifty years and in full knowledge of what became of the marriage about to be enacted – Munro is especially harsh on herself. This harshness stems from Munro's by now deeply felt sense that, when marrying Jim Munro in 1951, she withheld the needed full commitment to their marriage. An artist first and foremost, she felt ever directed away from their relationship into her writing. Given her history this is not surprising, but she returns to the writer she was even back in 1951 in a striking way. At one point in "The Ticket," as she is writing her life, she recalls herself wanting to avoid her grandmother and great-aunt's house because "the town was enticing to me, it was dreamy in these autumn days. It was spellbound, with melancholy light on the gray or yellow brick walls, and a peculiar stillness, now that the birds had flown south and the reaping machines in the country round about were silent." She continues: "One day," as she approached her grandmother's house, "I heard some lines in my head, the beginning of a story. *All over the town the leaves fell. Softly, silently the yellow leaves fell – it was autumn.* And I actually did write a story, then or sometime later, beginning with these sentences – I can't remember what it was about."

In fact, the fragment of that story in her papers begins differently: "All over the town the leaves fell; it was autumn. Carelessly, softly, the leaves fell, for there was no wind." But close enough. Written in the summer of 1951 – the very time Alice Laidlaw was home from university and beginning preparations for her December wedding and so a new life – "The Yellow Afternoon" is about the efforts of a high school teacher, a single woman who wishes to encourage in one of her students a devotion to the life of mind, to poetry and aesthetics, and to a commitment to university studies. The teacher, Miss Levinston, wants also to warn young Frances, who shows sparks of such potential, away from her likely alternative: getting married to a local boy. Frances, for her part, decides to do just that, and the story details her efforts to tell Miss Levinston of her intentions in a rather cruel way. "The Yellow Afternoon" was broadcast on the CBC program *Anthology* in February 1955 but never published.

It is interesting to see that Munro returned here in "The Ticket" to one of her very early stories, one written during and derived from the very time in her life she was thinking about as she was trying to bridge the biographical gap between "Hired Girl" and "Home" for *The View from Castle Rock*. Interesting both for this book and as an example of Munro's characteristic artistic practice: she is, as ever, writing her lives. Turning back to her younger self at a critical juncture in her own life – to the moment when marriage to Jim Munro "rescued" her (a word used in "The Ticket") – Munro assesses her own heartlessness. Marriage got her out of Lower Town, Wingham, got her away from her mother's illness and the family's struggles for survival, and so got her away from the "calamity" that had "arrived with the end of childhood." So Alice Munro is seen in *Castle Rock* completing the whole of her own life story as she, once again, writes her own life as it is inextricably connected to the lives of her Laidlaw ancestors, to their emigration to Canada and to Illinois (and thence to Canada), and to Huron County, her own ancestral home place. The place she has used continually from the beginning of her career to write her lives. Long envisioned and pondered, *The View from Castle Rock* is a critical book in Munro's *oeuvre;* in fact, it is like nothing else she has written before or since.[12]

☙

The Everyman's Library edition of Munro's stories, *Carried Away,* which Knopf published alongside *The View from Castle Rock,* and which was later published in Canada in hardcover as *Alice Munro's Best* and in paper as *My Best Stories,* contains what Alison Lurie in the *New York Review of Books* called a "generous and perceptive" introduction by Margaret Atwood. There, Atwood begins with this assertion: "Alice Munro is among the major writers of English fiction of our time." Lurie's own perceptive and extended review of Munro's *oeuvre* and Atwood's matter-of-fact and sharply incisive introduction – these together encapsulate the critical reception accorded *Castle Rock.* With that book as its final text (but also treating the 2005 edition of this biography, Sheila Munro's *Lives of Mothers and Daughters,* and the Everyman *Carried Away*), Lurie's review essay of *The View from Castle Rock* constitutes clear recognition of Munro's import and stature in late 2006. Her reading of Munro and her work is ample and informed, thoughtful and precise. As many reviewers of *Castle Rock* did, Lurie concludes by offering some lines from the cemetery scene toward the end of Munro's epilogue, "Messenger." The full passage reads, "We can't resist this rifling around in the past, sifting the untrustworthy evidence, linking stray names and questionable dates and anecdotes together, hanging on to threads, insisting on being joined to dead people and therefore to life." Connecting this with the final scene in "What Do You Want to Know For?," Lurie writes: "The narrator and her husband wonder if there is oil in the lamp inside the mausoleum" that they have discovered, "so that it might somehow, one day, shine forth. Metaphorically, in this book, it already does." Ending her review, which is called "The Lamp in the Mausoleum," with these words, Lurie points to an essential element in Munro's writing, asserting that "even in these stories, which are closest to her own history, Alice Munro's commitment to indeterminacy and the essential confusion and mystery of life remains." Citing the initial scene in "The View from Castle Rock," when young Andrew and his grandfather look out from Castle Rock in Edinburgh, Lurie maintains that it "contains the message of the whole book: what you imagine as your future is not what you will get: the real future is always farther away and stranger, better and worse."

Another indicative long review in another august foreign publication, "The Sense of an Ending" by Stephen Henighan in the *Times Literary Supplement,* stands in sharp contrast to Lurie's. It, too, is a wide-ranging overview of Munro and her career, but while the American shows herself generous, perceptive, and appreciative, Henighan comes across as dour, picky, and even petulant. Although writing after the flap in Canada over Munro's announcement that *Castle Rock* would be her last book, and so in a position to be aware of the equivocal quality of that announcement, Henighan begins by taking the announcement as fact. He then proceeds to summarize Munro's career, preferring her early, presumably more Canadian, work over that first published in the *New Yorker,* where, he nitpicks, there are many signs of a creeping Americanization ("college" for "university," while the CBC becomes "the national radio network"). Ultimately he pronounces the book at hand "a disappointment" and sadly asserts as he ends that as "the concluding work in a remarkable career, *The View from Castle Rock* is not the ending for which Alice Munro would have wished."

Any reviewer is entitled to a sustained response to a book, certainly, so in that sense Henighan's carpings are fair enough. As another

Canadian reviewer of *Castle Rock,* John Moss, asserted in his review, "Nothing separates reviewers and critics like a new book by Alice Munro. The former, exercising taste in the present tense, is challenged to find fresh accolades to heap on the author. The latter, whose job is the exercise of judgement informed by an educated imagination, who writes with a sense of historical context, is charged with the task of explaining 'why.' Why is Munro so good, how does she do it, what makes her writing so stunning in its casual complexity, its intense directness?" Both Lurie and Henighan combine the two perspectives Moss reasonably defines here, although each comes to different conclusions and each, too, is representative of the poles of response *Castle Rock* garnered. Most reviewers, just as Moss maintains, responded favorably to the book and struggled to find more laudatory things to say, while a few – like Henighan, proceeding from other aesthetic expectations and either unwilling to understand the book's unusual position between memoir and fiction or rejecting its effects – chose to find fault and dismiss. That such treatment would eventually come to a writer as celebrated as Munro is certainly not surprising. Nor, given literary values passing from one generation to the next and the jealousy born of long reputation, is it anything other than human.

Surveying the reviews of *Castle Rock,* what is surprising is how little of this hostile treatment the book actually received. In that vein, Darryl Whetter offers a review in the *Toronto Star* (where the subheading asserts that "the failure of this new collection – a kind of fictional family tree – comes as a shock") and writes that "sadly, Munro's normally enviable skills simply do not transform what ultimately remains a private history." Like Henighan, this reviewer sees "Hired Girl" as what he calls "the collection's one gem" – and before that, "we have a narrator-character wedged between these ancestral characters and us. The narrator's own story doesn't emerge fully until late in the book. . . ." Whetter sees that happening in "Hired Girl" and, apparently, manages to miss Munro's subsequent transformation in "The Ticket," "Home," and the balance of her text.

By way of contrast we see Hilary Mantel, writing in *The Guardian,* discussing Munro's ancestor, James Hogg, the Ettrick Shepherd, author of *The Confessions of a Justified Sinner,* and the man who helped Sir Walter Scott "steal" the ballads he published in *The Minstrelsy of the Scottish Border* (1802). Following Munro, Mantel writes that "It's difficult to draw a line between the objective truth and the truth in his head; and some readers are uncomfortable if they can't draw the lines between genres." Such readers as Henighan and Whetter, certainly. Mantel asserts that *The View from Castle Rock* is "an act of salvage rather than appropriation. It is a memoir that has taken a breath, and expanded itself beyond genre and beyond the confines of one life. . . . Just as there is no real division here between fiction and non-fiction, there is no turning point at which the epic story of emigration gives way to observation of the nuance and detail of settled lives."

And John Moss, for his part, asserts that *Castle Rock* is not just a memoir; "it is something else, a major achievement, and an exciting revitalisation of a somewhat exhausted genre. . . . It is a memoir as only Alice Munro could write it. Are there stories in it? Is it fiction? Well, of course. . . . The difference is, the fiction here is neither subterfuge nor self-enhancing. It is an essential element of an intimate past, both ancestral and remembered, that is transformed by the author into shared revelation." With this book, Moss concludes, "Munro proves herself once again one of those rare writers whose work changes the lives of her readers."

Seen together, a large grouping of the reviews of *The View from Castle Rock* most frequently take up, as Mantel and Moss do, the numerous ways in which the historical interacts with the fictive in the book to create the numinous. Neil Besner, a sharp, longstanding, and well-informed critic of Munro's work, especially notes the book's second section, "Home." In his review in the *Winnipeg Free Press* he maintains that "there is everywhere a deeply felt sense of connection to the climate of feeling inhabited by her father – not only his beliefs, expressed and more often silent, but to his habits of thought. In this collection, Munro follows that sense of connection more strongly and widely than she has before. And she does so incomparably." He speaks of Munro's "more intimately focused returns, guided by a writer always aware of, and inquiring into her own pastward gaze, with its moments of deception or deceit – and of revelation." Surveying the stories making up the second section of *Castle Rock* within the context of the stories contained in *Carried Away,* A.O. Scott writes in the *New York Times* that "Whether they are the literal truth is beyond irrelevant. The point of storytelling, as Munro practices it, is to rescue the literal facts from banality, from oblivion, and to preserve – to create – some sense of continuity in the hectic ebb and flow of experience."

Perhaps the best single review of *The View from Castle Rock* appeared in the review section of *The Guardian,* written by Karl Miller. This is the Scottish critic who once hailed Alistair MacLeod and Alice Munro, though born and bred in Canada, as among Scotland's greatest authors of all time. In addition Miller has written a biography of James Hogg. As a result, his review is suffused with his own knowledge of Ettrick and with a deep appreciation of just what Munro was about as she shaped this, her long-contemplated family book that she hoped would achieve something unexpected. In a long passage that synthesizes the whole of her accomplishment, Miller first cites one of Munro's comments from her foreword and then writes at some length:

> This leaves you feeling that these stories are like the others after all, being at once her life and her art. Old questions, including James Laidlaw's, about art's lies and feigning arise here, as they do elsewhere in the book, when Munro alludes, cannily enough, to "canny lying of the sort you can depend on a writer to do."
>
> The new stories make use of family papers and public records. Munro once spent time looking and learning in Selkirkshire, with its heritage of battles and ballads and the spirits of the glen. There were those in her earlier life who thought writing meant handwriting; her stepmother assured her that her father wrote better than her. But he was also a writer in the other sense: late in life, after his years as a fox farmer and night watchman, he wrote about the pioneer life of his forebears, and he was not the only family member who could, in a sense, write. The diary of young Walter Laidlaw, James's son, lends quotations. The archives offered her plenty of stuff to

incorporate and supplement, including items unfamiliar to me as a biographer of Hogg. The high house of Phaup, up on the hills above Ettrick kirk, near the burial place of Hogg's sinner, is identified – correctly, I think – as the place where Hogg's shepherd friends met for debates and were held to have caused the disastrous storm of 1794 by trying to raise the Devil.

Offering such knowledge and such a perspective, Miller ultimately provides this assessment of the whole of Munro's "family book":

> The collection, which has opened in Ettrick and gone with the pioneers to Illinois and on their great trek north to Ontario, ends with a return to the genealogy of the pioneers and with the author up to her ankles in poison ivy as she searches for a forgotten grave. This is a rare and fascinating work, in which the past makes sense of the present and the present makes sense of the past, and the two are both a continuum and a divorce. It is very much a memoir, as well as a set of fictions. But then the whole corpus of Munro's stories is a memoir, the novel of her life. It is silly to complain, as some once did, that she writes not novels but stories. The book says barely anything about Hogg's *Confessions,* but it's more than likely that the novel has been an influence on what she has done. She is the cooler, the more deliberate artist of the two, her tales plainer. But they can be drawn all the same to uncertainty and contradiction. "When you write about real people you are always up against contradictions."

"A Strangeness and Strength, Sometimes Harshness": *Away from Her,* the Man Booker International Prize, *Too Much Happiness*

During the four years since the publication of *The View from Castle Rock,* Munro has continued to live the life she has long preferred. Health issues – most especially a bout of cancer during 2009 – have been a fact of life for her, as they are for any person her age. She has mostly stayed in Clinton; her trips to Comox have been fewer, the last one something of a valedictory journey, saying farewell to friends there. She seems to be travelling for purposes connected to her celebrity, if anything, more frequently. For instance, she was in Toronto in November 2007 to participate in a celebration of the fiftieth anniversary of McClelland & Stewart's New Canadian Library series, for which she has long served on the Editorial Board. In 2008, she went to Italy as one of three finalists for the Flaiano Prize – along with Alberto Arbasino and Ismail Kadare – and was selected as the winner after a round of public voting, a potentially embarrassing process that the three contenders solved by turning the voting into a great joke. In October of 2008 she went to New York to be interviewed on stage by her *New Yorker* editor Deborah Treisman as part of the magazine's annual festival. The highlight of 2009 was a trip to Dublin to receive the Man Booker International Prize and, that fall, she was slated to attend "A Tribute to Alice Munro" at the opening of the Vancouver International Writers Festival, although she did not make the trip for health reasons.

She did participate in "Too Much Happiness!" – an event billed as "Diana Athill in Conversation with Alice Munro," the opening gala of Toronto's International Festival of Authors and a PEN Canada benefit. Athill is a well-known British editor and writer whom Munro had never met. The two women hit it off and have corresponded since – that night they had a wide-ranging conversation, chatting, as one news report put it, "about everything from sex, to Canadian literature, to how times have changed since they began their writing careers." During that conversation, too, Munro acknowledged that she had had cancer – and, as with her earlier public musing that *Castle Rock* might be her last book, the revelation made headlines. Above all, throughout these years Munro wrote. *Too Much Happiness* was published in the fall of 2009, the *New Yorker* published "Corrie" in October 2010 and "Axis" in January 2011. *Harper's* has two others forthcoming. Alice Munro writes on.[13]

One of the American reviews of *Castle Rock,* by Sigrid Nunez, comments that with this book Munro "has given us something much closer to autobiography," and that "though Munro is temperamentally unsentimental the mood is often elegiac." The place of autobiography in Munro's work, especially after *Castle Rock,* is inarguable, and Nunez's point about the elegiac is backed by the images of Munro seeking after facts in cemeteries, and also by such stories as "What Do You Want to Know For?", with the looming presence of mortality. Not at all unusual in an introspective writer approaching her ninth decade, certainly, but since her family book there has been a deepening of such elegiac tendencies and, in significant ways, a sharpening of the insight that has long been present in Munro's stories. But with *Too Much Happiness* this observation has become even more acute. Claire Tomalin, an earlier British reviewer of Munro, has recently said that Munro "is a greater writer than" Katherine Mansfield, the subject of one of Tomalin's books, "with a wider range, and a strangeness and strength, sometimes harshness, that I admire."

An early title for Munro's "The Bear Came Over the Mountain" was "Papa Bear, Mama Bear, Baby Bear." That story closes *Hateship, Friendship, Loveship, Courtship, Marriage,* and the rejected nursery rhyme title seems to catch exactly what is going on there, for Munro and for each and every one of us: the progression of a life from birth through vibrant life to inevitable decline and a surrendering of our being to the next generation. This inescapable reality is just what Munro sees "with strangeness and strength" and "sometimes harshness," just as Tomalin said.

"The Bear Came Over the Mountain" is a notable story too because in 2007 the Canadian actress Sarah Polley transformed it, as director and writer, into *Away from Her,* a feature film starring Julie Christie, Gordon Pinsent, and Olympia Dukakis. This title is actually Munro's line, lifted from the story for the film. David Denby, reviewing the film in the *New Yorker,* called it "a small-scale triumph that could herald a great career" for Polley as a director. It captures Munro's insight since, as Denby also writes, in it "Grant finds a way for personal survival and love for someone lost to flourish together." And as A.O. Scott wrote in another review, there is "in Ms. Munro's mature work, a flinty wisdom about heterosexual love, a skepticism about romantic ideals that does not altogether deny their power or necessity. Ms. Polley, rather remarkably for someone still in her twenties, shows an intuitive grasp of this wisdom and a welcome, unsentimental interest in the puzzles and pleasures of a long, imperfect marriage." Scott also said, "I can't remember the last time the movies yielded up a love story so painful, so tender and so true."

Faced with this welcome event, Penguin in Canada, and Vintage in the United States, issued a paperback book version of "The Bear Came Over the Mountain" with a preface by Polley, as *Away From Her*, with cover images from the film. The cover and packaging notwithstanding, the title inside remains Munro's; that is, she did not concede her story's title to the film's. While Munro's stories have been used as bases for dramatic forms for some time – the longstanding popularity of "How I Met My Husband" as a play is notable – the critical success of *Away from Her* as a feature seems to portend more such transformations from her large body of fictional work. In 2008 the Blyth Festival produced *Courting Johanna,* Marcia Johnson's adaptation of "Hateship, Friendship, Courtship, Loveship, Marriage," a fine rendering of that story on the stage. According to Munro's agent, Jennifer Rudolph Walsh, that same story has been optioned for a film and there has been interest in other stories from Hollywood too: "Runaway" was optioned in 2008 by Jane Campion and the Juliet triptych has been optioned by Pedro Almodóvar's production company.[14]

On May 27, 2009, Munro was announced as winner of the third Man Booker International Prize, following Albanian Ismail Kadare (2005) and Nigerian Chinua Achebe (2007). Although *The Beggar Maid* was among the shortlisted books for the 1980 Booker-McConnell Prize, which is awarded annually to a single novel, and her British editor at Chatto & Windus, Alison Samuel, tried valiantly to have her subsequent books considered for that award, their status as collections of stories has precluded her work's participation in that competition since then. The Man Booker International Prize, however, is awarded "for a body of work that has contributed to an achievement in fiction on the world stage." The creation of this second and larger award – it brings with it a prize of sixty thousand pounds – may well have been designed with a short story writer like Munro in mind, since she had been so long frozen out of consideration for the older Booker Prize.

While, like the annual Man Booker Prize for Fiction, "literary excellence [is] its sole focus," the Man Booker International Prize "is significantly different" from its predecessor "in that it highlights one writer's overall contribution to fiction on the world stage. In seeking out literary excellence the judges consider a writer's body of work rather than a single novel." The prize aims at recognizing literary excellence by maintaining an open competition – Munro was selected from a shortlist of fourteen – and by defining that excellence broadly: writers writing in any language are eligible, although they must have had at least three books translated into English.

Before taking up the specifics of the prize, the details of the judges' deliberations, and the ultimate import of Munro's selection, it seems useful to say something about her reputation in Britain. When Barber began representing Munro in the late 1970s, she worked through Abner Stein, a British agent who represented all of her authors there – he placed the British editions of *The Beggar Maid* and *The Moons of Jupiter* with Allen Lane. During this period, Barber had met and become friends with Carmen Callil, who had founded Virago Press – an avowedly feminist publisher. In 1982, Callil moved to Chatto & Windus as Managing Director and when it became available, she acquired *The Progress of Love*. This was an appropriate pairing since Chatto then published "the big women writers" – A.S. Byatt, Toni Morrison – according to Munro's editor there, Alison Samuel. Recalling this move, Callil said that the growth of Munro's readership in the U.K. was very slow, happening by word of mouth. For her part, Callil made sure that Munro had good covers and that she was presented in a literary fashion; "not vulgarized," she has said. "Gradually," she continued, Munro "did it herself." Callil went on to say that "When you're publishing a genius" the publisher's role is none too difficult.

Munro came over to Britain a couple of times during the 1980s and early '90s to promote her books – Samuel recalls one tour that included Scotland, during which Munro was looked after by Ben Macintyre, now a novelist and a journalist with the *Times* of London. Munro told him of her connections to James Hogg and to Scotland, and she spoke also about the family book she wanted to do. As well,

Samuel recalls her own special need for the *Selected Stories* in her market, and the role she played in putting that volume together.

There are no U.K. sales figures for *The Progress of Love,* but *Friend of My Youth, Open Secrets,* and *Selected Stories* each sold about 4,000 hardback copies and 20,000 to 30,000 (with *Open Secrets* jumping to 46,000) in paper. *The Love of a Good Woman* sold almost 6,000 hardbacks while *Hateship* reached toward 7,000 – and the former sold just under 34,000 in paper, the latter almost 40,000. Seen through sales, *Runaway* was Munro's breakthrough in the U.K. – it sold 7,200 in hardback but over 70,000 in paper. Given its subject, *The View from Castle Rock* did even better, selling almost 11,000 in hardback, although just under 30,000 in paper. *Too Much Happiness,* no doubt driven in part by the Man Booker International Prize publicity, had sold about 16,500 hardbacks by late August 2010.[15] This book-by-book progress in Britain set the stage for her Man Booker International Prize win in May 2009.

The award Munro received in Dublin in June 2009 was the result of a thorough process, one open to scrutiny and intended to excite both interest and some controversy through its selections. The longstanding Nobel Prize – with which the Man Booker International Prize is often compared – emerges from a closed process and there is often a perception that politics – of both the small *p* and capital *P* variety – play a role there. (One notes in passing that Mario Vargas Llosa, one of those in play in the final voting for the Man Booker International in 2009, has just won the Nobel.) The Man Booker International recognizes "one writer's overall contribution on the world stage"; there are no submissions from publishers; the recipient has to be living; and, above all, it is an *international* award. Both Fiammetta Rocco, literary editor of the *Economist* and administrator of the Man Booker International Prize, and Jane Smiley, chair of the three-person panel of judges, have insisted on this international quality, on its translinguistic recognition, and on its emphasis on literary merit alone. The other two judges working with Smiley were Andrey Kurkov and Amit Chaudhuri. Born of Ukrainian extraction in the U.S.S.R. to a Soviet military officer, Kurkov speaks Russian as his first language but has learned nineteen languages. He is among the biggest-selling writers in Russia and is known for his mordant black humour; he writes in exile. Chaudhuri is a Bengali from Calcutta, although educated in English at University College London and then at Balliol College, Oxford. He is a person, Rocco has said, of "fierce views."

The judges met four times in all. First in Washington, D.C., in the spring of 2008, where they agreed on a list of about seventy possible writers. The idea at that point was that each judge would go away and read one book by each person. A second meeting was held in England in January 2009, where they arrived at a long shortlist or a short longlist of forty – at that point each judge was to read two books by each author. After that, they met again by teleconference and refined the list – agreeing that they would each be reading three books by each author.

In March 2009 the judges met at the New York Public Library and agreed upon the shortlist of fourteen authors that was made public. They wanted the list to attract attention and to be controversial – they wanted people to pay attention. It did, it was, and they did. The list was quite diverse, which was what they were aiming at: there were the expected (Munro, V.S. Naipaul, Joyce Carol Oates, Mario Vargas Llosa) and the unexpected (Antonio Tabucchi, James Kelman, Ludmila Ulitskaya) – and another seven too.

During their final deliberations and voting, the survivors from the announced list of fourteen had become just four: E.L. Doctorow, James Kelman, Mario Vargas Llosa, and Munro. For her part, Smiley was direct and determined in convincing her colleagues of her sense that Munro was their clear choice. Reading Munro, as she had done with each of her books since the 1970s, Smiley had come to see that every Munro story is a surprise, a quiet surprise. And that there is nobody else like her: the historical fiction is absolutely true and her insights about women are too – she never makes a wrong move as a woman writer. Most of all, Smiley saw Munro as a writer who creates on the page an intimate sense of the human condition, for she is both quiet and ruthless; to trace the development of Munro's consciousness is to learn about the cruelty of the world. While others under their consideration showed some of these same qualities, and were adventurous writers too, Smiley felt Munro's was the greatest achievement.

❧

Once she had convinced her fellow judges, Smiley elaborated these sentiments in her chair's speech at the award ceremony that took place, amid the elegant eighteenth-century surroundings of Trinity College, Dublin, on June 25. She began her remarks with a list of places drawn from the books the judges had read, commencing with "the brow of Castle Rock, with a view across the Atlantic Ocean, in Edinburgh, in 1818," and ended her list with a comment which resonates throughout the prize-winner's *oeuvre:* "Fiction, as Cervantes would have been happy to tell you, is and must be geographical."

Munro was accompanied to Dublin by her daughter Jenny Munro and by her goddaughter Rebecca Garrett, Jenny's good friend. Alison Samuel was there as Munro's editor at Chatto & Windus. But inevitably, given the occasion and their long-shared history, there too, beaming throughout at the utter rightness of all this, was Munro's longtime editorial triumvirate – Virginia Barber, Ann Close, and Douglas Gibson, who turned into an instant journalist and wrote and published a detailed account of the evening's festivities for the Toronto *Globe and Mail.* It carried the subtitle "Oscar Wilde's alma mater 'gets it right' with fete for Our Lady Alice."

Slowed by the effects of her ongoing medical treatments, Munro took things as easily as was possible during her time in Dublin. She paced herself, noting Jenny and Rebecca's busy activities while they were there in the Irish capital, during which time she rested at the hotel. She fulfilled her obligations as the winner, appearing also at a public event/press conference that morning in connection with the prize – about two hundred people who were interested in it and in her writing just came to see her. The journalists present were uncharacteristically shy (Gibson had to ask a question to move things along) but that hesitancy seemed to draw Munro out. She was charming and funny as she answered questions, talking about her childhood, her mother, and her writing career over the years. According to Rocco, there was a general tone suggesting that the people there were *very* pleased that Munro had won. As Gibson noted in his account, James Wood, who writes for both the *Guardian* and the *New Yorker,* and knows the writing scene on both sides of the Atlantic, had some weeks earlier quietly expressed his approval of Alice's win. "'Sometimes,' he said, 'they get it right.'"

Smiley, pressing on in her speech to give details of the judges' sense of the quality of the writing, spoke of Munro's "capacity for empathy." She also spoke about another quality she cherishes about her work: "No woman in an Alice Munro story is ever less than the agent of her own existence, no matter how impoverished or powerless her circumstances, and no woman's circumstances, in an Alice Munro story, are seen to be trivial."[16]

☙

When Smiley argued for Munro as the writer who most deserved the prize, she ended by saying that the trajectory of Munro's work teaches us "about the cruelty of the world." In the same way, "The Bear Came Over the Mountain," become *Away from Her,* is, as the film critic A.O. Scott asserts, "a love story so painful, so tender and so true." Claire Tomalin saw in Munro "a strangeness and strength, sometimes harshness" that she admires. And after a long and close association with Munro and her work from the late 1970s through the mid-1990s, Daniel Menaker once maintained that

> a Munro story . . . consists of a number of versions or visions of the same incident or drama which pull sets of inaccurate or only partly accurate "facts" aside like curtains, to reveal deeper truths about character, motivation, and even the event itself, and often, when the story penetrates to the ultimate truth or emotion she is capable of, it takes the form of something about human behavior that is asocial, amoral, almost bestial but that will not be denied.

As she begins her wending and ruminative review of Munro's career and of *Too Much Happiness* in the *New York Review of Books,* Joyce Carol Oates comments that this thirteenth collection's title is "both cuttingly ironic and passionately sincere." Another reviewer, Karen R. Long, in the Cleveland *Plain Dealer,* compares Munro to some of her contemporaries also writing into their old age, maintaining that E.L. Doctorow's "last novel led into bleakness, and Philip Roth . . . now flirts with fetishizing decay and death." Munro, in contrast, "is still turning the seams inside out on her characters to unpredictable and pleasurable surprise." Continuing that the book's stories "take up home invasion, child murder (twice), and creepy perversion of the old-man/young schoolgirl variety," Long notes the collection's "jolting" qualities and writes of "the tabloid grubbiness of the lives in *Too Much Happiness.*" Munro is a writer who "can make the lurid sing with nuance and explicability, particularly in her opening story, 'Dimensions,' about a young chambermaid living quietly several years after the trauma of a triple homicide," one that killed her children.

Just as Munro returned to the name "Willens," which she had given to a character in one of her earliest published stories when she created the adulterous optometrist who is murdered in "The Love of a Good Woman," with this opening story, "Dimensions," harrowing and surprising, she echoes her younger self once again: "The Dimensions of a Shadow" was her first published story in *Folio* in 1950. That story, too, characteristically (and also obviously, in ways that reveal a young writer still very much grasping, even groping, toward her craft), moves toward a character's innermost desires. Those desires – very much indicative of "the cruelty of the world" – are quite harsh, and suggest, as Menaker said, a view of "human behavior that is asocial, amoral, almost bestial but that will not be denied." Munro, for her part, commented at the Toronto "Too Much Happiness!" event, when she was interviewed with Diana Athill, "I don't understand the concept 'ordinary people.'" To her, each of us is unique, often "touchable and mysterious" and also prone to frightening acts. Her stories unfurl, again and again, to reveal human beings being human. As so many reviewers and critics have written, and so many readers have paused to think: *This is what it feels like to be, to be alive, to be a human being.*

Her "family book" done and published, Munro returned with *Too Much Happiness* to another collection of stories of the sort that has been her hallmark since the 1980s. Most of its ten stories had been first pub-lished in the *New Yorker* in recent years – here there was some overlap, though, because of the historical and autobiographical cast of the pre-vious book; two stories in *Too Much Happiness,* "Wenlock Edge" and "Dimensions," appeared before *Castle Rock.* Three stories appeared first in *Harper's,* confirming that the *New Yorker* editors had passed on them – the title story for reasons of length, certainly. As with every collection since *The Love of a Good Woman,* Munro includes a very long story that is also in some way surprising. In the case of "Too Much Happiness," she offers another piece of historical fiction, but this one is focused on a real historical figure, a famous Russian mathematician named Sophia Kovalevsky. Almost as if she were sneering at those critics who have claimed that Munro focuses too exclusively on her own time, her own class, and her own place, here she offers a moving title story from the nineteenth century that never so much as mentions Canada, let alone Huron County, Ontario.

A final story remains to be noted: "Wood." First published in the *New Yorker* in November 1980, it had awaited inclusion in a collection ever since, almost thirty years. Unlike the fugitive pieces Munro incor-porated into *Castle Rock,* "Wood" had no autobiographical cast to it – she and her editorial triumvirate just never agreed that it fit into a col-lection, as new collections were assembled and published (indeed, Ann Close was not sure it would make this one, where it appears just before the long title story, the last in the book).[17] The story of Roy Fowler, a sign painter whose overriding passion is different kinds of hardwood, the original 1980 version – for which Munro gleaned considerable information from Gerry Fremlin – originally focused on a serious acci-dent that Fowler had in the woods as he felled a tree, and how he saved himself. Now, almost thirty years later and doubtless having thought about what the story needed many, many times since, Munro the per-petual reviser has expanded Roy's relationship with his wife, developed her character, extended the accident and the action, and so trans-formed it into a much deeper, much richer, and ultimately much more satisfying story of both surprise and redemption. Munro has, as always, continued to think the story through, to probe its heart, to catch its essential beat. Looking at the first version of "Wood" and at its transformation into the much better version found in *Too Much Happiness,* a reader sees Munro's transforming vision in microcosm. As Oates writes, the story "comes to a plausibly happy ending, where the reader has been primed to expect something quite different, as in one of Jack London's gleefully grim little allegories of men succumbing to the wild."

The reviews of *Too Much Happiness,* already mentioned briefly, do have something of a valedictory air to them. But now there is a continuing meditation on just how Munro does what she does. Leah Hager Cohen, in yet another cover review in *The New York Times Book Review,* begins wondering if the Germans "have a term for it. *Dopplegedanken,* perhaps: the sensation, when reading, that your own mind is giving birth to the words as they appear on the page. Such is the ego that in these rare instances you wonder, 'How could the author have known what I was thinking?' Of course, what has happened isn't this at all, though it's no less astonishing. Rather, you've been drawn so deftly into another world that you're breathing with someone else's rhythms, seeing someone else's visions as your own." Thus Alice Munro's *Too Much Happiness.* Cohen continues to talk of this story or that, expressing amazed reaction to what Munro accomplishes. ("The real story keeps turning out to be larger than, and at a canted angle to, what we thought it would be. The effect is initially destabilizing, then unexpectedly affirming.") Taking on the perennial and by now quite clichéd Ozick exclamation of Munro as "our Chekhov," Cohen concludes: "And at this point in Munro's career, how much can [such comparisons] add? What is certain is this: She is our Munro. And how fortunate we are to call her that."

ॐ

Although less concerned with Munro's effects than Cohen is, Anne Enright considers Munro's presence as a model, and in the *Globe and Mail* asserts that "The most salutary thing, for her fellow writers, is the way that Munro, buffeted by our adulation, has carried on doing exactly what she has always done, with scarcely a wobble on the high wire. Of course, she might deny that there is a wire, she might say that she is just walking on the ground. But it is a mistake to say that writers do not know what they are doing; in my experience, they know very well."

As the entire trajectory of Munro's career has shown, and as has been detailed here, Enright's discerning assertion applies utterly to Alice Munro. W.P. Kinsella, who himself stopped writing fiction in his sixties, marvels at this in a review titled "Everything is Funny" (a remark that Munro once made to him when he noticed for the first time that one of her stories was funny – even, one adds, ironic titles like "Too Much Happiness"). Reading this collection, he sees Munro still writing at the highest level: these stories are "as good as anything she written in her long career. . . . The language is always crisp and clear, like the tinkling of bells. Reading becomes a compulsion: one has to find out what is going to happen."

Surveying the reviews of *Too Much Happiness,* one finds apt phrasings, sharp insights, and evidence of great care in reading wherever one looks. Philip Marchand, who in 2007 published an essay entitled "The Problem with Alice Munro" where he bewails the sameness of Munro's vision, takes up *Too Much Happiness* in the spirit of something of a deathbed conversion; he begins his review in the *National Post* by asserting that "If Alice Munro had never existed, part of the soul of Canada would have remained inarticulate, forgotten, submerged. . . . It has always been Munro's aesthetic to 'tell stories to make your hair curl.'"[18] Christopher Taylor, writing in the *Guardian,* offers this clear summation: "Rural or puritanical suspicions of pretension, which often oppress her characters, have left their impress on her writing style, too. Her prose is clean, precise and unmannered; her stories are attentive to emotion but almost witheringly unsentimental. She is also a storyteller rather than a maker of atmospheric vignettes, not afraid to shift chronology around or have dramatic things happen." Like many readers, Taylor pays especial attention to "Fiction," one of the volume's very best, along with the title story. After describing it, he writes: "Laid out in a short summary, the story's workings – the lessons and counter-lessons in fiction making; the fluent, dramatic changes of perspective; the approach to, and retreat from, generalising wisdom – inevitably seem a bit squashed. On the page, though, they hang together beautifully, without strain; and the same holds true for many of the other pieces in the book." Munro's stories, just as Cohen mused, "create a powerful illusion of bringing their readers up against unmediated life. . . ."

Michael Gorra, in perhaps the best single review of *Too Much Happiness* to be found, writes in the *Times Literary Supplement* of Munro's effects at length and with what seems stunning insight. Looking back to *Castle Rock,* he acknowledges the notion of it being her last book but maintains that "with time [it] will stand as something like her Enigma of Arrival." By this he means that the book will be seen as a critical text for Munro, capturing her own explanations and wonderings over her ancestry. More than that, her work's singularity "lies in the fact that it has never seemed to be about her" – by this he seems to mean not that it is without autobiographical material, but rather that she has been able to rise beyond the descriptive to the universal, since "this collection does show the blend of continuity and change that one wants and hopes to find in a late book by a master." Focusing closely on "Some Women" (Munro's story that begins, "I'm amazed sometimes to think how old I am" before it tells a story from the narrator's teenaged girlhood), Gorra asks, "What did the narrator learn that summer that has to do with the fact of her own old age? What prompts her memory? It's too easy to say that its last words ["I grew up, and old"] make the narrator herself into the subject of the tale, and these questions must remain unanswered. The fact that we ask them is, however, one mark of Munro's power. We ask, and trust the narrator precisely because she gives no answers; trust that she herself knows, even if she can't or won't tell us."

Gorra then argues that "Many great poets have lived and worked to a fine age; few fiction writers have. . . . Unlike Philip Roth [Munro] does not seem to rage at the indignity of years, and yet if I had to reduce the concerns of *Too Much Happiness* to a single word, it would be 'mortality.'"

Moving through "Dimensions," Gorra spends considerable attention on "Free Radicals" – its "conclusion is even terser than that of

'Some Women,' a two-word paragraph which feels like no ending at all: 'Never know.' It leaves Nita physically safe but with her situation unresolved; only death will do that. Munro has always had an ability to take a narrative corner at speed, to whip a story into a new direction at the last minute. But the corners are now tighter than ever, single words or sentences that seem marked by an epigrammatic impatience with the whole business of endings; as though every tale might allow for an alternative version and no story is ever really over."

Presumably, Gorra has not studied the proof materials in the *New Yorker* files, or even Munro's proof pages for *Too Much Happiness* at the Alice Munro Fonds at the University of Calgary. There, not at all surprisingly, anyone can see Munro working on her endings – perpetually, as she always has, sometimes in concert with an editor, sometimes in defiance of an editor screaming for final delivery of a perfectly fine existing ending, sometimes alone: the endings of her stories always matter, they get the most attention, the most frequent changes. Gorra is right about Munro's writing. Continuing to wonder over Nita in "Free Radicals," Gorra writes tellingly about Munro's ongoing effects on her readers, saying that "the drama of her situation will remain in my head long after I have forgotten the story's precise ending. I will remember its emotional terrain as I remember lines and fragments from this Yeats poem or that; a twist of the voice, an intonation separate, perhaps, from any actual words. Each of these is like a chip off some massy substance, a piece that implies the whole. Every one of them seems reinforced by the echoes of another, and to read Munro now, to visit and revisit this house or that marriage, seems like immersing oneself in a great poet's collected works, a chance to inhabit a mind, a sensibility, that is larger than any of its individual iterations." This fine review concludes by suggesting that Chekhov is not the Russian that Munro should be compared to – rather, "Turgenev is a different matter." Wryly too, Gorra notes that Munro's work "has been translated into thirteen languages. That's not enough; but one of them is Swedish."

In August 2009, just as *Too Much Happiness* was being published, Alice Munro announced that she was withdrawing it from the Giller Prize competition – one of her private reasons was that a head-to-head competition was shaping up between her and her good friend Margaret Atwood and, not surprisingly, Munro decided not to let it happen. Equally important to her, having won the Giller Prize twice already, her absence would clear the field for younger writers. At this, the *Globe and Mail* published a head-shaking editorial called "Too Much Generosity." Such comments remind us of a point made by W.P. Kinsella in his review: describing what he calls "the CanLit scene," Kinsella sees it as "an industry rife with jealousies, feuds and petty backbiting" yet announces categorically, "I have never heard anyone say anything unkind about Alice Munro, personally or professionally. When Alice wins a prize other writers and critics are not lined up to name ten books that should have won." To Gibson's relief (he knew how her Giller Prize withdrawal would cut her sales) Munro forgot to withdraw her book from the Governor General's Award competition – *Too Much Happiness* was shortlisted but it did not win. Having just published another story, "Axis," in the *New Yorker*, Munro now has two more awaiting publication at *Harper's*. Its literary editor, Ben Metcalf, is delighted to have a story from her whenever he is able to get one. One of the two he has, "Train," seems to have returned to material Munro worked on in the 1960s. She has a contract for another book of stories with Knopf, and the issue of the *New Yorker* including "Axis" announced that collection for the fall of 2012. She continues to write into her ninth decade, for she turns eighty next July.

Seen by Gorra as akin to Yeats – a comparison that pleases her – compared perpetually to Chekhov, Alice Munro continues to do "exactly what she has always done," as Anne Enright said.[19] She continues to write her lives – the life she has lived, the lives she has read about, researched, and studied; the lives she has imagined. Like her much-admired William Maxwell, Munro has demonstrated time and time again that she knows exactly how it should be done. Ever revising, ever hoping to do it better, she remains her readers' Alice Munro, writing on. . . .

EPILOGUE

Alice Munro

Writing Her Lives, Writing Home, Writing On . . .

I worry the story.
— AM to Peter Gzowski, October 22, 1982

Something happened here. In your life there are a few places, or maybe only one place, where something happened, and then there are all the other places.
— "Face" (2009)

Just before Richard Avedon's gallery of the magazine's best-known authors and Munro's "The Albanian Virgin," the *New Yorker's* 1994 fiction celebration ran an essay by Roger Angell, "Storyville." A fiction editor and writer at the magazine since the mid-1950s, Angell took a long view of the *New Yorker's* record as a venue for short fiction, trying to define the qualities needed to make it into its pages. He saw Munro in the line of the magazine's mainstays: "Now and then, a writer stakes out an entire region of the imagination and of the countryside – one thinks of Cheever, Salinger, Donald Barthelme, and Raymond Carver, and now Alice Munro and William Trevor – which becomes theirs alone, marked in our minds by unique inhabitants and terrain. Writers at this level seem to breathe the thin, high air of fiction without effort, and we readers, visiting on excursion, feel a different thrumming in our chests as we look about at a clearer, more acute world than the one we have briefly departed." Reading Munro, he continued, "brings back for me, every time, the mood of thrilling expectancy with which I read the entrancing events in all those variously tinted fairy-story collections of my childhood – 'The Blue Fairy Book,' 'The Yellow Fairy Book,' 'The Grey Fairy Book,' and the rest." When he came to read "Silence" in manuscript, Angell remarked to his colleagues that "these lives seem thick with detail and events and other people, in a way that only Munro seems able to get down, and sad with the sadness of life."

In the magazine's 2004 triptych, Juliet's life is "thick" with the precise details that Munro has spent her entire life observing, living, imagining, and shaping herself. Riding across Canada by train toward British Columbia and a new life in "Chance," Juliet recalls Munro's own such trips – in emotion, most probably, Juliet's expectations of a new life are rooted in Munro's own journey west with her new husband in December 1951, leaving Ontario. "Soon" draws upon another trip, that one back home to Ontario in 1954 with her new daughter, Sheila, and also meditates on the Chagall print she has been long drawn to, *I and the Village.* That story too, in Sara's unacknowledged reassurance – *"Soon I'll see Juliet"* – reveals Munro writing her lives whole. As she makes clear in "Soon" and emphatic in "Silence," Juliet's eager self-assured youthful certainty over her own life, and the ways of being she

thinks superior to Sara's hopeful though empty delusions, will ultimately founder against the rock of Penelope's silence. "Sad with the
sadness of life," Alice Munro writes Juliet's life through Sara's: "*Soon I'll
see Juliet*" is a hopeful sign which resonates throughout the triptych.
Juliet becomes a creature bereft, like her mother before her whom she
was then able to dismiss, and not even answer with a reassuring "Yes";
in Penelope's silence she becomes the worse, the one even more bereft.
"Sad with the sadness of life," Munro encapsulates the daughter's vision
felt and understood concurrent with the mother's – each both remembered and, as one generation gives way to the next, lived.

"Sad with the sadness of life," happy in its humour, aware of life's
ironies, knowing always that this life is "touchable and mysterious,"
Alice Munro has written her lives and continues to write them in just
the ways she always has done – as Anne Enright wrote in her review of
Too Much Happiness. "There is always a starting point in reality," Munro
told Harry Boyle in August 1974. For her, reality is the life she has lived,
the people she has known and, perhaps above all, the place she has felt:

> Whichever road you take, on your way out of Jubilee, you
> will have to cross a bridge, narrow and high above the Wawanash
> River, and painted with silver paint that glimmers in the dark.
> If you are going west, towards Lake Huron, you will see that
> on the other side of the bridge there are several houses, a
> school, a grocery store and gas pump and a couple of buildings
> which look as if they may have been places of business at one
> time, but now are closed up and rented as living-quarters. The
> town itself does not extend this far; the last street light shines
> on the approach to the bridge, and on the place where the
> sidewalk changes to plain dirt path, bordered in the summer-
> time by waist-high grass. The community across the bridge,
> which straggles out along some short, intersecting dirt roads, is
> not part of the town, nor of the country either; it is a place by
> itself, known as The Flats; this name it takes from the old fair-
> grounds, which is certainly the most interesting thing to be seen
> there, with its tumbled ruin of a grandstand and the handsome

stone pillars at the gate, supporting a sign that says: TO THE F LLEN H ROES O JUBI EE. A sign like that, hanging boldly against the northern sky, with nothing on the other side of it but that grandstand, and a great field blooming with milkweed and showing some traces of a harness track – a sign like that has such superb irrelevance and finality about it that you do not bother supplying, in your mind, the letters that have fallen away.

What this is, apart from a fragment dating probably from the 1960s, is a description of one of the scenes Munro saw walking home from school from Grade 4 on – walking from Wingham to Lower Wingham, walking from town to home, out through Lower Town to the Laidlaw farm by the river. "Home." Passing by the old fairgrounds now, there are in fact stone pillars that do support a sign, though it says "To the Fallen Heroes of Turnberry Twp." and no letters are missing – there is no grandstand. "There is always a starting point in reality."

A draft of "Everything Here Is Touchable and Mysterious" begins nearby, describing the river, and offers a confession:

> I always call this river the Wawanash, when I write about [it] in stories. That is just because I like the name. There is no real Wawanash river, no Wawanash county. There are two townships, East and West Wawanash, in northern Huron County. The river's name is really the Maitland. It rises at Flesherton and flows into Lake Huron at Goderich. West of Wingham it flows through what used to be, and maybe still is, called Lower Town (pronounced Loretown) and passed my father's land and Cruikshank's farm and loops up, in what is known as the Big Bend, before flowing south under Zetland bridge.

Some of this was in the published essay, but after the final phrase here Munro added "and that is the mile or so I know of it." This mile or so along the river, like Munro's recurring walk down "the Flats Road," became the scene of remembering, in early stories like "Images" or more recently in "The Love of a Good Woman" or "Nettles." Or as a point of comparison as Munro recalls first looking at Ettrick Water in "No Advantages" as she begins *The View from Castle Rock,* the family book in which she writes herself, her inheritances, her *own* lives. "This ordinary place" has been so much more than sufficient for Alice Munro: that mile or so along the Maitland has been a place where, truly, everything is touchable and mysterious. "Until she came along," James Reaney once wrote of Munro, southwestern Ontario "had no voice – she gave it a voice and that has made such a difference. I don't know what we'd have done without her."[1] Sad with the sadness of life, Alice Munro, writing her lives in Huron County, the home place that is hers alone. Our Alice Munro, writing on . . .

Acknowledgements

Though such things are hard to place exactly, this book probably had its beginning sometime in the 1970s. After graduating university in 1973, I took a year off to work, read, get married, and figure out what I was going to do next. One of the possibilities was to go to Canada for graduate school to study Canadian literature, so I began a subscription to the *Tamarack Review*. As it happened, the first piece in the first issue I received was Alice Munro's "Material." After reading it, I decided that if this is Canadian literature, sign me up. I signed, moving to the University of Waterloo where it was my excellent fortune to study with Stanley E. McMullin – I kept reading Munro and he encouraged me to write an M.A. thesis on her early stories and *Dance of the Happy Shades*. Though some in the English department thought it premature – Munro had just three books at the time – the project was approved and completed. By then I was hooked. Like Mr. Stanley on Cather in "Dulse," "I read and reread" Munro "and my admiration grows. It simply grows."[1]

I then went off to the University of Manitoba for a Ph.D. There I had more excellent fortune to become the late Evelyn J. Hinz's first doctoral student and to work closely with John J. Teunissen – together, they modelled a scholarly teaching life for which I remain profoundly grateful. Though my work there was focused on other matters, I went from Manitoba during those years to give my first conference papers, one of which drew from my thesis on Munro. It eventually appeared in *Probable Fictions*. By then I had returned to the States to teach Canadian literature, and Munro's fiction remained a primary, and continuing, critical focus.

Working on the annotated bibliography of Munro for ECW Press in 1983, I had occasion to meet Alice Munro to ask some related questions. After saying hello, she looked me straight in the eye and said, with a clarity that still rings, "I'm not dead yet." I saw her for a day five years later when we both attended Trent University's tribute to Margaret Laurence and once, in between, we talked on the phone about "Dulse" and Cather's presence there. As a critic, I thought Munro should simply be left alone to write, so that's what I did. I did not see her again until August 2001, by which time she had decided to cooperate with me on this book, "doing penance," she wrote me in March 2000, "for all those literary biographies I have devoured."

My first and foremost acknowledgement is to Alice Munro. While it has been clear to me throughout that she takes no relish in what she called in the same letter "being 'biographied,'" she has been candid, precise, and helpful throughout – answering questions, wondering over lost memories, stewing a bit, and opening doors.[2] As the references here show, our contacts have not been numerous – three long sessions each over two days and some phone calls – but they have been just what was needed. In no sense an "official" biography, *Alice Munro: Writing Her Lives* benefited enormously from its subject's cooperation.

Once the idea was broached and the work begun, those to acknowledge and thank became legion. During the 1990s, when I was contemplating the possibility, Douglas Gibson was both discouraging and encouraging. That was just what was needed then, since while Munro was not yet prepared to cooperate it was clear, he wrote, that such a book as this would be called for eventually. When Munro decided to cooperate, Gibson made it happen, as did Michael Levine. I am grateful to them both and proud that this is a Douglas Gibson Book.

Since 1983, my career as a scholar-teacher has been effected by St. Lawrence University and by its Canadian Studies Program. There, a succession of deans, presidents, and faculty colleagues have supported my work on Munro. I am particularly grateful to Grant Cornwell and to Daniel Sullivan, whose imaginative leadership and initiative provided me with a research leave at a critical time. That leave was funded by the Lincolnshire Foundation, so I am equally grateful to Eric and Jane Molson. Early on, they saw this book as an important project and arranged the time and resources I needed to research and write it. Throughout, they have followed its progress with interest and enthusiasm. I am deeply grateful for this, as well as for the Molsons' support of Canadian Studies at St. Lawrence.

The author of any book that rests on archival research has many organizations and people to thank. The support of the Government of Canada has been critical to this project. Beginning in the late 1980s, through a Senior Fellowship and a succession of smaller grants, Foreign Affairs Canada has supported this work. Its Research Grant Program administered by the Canadian Embassy in Washington has funded my travel to the Alice Munro Fonds at the University of Calgary and to other archives. Speaking as someone long involved in Canadian Studies in the United States, I know without question that these programs have had significant effect on Canada-U.S. understanding.

My visits to the University of Calgary to read the Munro papers began in January 1988. I have been back several times since, including a semester-long stay as a visiting scholar at the Calgary Institute for the Humanities during fall 2003. People at the university have been uniformly welcoming and gracious. Particularly, Apollonia Lang Steele and Marlys Chevrefils of the Archives and Special Collections section have each been singular in their myriad assistances to this project. Every request and question, whether on-site or across the continent, has been attended promptly and with interest. Each of them has handed me a "Eureka!" more than once, so I am especially grateful to them for all their help, and to the University of Calgary for its Special Collection of Canadian Authors' Papers. It is a singular place for scholarly work. For similar assistance at other archives, I am grateful to the staff of those institutions I have listed in the Select Bibliography. Of these, McMaster University should be singled out – its collection of papers from Canadian publishers is another key resource. Also, Kip Jackson of CBC Archives, along with his colleagues, guided my work there.

The research involved in discovering Munro's ancestors led me, for the first time, into the world of genealogy. There I discovered many people with relevant information who were much more than happy to share it. Arlyn Montgomery of Belgrave, Ontario provided much information from her own work on the Laidlaw side of the family and sent photographs too. Eleanor Henderson, of Carleton Place, Ontario, did exactly the same for the Chamney side and also spent most of a glorious spring day giving me an extended tour of Scotch Corners. And as I gathered archival confirmations from Ottawa Valley newspapers, Ann MacPhail of Algonquin College helped in many ways, even transcribing almost illegible microfilm.

Although a blanket acknowledgement, I want to thank all those who agreed to talk to me (or in some cases, e-mail me), those whose interviews I cite here. A bit perversely, too, I thank those who refused to talk to me – their refusals occasioned considerable thinking about just what is involved in the writing of the biography of a living subject, thinking which doubtless helped this book. Among those who helped me, cited and not, I would' like to mention a few people in particular. Helen Hoy, who has written some of the most important articles on Munro, generously shared her research into the making of *Who Do You Think You Are?;* without it, I would not have known some of the details of that story. Walter Martin, author of the first real critical book on Munro, was encouraging and provided necessary information about Robert Laidlaw. Catherine Ross told me about the writing of her own Munro biography and arranged for me to see the late Thomas Tausky's excellent 1984 interview with Munro (for that, too, I thank Nancy Tausky). Ben Sonnenberg told me a great deal about how Munro was seen in New York in the early 1980s. In particular, Earle Toppings has been gracious, interested, and very helpful beyond his own memories of working with Munro. To my considerable regret, I never managed to speak to the late Harry J. Boyle about Munro, but I appreciate his daughter Patricia's efforts to make that happen. I believe he did know just how important that interview was to Munro's career.

Closer to my home, there are several others to acknowledge. At St. Lawrence, Joan Larsen, Head of Reference and Instructional Services at the Owen D. Young Library, helped this project in countless ways – she is a great friend and a "friendly librarian" indeed, as so many of us here know and appreciate. I hope this book meets the advice she gave me years ago. Then there is Nancy Alessi, Canadian Studies Program Assistant – she has helped this project in more ways than I can recount, and has done so precisely and with interest. Here too Bonnie Enslow undertook the work of transcribing hours and hours of interviews with diligence and interest. Graphic designer Ken Alger led me through the details of scanned photographs with precision and knowledge, teaching me a good deal as he produced the images that appear here.

Finally, there is Michael Peterman of Trent University, one of the trio to whom this book is dedicated. Since we met in the late 1970s, we have shared the details of the academic life and of Canadian writing continually – working on projects together, travelling to conferences, keeping up with what's going on. Michael is in many ways the spiritual godfather to this project – he has known about it as long as anyone, has always been encouraging, and he read the whole thing straight through, hammering the prose and my assumptions at every turn. Thanks are not really enough.

➷

Reviewing Joan Acocella's *Willa Cather and the Politics of Criticism* in the *New York Review of Books,* A.S. Byatt remarked that "biographical critics undo the artist's work, and may kill the life of the art." Throughout *Alice Munro: Writing Her Lives,* I have kept Byatt's comment in mind and, probably more urgently, I have thought too about the exception Munro took to the "Toronto critic" who saw the house in the ground in "Images" as "symbolizing death, of course, and burial." "What you write is an offering," she conceded in the same essay, "anybody can come and take what they like from it." This offering has consciously avoided discussion of Munro criticism, a subject that was a particular interest of mine in the 1990s. Now it is better to get at the biographical facts and individual interpretations of Munro's career and her writing's progress – as revealed by archival holdings and published sources – than to belabour interpretation. That, doubtless, will continue unimpeded. I hope, though, in closing this biography, that I have not too much displayed what Janet Malcolm recently enumerated as a "crucial biographer's trait: the arrogant desire to impose a narrative on the stray bits and pieces of a life that wash up on the shores of biographical research." I may have – that is for others to judge – but if so it has been in ongoing fascination over the trajectory and utter artistry of Alice Munro's life and career. When she talked to Peter Gzowski on *Morningside* in October 1982 about *The Moons of Jupiter* – "I worry the story" – Munro also remarked that she hoped she would still be writing, and wanting to write, twenty years from now. More than twenty years, now, in fact. As she wrote in "Material," my very first Munro story, this fact is most emphatically "A fine and lucky benevolence."3

R.T.

Canton, New York

June 6, 2005

A Note on the Revised Edition:

In preparing this updated edition, I have added a chapter, revised the epilogue, updated the select bibliography, and revised the index. There are also some silent corrections of small errors and omissions in the first edition. By way of acknowledgement, I thank Alice Munro once more: she has met with me and responded to my various entreaties, as always, graciously and thoughtfully. Her "literary triumvirate" – Virginia Barber, Ann Close, and (especially) Douglas Gibson – has helped these revisions in numerous ways. I wish also to acknowledge Deborah Treisman particularly. She has been prompt and proficient, both for the first edition and for this revision. Others, cited here, have been equally generous with their time and interests. Keeping up with Alice Munro as she continues to write on is both an adventure and a joy and, speaking as one is still doing so, I remain profoundly grateful for the chance.

R.T.

Canton, New York

December 7, 2010

A Note on the Sources

All citations from Alice Munro's fiction are from the first Canadian book publication unless otherwise indicated; book titles are abbreviated. Except for some newspaper articles from the *Wingham Advance-Times* and other newspapers, references to print materials refer to the items in the Select Bibliography. Single-page items are listed in the Select Bibliography only. Authors and titles of book reviews are listed here only when page references for quotations are needed; otherwise, the citations are in the Select Bibliography. Interviews with Alice Munro are mine unless another interviewer is named. Interviews listed as "Interview [name]" refer to my own interviews with others. Regarding archival sources, those items followed by a number alone are in the Alice Munro Fonds, Special Collections, University of Calgary. All others, including other collections held at the University of Calgary, are cited with details specific to the archive or owner. In most cases, a box number is followed by a file number. Alice Munro is abbreviated AM throughout. So too Virginia Barber, VB; Ann Close, AC; Douglas M. Gibson, DG; Charles McGrath, CM; John Metcalf, JM; and Robert Weaver, RW. M&S is used here to identify location of papers in the files of McClelland & Stewart. NYPL indicates *New Yorker* files at the New York Public Library.

References

Back dust jacket: AM, June 19, 2003.

Epigraphs and Prologue
  1. "A Real Life," *Open*: 80. "Introduction," *Moons*: xiii. "Golden Apples": 24.
     "Everything Here Is Touchable and Mysterious," *Weekend Magazine*
     [*Toronto Star*], May 11, 1974: 33. "Nettles," *Hateship*: 167.

2. "Foreword." *Anthology Anthology:* ix. "wooing," "real work": "Miles City, Montana," *Progress:* 88. "Alice was known": Interview George Cuomo, February 3, 2004.
3. "Material," *Something:* 43.
4. "The Ottawa Valley," *Something:* 244, 246. Boyle interview.
5. "Home": 152.
6. "Home": 143, 152. "Material," *Something:* 31. "Cortes Island," *Love:* 144.
7. "Home": 134, 136.
8. AM, August 22, 2001. Audrey Coffin to AM, October 7, 1974: 37.2.25.5. DG to AM, August 26, 1974: 37.2.20.2.
9. Barber's initial approach to Munro: Phoebe Larmore to Toivo Kiil, December 22, 1975. VB to Toivo Kiil, January 23, 1975: Private collection. VB to AM, March 11, 1976: 37.2.47.2.

Chapter I

1. "Changing Places": 192.
2. James Hogg and James Laidlaw, "Letter from the Ettrick Shepherd": 630, 632.
3. "Changing Places": 204, 205.
4. "Powers," *Runaway:* 330. "Introduction," *Selected Stories:* xvi.
5. "Lying Under the Apple Tree," *New Yorker,* June 17 and 24, 2002: 88. Deborah Treisman to AM, May 30, 2002: *New Yorker* Files.
6. CM to VB, March 28, 1979, April 9, 1980: *New Yorker* (NYPL): 916:17, 927:17.
7. "Material," *Something:* 42.
8. Jean S. McGill, *A Pioneer History of the County of Lanark,* 61–78, 238, *passim.*
9. See Akenson, *passim.* Akenson notes that "a massive restudy" of the 1871 Census of Canada by A. Gordon Darroch and Michael D. Ornstein "revealed that in the province of Ontario 48.1 percent of Catholics of Irish descent and 59.4 percent of Protestants of Irish descent were farmers" (337–38).
10. Thomas Dougherty, Registered Will Dated June 6, 1853. Registered County of Lanark, November 24, 1855: Private collection.
11. 1871 Census of Canada, Ontario, District 82, Sub-District East Pembroke Village. John, twenty-eight, is listed as a "Wagon-Maker," his origin is listed as "English" (he was born in Drummond Township, Lanark County, Ontario); Catherine, twenty-nine, is "Irish" and their daughters, Bertha Ann and Blanche M., are four and two, respectively. The family's religion is Church of England.
12. Pembroke *Observer and Upper Canada Advertiser,* March 12, 1875; there follow five more insertions of this ad. "Full Blast": May 21, 1875, and almost

weekly through November; "Removal J.M. Stanley & Co." December 10, 17, 24, and 31, 1875. AM's comments, April 3, June 20, 2003.

13. Catherine's age was listed as forty-two in obituaries and on the death notice; the difference made her the same age as her husband. The funeral was on Sunday, October 14.

14. John McLenaghan Stanley to Mary Stanley Legerwood, July 15, 1888; to Blanche Stanley, no date; to George Legerwood, May 26, 1891. T. O'Meara to Blanche Stanley, August 14, 1891. Charles H. Burggraf, Albany, Oregon, to Blanche Stanley, June 14, 1904. William R. Mealey, Albany, Oregon, to Blanche Stanley, February 5, 1906: Private collection.

15. "Wedding Bells," Carleton Place *Central Canadian* [n.d.], Perth *Courier*, January 9, 1891. Bertha Stanley's attendance at the Renfrew Model School and her teaching at the Scotch Corners schools are specified in her obituary, Carleton Place *Canadian* and Perth *Courier*, March 15, 1935. AM mentioned Bertha's teaching at Scotch Corners, June 20, 2003.

16. The scrapbook is in the possession of Mrs. Eleanor Chamney Henderson, Carleton Place, Ontario. AM, June 20, 2003. McGill, *A Pioneer History of the County of Lanark*, 26.

17. "The Ottawa Valley," *Something*: 246.

18. Robert B. Laidlaw, "Diary of Robert B. Laidlaw," in *Blyth: A Village Portrait*: 17–20. Also James Scott, *The Settlement of Huron County*: passim.

19. See *Illustrated Atlas of Huron County*, Morris Township.

20. The *Illustrated Atlas of Huron County* (1879) shows William Black across the road from Thomas Laidlaw. After Black's death, Munro's grandfather inherited fifty acres of land from him; when he sold his farm and moved into Blyth they retained it, since they had no proper title to it. "Chaddeleys and Flemings: 2. The Stone in the Field," *Moons*: 30–31. "Changing Places": 205–6.

21. Transcript obituary. No reference given: Private collection.

22. Transcript of interview with AM, Sheila Munro, March 1997. AM, June 20, 2003.

23. "Working for a Living": 14, 15. "The Peace of Utrecht," *Dance*: 208–9.

24. "Working for a Living": 17.

25. Robert M. Stamp, *The Schools of Ontario*, 123. 1916 enrolment figure from Molly Jordan and Florence Theobald, "Our School Year," in *Yearbook of the Ottawa Normal School, 1915–16*: 4. Library and Archives Canada, Ottawa.

26. Ottawa Normal School Register, 1898–1919; Provincial Normal Schools Training Register, 1915–16, 1916–17; Ottawa Normal School First-, Second-Class and Extra-Mural Final Examinations, 1910–11 to 1929–30. RG2-368, vols. 456, 484, 462. Archives of Ontario, Toronto. AM to Eleanor Chamney

Henderson, November 23, 1995: Private collection. *Public and Separate Schools and Teachers in the Province of Ontario, November 1917*: 57. *Schools and Teachers, November 1918*: 57.

27. Daily Record, S.S. #12, Lanark Township (1921), Archive of Ontario. Alberta Teachers Indexes, Accession 75.602. Annie Chamney appears, along with teachers named Knight, Hines, and Matheson, in *The Pleasant Country: Killam and District, 1903–1993*: 207. A 1909 photograph of the school appears on 201. AM, June 19, 2003.

28. AM to Eleanor Chamney Henderson, November 23, 1995: Private collection. Interview W. Clyde Bell, March 4, 2003.

29. AM, June 20, 2003.

30. "Working for a Living": 10. 396/87.3: 5.11: 3.

31. "Working for a Living": 13. 396/87.3: 3.4.

32. "Working for a Living": 15. 396/87.3: 5.11: 8a-b.

33. AM, June 20, 2003. 396/87.3: 5.11: 9. AM, April 22, 2004.

34. "Laidlaw – Chamney," Perth *Courier*, August 12, 1927.

35. "Working for a Living": 23, 18.

36. "Distressing Impression." 396/87.3: 5.11: 18. The *Globe and Mail* profile was the unsigned "'Writing's Something I Did, Like the Ironing.'"

37. "Material," *Something*: 43.

38. M. Alice Aitken and John Underwood, *The Book of Turnberry*: 41. Scott, *The Settlement of Huron County*: 275, *passim*, 271–77. See also Jodi Jerome, *The Evolution of Wescast*: 102 and *passim*, and *1984 Huron County Historical Atlas*: 90–93.

39. *Wingham Advance-Times*: August 4, 1927.

40. Twigg interview: 18. Munro's comments here were quoted by Wayne Grady, "Story Tellers to the World": 10, a piece that caused the *Wingham Advance-Times* to publish an anti-Alice Munro editorial in its December 16, 1981, issue. Munro's characterization of Lower Town confirmed by Julie Cruikshank, who grew up in Lower Town across the road from the Laidlaws, and for whom Munro babysat. Interview April 20, 2004. "Highway Flooded South of Town." *Wingham Advance-Times*, April 11, 1940: 1.

41. Welty, "Some Notes on River Country": 286. AM, "Everything Here Is Touchable and Mysterious": 33. Robert E. Laidlaw to AM, February 10, 1974. 38.1.65a. AM consulted her father for details for this essay; she shared the money she was paid with him: August 22, 2001.

Chapter 2

1. "An Open Letter": 6, 5. *Real Life* was not used as a title because another book, a novel by Deborah Pease, was announced for 1971 publication by Norton.

2. *Wingham Advance-Times*, July 16, 1931: 4. Catherine Sheldrick Ross, *Alice Munro: A Double Life*: 34. AM, April 3, 2003.

3. AM, April 23, 2004. Wachtel interview: 48.

4. "Home": 152–53. Italics in original.

5. "Walker Brothers Cowboy," *Dance*: 5. AM, April 23, 2004.

6. AM, June 19, 2003.

7. "A Real Life": *Open Secrets*: 80. AM, June 19, 2003. McCulloch and Simpson interview: 229. Hancock interview: 100.

8. "Home": 134–35, 136.

9. Interview Mary Ross Allen, January 28, 2004. Stapleton, "Alice Munro – Friend of Our Youth": 10.

10. AM, June 19, 2003. "Privilege," *Who*: 23–25. Hancock interview: 93. Twigg interview: 18. 2004 Wachtel interview.

11. Ross, *Alice Munro*: 34. AM, June 19, 2003.

12. Ross, *Alice Munro*: 33. 37.18.6.3.

13. "Working for a Living": 17. "Mrs. George Chamney," *Carleton Place Canadian*, March 15, 1935. *Wingham Advance-Times*: as indicated: all items: 1.

14. "Institute Held Annual Meeting," *Wingham Advance-Times*, April 27, 1939: 1. AM, June 20, 2003.

15. Interview Mary Ross Allen, January 28, 2004. Interview Audrey Boe Tiffin Marples, January 29, 2004. Interview Donna and James Hall, June 11, 2004. "School Children Missed Seeing King and Queen," *Wingham Advance-Times*, June 8, 1939: 1. AM, June 20, 2003. AM, August 5, 2004. "Changes and Ceremonies": 37.4.9.3.f3.

16. AM, August 22, 2001.

17. "Going to the Lake," *Ontario: A Bicentennial Tribute*: 51–52. Draft versions: 396/87.3: 8.4.

18. 396/87.3: 7.5. *Wilderness to Wawanosh 1867–1992*: 413. AM, June 19 and 20, 2003. Movie star: 2004 Wachtel interview.

19. "Blyth," *Wingham Advance-Times*, July 26, 1939, May 23, 1940. "Chaddeleys and Flemings: 1. Connection," *Moons*: 6.

20. "L.M. Montgomery Well Received," *Wingham Advance-Times*, November 16, 1939: 1.

21. AM, June 20, 2003. "Afterword," *Emily of New Moon*: 357, 359, 361.

22. AM, April 24, 2004, June 20, 2003.

23. AM, June 20, 2003.

24. "Remember Roger Mortimer: Dickens' 'Child's History of England' Remembered": 34, 37.

25. Tausky interview. "Boys and Girls," *Dance*: 113–14.

26. Tausky interview. Interview Audrey Boe Tiffin Marples, January 29, 2004. "Introduction," *Selected Stories*: xvi–xvii. 396/87.3: 6.5.

27. AM, "Stories": 1.

28. "Cows Electrocuted Entering Barn," *Wingham Advance-Times*, June 3, 1943: 1.

29. "The Ottawa Valley," *Something*: 237, 244.

30. "The Ottawa Valley," *Something*: 236. Italics in original. Munro called "The Peace of Utrecht" her first "painful autobiographical story" in her interview with John Metcalf: 58. Ross, *Alice Munro*: 38. AM, June 20, 2003.

31. AM, June 20, 2003. Redekop interview.

32. *Wingham Advance-Times*, April 6, 1944: 1, 5. *Lives*: 129.

33. "Entrance to High School Results," *Wingham Advance-Times*, July 23, 1944: 1. "High School Held Easter Literary," *Wingham Advance-Times*, March 15, 1945: 1.

34. "Red Dress – 1946," *Dance*: 150–51, 147, 160. Interview Audrey Boe Tiffin Marples, January 29, 2004.

35. AM, June 20, 2003. Interview Mary Ross Allen, January 28, 2004. "Changes": 37.4.8.3. 38.10.41.f25 (verso). Interview Audrey Boe Tiffin Marples, January 29, 2004. Interview Eleanor Chamney Henderson, May 21, 2003. AM, June 20, 2003. "Sunday Afternoon," *Dance*: 170, 171. AM, April 23, 2004. "Hired Girl": 82, 88, 84. Interview Julie Cruikshank, April 20, 2004.

36. AM, August 22, 2001. Interview Mary Ross Allen, January 28, 2004. Interview Audrey Boe Tiffin Marples, January 29, 2004. Mary Ross, "Prophet's Address," *Wingham Advance-Times*, May 4, 1949: 4.

37. AM, June 20, 2003, August 22, 2001, August 5, 2004. "Wingham H. S. Upper S. Results," *Wingham Advance-Times*, August 17, 1949: 1.

38. AM, June 20, 2003. "Won Scholarship at Western Univ.," *Wingham Advance-Times*, August 31, 1949: 1. "The Commencement Exercises of the Wingham High School," *Wingham Advance-Times*, December 14, 1949: 7. "Splendid Program at Commencement," *Wingham Advance-Times*, December 28, 1949: 1, 8. AM, August 5, 2004.

39. 38.10.36.2.f2, 1. "An Open Letter": 7.

Chapter 3

1. 37.6.26.3.f3. Gardiner interview: 174. Ellipsis in original. Interview Diane Lane Bessai, May 27, 2004. Interview Audrey Boe Tiffin Marples, January 29, 2004. Tausky interview. AM, August 22, 2001. Alice Laidlaw, "The Dimensions of a Shadow," Gerald Fremlin, "An Ear to a Knot Hole" [story], "Pspring Psong for Psychologists," "Death's Twilight Kingdom" [poems], "The Contributors," *Folio*, April 1950: n.p. Interview James Munro, July 9, 2002.

2. RW to Alice Laidlaw, May 18, 1951. AM to RW, May 25, 1952. National Archives Manuscript Group (MG) 31 D162. "Canadian Short Stories," *CBC Times* 4, no. 47 (June 8–14, 1952).

3. James and Ruth Davis Talman, *"Western" – 1873–1953*: 163. McKillop, *Matters of Mind*: 553–56.

4. Interview Diane Lane Bessai, May 27, 2004. Ross, *Alice Munro*: 47. "The Contributors," *Folio*, April 1951: n.p. 37.14.17. AM, April 23, 2004.

5. AM, August 22, 2001. AM, June 20, 2003. AM, August 5, 2004. Interview Joan Lawrence, January 21, 2005.

6. Interview James Munro, July 9, 2002.

7. Doug Spettigue, "Alice Laidlaw Munro: A Portrait of the Artist": 5. Interview Diane Lane Bessai, May 27, 2004. Sheila Munro, *Lives of Mothers and Daughters*: 6–8. Interview Gerald Fremlin, August 4, 2004. AM, August 5, 2004.

8. AM, August 22, 2001. Sheila Munro, *Lives of Mothers and Daughters*: 6–7. Interview Diane Lane Bessai, May 27, 2004. Alice Laidlaw, "The Dimensions of a Shadow": n.p. [4, 7, 9, 10]. AM, June 20, 2003, April 23, 2004.

9. Alice Laidlaw, "Story for Sunday": n.p. [7, 4, 5, 8].

10. "The Love of a Good Woman," *Love*: 3. 37.13.10. "Wild Swans," *Who*: 57.

11. "Is She as Kind as She Is Fair?": 37.15.26. 37.15.27.

12. Metcalf interview: 55. The waitresses are reading romance magazines in 37.15.30.8.f2. This story exists in several fragments totalling sixty-six pages, all beginnings – thus there is not a completed version of the story. Munro later drew on her Muskoka experience, she has said, when writing "The Turkey Season" (*Moons*) during the early 1980s.

13. "Munro-Laidlaw." *Wingham Advance-Times*, January 2, 1952. Interview Diane Lane Bessai, May 27, 2004.

14. Ross, *Alice Munro*: 52. "Old Mr. Black": 37.17.6.f17–19.

15. Mark Everard, "Robert Weaver's Contributions to Canadian Literature": 10, 13, 100. Interview Robert Fulford, October 16, 2003.

16. RW to Alice Laidlaw, May 18, 1951. Alice Laidlaw to RW, May 25, 1951: National Archives MG 31 D162.

17. AM to Marian Engel, August 29, 1984. Marian Engel Fonds: 31.67. Mark Abley, "Bob's Our Uncle": 9. "The Strangers": 37.16.9.

18. RW to Alice Laidlaw, June 1, 1951, July 20, 1951. Alice Laidlaw to RW, June 8, 1951: National Archives MG 31 D162. "The Liberation": 37.15.39.

19. Everard: 32–33. JM [Joyce Marshall], Reading of Alice Laidlaw's "The Shivaree" and "The Man from Melbury," RW to AM, October 3, 1952. National Archives MG 31 D162.

20. AM, August 5, 2004. AM, "Foreword." *Anthology Anthology*: ix. Interview Robert Weaver, June 17, 2004.

21. 38.12.15.1.f1. Sheila Munro, *Lives of Mothers and Daughters*: 15–16. "Cortes Island," *Love*: 117, 144, 140, 124. "Home": 136. Joyce Wayne, "Huron County Blues": 11. AM, August 22, 2001.

22. Interview James Munro, July 9, 2002. AM, August 22, 2001.

23. 38.12.15.1.f2. 38.11.6.f2–3. Interview James Munro, April 22, 2004. AM, April 23, 2004.

24. "The Beggar Maid," *Who*: 87. "Chaddeleys and Flemings 1. Connection," *Moons*: 17. "Miles City, Montana," *Progress*: 92.

25. AM, August 22, 2002. Interview Robert Weaver, June 23, 2004. AM, April 23, 2004.

26. "Cortes Island": 124–25, 142. Interview James Munro, July 9, 2002. "About Ourselves," *Mayfair*, November 1953.

27. Struthers interview: 21, 20.

28. Sheila Munro, *Lives*: 21. AM, August 22, 2003, April 23, 2004. "Material," *Something*: 31, 36–41. "The Moons of Jupiter," *Moons*: 222–23.

29. Ross, *Alice Munro*: 53. Poem: 37.20.13.17.f1–2. "S. B." ["Shoebox Babies"]: 38.11.4. "Miles City": 396/87.3: 7.3.

30. Sheila Munro, *Lives*: 22. AM, June 20, 2003. Interview James Munro, July 9, 2002.

31. Interview James Munro, July 9, 2002. "Material," *Something*: 35.

32. "The Moons of Jupiter," *Moons*: 222. Interview Daphne Cue, April 19, 2004. AM, April 23, 2004. Sheila Munro, *Lives*: 78.

33. "Miles City, Montana," *Progress*: 88. "S. B." ["Shoebox Babies"]: 38.11.4. AM, August 22, 2001. "Jakarta," *Love*: 99.

34. "The Return of the Poet": 37.16.5. "The Yellow Afternoon": 37.16.34. Munro identified these stories as dating from summer 1951. Struthers interview: 21, 22.

35. AM, April 23, 2003. "At the Other Place": 131.

36. "The Edge of Town": 368, 371. Gardiner interview: 174. Ellipsis in original. "Pastime of a Saturday Night": 37.1552.f1. Also 37.15.53. Unsigned stories: AM, August 5, 2004.

37. RW to AM, January 24, 1956, RW to Robert Patchell, May 31, 1955: National Archives MG 31 D162. Interview Robert Weaver, June 17, 2004.

38. Weaver to Patchell, May 31, 1955. RW to AM, January 24, 1956. National Archives MG 31 D162. "Chatelaine Centre," *Chatelaine*, March 1956: 1.

39. RW to AM, May 16, 1957: National Archives MG 31 D162.

40. JM [Joyce Marshall], CBC Critique, "Thanks for the Ride" and "The Chesterfield Suite." RW to Robert Patchell, May 31, 1955: National Archives MG 31 D162.

41. RW to AM, January 24, 1956: National Archives MG 31 D162. "Thanks for the Ride": 37.6.60 (earliest version, signed by Weaver); 37.6.61.1–2 (revision, also signed by Weaver); 37.6.62. AM, April 23, 2004. AM, August 22, 2001. "Chaddeleys and Flemings: 1. Connection," *Moons*: 6.

42. AM to Mary McAlpine, October 14, 1980: Mary McAlpine Fonds, University of British Columbia.

43. James King, *The Life of Margaret Laurence*: 158. AM, June 20, 2003. Interview James Munro, July 9, 2002. Moira Farrow, "Housewife Finds Time to Write Short Stories."

44. "Funorama": 38.11.5. Patrick, Rose's husband in *Who*, is at one point referred to as "a man who wouldn't let me hang up a ten-dollar Chagall print": 37.11.14.14.f1. Munro remembered and described this print again at the beginning of "Soon."

45. AM, August 22, 2001. "Golden Apples": 23.

46. In the Alice Munro Fonds there are numerous versions of stories featuring Franklin, coming home from the war, getting off the train early. See, for example, a story called "The Boy Murderer," or "The War Hero," 37.16.28. Although the Fonds identify these as short stories, Munro has said "The Boy Murderer" was an attempted novel. AM, April 23, 2004. "Death of a White Fox": 37.3.1.3, 37.3.6.3.f 18–19. See also 37.3.1–11. AM, April 23, 2004.

47. RW to AM, March 28, 1958, December 8, 1958, December 12, 1958, December 17, 1958 (telegram), January 21, 1959. AM to RW, January 4, 1959: National Archives MG 31 D162. Original December 12, 1958: 37.2.8.3.

48. "Funeral Friday for Mrs. Robert Laidlaw," *Wingham Advance-Times*, February 18, 1959: 1. Interview Julie Cruikshank, April 29, 2004.

49. AM, June 20, 2003. "The Peace of Utrecht," *Dance*: 209.

50. Metcalf interview: 58. Struthers interview: 21.

51. "Places at Home" ["The Peace of Utrecht"] 37.6.26.f3. "The Peace of Utrecht," *Dance*: 196, 201, 199, 195. "The Ottawa Valley," *Something*: 246.

52. "The Peace of Utrecht": 37.6.28.f1, 37.6.33.1–3. AM to RW, n.d. [1959], October 13, 1959, October 24, 1959, December 5, 1959: National Archives MG 31 D162.

53. Irving Layton, "Keine Lazarovitch 1870–1959," *Tamarack Review*: 22.

Chapter 4

1. "I was trying to find a meaning": Gardiner interview: 174. "You don't really": AM to Audrey Coffin, April 3, 1968, transcript copy: Private collection. Robert E. Laidlaw to John Chamney, November 20, [1960]: Private collection.

2. "The Time of Death," *Dance*: 89, 90, 94, 98–99.

3. Gardiner interview: 173–74. Struthers interview: 23. RW to AM, March 28, 1958. National Archives MG 31 D162. Earle Toppings to AM, March 3, 1967: Private collection. Giose Rimanelli, Introduction, *Modern Canadian Stories*: xxvii. Robert Weaver, Introduction, *Ten for Wednesday Night*: xvii.

4. *Ten for Wednesday Night*: 74. Farrow, "Housewife Finds Time to Write Short Stories." AM to RW, n.d. [1959], December 5, 1959: National Archives MG 31 D162.

5. Struthers interview: 20. Interview James Munro, July 9, 2002.

6. AM to RW, January 4, 1959. National Archives MG 31 D162. Maria Taaffe, "*The Montrealer* and Canadian Short Stories": 8–14 and *passim*. Interview Gerald Taaffe, May 9, 2003. AM, August 5, 2004.

7. Struthers interview: 23. Gerald Taaffe to AM, August 17, 1961, November 15, 1961, June 8, 1962: 37.2.27.1–3.

8. 37.7.22. This file contains sixteen photocopied reviews of *The First Five Years*; while some of them single Munro out, most do not.

9. Interview Gerald Taaffe, May 9, 2003. E-mail from him, July 22, 2004.

10. RW to AM, August 24, 1961: 37.2.8.4. Theodore M. Purdy to AM, September 26, 1961: 37.2.1. J.G. McClelland to AM, October 12, 1961: 37.2.22.1. Hugh Kane to AM, November 15, 1961: 37.2.22.2.

11. RW to AM, November 22, 1961: 37.2.8.8. AM, August 22, 2001. John Robert Colombo to AM, n.d.: 37.2.39.1. Because Colombo begins this letter referring to John Webster Grant's letter of "a year ago," and he concludes with a reference to a recent story in the *Montrealer* that could only have been "The Office" (September 1962), this letter was likely written late in 1962. E-mail John Robert Colombo, February 4, 2003.

12. Interview Earle Toppings, January 3, 2003.

13. Interview Sheila Munro, July 11, 2002. Interview Jenny Munro, January 8, 2003. AM, "An Appreciation": 33. AM, April 24, 2004. Early version of Miles City incident connected with *Who*: 37.9.9.1. Cather, "Miss Jewett": 76.

14. "In the spring of 1963. . . .": 396/87.3: 6.2. "On Writing 'The Office'": 260, 261. "The Office," *Dance*: 59, 60–61, 74. "An Appreciation": 32. Interview James Munro, July 9, 2002. Interview Jenny Munro, January 8, 2003. Interview Daphne Cue, April 19, 2004.

15. "In the spring of 1963. . . .": 396/87.3: 6.2. AM, June 20, 2003. AM, August 22, 2001. Interview James Munro, July 9, 2002 and April 22, 2004. Interview Daphne Cue, April 19, 2004. MacSkimming, *The Perilous Trade*: 35–36 and "The Great Original": 13.

16. "Then at the beginning. . . .": 396/87.3: 6.2.

17. *Victoria Daily Times*, September 14, 1963: 12, October 12, 1963: 8, October 19, 1963: 6. Ross, *Alice Munro*: 61. AM, June 20, 2003. "Save on wage bill": AM to Earle Toppings, March 21, 1967: Private collection. Interview Craig Barrett and Ernest Hunter, October 17, 2003. E-mail George Cuomo, January 31, 2004. 396/87.3: 6.2.

18. AM to Earle Toppings, November 30, 1964. Earle Toppings to AM, December 2, 1964. AM to Earle Toppings, October 28, 1965: Private collection. Interview Earle Toppings, January 3, 2003.

19. AM to Earle Toppings, February 23, 1967: Private collection. AM, August 22, 2001. Ross, *Alice Munro*: 64. Tudor house: 37.19.28.4.f4.

20. Earle Toppings to AM, March 3, 1967. AM to Earle Toppings, March 14, 1967, March 21, 1967: Private collection. There is a manuscript of "The Office" in Alice Munro Fonds with AM's annotation, "Dear Earle – Here it is in manuscript – I lost the magazine": 37.6.20. Ross, *Alice Munro*: 64. Interview James Munro, April 22, 2004. AM, June 20, 2003.

21. Original contract for *Dance of the Happy Shades*. McGraw-Hill Ryerson, Whitby, Ontario. AM, August 22, 2001. Order of composition: Struthers interview: 20. "Postcard" was first published in the *Tamarack Review* in its spring 1968 issue; initially they were going to publish "Walker Brothers Cowboy" as well, but did not. RW to Earle Toppings, January 26, 1968: Private collection. Author visit to Rockland house, July 9, 2002. A 1969 profile in the *Victoria Daily Times* mentions that Munro's typewriter "sits in an upstairs room in proximity to domestic necessities such as a washing machine and a sewing machine." Jan Gould, "Memory, Experiences of 'Normal Life' Feed Her Fiction."

22. Earle Toppings to AM, March 5, 1968, January 15, 1968 (two letters). AM to Audrey Coffin, March 27, 1968 (transcript): Private collection.

23. Georgeanna [Hamilton] to Hugh Garner, March 13, 1968. Robin M. Farr to Georgeanna Hamilton, March 13, 1968. Audrey Coffin to Hugh Garner, March 28, March 29, April 4, May 10, 1968. Hugh Garner to Audrey Coffin, May 11, 1968. "The Stories of Alice Munro" (carbon of original submission). Correspondence, January–May 1968: Hugh Garner Fonds, Queen's University.

24. AM to Audrey Coffin, April 3, 1968 (transcript). Earle Toppings to Audrey Coffin, April 8, 1968. Here Toppings comments on "Images," which he has read in manuscript, Garner's foreword, and approves the idea of having Robert Weaver write the blurb for the back of the dust jacket. He also makes suggestions as to the book's design, and how to handle the designer. Earle Toppings to Audrey Coffin, April 10, 1968, transcript copy: Private collection. Here he advocates *Dance of the Happy Shades* over *Walker Brothers Cowboy* for the book's title. Date of publication: Frank Flemington to Hugh Garner, September 24, 1968. Correspondence, June–December 1968: Hugh Garner Fonds, Queen's University.

25. E-mail George Cuomo January 31, interview February 3, 2004. "My almost only": 396/87.3: 6.6. This is an earlier draft of "On John Metcalf: Taking Writing Seriously," where the passage has become "A creative writing teacher at the University of Victoria had told me that I wrote the kind of things he used to write when he was fifteen" (6). Russell did not join the faculty until after this incident. Sheila Munro, *Lives of Mothers and Daughters*: 191. AM, April 23, 2004. E-mail Lawrence Russell, August 13, 2003.

26. Advertisement for *Dance of the Happy Shades*, one of "the Ryerson Collection of Fine Canadian Books," *Globe and Mail, Globe Magazine*, n.d. [1968]. Dorothy Bishop, "A Novel of the Week." Kent Thompson, radio script review of *Dance of the Happy Shades* by Alice Munro, CBZ Fredericton. Leo Simpson, radio script review of *Dance* and *Miracle at Indian River* by Alden Nowlan. *Anthology*. All items 37.7.18.

27. All reviews 37.7.18.

28. Hilda Kirkwood, rev. of *Dance*: 260. Kent Thompson, *Fiddlehead* rev. of *Dance*: 71. Audrey Thomas, "'She's Only a Girl,' He Said": 91, 92. David Helwig, "Canadian Letters": 128. Beth Harvor, "The Special World of the WW's": 3.

29. Robin Farr to AM, March 18, 1969 and advance press release on Governor General's Award nominees (March 18, 1969) by Gerald Taaffe and Mario Lavoie: 37.2.39.4. John Peter: 126. AM, April 23, 2004. "Literary Fame Catches City Mother Unprepared." *Victoria Daily Times*, April 22, 1969. William French, "The Establishment Beware! These Awards Are With It." *Globe and Mail*, April 22, 1969: 13. "B. C. Mother of Three Wins Top Literary Award." *Vancouver Sun*: 1, 13. "Victoria Woman's Book Wins Literary Award." *Victoria Daily Colonist*, April 22, 1969: 1–2. "Ex-Wingham Resident Wins Literary Award." *London Free Press*, April 22, 1969. Newspaper stories 37.20.22. "Oakville Wife Wins Literary Prize": 709/01.15:5.1. Mrs. P. Schwantje to AM, April 23, 1969: 37.2.55.4.

30. William French, "Leonard Cohen Wants to Be Governor-General." *Globe and Mail*, May 17, 1969: 25. Mordecai Richler, "A Little Noblesse Oblige Goes a Long Way at the Top." *Victoria Daily Times*, June 21, 1969: 5. Interview Robert Weaver, July 3, 2001. Connolly, Freake, Sherman interview: 10.

31. Toppings interview. Jan Gould, "Memory, Experiences of 'Normal Life' Feed Her Fiction": 37.20.22. AM, August 5, 2004. "Woman Author Wins Award." *Toronto Star*, February 3, 1973: 37.20.22. This was a Canadian Press story, so it was syndicated. Munro mentioned this incident often in interviews.

32. Interview John Metcalf, June 17, 2002. AM, "On John Metcalf": 6.

33. "Author's Commentary": 126. "The Colonel's Hash Resettled": 183.

34. E-mails Audrey Thomas, August 1 and 2, 2004. Interview Margaret Atwood, January 27, 2004. Phoebe Larmore to Toivo Kiil, December 22, 1975: Private collection.

35. John Morgan Gray, "Canadian Books," Earle Birney, "Canadian Publishing," in "Publishing in Canada," *Canadian Literature*: 27, 12. My "Gazing Through the One-Way Mirror" develops these contexts as they affect Canadian literature in more detail; see also MacSkimming and, for a contemporary assessment of book publishing, Robert Weaver's "Books."

36. Peter Sypnowich, "It Was a Sad, Sad Day for Ryerson Press Staff," *Toronto Star*, November 3, 1970: 34. George Parker, "Sale of Ryerson Press": 29. "McGraw-Hill Takes Over Ryerson," *Quill & Quire*, December 11, 1970: 1.

37. AM to Earle Toppings, November 24, December 16, 1970. Audrey Coffin to Earle Toppings [January 1970]: Private collection.

38. Margaret Laurence to Audrey Coffin, December 30, 1968: Private collection. Margaret Laurence to Judith Jones, February 10, 1969. Also Laurence to Jones, February 25, March 8, and July 19, 1969. Jones to

Laurence, February 19, 1969. Alfred A. Knopf Archive. E-mail Judith Jones, May 3, 2004.

39. "On Writing 'The Office'": 261. AM, August 5, 2004. AM to Audrey Coffin, October 22, 1970: Private Collection. AM to Audrey Coffin, December 10 and 22, 1970: 396/87.3: 1.119. Audrey Coffin to AM, December 14, 1970: 37.2.24.1.

40. *Lives*: [iv, vii]. Tausky interview. 37.4.40–41. 396/87.3: 1.119. Struthers interview: 25. Tausky, "'What Happened to Marion?'."

41. Miss Musgrave: 37.4.22. "Walker Brothers Cowboy" and *Lives*: 37.3.12. 396/87.3: 1.119. Tausky interview. *Lives*: 253.

42. 37.4.17.f4. Interview Toivo Kiil, January 7, 2003. Toivo Kiil to AM, March 10 and 23, 1971: 37.2.24.2-3. VB to John Diamond, January 17, 1983: 396/87.3: 2a.1. All materials connected with the production of *Lives* and *Something I've Been Meaning to Tell You* at McGraw-Hill Ryerson, including contracts, appear to have been destroyed by the firm.

43. E.D. Ward-Harris, rev. of *Lives*. Quoted from ad *Victoria Daily Times* December 11, 1971: 23. 37.5.14.

44. Irene Howard, "An Elegant Look at the World of Women": 23. 37.5.14. Clara Thomas, "Woman Invincible": 96. James Polk, "Deep Caves Paved with Kitchen Linoleum": 102–04.

45. "Alice Munro Wins CBA Award": 8. Bryan L. Bacon (British Columbia Library Association) to AM, September 29, 1972: 37.2.6. Toivo Kiil to AM, October 13, and November 13, 1972: 37.2.25.1–2.

Chapter 5

1. *Lives*: 240. Connolly, Freake, Sherman interview: 8. "Soon," *Runaway*: 87, 88. In between these two instances, Munro also used Chagall's *I and the Village* in draft material connected to *Lives*; as in "Soon," a print of it is a character's present to her mother: 37.4.40.1. "Funorama": 38.11.5. AM, August 5, 2004. "The Author," *Dance* dust-jacket flap.

2. Sheila Munro, *Lives*: 199, 201. Interview James Polk, June 8, 2004.

3. Ross, *Alice Munro*: 64. Sheila Munro, *Lives*: 82–84. AM, June 20, 2003.

4. AM, June 20, 2003. "Jakarta," *Love*. Sheila Munro, *Lives*: 208–9, 83, 84, 219–20, 82. AM, April 23, 2004.

5. "Material," *Something*: 42, 35, 43. "Chaddeleys and Flemings: 1. Connection," *Moons*: 18. "Miles City, Montana," *Progress*: 91–92.

6. AM to JM, November 26, 1969, June 11, 1971, John Metcalf Fonds: 24.24.1.5, 24.21.10.28. AM, April 23, 2004. AM to Marian Engel, August 29, 1984, Marian Engel Fonds: 31.67.

7. AM to Earle Toppings, June 8, July 26, August 31, September 12, 1972. Earle Toppings to AM, July 11, 1972: Private collection. He "looked bad enough": 12 September.

8. Ross, *Alice Munro*: 75. Thomas, "Initram." AM, April 23, 2004.

9. RW to AM, November 27, [1971 or '72?]: 37.1.29. Earle Toppings to AM, March 5, 1968: Private collection. AM to JM, February 5, 1973, John Metcalf Fonds: 24.13.32.17. 1973 income tax return: 38.2.75. RW to AM, April 18, 1973: 37.2.8.11.

10. JM to Desmond [Pacey], March 6, 1973: 24.13.32.25. AM to JM, January 15, February 5, August 12, 1973. John Metcalf Fonds: 24.13.32.12-13, 87.

11. Interview Margaret Atwood, January 27, 2004. Details of teaching appointment: L.A.D. Morey to AM, March 6, April 2, 1973: 37.2.33.1-2. E.D. Baravale to AM, May 4, 1973: 37.2.33.3.

12. "Creative Writing": 37.19.27.3, 10, 8. "Eternal Springs" is the version of the story in which the husband teaches at the college: 37.14.46. "Red Dress – 1946," *Dance*: 160. AM, April 23, 2004.

13. D.R. Ewen to AM, January 18, 1974: 37.2.52. E-mail Mary Swan, February 24, 2004. AM, June 20, 2003.

14. John Metcalf Fonds: 24.48.17.f23. The version in *New Canadian Stories* is dated November 12, 1973, the dedication remains though "with love" has been omitted.

15. William French. "Script for CBC on Writers' Union." Broadcast November 11, 1971. William French Collection. Toivo Kiil to AM, November 13, 1972: 37.2.25.2. Interview Toivo Kiil, January 7, 2003.

16. Geoffrey Wolff, "Call It Fiction": 66. The Denise Levertov review of *Lives* is an unidentified proof copy in the Alice Munro Fonds; its published source has not been identified. See 37.5.15.

17. See 37.15.16.

18. See 37.7.19–20.

19. Toivo Kiil to AM, November 13, 1972: 37.2.25.2. Interview Toivo Kiil, January 7, 2003. AM, April 23, 2004.

20. Toivo Kiil to AM, August 23, 1973: 38.1.80.2. McGraw-Hill Ryerson Royalty Statement January–June 1974 shows a $5,000 advance for *Something*: 38.1.80.4 a–c.

21. Robert Fulford, "Tamarack Review Returns to Offer Good Writing." "Material," *Something*: 42. AM, April 23, 2004. "Real People": 37.8.8. Munro identified this as dating from the 1960s.

22. These generalizations are supported by draft materials in the Alice Munro Fonds (37.7-9). Alice Kelling, Chris's fiancé in "How I Met My Husband," was in the same position in "Death of White Fox" (see 37.3.6.3.f1). And Robina, in "Executioners," was from a family connected to the Frenches in *Lives*. The double murder Mr. Lougheed dreams about in "Walking on Water" is related to "The Boy Murderer," which was in *Lives*, as was Miss Musgrave, who used to own the house in which he lives. In one fragment a Mr. Lougheed plays cards with her in Mock Hill, a place name Munro used in *Something* (37.14.2-0-22, 37.4.21.26).

23. AM, June 19, 2003. AM, April 23, 2004. "Mrs. W.C. Laidlaw Dies in 90th Year," *Wingham Advance-Times*, January 13, 1966. "Winter Wind," *Something*: 195, 204, 206, 201. "The Ottawa Valley," *Something*: 246.

24. "The Ottawa Valley," *Something*: 244–46. AM, "A Walk on the Wild Side": 38, 41. "Home": 153.

25. Interview Jack Hodgins, April 21, 2004. AM, June 20, 2003. Struthers interview: 26–28. John Metcalf Fonds, 24.20: *passim*. "Home": 152.

26. Interview Toivo Kiil, January 7, 2003. The manuscript of *Something* used for typesetting is in the Alice Munro Fonds (37.9.1–2) and, in addition, there are manuscript pages connected with individual stories showing Munro rejecting proposed changes. See for example, 38.3.3, from "Executioners."

27. David Stouck, rev. of *Something*: 46. E.D. Blodgett, rev. of *Something*: 100. See also *passim*.

28. Bette Howland, "Tricks, Trap-Doors, a Writer's Craft." Frederick Busch, "A Trio of Fictions": 54. Susan Cushman, "Munro's Story Collection Is her Weakest So Far." 37.9.4, *passim*.

29. Joanna Beyersbergen, "No Bitterness or Anxiety for Writer": 70.

30. John Metcalf Fonds: 24.20, *passim*. Fred Bodsworth to AM, October 31, 1974: 37.2.5. AM, June 20, 2003.

31. Elizabeth Christman (Coordinator, Great Lakes College Association) to AM, May 28, 1974: 37.2.17. Paul Vasey, "Alice Has a Lot of Reasons to Be Happy": 38.13.5. AM, August 22, 2001. Audrey Coffin to AM, October 7, 1974: 37.2.25.5.

32. John Metcalf Fonds: 24.20, *passim*. Rehearsal of "Home": 24.45.6. Loyola Reading: 24.43.2.

33. Draft "Married People": 38.11.4. Interview John Metcalf, June 17, 2002. "Married People," John Metcalf Fonds: 24.48.16.f2, 21.

34. Audrey Coffin to AM, October 7, 1974: 37.2.25.5. Douglas Gibson to AM, August 26, 1974, January 23, 1975: 37.2.20.2-3. Interview Douglas M. Gibson, October 16, 2003.

35. Interview Peter D'Angelo, October 3, 2003. DG to AM, February 4, 1976: 37.2.20.6. *The McGregors*: Gibson to AM, April 21, 1977: Macmillan Canada Archive. Toivo Kiil to AM, March 7, 1975: 37.2.25.6.

36. AM to Audrey Thomas, March 3, 1974: Audrey Thomas Papers 3: 6. Stan Dragland, "Alice Munro at the University of Western Ontario." Unpublished memoir. July 1, 2003. John Metcalf Fonds, 24.20: *passim*. Letter James Reaney, March 24, 2003. E-mail Mary Swan, February 24, 2004. Interview Leo Simpson, August 20, 2004.

37. Interview Gerald Fremlin, August 4, 2004. AM, August 22, 2001. John Metcalf Fonds, 24.20: *passim*. AM to DG, September 16, 1975: Macmillan of Canada Archive. AM to Audrey Thomas, March 20, 1975: Audrey Thomas Papers 3: 6.

Chapter 6

1. Alice Quinn to VB, July 7, 1977: 37.2.47.15c. "Who Do You Think You Are." Advance proof of supplanted *Who Do You Think You Are?* (August 11, 1978): 229. John and Myrna Metcalf Collection: item 6000. Menaker quotation: CM to VB, February 28, 1977: 37.2.47.6b. "Privilege," "Royal Beatings," *Who*: 36–37, 5. "The Ottawa Valley," *Something*: 246. "Introduction," *Selected Stories*: xv–xvi.

2. "Places at Home": 37.13.10.1–4, 13. *Lives*: 253. "Names": 37.13.9.4. "Churches and Lodges": 37.13.10.13. "Kill a Chicken": 37.13.10.17.

3. "Places at Home": 37.13.10.5–8, 11–12, 14–19.

4. "Notes on Mame Pinning" (April 19, 1975): 37.9.18. AM identified this as Fremlin's writing, April 23, 2004. "Visitors" in "Places at Home": 37.13.11.f25–26. AM to DG, September 16, 1975: Macmillan: 429: 4.

5. AM to DG, n.d. [July–August 1975?], September 16, December 30, 1975: Macmillan: 429: 4. DG to AM, July 22, 1975: Macmillan: 429: 4, October 9, 1975: 37.2.20.4, December 23, 1975: 37.2.20.5. Interview Peter D'Angelo, October 3, 2003.

6. *Lives*: 246–47. "Clues," "Places at Home": 37.13.10.23.f1–2.

7. John Metcalf Fonds: 24.20. AM to DG, December 30, 1975, March 6, 1976, DG to AM, July 22, 1975, March 10, 1976: Macmillan: 429: 4. DG to AM, February 4, 1976: 37.2.20.

8. AM, June 20, 2003. "Places at Home" title sheet: 37.12.23.2.

9. AM, April 23, 2004. Notes on Treatment: 37.20.3.3. John Metcalf Fonds: 24.20. AM, August 5, 2004.

10. "The Stories of Alice Munro" (carbon of original submission): 2. Correspondence January–May 1968: Hugh Garner Fonds, Queen's University. Interview Margaret Atwood, January 27, 2004. Phoebe Larmore to Toivo Kiil, December 22, 1975. VB to Toivo Kiil, January 23, 1976: Private collection. Interview Toivo Kiil, October 12, 2004.

11. Blaise: VB to AM, March 14, 1977: 37.2.47.7, March 11, March 22, 1976: 37.2.47.2–3. Interview VB, January 14, 2003.

12. John Metcalf Fonds: 24.20. Leslie Peterson, "Nothing to Tell Us."

13. "Alice Laidlaw Munro": 113. D.C. Williams to AM, February 12, 1976: 37.2.45. "Seven to Receive Honorary Degrees" [*London Free Press*? n.d.]: 37.20.22. Order of Canada: AM, June 19, 2003.

14. John Metcalf Fonds: 24.20. "Robert Laidlaw Dies in London": *Wingham Advance-Times*, August 19, 1976: 10. AM, August 22, 2001. Sheila Munro quotes these letters from Laidlaw to Munro, *Lives of Mothers and Daughters*: 223, 114. Ellipsis in original. 396/87.3: 3.4.

15. Struthers interview: 21. "Miles City, Montana," *Progress*: 93, 94. *Who*: 5. CM to VB, December 13, 1984: 396/87.3: 2.13.

16. Interview James Munro, July 9, 2002. VB to AM, October 4, 1976, October 19, 1976. November 1, [1976]: 38.2.63.2–4. Interview CM, January 14, 2003. E-mail Daniel Menaker, August 10, 2003.

17. The *New Yorker*, Ross, and Shawn have a considerable literature surrounding them. In understanding the magazine's history and personalities, books by Bodsford, Gill, Kunkel, Mehta, and Yagoda are useful to varying degrees. There are also numerous articles, particularly connected with Shawn's dismissal in 1987. Throughout this writing, Shawn's motives, mien, and significance are continual questions.

18. Interview CM, January 14, 2003. CM to VB, November 17, 1976: 38.2.63.6. VB to AM, November 17, 1976: 37.2.47.3. CM to AM, November 18, 1976: 37.2.30.1. Munro received just under $3,300 for "Royal Beatings": VB to AM, January 27, 1977: 38.2.63.8.

19. CM to AM, January 11, 1977: 37.2.30.3. Interview VB, January 14, 2003. CM to VB, February 28, 1977: 37.2.47.6b, December 21, 1976: 37.2.47.4.

20. VB to AM, March 2, 1977: 37.2.47.6a, March 22, 1977: 37.2.47.8. Kate Medina to VB, March 8, 1977: 37.2.47.8. Gordon Lish to Mary Evans, May 13, 1977: 37.2.47.11. Anne Mollegen Smith to VB, April 6, 1977: 37.2.47.10. VB to AM, June 15, 1977: 37.2.47.13.

21. Alice Quinn to VB, July 7, 1977: 37.2.47.15c.

22. VB to AM, December 12, 1977: 38.2.63.9. CM to AM, December 8, 1977: *New Yorker* files (NYPL): 897:12.

23. "Who Do You Think You Are?" Advance proof of supplanted *Who Do You Think You Are?* (August 11, 1978): 229. John and Myrna Metcalf Collection: item 6000. Living with the man's mother: 37.19.63. AM, April 24, 2004. CM to AM, August 3, 1977: 37.2.30.4. Four-part "Simon's Luck": 37.11.20. CM to VB, December 5, 1977: 38.2.63.9. CM to VB, April 12, 1978: *New Yorker* (NYPL): 907:5. Shift to first person: 38.3.21.

24. John Metcalf Fonds: 24.20. William French, "Richler and Munro Are Alive and Well Between Books": 15.

25. "Munro Awarded Literary Prize," *Globe and Mail*, January 23, 1977: 13.

26. "Novelist Fights Book Banning," *Montreal Star*, May 25, 1978: B11. AM to Margaret Laurence, February 23, 1976: Margaret Laurence Fonds: 1980–001/008 (098). "Writer Uses Bible to Thwart Banning of Books," *Globe and Mail*, June 14, 1978: 9. Turnberry Township: "Drive to Ban Books 'Like Nazi Censorship,'" *London Free Press*, May 27, 1978: D1. William French, "The Good Book Versus Good Books": 16. Jeff Seddon, "Book Debate Attracts 500 to CHSS," *Clinton News-Record*, June 15, 1978: 1. Munro speech text: 38.12.33.1.f2–4. "Ultimately": Carol Off, "Munro Speaks Out On Rights," [UWO] *Gazette*, January 13, 1979. AM to Margaret Laurence, July 16, 1978: Margaret Laurence Fonds: 1980–001/008 (098). See also

Paul Stuewe, "Better Dead Than Read": 3–7, and Timothy Findley, "Better Dead Than Read? An Opposing View": 3–5. Also AM, "On Stuewe and Censorship": 39–40.

27. "A Concerned Mother of Two Sons" from Clinton to AM, May 23, 1978: 38.2.74.9. Another such letter, also anonymous though from Alberta, is 38.2.74.11. [Barry Wenger,] "A Genius of Sour Grapes": 3. E-mail Henry Hess (then editor, *Wingham Advance-Times*) June 14, 2004. Joyce Wayne, "Huron County Blues": 9.

28. VB to AM, December 12, 1977: 38.2.63.9. VB to Robin Brass, Jack Stoddard, January 20, 1977: 37.2.47.5a–d. VB to Bella Pomer, May 17, 1977: Macmillan 429: 4. John Pearce to VB, July 4, 1977: 37.2.47.15b. Robin Brass to VB, November 16, 1977: 37.2.47.19.

29. VB to AM, October 7, 1977: 37.2.47.18. DG to AM, April 21, 1977, AM to DG, January 22, 1978, DG to AM, February 7, 1978, Robert Stuart to DG, February 23, 1978: Macmillan 429: 4.

30. AM to DG, February 22, 1978, VB to DG, March 8, 1978, Charlotte Weiss to DG, Jan Walter, and Robert Stuart, April 6, 1978, Bill Baker to DG, April 10, 1978, DG to AM, April 25, 1978, VB to DG, May 3, 1978: Macmillan 429: 4.

31. Kate Medina to AM, December 19, 1978: 38.1.35.1. "Knopf, Norton, and Viking": R.J. Stuart to Herbert K. Schnall (president, New American Library), May 19, 1977: Macmillan 429: 4. Interview Virginia Barber, January 14, 2003. AM to Sherry Huber (two letters), May 19, 1977: 38.2.64.4–5.

32. "Rose and Janet," Pratt's *Young Woman in a Slip*: DG to Rick Miller, May 23, 1978; "exciting": returned annotated copy. "Who": AM to DG [n.d. May 1978?] "Disgust and dismay": DG to Trade Division, May 26, 1978. DG to VB, June 15, 1978. VB to DG, June 9, 1978. "Danby": DG to W.H. Clarke, August 31, 1978. Macmillan 429: 4.

33. "'Rose and Janet': Alice Munro's Metafiction": 67, 68. See also Linda Leitch: *passim*, 150–71. Helen Hoy, Interview Sherry Huber: February 22, 1988. [Sherry Huber,] Notes 11 June 1978: 38.2.64.7. AM to Sherry Huber, August 21, 1978: 38.2.64.8. Sherry Huber to AM, August 25, September 12, 1978: 38.2.64.9–10. Contents: 38.5.4.f5. Shift to past tense: "Royal Beatings": 38.5.1. "True Enemies": 38.5.5. "Privilege," *Who*: 36–37. [Sherry Huber] Draft Norton flap copy: 38.5.9.f1. AM to Sherry Huber, September 16 and 19, 1978: W.W. Norton.

34. Interview DG, July 3, 2001. DG to Trade Division, Macmillan, September 21, 1978: Macmillan 429: 4. AM to Sherry Huber, September 19, 1978: W.W. Norton. B. Hamilton to DG, September 18, 1978. DG to R.J. Stuart, September 22, 1978. R.J. Stuart to AM, September 22, 1978: Macmillan 429: 4. See also Martin Knelman, "The Past, the Present, and Alice Munro."

35. DG to VB, October 25, 1978: Macmillan 429: 4. Interview Virginia Barber, January 14, 2003. VB to AM, November 7, 1978: 38.2.63.16. AC to AM, November 13, 1978: 38.1.3.5. DG to AC, DG to Robert Gottlieb, November 22, 1978: Macmillan 429: 4. AC to AM, January 19, 1979: 38.1.3.6. AC to DG, December 11, 1978: Macmillan 429: 4.

36. DG, "Alice Munro." Reprinting: Jan Walter to Carol McCarthy, January 9, 1979. DG to Linda Taylor (Trade Promotion, Macmillan), August 16, 1978: Macmillan: 429: 4.

37. Wayne Grady, "Alice Through a Glass Darkly": 15. *Who* review file: Macmillan: 401:1.

38. Sam Solecki, "Letters in Canada 1978": 319, 320. Gerald Noonan, rev. of *Who*: 151. Michael Taylor, rev. of *Who*: 126, 127.

39. Urjo Kareda, "The War Within Alice Munro's Heroine": 62, 63. DG to VB, November 24, 1978: Macmillan 429: 4. Chair: Margaret Laurence to Judith Jones, June 28, 1979: 38.1.3.11. Robert J. Stuart to AM, March 27, 1979: 38.1.75.8. VB to DG, March 5, 1979, February 13, 1979. Australia visit: Paul Myer to DG, April 10, 1979: Macmillan 429: 4.

40. AC to AM, January 19, 1979: 38.1.3.6. AM to AC, January 24, 1979: Private collection. Fact sheet: 38.1.3.8b. Planned Norton cover: Helen Hoy, Interview Sherry Huber: February 22, 1988. "The Beggar Maid," *Who*: 77. Linda Xiques, "The Beggar Maid." *The Beggar Maid* reviews file (U.S.): 38.7.2.

41. Joyce Carol Oates, "Books": 72, 74. Ted Morgan, "Writers Who Happen to Be Women": 78. Thomas R. Edwards, "It's Love!": 44. Paul Wilner, "Virtue Wins": 43. Joanna Higgins, "To Bridge Gulfs and Make Connections": 29.

42. AC to AM, June 19, 1980: 38.1.3.21. Knopf Royalty Sheet, March 31, 1981: 38.1.3.24.

43. Alan Hollinghurst, "Elapsing Lives": 830, 831. One of the judges of the 1979 described the group's work on their decision: Margaret Forster, "Secrets of a Glittering Prize." *The Beggar Maid* reviews file (U.K.): 38.7.3. Sales: VB to AM, April 15, 1982: 38.2.63.84. Timothy Findley, "The McGregors."

Chapter 7

1. "Chaddeleys and Flemings: 1. Connection," *Moons*: 6–7. "Circle of Prayer," *Progress*: 273. David Macfarlane, "Writer in Residence": 56. DG to AM, September 5, 1980. AM to DG, October 13, 1980. Macmillan: 429: 4. Margaret Smith, "Telling Life as It Is." Family book: AM, April 24, 2004. CM to AM, November 1, 1977: 37.2.30.5. CM to VB, April 9, 1980: *New Yorker* (NYPL): 927:17. "Munro bonanza": CM to VB, December 13, 1984: 396/87.3: 2.13.

2. VB to AM, June 24, 1980: 38.2.63.46. VB to AM, March 27, 1980: 38.2.63.43. CM to AM, October 15, 1984: 396/87.3: 2.13. David Macfarlane, "Writer in Residence": 56.

3. Ending cut off and moved to "Connection": 396/87.3: 4.6. "Chaddeleys and Flemings: 2. The Stone in the Field," "Chaddeleys and Flemings: 1. Connection," *Moons*: 35, 18. [Robert Fulford,] "This Month: The Past, the Present, and Alice Munro": 11.

4. Martin Knelman, "The Past, the Present, and Alice Munro": 18, 22. CM to VB, December 13, 1984: 396/87.3: 2.13. Hilda Kirkwood to AM, February 17, 1981: 38.1.19.2. Elizabeth Spenser to AM, March 18, 1981: 38.2.33.

5. Alan Twigg, "Alice Doesn't Live Here Any More – But She's a Distinguished Visitor." *Province* (Vancouver), March 9, 1980: 12. AM to JM, December 31, 1980, October 16, 1981: John Metcalf Fonds: 24.8.9.1–2. "Through the Jade Curtain": 51, 55.

6. Wayne Grady, "Story Tellers to the World": 10. [Barry Wenger,] "A Genius of Sour Grapes." Wenger wrote editorial, general feelings in Wingham about AM: e-mail, Henry Hess (then editor, *Wingham Advance-Times*) June 14, 2004. Joyce McDougall, "The Truth Behind Alice Munro's Tales." AM, "Writer Denies Her Books Were Based on Wingham," AM, "A Leaven of Alice." AM, "Distressing Impression." Barry Wenger to AM, December 21, 1982: 396/87.3:2a.6. "Material," *Something*: 43.

7. AM to JM, November 27, 1983: John Metcalf Fonds: 24.8.9.10. John Metcalf, "What Happened to CanLit?" W.P. Kinsella, "CanLit Clique for Metcalf?" AM to JM, August 28, 1987: John Metcalf Fonds: 24.20.2.63.

8. Price paid for "Working": Mary Evans to AM, March 13, 1981: 38.2.63.56. Jack McClelland to AM, July 11, 1980: 38.1.78.7. DG to VB, December 14, 1981, DG to AM, January 11, 1982: Macmillan: 429: 4. VB to AM, January 14, 1981: 38.2.63.73. VB to DG, January 21, 1981: Macmillan: 429: 4.

9. CM to VB, April 10, 1978: *New Yorker* (NYPL): 907: 5. "Working for a Living": 396/87.3: 5.11. CM to AM, January 9, [1978]: 38.2.4.1. "Taking Chances": 37.14.14. "Simon's Luck": 37.11.20. AM, April 29, 1987. In May 1995 I met and talked to this woman on Grand Manan. CM to AM, September 17, 1980: 396/87.3: 2.13. See also my "Alice Munro's Willa Cather."

10. Scobie interview: 13. [Joe Radford,] "Eviscerating Poultry: Techniques and Impressions": 38.9.25. Munro's notes on different types of wood, with diagrams of cuts in another hand: 38.12.1. CM to AM, June 17, 1980: 38.2.4.8. Interview Charles McGrath, January 14, 2003. "The Turkey Season," *New Yorker* galley proofs (June 9, 1980): 38.9.30. Telegrams to legal: CM to AM, December 11, [1980]: 38.2.4.13. A present to our readers: CM to AM, December 1, 1980: 38.2.4.12.

11. Undated titles: 38.9.35. Second "Bardon Bus": 396/87.3: 4.5. "Ferguson Girls" submissions: Mary Evans to AM, January 12, 1982: 38.2.63.71. Submission: VB to DG, March 18, 1982: Macmillan: 429.2. Confirmation of submissions: VB to AM, March 19, 1982: 38.2.63.79. Ordering: DG to AM,

April 6, 1982: 38.1.75.18. Knopf confirmed: AC to AM, May 17, 1982: 38.1.3.27.

12. Changes in contract (DG's acceptance annotated): VB to DG, April 12, 1982. Macmillan contract for *Moons of Jupiter*, May 10 [or 11?], 1982; annotation: "Original to AM." Pratt images: W.E. Smillie to DG, May 10, 1982, DG to Mira Godard, June 2, 1982: Macmillan: 429.2. "Rights," *Quill & Quire* November 1982.

13. Publicity tour: Macmillan: 400: 15. *Anthology:* CBC archives. Profiles: Macmillan: 400: 15. Wayne Grady, "A House of Her Own": 14. Sam Solecki, "Lives of Girls and Women": 24.

14. Urjo Kareda, "Double Vision": 63, 63–64. John Faustman, "Two Alices": 64, 63.

15. Cynthia Ozick to AC, March 9, 1983, Bobbie Ann Mason to AC, March 7, 1983: 396/87.3: 1.9. There are also notes here from Hazzard, McDermott, and O'Brien. Patricia Blake, "Heart-Catching": 71, 73. Ann Hurlbert, "The Country and the City": 37. Benjamin DeMott, "Domestic Stories": 1, 26. David Lehman, "When Short Is Beautiful": 85.

16. "Accident," "The Moons of Jupiter," "Hard-Luck Stories," *Moons*: 81, 82, 223, 197. "A Perfect Story": 38.9.2.3. VB to AM, August 24, 1984: 396/87.3: 2a.1. "Alice Munro Finds Writing a Struggle," *News* (Prince Rupert), May 18, 1983. Also in *Cape Breton Post*, May 24, 1983. Linda Matchan, "Alice Munro: From the Ontario Hinterland to 'The Moons of Jupiter.'" This was reprinted, at least, in the Montreal *Gazette* (June 4, 1983) and *Vancouver Sun* (May 27, 1983). Interview Ann Close, January 15, 2003.

17. VB to AM, August 4, 1980: 38.2.63.49. Knopf Royalty Statement (March 31, 1981): 38.1.3.24. VB to John Diamond, January 17, 1983, VB to AM, January 26, 1983. VB to Martha Clark, November 19, 1982: 396/87.3: 2a.1. VB to AM, September 12, 1983: 396/87.3: 2a.2.

18. VB to DG, December 1, 1983, DG to VB, January 4, 1984, VB to DG, January 12, 1984, VB to AM, February 7, February 27, 1984: 396/87.3: 2a.2. Virginia Barber, Text of Remarks at Alice Munro Garden Dedication, July 10, 2002.

19. Specifics for these examples are from correspondence files in the Alice Munro Fonds. Edna O'Brien blurb: Pat Strachan to AM, December 5, 1984: 396/87.3:1.66. CBC profile: *Sunday Morning*, October 17, 1982. Patrick Watson, *Gzowski on FM*, February 19, 1976. Anne Holloway and DG to AM, July 17 and 18 1984:, 396/87.3: 1.111. AM draft foreword: 396/87.3: 3.3. Eithne Black to AM, August 22, 1984: 396/87.3:1.36. Also Ken Adachi, "Writers Pay Tribute to Beautiful Man." *Toronto Star*, October 29, 1984: C3. AM, "On John Metcalf."

20. "Gold": 396/87.3: 2.11. Raymond Carver, "Introduction": xvi. CM to VB, September 26, 1984, VB to AM, October 2, 1984: 396/87.3: 2a.1. CM to AM,

October 15, 1984: 396/87.3: 2.13. VB to AM, September 27, 1984: 396/87.3: 2a.1.

21. VB to AM, October 2, 1984: 396/87.3: 2a.1. CM to AM, December 26, 1984: 396/87.3: 2.13. CM to VB, December 13, 1984: 396/87.3: 2a.1. AC to AM, January 10, [1985]: 396/87.3:1.9. CM to AM, November 9, 1984: 396/87.3: 2.13, CM to VB, February 15, 1985: 396/87.3: 2a.1. AM to JM, August 28, 1987: John Metcalf Fonds: 24.20.2.63. Interview Virginia Barber, January 14, 2003.

22. AM, "Introduction": xiii, xv–xvi. AM, April 24, 2004. Narrator and Hugh: 37.9.9.1. "Shoebox Babies": 38.11.4. "Miles City": 396/87.3: 7.3. Scanlon Lake: Interview James Polk, June 8, 2004. "Miles City, Montana," "The Progress of Love," *Progress*: 105, 26, 31. "Chaddeleys and Flemings: 2. The Stone in the Field," *Moons*: 33.

23. AM to DG, August 22, 1985: Macmillan: 429.3. CM to AM, September 12, 1985: 396/87.3: 2.13. AC to AM, September 20, 1985: 396/87.3:1.9. VB to AM, October 2, 1984: 396/87.3: 2a.1. VB to DG, July 15, 1985: Macmillan: 429:3. AC to AM, July 8, 1985: 396/87.3: 1.9. DG to VB, September 13, 1985, Macmillan contract (receipt stamped December 2, 1985), *The Progress of Love*, DG to Irene DeClute, December 24, 1985, January 31, 1986: Macmillan: 429.3.

24. AM to DG, November 30, 1985, "Please call Ginger. Urgent": Telegram AM to DG, February 20, 1986, Linda McKnight to file, February 25, 1986, Linda McKnight to VB, March 4, 1986, VB to Linda McKnight, March 14, 1986, AM to Linda McKnight, March 7, 1986, Linda McKnight to Ron Besse and Arnold Gosewich, April 11, 1986, Peter Waldock to Avie Bennett [n.d. April 15, 1986], Marge Hodgeman to Avie Bennett, Peter Waldock, Jan Walter, Doug Gibson, April 16, 1986, VB to DG, April 17, 1986, Memorandum of Agreement, April 29, 1986, Press release [n.d. April 29, 1986]: Macmillan: 429.3. Ken Adachi, "Munro Follows Publisher Gibson from Macmillan," *Toronto Star*, April 30, 1986. Salam Alaton, "CanLit Luminaries Stick with Gibson," *Globe and Mail*, May 1, 1986: D5.

25. Galleys: Invoice, Crane Duplicating Service, Barnstable, MA: M&S. Knopf author's proof: 396/87.3: 14.1. Penguin: Peter Waldock to Ann Nelles, August 21, 1986, DG to AM, August 27, 1986, DG to VB, August 27, 1986: M&S. "Distinguished": Ken Adachi, "Alice Munro Honored with First Marian Engel Award," *Toronto Star*, October 21, 1986: H1. "Hometown": VB to DG, September 16, 1986: M&S. AM to JM [n.d. received November 6, 1986: JM], AM to JM, November 21, 1986: John Metcalf Fonds: 24.8.9.19, 24.8.9.21. "Accident," *Moons*: 109.

26. Beverly Slopen, "Alice Munro's Audience Grows," *Toronto Star*, August 3, 1986. "Darling": Sumi. "Not doing anything *new*": "Writer's Writers": 10.

27. Beverly Slopen, "PW Interviews Alice Munro": 76. Joyce Carol Oates, "Characters Dangerously Like Us": 7, 9. Anne Tyler, "Canadian Club": 54.

"Size reported": Ken Adachi, "J.D. Salinger's Biography Too Tame to Cause Ripples," *Toronto Star*, February 2, 1987: D2.

28. *Book-of-the-Month Club News* November 1986: 1– 4. "Editor's Choice: Best Books of 1986," *New York Times Book Review*, December 7, 1986: 3, 37, 40. "Atwood and Munro Touted by Times," *Globe and Mail*, December 8, 1986: D9. M&S Royalty statement: May 1, 1987 (July–December 1986). Lisa Rochon, "Munro Wins Top Literary Prize," *Globe and Mail*, May 28, 1987: D1. David Macfarlane, "Writer in Residence": 56.

29. Norman Mailer to AM, April 22, 1985, Karen Kennerly (P.E.N. International) to AM, April 22, 1985: 396/87.3: 2.27.

30. Judith Timson, "Merciful Light": 66. "CBC Radio Asks Robert Weaver to Retire Early," *Globe and Mail*, January 17, 1985: E1. AM to JM, March 24, 1985, March 28, 1988: John Metcalf Fonds: 24.8.9.13, 22. "The Ottawa Valley," *Something*: 246. "Friend of My Youth," *Friend*: 3, 26.

31. AM, "Contributors Notes," *Best American Short Stories 1989*: 322. Here Munro mentions Clinton's "Miss Mountcastle" and Goderich's "Sweet Songstress of Le Mer Douce." See Nerissa Arch McInnes, "The Clever Mountcastle Family," Godard, and "Eloise Skimings." Joynt: *Wingham Advance-Times*, March 10, 1938: 2. "Meneseteung" typescript: 396/87.3:3.2. "Meneseteung" Knopf setting text: 396/87.3: 3.4. "Meneseteung," *Friend*: 73, 68–69, 70. "Circle of Prayer," *Progress*: 273.

32. DG to Kelly Hechler, Janet Heisey, Bill Hushion, Don Sedgwick, December 8, 1989: M&S. D.J.R. Bruckner, "An Author Travels to Nurture Ideas About Home." Harbourfront: Kelly Heckler to AM, February 14, 1990. Mary Pratt's *Wedding Dress*: DG to file, January 5, 1990. Sales figures: DG to Bill Hushion, Lynn Shannon, July 19, 1990. DG to Alison Samuel, June 6, 1990: M&S.

33. M&S ad: *Globe and Mail*, April 28, 1990: C8. Bharati Mukherjee, "Hometown Horrors": 1, 31. Malcolm Jones, Jr., "The Glory of the Story": 56, 57. Philip Marchand, "Telling Stories": M13. Mary Jo Salter, "In Praise of Accidents": 51, 52, 53. Robert Towers, "Short Satisfactions": 38. Maria Russo, "Final Chapter": 34. Carol Shields, "In Ontario": 22, 23.

Chapter 8

1. "Carried Away," *Open*: 50. "What Do You Want to Know For?": 220. Ozick, "A Short Note on 'Chekhovian'": 88, 89. E-mail AC, December 16, 2004. Diane Turbide, "The Incomparable Storyteller": 46, 47. Trillium Award: "Munro Honoured," *Globe and Mail*, August 28, 1991: A11. Air Lingus: DG to Kelly Hechler, September 7, 1990: M&S. Molson: "Cultural Award Winner," *Toronto Star*, April 4, 1991: A4. Commonwealth: DG to AM, November 7, 1991. W.H. Smith: DG to AM, January 11, 1995: M&S. "Lannan Gives 10 Writers $500K," *Publishers Weekly*, September 25, 1995: 10.

2. AM to JM, March 28, 1988: John Metcalf Fonds: 24.8.9.22. Daniel Menaker, "Authors! Authors!": 117. *New Yorker*, June 27, July 4, 1994: *passim*. E-mail Daniel Menaker, August 10 and 17, 2003. AM to Daniel Menaker, November 21, 1991, two n.d., and July 26, 1993: Private collection.

3. Gzowski interview (1994). "The Albanian Virgin," *Open*: 50. Description of tobacco work: AM, June 19, 2003. Interview Reg Thompson, June 10, 2004.

4. Val Ross, "A Writer Called Alice": C1. Daniel Menaker, "Authors! Authors!": 117. Ann Hulbert, "Writer Without Borders": 59. DG to AC, January 20, February 7, 1994: M&S. *Open Secrets* proof: 752/04.3: 6.2. "Open Secrets," *Open*: 153–44. *New York Times* Bestseller Listing, *New York Times Book Review*, October 2, 1994: 38. David Helwig, "Alice in Wonderland": I1.

5. Josephine Humphreys, "Mysteries Near at Hand": 1, 36, 37. "The two stories combined": Alinda Becker, "Sex and Self-Defense." J.R. (Tim) Struthers, "How Real, How Magical": 33, 32. Ann Hulbert, "Writer Without Borders": 59, 60. Ted Solotaroff, "Life Stories": 665, 666. "Vandals," *Open*: 268–69. Wendy Lesser, "The Munro Doctrine": 53, 51, 52. Lesser is quoting from the McCulloch-Simpson interview. Merna Summers, "An Entertainer of the Spirit": 39.

6. Harbourfront Reading Series Press Release (August 12, 1994): M&S. "Munro, Davies Read Together," *Toronto Star*, August 9, 1994: C4. Vancouver reading: Alma Lee to Kelly Hechler, December 12, 1994: M&S. David Staines, Introduction, *Prize Writing*: 17–19. Interview David Staines, January 15, 2004. DG to AM, January 11, 1995. Final sales: DG sales meeting notes for *Selected Stories* (1996): M&S. Translations: Laura Nolan (Barber Literary Agency) to Kelly Hechler, September 13, 1994: M&S. Thirteen languages: Draft promotional material for *Selected Stories*: M&S.

7. David Creighton, "In Search of Alice Munro": 19. Elizabeth Campbell and Sandra Molloy, "Self-Guided Tour of Points of Interest in the Town of Wingham Relating to Alice Munro." Wingham: North Huron District Museum, 2000. 17" x 11" sheet. "This tour is in no way connected to Alice Munro."

8. VB to AM, May 10, 1984: 396/87.3: 2a.1. VB to DG, March 9, 1995. DG to AM, March 4, 1996. DG to VB, June 22, 1995. David Staines to DG, December 3, 1995: M&S. AM "Good Woman in Ireland": 27. AC to VB, DG, and Alison [Samuel], February 16, 1996. AC to DG, March 1, 1996. M&S. Knopf first printing: Review of *Selected Stories*, *Publishers Weekly*.

9. [DG], Draft catalogue copy. "Same memorandum": Gail [Stewart] to Valerie [Jacobs], November 30, 1995: M&S. A.S. Byatt, "Alice Munro: One of the Great Ones": D18, D14. John Updike, "Magnetic North": 11, 13. Dennis Duffy, "Something She's Been Meaning to Tell Us": 8, 9. James Wood, "Things Happen All the Time": 31, 32. John Banville, "Revelations": 20.

10. DG to Avie Bennett and Valerie Jacobs, January 7, 1997. "Product Summary Report," December 4, 1997. DG to Ken [Thomson], October 16, 1997. DG to AM, November 24, 1997. "Alice Munro Wins PEN-Malamud Award," *Globe and Mail*, November 15, 1997: C8. Robert MacNeil: As quoted in DG, "Editor's Note"on *The Love of a Good Woman*: M&S. *Selected Stories* withheld: DG to Diana Massiah, August 19, 1996: M&S. "Walker Brothers Cowboy," *Dance*: 3. "What Do You Want to Know For?": 220.

11. "Bill's Story," *Weekend Australian*, July 22, 1995. AM, "Good Woman in Ireland." VB to Bill Buford, May 9, 1996, May 28, 1996: *New Yorker* files. VB to DG, May 28, 1996: M&S. Bill Buford to AM, August 20, 1996, VB to Bill Buford, September 18, 1996, Bill Buford to VB, September 23, 1996, VB to Bill Buford, September 24, 1996, Bill Buford to VB, September 25, 1996: *New Yorker* files.

12. Carol Beran, "The Luxury of Excellence": 219, 213, *passim.* "Author's Note," *Love*: [x]. Cuts to "Love": Dennis Duffy, "'A Dark Sort of Mirror'": 188–89. AM, June 19, 2003. Interview Alice Quinn, March 8, 2004. Interview Virginia Barber, January 14, 2003. Interview Charles McGrath, January 14, 2003. "The Face and Place of Poetry: Alice Quinn – The New Yorker": www.csmonitor.com/atcsmonitor/specials/poetry/p-quinn.html. Roger Angell: Alice Quinn, "The 'Wholly Original' Alice Munro." VB to Bill Buford, October 30, 1997: *New Yorker* Files. Ellen Vanstone, "Saturday Night Scores Coup with Munro Tale 'Jakarta,'" *Globe and Mail*, January 12, 1998: C5.

13. AM, "Contributor's Note," *Prize Stories 1997*: 443. "Cortes Island," *Love* 117, 140. DG to AC, May 6, 1998: M&S. DG to VB, February 12, 1998, VB to DG, March 9, 1998: M&S. Interview Jack Hodgins, April 21, 2004. Judy Stoffman, "Celebrating Alice Munro," *Toronto Star*, November 1, 1998: D9. Judy Stoffman, "Munro Wins Giller," *Toronto Star*, November 4, 1998: D1, D4. National Book Critics: Kelly Heckler to "Everyone": March 9, 1999: M&S.

14. Aritha van Herk, "Between the Stirrup and the Ground": 49, 50, 52. Michael Gorra, "Crossing the Threshold": 6, 7. Frank, "Fiction in Review": 168, 173–74. Following Updike, Frank also comments that Munro's *Selected Stories* "seemed to come out of nowhere, with no explanation of why the stories were selected and without any attempt to present them within the context of her extraordinary development as a writer" (166). Barbara Croft, "Indirect Objects": 15, 16. "Less Is More": 14. Tamsin Todd, "The Love of a Good Woman": 54, 55.

15. AM to Helen Hoy, November 9, 1987: Private collection. AM, "Introduction," *Selected Stories*: *passim.* "Spaceships Have Landed," *Paris Review*: 276–77. *Open Secrets* proof: 752/04.3: 6.3. "Working for a Living": 38.10.36.4.f4.

Chapter 9

1. "Introduction," *Selected Stories*: xiii–xiv. Gzowski *Globe and Mail* interview: F4. "Home": 153. A.S. Byatt, "Justice for Willa Cather": 53. Judy Stoffman, "Munro Wins Giller," *Toronto Star*, November 4, 1998: D1, D4. Judy Stoffman, "Authors Fest Numbers Rise," *Toronto Star*, November 1, 2004: F2. Andrea Baille, "Munro Awarded Second Giller," *Toronto Star*, November 12, 2004: A3.

2. "The Albanian Virgin," *Open*: 105. Gzowski *Globe and Mail* interview: F4. Prize information: M&S. Health: Douglas Gibson, "A Very Canadian Celebrity": 10. AM, August 22, 2001.

3. Buford proofs: "Post and Beam," "Family Furnishings," "Lying Under the Apple Tree." Deborah Treisman to AM, July 9, 2001: *New Yorker* Files. Interview Deborah Treisman, March 10, 2004. "Best fiction out there": Jonathan Bing, "The Write Stuff," *Variety*, October 30, 2002.

4. Douglas Gibson, "A Very Canadian Celebrity": 9–10. M&S print run: DG to VB, January 7, 2002. Bestseller: *Globe and Mail*, October 13, 2001: M&S. Mona Simpson, "A Quiet Genius": 128, 133, 134, 135. "Family Furnishings," *Hateship*: 117. Ann Beattie, "Alice Munro's Amazing Ordinary World": D3. Merilyn Simonds, "Munro's Wit Is Undiminished": I1. Philip Marchand, "The Way Things Are": D12. Catherine Lockerbie, "The Loving Literature of Alice Munro": C15. Lorrie Moore, "Artship": 41, 42. Tom Deignan, "Life in a Sentence": 26, 27. Franklin, "Assent and Lamentation": 33, 36, 37. Michael Ravitch, "Fiction in Review": 160, 161, 164, 165, 170. Benjamin Markovits, "Suspicion of Sentiment": 26. John McGahern, "Heroines of Their Lives": 23, 24.

5. Patricia Hluchy, "Alice Munro": 67. Ross and Carol Hamilton, "Story of Munro's Early Life Indicates Star in the Making," *Wingham Advance-Times*, December 23, 1998. Brenda Burke, "Alice Munro Collection Planned for Museum," *Wingham Advance-Times*, January 13, 1999. Catherine MacDonald, "More Suggestions Received on Ways to Recognize Alice Munro," *Wingham Advance-Times*, January 20, 1999. Program, Dedication of "Alice Munro Literary Garden," July 10, 2002. Judy Stoffman, "Jubilation in Jubilee," *Toronto Star*, July 11, 2002: A28. Bennett: Stoffman and also Jessica Leeder, "Friends, Family Salute Munro's Literary Garden," *National Post*, July 11, 2002: A7. Virginia Barber, Remarks at Dedication of Alice Munro Literary Garden, July 10, 2002. AM, June 20, 2003.

6. Barber quotation: Leeder, "Friends, Family Salute Munro's Literary Garden." Excised passage: "Lying Under the Apple Tree" proofs May 15, 2002. Deborah Treisman to AM, May 30, 2002. Photograph: *New Yorker* Files. "Lying Under the Apple Tree": 88. "What Do You Want to Know For?": 215. Simpson, "A Quiet Genius": 131. AM, "Foreword," *Castle Rock*: x. "Last book": AM, April 23, 2004.

7. DG to VB, August 17, 2000. VB to DG, August 25, 2000. DG to VB, October 28, 2002. VB to DG, November 5, 2002: M&S. Story Selection: e-mail David Staines, December 28, 2004. Jane Urquhart, "Afterword": 416.

8. Knopf first printing: Rev. of *Runaway, Publishers Weekly*. Philip Marchand, "Time Passing": D13. Bruce Erskine, "Mastery of Munro": NS11. A. Alvarez, "Life Studies": 23. Jonathan Franzen, "Alice's Wonderland": 1, 14, 15, 16. Lorrie Moore, "Leave Them and Love Them": 125, 127, 128.

9. Mary Hawthorne, "Disconnected Realities": 17, 18. Karl Miller, "Not Bad for a Housewife": 18. 2004 Rogers Writers' Trust Citation: M&S. Munro mania in New York: Rebecca Caldwell, "Alice Munro," *Globe and Mail*, December 27, 2004: R6-7. Trip home with Sheila: AM, April 23, 2004. "Soon," *Runaway*: 124–25. "Originally": "Soon" mss. "July 30/03": *New Yorker* Files. *Lives*: 254. "A Real Life," *Open*: 80.

Chapter 10

1. Judy Stoffman, "Making a Short Story Long": H10. AM, "Maxwell": 40, 47. AM, "Writing. Or, Giving Up Writing": 300. "A Conversation with Alice Munro": www.reading-group-cnter.knopfdoubleday.com/2010/01/08/alice-munro-interview/. July 16, 2010. "Doubtful": AM, August 21, 2001. E-mail Charles Baxter, September 10, 2010. AM, "The Novels of William Maxwell": 31. AM, "Maxwell": 47.

2. AM, "Maxwell": 35. Stoffman, "Making a Short Story Long": H10. AM, June 14, 2010.

3. Lorrie Moore, "Leave Them and Love Them": 128. A revised version of "Home" was published in Britain in the *New Statesman* in late 2001, a fact not noted in the first version of this biography.

4. *Runaway* sales figures: E-mail Alison Samuel, August 25, 2010; McClelland & Stewart; Interview Ann Close, July 21, 2010.

5. This book was published concurrently in Canada by McClelland & Stewart, without Everyman's select bibliography and chronology but with Atwood's introduction, as *Munro's Best*. It was published as *Carried Away* by Everyman in Britain in October 2008.

6. AM, April 24, 2004. "The Mount Honors Women of Achievement." *The Mount* 24 (Winter 2004): 8. "Alice Munro Given Lifetime Achievement Honour." Cbc.ca, December 3, 2007. "The Tyranny of Library Hierarchy": http://librarysupporter.blogspot.com/2005/05/tyranny-of-library-hierarchy.html. August 30, 2010. Ben Marcus, "Why Experimental Fiction Threatens to Destroy Publishing, Jonathan Franzen, and Life as We Know It: A Correction." *Harper's*, October 2005: 39–52. David Laskin, "Tales of Love and Sorrow in a Singular City: Alice Munro's Vancouver." *New York Times*, June 11, 2006: TR 9, 12.

7. "Alice Munro Given Lifetime Achievement Honour." Richard Helm, "Literary Icon Alice Munro Expected to Retire Tonight." *Winnipeg Free Press,* June 20, 2006: D4. Richard Helm, "Editor Insists New Book Won't Be Munro's Last." *Edmonton Journal,* June 22, 2006: D4.

8. AM to DG, October 13, 1980: Macmillan: 429.3. AM, VB, "2006 Medal Day." *The MacDowell Colony* 25.2 (Winter 2006): 10, 11.

9. Central Subject: Eleanor Wachtel, "Alice Munro: A Life in Writing: A Conversation": 278. Munro made the same point when she was interviewed by Deborah Treisman on October 3, 2008. A summary of this interview: www.newyorker.com/online/blogs/festival/2008/10/things-you-may.html. December 3, 2010. Notebook drafts: 38.12.3, 38.10.39.f13. AM, "No Advantages," *Castle Rock*: 6, 7.

10. Robert Thacker, "A 'Booming Tender Sadness': Alice Munro's Irish." AM, June 19, 2003. AM, "Meneseteung," *Friend*: 73. Jim Dills and Gloria (Stark) Brown, *Halton's Scotch Block*: 54. AM, "Messenger." *Castle Rock*: 347, 348–49.

11. AM, "Chaddeleys and Flemings: 1. Connection." *Moons*: 6. Jennifer Rudolph Walsh to Deborah Treisman, March 7, 2005. "Laidlaws II: The View from Castle Rock" (140 pp., dated by AM February 7, 2005). Deborah Treisman to David Remnick, March 24, 2005. *New Yorker* files. AM, "Foreword," *Castle Rock*: x.

12. AM, "The Ticket," *Castle Rock*: 258–59, 281, 283, 261, 260. "The Yellow Afternoon": 37.16.34. f1–11. "The Ticket" was submitted to the *New Yorker* – along with "Dimensions" and "What Do You Want to Know For?"; its editors bought only "Dimensions." Shannon Firth (assistant to Jennifer Rudolph Walsh) to Deborah Treisman, November 30, 2005. *New Yorker* files.

13. AM, August 18, 2008. Interview with Treisman at *New Yorker* Festival, October 3, 2008. "Alice Munro Reveals Cancer Fight." October 22, 2009. www.cbc.ca/arts/books/story /2009/10/22/alice-munro-cancer.html. October 25, 2009.

14. E-mail Claire Tomalin, August 11, 2010. Megan Hoak (VB assistant) to DG November 28, 2000. *New Yorker* files. *Courting Johanna* (June 18–September 6, 2008): 2008 Blyth Festival Program. Interview Jennifer Rudolph Walsh, July 20, 2010.

15. Interview Carmen Callil, August 9, 2010. Interview Alison Samuel, July 28, 2010. Sales figures: E-mail Alison Samuel, August 25, 2010.

16. Interview Fiammetta Rocco, August 9, 2010. Interview Jane Smiley, August 30, 2010. Douglas Gibson. "Dublin College Honours Alice Munro." *Globe and Mail:* www.theglobeandmail.com/news/arts/dublin-college-honours-alice-munro/article1198858/. June 30, 2009. Jane Smiley, "Chairs Speech 2009": www.themanbookerprize.com/prize/mbi-archive/chairsspeech2009. August 2, 2010.

17. E-mail Daniel Menaker, August 17, 2003. Interview Ann Close, July 21, 2010.
18. For a brief discussion of Marchand's "The Problem of Alice Munro," see my own review of *Too Much Happiness.*
19. "Too Much Generosity." *Globe and Mail,* September 1, 2009: A12. Interview Ben Metcalf, July 27, 2010. Interview Jennifer Rudolph Walsh, July 20, 2010. AM, June 14, 2010.

Epilogue

1. Roger Angell, "Storyville": 107. Roger Angell, Internal Critique of "Silence," by AM: *New Yorker* Files. "Soon," *Runaway:* 125. Boyle interview. Fragment: 37.18.10.1. Draft "Everything": 38.12.31. Letter James Reaney, March 24, 2003.

Acknowledgements

1. "Dulse," *Moons:* 39.
2. Letter, AM, March 9, 2000: Private collection.
3. A.S. Byatt, "Justice for Willa Cather": 53. AM, "The Colonel's Hash Resettled": 181. Janet Malcolm, "Gertrude Stein's War": 70. "A fine and lucky benevolence": "Material," *Something:* 43.

Archival and Unpublished Sources

Alfred A. Knopf Archive. Harry Ransom Humanities Research Center, University of Texas at Austin.

Alice Munro Fonds. Special Collections Division, University of Calgary Libraries.

Archives of Ontario, Toronto.

Audrey Thomas Papers. National Archives of Canada, Ottawa.

CBC Archives, Toronto.

Canadian Fiction Magazine Archive. William Ready Division of Archives and Research Collections. McMaster University.

Carol Shields Papers. National Archives of Canada, Ottawa.

Ernest Buckler Papers. Thomas Fisher Rare Book Library. University of Toronto.

Hugh Garner Fonds. Queen's University Archives.

John and Myrna Metcalf Collection. Rare Books and Special Collections. McGill University Library.

John Metcalf Fonds. Special Collections Division, University of Calgary Libraries.

Mary McAlpine Fonds. Rare Books and Special Collections. University of British Columbia.

Macmillan Company of Canada Archive. William Ready Division of Archives and Research Collections. McMaster University.

McClelland & Stewart Archive. William Ready Division of Archives and Research Collections. McMaster University.

McClelland & Stewart Files. 75 Sherbourne Street, 5th Floor, Toronto.

McGraw-Hill Ryerson Files. 300 Water Street, Whitby, Ontario.

Margaret Laurence Fonds. University Archives and Special Collections. Scott Library. York University.

Marian Engel Fonds. William Ready Division of Archives and Research Collections. McMaster University.

Mordecai Richler Fonds. Special Collections Division, University of Calgary Libraries.

New Yorker Files. 4 Times Square, New York, New York.

New Yorker Records. Center for the Humanities. Manuscripts and Archives. New York Public Library.

Robert Kroetsch Fonds. Special Collections Division, University of Calgary Libraries.

W.W. Norton & Company. 500 Fifth Avenue, New York, New York.

Robert Weaver Papers. National Archives and Library of Canada, Ottawa.

William French Collection. James Alexander and Ellen Rea Benson Special Collections. D.B. Weldon Library. University of Western Ontario.

Select Bibliography

1. Works by Alice Munro (By Publication Date)

A. Books

Dance of the Happy Shades. Foreword Hugh Garner. Toronto: Ryerson, 1968.

Lives of Girls and Women. Toronto: McGraw-Hill Ryerson, 1971.

Something I've Been Meaning to Tell You: Thirteen Stories. Toronto: McGraw-Hill Ryerson, 1974.

Who Do You Think You Are? Toronto: Macmillan, 1978.

The Beggar Maid. New York: Knopf, 1979.

The Moons of Jupiter. Toronto: Macmillan, 1982

The Progress of Love. Toronto: McClelland & Stewart, 1986.

Friend of My Youth. Toronto: McClelland & Stewart, 1990.

Open Secrets. Toronto: McClelland & Stewart, 1994.

Selected Stories. Toronto: McClelland & Stewart, 1996.

The Love of a Good Woman. Toronto: McClelland & Stewart, 1998.

Hateship, Friendship, Courtship, Loveship, Marriage. Toronto: McClelland & Stewart, 2001.

No Love Lost. Selected with an Afterword by Jane Urquhart. Toronto: McClelland & Stewart/New Canadian Library, 2003.

Runaway. Toronto: McClelland & Stewart, 2004.

The View from Castle Rock: Stories. Toronto: McClelland & Stewart, 2006.

Alice Munro's Best. Introduction Margaret Atwood. Toronto: McClelland & Stewart, 2006. [*Carried Away* in Britain and the United States.]

Away From Her. Foreword Sarah Polley. Toronto: Penguin Canada, 2007. ["The Bear Came Over the Mountain."]

Too Much Happiness: Stories. Toronto: McClelland & Stewart, 2009.

B. Broadcast Stories

"The Strangers." *Canadian Short Stories*. CBC Radio. October 5, 1951.

"The Liberation." *Canadian Short Stories*. CBC Radio. June 13, 1952.

"The Idyllic Summer." *Anthology*. CBC Radio. March 22, 1954.

"The Yellow Afternoon." *Anthology.* CBC Radio. February 22, 1955.
"The Green April." *Anthology.* CBC Radio. 1956.
"The Trip to the Coast." *CBC Wednesday Night.* 1960.
"Dance of the Happy Shades." *CBC Sunday Night.* October 30, 1960.
"The Shining Houses." *CBC Wednesday Night.* June 6, 1962.
"Images." *CBC Tuesday Night.* September 17, 1968.
"Forgiveness in Families." *Anthology.* March 10, 1973.
"The Found Boat." *Anthology.* April 6, 1974.
"Providence," CBC International Service. April 9, 1977.
"The Turkey Season." *Anthology.* October 16, 1982.
"Wild Swans." CBC International Service. April 7, 1984.

C. Stories First Published in Periodicals (Included in Books – Most Revised)

[Laidlaw, Alice.] "The Time of Death." *Canadian Forum.* June 1956: 63–66.
"Good-By, Myra." *Chatelaine.* July 1956: 16–17, 55–58. ("Day of the Butterfly")
"Thanks for the Ride." *Tamarack Review* 2 (Winter 1957): 25–37.
"Sunday Afternoon." *Canadian Forum.* September 1957: 127–30.
"The Peace of Utrecht." *Tamarack Review* 15 (Spring 1960): 5–21.
"The Trip to the Coast." *Ten For Wednesday Night.* Ed. Robert Weaver. Toronto: McClelland & Stewart, 1961: 74–92. ("A Trip to the Coast")
"Dance of the Happy Shades." *Montrealer.* February 1961: 22–26.
"An Ounce of Cure." *Montrealer.* May 1961: 26–30. Also *McCall's.* October 1973: 92–93, 130, 132–34.
"The Office." *Montrealer,* September 1962: 18–23.
"Boys and Girls." *Montrealer.* December 1964: 25–34.
"Red Dress – 1946." *Montrealer.* May 1965: 28–34. Also *McCall's.* March 1973: 66–67, 138–41, 146.
"Postcard." *Tamarack Review* 47 (Spring 1968): 22–31, 33–39.
"Material." *Tamarack Review.* 61 (November 1973): 7–25.
"Home." *New Canadian Stories: 74.* Ed. David Helwig and Joan Harcourt. Ottawa: Oberon, 1974: 133–153.
"Royal Beatings." *New Yorker.* March 14, 1977: 36–44.
"The Beggar Maid." *New Yorker.* June 27, 1977: 31, 35–41, 44–47.
"Providence." *Redbook.* August 1977: 98–99, 158–59, 160–63.
"Accident." *Toronto Life.* November 1977: 60–61, 87–88, 90–95, 149–50, 153–56, 159–60, 162–65, 167, 169–73.
"Privilege." *Tamarack Review* 70, November 1977: 14–28.
"The Honeyman's Granddaughter." *Ms.* October 1978: 56–57, 75–76, 79.
"Mischief." *Viva.* April 1978: 99–109.
"Wild Swans." *Toronto Life.* April 1978: 52–53, 124–25.
"Half a Grapefruit." *Redbook.* May 1978: 132–22, 175, 178, 180, 182, 183.
"The Moons of Jupiter." *New Yorker.* May 22, 1978: 32–39.

"Spelling" [excerpt]. *Weekend Magazine.* June 17, 1978: 24, 26–27.

"Emily." *Viva.* August 1978: 99–105.

"Connection." *Chatelaine.* November 1978: 66–67, 97–98, 101, 104, 106.

"The Stone in the Field." *Saturday Night.* April 1979: 40–45.

"Dulse." *New Yorker.* July 21, 1980: 30–39.

"Wood." *New Yorker.* November 24, 1980: 46–54.

"The Turkey Season." *New Yorker.* December 29, 1980: 36–44.

"Mrs. Cross and Mrs. Kidd." *Tamarack Review* 82 and 83 (Winter 1982): 5–24.

"Miles City, Montana." *New Yorker.* January 14, 1985: 30–40.

"Monsieur les Deux Chapeaux." *Grand Street* 4, no. 3 (Spring 1985): 7–33.

"Lichen." *New Yorker.* July 15, 1985: 26–36.

"The Progress of Love." *New Yorker.* October 7, 1985: 35–46, 49–50, 53–54, 57–58.

"A Queer Streak. Part One: Anonymous Letters." *Granta* 17 (Autumn 1985): 187–212.

"Secrets Between Friends." *Mademoiselle.* November 1985: 116, 118, 120, 122, 124, 126, 128, 130, 228, 230. "Jesse and Meribeth."

"Eskimo." *GQ – Gentleman's Quarterly.* December 1985: 262–66, 301–02, 304.

"A Queer Streak. Part Two: Possession." *Granta* 18 (Spring 1986): 201–19.

"The Moon in the Orange Street Skating Rink." *New Yorker.* March 31, 1986: 26–36, 38–41, 44.

"White Dump." *New Yorker.* July 28, 1986: 25–39, 42–43.

"Circle of Prayer." *Paris Review* 28 [No. 100] (Summer/Fall 1986): 31–51.

"Fits." *Grand Street* 5.2 (Winter 1986): 36–61.

"Oh, What Avails." *New Yorker.* November 16, 1987: 42–52, 55–56, 58–59, 62, 64–65, 67.

"Meneseteung." *New Yorker.* January 11, 1988: 28–38.

"Five Points." *New Yorker.* March 14, 1988: 34–43.

"Oranges and Apples." *New Yorker.* October 24, 1988: 36–48, 52, 54.

"Hold Me Fast, Don't Let Me Pass." *Atlantic Monthly.* December 1988: 58–66, 68–70.

"Differently." *New Yorker.* January 2, 1989: 23–36.

"Goodness and Mercy." *New Yorker.* March 20, 1989: 38–48.

"Wigtime." *New Yorker.* September 4, 1989: 34–46, 48, 50.

"Pictures of the Ice." *Atlantic Monthly.* January 1990: 64–73.

"Friend of My Youth." *New Yorker.* January 22, 1990: 36–48.

"Carried Away." *New Yorker.* October 21, 1991: 34–46, 48–51, 54–58, 60–61.

"A Real Life." *New Yorker.* February 10, 1992: 30–40.

"A Wilderness Station." *New Yorker.* April 27, 1992: 35–46, 48–51.

"Open Secrets." *New Yorker.* February 8, 1993: 90–101.

"The Jack Randa Hotel." *New Yorker.* July 19, 1993: 62–70.

"Vandals." *New Yorker.* October 4, 1993: 179–82, 184–90.

"Spaceships Have Landed." *Paris Review* 131 (1994): 265–94.

"Hired Girl." *New Yorker.* April 11, 1994: 82–88.

"The Albanian Virgin." *New Yorker.* June 27 and July 4, 1994: 118–21, 123–27, 129–34, 136–38.

"The Love of a Good Woman." *New Yorker.* December 23 and 30, 1996: 102–05, 107–08, 110–14, 116–22, 124–32, 134–38, 140–41.

"The Children Stay." *New Yorker.* December 22, 1997: 90–96, 98–100, 102–03.

"Jakarta." *Saturday Night.* February 1998: 44–60.

"Save the Reaper." *New Yorker.* June 22 and 29, 1998: 120–28, 130–32. 134–35.

"Queenie." *London Review of Books.* July 30, 1998: 11–16. Also London: Profile Books, 1999.

"Before the Change." *New Yorker.* August 24 and 31, 1998: 132–36, 138–43.

"Cortes Island." *New Yorker.* October 12, 1998: 72–80.

"The Bear Came Over the Mountain." *New Yorker.* December 27, 1999 and January 3, 2000: 110–21, 124–27.

"Nettles." *New Yorker.* February 21 and 28, 2000: 254–56, 258–59, 262–64, 266–69.

"Floating Bridge." *New Yorker.* July 31, 2000: 64–72.

"Post and Beam." *New Yorker.* December 11, 2000: 96–106, 108.

"What Is Remembered." *New Yorker.* February 19 and 26, 2001: 196–207.

"Family Furnishings." *New Yorker.* July 23, 2001: 64–70, 72–77.

"Comfort." *New Yorker.* October 8, 2001: 66–77.

"Home." *New Statesman.* December 17, 2001–January 7, 2002: 84–93.

"Fathers." *New Yorker.* August 5, 2002: 64–7.

"Runaway." *New Yorker.* August 11, 2003: 62–75.

"Passion." *New Yorker.* March 22, 2004: 76–89.

"Change," "Soon," "Silence." *New Yorker.* June 14 and 21, 2004: 130–49, 150–58, 160, 163–64, 166, 168–72, 175–76, 178–80, 183. "Change," 130–42. "Soon," 142–49, 150–57. "Silence," 157–58, 160, 163–64, 166, 168–72, 175–76, 178–80, 183.

"The View from Castle Rock." *New Yorker.* August 29, 2005: 64–77.

"Wenlock Edge." *New Yorker.* December 5, 2005: 80–91.

"Dimension." *New Yorker.* June 5, 2006: 68–79.

"Home: A Story." *Virginia Quarterly Review.* 82.3 (Summer 2006): 108–28.

"What Do You Want to Know For?" *American Scholar.* 75.3 (Summer 2006): 94–105.

"Child's Play." *Harper's.* February 2007: 73–84.

"Fiction." *Harper's.* August 2007: 71–80.

"Free Radicals." *New Yorker.* February 11 and 18, 2008: 136–43.

"Deep-Holes." *New Yorker.* June 30, 2008: 66–73.

"Face." *New Yorker.* September 8, 2008: 58–66.

"Some Women." *New Yorker.* December 22 and 29, 2008: 69–77.
"Too Much Happiness." *Harper's.* August 2009: 53–72.

D. Uncollected Stories

[Laidlaw, Alice.] "The Dimensions of a Shadow." *Folio* 4, no. 2 (April 1950): [4–10].
[Laidlaw, Alice.] "Story for Sunday." *Folio* 5, no. 1 (December 1950): [4–8].
[Laidlaw, Alice.] "The Widower." *Folio* 5, no. 2 (April 1951): [7–11].
"A Basket of Strawberries." *Mayfair.* November 1953: 32–33, 78–80, 82.
[Munro, Alice Laidlaw.] "The Idyllic Summer." *Canadian Forum.* August 1954: 106–07, 109–110.
[Laidlaw, Alice.] "At the Other Place." *Canadian Forum.* September 1955: 131–33.
"The Edge of Town." *Queen's Quarterly* 62 (Autumn 1955): 368–80.
[Munro, Alice Laidlaw.] "How Could I Do That?" *Chatelaine.* March 1956: 16–17, 65–70.
"The Dangerous One." *Chatelaine.* July 1957: 48–51.
"Characters." *Ploughshares* 4, no. 3 (Summer 1978): 72–82.
"The Ferguson Girls Must Never Marry." *Grand Street* (Spring 1982): 27–64.
"Corrie." *New Yorker.* October 11, 2010: 94–101.
"Axis." *New Yorker.* January 31, 2011: 62–69.
"Train." Forthcoming *Harper's.*
"Pride." Forthcoming *Harper's.*

E. Essays, Memoirs, Letters, Poem, and Occasional Pieces by Alice Munro

"Remember Roger Mortimer: Dickens' 'Child's History of England' Remembered." *Montrealer.* February 1962: 34–37.
"Poem (Untitled)." Pseudonym Anne Chamney. *Canadian Forum.* February 1967: 243.
"Author's Commentary." *Sixteen by Twelve.* Ed. John Metcalf. Toronto: Ryerson, 1970: 125–26.
"The Colonel's Hash Resettled." *The Narrative Voice.* Ed. John Metcalf. Toronto: McGraw-Hill Ryerson, 1972: 181–83.
"An Open Letter." *Jubilee* 1 [1974]: 5–7.
"Everything Here Is Touchable and Mysterious." *Weekend Magazine* [*Toronto Star*] May 11, 1974: 33.
"On Writing 'The Office.'" *Transitions II: Short Fiction.* Ed. Edward Peck. Vancouver: Commcept, 1978: 259–62.
"On Stuewe and Censorship." Letter. *Books in Canada.* December 1978: 39–40.
"Working for a Living." *Grand Street* 1, no. 1 (1981): 9–37.
"Through the Jade Curtain." *Chinada: Memoirs of the Gang of Seven.* Dunvegan, Ont.: Quadrant, 1982: 51–55.

"Writer Denies Her Books Were Based on Wingham." *Wingham Advance-Times.*
    January 13, 1982: 4.
"A Leaven of Alice." Letter. *Today.* February 27, 1982: 2.
"What Is Real?" *Canadian Forum.* September 1982: 5, 36.
"Distressing Impression." Letter. *Globe and Mail.* December 22, 1982: 6.
"Going to the Lake." *Ontario: A Bicentennial Tribute.* Toronto: Key Porter, 1983:
    51–52.
"An Appreciation [of Marian Engel]." *Room of One's Own* 9.2 (1984): 32–33.
"Foreword." *The Anthology Anthology: A Selection from 30 Years of CBC Radio's
    "Anthology."* Ed. Robert Weaver. Toronto: Macmillan, 1984: ix–x.
"On John Metcalf: Taking Writing Seriously." *Malahat Review* 70 (1985): 6–7.
"Introduction." *The Moons of Jupiter* by Alice Munro. Markham, Ont.: Penguin,
    1986: vii–xvi.
"The Novels of William Maxwell." *Brick* 34 (Fall 1988): 28–31. Also *Brick* 65/66
    (Fall 2000): 23–29.
"Afterword." *Emily of New Moon* by Lucy Maud Montgomery. Toronto:
    McClelland & Stewart/New Canadian Library, 1989: 357–61.
"Contributor's Note." *Best American Short Stories 1989.* Ed. Margaret Atwood
    and Shannon Ravenel. Boston: Houghton Mifflin, 1989: 322–23.
"Take a Walk on the Wild Side." *Canadian Living.* October 1989: 38, 41–42.
"What Do You Want to Know For?" *Writing Away: The PEN Canada Travel
    Anthology.* Ed. Constance Rooke. Toronto: McClelland & Stewart, 1994:
    203–20.
"About This Book." ["Introduction" to *Selected Stories*] "Alice Munro: *Selected
    Stories*: A Tribute." Toronto: McClelland & Stewart, 1997: 1–7.
"Changing Places." *Writing Home: A PEN Canada Anthology.* Ed. Constance
    Rooke. Toronto: McClelland & Stewart, 1997: 190–206.
"Contributor's Note." *Prize Stories 1997: The O. Henry Awards.* Ed. Larry Dark.
    New York: Anchor, 1997: 442–43.
"Introduction." *Selected Stories* by Alice Munro. New York: Vintage, 1997:
    xiii–xxi.
"Golden Apples." *The Georgia Review* 53 (1999): 22–24.
"Alice Munro Writes." *National Post.* June 29, 2000.
"Stories." Speech to O. Henry Awards Tribute to AM, November 19, 2001.
    www.randomhouse.com/knopf/authors/munro/desktopnew.html.
    November 27, 2002.
"Lying Under the Apple Tree." *New Yorker.* June 17 and 24, 2002: 88–90, 92,
    105–08, 110–14.
"The Sweet Second Summer of Kitty Malone." *Uncommon Ground: A
    Celebration of Matt Cohen.* Ed. Graeme Gibson et al. Toronto: Knopf
    Canada. 2002: 91–94.

"Good Woman in Ireland." *Brick* 72 (2003): 26–30. Also *Prize Writing*. Ed.
　　Gary Stephen Ross. Toronto: Giller Prize Foundation, 2003: 57–64.
"Maxwell." *A William Maxwell Portrait: Memories and Appreciations*. Ed. Charles
　　Baxter, Michael Collier, and Edward Hirsch. New York: Norton, 2004.
　　24–47.
"Writing. Or, Giving Up Writing." *Writing Life: Celebrated Canadian and
　　International Authors on Writing and Life*. Ed. Constance Rooke. Toronto:
　　McClelland & Stewart, 2006: 297–300.

F. Notable Anthology Inclusions

"The Time of Death." *Canadian Short Stories*. Ed. Robert Weaver. London and
　　New York: Oxford UP, 1960: 398–410.
"The Trip to the Coast." *Ten for Wednesday Night*. Ed. Robert Weaver. Toronto:
　　McClelland & Stewart, 1961: 74–92.
"The Peace of Utrecht." *The First Five Years: A Selection from* The Tamarack
　　Review. Ed. Robert Weaver. Foreword. Robert Fulford. Toronto: Oxford
　　UP, 1962: 149–64.
"Sunday Afternoon." *A Book of Canadian Stories*. Ed. Desmond Pacey. Rev. ed.
　　Toronto: Ryerson, 1962: 327–36.
"The Time of Death." *Modern Canadian Stories*. Ed. Giose Rimanelli and
　　Roberto Ruberto. Foreword. Earle Birney. Toronto: Ryerson, 1966: 314–23.
"An Ounce of Cure," "Boys and Girls." *Sixteen by Twelve*. Ed. John Metcalf.
　　Toronto: Ryerson, 1970: 103–24.
"Images," "Dance of the Happy Shades." *The Narrative Voice*. Ed. John Metcalf.
　　Toronto: McGraw-Hill Ryerson, 1972: 161–80.
"Wood." *81: Best Canadian Stories*. Ed. John Metcalf and Leon Rooke. Ottawa:
　　Oberon, 1981: 93–110.
"Prue." *82: Best Canadian Stories*. Ed. John Metcalf and Leon Rooke. Toronto:
　　Oberon, 1982: 74–79.
"Oranges and Apples" and "Oh, What Avails." *The Second Macmillan Anthology*.
　　Ed. John Metcalf and Leon Rooke. Toronto: Macmillan, 1989: 63–123.

G. Television and Film Adaptations

"How I Met My Husband." Dir. Herb Roland. *The Play's the Thing*. Prod.
　　George Jonas. CBC-TV. January 17, 1974. Printed in *The Play's the Thing:
　　Four Original Television Dramas*. Ed. Tony Gifford. Toronto: Macmillan,
　　1976: 15–34.
"1847: The Irish." *The Newcomers/Les arrivants*. Dir. Eric Till. CBC-TV.
　　January 8, 1978. Published as "A Better Place Than Home." *The Newcomers:
　　Inhabiting a New Land*. Ed. Charles E. Israel. Toronto: McClelland &
　　Stewart, 1979: 113–24.

H. Interviews by Others (Alphabetical listing)

Boyle, Harry. Interview with Alice Munro. *Sunday Supplement.* CBC Radio. August 18, 1974. CBC Archives.

Connolly, Kevin, Douglas Freake, and Jason Sherman. "Interview: Alice Munro." *What* September-October 1986: 8–10.

Gardiner, Jill. Interview. Appendix. "The Early Short Stories of Alice Munro." M.A. Thesis. University of New Brunswick, 1973: 169–82.

Gibson, Graeme. "Alice Munro." *Eleven Canadian Novelists.* Toronto: Anansi, 1973: 241–64.

Gzowski, Peter. *Morningside.* October 18–22, 1982, CBC Archives.

———. *Morningside.* September 30, 1994. CBC Archives.

———. "'You're the Same Person at 19 That You Are at 60.'" *Globe and Mail.* September 29, 2001: F4–5.

Hancock, Geoff. "An Interview with Alice Munro." *Canadian Fiction Magazine* 43 (1983): 74–114.

McCulloch, Jeanne, and Mona Simpson. "Alice Munro: The Art of Fiction CXXXVII." *Paris Review* 131 (1994): 226–64.

Metcalf, John. "A Conversation with Alice Munro." *Journal of Canadian Fiction* 1.4 (1972): 54–62.

Quinn, Alice. "Go Ask Alice." February 12, 2001. http://www.newyorker.com/ON-LINE_ONLY/Q_A/?010219on_online_munro.

Redekop, Magdalene. Interview with Alice Munro. July 17, 1999. Stratford, Ontario. Unpublished.

Scobie, Stephen. "A Visit with Alice Munro." *Monday* [Victoria, B.C.] November 19–25, 1982: 12–13.

Stainsby, Mari. "Alice Munro Talks with Mari Stainsby." *British Columbia Library Quarterly* 35 (1971): 27–30.

Struthers, J.R. (Tim). "The Real Material: An Interview with Alice Munro." *Probable Fictions: Alice Munro's Narrative Acts.* Downsview, Ont.: ECW Press, 1983: 5–36.

Tausky, Thomas. Interview with Alice Munro. July 20, 1984, London, Ontario. Unpublished. Transcribed by Catherine Sheldrick Ross.

Toppings, Earle. Audio Interview with Alice Munro. Distributed to Canadian radio stations by The Ryerson Press. 1969.

Twigg, Alan. "What Is." *For Openers: Conversations with 24 Canadian Writers.* Madiera Park, B.C.: Harbour, 1981: 13–20.

Wachtel, Eleanor. "An Interview with Alice Munro." *Brick* 40 (1991): 48–53.

———. *Writers and Company.* November 7, 2004.

———. "Alice Munro: A Life in Writing: A Conversation." *Queen's Quarterly* 112 (2005): 266–80.

2. Works by Other Authors (Alphabetical)

A. Books, Journals, and Theses

Aitken, M. Alice, and John Underwood. *The Book of Turnberry, 1857–1982.* [Wingham, Ont.: n.d.].

Akenson, Donald Harman. *The Irish in Ontario: A Study in Rural History.* 2nd ed. Montreal and Kingston: McGill-Queen's UP, 1999.

The Alice Munro Papers: First Accession. Ed. Apollonia Steele and Jean F. Tener. Biocritical Essay Thomas E. Tausky. Calgary: U Calgary P, 1986.

The Alice Munro Papers: Second Accession. Ed. Apollonia Steele and Jean F. Tener. Calgary: U Calgary P, 1987.

Botsford, Gardner. *A Life of Privilege, Mostly: A Memoir.* New York: St. Martin's, 2003.

Brown, Jim, and Gloria (Stark) Brown. *Halton's Scotch Block: The People and Their Stories.* Milton, Ont.: Milton Historical Society, 2009.

Everard, Mark. "Robert Weaver's Contributions to Canadian Literature." M.A. Thesis. University of Toronto, 1984.

Gill, Brendan. *Here at the New Yorker.* New York: De Capo, 1997.

Illustrated Atlas of Huron County. Toronto: H. Belden, 1879.

Jerome, Jodi. *The Evolution of Wescast: People Moulding a Legacy.* [Wingham, Ont.]: Pinpoint Publications, 2002.

King, James. *The Life of Margaret Laurence.* Toronto: Knopf Canada, 1997.

Kunkel, Thomas. *Genius in Disguise: Harold Ross of* The New Yorker. New York: Random House, 1995.

Laidlaw, Robert E. *The McGregors: A Novel of an Ontario Farm Family.* Introd. Harry J. Boyle. Toronto: Macmillan, 1979.

Leitch, Linda Margaret. "Alice Munro's Fiction: Explorations of Open Forms." M.A. Thesis. University of Guelph, 1980.

McGill, Jean S. *A Pioneer History of the County of Lanark.* Bewdley, Ont.: Clay, 1968.

McKillop, A.B. *Matters of Mind: The University in Ontario, 1791–1951.* Toronto: U Toronto P, 1994.

MacSkimming, Roy. *The Perilous Trade: Publishing Canada's Writers.* Toronto: McClelland & Stewart, 2003.

Mehta, Ved. *Remembering Mr. Shawn's* New Yorker: *The Invisible Art of Editing.* Woodstock, N.Y.: Overlook, 1998.

Morris, Wright. *The Home Place.* 1948. Lincoln: U Nebraska P, 1972.

Munro, Sheila. *Lives of Mothers and Daughters: Growing Up With Alice Munro.* Toronto: McClelland & Stewart, 2001.

1984 Huron County Historical Atlas. Goderich: County of Huron, 1984.

The Pleasant Country: Killam and District, 1903–1993. Killam, Alta.: Killam Historical Society, 1993.

Probable Fictions: Alice Munro's Narrative Acts. Ed. Louis K. MacKendrick.
    Downsview, Ont.: ECW Press, 1983.
Public and Separate Schools and Teachers in the Province of Ontario. Toronto:
    Legislative Assembly, 1917–26.
"Publishing in Canada: A Symposium." *Canadian Literature* 33 (1967): 3–62.
The Rest of the Story: Critical Essays on Alice Munro. Ed. Robert Thacker.
    Toronto: ECW, 1999.
Ross, Catherine Sheldrick. *Alice Munro: A Double Life.* Toronto: ECW, 1992.
Scott, James. *The Settlement of Huron County.* Toronto: Ryerson, 1966.
Stamp, Robert M. *The Schools of Ontario, 1876–1976.* Toronto: U Toronto P, 1982.
Taaffe, Maria. "The *Montrealer* and Canadian Short Stories." M.A. Thesis.
    University of Montreal, 1998.
Talman, James J., and Ruth Davis. *"Western" – 1873–1953.* London: University of
    Western Ontario, 1953.
Wilderness to Wawanosh: East Wawanosh Township 1867–1992. Ed. Lori Jamison.
    Belgrave, Ont.: Township of East Wawanosh, 1992.
Yagoda, Ben. *About Town: The* New Yorker *and the World It Made.* New York:
    De Capo, 2001.

B. Articles, Introductions, Poems, and Stories
Abley, Mark. "Bob's Our Uncle." *Books in Canada.* May 1979: 4–9.
"Alice Laidlaw Munro." *They Passed This Way: A Selection of Citations.* Ed.
    Robert N. Shervill. London: University of Western Ontario, 1978: 113.
Angell, Roger. "Storyville." *New Yorker.* June 27 and July 4, 1994: 104–09.
Becker, Alinda. "Sex and Self-Defense." *New York Times Book Review.*
    September 11, 1994: 36.
Beran, Carol. "The Luxury of Excellence: Alice Munro in the *New Yorker.*"
    The Rest of the Story: Critical Essays on Alice Munro. Ed. Robert Thacker.
    Toronto: ECW, 1999: 204–31.
Beyersbergen, Joanna. "No Bitterness or Anxiety for Writer." *London Free Press.* s
Bruckner, D.J.R. "An Author Travels to Nurture Ideas About Home." *New York
    Times.* April 17, 1990: C13.
Byatt, A.S. "Justice for Willa Cather." Rev. of *Willa Cather and Politics of
    Criticism* by Joan Acocella. *New York Review of Books.* November 30, 2000:
    51–53.
Carver, Raymond. "Introduction." *Best American Short Stories 1986.* Ed.
    Raymond Carver and Shannon Ravenel. Boston: Houghton Mifflin, 1986:
    xi–xx.
Cather, Willa. "Miss Jewett." *Not Under Forty.* Lincoln: U Nebraska P, 1988:
    76–95.
"The Clever Mountcastle Family." *Huron Historical Notes* (1986): 24–28.

Creighton, David. "In Search of Alice Munro." *Books in Canada.* May 1994:
19–24.

Dafoe, Christopher. "Books and Bookmen." *Vancouver Sun.* May 2, 1969.

Dahlie, Hallvard. "Unconsummated Relationships: Isolation and Rejection in
Alice Munro's Stories." *World Literature Written in English* 11 (1972): 43–48.

Duffy, Dennis. "'A Dark Sort of Mirror': 'The Love of a Good Woman' as
Pauline Poetic." *The Rest of the Story: Critical Essays on Alice Munro.* Ed.
Robert Thacker. Toronto: ECW, 1999: 169–90.

"Eloise Skimings." *Huron Historical Notes* (1986): 33–34.

Farrow, Moira. "Housewife Finds Time to Write Short Stories." [North
Vancouver] *Citizen.* August 10, 1961.

Findley, Timothy. "Better Dead Than Read? An Opposing View." *Books in
Canada.* December 1978: 3–5.

———. "The McGregors." Rev. of *The McGregors* by Robert Laidlaw. *Globe
and Mail.* May 19, 1979: 45.

Forester, Margaret. "Secrets of a Glittering Prize." *Sunday Times.* October 26,
1980: 13.

French, William. "In Alice Land." *Globe and Mail.* June 19, 1973.

———. "Richler and Munro Are Alive and Well Between Books." *Globe and
Mail.* March 22, 1977: 15.

———. "The Good Book Versus Good Books." *Globe and Mail.* June 15, 1978:
16.

Fulford, Robert. "Tamarack Review Returns to Offer Good Writing." *Toronto
Star.* January 12, 1974: H5.

[———]. "This Month: The Past, the Present, and Alice Munro." *Saturday
Night.* April 1979: 11.

Gibson, Douglas. "A Very Canadian Celebrity." *Read,* 2, no. 2 (2001): 8–10.

Givner, Joan. "Mysteries of the Severed Head." *Thirty-Four Ways of Looking at
Jane Eyre.* Vancouver: New Star, 1998: 149–60.

Godard, Barbara. "Mountcastle, Clara H." *Dictionary of Canadian Biography.*
Vol. 13. Ed. Ramsay Cook. Toronto: U Toronto P, 1994: 722–24.

Gould, Jan. "Memory, Experiences of 'Normal Life' Feed Her Fiction." *Victoria
Daily Times.* August 9, 1969.

Grady, Wayne. "Story Tellers to the World." *Today.* December 10, 1981: 10–12.

Hluchy, Patricia. "*Maclean's* Honour Roll 1998: Alice Munro." *Maclean's.*
December 21, 1998: 67.

Hogg, James, and James Laidlaw. "Letter from the Ettrick Shepherd."
Blackwood's Magazine 6 (March 1820): 630, 632.

Hoy, Helen. "'Rose and Janet': Alice Munro's Metafiction." *Canadian Literature*
121 (1989): 59–83.

Kinsella, W.P. "CanLit Clique for Metcalf?" *Globe and Mail.* December 7, 1983: 7.

Knelman, Martin. "The Past, the Present, and Alice Munro." *Saturday Night.*
    November 1979: 16–18, 20, 22.

Laidlaw, Robert B. "The Diary of Robert B. Laidlaw." *Blyth: A Village Portrait.*
    Ed. Susan Street. Blyth, Ont.: [n.p.], 1977: 17–21.

Laidlaw, Robert E. "The Boyhood Summer of 1912." [Blyth, Ontario *Citizen*]
    Village Squire. July 1974: 15–19.

Laskin, David. "Tales of Love and Sorrow in a Singular City: Alice Munro's
    Vancouver." *New York Times.* June 11, 2006: TR 9, 12.

Layton, Irving. "Keine Lazarovitch, 1870–1959." *Tamarack Review* 15 (Spring
    1960): 22.

Macfarlane, David. "Writer in Residence." *Saturday Night.* December 1986:
    51–52, 54, 56.

MacSkimming, Roy. "The Great Original: Jack McClelland Reinvented
    Canadian Publishing." *Quill & Quire.* August 2004: 12–13.

McDougall, Joyce. "The Truth Behind Alice Munro's Tales." *Wingham Advance-
    Times.* December 22, 1981: 4.

McInnes, Nerissa Archer. "The Clever Mountcastle Family." *Huron Historical
    Notes* (1986): 24–25.

Malcolm, Janet. "Gertrude Stein's War." *New Yorker.* June 2, 2003: 58–81.

Marchand, Philip. "The Problem with Alice Munro." *Canadian Notes & Queries*
    72 (Fall/Winter 2007): 10–15.

Marcus, Ben. "Why Experimental Fiction Threatens to Destroy Publishing,
    Jonathan Franzen, and Life as We Know It: A Correction." *Harper's.*
    October 2005: 39–52.

Matchan, Linda. "Alice Munro: From the Ontario Hinterlands to 'The Moons
    of Jupiter.'" *Boston Globe.* May 25, 1983: 69, 73.

Menaker, Daniel. "Authors! Authors!" *New Yorker.* June 27 and July 4, 1994:
    110, 117.

Metcalf, John. "What Happened to CanLit?" *Globe and Mail.* November 19,
    1983: B1.

Ozick, Cynthia. "A Short Note on 'Chekhovian.'" *Metaphor and Memory.* New
    York: Knopf, 1989: 88–89.

Parker, George. "Sale of Ryerson Press: The End of the Old Agency System and
    Conflicts Over Domestic and Foreign Ownership in the Canadian
    Publishing Industry, 1970–1986." *Papers of the Bibliographic Society of
    Canada* 40 (2002): 7–56.

Peterson, Leslie. "Nothing to Tell Us." *Vancouver Sun.* February 13, 1976.

Quinn, Alice. "The 'Wholly Original' Alice Munro." *National Post.*
    November 18, 2000: B11.

Ross, Val. "A Writer Called Alice." *Globe and Mail.* October 1, 1994: C1, 21.

Russo, Maria. "Final Chapter." *New York Times Magazine.* April 14, 2002: 32–35.

Simpson, Mona. "Alice Munro: Conveying Our Dreams." *Time*. April 18, 2005: 116.

Slopen, Beverly. "PW Interviews Alice Munro." *Publishers Weekly*. August 22, 1986: 76–77.

Smith, Margaret. "Telling Life As It Is." *Weekly Australian Magazine*. February 14–15, 1981.

Spettigue, Doug. "Alice Laidlaw Munro: A Portrait of the Artist." University of Western Ontario *Alumni Gazette*. July 1969: 4–5.

Staines, David. Introduction. *Prize Writing: The 10th Anniversary Collection*. Ed. Gary Stephen Ross. Toronto: Giller Prize Foundation, 2003: 15–21.

Stapleton, Margaret. "Alice Munro – Friend of Our Youth." *Wingham Advance-Times*. December 16, 1998: 10–11.

Stuewe, Paul. "Better Dead Than Read." *Books in Canada*. October 1978: 3–7.

Tausky, Thomas. "'What Happened to Marion?': Art and Reality in *Lives of Girls and Women*." *Studies in Canadian Literature* 11 (1986): 52–76.

Thacker, Robert. "Alice Munro's Willa Cather." *Canadian Literature* 134 (1992): 42–57.

———. "A 'Booming Tender Sadness': Alice Munro's Irish." *Canada: Text and Territory*. Ed. Máire Áine Ní Mhainnín and Elizabeth Tilley. Cambridge: Cambridge Scholars Press, 2008. 132–40.

———. "Gazing Through the One-Way Mirror: English-Canadian Literature and the American Presence." *Colby Quarterly* 29 (1993): 74–87.

Thomas, Audrey. "Initram." *Ladies and Escorts*. Toronto: Oberon, 1977: 88–107.

Timson, Judith. "Merciful Light." *Maclean's*. May 7, 1990: 66–67.

Turbide, Diane. "The Incomparable Storyteller." *Maclean's*. October 17, 1994: 46 49.

Urquhart, Jane. "Afterword." *No Love Lost* by Alice Munro. Toronto: McClelland & Stewart/New Canadian Library, 2003: 416–21.

[Wenger, Barry.] "A Genius of Sour Grapes." *Wingham Advance-Times*. December 16, 1981: 4.

"'Writing's Something I Did, Like the Ironing.'" *Globe and Mail*. December 11, 1982: E1.

Vasey, Paul. "Alice Has a Lot of Reasons to Be Happy." *Windsor Star*. September 27, 1974.

Wayne, Joyce. "Huron County Blues." *Books in Canada*. October 1982: 9–12.

Weaver, Robert. "Books." *Mass Media in Canada*. Ed. John Irving. Toronto: Ryerson, 1962: 31–50.

Welty, Eudora. "Some Notes on River Country." *The Eye of the Story: Selected Essays and Reviews*. New York: Vintage, 1979: 286–99.

"Writer's Writers." *Books in Canada*. January/February 1987: 8–11.

C. Reviews Mentioned (Grouped by Book Title, Alphabetically Within Group)

Dance of the Happy Shades

Bishop, Dorothy. "A Novel of the Week." *Ottawa Journal.* December 11, 1968.

Byrd, Martha. "Art of Short Stories Revived in Collection." Kingsport [Tenn.] *Times-News.* January 27, 1974.

Cheney, Francis Neel. "Short Stories Please Critic." *Tennessean* (Nashville). October 7, 1973.

Engel, Allison. "Fine Collection – Fresh and Honest!" *Des Moines Register.* September 16, 1973.

Fischman, Sheila. "To Maturity Along a Rural Route." *Globe Magazine* [*Globe and Mail*]. October 19, 1969: 24.

Harvor, Beth. "The Special World of the W[omen] W[riter]s." *Saturday Night.* August 1969: 3.

Heald, Tim. "Recent Fiction." *Daily Telegraph* [n.d.].

Helwig, David. "Canadian Letters." *Queen's Quarterly* 77 (1970): 127–28.

Kirkwood, Hilda. Rev. of *Dance, Canadian Forum.* February 1969: 259–60.

Lawrence, R.G. "Mental Ghosts Delicately Exorcised." Victoria *Daily Times.* November 2, 1968.

Levin, Martin. "New & Novel." *New York Times Book Review.* September 23, 1973: 48.

Peter, John. *Malahat Review* 11 (July 1969): 126.

Philips, Joan. "First Stories by Alice Munro Show Real Talent." *Standard* (St. Catharines). December 7, 1968.

Portman, Jamie. "Ordinary People, Ordinary Situations, Ordinary Lives." *Calgary Herald.* March 21, 1969.

Prince, Peter. "Paragons." *New Statesman.* May 3, 1974: 633.

Rev. of *Dance. New Yorker.* November 5, 1973: 186.

Richardson, Jean. "New Fiction." *Birmingham Post.* May 4, 1974.

Roper, Gordon. "Letters in Canada 1968: Fiction." *University of Toronto Quarterly* 38 (1969): 363.

Simpson, Leo. Radio review of *Dance* and *Miracle at Indian River* by Alden Nowlan. *Anthology.* CBC Radio. October 19, 1968.

"Small Town Tales." *Leader-Post* (Regina). October 26, 1968.

Tench, Helen. "Turning-Points in Young Lives Turning Points in Fine Short Stories." *Ottawa Citizen.* January 4, 1969.

Thomas, Audrey. "'She's Only a Girl,' He Said." *Canadian Literature* (Winter 1969): 91–92.

Thompson, Kent. Radio review. Music and Arts. CBC Radio Fredericton. May 1969.

———. *Fiddlehead* 82 (1969): 71–72.

Vale, Adrian. "Private Lives." *Irish Times* [n.d.].

Ward-Harris, E.D. "These Stories Have the Maugham Touch." *Victoria Daily Colonist.* November 10, 1968: 14.

Lives of Girls and Women

Anderson, Patrick. "Falling in Love with a Thud." *Sunday Telegraph.* November 4, 1973.

Beer, Patricia. "Beside the Wawanash." *Times Literary Supplement.* March 17, 1978: 302.

Blythe, Ronald. "Blob." *Listener.* November 29, 1973: 752.

Barrett, Mary Ellin. "Cosmo Reads the New Books." *Cosmopolitan.* March 1973: 26.

Brasier, Virginia. "Alice Munro Called 'Writer to Watch.'" *Sun-Telegram* (San Bernardino). November 19, 1972.

Burroway, Janet. "Variety Justifies 'Lives of Girls.'" *Tallahassee Democrat.* November 19, 1972: 12E.

Coldwell, Joan. "A Small World Re-Created." *Victoria Times* [October-November 1971].

Dafoe, Christopher. "The Causerie": rev. of *Lives. Vancouver Sun.* November 26, 1971.

Dobbs, Kildare. "This First Novel Is Solid, Beautiful." *Toronto Star.* October 30, 1971.

Ferrari, Margaret. "Lives of Girls & Women." *America.* February 24, 1973: 168.

Foote, Audrey C. "Nostalgia for Jubilee." *Washington Post.* January 4, 1973.

Grosskurth, Phyllis. "A Delight. Goodbye to Inhibitions." *Globe Magazine* [*Globe and Mail*]. October 30, 1971: 17.

Howard, Irene. "An Elegant Book About Women." *Monday Morning* [Vancouver]. February 1972: 22–23.

Johnson, Marigold. "Mud and Blood." *New Statesman.* October 26, 1973: 618–19.

Levertov, Denise. Rev. of *Lives.* [No publication information].

Metcalf, John. "Growing Up." *Montreal Star.* November 20, 1971.

Peterson, Kevin. "A Penetrating Look at the World of Women." *Calgary Herald Magazine.* February 4, 1972.

Polk, James. "Deep Caves Paved with Kitchen Linoleum." *Canadian Literature* 54 (1972): 102–04.

Rev. of *Lives. New Yorker.* January 6, 1973: 75.

———. *Publishers Weekly.* July 31, 1972: 68.

Rex, Barbara. "The Canvas Is Small, the Talent Is Large." *Philadelphia Inquirer.* February 18, 1973.

Symons, Julian. "Scenes from Provincial Life." *Sunday Times.* October 14, 1973.

Thomas, Clara. "Woman Invincible." *Journal of Canadian Fiction* 1, no. 4 (1972): 95–96.

Tomalin, Claire. "Harvest and Holocaust." *Observer*. October 21, 1973: 40.

Walfoort, Mary. "A Girl in Canada Finds a Universe in a Village." *Milwaukee Journal*. January 28, 1973.

Ward-Harris, E.D. Rev of *Lives*. *Victoria Daily Colonist* [October-November 1971].

Wolff, Geoffrey. "Call It Fiction." *Time*. January 15, 1973: 64, 66.

Something I've Been Meaning to Tell You

Blodgett, E.D. Rev. of *Something*. *Canadian Fiction Magazine* 16 (Winter 1975): 99–101.

Busch, Frederick. "A Trio of Fictions." *New York Times Book Review*. October 27, 1974: 52–54.

Cusham, Susan. "Alice Munro's Story Collection Is Her Weakest Book So Far." *Minneapolis Star*. November 7, 1974.

Dobbs, Kildare. "New Direction for Alice Munro." *Saturday Night*. July 1974: 25.

French, William. "Beautiful. Her Talent's Transportable." *Globe and Mail*. May 25, 1974: 32.

Fulford, Robert. "Solemn Style." *Toronto Star*. May 25, 1974: F5.

Hosek, Chaviva. Rev. *Something*. *Quill & Quire*. June 1974: 11.

Howland, Bette. "Tricks, Trap-Doors, a Writer's Craft." *Chicago Tribune*. October 6, 1974.

James, Geoffrey. "Moving Miniaturist." *Time* Canada. June 17, 1974: 10.

Kirkwood, Hilda. "Tell Us Again." *Canadian Forum*. June 1975: 42.

Powell, Dorothy M. Rev. of *Something*. *Canadian Author and Bookman* (Fall 1974).

Stouck, David. Rev. of *Something*. *West Coast Review* 10 (1975): 46–47.

Struthers, J.R. (Tim). "Exciting Collection." *London Free Press*. June 22, 1974: 10.

Who Do You Think You Are?

Abley, Mark. "Growing Up Sad in Southern Ontario." *Maclean's*. December 11, 1978: 62.

Bartlett, Brian. "New Severity." *Gazette* (Montreal). January 13, 1979: 53.

Follis, Sheila Robinson. Rev. of *Who*. *Quill & Quire*. October 1978: 43.

French, William. Rev. of *Who*. *Globe and Mail*. November 11, 1978: 40.

Grady, Wayne. "Alice Through a Glass Darkly." *Books in Canada*. October 1978: 15–16.

Harrison, Claire. "Brilliant Collection." *Ottawa Journal*. December 16, 1978.

Kareda, Urjo. "The War Within Alice Munro's Heroine." *Saturday Night*. January-February 1979: 62–63.

Leitch, Linda. Rev. of *Who*. *Ontarion* (University of Guelph). January 16, 1979.

Mallet, Gina. "Alice Munro: The Mud Underneath the Manicure." *Toronto Star*. November 18, 1978: D7.

Noonan, Gerald. Rev. of *Who*. *Canadian Book Review Annual 1978*. Ed. Dean
    Tudor et al. [Toronto]: PMA Books, 1979: 150–51.
Porter, Helen. Rev. of *Who*. *Evening Telegram* (Newfoundland). March 24,
    1979.
Powers, Gordon. "Alice Munro: A New Darker Mirror of the Self." *Ottawa
    Revue*. February 8–14, 1979.
Solecki, Sam. "Letters in Canada 1978: Fiction." *University of Toronto Quarterly*
    48 (1978–79): 319–20.
Struthers, J.R. (Tim). "Munro's Latest Shows 'Astonishing' Maturity." *London
    Free Press*. December 16, 1978.
Taylor, Michael. Rev. of *Who*. *The Fiddlehead* 121 (1979): 125–27.
Williamson, David. "Alice Munro: Is She the Best Canadian Writer?" *Winnipeg
    Free Press*. February 17, 1979: Insert: 13.

The Beggar Maid

Balakian, Nona. "Books of the Times." *New York Times*. December 13, 1979: C21.
Beatty, Jack, Rev. of *The Beggar Maid*. *New Republic*. October 13, 1979: 40.
Cameron, Marsaili. "Who Do You Think You Are?" *Gay News* 191 [1980]: 22.
Edwards, Thomas R. "It's Love!" *New York Review of Books*. March 6, 1980:
    43–45.
Epps, Garrett. "Real Short Stories and Static Prose." *Washington Post*.
    December 21, 1979: C10.
Higgins, Johanna. "To Bridge Gulfs and Make Connections." *Lone Star Book
    Review*. February 1980: 9, 29.
Hollinghurst, Alan. "Elapsing Lives." *New Statesman*. April 25, 1980: 830–31.
Lothian, Andrew. *The Beggar Maid*. *Blackwood's Magazine*. August 1980: 159.
Morgan, Ted. "Writers Who Happen to Be Women." *Saturday Review*.
    October 13, 1979: 76–78.
Oates, Joyce Carol. "Books." *Mademoiselle*. October 1979: 72, 74.
O'Faolain, Julia. "Small-Town Snobbery in Canada." *New York Times Book
    Review*. September 16, 1979: 12.
Rabinowitz, Dorothy. "The Flash Floodings that Love Breeds." *Wall Street
    Journal*. November 7, 1979.
Reed, Nancy Gail. "We Can Find Ourselves, Like Rose." *Christian Science
    Monitor*. January 2, 1980: 17.
Rev. of *The Beggar Maid*. *Kirkus Reviews*. August 1, 1979: 882.
Rev. of *The Beggar Maid*. *Ms*. February 1980: 33.
Rev. of *The Beggar Maid*. *Paperback and Hardback Book Buyer*. April 1980.
Tucker, Eva. "Ancient Mariner Mannerisms." *Hampstead and Highgate Express*.
    October 17, 1980: 60.
Wilentz, Amy. Rev. of *The Beggar Maid*. *Nation*. December 29, 1979: 696.

Wilner, Paul. "Virtue Wins." *Village Voice.* October 15, 1979: 43.

Xiques, Linda. "The Beggar Maid." *Pacific Sun* (Mill Valley, Calif.). April 11, 1980.

The Moons of Jupiter

Allnutt, Gillian. Rev. of *Moons. City Limits.* April 29, 1983.

Bailey, Paul. "Martially Milled." *Standard* (Great Britain). May 18, 1983.

Bowden, Nina. "Love in an Irish Shadow." *Daily Telegraph.* April 28, 1983.

Black, Barbara. "Munro Delivers Yet Another Superb Collection." *Montréal Gazette.* October 16, 1982: A9.

Blake, Patricia. "Heart-Catching." *Time.* February 28, 1983: 71, 73.

Broyard, Anatole. "Books of the Times." *New York Times.* February 16, 1983: C27.

Crerar, Tom. "A Sentence to Life." *Brick* 18 (Spring 1983): 2.

DeMott, Benjamin. "Domestic Stories." *New York Times Book Review.* March 20, 1983: 1, 26.

Evenchik, Arthur. "A New Doubtfulness in Alice Munro's Stories." *Sun* (Baltimore). March 13, 1983.

Faustman, John. "Two Alices." *Western Living.* June 1983: 63–64, 66.

French, William. "The Moons of Jupiter." *Globe and Mail.* October 16, 1982: 15.

Grady, Wayne. "A House of Her Own." *Books in Canada.* October 1982: 12, 14.

Hollinghurst, Alan. "The Secrets of Failing Lives." *Times Literary Supplement.* May 6, 1983: 457.

Hurlbert, Ann. "The Country and the City." *New Republic.* March 7, 1983: 37–38.

Kareda, Urjo. "Double Vision." *Saturday Night.* November 1982: 63–64.

Kemp, Peter. "Making Connections." *Observer.* May 1, 1983.

Lehman, David. "When Short Is Beautiful." *Newsweek.* April 25, 1983: 85–86.

Manning, Margaret. "Stories of Women in a Harsh Climate." *Boston Globe.* February 21, 1983: 28.

McFall, Gardner. "Broken Hearts and Broken Homes." *Newsday.* March 6, 1983.

Mellors, John. "Canada Swans." *Listener.* June 9, 1983.

Mukherjee, Bharati. "Alice Munro's Visionary Lyricism Dazzles." *Quill & Quire.* October 1982: 57.

O'Faolain, Nuala. "Alice Munro: Soaring Clear." *Sunday Tribune* (Dublin). August 26, 1984.

Porter, Dorothy. "Pie in the Face for Superficial Judgers." *Herald* (Glasgow). July 2, 1983.

Quigly, Isabel. "When Auntie Came to Dinner." *Financial Times.* May 14, 1983.

Rev. of *Moons. Publisher's Weekly.* December 17, 1982: 63.

Robertson, William. "Short Stories That Check Up on Human Hearts." *Miami Herald.* February 27, 1983.

Seidenbaum, Art. "Canadian Stories Are Warmly Told." *Los Angeles Times.* February 13, 1983: V6.

Simpson, Leo. "Story by Story, a Stronger Collection Than Joyce's Dubliners."
  Hamilton Spectator. November 20, 1982.
Scanlan, Larry. "Believing Alice Munro." *Kingston Whig-Standard Magazine.*
  December 4, 1982: 21.
Solecki, Sam. "Lives of Girls and Women." *Canadian Forum.* October 1982:
  24–25.
Twigg, Alan. "The Flawless Alice Munro." [Vancouver *Sun* or *Province* ?] n.p.
Williamson, David. "Alice Munro at Her Best." *Winnipeg Free Press.* October 30,
  1982: 46.
Wordsworth, Christopher. "Dissolved in the Sludge." *Financial Guardian.*
  May 6, 1983.
Zeidner, Lisa. "Her Fine Short Stories Are Long on Insight." *Philadelphia
  Inquirer.* February 20, 1983. 6.

The Progress of Love

Andrews, Audrey. "Munro Plumbs Emotional Depths." *Calgary Herald.*
  October 19, 1986: C11.
Bradbury, Patricia. "The Realism of Munro and the Romance of Turner
  Hospital." *Quill & Quire.* August 1986: 42.
Craig, Patricia. "Minor Upheavals." *Sunday Times.* January 25, 1987.
Duchêne, Anne. "Respect for the Facts." *Times Literary Supplement.* January 30,
  1987: 109.
French, William. "Less is Much More in the Short Story." *Globe and Mail.*
  September 20, 1986: D19.
Gray, Paul. "Amplitudes." *Time.* September 22, 1986: 95.
Henderson, Heather. "Gently Unsettling Songs of Experience." *Maclean's.*
  September 22, 1986: 57.
Kakutani, Michiko. "Books of the Times." *New York Times.* September 3, 1986:
  C22. Also "Alice Munro: The True Art of Storytelling." September 6, 1986.
Oates, Joyce Carol. "Characters Dangerously Like Us." *New York Times Book
  Review.* September 14, 1986: 7, 9.
Rev. of *The Progress of Love. Canadian Churchman.* December 1986: 20.
Rev. of *The Progress of Love. Publishers Weekly.* July 4, 1986: 60.
Stewart, Robert. "Exploring Alice Munro Country." *Gazette* (Montreal).
  September 20, 1986: B1.
Sumi, Glenn. "Progressing at Fiction." *Varsity* (University of Toronto).
  October 9, 1986: 11.
Tomalin, Claire. "Generation to Generation." *Observer.* January 25, 1987.
Tyler, Anne. "Canadian Club." *New Republic.* September 15 and 22, 1986: 54–55.
Williamson, David. "Munro Excels at Short Story." *Winnipeg Free Press.*
  September 20, 1986.

Friend of My Youth

Craig, Patricia. "Pungent Connections." *Times Literary Supplement.* October 19, 1990: 1130.

French, William. "Just Folks." *Globe and Mail.* April 21, 1990: C17.

Jones, Malcolm, Jr. "The Glory of the Story." *Newsweek.* April 2, 1990: 56–57.

Marchand, Philip. "Telling Stories." *Toronto Star Saturday Magazine.* April 21, 1990: M12–13.

Mukherjee, Bharati. "Hometown Horrors." *New York Times Book Review.* March 18, 1990: 1, 31.

Salter, Mary Jo. "In Praise of Accidents." *New Republic.* May 14, 1990: 50–53.

Shields, Carol. "In Ontario." *London Review of Books.* February 7, 1991: 22–23.

Towers, Robert. "Short Satisfactions." *New York Review of Books.* May 17, 1990: 38–39.

Walbert, Kate. "Munro Doctrine." *Nation.* May 14, 1990: 678–80.

Open Secrets

Butala, Sharon. "A Walk on the Wild Side with Alice Munro." *Globe and Mail.* September 17, 1994: C30.

Holmstrom, David. "Compassion, Surprise Shape Work of Two Veteran Storytellers." *Christian Science Monitor.* October 11, 1994: 14.

Goldman, Marlene, and Teresa Heffernan. "Letters in Canada 1994: Fiction." *University of Toronto Quarterly* 65 (1995/6): 15.

Helwig, David. "Alice in Wonderland." *Gazette* (Montreal). September 24, 1994: I1,3.

Hulbert, Ann. "Writer Without Borders." *New York Review of Books.* December 22, 1994: 59–60.

Humphreys, Josephine. "Mysteries Near at Hand." *New York Times Book Review.* September 11, 1994: 1, 36–37.

Jones, Malcolm, Jr. "Ordinary People." *Newsweek.* September 26, 1994: 63.

Kakutani, Michiko. "Love, Found and Lost, Amid Sharp Turns of Fate." *New York Times.* September 6, 1994: C17.

Lesser, Wendy. "The Munro Doctrine." *New Republic.* October 31, 1994: 51–53.

O'Faolain, Julia. "In the Territory of Dreams." *Times Literary Supplement.* October 14, 1994: 24.

Rev. of *Open Secrets. Publishers Weekly.* August 1, 1994: 72.

Sheppard, R.Z. "Women on the Edge." *Time.* October 3, 1994: 80.

Solotaroff, Ted. "Life Stories." *Nation.* November 28, 1994: 665–68.

Struthers, J.R. (Tim). "How Real, How Magical." *Books in Canada.* October 1994: 32–33.

Summers, Myrna. "An Entertainer of the Spirit." *Canadian Forum.* January/February 1995: 38–39.

Woodcock, George. "The Secrets of Her Success." *Quill & Quire.* August 1994: 25.

Selected Stories

Archer, Bert. "Mavis and Alice." *Quill & Quire.* October 1996: 33.

Banville, John. "Revelations." *New York Review of Books.* February 20, 1997: 19–20, 22.

Byatt, A.S. "Alice Munro: One of the Great Ones." *Globe and Mail.* November 2, 1996: D18, D14.

Duffy, Dennis. "Something She's Been Meaning to Tell Us." *Books in Canada.* December, 1996: 8, 9.

Jones, Malcolm, Jr. "Genius in Disguise." *Newsweek.* October 21, 1996: 88.

Mars-Jones, Adam. "Histories of American Marriage." *Times Literary Supplement.* November 8, 1996: 26.

Rev. of *Selected Stories. Publishers Weekly.* August 12, 1996: 61.

Updike, John. "Magnetic North." *New York Times Book Review.* October 27, 1996: 11, 13.

Wood, James. "Things Happen All the Time." *London Review of Books.* May 8, 1997: 31–32.

The Love of a Good Woman

Byatt, A.S. "Munro: The Stuff of Life." *Globe and Mail.* September 26, 1998: D16.

Croft, Barbara. "Indirect Objects." *Women's Review of Books.* January 1999: 15–16.

Frank, Michael. "Fiction in Review." *Yale Review* 87, no. 2 (1999): 157–74.

Gorra, Michael. "Crossing the Threshold." *New York Times Book Review.* November 1, 1998: 6–7.

"Less Is More." *Economist.* December 12, 1998: 14–15.

Lowry, Elizabeth. "Getting Over Love." *Times Literary Supplement.* December 4, 1999: 22.

Sheppard, R.Z. "Quiet Virtues." *Time.* November 20, 1998: 119.

Todd, Tamsin. "The Love of a Good Woman." *New Statesman.* February 12, 1999: 54–55.

Urquhart, Jane. "Art of Alice Munro." *Ottawa Citizen.* September 20, 1998.

van Herk, Aritha. "Between the Stirrup and the Ground." *Canadian Forum.* October 1998: 49–52.

Hateship, Friendship, Courtship, Loveship, Marriage

Allardice, Lisa. "Small-Town Blues." *New Statesman.* November 19, 2001: 51.

Beattie, Ann. "Alice Munro's Amazing Ordinary World." *Globe and Mail.* September 29, 2001: D2–3.

Deignan, Tom. "Life in a Sentence." *Commonweal.* February 22, 2002: 26–27.

Drainie, Bronwyn. "Relationship Roulette." *Quill & Quire.* August 2001: 22.

Enright, Anne. "New Ways to Leave." *National Post.* September 29, 2001: RB7.

Fertile, Candace. "The Mistress of Style." *Vancouver Sun.* September 29, 2001.

Franklin, Ruth. "Assent and Lamentation." *New Republic.* February 25, 2002: 33–37.

Giles, Jeff. "The Heart of Her Matter." *Newsweek.* November 12, 2001: 66.

Kakutani, Michiko. "Home Is Where the Heart Is, An Independent One." *New York Times.* November 20, 2001: E8.

Lockerbie, Catherine. "The Loving Literature of Alice Munro." *Ottawa Citizen.* September 30, 2001: C11, 15.

Marchand, Philip. "The Way Things Are." *Toronto Star.* September 30, 2001: D12–13.

Markovits, Benjamin. "Suspicion of Sentiment." *London Review of Books.* December 13, 2001: 26–27.

McGahern, John. "Heroines of Their Lives." *Times Literary Supplement.* November 9, 2001: 23–24.

Moore, Lorrie. "Artship." *New York Review of Books.* January 17, 2002: 41–42.

Neufeld, K. Gordon. "Wondrous Tales from Munrovia." *Calgary Herald.* September 29, 2001.

Pritchard, William H. "Road Map Not Included." *New York Times Book Review.* November 25, 2001: 8.

Ravitch, Michael. "Fiction in Review." *Yale Review* 90. no. 4 (2002) 160–70.

Rev. of *Hateship. Economist.* November 24, 2001: 80.

Rev. of *Hateship. Publishers Weekly.* October 8, 2001: 41.

Simonds, Merilyn. "Munro's Wit Is Undiminished." *Montreal Gazette.* September 29, 2001: I1–2. Also *Kingston Whig-Standard.* October 13, 2001; and *Victoria Times-Colonist.* October 14, 2001.

Simpson, Mona. "A Quiet Genius." *Atlantic Monthly.* December 2001: 126–31, 133–36.

Wharton, Thomas. "Bits, Pieces of Everyday Life." *Edmonton Journal.* September 30, 2001. Also *Daily News* (Halifax). September 30, 2001; and *Windsor Star.* November 10, 2001.

Runaway

Aitken, Lee. Rev. of *Runaway. People.* November 15, 2004: 47.

Alvarez, A. "Life Studies." *New York Review of Books.* October 2, 2004: 23–24.

Bailey, Paul. Rev. of *Runaway. Independent.* January 28, 2005: 29.

Dhubhne, Éilís Ní. "A Cause for Celebration." *Irish Times.* January 29, 2005: 13.

Erskine, Bruce. "Mastery of Munro." *Chronicle Herald* (Halifax). September 26, 2004: NS11–12.

Fish, Maria. "Munro's 'Runaway' Hits Home." *USA Today.* November 18, 2004.

Franzen, Jonathan. "Alice's Wonderland." *New York Times Book Review.* November 14, 2004: 1, 14–16.

Gatti, Tom. "You Can Run, But You Can't Hide." *The Times.* February 5, 2005.

Goldberg, Carole. "Eight Tales of the Twists Women's Lives Take." *Hartford Courant.* December 19, 2004: G3.

Hawthorne, Mary. "Disconnected Realities." *London Review of Books.* February 17, 2005: 17–18.

Herford, Oliver. "The Impulse of Avoidance." *Times Literary Supplement.* February 18, 2005: 21.

Hollinghurst, Alan. "The Munro Doctrine." *Guardian.* February 5, 2005.

Kakutani, Michiko. "Realizing That Certainty Is Inevitably Uncertain." *New York Times.* December 7, 2004: E1.

Kritenbrink, Angie. Rev. of *Runaway. Identity Theory.* November 7, 2004. www.identitytheory.com. Accessed December 28, 2004.

Marchand, Philip. "Time Passing." *Toronto Star.* September 26, 2004: D12–13.

Messud, Claire. "Our Chekhov, Our Flaubert." *Globe and Mail.* September 25, 2004: D6.

Miller, Karl. "Not Bad for a Housewife." *Scottish Review of Books* 1, no. 2 (2005): 18–19.

Moore, Lorrie. "Leave Them and Love Them." *Atlantic Monthly.* December 2004: 125–28.

"Peripheral Visions." Rev. of *Runaway. Economist.* December 18, 2004: 134.

Rev. of *Runaway. Publishers Weekly.* October 11, 2004: 53.

Ridge, Mary Blanche. "Ripples in the Backwaters." *Tablet.* February 12, 2005.

Smee, Sebastian. "The Dangerous Edge of Things." *Spectator.* January 22, 2005: 32.

Timson, Judith. "Do Not Write Gently." *Maclean's.* October 4, 2004: 48.

Upchurch, Michael. "'Runaway': Challenging Journeys Through Women's Eyes." *Seattle Times.* October 31, 2004. www.seattletimes.nwsource.com. December 28, 2004.

Urquhart, Jane. "Master of Missed Clues." *National Post.* September 25, 2004.

Alice Munro's Best / Carried Away

Scott, A.O. "Native Ground." December 10, 2006. www.nytimes.com. December 11, 2006.

The View from Castle Rock

Besner, Neil. "Munro Collection Luminous." *Winnipeg Free Press.* September 24, 2006: B7.

Henighan, Stephen. "The Sense of an Ending." *Times Literary Supplement.* October 27, 2006: 21–22.

Lurie, Alison. "The Lamp in the Mausoleum." *The New York Review of Books.* December 21, 2006: 22, 24, 26, 28, 30.

Mantel, Hilary. "A Canny Kind of Lying." *The Guardian Review.* November 11, 2006: 16.

Miller, Karl. "Lives and Letters: Humble Beginnings." *The Guardian Review.* October 28, 2006: 21.

Moss, John. "Saving the Best for Last." *Books in Canada.* www.booksincanada.com. March 10, 2007.

Nunez, Sigrid. Rev. of *The View from Castle Rock. Publishers Weekly.* September 25, 2006: 42.

Whetter, Darryl. "Running in the Family." *Toronto Star.* September 17, 2006: D5, 8.

Too Much Happiness

Cohen, Leah Hager. "Object Lessons." *New York Times Book Review.* November 29, 2010: 1, 9.

Enright, Anne. "Come to Read Alice, Not to Praise Her." *Globe and Mail.* August 29, 2009.

Gorra, Michael. "The Late Mastery of Alice Munro." *Times Literary Supplement.* August 26, 2009.

Kinsella, W.P. "Everything is Funny." *BC BookWorld.* Autumn 2009: 23.

Long, Karen R. Rev. of *Too Much Happiness. Cleveland Plain Dealer.* December 6, 2009.

Marchand, Philip. "She'll Curl Your Hair." *National Post.* August 29, 2009: WP 10.

Oates, Joyce Carol. "'Who Do You Think You Are?'" *New York Review of Books.* December 3, 2009: 42–44.

Tayler, Christoper. "The Emotional Housekeeping of the World." *The Guardian Review.* August 15, 2009.

Thacker, Robert. "No Problem Here." *Literary Review of Canada.* September 2009: 19.

Index

Tara Freeman

ROBERT THACKER wrote his M.A. thesis on Alice Munro at the University of Waterloo in 1976 and has been writing about her stories, and Munro herself, ever since. He earned a Ph.D. at the University of Manitoba and is now Charles A. Dana Professor of Canadian Studies and English and Associate Dean at St. Lawrence University. He has been editor of *The American Review of Canadian Studies* and, as a result of his thirty-five years following Munro, he is now recognized as the leading academic authority on her fiction and career.